INTRODUCTION TO
Adobe® Flash® Professional CS6

Complete Coverage of the Adobe® Certified Associate Exam:
Rich Media Communication using Adobe® Flash® Professional CS6

AUTHOR	Fred Gerantabee
ADDITIONAL WRITING	Chad Chelius
PROJECT MANAGER	Cheri White
VIDEO PRODUCTION	Chris Leavey
VP & EXECUTIVE PUBLISHER	Don Fowley
EDITOR	Bryan Gambrel
DIRECTOR OF SALES	Mitchell Beaton
EXECUTIVE MARKETING MANAGER	Chris Ruel
ASSISTANT MARKETING MANAGER	Debbie Martin
EDITORIAL PROGRAM ASSISTANT	Jennifer Lartz
SENIOR PRODUCTION MANAGER	Janis Soo
ASSOCIATE PRODUCTION MANAGER	Joel Balbin
CREATIVE DIRECTOR	Harry Nolan
COVER DESIGNER	Georgina Smith
TECHNOLOGY & MEDIA	Tom Kulesa, Wendy Ashenberg
TECHNICAL EDITORS	Haziel Olivera, Sean McKnight
ART DIRECTOR	Jennifer Smith

This book was set in Bembo by Spoke & Wheel with production and development services provided by American Graphics Institute. It was printed and bound by Courier Kendallville. The covers were printed by Lehigh Phoenix.

Copyright © 2012 by John Wiley & Sons, Inc. All rights reserved.

Cover photo: © Marc Romanelli/Age Fotostock America, Inc.

No part of this publication may be reproduced, stored in a retrieval system or transmitted in any form or by any means, electronic, mechanical, photocopying, recording, scanning or otherwise, except as permitted under Sections 107 or 108 of the 1976 United States Copyright Act, without either the prior written permission of the Publisher, or authorization through payment of the appropriate per-copy fee to the Copyright Clearance Center, Inc. 222 Rosewood Drive, Danvers, MA 01923, (978) 750-8400, fax (978) 646-8600. Requests to the Publisher for permission should be addressed to the Permissions Department, John Wiley & Sons, Inc., 111 River Street, Hoboken, NJ 07030-5774, (201) 748-6011, fax (201) 748-6008.

Adobe Acrobat, Adobe Creative Suite, Adobe Dreamweaver, Adobe Flash Professional, Adobe InDesign, Adobe Photoshop, and Adobe Reader are either registered trademarks or trademarks of Adobe Systems Incorporated in the United States and/or other countries. Adobe product screenshot(s) reprinted with permission from Adobe Systems Incorporated. The Apple Logo is a registered trademark of Apple Inc. registered in the U.S. and other countries. Android is a trademark of Google Inc. The Android robot is reproduced or modified from work created and shared by Google and used according to terms described in the Creative Commons 3.0 Attribution License. Other product and company names mentioned herein may be the trademarks of their respective owners.

The example companies, organizations, products, domain names, e-mail addresses, logos, people, places, and events depicted herein are fictitious. No association with any real company, organization, product, domain name, e-mail address, logo, person, place, or event is intended or should be inferred.

The book expresses the author's views and opinions. The information contained in this book is provided without any express, statutory, or implied warranties. Neither the authors, John Wiley & Sons, Inc., nor their resellers or distributors will be held liable for any damages caused or alleged to be caused either directly or indirectly by this book.

Founded in 1807, John Wiley & Sons, Inc. has been a valued source of knowledge and understanding for more than 200 years, helping people around the world meet their needs and fulfill their aspirations. Our company is built on a foundation of principles that include responsibility to the communities we serve and where we live and work. In 2008, we launched a Corporate Citizenship Initiative, a global effort to address the environmental, social, economic, and ethical challenges we face in our business. Among the issues we are addressing are carbon impact, paper specifications and procurement, ethical conduct within our business and among our vendors, and community and charitable support. For more information, please visit our website: *www.wiley.com/go/citizenship*.

ISBN 978-1-1183-9407-6

Printed in the United States of America

10 9 8 7 6 5 4 3 2 1

Preface

Welcome to *Introduction to Adobe Flash Professional CS6*. Part of Wiley's Adobe courseware series, this book is designed as a complete introduction to Adobe Flash Professional for Creative Suite 6. With this series, we've set out to produce a series of textbooks that deliver compelling and innovative teaching solutions to instructors and superior learning experiences for students. Infused and informed by in-depth knowledge from Adobe Certified Experts and Flash professionals who have created many official training titles for Adobe Systems, and crafted by a publisher known worldwide for the pedagogical quality of its products, these textbooks maximize skills transfer in minimum time. Students are challenged to reach their potential by using their new technical skills as highly productive members of the workforce. This courseware was designed to ensure you receive the topical coverage that is most relevant to your personal and professional success.

Wiley's Adobe courseware Program

Wiley's Adobe courseware series is a complete program for instructors and institutions to prepare and deliver great courses on Adobe software technologies. With this courseware series, we recognize that—because of the rapid pace of change in the technology and curriculum developed by Adobe—there is an ongoing set of needs beyond classroom instruction tools for an instructor to be ready to teach the course. This courseware program endeavors to provide solutions for all these needs in a systematic manner in order to ensure a successful and rewarding course experience for both instructor and student via technical and curriculum training for instructor readiness with new software releases and a great set of tools for delivering instruction in the classroom and lab. All are important to the smooth delivery of a course on Adobe software, and all are provided with Wiley's Adobe courseware program. We think about this model as a gauge for ensuring that we completely support you in your goal of teaching a great course.

VIDEO TUTORIALS

Your *Introduction to Adobe Flash Professional CS6* textbook comes with access to approximately 2 hours of online video tutorials. The video tutorials are designed to supplement each lesson in the book. These video tutorials are created and presented by the authors and demonstrate topics covered in each lesson or related topics that enhance your understanding of each lesson.

Illustrated Book Tour

Pedagogical Features

The Wiley Adobe courseware and textbooks for Adobe Creative Suite 6 are designed as complete introductory textbooks on a particular Adobe software product. The books are also designed to cover all the learning objectives for that product's related Adobe Certified Associate (ACA) exam. The ACA exam is industry-recognized and identifies skills and topics expected for entry-level positions. Each ACA exam item is referred to as an exam objective, and these objectives are highlighted throughout the textbooks. Many pedagogical features have been developed specifically for this courseware. Unique features of our task-based approach include a Lesson Skill Matrix that correlates skills taught in each lesson to the ACA objectives; Certification Ready sidebars; Step-by-Step exercises; and two levels of increasingly rigorous lesson-ending activities—Competency Assessment and Proficiency Assessment.

Presenting the extensive procedural information and technical concepts woven throughout the textbook raises challenges for the student and instructor alike. The Illustrated Book Tour that follows provides a guide to the rich features contributing to Wiley's Adobe courseware pedagogical plan. Following is a list of key features in each lesson designed to prepare students for success on the certification exams and in the workplace:

- Each lesson begins with a **Lesson Skill Matrix**. More than a standard list of learning objectives, the skill matrix correlates each software skill covered in the lesson to the specific ACA exam objective.
- Each lesson features a real-world **Business Case** scenario that places the software skills and knowledge to be acquired in a real-world setting.
- Concise and frequent **Step-by-Step** instructions teach students new features and provide an opportunity for hands-on practice. Numbered steps give detailed instructions to help students learn software skills. The steps also show results and screen images to match what students should see on their computer screens.
- **Illustrations** provide visual feedback as students work through the exercises. The images reinforce key concepts, provide visual clues about the steps, and allow students to check their progress.
- When the text instructs a student to use a particular tool, **tool images** are shown within the text.
- Important technical vocabulary is listed in the **Key Terms** section at the beginning of the lesson. When these terms are used later in the lesson, they appear in bold italic type and are defined. The Glossary contains all of the key terms and their definitions.
- Engaging point-of-use **Reader Aids** located throughout the lessons tell students why this topic is relevant (*The Bottom Line*) and provide students with helpful hints (identified with the words *Take Note*) or ways to expand their skills (identified using the text *Learning More*). Reader aids also provide additional relevant or background information that adds value to the lesson.
- **Certification Ready** features throughout the text signal students where a specific certification objective is covered. They provide students with a chance to check their understanding of that particular ACA exam objective and, if necessary, review the section of the lesson where it is covered. This courseware provides complete preparation for ACA certification.

- Each lesson ends with a **Skill Summary**, recapping the ACA exam skills covered in the lesson.
- Accompanying **video tutorials** for each lesson provide a visual way to see selected content from the each lesson presented by the authors.
- The **Knowledge Assessment** section provides a total of 20 questions from a mix of True/False and Multiple Choice, testing students on concepts learned in the lesson.
- **Competency Assessment** and **Proficiency Assessment** sections provide progressively more challenging lesson-ending activities.
- Integrated **Circling Back** projects provide students with an opportunity to renew and practice skills learned in previous lessons.
- The student companion website contains the **online files** needed for each lesson.

Illustrated Book Tour

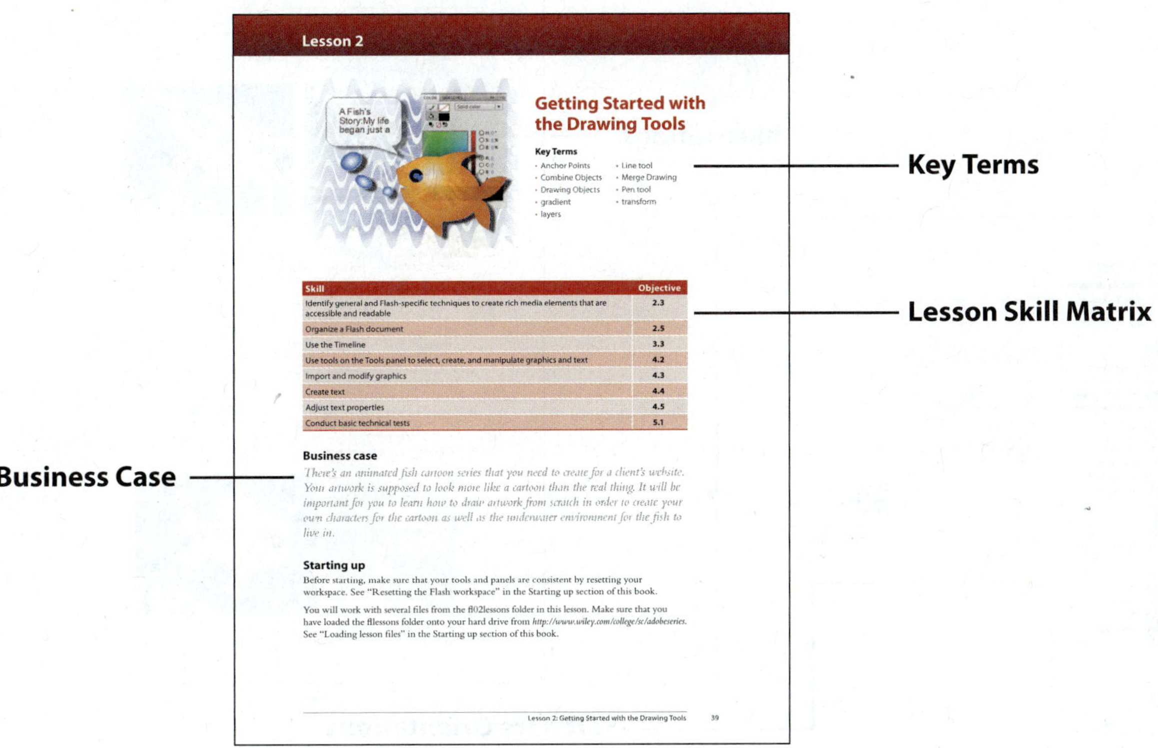

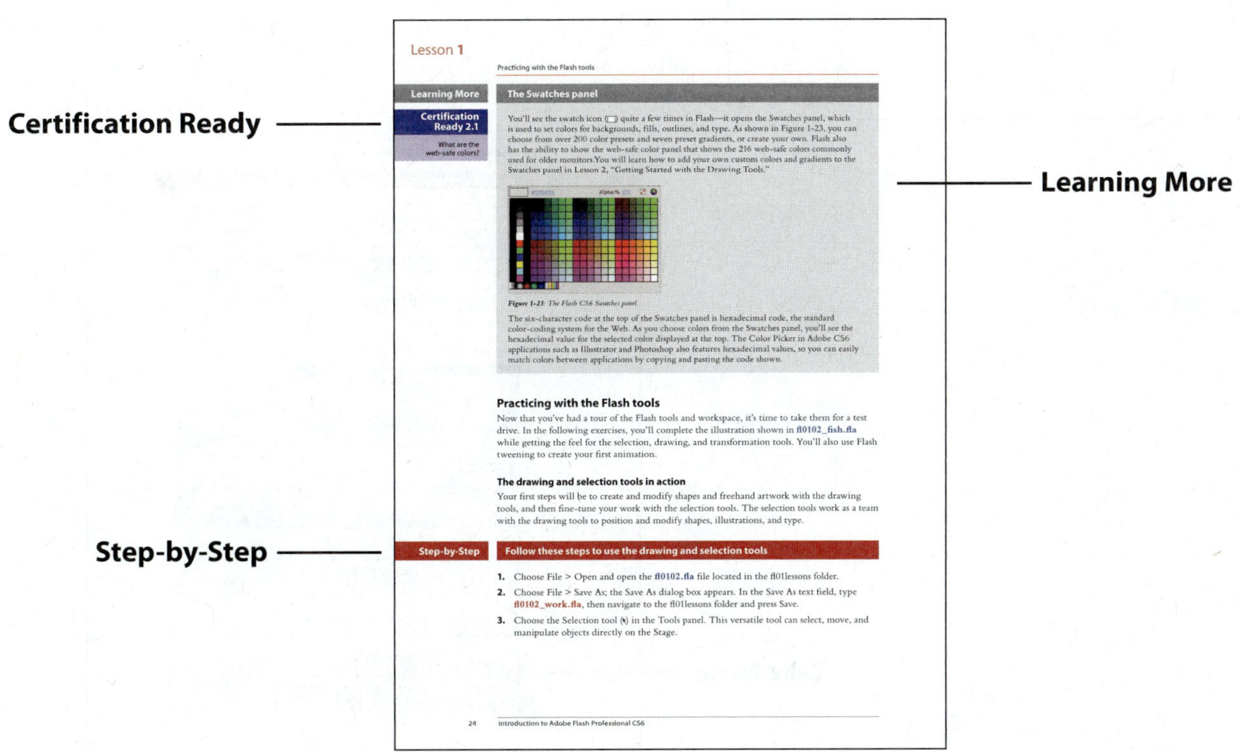

Illustrated Book Tour

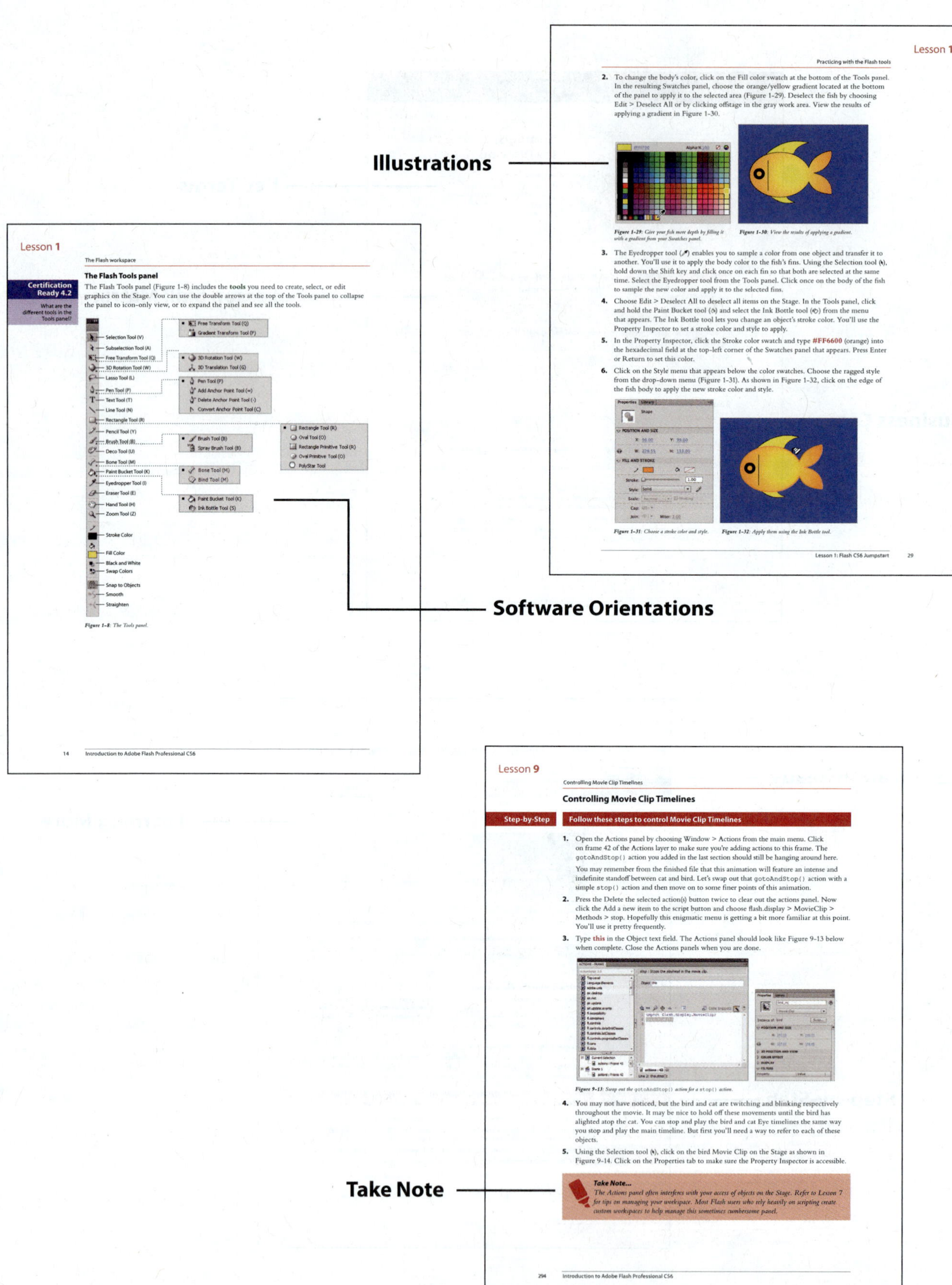

Illustrations

Software Orientations

Take Note

Skill Summary

Knowledge Assessment

True/False

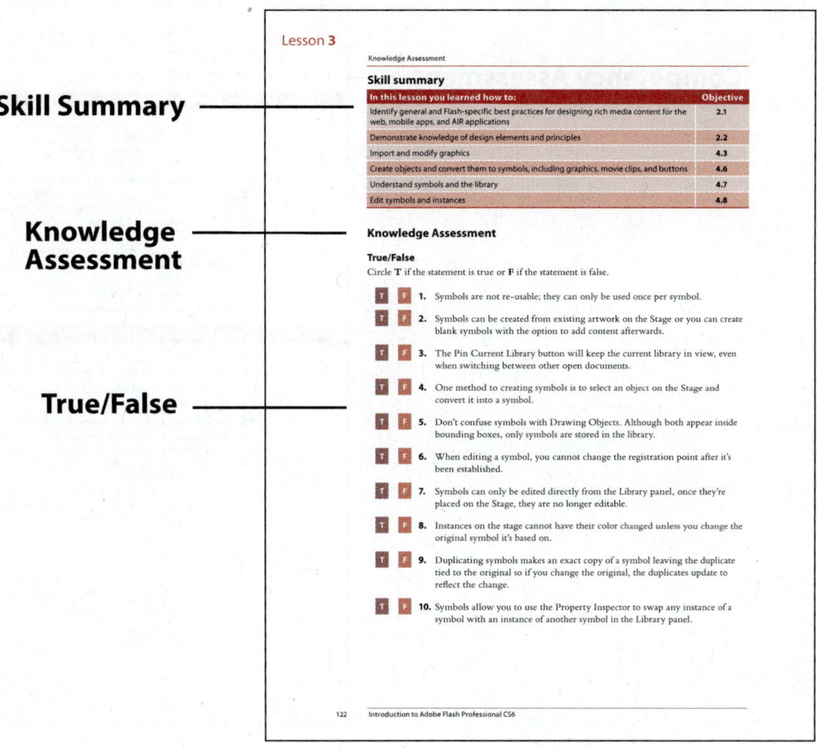

Lesson **3**

Knowledge Assessment

Skill summary

In this lesson you learned how to:	Objective
Identify general and Flash-specific best practices for designing rich media content for the web, mobile apps, and AIR applications	2.1
Demonstrate knowledge of design elements and principles	2.2
Import and modify graphics	4.3
Create objects and convert them to symbols, including graphics, movie clips, and buttons	4.6
Understand symbols and the library	4.7
Edit symbols and instances	4.8

Knowledge Assessment

True/False

Circle **T** if the statement is true or **F** if the statement is false.

1. Symbols are not re-usable; they can only be used once per symbol.

2. Symbols can be created from existing artwork on the Stage or you can create blank symbols with the option to add content afterwards.

3. The Pin Current Library button will keep the current library in view, even when switching between other open documents.

4. One method to creating symbols is to select an object on the Stage and convert it into a symbol.

5. Don't confuse symbols with Drawing Objects. Although both appear inside bounding boxes, only symbols are stored in the library.

6. When editing a symbol, you cannot change the registration point after it's been established.

7. Symbols can only be edited directly from the Library panel, once they're placed on the Stage, they are no longer editable.

8. Instances on the stage cannot have their color changed unless you change the original symbol it's based on.

9. Duplicating symbols makes an exact copy of a symbol leaving the duplicate tied to the original so if you change the original, the duplicates update to reflect the change.

10. Symbols allow you to use the Property Inspector to swap any instance of a symbol with an instance of another symbol in the Library panel.

122   Introduction to Adobe Flash Professional CS6

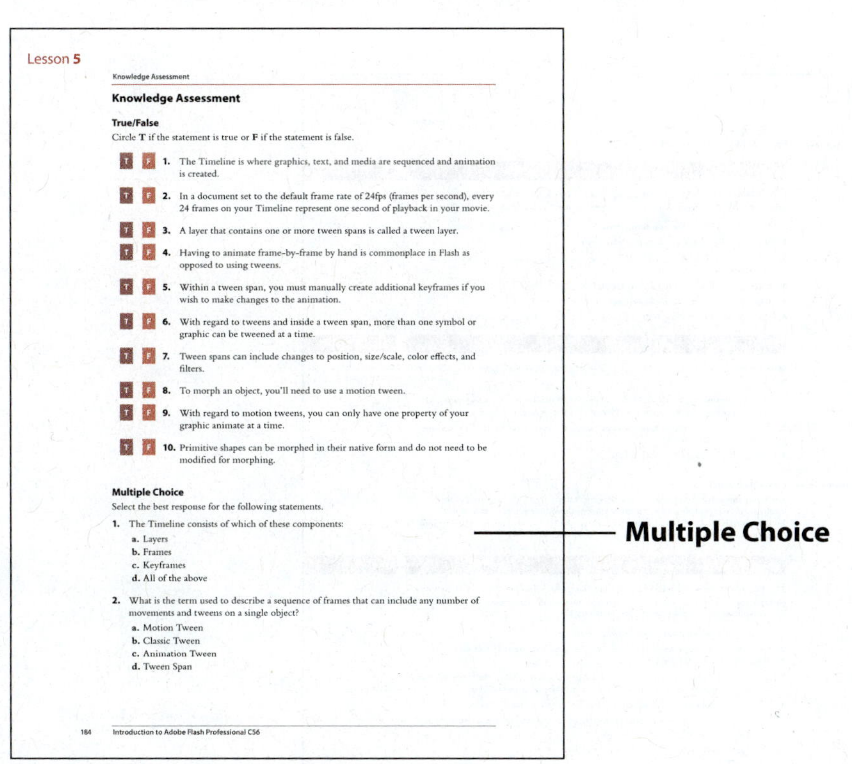

Lesson **5**

Knowledge Assessment

Knowledge Assessment

True/False

Circle **T** if the statement is true or **F** if the statement is false.

1. The Timeline is where graphics, text, and media are sequenced and animation is created.

2. In a document set to the default frame rate of 24fps (frames per second), every 24 frames on your Timeline represent one second of playback in your movie.

3. A layer that contains one or more tween spans is called a tween layer.

4. Having to animate frame-by-frame by hand is commonplace in Flash as opposed to using tweens.

5. Within a tween span, you must manually create additional keyframes if you wish to make changes to the animation.

6. With regard to tweens and inside a tween span, more than one symbol or graphic can be tweened at a time.

7. Tween spans can include changes to position, size/scale, color effects, and filters.

8. To morph an object, you'll need to use a motion tween.

9. With regard to motion tweens, you can only have one property of your graphic animate at a time.

10. Primitive shapes can be morphed in their native form and do not need to be modified for morphing.

Multiple Choice

Select the best response for the following statements.

1. The Timeline consists of which of these components:
  a. Layers
  b. Frames
  c. Keyframes
  d. All of the above

2. What is the term used to describe a sequence of frames that can include any number of movements and tweens on a single object?
  a. Motion Tween
  b. Classic Tween
  c. Animation Tween
  d. Tween Span

184   Introduction to Adobe Flash Professional CS6

Multiple Choice

Illustrated Book Tour

Competency Assessment ————

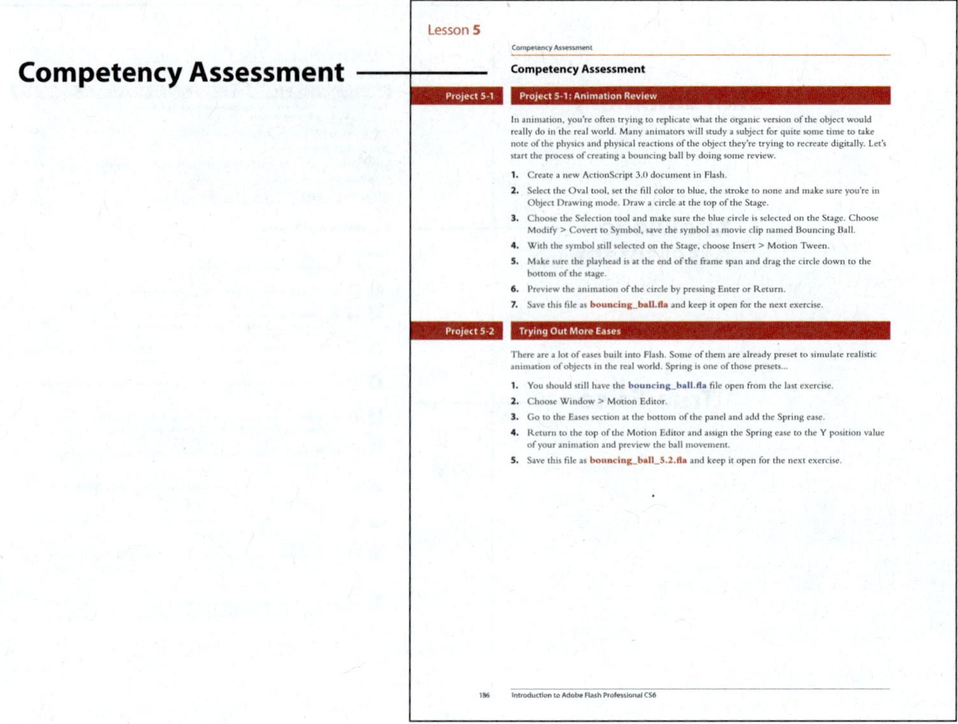

Proficiency Assessment ————

Circling Back ————

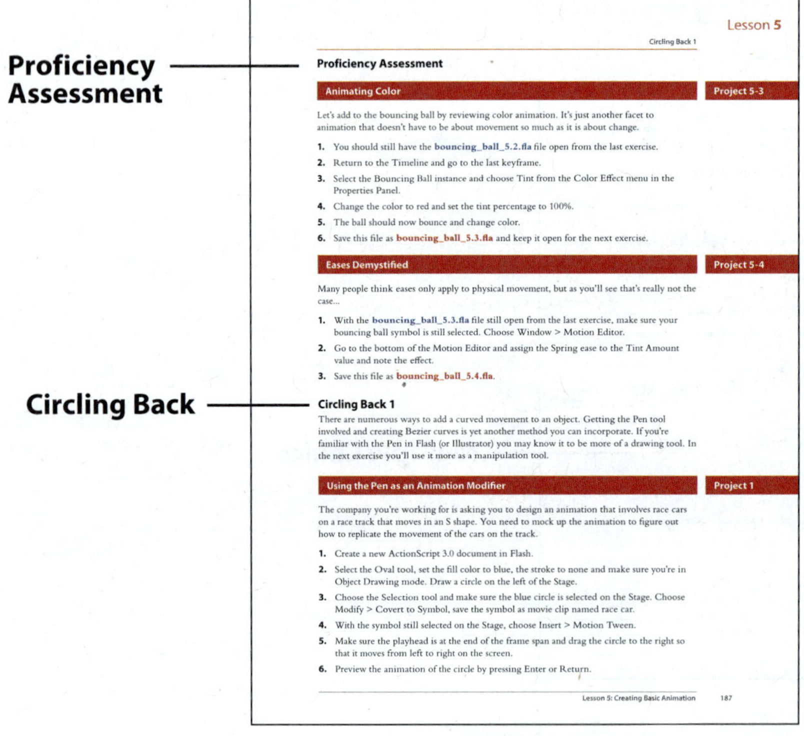

Conventions and Features Used in This Book

This book uses particular fonts, symbols, and heading conventions to highlight important information or to call your attention to special steps. For more information about the features in each lesson, refer to the Illustrated Book Tour section.

File > Open Text separated by the greater than symbol (>) indicates instructions for using a menu to perform a task—with the first item indicating the menu to use and the second item indicating the menu choice. If the menu includes additional choices, more than one greater than symbol will be used to indicate the additional choices, such as File > Open > Recent.

Certification Ready 4.12

What audio file types can be imported for use in a Flash document?

This feature signals the point in the text where a specific certification objective is covered. It provides you with a chance to check your understanding of that particular ACA objective and, if necessary, review the section of the lesson where it is covered.

Take Note reader aids provide helpful hints related to particular tasks or topics. These notes, set in red shaded boxes, provide pointers to information discussed elsewhere in the textbook or describe interesting features that are not directly addressed in the current topic or exercise.

ALT+Tab

A plus sign (+) between two key names means that you must press both keys at the same time. Keys that you are instructed to press in an exercise will appear in the font shown here.

Key Terms

Key terms appear in green.

Type My Name is

Any text you are asked to type on the keyboard appears in red.

fl0102.fla

The names of data files will appear in blue for easy identification.

Instructor Support Program

Wiley's Adobe courseware program is accompanied by a rich array of resources that incorporate the extensive textbook visuals to form a pedagogically cohesive package. These resources provide all the materials instructors need to deploy and deliver their courses. The following resources are available online for download.

- The **Instructor's Guide** contains solutions to all the textbook exercises as well as chapter summaries and lecture notes. The Instructor's Guide and Syllabi for various term lengths are available on the Instructor's Book Companion Site (*http://www.wiley.com/college/sc/adobeseries*).
- The **Solution Files** for all the projects in the book are available online on the Instructor's Book Companion Site (*http://www.wiley.com/college/sc/adobeseries*).
- A complete set of **PowerPoint Presentations** is available on the Instructor's Book Companion Site (*http://www.wiley.com/college/sc/adobeseries*) to enhance classroom presentations. Tailored to the text's topical coverage and the Lesson Skill Matrix, these presentations are designed to convey key Adobe Flash concepts addressed in the text.

  All images from the text are on the Instructor's Book Companion Site (*http://www.wiley.com/college/sc/adobeseries*). You can incorporate them into your PowerPoint presentations or create your own overhead transparencies and handouts.

  By using these visuals in class discussions, you can help focus students' attention on key elements of Flash and help them understand how to use it effectively in the workplace.
- The **Student Data Files** are available online on both the Instructor's Book Companion Site and for students on the Student Book Companion Site.
- To create a complete certification solution, this textbook can be bundled with Adobe **Certified Associate exam vouchers** and/or **ACA practice tests** from Certiport—available as a single bundle from Wiley. Providing your students with the ACA exam voucher is the ultimate workforce preparation.
- When it comes to improving the classroom experience, there is no better source of ideas and inspiration than your fellow colleagues. The **Wiley Faculty Network** connects teachers with technology, facilitates the exchange of best practices, and helps to enhance instructional efficiency and effectiveness. Faculty Network activities include technology training and tutorials, virtual seminars, peer-to-peer exchanges of experiences and ideas, personal consulting, and sharing of resources. For details, visit *www.WhereFacultyConnect.com*.

Wiley Faculty Network

VIDEO TUTORIALS

The *Introduction to Flash Professional CS6* textbook comes with access to approximately two hours of online video tutorials that accompany each lesson in the book. These video tutorials are designed to help your students to better understand certain topics covered within each lesson. The video tutorials do not replace the lessons and only cover select material the authors have selected to enhance the content being covered within the lesson. To obtain access to the video tutorials, go to *http://www.wiley.com/college/sc/adobeseries*.

Important Web Addresses and Phone Numbers

To locate the Wiley Higher Education Rep in your area, go to *www.wiley.com/college*, select Instructors under Resources & Events, and click on the Who's My Rep link, or call our toll-free number: 1+(888) 764-7001 (U.S. and Canada only).

Student Support Program

VIDEO TUTORIALS

Your *Introduction to Flash Professional CS6* textbook comes with access to approximately two hours of online video tutorials that accompany each lesson in the book. These video tutorials are accessible online and are hosted on Wiley's website. To obtain access to the video tutorials, go to *http://www.wiley.com/college/sc/adobeseries.* and search for Introduction to Flash Professional. A broadband Internet connection is required to view the video tutorials.

Book Companion Website

The Students' Book Companion Site for this textbook (*http://www.wiley.com/college/sc/adobeseries*) includes any resources, exercise files, and web links that will be used in conjunction with this course.

Wiley E-Text: Powered by VitalSource

Wiley E-Texts: Powered by VitalSource are innovative, electronic versions of printed textbooks. Students buy the Wiley E-Text for 50% off the U.S. price of the printed text and get the added value of permanence and portability. Wiley E-Texts provide students with numerous additional benefits that are not available with other e-text solutions.

Wiley E-Texts are NOT subscriptions; students download the Wiley E-Text to their computer desktops. Students own the content they buy and keep it for as long as they want. Once a Wiley E-Text is downloaded to the computer desktop, students have instant access to all of the content without being online. Students can also print the sections they prefer to read in hard copy. Students also have access to fully integrated resources within their Wiley E-Text. From highlighting their e-text to taking and sharing notes, students can easily personalize their Wiley E-Text as they are reading or following along in class.

CourseSmart

CourseSmart goes beyond traditional expectations providing instant, online access to the textbooks and course materials you need at a lower cost option. You can save time and hassle with a digital version of this book. The eTextbook option allows you to search for the most relevant content at the very moment you need it. To learn more go to: *www.coursesmart.com.*

WHY ACA CERTIFICATION?

The Adobe Certified Associate (ACA) credential has been upgraded to validate skills with the Adobe Creative Suite 6 system. The ACA certifications target information workers and cover the most popular business applications.

Adobe offers four areas in which to gain certification for entry-level skills: Web Communication using Adobe Dreamweaver, Rich Media Communication using Adobe Flash, Video Communication using Adobe Premiere Pro and Visual Communication using Adobe Photoshop. To learn more about becoming an Adobe Certified Associate and exam availability, visit *www.certiport.com/adobe.*

Preparing to Take an Exam

The workplace demand for digital media skills—creating, managing, integrating, and communicating information by using Adobe's dynamic multimedia, video, graphic, web, or design software—is on the rise. This new certification program will help educators effectively teach and validate digital communications skills while providing students with credentials that demonstrate real-world prowess to prospective employers.

What are the Benefits of Becoming Certified?

By certifying one's skills, individuals can validate their technical abilities and demonstrate proficiency. Adobe's associate-level certifications are based on research about digital communications skills required by industry, government, and education. The objectives reflect the foundation skills needed to be successful communicators in today's digital world.

In educational settings, industry-recognized certification programs ensure students and teachers are acquiring the knowledge and skills valued in today's workplace. For institutions seeking to keep curriculum vitalized and relevant, certification plays a critical role in bridging classroom learning to real-world application.

Preparing to Take an Exam

Unless you are a very experienced user, you will need to use a test preparation course to prepare for the test to complete it correctly and within the time allowed. Wiley's Adobe courseware is designed to prepare you with a strong knowledge of all exam topics. With some additional review and practice on your own, you should feel confident in your ability to pass the appropriate exam.

After you decide which exam to take, review the list of objectives for the exam. This list can be found in Appendix A at the back of this book. You can also easily identify tasks that are included in the objective list by locating the Lesson Skill Matrix at the start of each lesson and the Certification Ready sidebars in the margin of the lessons in this book.

To take the ACA test, visit *www.certiport.com/adobe* to locate your nearest testing center. Then call the testing center directly to schedule your test. The amount of advance notice you should provide will vary for different testing centers, and it typically depends on the number of computers available at the testing center, the number of other testers who have already been scheduled for the day on which you want to take the test, and the number of times per week that the testing center offers ACA testing. In general, you should call to schedule your test at least two weeks prior to the date on which you want to take the test.

When you arrive at the testing center, you might be asked for proof of identity. A driver's license or passport is an acceptable form of identification. If you do not have either of these items of documentation, call your testing center and ask what alternative forms of identification will be accepted. If you are retaking a test, bring your ACA identification number, which will have been given to you when you previously took the test. If you have not prepaid or if your organization has not already arranged to make payment for you, you will need to pay the test-taking fee when you arrive.

Test Format

All ACA certification tests are live, performance-based tests. There are no multiple-choice, true/false, or short-answer questions. Instructions are general: you are told the basic tasks to perform on the computer, but you aren't given any help in figuring out how to perform them. You are not permitted to use reference material other than the application's Help system.

Acknowledgments

Thank you to Nell Hurley, Tacy Trowbridge, Matt Niemitz, and Melissa Jones at Adobe for their encouragement and support in making this textbook the finest instructional materials for mastering the newest Adobe technologies for both students and instructors.

About the Author

Fred Gerantabee is an award winning interactive designer, web developer, and author based in New York City. He is a subject matter expert in Flash and ActionScript, standards-based web development and various scripting languages and platforms. Fred has worked with the AGI team for several years as a contributor to the Digital Classroom series, training events and currently leads the technology initiatives at Grey Worldwide in NYC. Fred is the author of several books in the Digital Classroom series on Flash and Dreamweaver, and co-author with AGI instructors Jennifer Smith and Christopher Smith of the *Creative Suite 6 Design Premium for Dummies*, also published by Wiley.

Starting up

Starting Adobe Flash Professional CS6

As with most software, Adobe Flash Professional CS6 is launched by locating the application in your Programs folder (Windows) or Applications folder (Mac OS). If you are not familiar with starting the program, follow these steps to start the Adobe Flash Professional CS6 application:

Windows

1. Choose Start > All Programs > Adobe Flash Professional CS6.
2. Close the Welcome Screen when it appears. You are now ready to use Adobe Flash Professional CS6.

Mac OS

1. Open the Applications folder, and then open the Adobe Flash CS6 folder.
2. Double-click on the Adobe Flash CS6 application icon.
3. Close the Welcome Screen when it appears. You are now ready to use Adobe Flash Professional CS6.

Menus and commands are identified throughout the book by using the greater-than symbol (>). For example, the command to print a document appears as File > Print.

Resetting the Flash workspace

To make certain that your panels and working environment are consistent, you should reset your workspace at the start of each lesson. To reset your workspace, choose Window > Workspace > Reset 'Essentials.'

Loading lesson files

The *Introduction to Adobe Flash Professional CS6* book includes files that accompany the exercises for each of the lessons. Please review the instructions below on downloading the lesson files to your desktop.

For each lesson in the book, the files are referenced by the file name of each file. The exact location of each file on your computer is not used, as you may have placed the files in a unique location on your hard drive. We suggest placing the lesson files in the My Documents folder (Windows), or at the top level of your hard drive (Mac OS), or on your desktop for easy access.

Copying the lesson files to your hard drive:

1. Use your web browser, navigate to *http://www.wiley.com/college/sc/adobeseries*. Follow the instructions on the web page to download the lesson files to your computer.
2. On your computer, navigate to the location where you downloaded the files and right-click (Windows) the .zip file you downloaded, then choose Extract All or double-click on the .zip file (Mac OS).

Brief Contents

Contents

Lesson 1: Flash CS6 Jumpstart   **1**

Contents

Lesson 3: Using Symbols and the Library   89

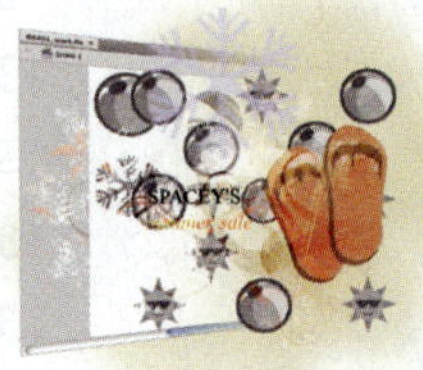

Contents

Lesson 6: Advanced Animation   **189**

Contents

Lesson 7: Customizing Your Workflow **217**

Lesson 8: Working with Imported Files **251**

Lesson 9: Introducing ActionScript   283

Contents

Lesson 12: Introducing Movie Clips   365

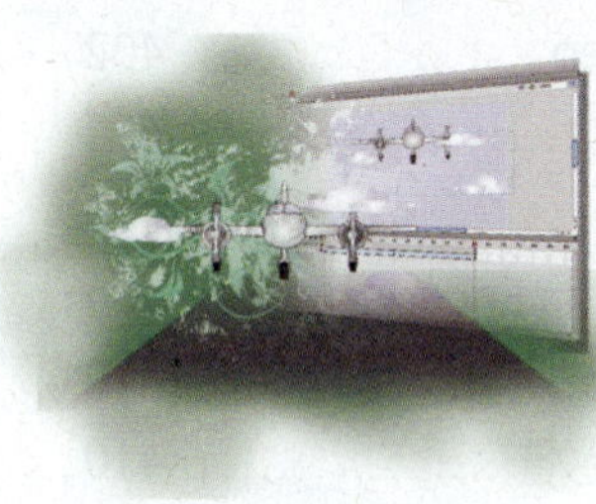

Contents

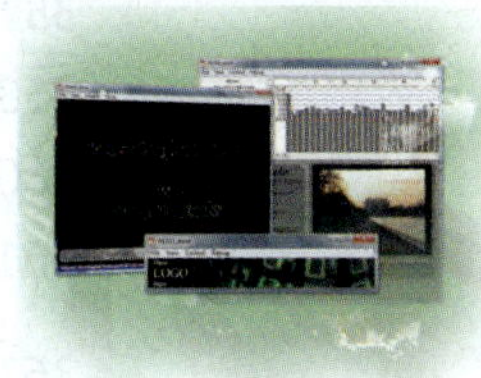

Lesson 14: Delivering Your Final Movie   419

Flash CS6 Jumpstart

Key Terms

- animation
- Flash
- Flash files
- Flash player
- panels
- Property Inspector
- Stage
- Timeline
- tools

Skill	Objective
Identify the purpose, audience, and audience needs for rich media content	1.1
Identify rich media content that is relevant to the purpose of the media in which it will be used (websites, mobile devices, and so on)	1.2
Understand options for producing accessible rich media content	1.3
Understand project management tasks and responsibilities	1.5
Communicate with others (such as peers and clients) about design and content plans	1.6
Identify general and Flash-specific best practices for designing rich media content for the web, mobile apps, and AIR applications	2.1
Use a storyboard to design rich media elements	2.4
Identify elements of the Flash interface	3.1
Use the Property inspector	3.2
Use the Timeline	3.3
Adjust document properties	3.4
Understand Flash file types	3.7
Make rich media content development decisions based on your analysis and interpretation of design specifications	4.1
Use tools on the Tools panel to select, create, and manipulate graphics and text	4.2

Business case

You've been assigned the task of creating a simple animation for a pet shop. The problem is, you're new to Flash and haven't had much time with the program yet. You'll start to explore the basic functions of the program, how to draw, how to do some basic animation and how to manipulate the workspace for your purposes.

Starting up

In this lesson, you will set up a new Flash document and work with several prepared files to explore Flash's tools and features. If you haven't done so already, install Flash Professional CS6 and the Adobe Media Encoder. Instructions for installation, system requirements, and information on how to use lesson files are in the Starting up section of this book.

Before starting, make sure that your tools and panels are consistent by resetting your workspace. See "Resetting the Flash workspace" in the Starting up section of this book.

You will work with several files from the fl01lessons folder in this lesson. Make sure that you have loaded the fllessons folder onto your hard drive from *http://www.wiley.com/college/sc/adobeseries*. See "Loading lesson files" in the Starting up section of this book.

What is Flash?

You may have heard about Flash and seen it on eye-catching websites, online and social games, and banner advertisements. But did you know that you can use **Flash** for more than creating animated graphics? With Flash CS6 Professional, you can also manipulate video and sound, and even connect to databases to build web-based applications, such as shopping carts, or display news feeds of continuously updated information.

There are four key feature areas in Flash CS6 Professional:

Drawing environment. Flash features a complete set of drawing tools to handle intricate illustration and typography. Like its cousin, Adobe Illustrator CS6, Flash is a native vector-drawing application where you'll create rich, detailed, and scalable digital illustrations. Flash supports Illustrator and Photoshop files in their native file formats, .ai and .psd, making it easy to work with your favorite applications. All the content you create in Flash or these other programs can be brought to life through animation and interactivity.

Animation. Flash creates lightweight **animation** that incorporates images, sound, and video, and can be quickly downloaded through the Web. It has become a favorite—and essential—tool among web designers and developers who want to take their creativity to a whole new level. Flash animation is featured on websites and social networks, and is a primary tool for developing interactive, web-based advertisements. Flash's capabilities also extend beyond the Web, with tools and options for creating applications and content for smartphones and tablets, too.

Flash supports traditional frame-by-frame animation as well as its own method of animation, known as tweening (Figure 1-1). With tweening, you specify an object to animate, create starting and ending frames, and Flash automatically creates the frames in between (hence *tween*) to create slick motion, color, and transformation effects. You'll design your own Flash animations in Lesson 5, "Creating Basic Animation."

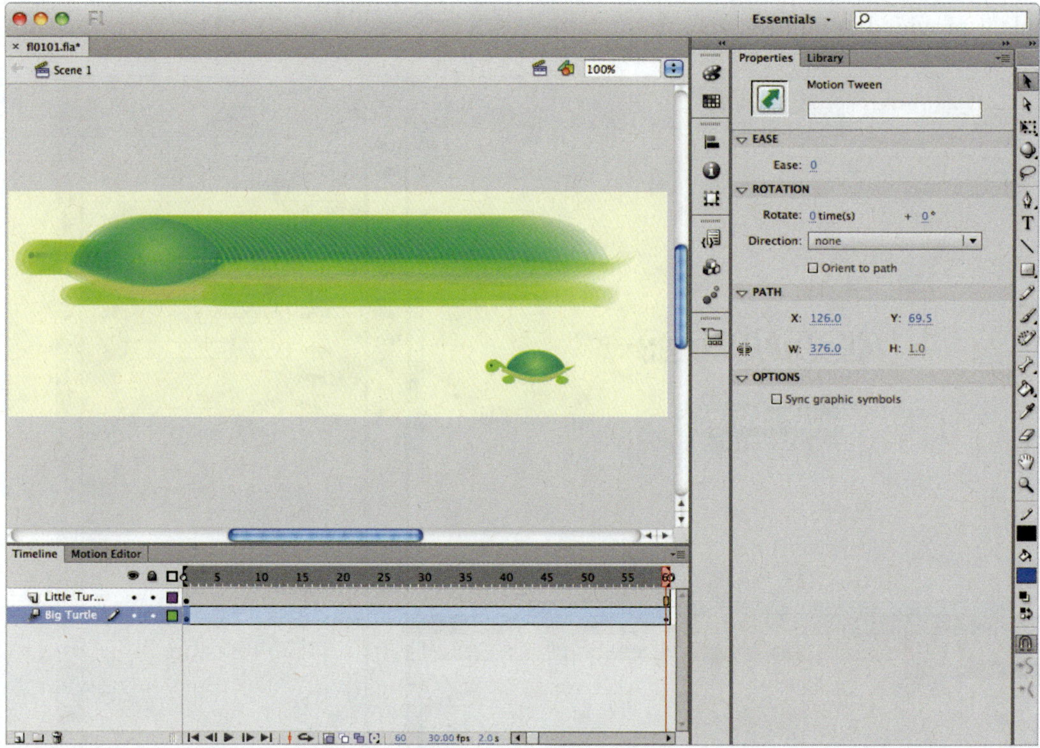

Figure 1-1: Flash's animation tweening easily generates animation between starting and ending frames.

Layout. The Flash stage gives you the flexibility to create extraordinary website layouts limited only by your creativity. You can position content anywhere on the Flash Stage with flexibility and precision, taking your layouts far beyond the "box" often associated with traditional web pages. Flash movies can also include any typefaces you choose, allowing you to use fancy typography and unusual fonts freely on your web pages, which is typically more involved and less consistent outside of Flash.

Programming. Hidden beneath the beauty of Flash Professional CS6 is the brain of ActionScript, a powerful, built-in scripting language that extends your capabilities beyond simple design and animation. With basic ActionScript, which you'll learn about in Lesson 9, "Introducing ActionScript," you can control movie playback or add functionality to buttons. If you venture deeper, ActionScript can turn Flash into a full-fledged, application-building environment to create shopping carts, music players, games, and mobile applications. An example is provided in Figure 1-2.

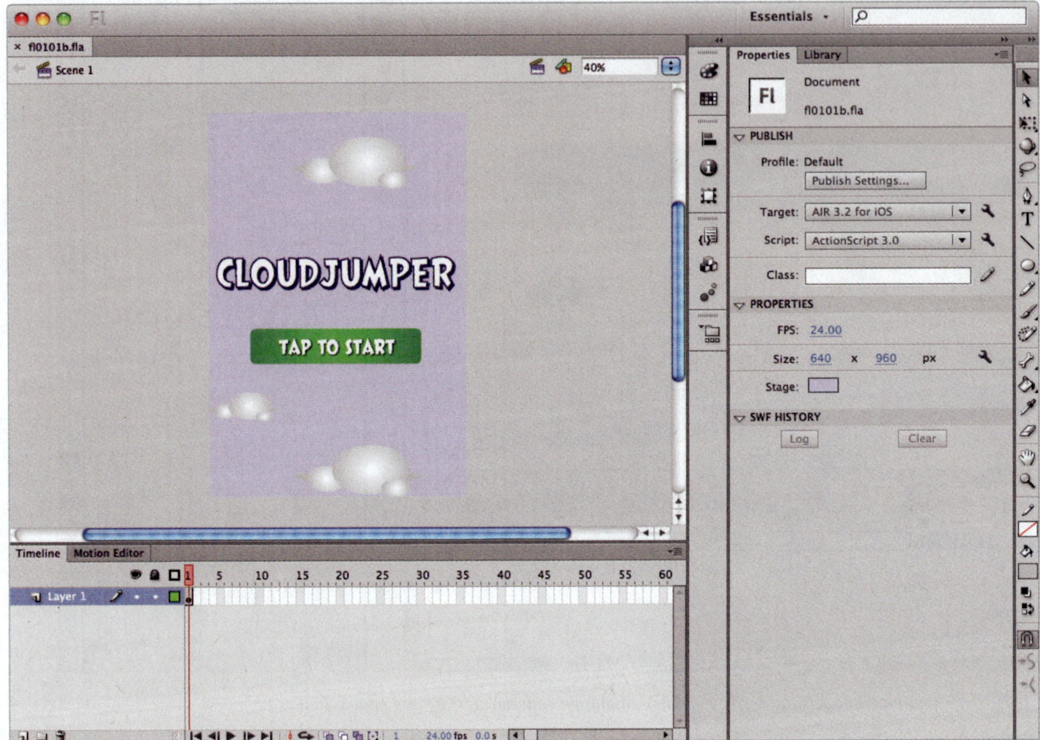

Figure 1-2: Flash can develop lightweight games for the Web and smartphones.

About Flash Player

The **Flash Player** is a stand-alone application found most often as a plug-in to such popular browsers as Internet Explorer, Safari, and Firefox. The Flash Player is required to play compressed Flash movies (.swf files), much like a movie projector is needed to play film reels.

The Flash Player is much more than just a playback machine, however. It is the platform that Flash content runs on and is the engine upon which ActionScript functions so you can incorporate rich interactivity within your movies.

As of this writing, the Flash Player is installed on more than 98 percent of Internet-enabled computers, so a majority of your online audience is already equipped to view your Flash creations. For users who do not have Flash Player installed, it is available as a free download from the Adobe website, *adobe.com*.

Flash Player 11 includes both a stand–alone application and browser plug–in, and is automatically installed with the Flash Professional CS6 application.

For environments where Flash player is not supported (such as on iPhones and iPads), you can publish Flash content as HTML and JavaScript, so it can run in nearly any device or browser.

Flash file types

You will encounter up to four types of **Flash files**: .fla, .xfl, .swf and .html. Each one has a very specific purpose in the process of creating or delivering Flash movies.

Flash work files are generally created and saved in the .fla (Flash authoring) format. These are the working documents you'll use to design, edit, and store resources such as graphics, images, sound, and video. Additionally, each .fla document stores its own unique settings for final publishing. Because they are intended for designing and editing, .fla files can't be viewed with the Flash Player or in a browser—they're only used as the foundation to publish your final movie files in the .swf file format. You can also save source files in the .xfl file format, which allows for open exchange between Flash and other authoring applications. The XFL format is a way to represent a Flash Pro document as an XML-based open folder of files. In Flash CS6, a document still uses the individual files that make up the projects. This offers improved cross-product integration and workflow productivity. If you replace the .fla extension with .zip, you can even unzip the file to view its contents.For nearly all examples in this book, however, it's assumed you are editing and saving to the .fla file format.

"Swiff", or .swf, files are completed, compressed movie files exported from your original .fla authoring files. These are played via the Flash Player in either a browser or your desktop. Although you can import .swf files into the Flash Professional CS6 application, you cannot edit them; you will need to reopen the original .fla files to make changes or additions. You can now also publish your movies to a variety of other formats, including HTML (for display in browsers and devices that don't support the Flash plug-in), AIR (for desktop applications), and popular mobile application formats for iOS and Android devices.

FLV and F4V are Flash video formats that provide a way to present motion graphics in a highly compressed, yet high quality formate for display on the web and within applications.

Now that you know what you're going to be working with, it's time to get your first Flash document started and begin exploring the Flash Professional CS6 workspace.

Take Note...
Another term you may hear when working in Flash is XMP. XMP (Extensible Metadata Platform) is a labeling technology that allows you to embed data about a file, known as metadata, into the file itself. This information can be used to help users find your file when searching on a computer or on the internet

Certification Ready 3.7

What are the differences between the different flash formats?

Certification Ready 3.7

What are the XMP and XFL file types in Flash?

Project Management

As you've read so far, Flash is an incredibly powerful and flexible application that can be used for a variety of different types of projects. Because of this, prior to diving into Flash and creating content, its very important that you determine the needs of the project first.

When developing the project concept, determine the purpose of the project. What is the project itself attempting to do and what are the goals of the client for this project? You'll want to develop a project plan that will identify the purpose and outline the criteria that is relevant to that purpose. The scope of a project plan should include work to be performed and should encompass the clients' expectations including tasks to be performed, due dates for different stages of the project, and resource allocation for the project. It's quite helpful to outline the phases of a project so that the client and the developer can easily measure the project status. Phases of a project plan might include:

- Planning and analysis
- Designing
- Building
- Testing
- Implementation or Launching

Determine your audience. This can often create limitations or open additional possibilities for your project. You need to know who your audience is in order to create a project that suits their needs. Know the age, occupation, gender, education, residence, ethnicity, and computer literacy of your target audience. Also find out if your audience will require that the project be accessible (able to be read on a screen reader by users with visual impairments) as content in Flash that is not made accessible will be unreadable to certain users. Knowing this information will set the project on the right track and create a realistic target for the goals of the project.

Establish deliverables. When working with a client, there will become points during the project in which expectations need to be met and deliverables will need to be presented to the client and in some cases, the client will have deliverables to provide to you. With rich media, content can be affected by end-user technical factors such as the target playback device, screen size and resolution, download speed, browser type, and operating system. Consider all of these factors when producing deliverables to the client. Some examples of deliverables you might be expected to provide could include:

- Storyboards (rough drawings of the stages of the animation for conveying information about the project. These often include animations, transitions, sequencing and timing, navigation, images, text, audio, buttons, interactions, link information, and placement of elements on the stage.)
- Comps
- Sketches
- Flowcharts
- A site map
- Prototypes
- Flash files (.fla or .swf)
- HTML files

During various phases of a project, you'll need to gather feedback on design and content plans from other users such as clients and even peers. You'll want to employ various techniques to obtain this information to stay on track and organized. Some techniques for gathering feedback might include:

- E-mail
- Questionnaires
- Collaborative review of a PDF document
- Meetings (online and in-person)

Finally, during any project you want to focus on keeping the project on task and adhering to the project plan. It's easy for a project to get off course or for the client to request items outside of the scope of the project (scope creep) at different phases of the project. Try to avoid a whimsical or off-the-cuff approach to project management. Adhere to the project plan, make modifications when necessary, but don't let the project go off course as you run the risk of not meeting the original project requirements or the expectations of the client. When making design and development decisions, always keep the end-user requirements in mind.

Creating a new document

Before you can draw or animate, you need to create a new document, or more specifically, an .fla file where all your work takes place. You can create and open documents from the Welcome Screen or from the File menu at the top of the screen.

The Welcome Screen (Figure 1-3) is the launch pad for creating and opening files, including handy, built-in sample templates for common project types, such as Flash movies, advertising banners, and mobile phone application templates. The Welcome Screen appears when Flash is first launched or when no documents are open in the application.

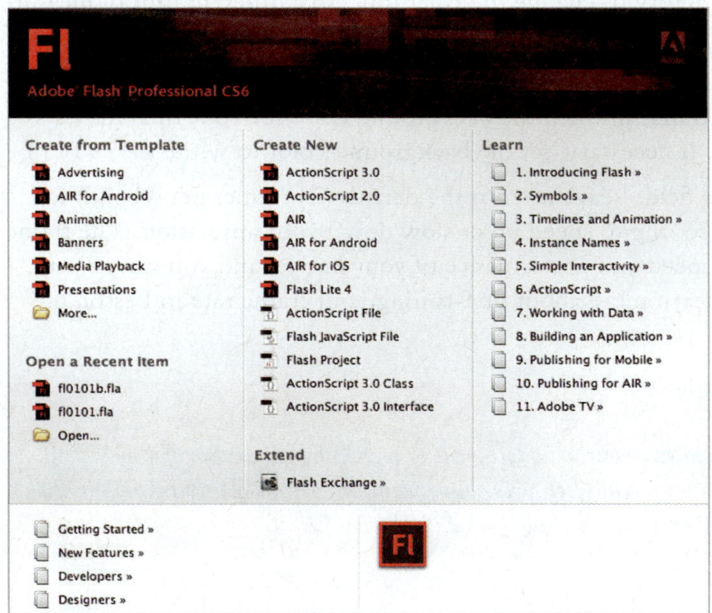

Figure 1-3: *The Welcome Screen is the launch pad for new documents, including many templates for common projects.*

Certification Ready 1.6

What are some techniques for gathering feedback on design and content plans?

Certification Ready 4.1

What is the relationship between end-user requirements and design and development decisions?

Certification Ready 1.5

What are some common problems and issues in project management?

Certification Ready 4.1

What rich content can be affected by end-user technical factors?

Certification Ready 1.3

Why does making content accessible in Flash matter to clients and the target audience?

Creating a new document

Follow these steps to create a new document

1. To create a new .fla document using the Welcome Screen, open Flash CS6 Professional. If the application is already open, close any files that are currently open using File > Close All.

2. From the Create New column in the middle of the Welcome Screen, select ActionScript 3.0. Your workspace, including the Stage, Timeline, and Tools panel, appears.

3. Alternatively, you can create a new .fla document using the File menu. If you already created a new document using the Welcome Screen, this is not necessary.

   To create a new document from the File menu, choose File > New. The New Document dialog box appears. Select ActionScript 3.0, and press OK to create the new document. Your workspace appears.

Setting up your new document

Now that you've created your new Flash file, take a moment to specify some important settings for it. These settings, or properties, will prepare your document before you get to work.

Step-by-Step

Follow these steps to change document settings

Certification Ready 3.3

How do you change the frame rate of a document?

Certification Ready 3.4

Which global settings can be adjusted using the Document Settings dialog box?

Certification Ready 3.4

How can you adjust the document properties?

1. Choose Modify > Document or use the keyboard shortcut Ctrl+J (Windows) or Command+J (Mac OS) to open the Document Settings dialog box. Note that many of the settings in the Document Settings dialog box can also be adjusted in the Properties inspector when nothing is selected on the stage.

2. Under the Dimensions section, locate the (width) and (height) fields and type **500** and **300**, respectively, to set the width and height of your stage in pixels. The size of the Stage is identical to the size of your final movie, so make sure the size accommodates the design you want to create. Note the ability to change the ruler units to a different unit of measure if desired.

3. Click on the Background Color swatch (▢) and the Swatches panel appears. This lets you choose the color of your Stage and, in turn, the background color for your final movie (.swf file) when it's published. If necessary, set the background color to white (#FFFFFF).

4. Note the Frame rate indicator field. Leave it set to the default (24 frames per second) for now but you can change this setting to speed up or slow down your animation. The frame rate determines the playback speed and performance of your movie, and you can adjust it later if you need to. You'll learn more about fine-tuning your frame rate in Lesson 6, "Advanced Animation."

Take Note...

The Match to Printer option sets your new document to match the paper size of your default system printer. This option is typically set to Default, requiring you to specify the width and height, or use the default Dimensions settings stored in Flash.

---

5. From the Ruler units drop-down menu, choose Pixels, if it is not already selected, to define the unit of measurement used throughout your Flash movie, including rulers, panels, and dialog boxes as shown in Figure 1-4.

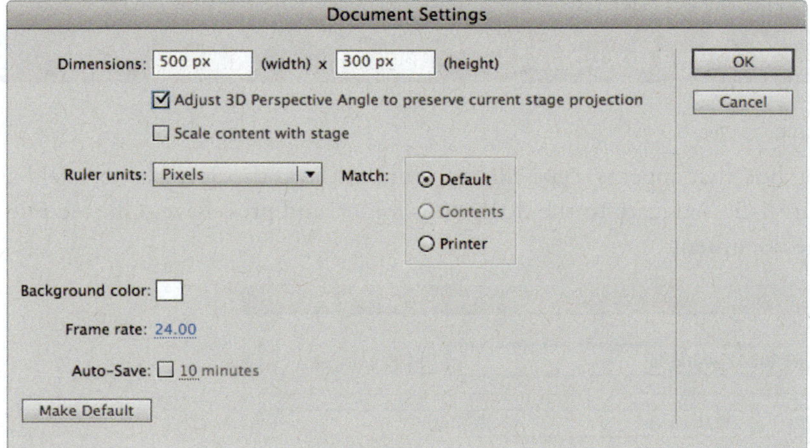

Figure 1-4: Use the Document Settings dialog box to specify settings.

> ### *Take Note...*
> *If you are new to designing for the screen, the concept of pixels may feel a bit alien to you. It helps to remember that there are generally 72 pixels in one inch for size calculation. If you prefer, you can use the Document dialog box at any time to change the Ruler units for your file to a different unit of measurement.*

6. Press OK to exit the Document Settings dialog box and apply these settings. Leave the new document open. You'll save it in the next part of this lesson.

Creating a new document

Saving your Flash document

Your new document should be saved before starting any work or adding any content. By default, the application saves documents in Flash CS6 (.fla) format.

<table>
<tr><td>**Step-by-Step**</td><td>**Follow these steps to save a document**</td></tr>
</table>

1. Choose File > Save.

2. In the Save dialog box that appears, type **fl0101_work.fla** into the Save As text field as displayed in Figure 1–5. Navigate to the fl01lessons folder, and press Save. Choose File > Close to close the document.

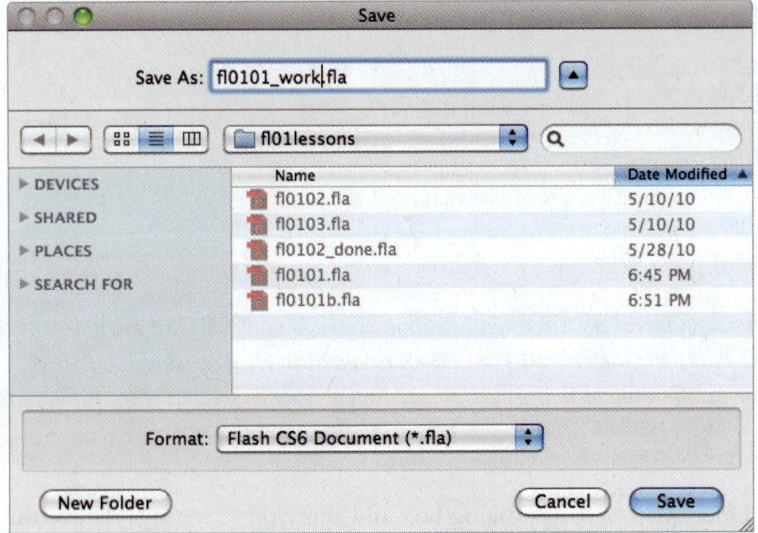

Figure 1–5: Use the Save dialog box to choose a name and location for your new file.

Take Note...
Always include the .fla extension at the end of your filename to make it easy to identify the file format.

To share your work with designers using Flash CS5, you can choose to save your document in Flash CS5 format. Flash Professional CS6 format files will not open in Flash CS5 or earlier. Flash CS6 Professional, however, can open files created in Flash CS5 or earlier.

Get started with sample templates

Flash includes a variety of sample templates to streamline the process of setting up common Flash projects. Creating files from these templates will pre-configure options such as document size and ActionScript version. Choose File > New and click on the Templates tab to view Flash's included templates.

In the Advertising section, templates include common banner sizes. Be aware that creating files from these templates sets the Flash player and ActionScript versions extremely conservatively for maximum compatibility. If you were planning on using the latest and greatest techniques and features in your project, this may be constricting.

New templates have been added for Animation, Banners, and Media Playback, and the Presentations templates have been enhanced for Flash Professional CS6. Sample Files, including animation examples, have been added as well. For more information on these new templates, see Lesson 15, "What's New in Adobe Flash CS6?".

Opening documents

Knowing how to open documents is as important as knowing how to save them. In addition to files created in Flash CS6 Professional, such as those included with this book, you can open documents created in previous versions of Flash. The steps are simple.

Follow these steps to open a document

1. Choose File > Open. Use the Open dialog box to locate the **fl0101_work.fla** file you previously saved into the fl01lessons folder.

2. Select the **fl0101_work.fla** file, then press Open. Leave this file open. You will be using it in the next exercise.

Take Note...
Don't confuse the Open command with the Import options also found in the File menu. To access files created in other applications, such as Photoshop or Illustrator, you must use the Import menu. Importing files from other applications is explored in detail in Lesson 8, "Working with Imported Files."

If you want to reopen a document on which you have recently worked, there's a shortcut. To list the last ten documents you've opened, and to reopen one, choose File > Open Recent, then select the file you need as shown in Figure 1-6.

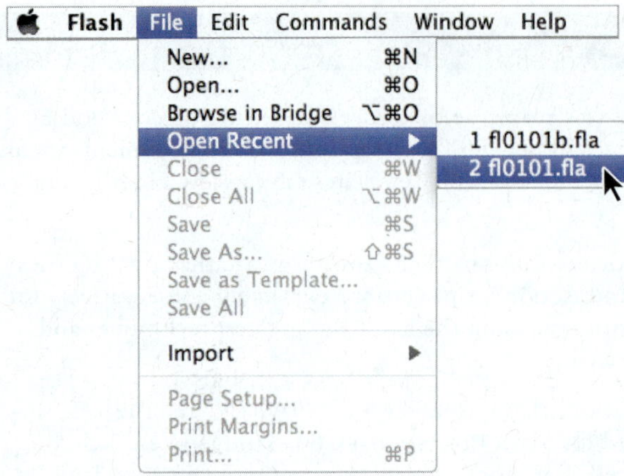

Figure 1-6: Choose File > Open Recent to access the last ten documents opened in Flash.

Take Note...
You can also open files using the Open button (📁) at the bottom of the Open Recent Items column on the Welcome Screen. Above this icon, you'll see the last several documents you worked on; this is a useful alternative to the Open Recent menu option.

The Flash workspace

Now that you know how to create, save, and open Flash documents, you're ready to get familiar with the workspace where you'll spend your time creating Flash content. The workspace is composed of the interface and all of the panels within Flash including but not limited to the Project panel, Tools panel, Timeline, Layers, Properties panel, Library panel, Output panel, Edit bar, Motion editor, and Accesibility panel.

The Stage and work area

After you create a Flash document, the center of your workspace, called the **Stage**, is where the action happens. The Stage is the visible area of your movie, where you place graphics and build animations and is also subdivided by scenes.. By default, the Flash Stage appears white, but, as you saw earlier, you can change its background color from the Document dialog box using the Modify > Document command.

The gray area surrounding the Stage is the *pasteboard*; artwork you place or create here is not included in your final movie. Think of this area as the *backstage*; for instance, you can animate a character to enter from the pasteboard onto the Stage. The pasteboard is also a good place to store objects that are not ready to appear in your movie. The Stage reflects the actual size of the movie you create when it is published. The pasteboard and stage are labeled in Figure 1-7 below.

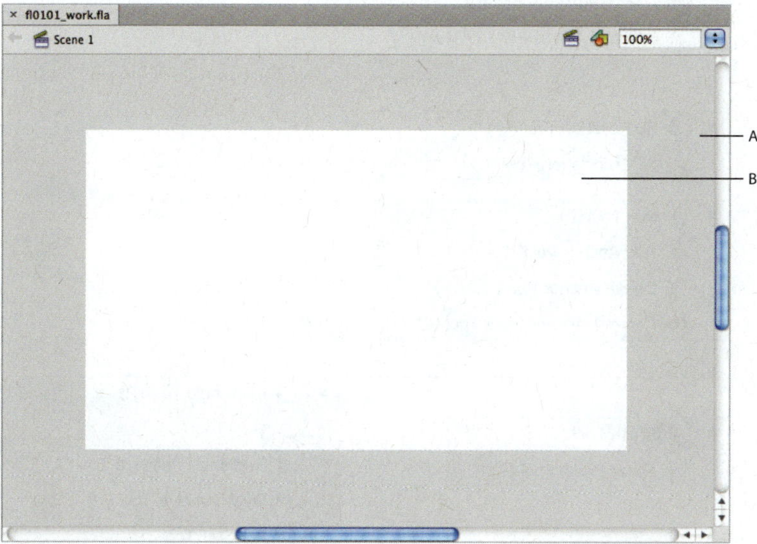

Figure 1-7

A. *Pasteboard.* **B.** *Stage.*

The Flash Tools panel

The Flash Tools panel (Figure 1–8) includes the **tools** you need to create, select, or edit graphics on the Stage. You can use the double arrows at the top of the Tools panel to collapse the panel to icon-only view, or to expand the panel and see all the tools.

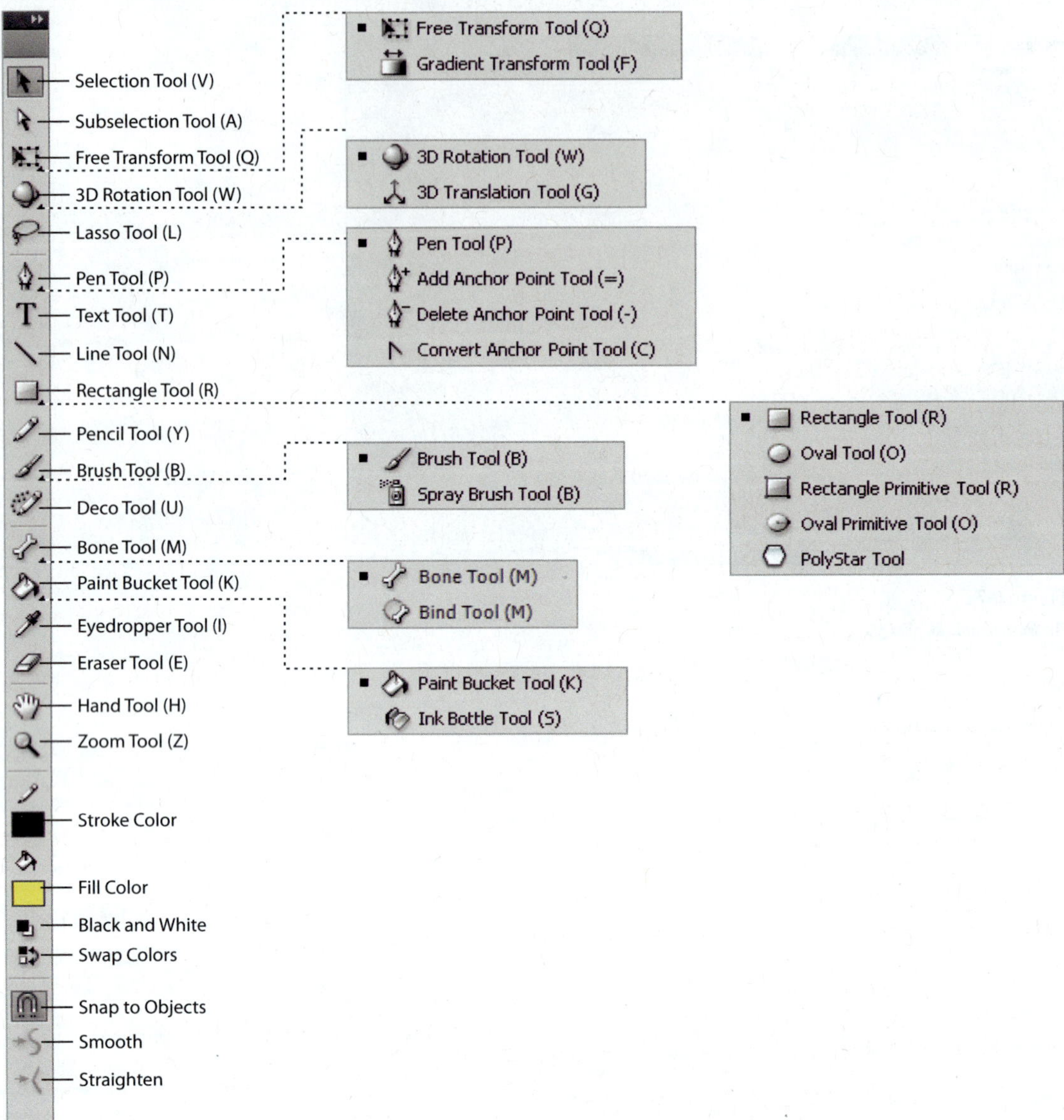

Figure 1–8: *The Tools panel.*

Selection tools

Icon	Tool Name	Use	Where It's Covered
	Selection	Moves selections or layers	Lessons 1, 2
	Subselection	Selects and moves points on a path	Lesson 2
	Free Transform	Resizes, rotates, and skews objects	Lessons 2, 4, 5, 8
	Lasso	Makes selections	Lesson 3
	3D Rotation	Rotates objects in 3D space	Lesson 6

Drawing and Text tools

Icon	Tool Name	Use	Where It's Covered
	Pen	Draws a vector path	Lesson 2
	Text	Creates a text box	Lesson 2
	Line	Draws straight lines	Lesson 2
	Shapes	Draws vector shapes	Lesson 2
	Pencil	Draws freehand paths	Lesson 2
	Brush	Draws freehand filled areas	Lesson 4
	Deco	Creates patterns using symbols	Lesson 4

Color tools

Icon	Tool Name	Use	Where It's Covered
	Ink Bottle	Applies or modifies strokes	Lessons 1, 2, 3
	Paint Bucket	Applies or modifies fills	Lessons 1, 2
	Eyedropper	Samples colors and styles	Lessons 1, 2
	Eraser	Erases artwork	Not referenced in this book
	Bone	Creates Inverse Kinematic objects	Lessons 4, 6

Navigation tools

Icon	Tool Name	Use	Where It's Covered
	Hand	Navigates the page	Lesson 7
	Zoom	Increases or decreases the relative size of the view	Lesson 6

The Flash workspace

Stroke and fill color selectors

Icon	Tool Name	Use	Where It's Covered
	Stroke Color	Selects stroke (outline) color	Lesson 3
	Fill Color	Selects fill (inside) color	Lesson 3
	Default Stroke/Fill	Sets stroke and fill to default colors: black and white	Lesson 3
	Swap Colors	Swaps stroke and fill colors	Lesson 3
	No Color	Sets selected color to none	Lesson 2

Tool options

Icon	Tool Name	Use	Where It's Covered
	Snap to Objects	Enables snapping between objects on the Stage.	Lesson 5

The Property Inspector

By default, the **Property Inspector** appears on the right side of your Flash workspace. Grouped with the Library panel, it displays properties and options for objects selected on the Stage, and also allows you to modify them. The Property Inspector is contextual, and so the information it displays is specific to the tool or object you select.

The Property Inspector is an essential part of the Flash workflow; it can display and set an object's properties, including width, height, position, and fill color for objects such as text, images, links, frames, shapes, actions, symbols, sound, tween, and the document itself. Let's take a look at the Property Inspector in action.

Step-by-Step | **Follow these steps to set an object's properties using the Property Inspector**

1. If the **fl0101_work.fla** file is not still open from the last exercise, choose File > Open to reopen it from inside the fl01lessons folder. Select the Rectangle tool (□) from the Tools panel.

2. At the bottom of the Tools panel, click the Fill Color swatch (⬚). When the Swatches panel appears, choose a yellow shade from the right side of the Swatches panel as shown in Figure 1-9.

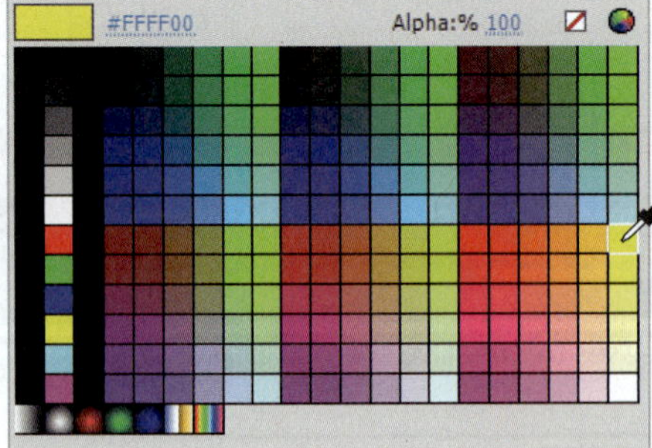

Figure 1-9*: Choose fill and stroke colors using the swatches at the bottom of the Tools panel.*

3. Move your cursor to the center of the Stage. As shown in Figure 1-10, click and hold, then drag to draw a new rectangle. Release the mouse button after you have created a rectangle at the center of the Stage.

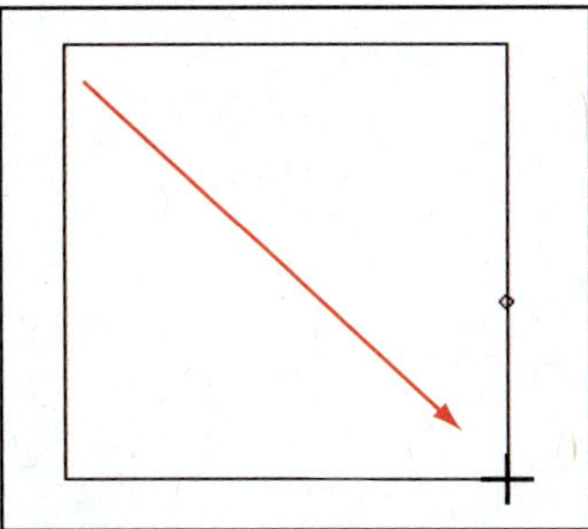

Figure 1-10: To draw shapes on the Stage, select a Shape tool, then click and drag.

4. Choose the Selection tool (▸) from the top of the Tools panel, and double-click the fill of the new shape to select it. If it's not already visible, click on the Property Inspector on the right side of the workspace to open it, and notice that it now displays the selected shape's width (W) and height (H) in pixels. Above the width and height, the object's X and Y positions on the Stage are also displayed.

5. As shown in Figure 1-11, click the underlined number next to W: to highlight the current value, then type **250** to set the rectangle's width. Press Enter (Windows) or Return (Mac OS). Use this same method to set the height to **150**.

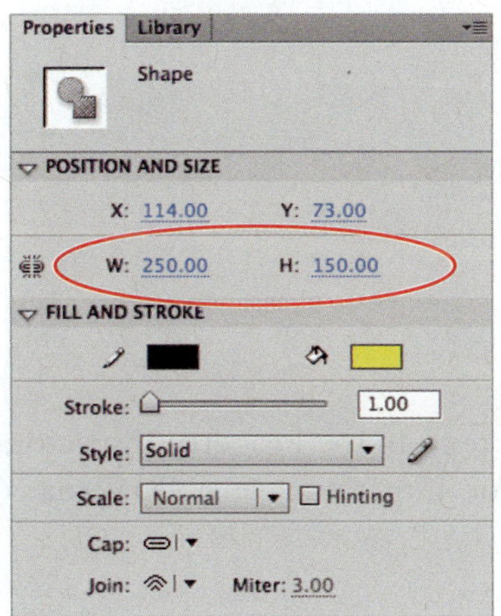

Figure 1-11: You can set properties for a selected shape using the Property Inspector.

6. Choose the Text tool (T) from the Tools panel. Click above the new rectangle you created and type the phrase **Flash CS6**. If it's not already visible, click to open the Property Inspector, and notice that it now displays text options such as font and size (Figure 1-12).

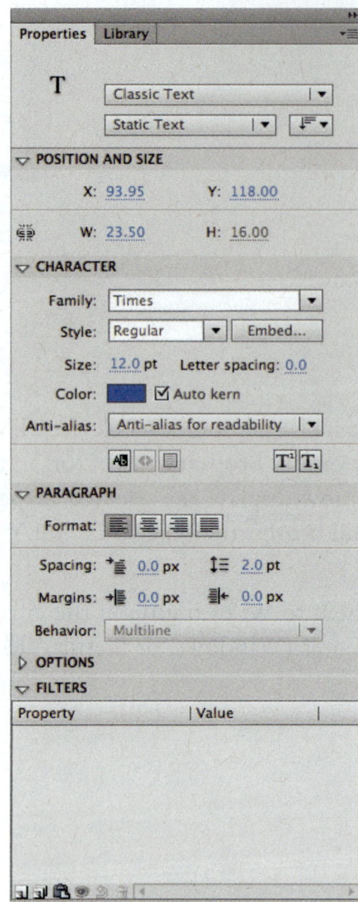

Figure 1-12: *When text is selected, the Property Inspector displays relevant options such as font and size.*

7. Click and drag inside the new text box to select all the text. In the Property Inspector, locate the Family drop-down menu and choose Arial (or, if that's unavailable, Verdana). Click on the Size and set the type size to **45**.

8. In the Property Inspector, click the Color swatch and choose a blue shade from the Swatches panel that appears to change the color of your type (Figure 1–13). In this exercise, the color #000099 was used.

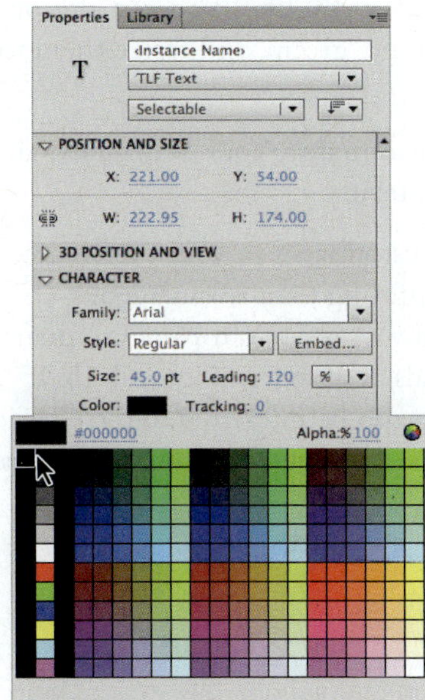

Figure 1–13: Select and format type directly from the Property Inspector.

9. Choose File > Save to save your work, then choose File > Close.

In addition to text and graphics, the Property Inspector also works with the Timeline, allowing you to set options and view information for specific frames (Figure 1–14). You will use this essential tool throughout the lessons to modify objects on the Stage, and frames in the Timeline.

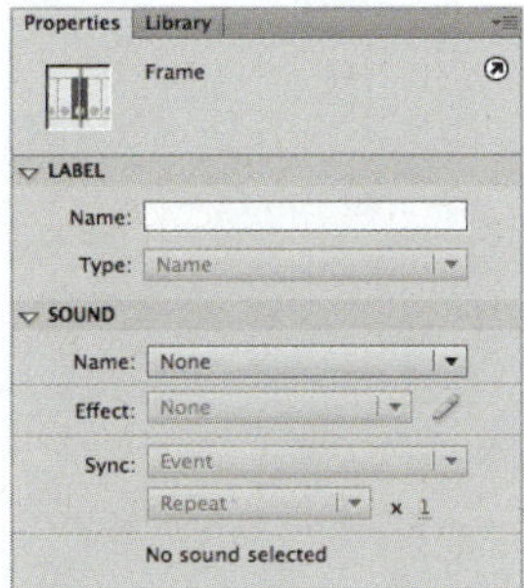

Figure 1–14: The Property Inspector shows options for an active tool or information about a selected object, including the document itself.

Panels and panel groups

The Flash workspace is extremely flexible. It is organized into a series of **panels**, many of which you'll become quite familiar with, including the Library panel, Property Inspector, and Timeline. You're free to arrange any of these panels however you like. You can also open panels that are not available in the default workspace and arrange, group, and resize them to suit your needs.

You'll explore the workspace in more detail in Lesson 7, "Customizing Your Workflow," but there are a couple things that you should be aware of in the interim.

Eventually you'll want to take control of your workspace and customize it to your preference, but for now, the flexibility of the workspace might be more confusing than advantageous. If you mistakenly drag panels around and start losing them, you can always reset your panels to their default positions by choosing Window > Workspace > Essentials as shown in Figure 1-15. If you're migrating to Flash CS6 from an earlier version, you may also be interested in the Classic option found in this menu. For the sake of consistency, this book uses the default CS6 workspace.

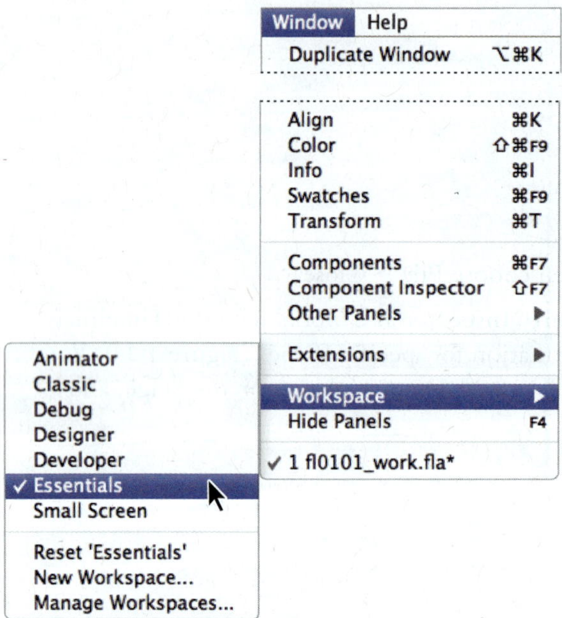

Figure 1-15: Choose Window > Workspace > Essentials, then choose Workspace > Reset 'Essentials' to reset your workspace to the Flash CS6 defaults.

It's also important to note that each panel features a panel menu that can be accessed from the button in the top-right corner as shown in Figure 1-16. This menu contains options that may or may not be available inside the panel. Sometimes this menu is superfluous; sometimes it's integral. Just remember to keep it in the back of your mind. This menu is usually the first place to look if you can't find an option that you're looking for.

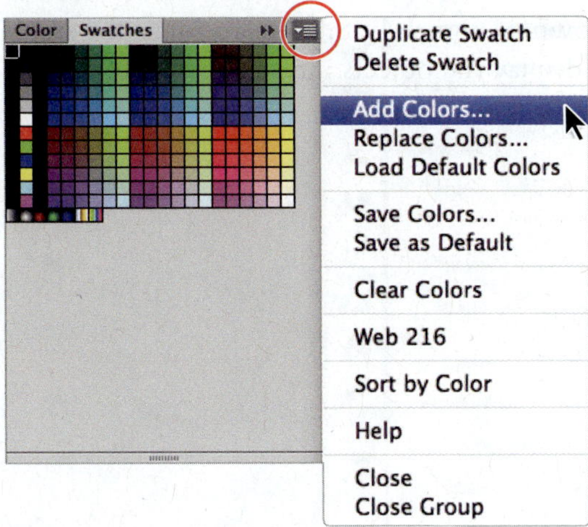

Figure 1-16: Panel menus are accessed using the button in the top-right corner.

The Timeline

The Flash **Timeline** (Figure 1-17) is the heart of the action, where you create animations and sequence graphics with sound, video, and controls. The Timeline comprises frames, each one representing a point in time, just like a historical timeline. Graphics and animations are placed at specific points, or keyframes, along the Timeline to create sequences, slide shows, or movies. You can place ActionScript on individual keyframes to control playback and add interactivity, or place sounds along the Timeline to add sound effects, music, and dialogue.

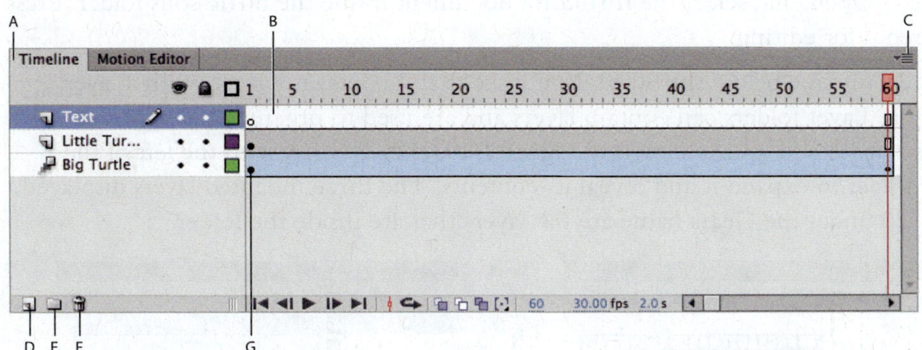

Figure 1-17

A. *Click and drag to undock the Timeline from the document window.* **B.** *Frames.* **C.** *Timeline panel menu.*
D. *Insert Layer.* **E.** *Insert Layer Folder.* **F.** *Delete Layer.* **G.** *Keyframe.*

The Timeline is composed of layers, which behave like transparent pieces of film stacked on top of one another. Each animation and piece of artwork can be placed on its own individual layer, which helps you organize and manage your work. If you've worked with other Adobe CS6 applications, such as Illustrator, Photoshop, or InDesign, you may already be familiar with the power and flexibility of layers.

Like all panels, the Timeline has a panel menu. Most of the options included in the Timeline's panel menu relate to customizing its display. As shown in Figure 1-18, you can adjust the size of layers and frames and turn on Preview mode to display the objects included on each layer as a thumbnail in the Timeline.

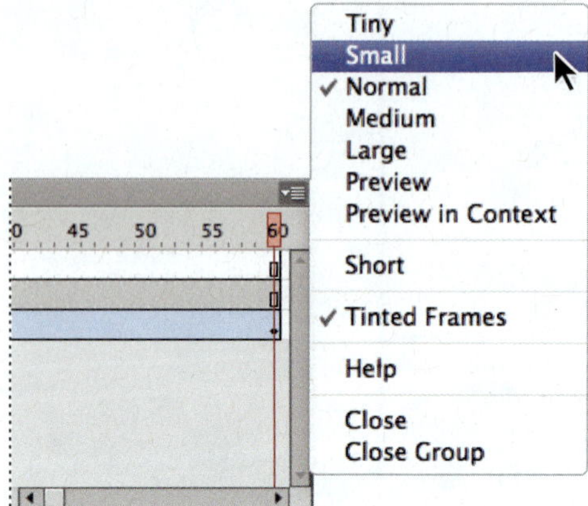

Figure 1-18: *Change the Timeline settings according to how you'd like it to appear.*

In this exercise, you'll explore a Timeline with multiple keyframes, animations, and layers to see how a typical Flash document looks.

Step-by-Step	**Follow these steps to explore the Timeline**

1. Choose File > Open, and select the **fl0103.fla** document inside the fl01lessons folder. Press Open to open it for editing.

2. Examine the Timeline below the Stage. You'll see that it contains a layer, with a layer folder above it. Layer folders can contain layers and are used to organize the Timeline when layers start to add up. As shown in Figure 1-19, click the arrow to the left of the Gears layer folder to expand it and reveal its contents. The three indented layers displayed in Figure 1-20 under the Gears name are the layers that are inside the folder.

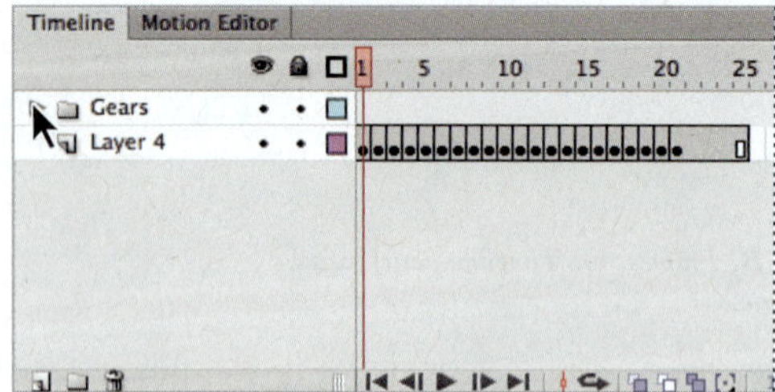

Figure 1-19: *Click the arrow to the left of a layer folder to expand it.*

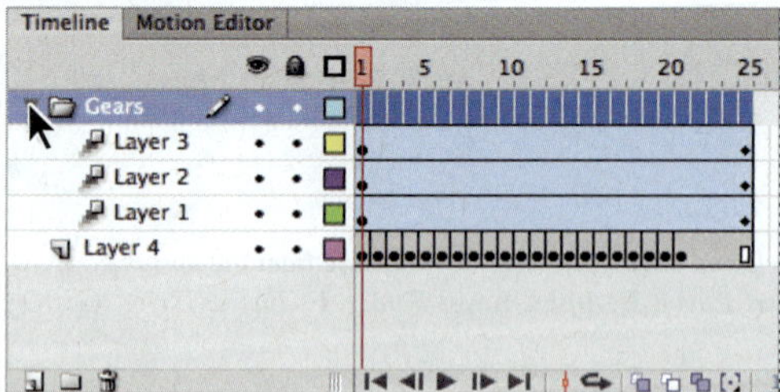

Figure 1-20: *View the layers in the Gears folder.*

3. Each of the three layers contains a separate animation that is marked at the beginning and end with a keyframe. Keyframes are special frames that are created along the Timeline where you want to introduce or remove a graphic, start or end an animation, or trigger something to happen with ActionScript. A blue background on frames indicates a Motion tween animation. Press Enter (Windows) or Return (Mac OS) to play the Timeline.

4. Look at Layer 4 in the Timeline, which contains several consecutive keyframes. Click once on each keyframe to jump to that frame and see what it displays at that specific point in time.

5. To shuttle through the Timeline, grab the playhead at the top (indicated by the red marker), and drag it in either direction as displayed in Figure 1–21.

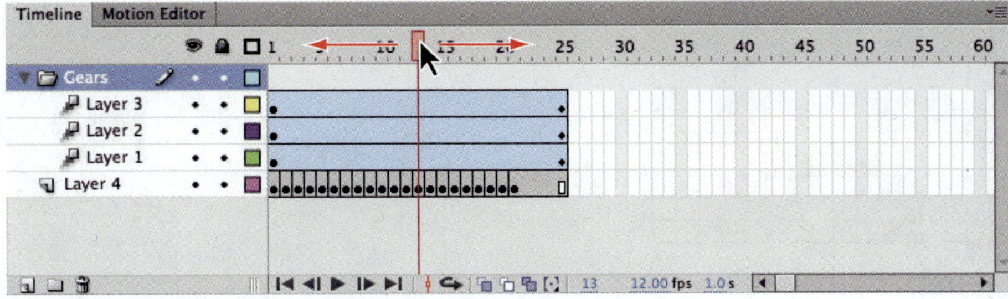

Figure 1–21: Scrub back and forth in the Timeline by dragging the playhead.

6. Choose File > Close to close the current document. If prompted to save any changes, press No (Windows) or Don't Save (Mac OS).

Tabbing between open documents

Learning More

When you have more than one document open at a time, each document displays its own tab at the top of the document window. Click on a document's tab to switch to it and bring it forward for editing (Figure 1-22). To close the active document, you can choose File > Close, or use the small *x* that appears at the top of the document's tab. To close all open documents at once, choose File > Close All.

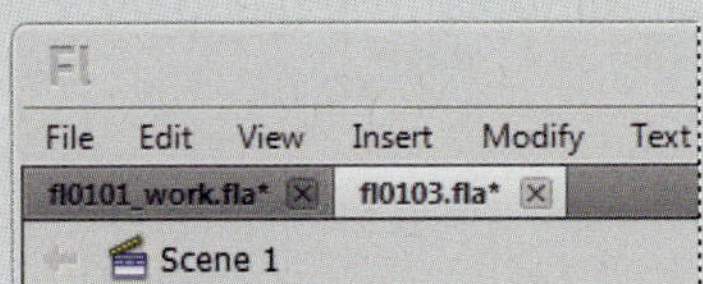

Figure 1–22: Tab easily between multiple documents at one time.

<table>
<tr><td>

</td><td>

The Swatches panel

You'll see the swatch icon (☐) quite a few times in Flash—it opens the Swatches panel, which is used to set colors for backgrounds, fills, outlines, and type. As shown in Figure 1-23, you can choose from over 200 color presets and seven preset gradients, or create your own. Flash also has the ability to show the web-safe color panel that shows the 216 web-safe colors commonly used for older monitors. You will learn how to add your own custom colors and gradients to the Swatches panel in Lesson 2, "Getting Started with the Drawing Tools."

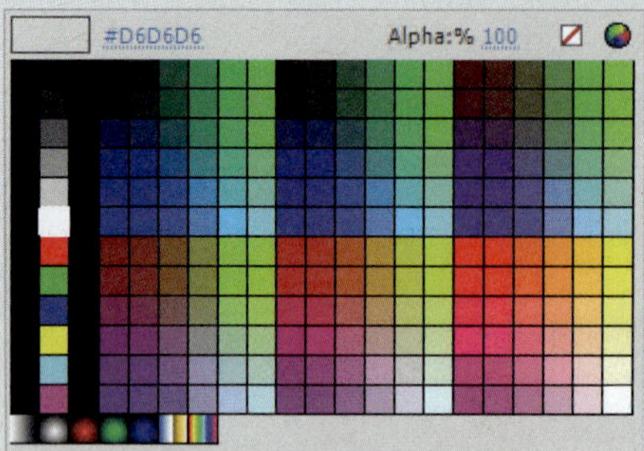

Figure 1-23: *The Flash CS6 Swatches panel.*

The six-character code at the top of the Swatches panel is hexadecimal code, the standard color-coding system for the Web. As you choose colors from the Swatches panel, you'll see the hexadecimal value for the selected color displayed at the top. The Color Picker in Adobe CS6 applications such as Illustrator and Photoshop also features hexadecimal values, so you can easily match colors between applications by copying and pasting the code shown.

</td></tr>
</table>

Practicing with the Flash tools

Now that you've had a tour of the Flash tools and workspace, it's time to take them for a test drive. In the following exercises, you'll complete the illustration shown in **fl0102_fish.fla** while getting the feel for the selection, drawing, and transformation tools. You'll also use Flash tweening to create your first animation.

The drawing and selection tools in action

Your first steps will be to create and modify shapes and freehand artwork with the drawing tools, and then fine-tune your work with the selection tools. The selection tools work as a team with the drawing tools to position and modify shapes, illustrations, and type.

Follow these steps to use the drawing and selection tools

1. Choose File > Open and open the **fl0102.fla** file located in the fl01lessons folder.

2. Choose File > Save As; the Save As dialog box appears. In the Save As text field, type **fl0102_work.fla**, then navigate to the fl01lessons folder and press Save.

3. Choose the Selection tool (⬆) in the Tools panel. This versatile tool can select, move, and manipulate objects directly on the Stage.

4. On the Stage, click once on the fin above the fish's body to select it. As shown in Figure 1-24, click and drag it downward, making sure that the registration circle appears on the lower corner as shown in the image below, until it joins with the body. Release the mouse button.

Figure 1-24: Use the Selection tool to select and move objects on the Stage.

5. You need to make a copy of this fin to use on the bottom of the fish. The easiest way is to clone it, or to drag a copy from the original. To do this, click the top fin once to select it, then, while holding the Alt (Windows) or Option (Mac OS) key, click and drag a copy away from the original fin as shown in Figure 1-25.

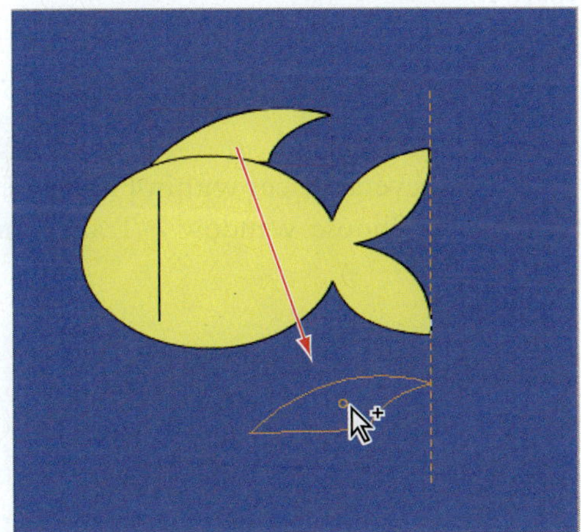

Figure 1-25: Hold down Alt (Windows) or Option (Mac OS) and drag an object to clone it.

6. Because the new copy will serve as the bottom fin, you'll need to flip it around so it's pointed in the proper direction. Click once to select the new fin copy, and as shown in Figure 1-26, choose Modify > Transform > Flip Vertical. This Transform menu command flips the fin so it's pointed in the right direction.

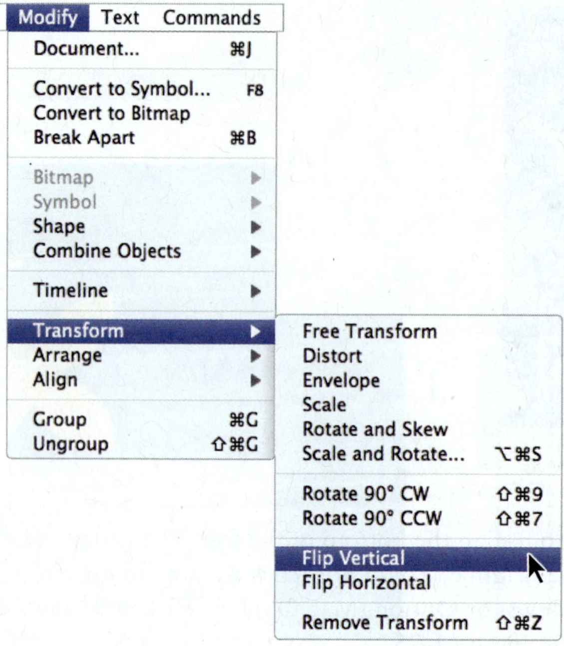

Figure 1-26: The Transform menu features commands that flip, skew, and rotate a selected object.

7. Still using the Selection tool, click and drag the new fin copy to the bottom of the fish's body, and leave it selected.

8. The new fin is almost there, but it's a bit big. There are several places within Flash where you can resize an object, including the Transform panel. Choose Window > Transform to open it.

9. With the new fin selected, type **60** in the horizontal and vertical Scale fields at the top of the panel and press Enter or Return to commit the change (Figure 1-27). The fin is reduced to 60 percent of its original size. If necessary, use the Selection tool to reposition the fin after reducing its size.

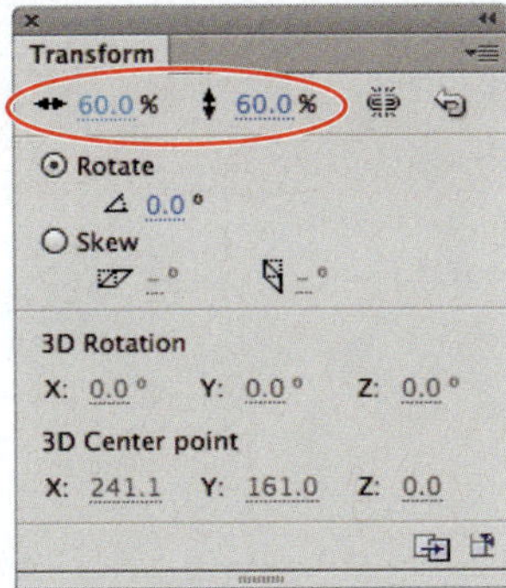

Figure 1-27: *The Transform panel precisely resizes objects by a set percentage.*

Take Note...

Notice the Constrain button (∞) next to the Transform panel's horizontal and vertical scale text fields. When you check this box, you can enter a size in only one field and Flash automatically resizes the selected object proportionally. A Reset button (↻) is also included to allow you to reset the selected object to its original proportions.

10. To add an eye to your fish, select the Oval tool (○) from the Tools panel. You may need to click and hold on the Rectangle tool (□) to access this tool. At the bottom of the Tools panel, click on the Fill color swatch and choose black as the fill color.

11. The Oval Tool Properties let you manipulate shapes even further; here, you'll add an inner radius to ovals to create ring-style shapes. In the Property Inspector, type **50** in the Inner radius text field and press Enter or Return.

12. Select Layer 1 in the Timeline by clicking on the name, and click and drag on the left side of the fish to draw a small oval, which will serve as the fish's eye (Figure 1-28). After you finish drawing the eye, make sure it is de-selected to avoid removing color from the fish below.

Take Note...
To create perfect circles, hold down the Shift key while drawing ovals.

Figure 1-28: *Use the Oval tool with an inner radius to add an eye to your fish.*

Congratulations! You've designed your first graphic object in Flash. However, this fish is rather basic.

Using gradient and color tools

Now you'll add some depth and more vibrant color to your fish, using the gradient colors and artistic stroke styles.

<table>
<tr><td>**Step-by-Step**</td><td>**Follow these steps to use the gradient and color tools**</td></tr>
</table>

1. Choose the Selection tool (⬚) from the Tools panel, and click once inside the body of the fish. A dotted pattern indicates the fill area is selected.

2. To change the body's color, click on the Fill color swatch at the bottom of the Tools panel. In the resulting Swatches panel, choose the orange/yellow gradient located at the bottom of the panel to apply it to the selected area (Figure 1-29). Deselect the fish by choosing Edit > Deselect All or by clicking offstage in the gray work area. View the results of applying a gradient in Figure 1-30.

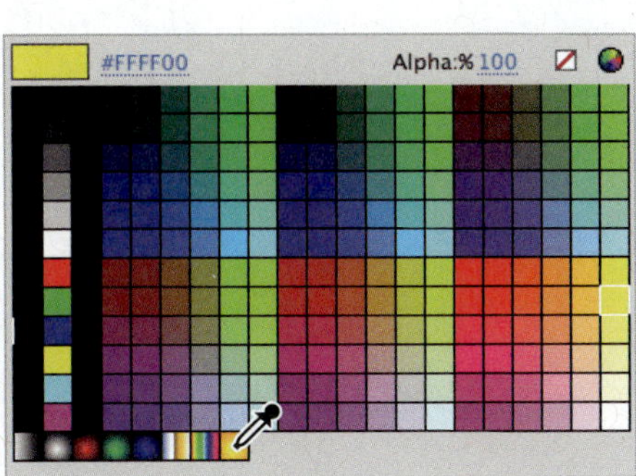

Figure 1-29: Give your fish more depth by filling it with a gradient from your Swatches panel.

Figure 1-30: View the results of applying a gradient.

3. The Eyedropper tool (✐) enables you to sample a color from one object and transfer it to another. You'll use it to apply the body color to the fish's fins. Using the Selection tool (➤), hold down the Shift key and click once on each fin so that both are selected at the same time. Select the Eyedropper tool from the Tools panel. Click once on the body of the fish to sample the new color and apply it to the selected fins.

4. Choose Edit > Deselect All to deselect all items on the Stage. In the Tools panel, click and hold the Paint Bucket tool (⬧) and select the Ink Bottle tool (⬧) from the menu that appears. The Ink Bottle tool lets you change an object's stroke color. You'll use the Property Inspector to set a stroke color and style to apply.

5. In the Property Inspector, click the Stroke color swatch and type **#FF6600** (orange) into the hexadecimal field at the top-left corner of the Swatches panel that appears. Press Enter or Return to set this color.

6. Click on the Style menu that appears below the color swatches. Choose the ragged style from the drop-down menu (Figure 1-31). As shown in Figure 1-32, click on the edge of the fish body to apply the new stroke color and style.

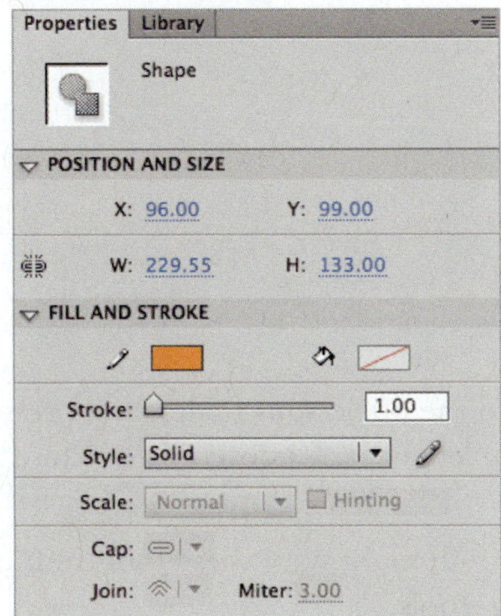

Figure 1-31: Choose a stroke color and style.

Figure 1-32: Apply them using the Ink Bottle tool.

7. Click on the edge of the remaining two fins and the gill line to apply the same color and stroke style to all three. Choose Edit > Deselect All to deselect any active items on the Stage.

8. Choose the Selection tool from the top of the Tools panel. Move the pointer slightly to the right of the gill line without touching it; a small curve appears below your pointer. As shown in Figure 1-33, click and drag slightly to the right to bend the gill line into a curve.

Figure 1-33*: The Selection tool can bend straight lines or distort shapes.*

9. Click the Oval tool (○) in the Tools panel and select the Oval Primitive tool (⊖). Click the Fill color swatch at the bottom of the Tools panel, and choose a light blue color; #6699FF was used in this example. Click the Stroke color swatch and set your stroke color to No color (☒). Set the Inner Radius to **50** in the Property Inspector.

10. While holding down the Shift key, draw several ovals in front of the fish to create bubbles (Figure 1-34).

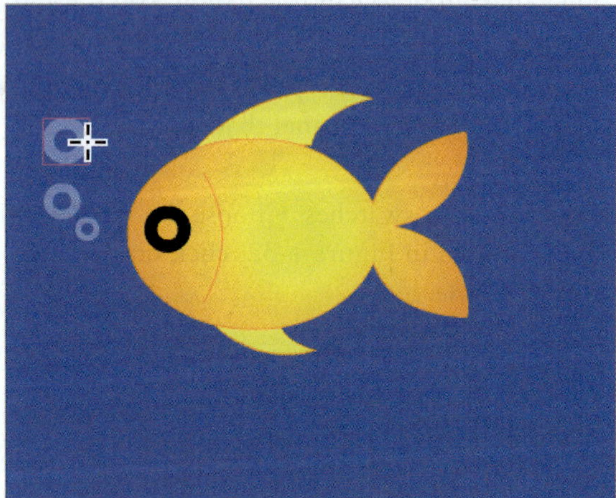

Figure 1-34*: Use the Oval Primitive tool to draw bubbles in front of your fish.*

11. Choose File > Save to save your work.

12. Choose File > Open, select the **fl0102_done.fla** file in the fl01lessons folder, and press Open to open it. Compare your work against the completed file. Choose File > Close All to close all currently open documents.

You're off to a good start with the drawing tools. You will work with these tools in more depth in Lesson 2, "Getting Started with the Drawing Tools."

Animation in action

Flash is known for powerful, yet easy-to-use animation that you create directly in the Timeline. The Timeline displays content over periods of time, represented on the Timeline in frames. Each frame can be set as a keyframe, where items can be placed and animation can start or end.

Flash can generate animation with little more than a starting point and ending point; this method is known as tweening. You tell Flash where you want an object to start and stop its animation, and it figures out the frames in between.

Follow these steps to add animation to an object | **Step-by-Step**

1. Choose File > Open and, when prompted, select the **fl0101.fla** file in the fl01lessons folder. Press Open. Two tortoises appear on the Stage. In the next steps you'll animate the big turtle crossing the Stage.

2. Using the Selection tool (↖), click on the big turtle. Notice that the Big Turtle layer in the Timeline is highlighted in blue, along with the 60 frames included in the Big Turtle layer. Right-click (Windows) or Ctrl+click (Mac OS) on the big turtle and choose Create Motion Tween from the context menu (Figure 1-35).

Figure 1-35: Right-click/Ctrl+click on the Big Turtle and choose Create Motion Tween from the context menu.

Motion tweens allow you to easily create animations by simply adjusting an object's properties at different points on the Timeline. Flash takes care of all the heavy lifting.

3. As shown in Figure 1-36, click and drag the playhead to frame 60.

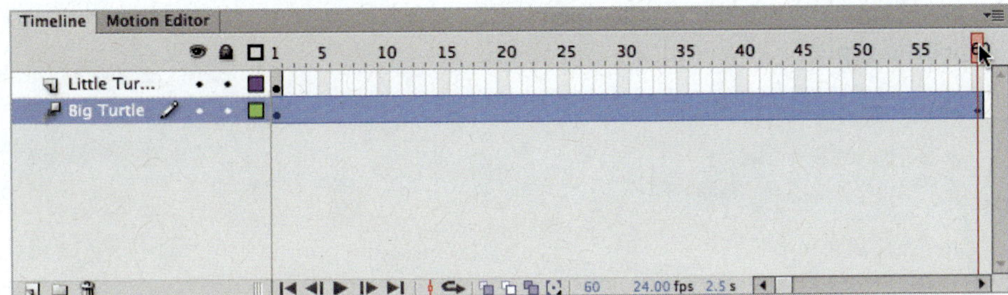

Figure 1-36: Drag the playhead to frame 60.

4. Click and drag the big turtle to the left side of the Stage (just before the head reaches the edge). When you release the mouse, you will see a green motion path appear between his old location and his new one (Figure 1-37).

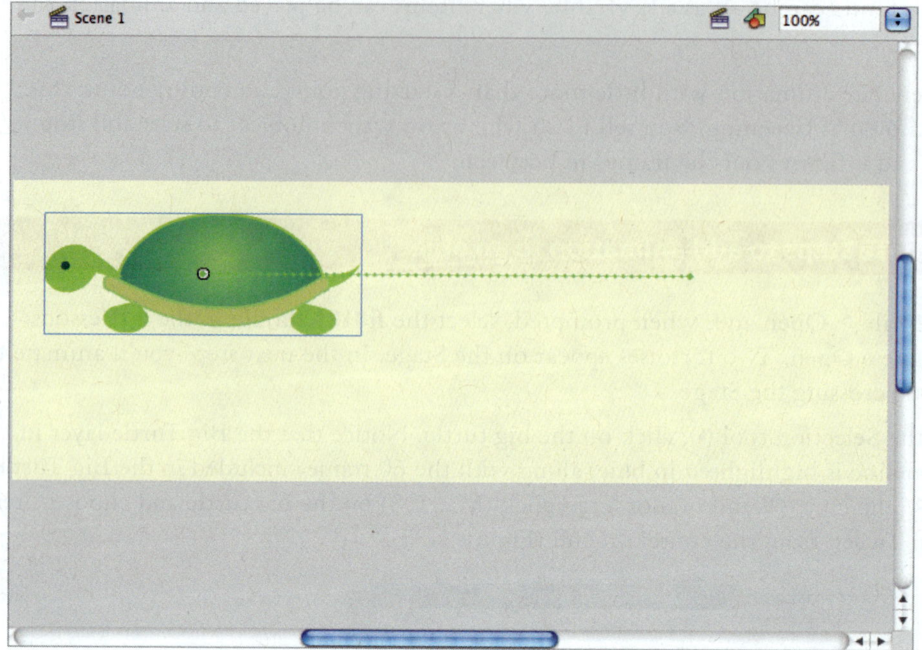

Figure 1-37: *The big turtle repositioned.*

5. Press Enter or Return to preview your first animation. It feels good, doesn't it?

Getting help

If at any point you can't find a specific command, want to know how a tool works, or want to learn how to complete a certain task, you can always consult the Flash Help menu. The Help menu launches the Help viewer (an all-in-one glossary, troubleshooter, and reference manual), and also provides links to key Adobe forums and support centers.

The Flash Help viewer is a good source for quick answers.

Step-by-Step	Follow these steps to learn how to find help using the Help viewer

1. Choose Help > Flash Help.

2. When the panel appears, use the categorized list on the left, or type in a search term to get help on a specific topic or keyword.

Support forums

Adobe's Flash forums can be a rich source of answers, ideas, and tips from experts and other avid Flash users. You can search for answers to common questions or post your own topics and questions.

Follow these steps to learn how to find help using the Flash Support Center

Step-by-Step

1. Choose Help > Flash Support Center. The Support forum launches in your system's default browser.

2. In the search text field in the upper-left corner, enter terms you want to explore, and then press the arrow to the right of the text field to select your desired application from the Adobe Community Help drop-down menu.

3. To post topics, questions, or replies, click the Account menu at the top of the page to log in with your Adobe ID.

Take Note...
You must register to post questions or replies to Adobe's Flash forums.

Moving forward

In the next chapter, you'll put pen to paper (or mouse to Stage, rather) to get your creativity flowing with the Flash drawing tools. Now that you've become familiar with the workspace, things should be just a bit easier. Don't hesitate to reference this chapter again to refresh your memory.

Going beyond Flash with HTML5

Learning More

Many Flash designers are expanding their skills to also include HTML5, CSS3 and JavaScript for building highly interactive web pages and applications. This is especially necessary when targeting content for devices that don't support the Flash plug-in, such as the iPhone, iPad, and Windows Phone, and likely future releases of the Android OS.

Flash will continue to serve as a platform for gaming, video content delivery and web applications. Broadening your skills to include HTML5 and related technologies makes you more versitile as a designer or developer, and allows you to understand how to target your content for a wide range of browsers and devices. As a next step in your learning, after developing skills with Flash, you may want to look the *HTML5 Digital Classroom*, created by the same team that developed the *Flash CS6 Digitial Classroom*.

Skill summary

In this lesson you learned how to:	Objective
Identify the purpose, audience, and audience needs for rich media content	**1.1**
Identify rich media content that is relevant to the purpose of the media in which it will be used (websites, mobile devices, and so on)	**1.2**
Understand options for producing accessible rich media content	**1.3**
Understand project management tasks and responsibilities	**1.5**
Communicate with others (such as peers and clients) about design and content plans	**1.6**
Identify general and Flash-specific best practices for designing rich media content for the web, mobile apps, and AIR applications	**2.1**
Use a storyboard to design rich media elements	**2.4**
Identify elements of the Flash interface	**3.1**
Use the Property inspector	**3.2**
Use the Timeline	**3.3**
Adjust document properties	**3.4**
Understand Flash file types	**3.7**
Make rich media content development decisions based on your analysis and interpretation of design specifications	**4.1**
Use tools on the Tools panel to select, create, and manipulate graphics and text	**4.2**

Knowledge Assessment

True/False

Circle **T** if the statement is true or **F** if the statement is false.

T F 1. Javascript is the name of the built-in scripting language of Flash.

T F 2. Flash Player is installed on more than 98% of Internet-enabled computers.

T F 3. When designing for the screen, the default ruler units are set up to measure in centimeters.

T F 4. If you place artwork in the pasteboard area (but not on the stage), that artwork is not included in your final movie.

T F 5. The Properties panel shows options for an active tool or information about a selected object. This does not include information about the document itself, that is only available through Modify > Document.

T F 6. In the Timeline, each animation and piece of artwork can be placed on its own individual layer, which helps you organize and manage your work.

T F 7. Motion tweens allow you to easily create animations by adjusting an object's properties at different points on the Timeline.

T F 8. The Selection tool can be used to modify the shape of lines and objects simply by hovering over them and clicking and dragging on them.

T F 9. The Ink Bottle tool allows you to change an object's fill color.

T F 10. The Paint Bucket tool allows you to change an object's fill color.

Multiple Choice

Select the best response for the following statements.

1. What is the name of the term used to describe when Flash automatically creates frames in between start and end keyframes to generate an animation?

    a. Keying

    b. Tweening

    c. Keyframing

    d. Auto-animate

2. Which of the following file types is considered the Flash authoring format?

    a. .html

    b. .swf

    c. .fla

    d. .xfl

3. Which of the following file types is considered the completed, compressed final export of your Flash project?

   a. .fla

   b. .xfl

   c. .swf

   d. .html

4. Which of the following is not a setting in the Document Settings window?

   a. Dimensions

   b. Volume control

   c. Ruler units

   d. Frame rate

5. Which panel displays properties and options for objects selected on the Stage and also allows you to modify them?

   a. Info

   b. Library

   c. Properties

   d. Timeline

6. When text is selected on the Stage, which of the following properties is available for modification in the Properties panel?

   a. Position and Size

   b. Character

   c. Paragraph

   d. All of the above

7. Which tool enables you to sample a color from one object and transfer it to another?

   a. Eyedropper

   b. Selection

   c. Free Transform

   d. Subselection

8. Which of the following is not a choice under Modify > Transform >?

   a. Free Transform

   b. Perspective

   c. Rotate and Skew

   d. Flip Vertical

9. What is the name of the line that appears when showing an animated object's starting location and ending location?

   a. Motion path

   b. Animation line

   c. Keyframe path

   d. None of the above

10. #FF6600 is what type of value when it comes to selecting color?

    a. RBG values

    b. CMYK values

    c. Hexadecimal values

    d. HDTV values

Competency Assessment

| **Modifying Your Document** | **Project 1-1** |

Your best course of action is to always know what your output intent is for your project when it's finished. Resizing and changing the Stage after you've got all your elements in place can be quite a pain, so perhaps taking some time to re-familiarize yourself with modifying your Flash project is a good idea to make sure you set everything up the right way the first time.

1. Open Flash.

2. Choose File > New and create a new ActionScript 3.0 document.

3. Set your background color to white.

4. Choose Modify > Document.

5. Set the Stage size to 750 px width and 450 px height.

6. Change the background color to a light-blue.

7. Save the file as **modifying.fla**.

| **New from Template** | **Project 1-2** |

If you're new to creating interactive projects and working with Flash you may be looking for a starting point for your project but are unsure where to start. A nice way to kick things into gear is to examine the templates to get the ball rolling.

1. In the Flash CS6 application, choose File > New.

2. Click on the Templates tab located in the New Document window to start to learn more about the pre-built templates that are at your disposal.

3. Click on the Advertising category, then select the 234 x 60 Half Banner, and click OK. As you can see, the size is preset but can easily be changed if necessary.

4. Save the file as **banner.fla**.

Proficiency Assessment

| **Project 1-3** | **Drawing with Strokes** |

You were briefly introduced to drawing some standard shapes in Flash, now let's have some fun with the Stroke tools.

1. Create a new ActionScript 3.0 document in Flash.

2. Select the Line tool in the Tools panel. Before drawing with it, go to the Properties panel and change its color to blue, the size to 3, and the Style to Dashed.

3. Draw and experiment as you like. Create an interesting design to your liking. Remember that when drawing with this tool, if you hold down the shift key on your keyboard before you draw, it will constrain the line to 45 and 90 degree increments.

4. Save your file as **line.fla**.

| **Project 1-4** | **Workspace Options** |

You're going to get further into configuring your workspace later in this book, but that doesn't mean you shouldn't pick the space that is right for you along the way.

1. Create a new ActionScript 3.0 document in Flash.

2. Go to Window > Workspace and start to take a look at each of the workspace configurations that Flash has available.

3. Modify the workspace extensively. Don't be afraid, you can easily undo it by choosing another workspace and choosing reset workspace.

4. Once you've modified the workspace to your liking, choose Window > Workspace > New Workspace and save the workspace as **Project 1-4**.

Getting Started with the Drawing Tools

Key Terms

- Anchor Points
- Combine Objects
- Drawing Objects
- gradient
- layers
- Line tool
- Merge Drawing
- Pen tool
- transform

Skill	Objective
Identify general and Flash-specific techniques to create rich media elements that are accessible and readable	**2.3**
Organize a Flash document	**2.5**
Use the Timeline	**3.3**
Use tools on the Tools panel to select, create, and manipulate graphics and text	**4.2**
Import and modify graphics	**4.3**
Create text	**4.4**
Adjust text properties	**4.5**
Conduct basic technical tests	**5.1**

Business case

There's an animated fish cartoon series that you need to create for a client's website. Your artwork is supposed to look more like a cartoon than the real thing. It will be important for you to learn how to draw artwork from scratch in order to create your own characters for the cartoon as well as the underwater environment for the fish to live in.

Starting up

Before starting, make sure that your tools and panels are consistent by resetting your workspace. See "Resetting the Flash workspace" in the Starting up section of this book.

You will work with several files from the fl02lessons folder in this lesson. Make sure that you have loaded the fllessons folder onto your hard drive from *http://www.wiley.com/college/sc/adobeseries*. See "Loading lesson files" in the Starting up section of this book.

Drawing in Flash

Adobe Flash Professional CS6 has many powerful tools to help you create vector-based shapes, paths, colors and patterns. Although Flash can work with pixel or bitmap images, the drawing tools in Flash create vector-based artwork that are much more flexible to work with. Whatever you create with the drawing tools can then be animated using the Timeline. Tools used for drawing and creating shapes in Flash include Rectangle, Oval, Primitive shapes, Line, Pen, Pencil, PolyStar, 3D Rotation and Translation, Bone, and Bind. The Deco tool includes drawing effects such as Particle System, 3D Brush, Decorated Brush, Grid Fill, Tree Brush, Lightening brush, and Building Brush. In this lesson, you will experiment with two different drawing models that you can use to create artwork in Flash: the Merge Drawing mode and the Object Drawing mode.

Using the Merge Drawing mode

The default mode is the Merge Drawing mode. At first, this mode may be difficult for new users to grasp, especially those already familiar with the drawing tools in Adobe Illustrator. In this lesson, however, you'll see how the Merge Drawing mode offers some unique benefits over traditional drawing tool behaviors. To view the finished project as shown in Figure 2–1, choose File > Open within Flash CS6. In the Open dialog box, navigate to the fl02lessons folder and select the file, **fl0202_done.fla**, then press Open. Keep this file open for reference or choose File > Close to close the file.

Figure 2–1: *The finished project.*

Creating artwork in Merged Drawing mode

In **Merge Drawing** mode, shapes can be easily torn apart like clay—strokes can be separated from fills (and vice versa) and you can create partial selections to break up your shapes even further. Most importantly, two shapes drawn in this mode will automatically merge when they overlap, making it easy to create complex combined shapes. Mergeable artwork is easily distinguishable on the Stage by its stippled (dotted) appearance.

You'll first get familiar with how this unique mode behaves before diving into a more complex drawing lesson.

Follow these steps to create artwork in Merged Drawing mode

Step-by-Step

1. Launch Flash CS6 Professional, if it is not already open.

2. Choose File > Open and navigate to the fl02lessons folder that you copied onto your computer. Select and open the file named **fl0201.fla**. You'll start your artwork off with a basic shape drawn in Merge Drawing mode. First, you'll need to make sure you're in the right drawing mode.

3. As shown in Figure 2-2, select the Oval tool (○) from the Flash Tools panel. This tool is grouped with the other shape tools, and you may need to click and hold down the mouse button on currently selected shape tool to select it.

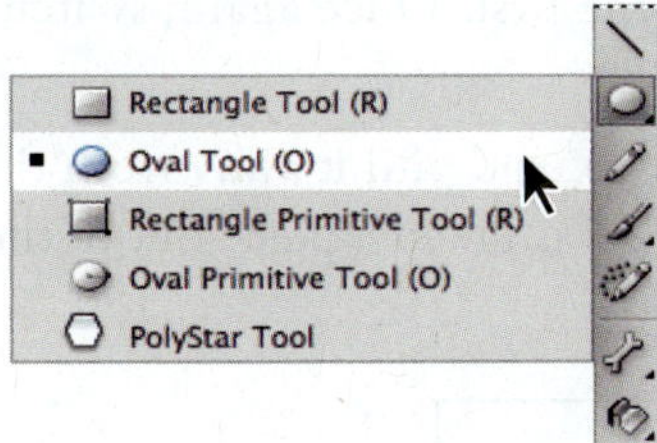

Figure 2-2: Click your mouse button to reveal more shape tools under the Rectangle tool.

4. At the bottom of the Flash Tools panel, locate the Object Drawing button (◎) and make sure it's *not* selected. This button controls whether or not you're drawing in Merge or Object Drawing mode. When selected, the button appears shaded.

5. Next, you'll choose your fill (inside) and stroke (outline) colors. At the bottom of the Flash Tools panel, locate the color swatch marked with a pencil icon (✐) and click it. The Swatches panel appears—select black as your stroke color. Below it, click the color swatch marked with a paint bucket icon (⬧)—from the Swatches panel, select a light orange for your fill color. Click the Reset button at the bottom of the Property Inspector to make sure the Oval Options are all set at 0.

6. Click and drag in the middle of your Stage to draw an oval—once you're satisfied with the size and shape, release the mouse button. Switch to your Selection tool (▶) at the top of the Tools panel; this tool allows you to select, move, and manipulate items on the Stage.

7. Click once on the fill (inside) area of your shape and the fill becomes selected without the stroke (outline). Double-click the fill, and both the stroke and fill become selected. You can now move or manipulate the shape as one whole object. Deselect the shape by clicking on the Stage.

8. Off to the upper-left corner, click and drag to create a marquee (selection area) shown in Figure 2-3, and release it once it partially overlaps your new shape. You'll notice that the shape becomes partially selected; you can now use the Selection tool (k) to click and drag the selected portion away from the rest (Figure 2-4).

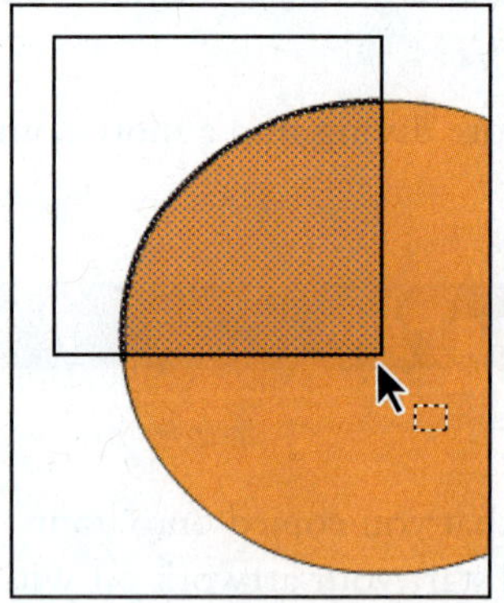
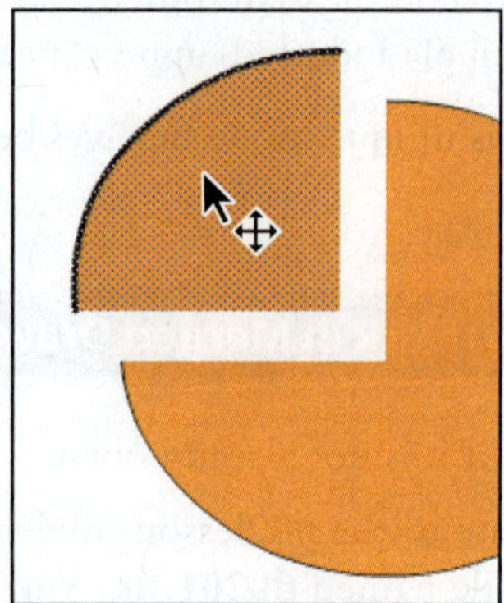

Figure 2-3: Create a marquee in the top-left corner of object.

Figure 2-4: Using the selection tool, click and drag selection away from the original object.

9. Next, you'll draw a new shape that overlaps the current one. Reselect the Oval tool (○) from the Tools panel on the right. You can leave your current color settings the same. Click and drag to draw a new shape that partially overlaps the first. Once again, switch to the Selection tool.

10. Double-click the fill of the new shape to select it (Figure 2-5), and pull it away from the existing one. You'll notice in Figure 2-6 that the new shape has taken a piece out of the old one where the two overlapped!

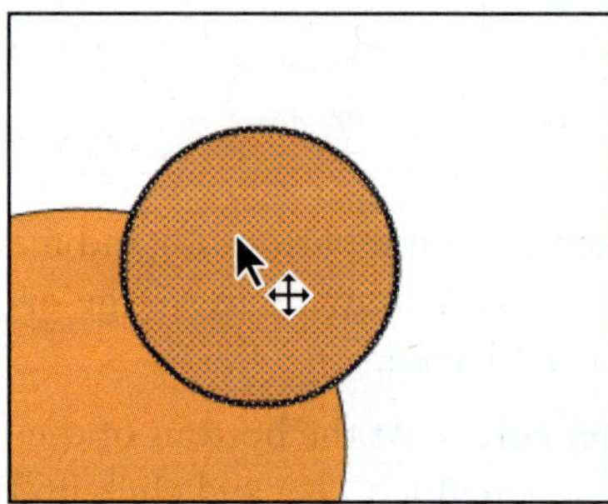
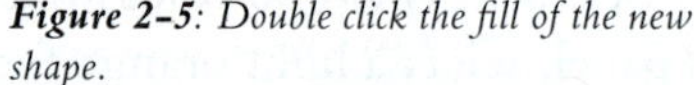
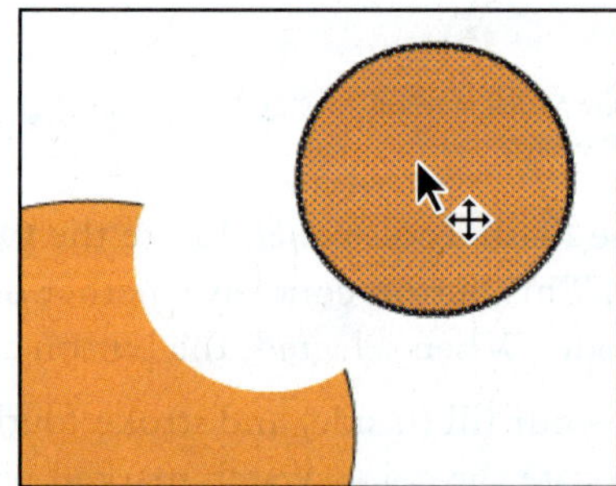

Figure 2-5: Double click the fill of the new shape.

Figure 2-6: Dragging it away from existing shape shows the new shape took a piece out.

11. Choose File > Save As. In the Save As dialog box, navigate to the fl02lessons folder, then type **fl0201_work.fla** into the Save As text field. Press Save.

Learning More	**Keeping panels open**

As a default, Flash collapses panels after it thinks you are done working with them.

You may find this to be inconvenient if you will be frequently using a panel. To have your panels remain open, choose Flash > Preferences (Mac) or Edit > Preferences (Windows) then uncheck the Auto-Collapse Icon Panels option.

Working with Drawing Objects

In contrast to artwork created in Merge Drawing mode (referred to simply as *shapes*), Object Drawing mode provides more rigid control over artwork created on the Stage. Much like drawing shapes in Illustrator CS6, shapes drawn in this mode group their stroke and fill together to avoid separation, and so partial selections are prevented. **Drawing Objects** give you the ability to stack and arrange shapes within a single layer, providing a deeper level of ordering amongst multiple pieces of artwork.

<table>
<tr><td>**Follow these steps to work with Drawing Objects**</td><td>**Step-by-Step**</td></tr>
</table>

1. Select a green shade from the Fill color swatch on the Tools panel. Click and hold your mouse button on the Oval tool (○) to reveal the other shape tools, and select the Polystar tool (⬠).

2. Locate the Object Drawing button (◉) at the bottom of the Tools panel, and click to select it. The button should be pressed in at this point, indicating that Object Drawing mode is enabled.

3. Click and drag to draw a new polygon on the Stage. As shown in Figure 2-7, you'll notice the shape appears inside a bounding box. Switch to the Selection tool (➤) and choose Edit > Deselect All.

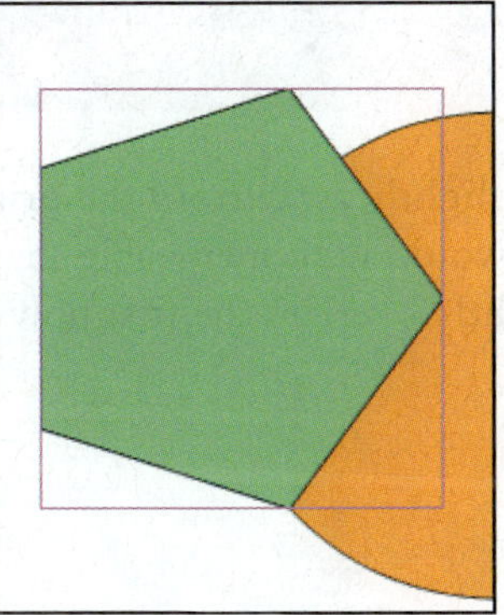

Figure 2-7: Drawing Objects appear inside of bounding boxes, and their strokes and fills can't be separated.

4. If you click once on the fill or stroke of the shape, the bounding box around the entire shape appears selected. Click and drag to draw a selection area (marquee) around part of the polygon, and you'll see that partial selections also result in the entire shape becoming selected.

5. Double-click the fill of the shape (Figure 2-8)—you'll be brought inside the Drawing Object to edit its contents. Interestingly enough, the contents of the Drawing Object are simply the same, mergeable shapes you worked with in the last lesson. You can think of a Drawing Object as a container around a mergeable shape that keeps its parts grouped together.

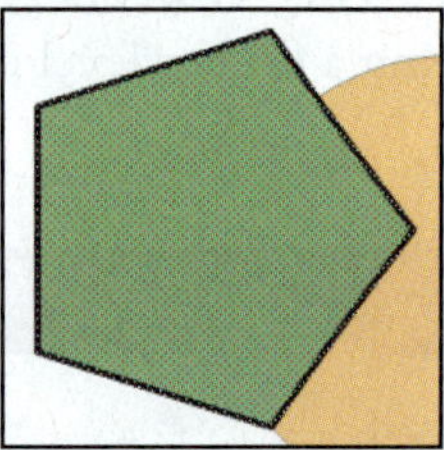

Figure 2-8: Double-click inside the Drawing Object.

6. Exit the Drawing Object by double-clicking on the Stage. Once again, return to the Tools panel and select the Polystar tool (○). Click and drag to draw another shape on the Stage that overlaps the polygon you drew in Step 3.

> ***Take Note...***
> *You can also exit a Drawing Object's Edit mode using the links shown above the Stage. Click on the Scene 1 link to return to the main Timeline, and you should no longer see the words Drawing Object appear to its right.*

7. Choose the Selection tool and select the new shape. Pull it slightly away from the original shape—you'll notice the two shapes did not merge as they would with mergeable shapes. Leave the new shape selected and make sure that it still slightly overlaps the first polystar.

8. Next, you'll see how Drawing Objects can be meticulously stacked and arranged, even on the same Timeline layer. With the new shape selected, choose Modify > Arrange > Send to Back (Figure 2-9). As shown in Figure 2-10, the new shape is pushed behind the first. The Arrange menu allows you to restack Drawing Objects, groups, and symbols. Symbols are covered in more detail in Lesson 3, "Using Symbols and the Library."

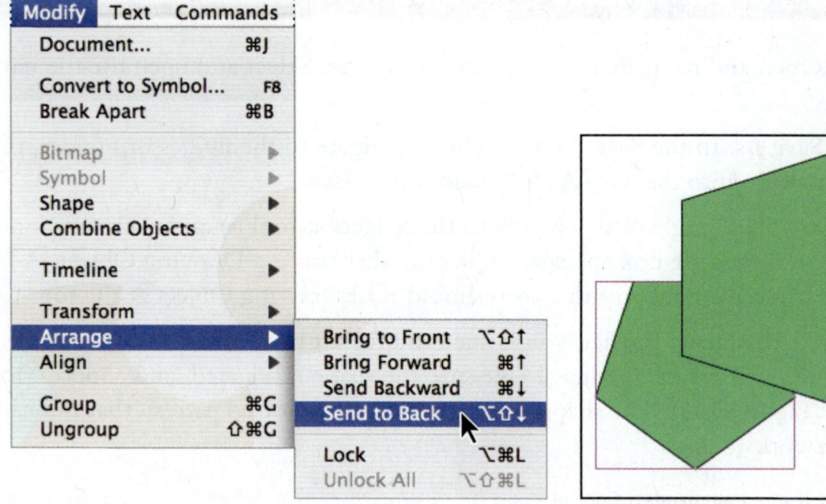

Figure 2-9: *Choose Modify > Arrange > Send to Back.*

Figure 2-10: *View the results of moving the selected object to the back.*

Take Note...
Mergeable shapes always fall below Drawing Objects, groups, or symbols on the Stage. To have a mergeable shape appear above other items, you need to place it on its own layer and move that layer to the top of the stack.

9. Choose File > Save, then choose File > Close.

Putting it all together

Now that you have a feel for how the two drawing modes work, you'll complete a piece of artwork using your new skills and become familiar with additional drawing tools.

Step-by-Step

Follow these steps to create and modify shapes

1. Choose File > Open and navigate to the fl02lessons folder. Select and open the file named **fl0202.fla**.

2. Choose File > Save As. In the Save As dialog box, navigate to the fl02lessons folder, then type **fl0202_work.fla** into the Save As text field. Press Save.

3. On the Stage, you see a single oval—switch to the Selection tool (✹) and click once on the oval to select it. A bounding box appears, indicating that this is a Drawing Object. A look at the Property Inspector confirms this, as it should read Drawing Object at the top.

4. In order to dissect this shape further, you'll need to break it back down to a mergeable shape like the ones you created earlier. Make sure the shape is selected, and choose Modify > Break Apart (Figure 2-11). The shape now appears with a dotted pattern that indicates it is mergeable artwork.

Figure 2-11: *The Break Apart command allows you to break any artwork down to its next most basic form.*

5. Deselect the oval shape by clicking on the pasteboard or a different area of the Stage. To create the mouth of your fish, click and drag with your Selection tool to create a partial selection that overlaps the left edge of the oval, as illustrated in Figure 2-12. Delete the selected portion by using the Backspace (Windows) or Delete (Mac OS) key (Figure 2-13). With mergeable shapes, you can delete partial selections to dissect shapes in unusual ways.

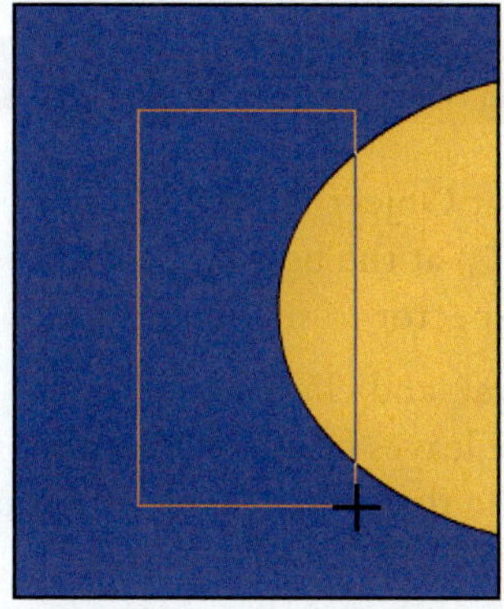 

Figure 2-12: *Create a partial selection that overlaps with the left edge.*   **Figure 2-13**: *Delete this portion.*

6. With the Selection tool active, move your cursor close to the open-ended stroke at the top of the oval. When an L-shaped angle icon (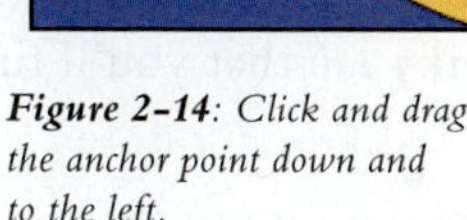) appears below your pointer, click and drag the anchor point down and to the left as shown in Figure 2-14

7. Continue using the Selection tool to click and drag the bottom anchor point up to meet the first anchor point as shown below.

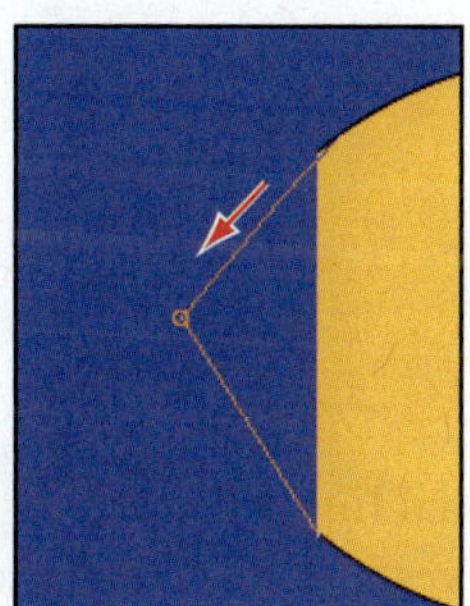 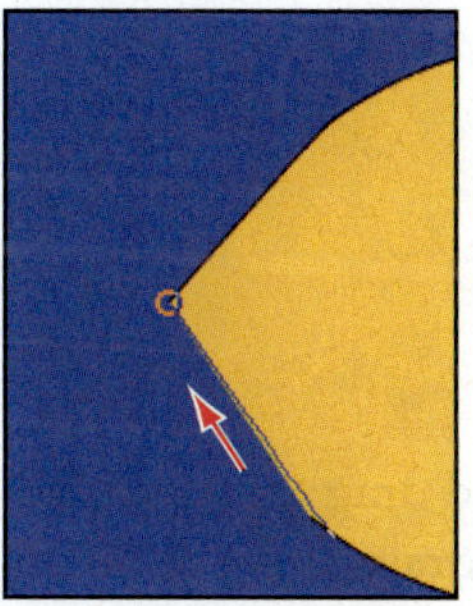

Figure 2-14: *Click and drag the anchor point down and to the left.*   **Figure 2-15**: *Click and drag the bottom anchor point up to meet the first.*

8. Choose File > Save to save your file.

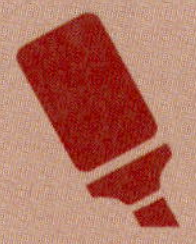

Take Note...

Paths on mergeable shapes automatically join when Snap to Objects is enabled. Snap to Objects can be enabled using View > Snapping > Snap to Objects, or by using the Snap to Objects button (⋒) at the bottom of the Tools panel.

Using the Line tool

Most illustration programs have a Line tool, and while it's not the most creative tool in the box, you can use Flash's Selection tool to make it more useful. Flash's **Line tool** allows users to draw straight lines in any number of directions.In the following steps, you'll form the tail of your fish using a few simple moves.

| Step-by-Step | Follow these steps to use the Line tool |

1. Select the Line tool (\) from the Tools panel. Make sure that Object Drawing mode is disabled (if necessary, deselect the Object Drawing button (◯) at the bottom of the Tools panel). Select Solid from the style menu on the Property Inspector to set a solid line.

2. Move your crosshair cursor close to the right edge of the oval, and click and drag to draw an upward diagonal line. Starting where your first line leaves off, click and drag to draw a second line that meets the oval again below where the first line began as shown in Figure 2-16.

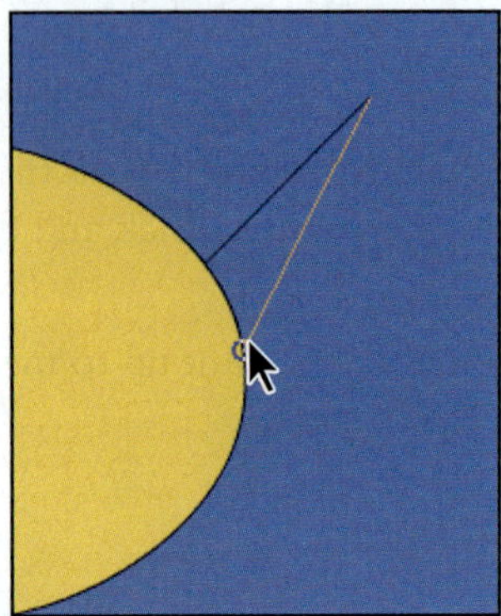

Figure 2-16: With Snap to Object enabled and Object Drawing disabled, diagonal lines automatically join if drawn close enough together.

3. Where the last line meets the oval, click and drag to draw a diagonal line moving downward. As you did in step 2, click and drag where the line leaves off to draw a second line that meets the oval again. These steps should have formed a spiky *tail* that you'll fine-tune in the next steps.

4. To change this from a spiky tail to a rounded, more appropriate one, you'll use the Selection tool. Choose the Selection tool (⬆), and move your cursor toward the middle of the first diagonal line you created. Once you are close enough, a curved icon appears (⬆) below your pointer. Click and drag upward to bend the line into a curve. As you can see, the Selection tool can also bend or reshape straight lines and curves.

5. As shown in Figure 2-17, repeat step 4 for each of the three remaining lines until the tail is formed.

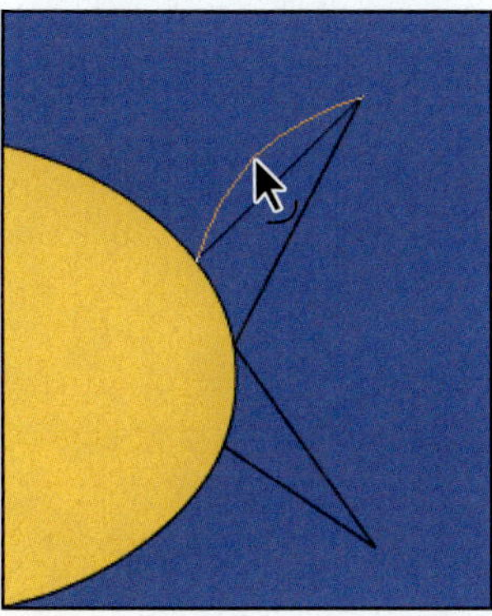

Figure 2-17: The Selection tool can be used to easily reshape lines and curves.

6. Next you'll need to fill the two sides of your new tail. By default, shapes drawn with path-centric tools such as the Line, Pen, and Pencil tools do not automatically fill. To fill these shapes, click and hold the Ink Bottle tool (⬙), if necessary, to locate and choose the Paint Bucket tool (⬙) from the Tools panel.

The Paint Bucket tool allows you to add fills where none exist, or to change the color of an existing fill.

7. Click on the Fill color swatch at the bottom of the Tools panel. Choose the light orange color marked #FFCC00. (You can also type this in the text field at the top of the Swatches panel to select the specified color.) As demonstrated in Figure 2-18, click inside of the tail fins to fill them with the selected color.

Figure 2-18: Add fills to empty paths using the Paint Bucket tool.

8. Switch back to the Line tool, and click and drag to draw two close, parallel, vertical lines in the middle of the oval. You will use these to form the gills for your fish.

9. Switch to the Selection tool (⬉), and use the technique shown in steps 4 and 5 (Figure 2-19) to bend each line into a slight curve in the same direction. The gills should resemble Figure 2-20.

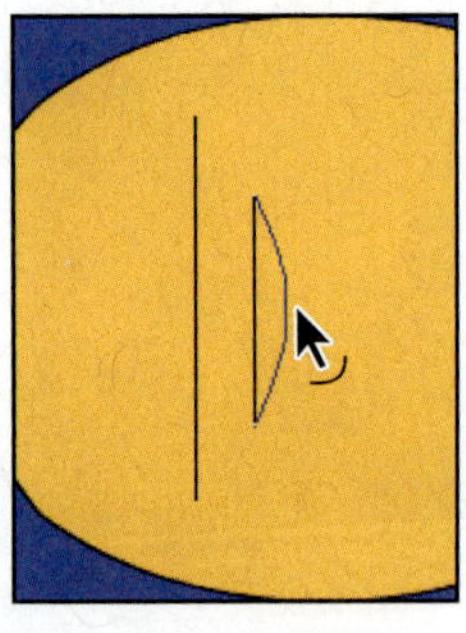 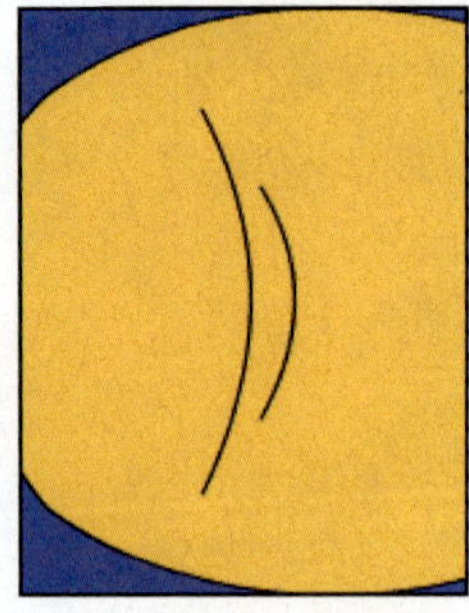 

Figure 2-19: *Use the same technique used to create the tail.*

Figure 2-20: *Bend out the lines to create gills.*

10. With the Selection tool active, click and select each of the two overlapping lines that separate the tail from the fish body. Press Backspace (Windows) or Delete (Mac OS) to clear the lines away.

11. Choose File > Save to save your file.

> **Take Note...**
> *You can easily switch from any tool to the Selection tool by pressing the V key, without having to go over to the Tools panel.*

Learning More

What the hex is a hexadecimal code?

You may have noticed that each color you choose (including colors referenced in these lessons) is marked with a hexadecimal code, a 6-character code preceded by a pound (#) sign. A hexadecimal code is a binary representation of an RGB color, used to indicate colors within web-specific languages and applications (such as HTML, Dreamweaver, and Fireworks).

Each byte, or pair of two digits, represents the red, green, and blue values for that color, respectively, from 00 to FF (in decimal notation, the values 0 to 255). For example, white in standard RGB values is notated as 255,255,255—in hexadecimal notation, #FFFFFF.

While it's not at all necessary (and somewhat impossible) to memorize the hexadecimal values for every popular color, becoming comfortable with this notation will help you work your way through Flash's color panels as well as those of other applications.

A helpful hint: the Photoshop and Illustrator color pickers also display a hexadecimal code for any color selected, making it easy to match colors between applications.

Using the Pen tool

For precision illustration tasks, you will most likely want to use the Pen tool. The **Pen tool** allows for point-to-point drawing, and precise control over curves and lines in between. You can even add or remove points to fine-tune your work. If you've used the Pen tool in Illustrator CS6, you'll already be familiar with the Pen tool and its related tools.

You'll use the Pen tool to create fins for your new fish in the following steps.

<table><tr><td>**Follow these steps to use the Pen tool**</td><td>**Step-by-Step**</td></tr></table>

1. Select the Pen tool (✎) from the Tools panel. In the Properties Panel or Tools panel, set your stroke color to black (#000000).

2. In the space above your oval, click and release the mouse pointer on the Stage to create a new point. Move your pointer to the left of the point you just created, and click and release again to create a second point. This point is joined to the first by a new path (line).

3. Position your cursor above and to the right of your last point. Click and hold down your mouse button, and then drag to the right (Figure 2-21). This forms a curve between your new point and the last one. Once you've gotten the curve just right, release the mouse button.

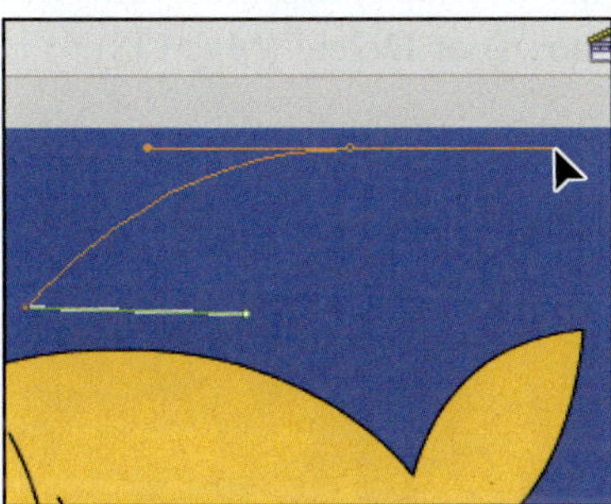

Figure 2-21: Creating precision lines and curves using the Pen tool.

Take Note...
You can create curves from any new point by holding down the mouse button and dragging in the direction you want to form the curve. (Be sure not to release the mouse button first!)

4. Next, you'll close up the shape. The next time you create a point, however, the Pen tool will attempt to draw a curve in the same direction as the last. To reset the last point drawn so that you can control the curve, click on the last point you created.

5. Move your pointer over the first point you created, and you should see a small loop appear below the pen cursor. Click and hold down your mouse button; drag to the right to form the final curve, and release the mouse to complete the shape.

6. As with other path-based tools, shapes created with the Pen tool do not automatically fill. To fill the new shape, choose the Paint Bucket tool (⬦) from the Tools panel. In the Tools panel, make sure the Fill color is still set to the orange color labeled #FFCC00.

7. Click once inside your new shape to fill it with the currently active fill color.

8. Now you'll move the fin into place and connect it with the rest of the body. Choose the Selection tool (▶), and double-click the fill of the fin to select the entire shape. Drag it into place at the top of the oval, slightly overlapping it as displayed in Figure 2-22. Click the Stage to deselect the shape; when you deselect the shape, the two become merged.

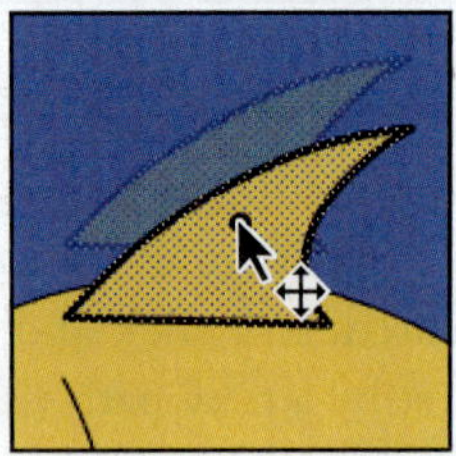

Figure 2-22: Move your new fin into place above the fish body.

9. The fin should now be merged with the oval. As shown in Figure 2-23, use the Selection tool and click once to select the portion of the stroke that overlaps onto the oval. Only that portion should become selected. Press Backspace (Windows) or Delete (Mac OS) to clear away the selected stroke (Figure 2-24).

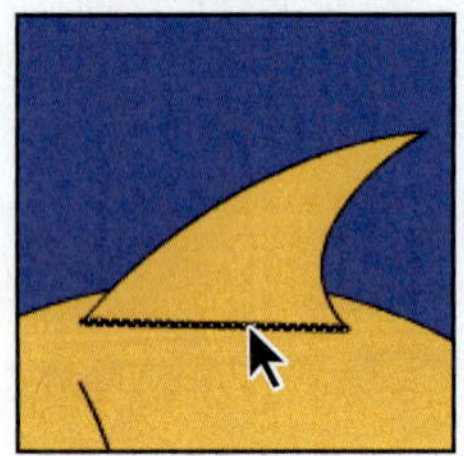
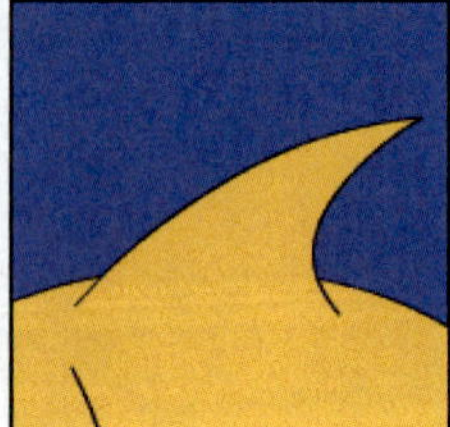

Figure 2-23: Select the portion of the stroke that overlaps onto the oval.

Figure 2-24: Delete the selected stroke.

Take Note...

By default, strokes that overlap between two merged shapes become segmented, and individual portions can be selected and removed.

10. Choose File > Save to save your file.

Using the Add and Delete Anchor Point tools

You can add or remove **Anchor Points** along existing paths with the Add and Delete Anchor Point tools. These tools are found under the Pen tool and enable you to further fine-tune your illustrations. Vector-based objects are composed of paths that are connected using anchor points. You'll add a bottom fin to your fish by manipulating the existing oval shape that forms its body.

| **Follow these steps to use the Add and Delete Anchor Point tools** | **Step-by-Step** |

1. Choose the Subselection tool (⟨) from the Tools panel. As shown in Figure 2-25, click on the edge of the oval; this reveals the points and paths that form this shape. From here, you can manipulate, add, or remove points along this path.

Figure 2-25: *Use the Subselection tool to activate the points and paths that compose a shape.*

2. Click and hold down your mouse pointer on the Pen tool (◊)—this reveals the Add, Delete, and Convert Anchor Point tools. Choose the Add Anchor Point tool (◊⁺).
Note: You can also use the = and - keys to toggle between the Add and Delete anchor point tools.

3. At the bottom center of the oval, you'll notice a single anchor point. Using the Add Anchor Point tool, click once to the left and once to the right of that point to add two new anchor points (Figure 2-26).

If you add the anchor point(s) in the wrong place, or add too many, choose the Delete Anchor Point tool (✎) and click on any point to remove it.

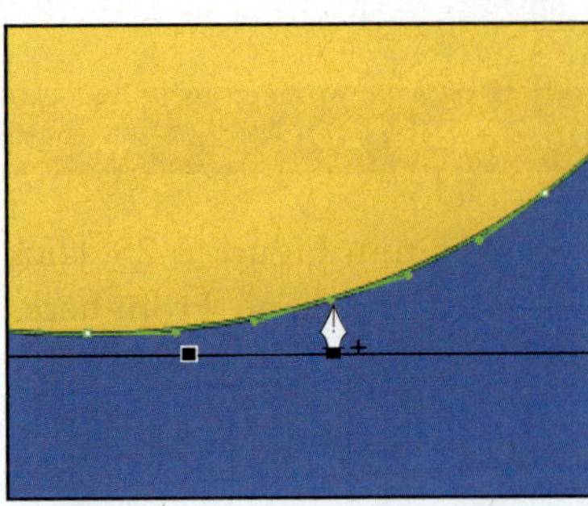

Figure 2-26: *Use the Add Anchor Point tool to add two additional points surrounding the bottom point.*

4. Choose the Subselection tool and, if necessary, click on the outline of your oval to reactivate the points and paths. Click the point at the very bottom of the oval to activate it—the point now appears solid instead of hollow.

5. Click and drag the point down and to the right, which extends that portion of the oval into a fin-like shape, as shown in Figure 2-27.

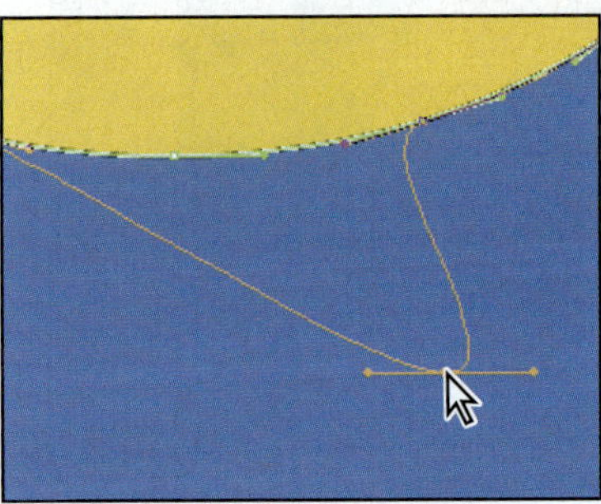

Figure 2-27: *With more points in place, you can easily pull out and extend a fin from the existing shape.*

6. Choose File > Save to save your file, and leave the file open.

Using the Combine Objects menu

If you need to create more complex combinations of shapes, you can use the **Combine Objects** menu, found at Modify > Combine Objects. This menu enables you to create punches, crops, or intersections between overlapping shapes, and even lets you convert mergeable artwork into Drawing Objects.

Before you can perform any Combine Objects menu commands on a piece of artwork, it first must be converted to a Drawing Object. To do this, you'll use the Union command to convert your fish from mergeable artwork to a Drawing Object.

Follow these steps to use the Combine Objects menu	Step-by-Step

1. Select the entire fish by choosing Edit > Select All. You can also use the Selection tool (▶) to draw a selection area around the artwork if you prefer.

2. As shown in Figure 2-28, choose Modify > Combine Objects > Union. This command converts the selected artwork to a Drawing Object, and a bounding box appears around your fish and its parts. Choose Edit > Deselect All.

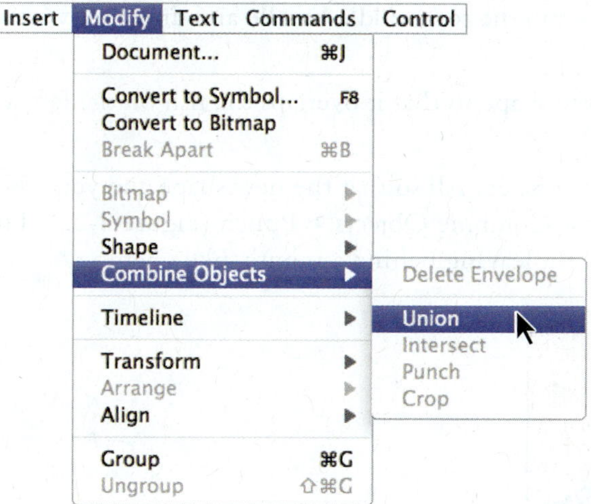

Figure 2-28: *Convert mergeable artwork to Drawing Objects using Modify > Combine Objects > Union.*

3. Select the Polystar tool (◯), and enable Object Drawing mode by selecting the button at the bottom of the Tools panel. From the Properties Panel, press the Options button. This opens the Tool Settings dialog box for the Polystar tool.

4. In the Tool Settings dialog box, type **3** for the number of sides. Leave the Star point size at its default setting as shown in Figure 2-29, and press OK to exit the dialog box. On the Stage, while holding your Shift key (to constrain the angle), click and drag to draw a right-pointing triangle (Figure 2-30).

If the new triangle appears unfilled, select any fill color from the Tools panel, and use the Paint Bucket tool to fill it.

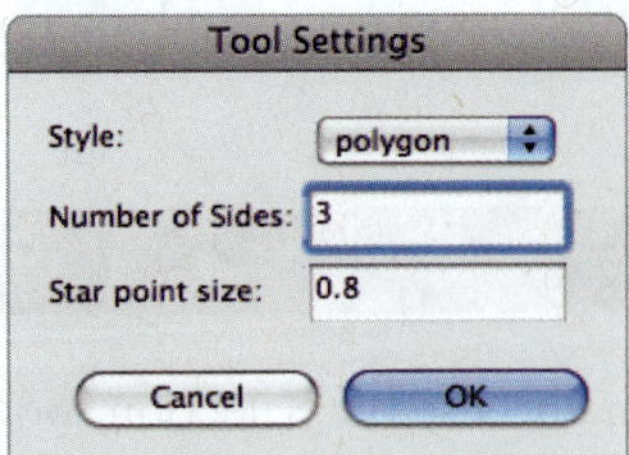

Figure 2-29: Use the Tool Settings dialog box to set the number of sides to 3.

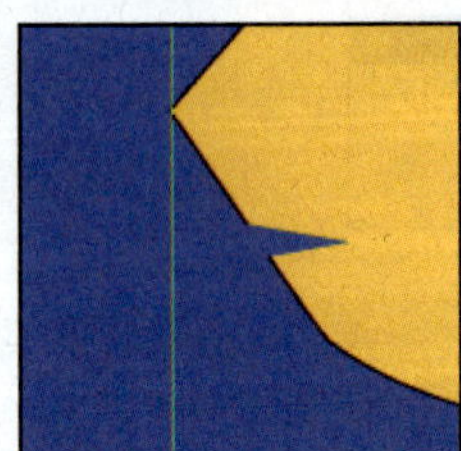

Figure 2-30: Draw a right-pointing triangle.

5. With the shape still selected, choose the Free Transform tool (⬚) from the Tools panel. A bounding box with handles appears—grab the top middle handle and drag it downward to scale the shape down vertically.

Choose the Selection tool and move the shape so that it overlaps the fish on the left where a mouth should be.

6. As shown in Figure 2-31, choose Edit > Select All so that the new shape and your fish both appear selected. Choose Modify > Combine Objects > Punch (Figure 2-32). The new shape is knocked out from your fish, leaving behind a mouth-like opening.

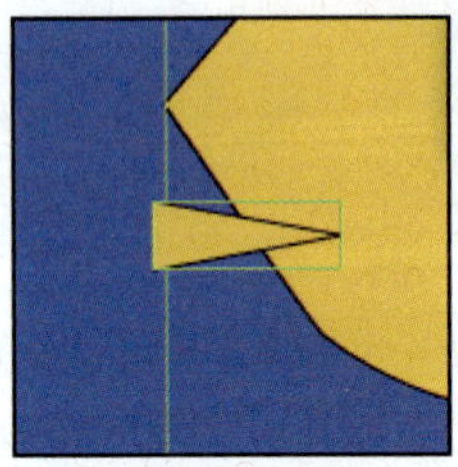

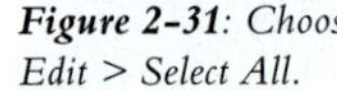

Figure 2-31: Choose Edit > Select All.

Figure 2-32: Use Modify > Combine Objects > Punch to subtract one shape from another.

7. Select the Oval tool from the Tools panel. Make sure you have a fill color selected (any color will do). With the Shift key held down, click and drag to draw a small, perfect circle. To match the figure shown in this example, use your Property Inspector to set the circle to a width and height of **50**. Switch to your Selection tool and position the circle on top of your fish above the mouth you created.

8. As displayed in Figure 2-33, choose Edit > Select All. With both the circle and fish selected, choose Modify > Combine Objects > Punch. This punches the circle into the body of the fish, making space for an eye as shown in Figure 2-34.

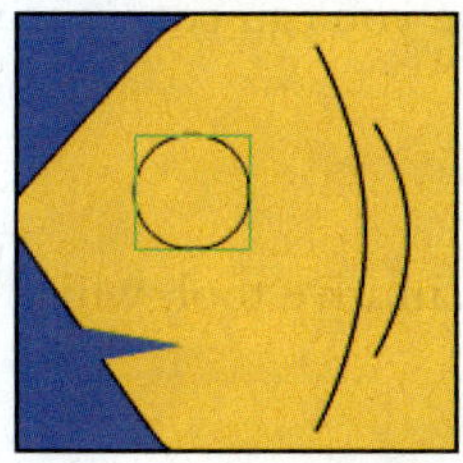

Figure 2-33: Select the circle and fish.

Figure 2-34: Use the Punch command to remove the circle from the fish.

9. Choose File > Save to save your file.

The Combine Objects menu

There are several commands available at Modify Combine Objects, not all of which you may use right away. Here's an overview of what each menu command does so that you can decide for yourself when and whether to use them.

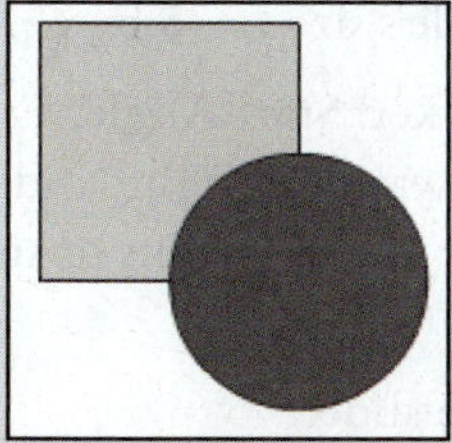
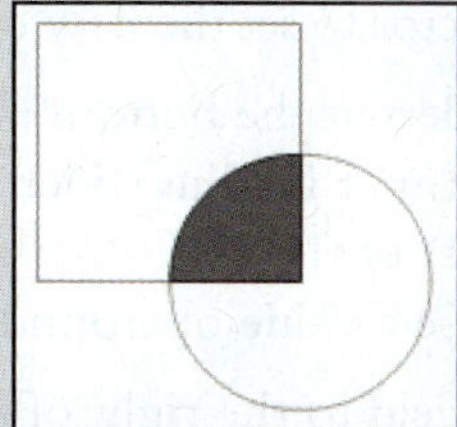
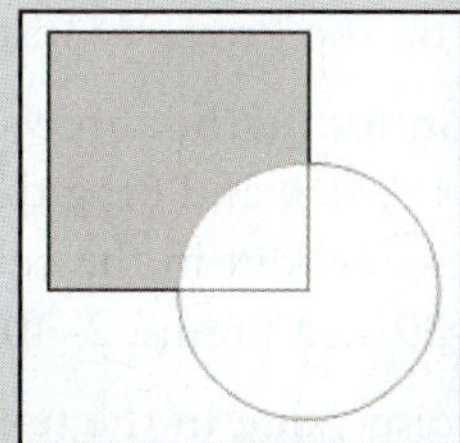
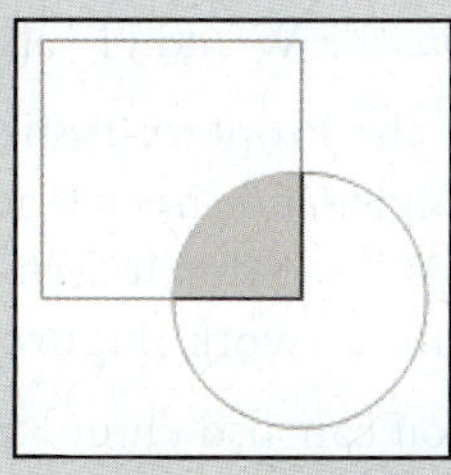

Figure 2-35: Union.   *Figure 2-36: Intersect.*   *Figure 2-37: Punch.*   *Figure 2-38: Crop.*

Union: Converts mergeable shapes into Drawing Objects. You can group several shapes into a single Drawing Object. In addition, shapes that are part of an Intersect, Punch, or Crop operation must all be Drawing Objects.

Intersect: Leaves behind only the overlapping area of two shapes.

Punch: Knocks out the top shape from the bottom shape.

Crop: Crops the bottom shape to conform to the top shape.

Using the Primitive tools (Smart Shapes)

The Rectangle and Oval Primitive tools provide you with an easy and time-saving way to create common variations on these basic shapes. From rounded or scalloped rectangles, to double-radius ovals, these smart shapes are especially powerful, because you can continue to modify them long after they've been created.

Using the Oval Primitive tool

Your new fish needs an eye, and the best tool for the job is the Oval Primitive tool, which allows you to create complex variations on ovals and circles.

<table><tr><td>**Step-by-Step**</td><td>**Follow these steps to use the Oval Primitive tool**</td></tr></table>

1. Select the Oval Primitive tool (⊖) from the Tools panel. This tool can be found underneath the existing shape tools. From the Tools panel, choose black (#000000) for your fill color, and set the stroke to None (☑).

2. Choose View > Snapping, and select Snap to Objects to temporarily disable object snapping. While holding your Shift key (to constrain width and height), click and drag to draw a small circle on the Stage. Switch to your Selection tool (⬏), and position the circle above the spot where the eye should appear on your fish (a hole should appear there from the last exercise).

   Use the W and H values on the Property Inspector to set the new circle's size to **45** by **45**.

3. In the Property Inspector, locate the three sliders at the bottom marked Start Angle, End Angle, and Inner Radius. Click and drag the Inner Radius slider toward the right, and you'll see that it forms a knockout in the center of the circle. Set the Inner Radius to suit your artwork (Figure 2-39 and Figure 2-40 use a value of around 49).

   You can also enter a precise value in the text field to the right of the slider.

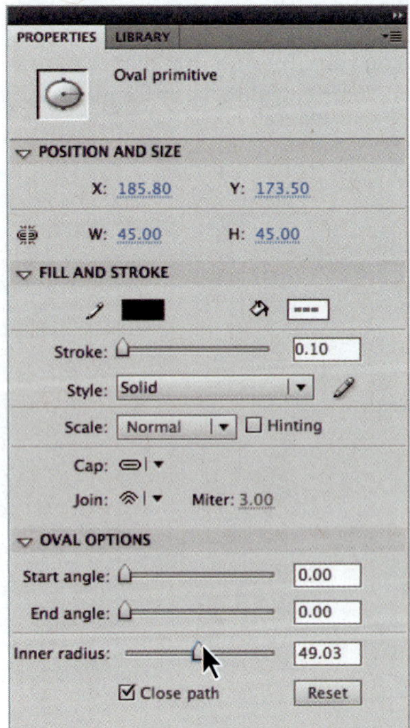

Figure 2-39: Drag the Inner Radius slider toward the right.

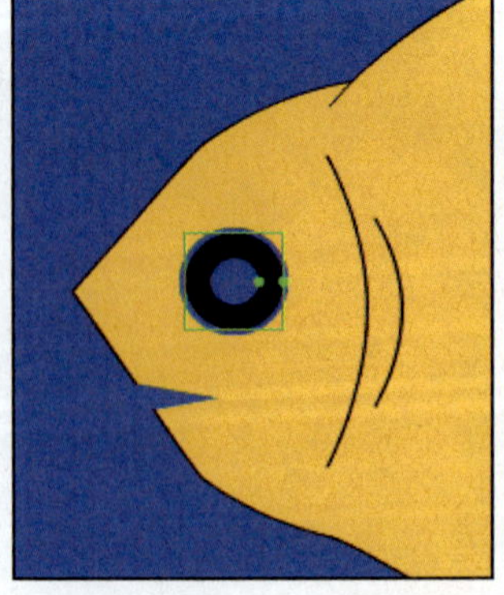

Figure 2-40: Composition shows the Inner Radius value set to 49.

4. Locate the Start Angle and End Angle sliders in the Property Inspector. Click and drag the Start Angle slider until its value reads somewhere between 40 and 45. You'll notice that as you increase the angle, the circle forms a *C* shape—this slider tells the circle to begin its circumference (shape) at a different angle, resulting in a partial shape!

5. You'll now perform the same action for the End Angle. Grab the End Angle slider and drag it to the right until the value reads about 330 (Figure 2-41). The circle now ends at a different location as well. As you can see in Figure 2-42, this can be very powerful in any situation where you need to create wedges or partial circle shapes without the need for complex punch or knockout commands.

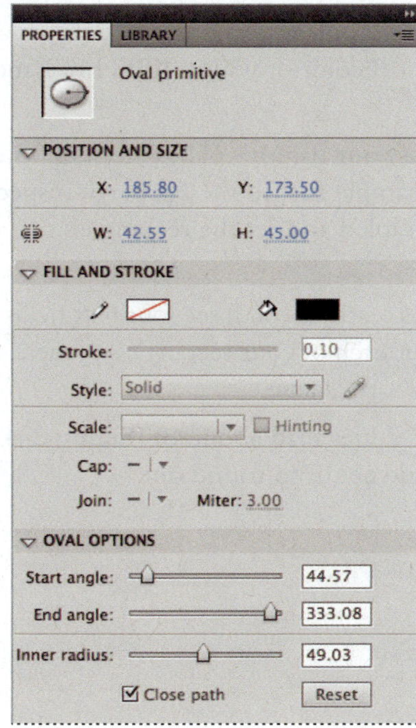

Figure 2-41: Use the sliders to affect your smart shape at any point.

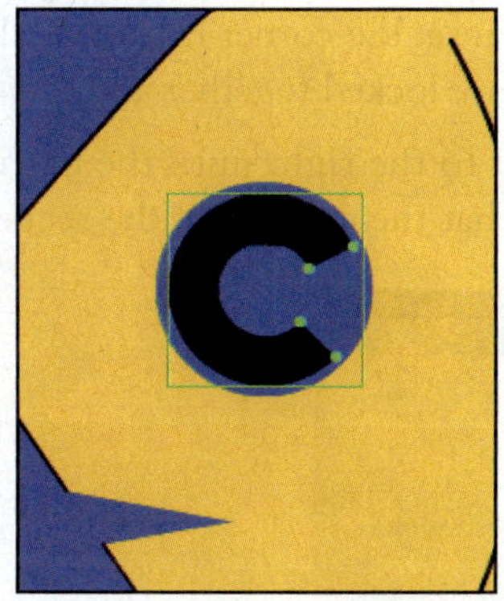

Figure 2-42: You can even deselect and return to the shape later on to edit its settings.

6. Choose View > Snapping > Snap to Objects to re-enable object snapping.

Oval Primitive shapes

For each oval primitive shape drawn, you'll see a discrete handle (it looks like an anchor point) on its right side (Figure 2-43). As an alternative to the Start and End Angle sliders, you can click and drag this handle in a clockwise or counter-clockwise motion to manually alter the start or end angle of the shape.

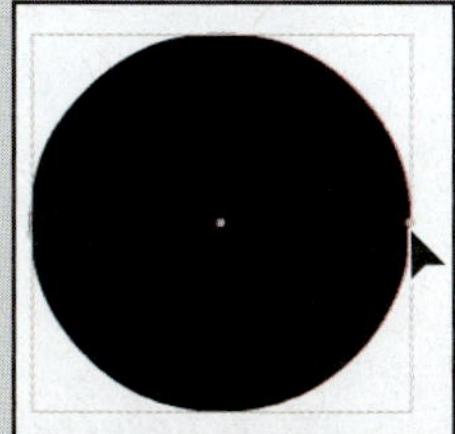
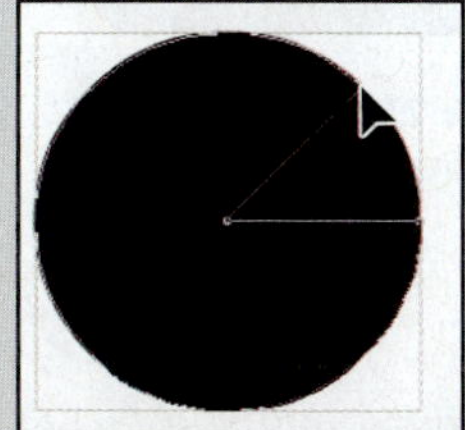

Figure 2-43: Oval primitive shapes have a discrete handle to manually alter the start or end angle of the shape.

The Rectangle Primitive tool

The close cousin of the Oval Primitive tool is the Rectangle Primitive tool, which gives you control over corner radii on rectangles and squares. Like the Oval Primitive tool, you can easily set values for a new primitive shape, and return to edit it at any time.

It's time to give your fish a way to speak its mind, so you'll create a basic word balloon using the power of the primitive.

<table><tr><td>**Step-by-Step**</td><td>**Follow these steps to use the Rectangle Primitive tool**</td></tr></table>

1. Choose the Rectangle Primitive tool (□) from the shape tools group on the Tools panel. From the Tools panel or the Property Inspector, set a fill color of white (#FFFFFF) and a stroke color of black (#000000).

2. Click and drag to draw a rectangle to the upper left of your fish. It's okay if it goes off the Stage into the pasteboard. If you'd like to match the sample file, in the Property Inspector make sure the Lock width and height button (∞) is disabled and set the rectangle's size to **200** pixels wide by **130** pixels high.

3. In the Property Inspector, locate the Rectangle Options section; you'll see four text fields and a slider. Here is where you set the corner radius for all or each of your rectangle's corners. By default, the four corners are locked together and use the same value.

    Click and drag the slider to the right until the corner values read about 40 (Figure 2-44)— you see in Figure 2-45 that the corners of the rectangle begin to round out.

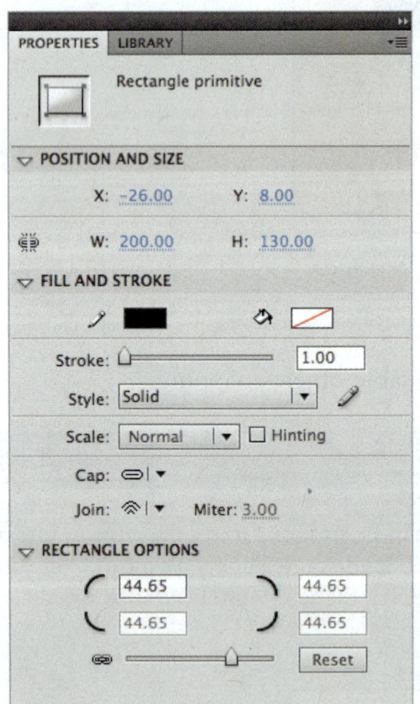

Figure 2-44: Add a corner radius to the rectangle primitive using the slider in the Property Inspector.   *Figure 2-45: The corners of the rectangle begin to round.*

Take Note...
To give each corner a unique value, click the chain link icon (∞) to the left of the slider to unlock the four corners. You can then type in a different value for each corner in its respective text field.

4. Next, you'll modify the corner radius using a slightly different technique. Instead of using the slider in the Property Inspector, you can grab the points adjacent to any corner and drag them to reshape the corner radius.

5. Switch to the Selection tool (⬂), then click and drag the point in the upper-left corner of your rectangle to the left and right. As you can see in Figure 2-46, this modifies the corners of your rectangle—move slightly to the right to reduce the corner radius.

Figure 2-46: Using the Selection tool can be a more tactile way to modify corners.

6. Choose File > Save to save your work.

You'll now add the stem to make this a true word balloon—however, you may have noticed that primitive shapes behave unlike any other shape you've used so far. While they appear to look and function much like Drawing Objects, they actually can't be modified in the way that Drawing Objects can.

Neither the Selection nor Subselection tool will allow you to modify them in the way you've been able to do with Drawing Objects and mergeable artwork. To accomplish this, you need to break the shape down to artwork that you can manipulate freely. Keep in mind, however, that doing this is a one-way street: You can't convert a shape or Drawing Object back into a primitive shape once it's been broken apart.

7. If it's not already active, switch to the Selection tool (⬂) and click once to select the rectangle primitive.

8. You'll now break this out of a primitive down to artwork you can manipulate further. As done with Figure 2-47, Modify > Break Apart, and the shape now appears with the dotted pattern that indicates it is now a mergeable shape. Keep in mind that you cannot go back.

Figure 2-47: Use Modify > Break Apart to convert the primitive shape to a mergeable shape.

Choose the Subselection tool (⬂) from the Tools panel and click once on the edge of the shape to reveal its points and paths.

9. Switch to the Add Anchor Point tool (✎). In the lower-right corner of the rectangle, click to create two new consecutive anchor points before the corner.

10. Switch to the Subselection tool, again, then click on the second point (the one closest to the corner) and drag it down and to the right to form the stem of your word balloon as shown in Figure 2-48.

Figure 2-48: *Form a stem by pulling out the second of the two new points you created.*

11. With the shape still selected, choose Modify > Combine Objects > Union to convert the shape to a Drawing Object, which you can easily move and stack later on.

12. Choose File > Save to save your work.

Adding text to your artwork

Flash allows you to create and style text to include in your movies, which can also be incorporated into animations or rendered in 3D (see Lesson 4, "Advanced Tools," and Lesson 6, "Advanced Animation" for more on this). There are three different text types that can be used in Flash: Static Text (regular text), Input Text (form fields), and Dynamic Text (dynamically changing text from another source). In addition, text is one of a few objects in Flash that can have filters applied to enhance its appearance.

When creating text in Flash, you may want to consider using screen or web fonts designed for being displayed on a pixel-based screen for improved readability. Keep in mind that font sizes will look different on each device so a minimum font size should be established. Sans-serif fonts tend to display better than serif fonts especially at smaller sizes. Other variables that affect readability are font color, alignment, placement of text, character spacing, line spacing, indentation, and anti-aliasing of fonts.

Flash Text: TLF & Classic Text

Flash uses two different types of text—TLF and "Classic" text. The TLF Text engine superseded the Classic text engine in Flash CS5, and vastly adds upon the capabilities of the "classic" Flash Text tool. TLF Text boasts features such as multi-column text and threaded text frames, which most designers have become accustomed to working with in other Adobe applications such as InDesign and Illustrator. In addition, many subtle but advanced text options such as character rotation, vertical orientation, ligatures, typographic case, digit case, digit width, advanced kerning, tracking, leading, duperscript and subscript, discretionary hyphens, hypertext and baseline shift are now available through an expanded character options panel in the Property Inspector. Even more advanced features are provided including support for multi-lingual typography, right-to-left scripts, using XML to dynamically style text, inline graphics, support for tabs, CFF anti-aliasing, and embedded font support.

You can continue to use Flash's Classic Text option in the Property Inspector, but for the purpose of the following exercises you'll be using the new TLF Text engine for all tasks.

In this lesson, you'll use the Text tool to add and style some cool text inside your fish's word balloon and alongside the edge of the Stage.

| **Follow these steps to add and style text using the Text tool** | **Step-by-Step** |

1. Select the Text tool (T) from the Tools panel. On the Property inspector, use the drop-down menu at the top to switch from Classic Text to TLF Text. Note that there are considerable differences in the options available in the Property inspector between classic text and TLF text.

2. Click once and drag within your word balloon to create a new text box that's slightly smaller than the balloon itself. The box appears with a blinking cursor in the upper-left corner, indicating that you're ready to type.

3. Type the words **A Fish's Story:** within the text box as shown in Figure 2-49. Click and drag across all the text within the box to select it.

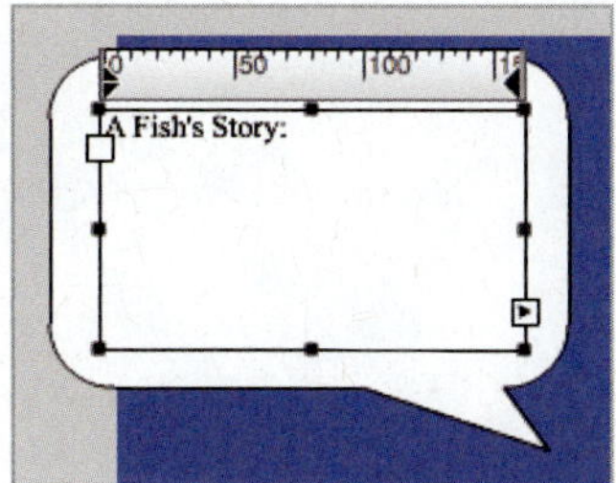

Figure 2-49: Use the Text tool to add some text to your word balloon.

Certification Ready 4.4

How do you create text using the TLF Text tool?

Certification Ready 4.5

Which text properties can be adjusted by using the Property inspector?

Certification Ready 4.5

How do you change the font and font size by using the Property inspector?

Certification Ready 4.5

How do you adjust text color?

Certification Ready 4.5

How do you change the anti-aliasing options for text?

Certification Ready 4.5

How do you change the alignment of static text?

4. In the Property Inspector, locate the Character options, which include options to set Family (font), Color, and Size. Choose Arial (or equivalent) from the Family menu to change the typeface. Move your cursor above the Size value, and drag to set the type size to 24 points. As shown in Figure 2-50, click the Color swatch and set the type color to black (#000000). If desired, you can experiment with the options in the anti-aliasing drop-down menu to modify how the text will appear in the document. In addition to the Character options, you'll also notice a Paragraph options section in the Property inspector where you can change the alignment of text as well as set indents and margins for the text.

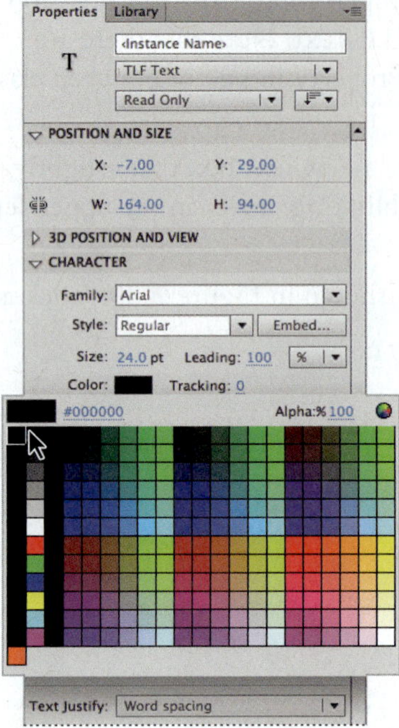

Figure 2-50: Specify typeface, size, and color options for your new text from the Property Inspector.

5. Press the Escape key twice to exit the current text box and make the Text tool active again. You'll now add some text along the left side of the Stage for more visual impact.

6. At the top of the Property Inspector, locate the Change orientation of text drop-down menu. Click it and select the Vertical option (Figure 2-51). This will create vertically-oriented text next time you use the Text tool.

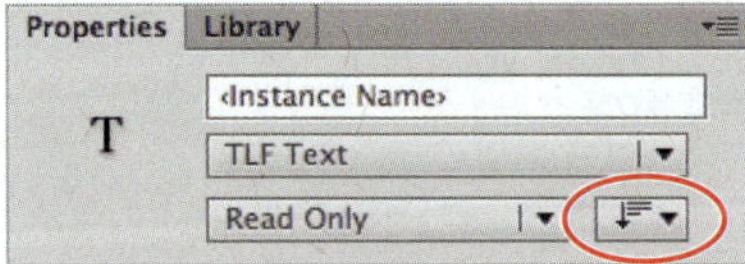

Figure 2-51: The Change orientation of text drop-down menu.

7. Click (but don't drag) near the left edge of the Stage to create a new text box, and type the words **Go Fish!** You'll see that the text now is created vertically alongside the left edge of the Stage.

Take Note...
You'll notice that you've created text on the Stage using two slightly different techniques: Clicking and dragging to create a fixed-width text box, or simply clicking on the Stage to create an expanding-width text block.. The former of the two will result in a text box that can take advantage of advanced type options and such as text-flow, multi-column text. The single click approach is a good way to create single lines of text for more basic and aesthetic purposes. You can convert expanding-width text to fixed-width text by double-clicking on the circle in the lower right corner of the text block. You can convert fixed-width text to expanding-width text by double-clicking on the out port located in the lower right corner of the text block.

New: Text Ruler

When you create text boxes on the Stage, you'll notice a handy ruler appears above it. As you can see in Figure 2-52, this shows you the width of your text field and allows you to set margins and other properties by dragging the available markers at the top.

Figure 2-52*: A helpful ruler appears on top of text fields to set margins and size.*

Working with Threaded and Multi-Column Text

Flash's TLF Text Engine brings a wealth of capabilities to type, many of which designers have become accustomed to in other Adobe applications, such as Illustrator and InDesign. This includes the ability to flow (thread) text across multiple text boxes, multi-column text and a variety of advanced character and paragraph options.

Next, you'll add more text to your fish's word balloon, and to catch the additional words you'll add a second text box on the Stage. You'll also take a look at splitting large blocks of type into columns for better presentation.

Follow these steps to work with threaded an multi-column text

1. Choose Edit > Deselect All. If it's not already active, select the Text tool (T) from the Tools panel. Also, make sure that the orientation of your text is set back to Horizontal (select Horizontal from the Change orientation of text drop-down menu toward the top of the Property Inspector).

2. Click and drag in the lower-right corner of the Stage to create a second, empty text box (it should take up roughly the entire lower-right quarter of the Stage).

Certification Ready 4.4

What is the difference between an expanding-width text block and a fixed-width text block?

Certification Ready 4.4

How do you create and convert expanding-width and fixed-width text blocks?

Certification Ready 4.5

How do you size a block of static text?

Step-by-Step

3. To resize the new text box, hover over any of the box handles on the sides or corners until you see a double-arrow. Click and drag to resize the text box until it's just right. The dimensions used in Figure 2-53 are 276px by 163px. You can also easily resize a text box by using the Property inspector or the Free transform tool.

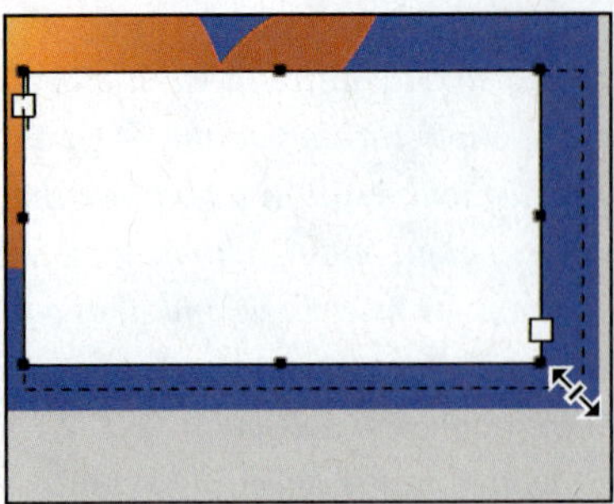

Figure 2-53: You can easily resize text boxes by dragging any of the four corners.

4. Now, you'll get some text to add to the first text box in the upper-left corner. Choose File > Open, and browse to this lesson's folder in the dialog box that appears. Select the **story.txt** file and click Open/Select to open it in Flash.

   You may need to make certain that All Files are set to display in the dialog box of the Open window in order to view and select a .txt file.

5. Select all the text within the text file you opened by triple-clicking within any point in the document, and choose Edit > Copy or Ctrl+C (Windows) or Command+C (Mac OS) to copy the selected contents.

6. Return to your Flash file by selecting its tab at the top of the workspace. Your text tool should still be active. Click within the first text box you created over the word balloon, and position your cursor following the words *A Fish's Story:*. Choose Edit > Paste or Ctrl+V (Windows) or Command+V (Mac OS) to paste the text into the frame.

7. You'll notice that the text is likely too long for the box, and gets cut off. You'll also note a small box with a red plus sign in the lower-right corner; this is the text frame's out port, and the red plus sign indicates an overrun, which means there's too much text for the box (Figure 2-54). You'll correct this by "flowing" the text from this box to the one you created on the bottom right corner of the Stage.

Figure 2-54: The newly added text overflows the text box, indicated by the red plus sign in the lower-right corner.

8. Click on the red plus sign, which is the out port of the text box; your icon should change to show a block of text attached. You are now carrying the overrun text, and can place it, or "flow" it to another text frame.

9. Locate the text box you created in the lower quarter of the Stage. Hover your cursor over the text box until you see a chain link icon (), and click. The text from the word balloon should now continue in this text frame, and you'll see a line going from one to the other to indicate the frames are threaded together.

The final touch will be splitting that new text box with some attractive columns. Displaying text in multiple columns is a clean, easy way to read large blocks of text, and a technique commonly used in print publications and websites.

10. Using your Text tool, click within the new text box you created on the lower–right corner of the Stage. In the Property Inspector, locate the Columns value under the Container and Flow options (the default value should read 1).

11. Click and drag over the columns value until the value reads 2. This will split your text box into two columns.

12. If you'd like to adjust the gap between the two columns, locate the gap width value directly to the right of the Columns value (the default value should read 20px). Click and drag to the left or right to decrease or increase the gap, respectively.

13. Choose File > Save to save your document.

Now, if you add text to the frame within the word balloon, the text in the lower corner of the Stage will continue to adjust as needed, and format the overflowed text into two nice columns!

> ***Take Note...***
> *Flash CS6 contains a powerful feature to help you check the spelling of text in a document. Simply choose Text > Check Spelling to begin spell checking the document. To refine the parameters that Flash uses to check spelling, choose Text > Spelling Setup to display the options available to control the behavior of the Check Spelling feature.*

Certification Ready 5.1

How do you check spelling in a Flash document?

Adding filters

To enhance the appearance of text, you can add popular live filters such as drop shadows, blurs, glows, and more. Filters can also be applied to other objects in your movie, such as button and movie clip symbols (covered later in this book). For now, you'll add some basic filters to make your text stand out.

Certification Ready 4.5

How do you add graphic filters to text?

Follow these steps to add a filter to text

Step-by-Step

1. Switch to the Selection tool (), and click once on your text box in the lower–right corner to select it.

> ***Take Note...***
> *Pressing the V key while editing text simply types a v in the text box; it doesn't switch to the Selection tool as anticipated. To exit a text box, use the Esc (escape) key, and then press the V key to jump to the Selection tool.*

2. At the bottom of the Property Inspector, locate and expand the Filters section. (Try collapsing the Container and Flow options to give your filter options more space.)

3. In the lower-left corner of the Filters section, press the Add Filter button (⬛) to add a new filter. A menu appears, showing you the various filters you can apply to your text. As shown in Figure 2-55, select the Drop Shadow filter.

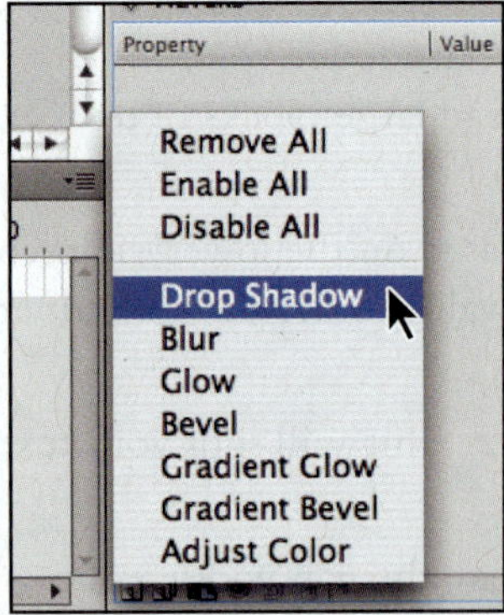

Figure 2-55: Apply filters to selected text from the Filters section of the Property Inspector.

4. Options appear for the new Drop Shadow filter, which you can fine-tune. To start, click and drag the Strength value to reduce the strength (opacity) to 30 percent.

5. As shown in Figure 2-56, click and drag the Distance value to increase the distance to 10 pixels. Under the Quality setting, select High. Filter quality settings are discussed further in Lesson 12, "Introducing Movie Clips."

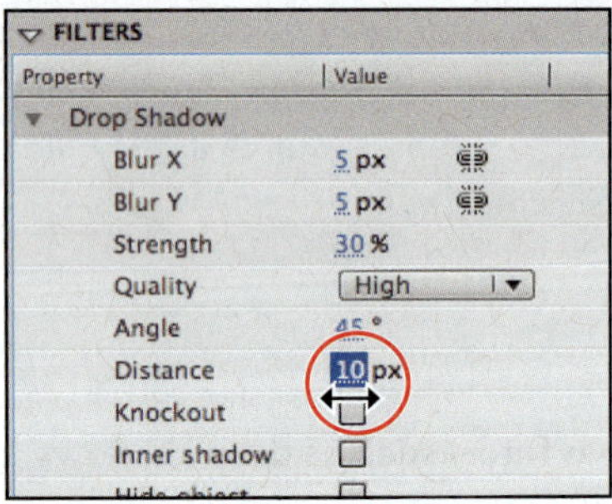

Figure 2-56: Set specific options for your filter, including color, strength, and distance.

6. Choose File > Save to save your file.

Working with colors

Flash offers a lot of options for creating, saving, and working with colors and gradients. In addition, the panels and workspace make it easy to choose and apply colors from virtually anywhere, or to save color sets that you can share between multiple Flash documents and projects.

Follow these steps to open the Color and Swatches panels

1. First you'll want to make sure that the Color and Swatches panels are visible. Choose Window > Color (Figure 2-57). By default, the Color and Swatches panels are already grouped together.

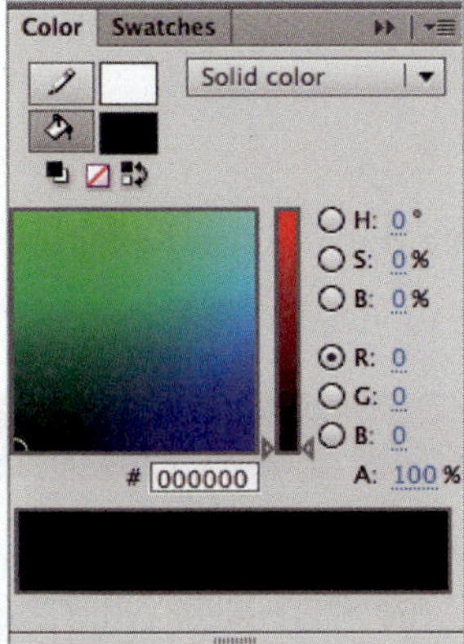

Figure 2-57: The Swatches and Color panels are grouped together by default.

2. As shown in Figure 2-58, drag the panel group by its title bar over the Property Inspector and Library panel on the right-hand side, releasing the mouse when you see a light blue line. The two panels should now appear docked in the panel group above the Property Inspector and Library panel (Figure 2-59).

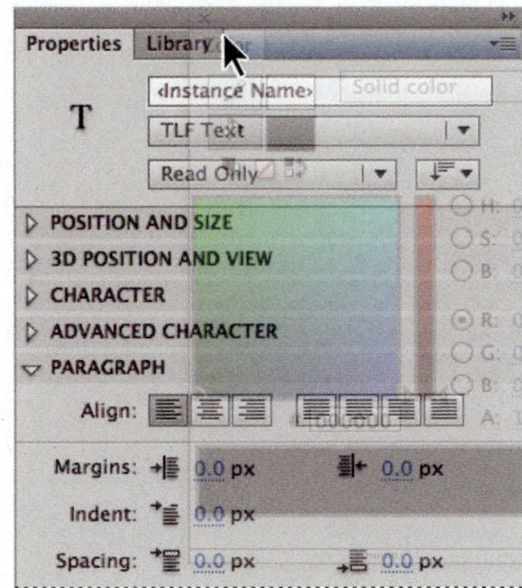

Figure 2-58: Move the Color and Swatches panel group to the Properties and Libraries panel group.

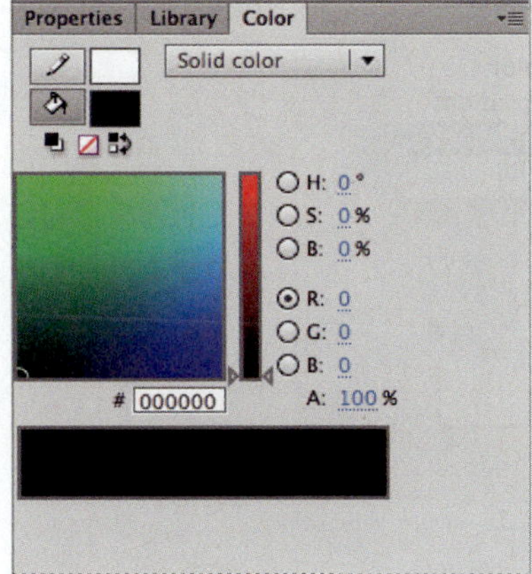

Figure 2-59: The Color panel now sits next to the Library panel.

Creating gradients

A **gradient** is a gradual blend between two or more colors, and is often used for complex color transitions or to imply lighting effects. You can create and save gradients and apply them to fills or strokes within your artwork. Flash supports *linear* gradients and *radial* gradients. Both types can include any number of colors.

Linear gradients (Figure 2-60) blend in a uniform manner and, as the name implies, in a straight line going in any direction or angle.

Radial gradients (Figure 2-61) blend in a circular manner, either from the inside out or the outside in (depending on your perspective, of course).

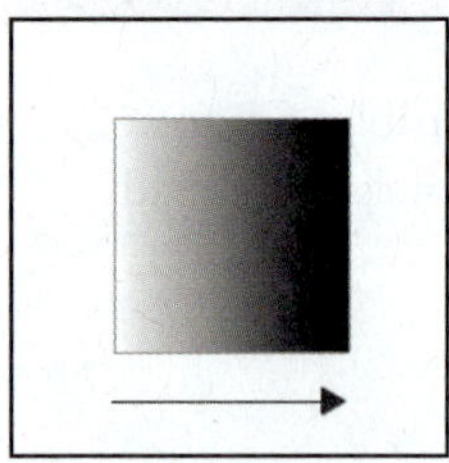 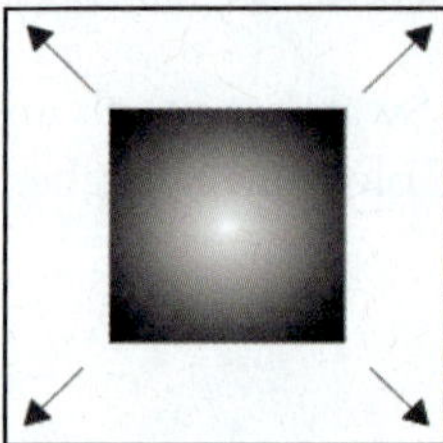

Figure 2-60: *Linear gradient.*   **Figure 2-61**: *Radial gradient.*

Your fish is almost complete, so it's time to bring it to life with some dynamic and exciting colors.

Follow these steps to add color to artwork

1. Choose your Selection tool (⬉), and click once on your fish to select it. Choose Modify > Break Apart to separate the fish and its parts, and then choose Edit > Deselect All. Click once on the body of the fish.

2. Locate the Color type drop-down menu at the top-right corner of the Color panel. This allows you to choose a solid color or gradient for the currently active color. Choose Radial gradient (Figure 2-62) to set a radial gradient to your fill. The fish displays the default black-to-white gradient.

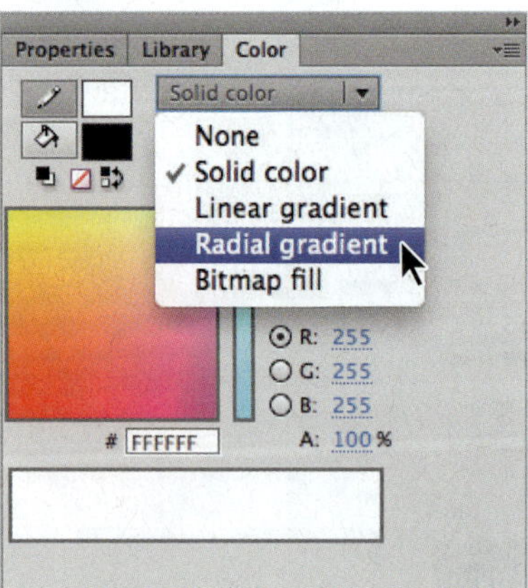

Figure 2-62: *Choose Radial to switch your shape's fill to a radial gradient.*

3. At the bottom of the Color panel, you see the color ramp, which now appears with two color stops (sliders), one for each color that forms your gradient. You'll need to assign a new color to each stop.

4. Double-click the right slider, and the Swatches panel appears. Choose the dark orange color marked #CC6600 (Figure 2-63). Double-click the left slider, and from the Swatches panel, choose the light orange color marked #FF9900 (Figure 2-64).

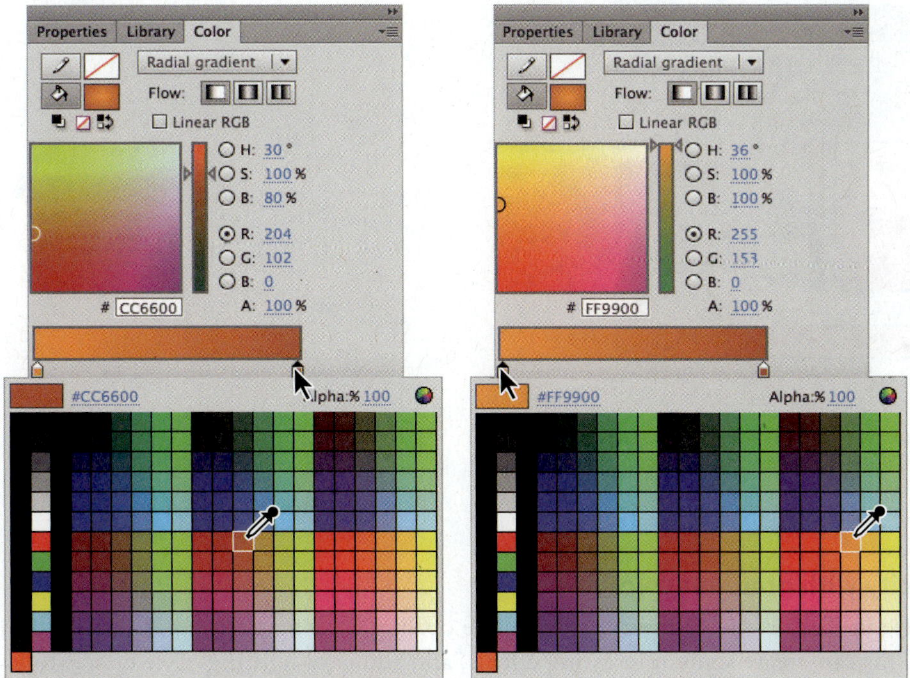

Figure 2-63: Set a darker color for the first color stop.   *Figure 2-64*: Set a lighter color for the other color stop.

5. The position and distance between the two sliders determines the blend point. Moving one slider closer to the other changes the balance between the two colors.

Click and drag the left slider slightly toward the middle—this makes the lighter orange more prominent than the dark orange.

6. To add colors to your gradient, you'll add more color stops. Add a new color stop by clicking on the far left edge of the color ramp. A new stop should appear below the color ramp. Double-click the stop, and choose white (#FFFFFF) from the Swatches panel.

Now, you'll save this gradient for use later on.

7. Locate and open the Color panel menu (▾≡) in the upper-right corner of the panel. As shown in Figure 2-65, choose Add Swatch to add your new gradient swatch to the existing swatch presets.

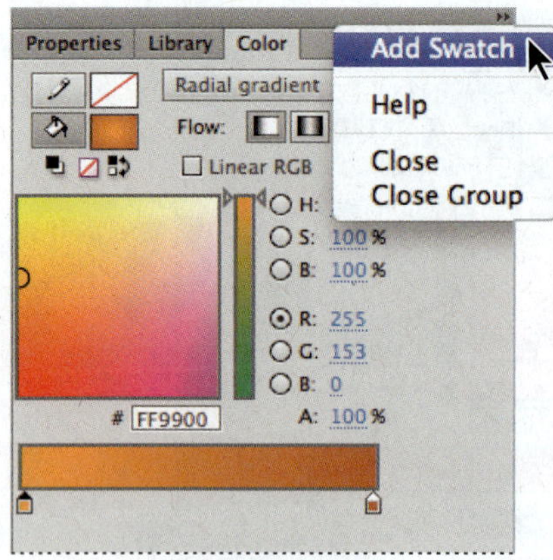

Figure 2-65: Save your new gradient as a preset that you can recall later on from the Swatches panel.

8. Choose File > Save to save your file.

Using opacity with gradient colors

A cool feature in Flash is the ability to set a unique opacity level for each individual color in a gradient. This can create some interesting effects, and add cool lighting-style effects to your illustrations. In this next exercise, you'll create and color some underwater bubbles using this interesting effect.

<table>
<tr><td>**Step-by-Step**</td><td>**Follow these steps to change the opacity of a color**</td></tr>
</table>

1. Choose the Oval tool (○) from the Tools panel. If it's not already enabled, activate Object Drawing mode by pressing the button at the bottom of the Tools panel.

2. From the bottom of the Tools panel, choose white (#FFFFFF) for your stroke color, and choose the black-to-white radial gradient preset for your fill color.

3. While holding the Shift key down (to constrain proportions), click and drag to draw a small circle to the left of your fish. Leave the circle selected.

4. If it's not already open, choose Window > Color to open the Color panel.

5. Double-click the black color stop to open the Swatches panel, and choose white (#FFFFFF).

6. With the stop still active, locate the Alpha slider; this sets the opacity of the selected color in the current gradient. Click and drag the slider downward (Figure 2–66) until the value reads 0 percent (Figure 2–67). This produces an interesting light flare effect inside the bubble.

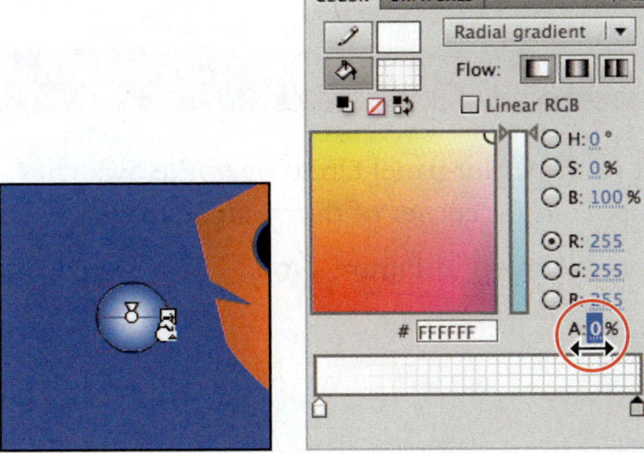

Figure 2–66: *Draw a new oval.*   *Figure 2–67*: *Use the Color panel to reduce the opacity of one of your oval's gradient colors.*

7. Choose File > Save to save your file.

Creating custom colors

As you may have discovered, creating and saving a solid color swatch is nearly identical to creating and saving a gradient swatch. In this case, you'll set specific RGB values to create a color that you can apply to your artwork, as well as add to your existing swatches.

Follow these steps to create custom colors   **Step-by-Step**

1. Choose the Selection tool (⬉) and double-click once on your fish to select it. In the Property Inspector, set the stroke color style to solid and the color to black (#000000).

2. Locate the R, G, and B text fields on the Color panel, click the stroke icon (✎ ■) to make certain the stroke (and not the fill) is selected, and type **250**, **100**, and **16**, respectively. This creates a dark orange color that is immediately applied to the stroke.

3. From the Color panel menu located in the upper-right corner, select Add Swatch to add your new color to the Swatches panel.

4. Choose File > Save to save your file.

Saving a custom color set

Once you've added new color swatches, you'll want to save that set for use with other projects and documents. If you've ever created and saved custom color swatches in applications like Photoshop or Illustrator, you'll find that saving color sets in Flash is very similar.

<table>
<tr><td>**Step-by-Step**</td><td>**Follow these steps to save a custom color set**</td></tr>
</table>

1. Press the Swatches panel tab located next to the Color panel tab to open the Swatches panel. Press the panel menu button (▾≡) in the upper-right corner of the Swatches panel.

2. From the panel menu, choose Save Colors as shown in Figure 2-68.

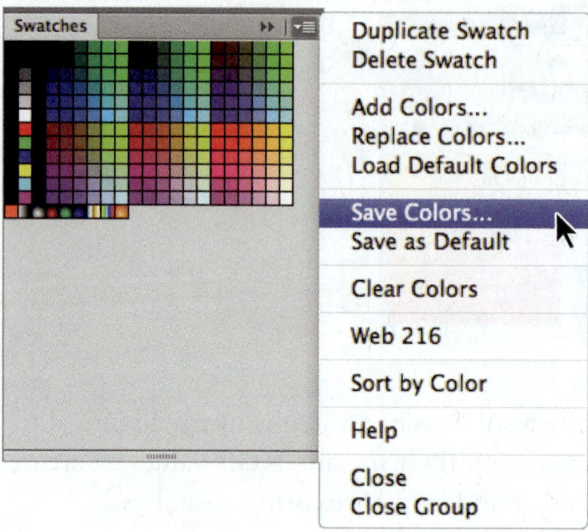

Figure 2-68: Save the current swatches as a new color set that you can recall at any time.

3. From the dialog box that appears, choose your Save location (for this lesson, you can choose the fl02lessons folder), and name the new file **fl02colors.clr**.

4. Press Save to save the color set into the selected folder. The color set appears in your destination folder as a single .clr (Flash Color Set) file.

Take Note...

You can also choose to save your swatches in .act (Adobe Color Table) format, which allows you to exchange it with Adobe applications such as Photoshop and Fireworks. You can even load .act color tables exported from Fireworks back into Flash if you'd like!

Organizing and layering graphics

As you build more complex graphics on the Stage, you'll want to position and layer them as needed to make your movie work for you, and to help you organize your movie. Some of these organizational elements include layers, folders, and labels. Flash gives you a lot of control over your Stage through a robust layer structure that you may already be accustomed to using in other Adobe design applications.

Working with layers

On a single layer, you have a great deal of flexibility to arrange Drawing Objects and grouped graphics—however, as your artwork becomes more complex, you'll want the power of **layers** to stack and arrange your artwork. In addition to controlling stacking order, layers let you hide specific graphics from view, and even lock those items from accidentally being edited or deleted.

You can think of layers as clear pieces of film that you can place graphics on and stack together; each layer sits above another, allowing you to reveal the items below, but also to control which items appear above or below another. Each layer and its contents can be isolated in view, toggled out of view, or locked to prevent editing.

In the next steps, you'll separate the graphics you've created so far onto individual layers for more control.

<table>
<tr><td>

Certification Ready 2.5

What structural elements can be used to organize a Flash document?

</td></tr>
<tr><td>

Certification Ready 3.3

How do you arrange content on the stage using layers?

</td></tr>
<tr><td>

Certification Ready 3.3

How do you add, delete, and rename layers?

</td></tr>
</table>

Follow these steps to add and name layers   **Step-by-Step**

---

1. To start, you'll make sure that each set of graphics you want to assign to a layer is grouped or converted to a Drawing Object. This will make them easier to move and distribute.

    Verify that your word balloon (leave the text separate) is a Drawing Object by selecting it and viewing its info in the Property Inspector. If not, use Modify > Combine Objects > Union to convert it to a Drawing Object.

2. Double-click to select your fish and the gills, then hold down the Shift key and select the eye. Convert them to a single Drawing Object by choosing Modify > Combine Objects > Union.

3. Shift+click to select the fish, the bubble, and the word balloon. Make sure to not select the text. Right-click (Windows) or Ctrl+click (Mac OS) on any of the selected items—a contextual menu appears.

4. At the bottom of the menu, locate and select Distribute To Layers (Figure 2-69). All the items on your Stage are placed onto several new layers, which appear on the Timeline panel at the bottom.

The layers are named generically (Layer 2, Layer 3, and so on). To fix this, you'll identify which graphics belong to which layers and rename them appropriately.

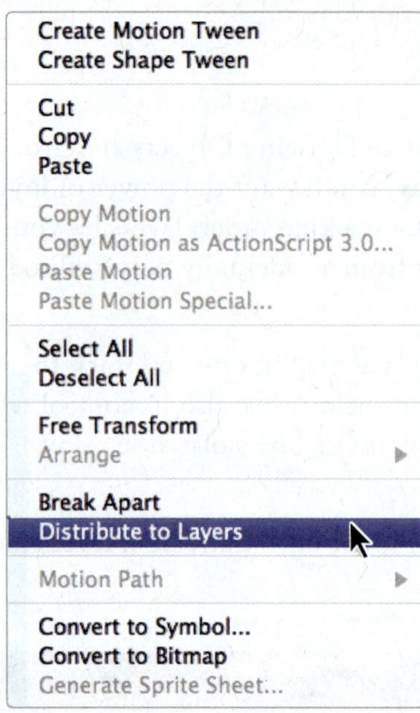

Figure 2-69: Use Distribute to Layers to separate multiple objects at once to their own layers on the Timeline.

5. Choose Edit > Deselect All. First, click on the fish on the Stage to select it, and look at the Timeline panel below. The layer that becomes selected is the one to which it belongs. Double-click directly on the layer's name to edit it, and type in the name **Fish**.

6. Repeat step 4 for the bubble and word balloon, naming them **Bubble** and **Word Balloon**, respectively (Figure 2-70). For Layer 1, rename this layer **Text** since all the text was left on this layer. Figure 2-71 shows all the renamed layers.

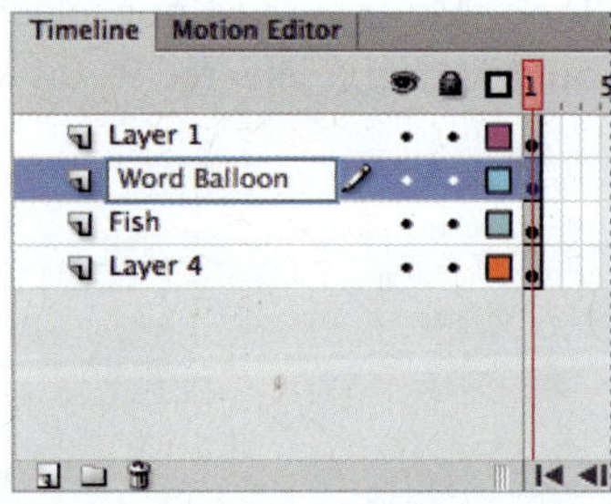

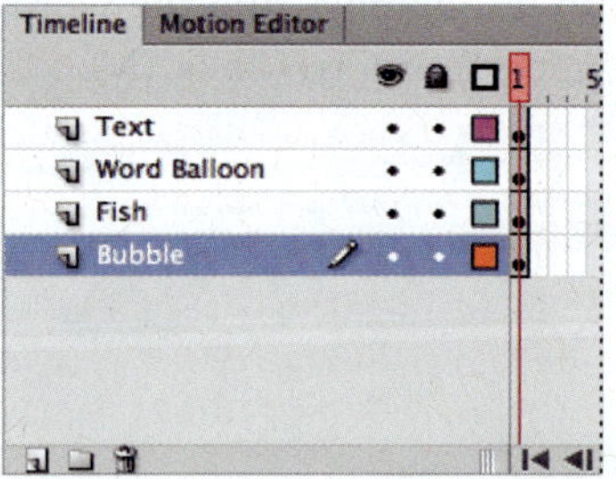

Figure 2-70:*Double-click a layer's name to edit it.*

Figure 2-71: *Rename your layers clearly so you know exactly what's on each one.*

7. Choose File > Save to save your file.

Arranging, locking, and hiding layers

Once you've arranged your artwork on individual layers, you can easily control which layers are visible (or invisible) and editable, and easily rearrange the order and appearance of items in your movie.

Follow these steps to work with layers **Step-by-Step**

1. Locate the layer titled Bubble, which contains the bubble you created earlier. Click to select it.

2. Click and drag upwards on the layer—you see in Figure 2-72 a black beam follow your cursor within the layers. This indicates where the layer will be moved when you release the mouse.

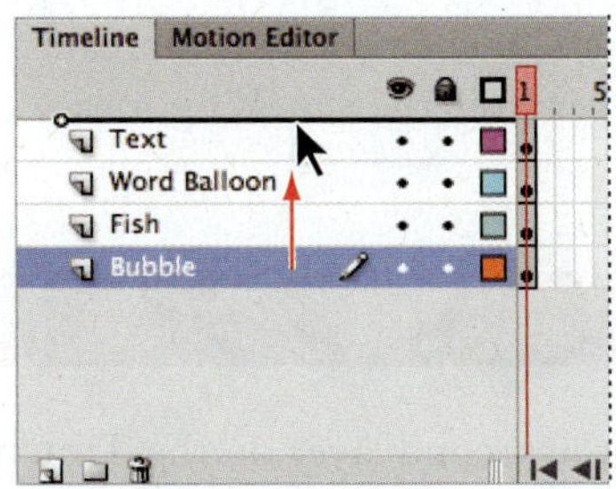

Figure 2-72: When dragging layers, follow the black beam to determine where your layer will be placed.

3. Drag the layer all the way up and release it at the top of the layer stack to move the bubble to the top.

4. Locate the two column headers above your layers—one appears with an visibility icon (👁) and one appears with a padlock icon (🔒), which means that it is locked. Under the padlock column, click on the Text, Word Balloon, and Bubble layers to lock those layers (a padlock icon should appear on the layer). Leave the Fish layer unlocked.

5. Click the Text layer below the visibility column—a red X appears (Figure 2-73)and the text disappears. Toggle the layer's visibility back on again by clicking the red X.

Certification Ready 3.3

How do you adjust the layer properties?

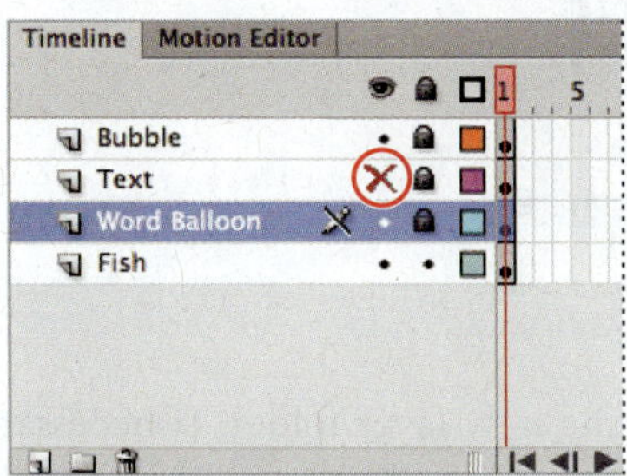

Figure 2-73: Click under the padlock or visibility icon to lock, hide, and show specific layers.

6. Double click the colored square to the right of the Text layer to open the Layer Properties dialog box. The Layer Properties allows you to change the type of layer, the outline color, the Layer height and whether the layer is locked or not. Leave these settings at the default and click OK.

Take Note...

To lock all layers except for the one you're targeting, hold down the Alt key (Windows) or Option key (Mac OS) and click on the target layer below the padlock column. All layers except for the one you clicked will lock. This also works for visibility!

Certification Ready 3.3

How do you add, name, arrange, delete, and organize layers into folders?

Creating layer folders

As you accumulate more layers on the Timeline, it makes sense to try and group them logically so that you can easily view, lock, and hide related layers with a few clicks. You can create layer folders on the Timeline that can group several related layers together, making it easy to collapse, hide, and lock them as needed.

Step-by-Step

Follow these steps to create layer folders

1. Click to select the Text layer, which should currently be the second layer on the Timeline.

2. Locate the New Folder button (📁) below the layer stack, and click it once to create a new folder above the current layer.

3. Double-click the Folder title, and type **Word Balloon and Text** as the new name.

4. Click and drag the Text layer up below the folder and to the right and release it—as shown in Figure 2–74, it should now appear indented below the folder, indicating it is now inside the new folder (Figure 2–75). (Follow the bar—it should appear indented below the layer folder before you release the mouse button.)

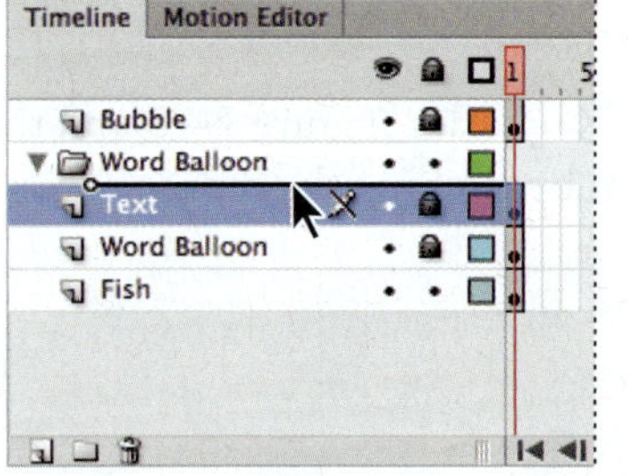

Figure 2–74: Move the Text layer below the Word Balloon folder.

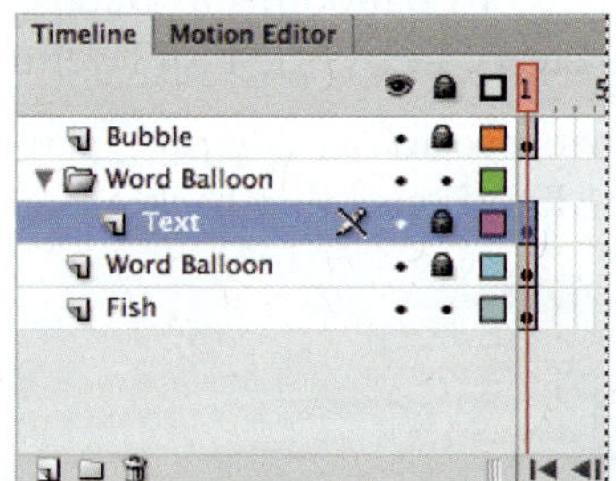

Figure 2–75: The Text layer should now appear indented below the folder.

5. Repeat step 4 with the Word Balloon layer to add it to the new layer folder. If necessary, rearrange the two layers within the folder so that the text appears above the Word Balloon.

6. Collapse the layer folder and hide its included layers by clicking the arrow that appears to the left of the folder name (Figure 2-76). The Word Balloon and Text layers temporarily disappear from view on the Timeline.

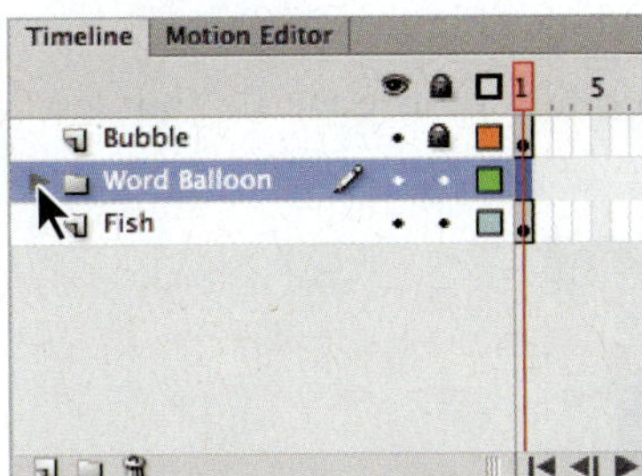

Figure 2-76: Collapse or expand a layer (and its contents) by using the arrow shown to the left of its title.

7. Choose File > Save to save your file.

    You can now lock or hide all layers under that folder at once by clicking the layer folder under the Padlock and Visibility columns, respectively. To access individual layers again, simply expand the layer folder.

Take Note...
Layer folders can be created several levels deep, allowing you a lot of organizational control when you need it. To create a nested layer folder, select any layer inside of a layer folder and click the New Folder button below the Timeline.

Transforming graphics

Once you've created artwork on the Stage, Flash gives you a lot of options to **transform**: scaling, rotating, skewing, and tweaking graphics and colors. Transforming existing graphics is as much a part of illustration as building them, so in the next steps you'll explore the various tools and panels at your disposal.

The Transform menu and Free Transform tool

The Modify menu at the top of your screen features a Transform menu, which provides shortcuts to many common transformation tasks as well as helpful dialog boxes. You'll use this menu in the next exercise to tweak the size and rotation of your fish.

Follow these steps to use the transform menu   **Step-by-Step**

1. Choose the Selection tool (k), and click once on the fish to select it (make sure its layer is unlocked).

2. Choose Modify > Transform > Scale and Rotate. This opens the Scale and Rotate dialog box (Figure 2-77), where you can enter values for Scale (in percentage) and Rotation (in degrees).

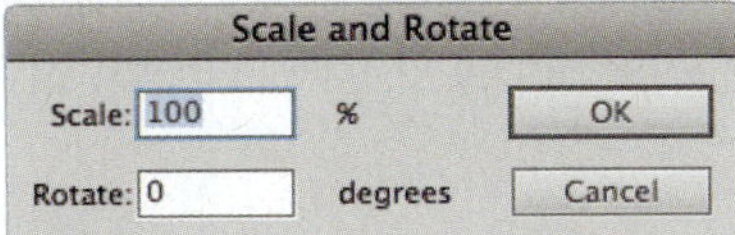

Figure 2-77: Choose Modify > Transform > Scale and Rotate to open the Scale and Rotate dialog box.

3. Type **75** for the Scale value, and **25** for the rotation value; then press OK to exit the dialog box.

4. Your fish now appears smaller and rotated slightly upward. Use the Selection tool to move your fish to the center of the Stage, closer to the word bubble (Figure 2-78).

    To fine-tune, you'll use the Free Transform tool, which offers a more tactile (but less precise) way of scaling and rotating your artwork.

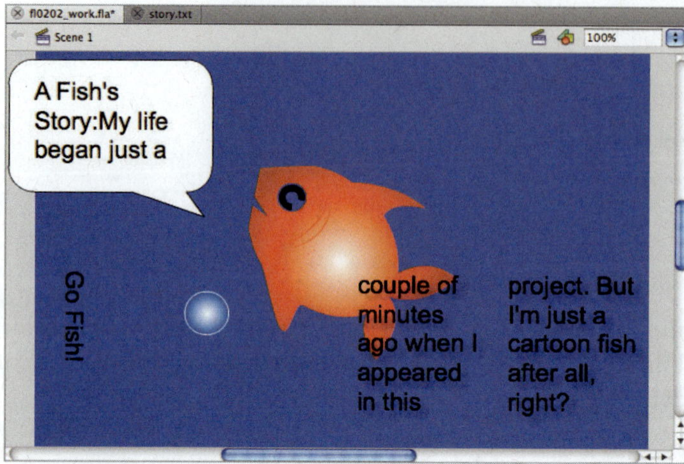

Figure 2-78: Rotate the fish.

5. Leave the fish selected, and choose the Free Transform tool (⬚) from the Tools panel. The fish now appears inside a black bounding box with eight handles.

6. Move your mouse pointer over the top-right handle of the bounding box until you see a double-arrow icon appear. While holding down the Shift key, click and drag the corner handle down and to the left to resize your fish slightly smaller (Figure 2-79). If the text box makes it difficult to select the fish, you may move the text to another location on the Stage.

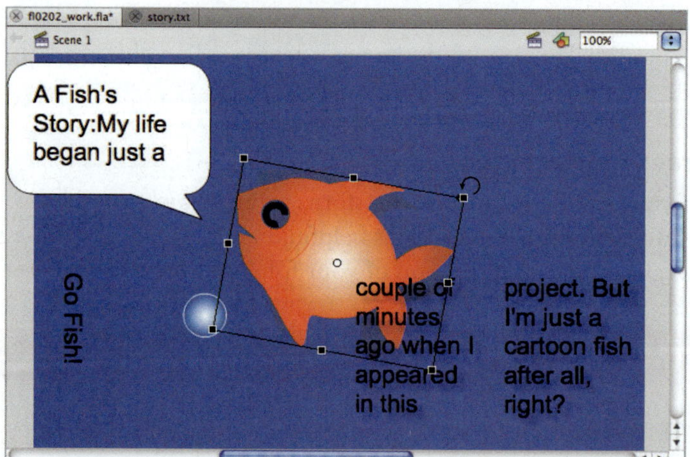

Figure 2-79: With the Free Transform tool, you can use corner handles to rotate or resize your artwork.

7. Move your cursor just above the same handle until you see the rotating arrow icon (↷). Once this icon appears, click and drag in a clockwise or counter-clockwise motion to adjust the rotation of your graphics to your liking.

8. Choose File > Save to save your file.

Getting the (transformation) point

What is that mysterious white dot that appears in the middle of your artwork when you use the Free Transform tool? That's your transformation point, which determines the point on a graphic from which scaling and rotation is set.

If you'd like to rotate a graphic around a different point than the center, for instance, you can move the transformation point to a different location within your graphic.

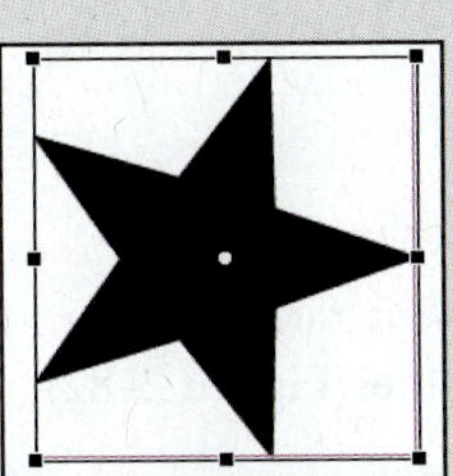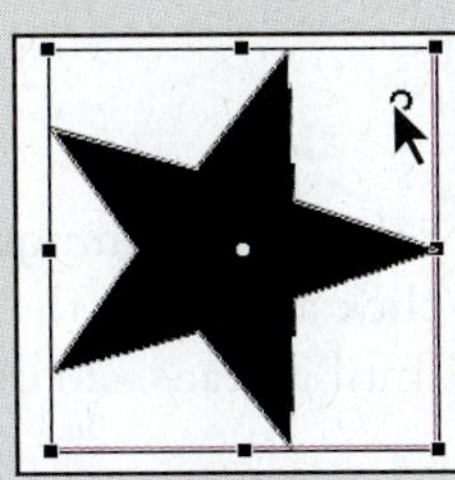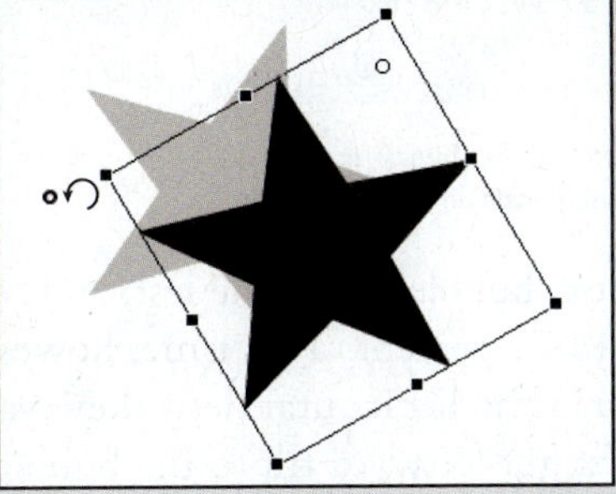

Figure 2–80: To do this, select your graphic with the Free Transform tool, locate the point, and click and drag it to a different part of your graphic.

The Transform panel

An alternative to the Free Transform tool and Transform menus is the Transform panel, which offers many of the same features plus some additional options for skewing and transforming graphics in the 3D plane.

Follow these steps to use the Transform panel

1. Choose Edit > Deselect All. If necessary, unlock the Bubble layer for editing. Use the Selection tool (▸) to select the bubble graphic.

2. Select Edit > Copy and then Edit > Paste in Center to make a copy of the bubble. Repeat this to make a third bubble. Use the arrow keys on your keyboard or the Selection tool to arrange the three bubbles vertically to the left of your fish's mouth.

3. Select the bottommost bubble. Choose Window > Transform to open the Transform panel. Locate the horizontal and vertical scale values at the top. Click the *Constrain* button (⬤) directly to the right, which will keep the horizontal and vertical values locked together.

4. Click and drag left over the horizontal value until the overall scale of the bubble is reduced to around 50 percent (Figure 2-81).

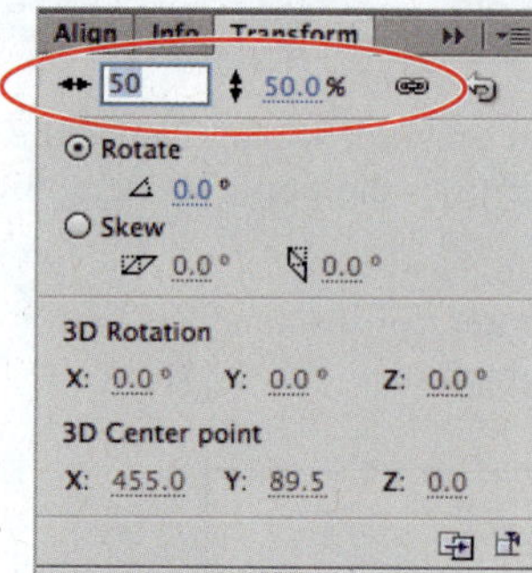

Figure 2-81: *Use the Transform panel to precisely scale an object.*

5. Select the next bubble above the last, and repeat the same technique from step 4 to reduce this bubble to 75 percent. This time, however, click and select the *Skew* radio button. Click and drag the horizontal (left) skew value until it reads –20 degrees(Figure 2-82). This adds a slight leftward tilt to the bubble.

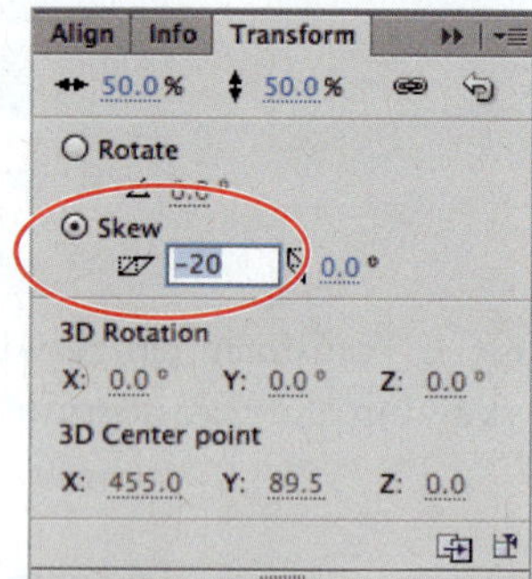

Figure 2-82: *Add skewing to an object by selecting it and using the Skew values on the Transform panel.*

6. Select the top bubble, and click to select the Skew radio button. Click and drag the horizontal (left) skew value until it reads 15 degrees. Close the Transform panel.

Take Note...

To remove all the transformation values from an object, select it and click the Remove Transform button (⬚) at the bottom of the Transform panel.

Transforming gradients

If you use gradients to fill or stroke graphics in your movie, you can precisely position, scale, and modify them using the Gradient Transform tool. Because your fish and bubbles both use gradient fills, you'll finalize your artwork with a little gradient tweaking.

Step-by-Step | **Follow these steps to transform gradients**

1. From the Tools panel, click and hold down your pointer on the Free Transform tool (⬚) to select the Gradient Transform tool (⬚), then click on the body of your fish to select it.

2. A circular bounding box appears around your fish. Move your cursor over the center point of the bounding box until a four-way arrow appears. You can click and drag this point to shift the center point of the gradient. As shown in Figure 2-83, click and drag the point up and to the left—this helps to imply a light source coming from the upper left.

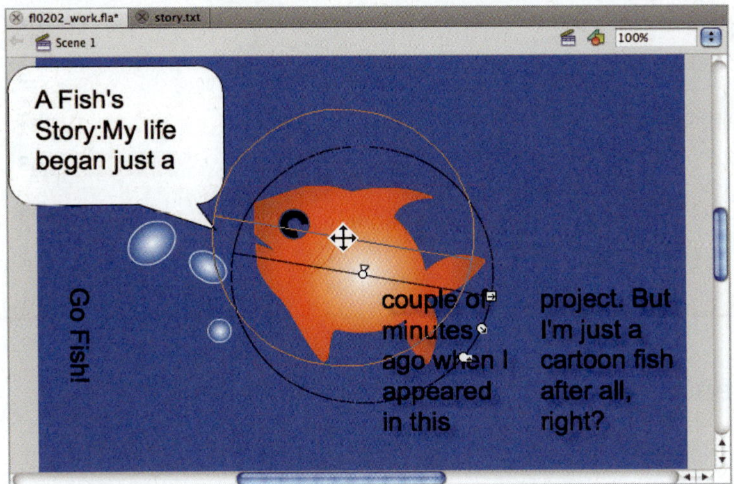

Figure 2-83: Move the point shown in a Gradient Transform bounding box to shift a gradient's center point.

3. Locate the scale handle in the lower-right corner of the bounding box. Click and drag it inward to scale the gradient down inside the fish (Figure 2-84). This increases the presence of the darkest color that makes up your fill.

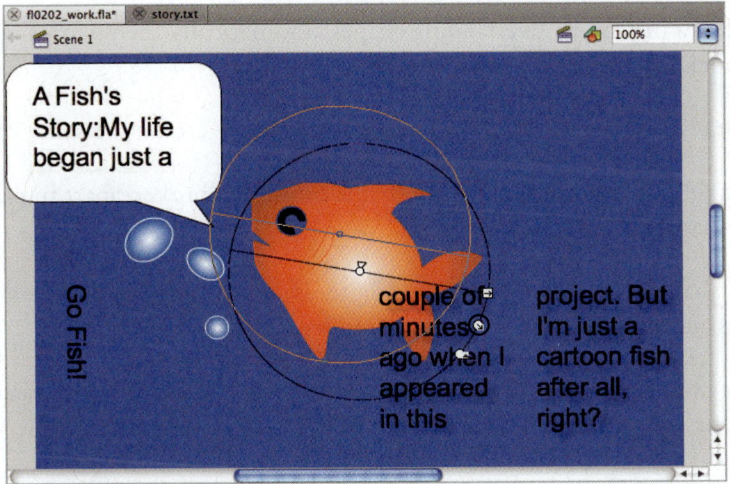

Figure 2-84: Scale down a gradient using the handle shown. This also changes the perceived balance of colors.

4. Choose File > Save to save your file.

Take Note...

For linear gradients, the rotate handle allows you to change the direction of the gradient. This also works for radial gradients if the center point is offset from the middle.

Skill summary

In this lesson you learned how to:	Objective
Identify general and Flash-specific techniques to create rich media elements that are accessible and readable	2.3
Organize a Flash document	2.5
Use the Timeline	3.3
Use tools on the Tools panel to select, create, and manipulate graphics and text	4.2
Import and modify graphics	4.3
Create text	4.4
Adjust text properties	4.5
Conduct basic technical tests	5.1

Knowledge Assessment

True/False

Circle **T** if the statement is true or **F** if the statement is false.

T   F   1. The default drawing mode for creating a shape is the Merge Drawing mode.

T   F   2. In Merge Drawing mode, strokes cannot be separated from fills, hence the reason for the name as objects remain merged after they're drawn.

T   F   3. In Merge Drawing mode, overlapping shapes automatically merge, causing one to "knock" the other one out when removed.

T   F   4. You cannot change the stacking order of images if they are on the same layer.

T   F   5. A Drawing Object is locked, meaning that it cannot be broken apart into a mergeable shape.

T   F   6. By default, shapes drawn with path-centric tools such as the Line, Pen, and Pencil tools automatically fill in color themselves.

T   F   7. Before you can perform any Combine Objects menu commands on a piece of artwork, it first must be converted to a Drawing Object.

T   F   8. With regard to the Combine Objects function, Intersect is defined as leaving behind only the overlapping area of the two shapes.

T   F   9. Despite the irony of its name, the Oval Primitive tool allows you to create complex variations on ovals and circles.

T   F   10. Flash uses one type of text only, referred to as "Classic" text.

Multiple Choice

Select the best response for the following statements.

1. Which of the following tools is not part of the other shape tools grouped together in the Tools panel?

    a. Rectangle Tool

    b. Oval Tool

    c. Line Tool

    d. PolyStar Tool

2. What is the name of the drawing mode that behaves more like Adobe Illustrator?

    a. Merge Drawing

    b. Object Drawing

    c. Object Editing

    d. Shape Drawing

3. Which of the following panels will display properties of a selected object on the Stage?

    a. Info

    b. Library

    c. Align

    d. Properties

4. Paths on mergeable shapes automatically join when which of the follow is enabled?

    a. Auto-Snap

    b. Snap To Guides

    c. Snap to Objects

    d. Snap to Pixels

5. Which tool is typically chosen to manipulate a shape after it's been drawn using one of the shape tools?

    a. Selection Tool

    b. Free Transform Tool

    c. Subselection Tool

    d. Lasso Tool

6. A hexadecimal code is a binary representation of which color mode?

    a. CMYK

    b. RGB

    c. LAB

    d. YBR

7. What is the name of the point that is created each time you click while using the Pen tool?

    a. Selection Point

    b. Transformation Point

    c. Anchor Point

    d. Pivot Point

8. Which tool is the best choice when trying to manipulate individual anchor points effectively?

    a. Selection Tool

    b. Subselection Tool

    c. Free Transform Tool

    d. Pen Tool

9. With one shape overlapping another, which of the following would you choose to knock out one shape to leave a stencil-like effect behind?

    a. Modify > Combine Objects > Union

    b. Modify > Combine Objects > Intersect

    c. Modify > Combine Objects > Punch

    d. Modify > Combine Objects > Crop

10. Start angle, End angle, and Inner radius are all properties of which shape?

    a. Oval Primitive

    b. Oval Shape Tool

    c. Line Tool

    d. All of the above

Competency Assessment

Project 2-1	Comparing Notes

As you've no doubt noticed, Flash can be a little tricky with regard to the various shapes included in the program as well as how it interacts with each. The best way to understand how Flash is going to do things is to continue to create and manipulate shapes and compare how one works versus the other.

1. Create a new ActionScript 3.0 document in Flash.

2. Select the Rectangle tool. Change the fill color to light blue and the stroke color to black.

3. Make sure that the Object Drawing at the base of the Tools panel is turned off.

4. Draw a rectangle on the Stage.

5. Return to the Properties panel and change the fill color to yellow.

6. Make sure that the Object Drawing at the base of the Tools panel is now turned on.

7. Draw a rectangle on the Stage.

8. Choose the Selection tool. Click and drag on each, double-click on each, note how they react and what else happens in response to your actions.

9. Save the file as **object_merge.fla**.

| **Practicing with Combine Objects** | **Project 2-2** |

The book provides a nice explanation as to how each of the options works under the Combine Objects menu. However, it's a bit more interesting to see how it works on Stage.

1. Create a new ActionScript 3.0 document in Flash.
2. Make sure that the Object Drawing at the bottom of the tools panel is turned on. Select the Rectangle tool, set the fill color as blue, set the stroke to None. Draw a rectangle.
3. Change the fill color to yellow and draw a second rectangle, make sure they overlap.
4. Select both using the Selection tool and choose Edit > Copy. Go to Modify > Combine Objects > Union.
5. Choose File > Paste to paste a new copy on the stage and apply a different Combine option.
6. Once you have an example of each combine type, save your file as **flash_combine.fla**.

Proficiency Assessment

| **Getting More Primitive** | **Project 2-3** |

Now that you understand the Primitives a bit more, let's unchain some of their settings and see what else we can draw with them...

1. Create a new ActionScript 3.0 document in Flash.
2. Select the Rectangle Primitive tool and draw a shape.
3. With the shape selected, select the Lock corner radius button in the Properties panels and try different corner settings.
4. Select the Oval Primitive tool and draw a shape.
5. With the shape selected, modify the oval options in the Properties inspector to see what shapes can be created.
6. Save the file as **flash_primitive.fla**.

| **Learning More About Type** | **Project 2-4** |

To understand some of the other capabilities of TLF text, you'll add some text to a document and change some of the properties.

1. Create a new ActionScript 3.0 document in Flash.
2. Select the Text tool, and in the Properties inspector, choose TLF text from the drop-down menu at the top.
3. Click and drag with the Type tool to create a text area and enter some text.
4. Select the text and spend some time modifying the settings in the Properties inspector to see the options that are available. Try creating several paragraphs of text. Maybe even link to text areas together.
5. When you are finished, save the file as **TLF_text.fla**.

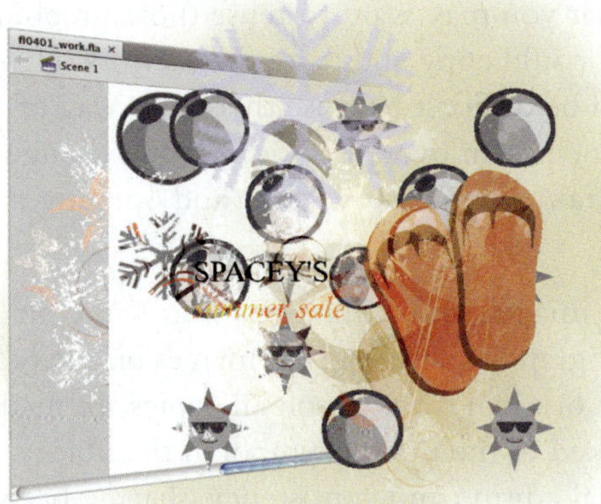

Using Symbols and the Library

Key Terms

- Library panel
- Move To
- swap
- symbols

Skill	Objective
Identify general and Flash-specific best practices for designing rich media content for the web, mobile apps, and AIR applications	**2.1**
Demonstrate knowledge of design elements and principles	**2.2**
Import and modify graphics	**4.3**
Create objects and convert them to symbols, including graphics, movie clips, and buttons	**4.6**
Understand symbols and the library	**4.7**
Edit symbols and instances	**4.8**

Business case

You need to create an animated ad for a department store. Part of the requirements of this assignment is that the ad will have to rotate year round so the artwork will have to change in order to reflect the appropriate season. You want to build this in an efficient enough way so that you don't have to create multiple Flash files, you'll just swap the artwork as needed and output separate files when finished.

Starting up

Before starting, make sure that your tools and panels are consistent by resetting your workspace. See "Resetting the Flash workspace" in the Starting up section of this book.

You will work with several files from the fl03lessons folder in this lesson. Make sure that you have loaded the fllessons folder onto your hard drive from *http://www.wiley.com/college/sc/adobeseries*. See "Loading lesson files" in the Starting up section of this book.

The project

You'll be learning how to create symbols from existing artwork and reuse those symbols throughout your movie to build a web banner for a department store's winter sale. After you build a layout for this season, you'll be able to easily modify it for other seasonal campaigns using the symbol's powerful swap and editing capabilities. Each exercise will introduce you to a new concept as you creatively evolve your ad campaign.

What are symbols?

As you create graphics on the Stage, you'll realize that you may want to reuse those graphics several times throughout your movie. Although you could copy and paste the artwork as many times as necessary, keeping track of each copy would be difficult because there's no way of letting Flash know they are related. Modifications, such as an overall color or shape change, would need to be applied to each copy individually, taking up creative time and opening the door to inconsistencies in your movie.

A better choice is to use **symbols:** reusable graphics, images, and animations stored in your document's library. You can create symbols from any graphics or imported images on the Stage, or from animations on the Timeline. A symbol is the original from which all copies are made; each copy of a symbol (called an *instance*) remains linked to the master symbol in the library. This allows for reduced file size, ease of editing, global editing and consistency, sharing between projects, and adding interactivity. Changes made to the original symbol in your library affect all instances of that symbol throughout your movie. Using symbols (along with templates at times) help to produce consistent elements in your Flash animations which improves usability for the user, and shorter development time and maintenance for you the developer.

As described in detail in the sidebar, "Symbol-ism: the symbol types," Flash uses three types of symbols:

- Graphic
- Button
- Movie clip

This lesson focuses on graphic symbols only: you'll be converting existing graphics to symbols as well as creating new symbols from the ground up. Lesson 10, "Creating Navigation Controls," explores buttons, while Lesson 12, "Introducing Movie Clips," covers the creation and use of movie clips—powerful symbols that can contain entire animations.

Certification Ready 2.1

What techniques can be used to produce consistent elements?

Certification Ready 2.1

What are the benefits of consistency?

Certification Ready 4.6

What are the characteristics of graphic, movie clip, and button symbols?

Certification Ready 4.7

What are the symbol types that are available in Flash?

Certification Ready 4.7

What are the benefits of using symbols in a movie?

    Introduction to Adobe Flash Professional CS6

Symbol-ism: The symbol types

Each symbol type has different attributes and a unique purpose within your movie. Everything from basic graphics to full-blown animations can be stored as symbols in the library, making it easy to manage and build even the most complex movies. Each symbol is represented in the library and in the Property Inspector by a unique icon, so you can easily identify which symbol belongs to which category. Here's a closer look at what makes each symbol unique:

Graphic (⬚): Graphic symbols are the most basic of the three types and can contain graphics, type, imported artwork, or bitmaps. Use graphic symbols to store your artwork in the library or to get graphics ready for animation. Graphic symbols can contain other graphics, so you can make more elaborate symbols by converting groups of graphic symbols into a single, new graphic symbol.

Button (⬚): These symbols are designed for use as controls, and they contain multiple states that react to a user's mouse interaction, including clicks and rollovers. You'll learn how to create and work with buttons in Lesson 10, "Creating Navigation Controls."

Movie clip (⬚): Movie clips can best be described as super-symbols. They can contain anything from other symbols to full animations, even sounds and video. In addition, movie clip symbols have their own independent timelines, so they are capable of housing elaborate animations that can be treated as movies themselves. You'll learn to create and work with movie clips in Lesson 12, "Introducing Movie Clips."

A look at the Library panel

Each Flash document contains its own Library, where you can find images, sounds and video files that are being used in your movie. The library's contents are displayed and managed in the **Library panel**. This powerful organizational tool lets you view, sort, edit, and return information on symbols. Located on the right side of the screen behind the Property Inspector in the default workspace, the Library panel is the store-all management system for symbols and imported assets. For a detailed list of the panel's features, see the sidebar, "Library panel options."

<table>
<tr><td>**Learning More**</td><td>**Library panel options**</td></tr>
</table>

As you've seen, the Library panel houses some additional features, and if you take a closer look at the Library panel in Figure 3-1, you'll see features that help you organize, sort, and view your symbols and assets.

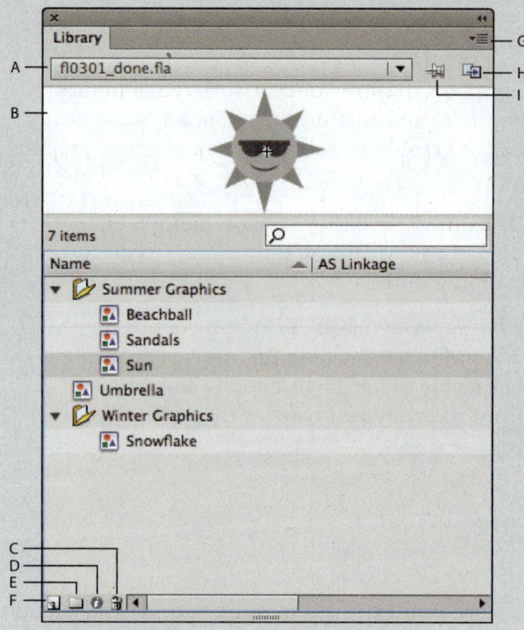

Figure 3-1

A. *Library selector.* B. *Preview window.* C. *Delete.* D. *Properties.* E. *New Folder.*
F. *New Symbol.* G. *Panel menu.* H. *New Library panel.* I. *Pin current library.*

Library selector: Allows you to navigate through the libraries of all currently open documents.

Preview window: Displays your symbol so you can see what it looks like. This is helpful if you have symbols with vague or similar names.

Delete: Deletes the currently selected symbol from the library. Choose Select Unused Items from the panel menu to highlight items that are not currently used by your movie or another symbol in the library.

Properties: Opens up the Symbol Properties dialog box for the currently highlighted symbol. From this dialog box, you can switch the symbol's type or assign it a new name.

New Folder: Creates a folder in the Library panel into which symbols can be sorted. Folders can go several levels deep, making fine-tuned organization possible.

New Symbol: Creates a new symbol in the library and is the same command as Insert > New Symbol or New Symbol from the Library panel's menu.

Panel menu: This menu features additional options for working with symbols or modifying the display of the Library panel. This contains advanced options for linking symbols to ActionScript or setting up shared libraries.

New Library Panel: Opens a duplicate Library panel. Use this if you want to display libraries from multiple open documents at once, or to create several different views of the library you're working on.

Pin Current Library: Keeps the current library in view, even when switching between other open documents. The default behavior is for the Library panel to display the library for the currently active document only. This is useful if you'd like to copy symbols between movies and need to keep a previous library view available while you switch documents.

The Library panel opens up further possibilities by letting you export symbols for direct interaction with ActionScript, or share library items across multiple .fla documents(Figure 3-2). To open the Library panel, choose Window > Library or use the keyboard shortcut Ctrl+L (Windows) or Command+L (Mac OS).

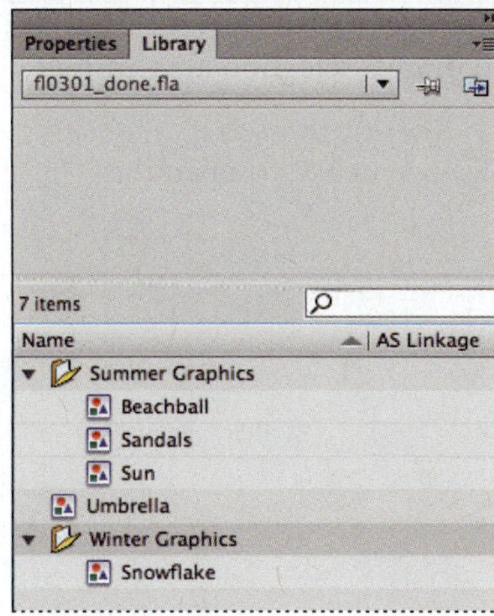

Figure 3-2: The Library panel is invaluable for managing symbols and imported assets.

Creating symbols

The first step toward taking advantage of symbols is to add some to the library. You can create symbols from existing artwork on the Stage, or you can create blank symbols with the option to add content afterwards by clicking on the New Symbol button at the bottom of the Library panel..

Converting a graphic to a symbol

Open the **fl0301.fla** file located in the fl03lessons folder, and select File > Save As. The Save As dialog box appears. In the Save As text field, type **fl0301_work.fla** and press Save As.

On the Stage, you'll find all the artwork you need to construct an ad banner for the fictional department store Spacey's (Figure 3-3). This document was created using the 500 × 500 (Popup) sample template found in the New Document dialog box under Templates > Advertising, which you learned about in Lesson 1, "Flash CS6 Jumpstart."

Figure 3-3: The lesson file contains all the basic artwork you need to get your ad banner started.

Certification Ready 4.6

How do you convert an existing object into a symbol?

In this exercise, you'll convert the six drawings on the Stage to symbols so you can store them in the library and reuse them several times throughout your movie.

<table><tr><td>**Step-by-Step**</td><td>**Follow these steps to convert a graphic to a symbol**</td></tr></table>

1. Using the Selection tool (⬆), click and drag on the Stage and draw a selection area around the entire snowflake to select it.

2. Choose Modify > Convert to Symbol, or use the keyboard shortcut F8, to open the Convert to Symbol dialog box (Figure 3-4).

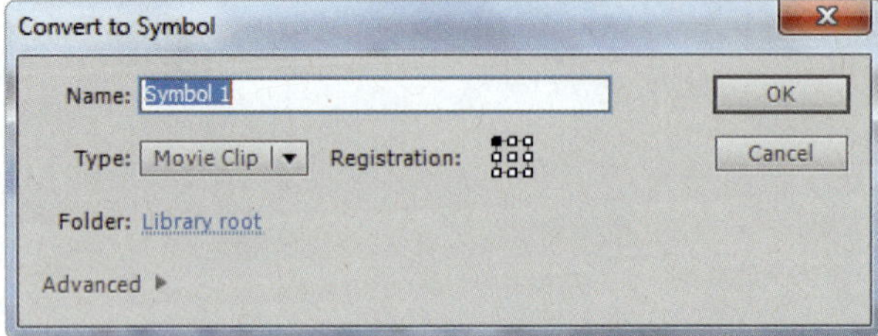

Figure 3-4: *Choose Modify > Convert to Symbol to save any artwork on the Stage as a symbol in your library.*

3. Assign the name **Snowflake** to the new symbol by typing it in the Name text field. You can name symbols just about anything you want, but try to keep names short and intuitive so you can easily figure out what's what when viewing the Library panel.

4. Choose Graphic from the Type drop-down menu.

5. Set the registration point for the new symbol by clicking the box in the center of the small grid shown on the right. Registration points serve as the *handles* by which you rotate and position symbols on the Stage. Registration point locations will vary, based on the shape of the artwork you're creating; here, a centered point works best.

6. By default, the Folder is listed as Library root (Figure 3-5). This means that your symbol will be in the main Library, not in any folders; you can leave this for now. Once you create folders, you'll be able to sort new symbols directly into a folder as you create them.

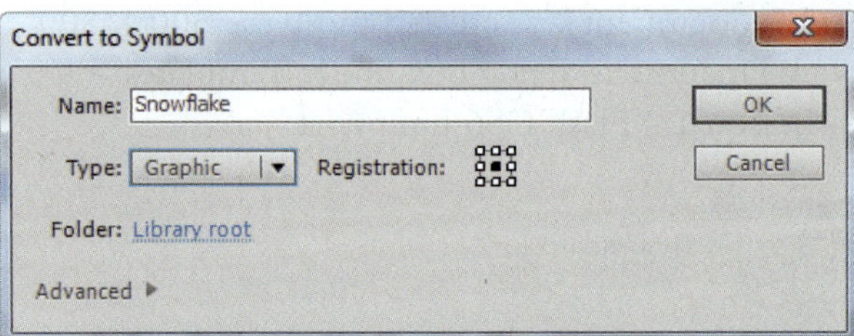

Figure 3-5: *The Convert to Symbol dialog box.*

7. Press OK. The new symbol appears in the Library panel, and the snowflake image remains exactly where you left it on the Stage (Figure 3-6). Click on the Properties tab to bring the Property Inspector forward. Click on the snowflake to select it. A special Graphic icon (🖾) in the top-left corner of the Property Inspector will confirm that the artwork is now an instance of the newly created Snowflake symbol (Figure 3-8). After it is converted to a graphic symbol, the snowflake should have a registration point in its center and a blue bounding box surrounding it (Figure 3-7).

Figure 3-6: The basic snowflake artwork.

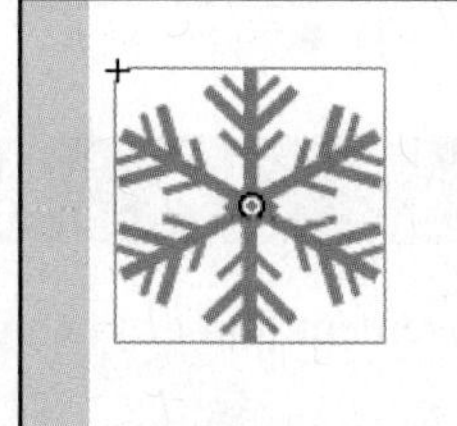

Figure 3-7: The artwork as a symbol.

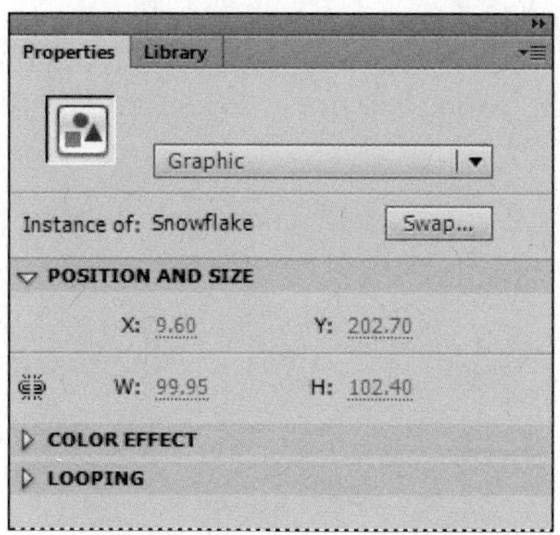

Figure 3-8: The Graphic icon and label verify that you have converted your symbol properly.

8. Repeat steps 1 to 7 for the Snowman, Beachball, Umbrella, and Sun designs on the Stage, using the corresponding names respectively. Leave the sandals design unconverted for now. When you're done, look at the Library panel in Figure 3-9 and you'll see that the artwork pieces have been added to your library as graphic symbols.

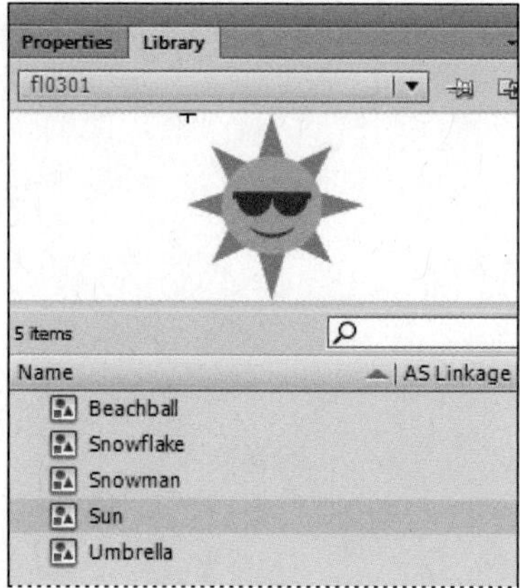

Figure 3-9: The new symbols in the library.

9. Choose File > Save to save your work, and keep the document open.

Take Note...
Don't confuse symbols with Drawing Objects. Although both appear inside bounding boxes, only symbols are stored in the library and have all the advantages discussed in this lesson. If you're unsure, select the artwork and use the Property Inspector to verify that what you're looking at is truly a symbol instance, and not a Drawing Object.

Learning More

What's the point of registration points?

A symbol's registration point determines the measurement point by which the symbol is positioned on the Stage.

You specify a registration point when you first convert an object to a symbol, and you should choose a point subjectively based on the shape of the object. It is common to set a centered registration point (Figure 3–10) for objects that are round or symmetrical (such as the beachball), or a top–left registration point for text or symbols that have no real point of symmetry (such as the snowman). When you edit your symbol, you can change the registration point by moving the artwork around relative to the crosshair that appears on the Stage in the symbol's Edit mode.

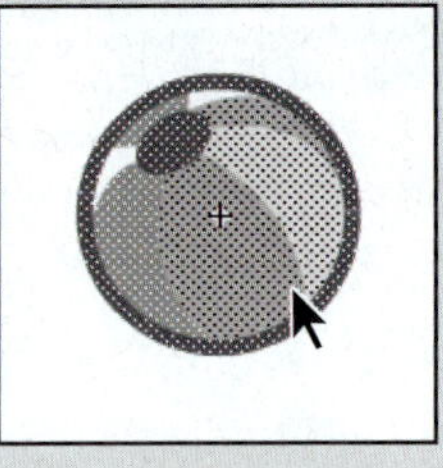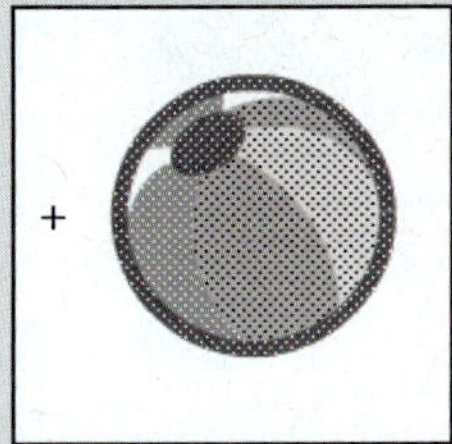

Figure 3–10: *Change the registration point.*

Certification Ready 4.6

How do you create a new symbol?

Creating blank symbols

You can create symbols of any type even when existing artwork isn't available. To do this, you can form an empty symbol, and add content later by drawing, pasting, or importing artwork into the new symbol. Here's how:

<table>
<tr><td>

Follow these steps to create a new symbol

</td><td>

Step-by-Step

</td></tr>
</table>

1. Select the entire drawing of the sandals on the Stage using the Selection tool (◣) as shown in Figure 3-11.

Take Note...

You can also draw a selection area around the sandals using the Lasso tool (⌀) to make sure you get all the pieces.

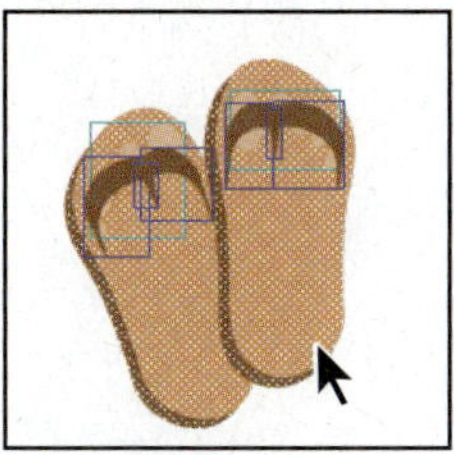

Figure 3-11*: Use the Selection tool to select the sandals drawing.*

2. Choose Edit > Cut to cut the artwork from the Stage and place it on the clipboard.

3. Choose Insert > New Symbol to open the Create New Symbol dialog box, which looks identical to the Convert to Symbol dialog box you used in the last exercise.

Type **Sandals** in the Name text field to name the new symbol.

4. Choose Graphic from the Type drop-down menu as displayed in Figure 3-12. Press OK to create the new symbol.

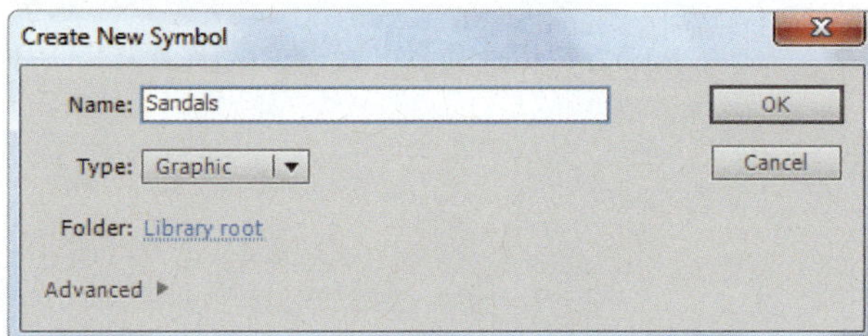

Figure 3-12*: The Create New Symbol dialog box.*

5. The new Sandals symbol appears in the Library panel, and you are presented with a blank Stage (Figure 3-13). You are now in Edit mode for the new symbol, where you can draw, paste, or import content for your symbol.

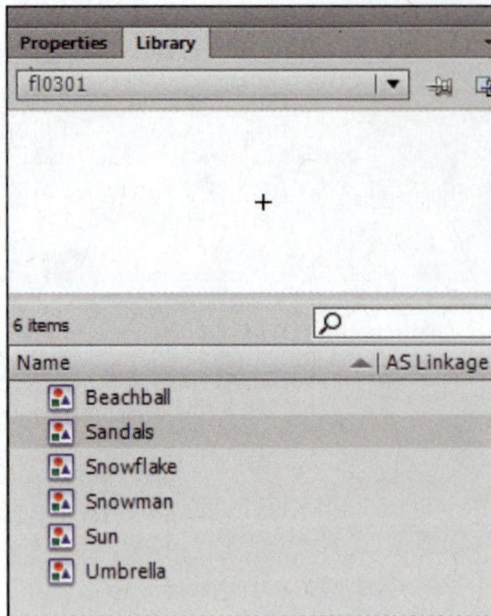

Figure 3-13: The Library now features your new Sandals symbol.

6. Select Edit > Paste in Center to paste the sandals artwork from the clipboard onto the symbol's Stage. This artwork is now included in your symbol, confirmed by the updated preview in the Library panel as shown in Figure 3-14.

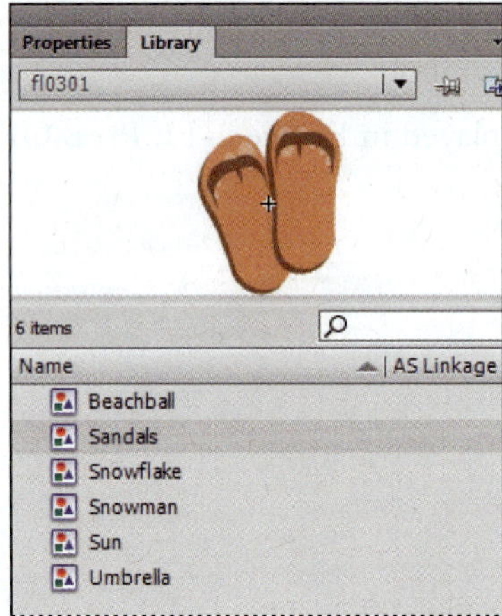

Figure 3-14: Paste the sandals onto the Stage in Edit mode.

7. Exit Edit mode by clicking the Scene 1 link above the Stage (Figure 3-15).

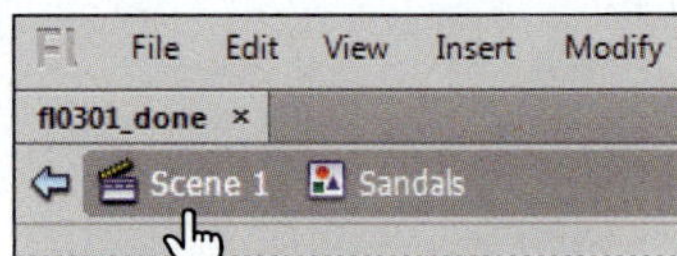

Figure 3-15: Select Scene 1 above the Stage to exit the symbol's Edit mode.

8. Choose File > Save to save your work.

You'll notice that the Create New Symbol dialog box didn't give you the option to specify a registration point. This is done when you paste, draw, or import artwork and position it relative to the crosshair in the symbol's Edit mode.

Whether you create blank symbols or convert existing artwork to symbols is completely up to you. Some designers prefer to have something tangible to work with before they create a symbol; others like to get symbols defined ahead of time.

Building artwork with symbol instances

With all the artwork added to the library as graphic symbols, you're ready to start building the layout for the banner advertisement. You'll find that working with symbols will be essential as the theme for your banner evolves. You'll soon discover how to easily place, swap, and update symbol instances to build and change the look and feel of your banner in a snap.

Positioning and snapping in symbol instances

To get the Spacey's ad banner started, you'll create a patterned background using some of your new symbols. The lesson is already sized and has visual guides to help you. To more accurately position symbols on the Stage, you'll use snapping. Snapping enables a magnet-like behavior, causing objects you move around the Stage to *snap* in place to guides, grids, or other objects when they are moved within a close–enough range of those objects.

Follow these steps to use snapping to position a symbol on the stage

1. Choose View > Snapping to open the Snapping submenu, and make sure the Snap to Grid and Snap to Guides options are checked (Figure 3-16).

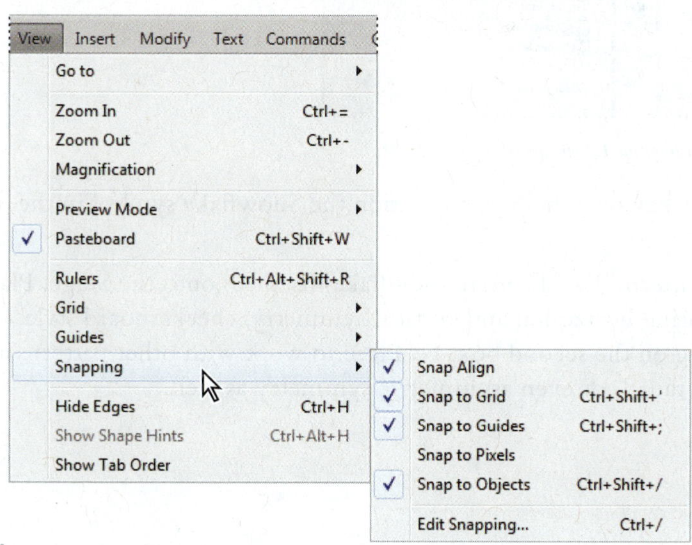

Figure 3-16: Set up your Snap options under View > Snapping.

2. Choose View > Grid > Show Grid to display the grid; in this document, it's set with the gridlines 50 pixels apart. You can store unique grid settings with each document.

Certification Ready 4.7
What is the difference between a symbol and a symbol instance?

Step-by-Step

3. Choose View > Guides > Show Guides. Vertical and horizontal guides appear, each one centered within the gridlines as shown in Figure 3-17. These will help center and position symbols inside each box formed by the grid.

Figure 3-17: The visible grid and guides will help you align artwork on the Stage.

4. Choose Edit > Select All, and press Backspace (Windows) or Delete (Mac OS) to delete any existing symbols from the Stage. Now you have a clean start for the layout.

5. With the Library panel open, locate and drag an instance of the Snowflake symbol from the library onto the Stage (Figure 3-18).

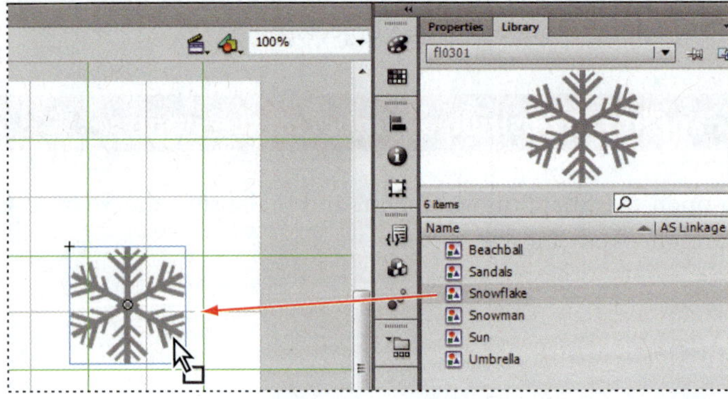

Figure 3-18: To place a symbol, drag it from the Library panel onto the Stage.

Certification Ready 2.2

What are some examples of horizontal, vertical, diagonal, radial, and asymmetric symmetry?

6. Using the snapping action behavior to help you, position the Snowflake symbol in the upper-left box.

7. To finish the background pattern, drag 12 more snowflake instances onto the Stage. Place one in every other box creating horizontal and vertical symmetry, checkerboard style, with the second row starting on the second box. Feel free to work with other patterns as well, try creating diagonal, radial, or even asymmetric symmetry as well.

8. Choose File > Save to save your work. See Figure 3-19 to view the completed background.

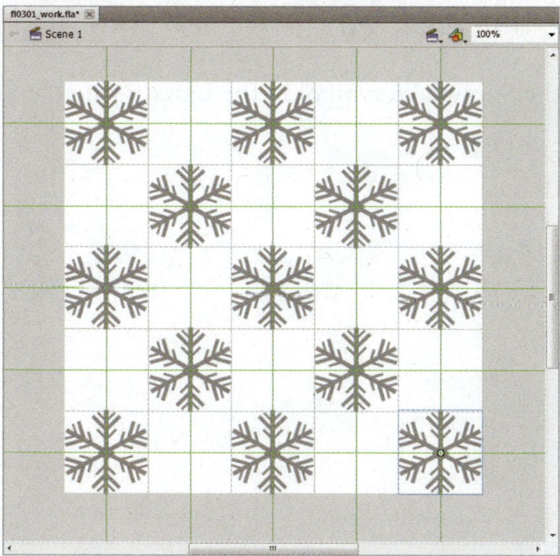

Figure 3-19: *The completed background for your ad banner.*

Editing and duplicating symbols

The beauty of working with symbols is that modifications to the master symbol automatically transfer to all instances throughout your movie. If you're not quite happy with the snowflake, for example, adjust it once and the entire background changes because all symbol instances are linked. You can update symbols in two places: from the master symbol in the Library panel or from any instance of that symbol on the Stage (Figure 3-20). In this exercise you'll explore both methods.

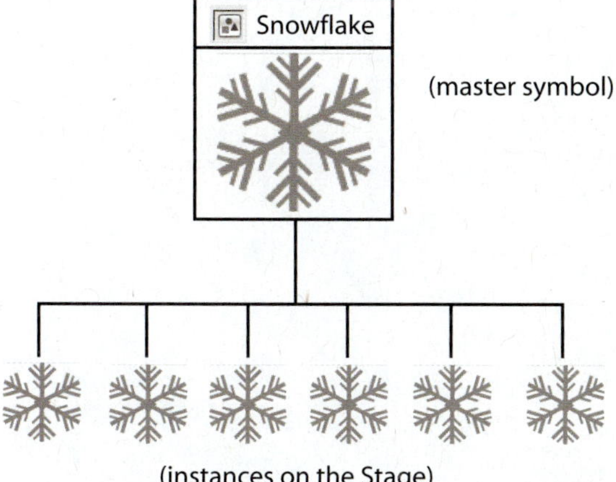

Figure 3-20: *A master symbol controls all its instances throughout a movie.*

Certification Ready 4.8

How do you edit symbols from both the Stage and the Library?

Certification Ready 4.8

What is the difference between editing a symbol and editing an instance of a symbol?

Building artwork with symbol instances

To edit a symbol directly from the Library panel:

<table><tr><td>Step-by-Step</td><td>Follow these steps to edit a symbol from the Library panel</td></tr></table>

1. As shown in Figure 3-21, double-click the Snowflake symbol in the Library panel to enter the symbol's Edit mode.

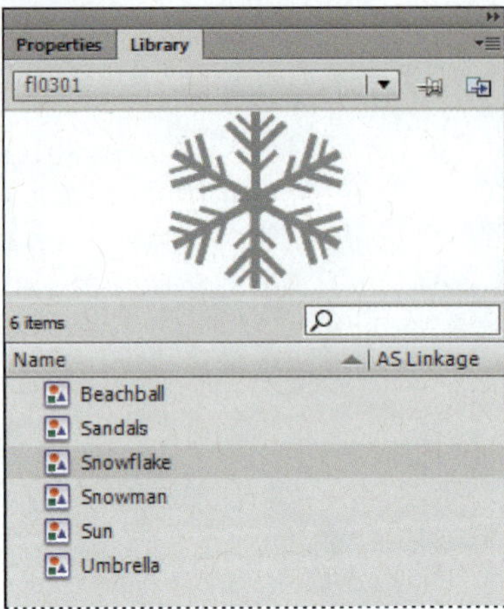

Figure 3-21: *Double-click a symbol in the Library panel to edit it.*

It now appears on the Stage in basic form (Figure 3-22), as it was before you added it to the library.

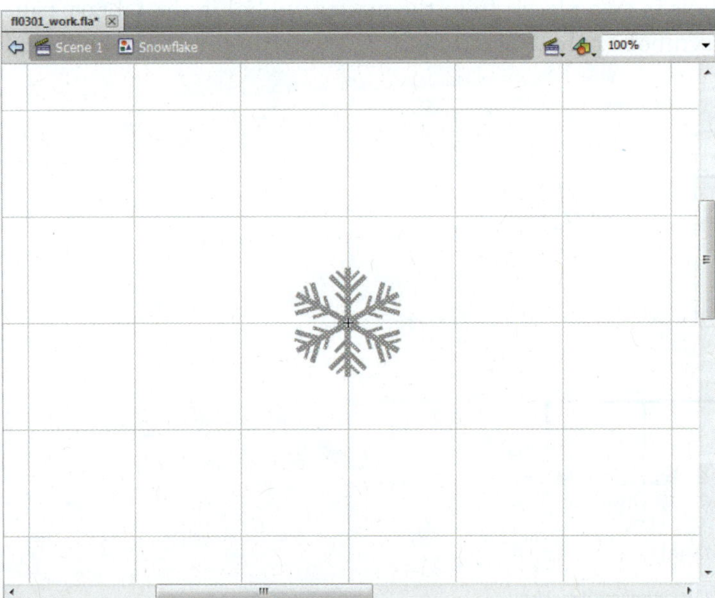

Figure 3-22: *Inside the Snowflake symbol's Edit mode.*

2. Select the snowflake with the Selection tool (⬉), if it is not already selected. From the Fill color swatch in the Tools panel, select the light blue color labeled #CCCCFF (Figure 3-23).

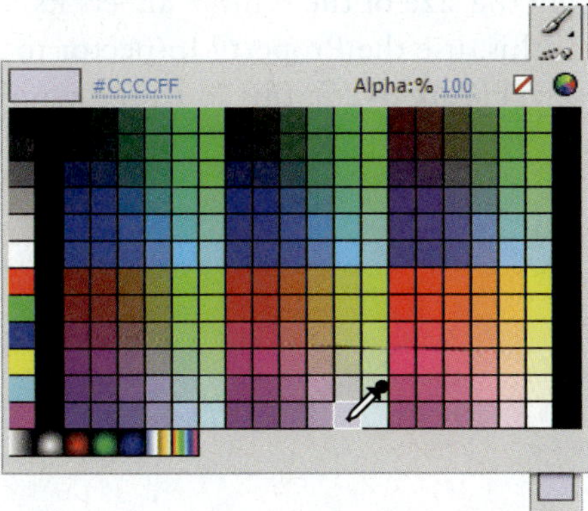

Figure 3-23: *Select a new color for your symbol.*

3. Exit the symbol's Edit mode by clicking the Scene 1 link above the Stage. Flash returns you to the main Stage. As displayed in Figure 3-24, all 13 instances of the Snowflake symbol on the Stage now reflect the color change that you applied.

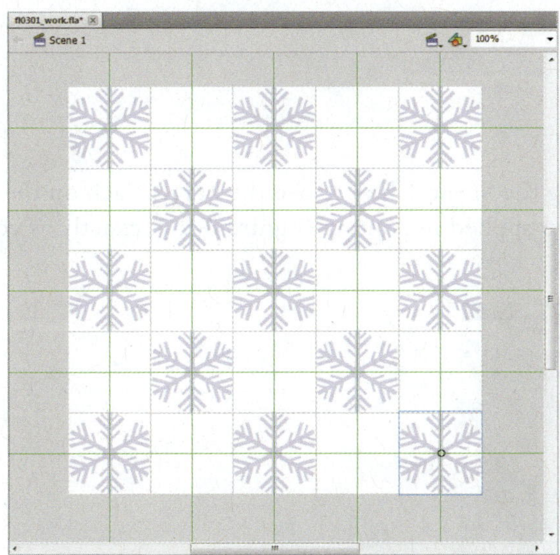

Figure 3-24: *All snowflakes adopt changes made to the master symbol.*

Editing symbols in place

The advantage to editing symbols directly from the Library panel is that you can focus on the symbol itself without the interference of other artwork on the Stage. Sometimes, however, you need to modify a symbol to better fit with the artwork surrounding it. In these cases, you can edit the symbol in-place on the Stage to see it in context as you make changes.

Certification Ready 4.8

How do you edit an instance of a symbol?

Follow these steps to edit a symbol in place　　　　　　　　　　**Step-by-Step**

1. Double-click one of the snowflake instances on the Stage. The other instances *dim out* because they are no longer selectable. The snowflake you chose, however, is editable as basic artwork, just as it was in the previous exercise.

2. Click on the Properties tab to bring the Property Inspector forward. In the Property Inspector, type **80** in both the width (W) and height (H) text fields to set the width and height of the snowflake to 80 pixels. Notice that changes also affect the dimmed instances that are visible in the background and that changing the size of the symbol affects its alignment relative to your grid. To compensate for this, use the Property Inspector to set the X and Y positions of the graphic to **–40** each (Figure 3-25); this shifts the symbol instances enough to keep them each in their respective grid boxes.

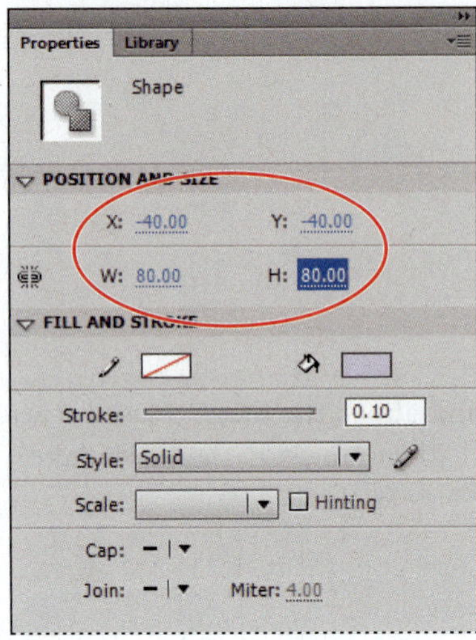

Figure 3-25: *Reposition the Snowflake symbol to compensate for its size change.*

3. Exit the symbol's Edit mode by clicking the Scene 1 link above the Stage. Back on the main Stage, you can see the changes you applied in context (Figure 3-26), exactly as you saw them when you were editing.

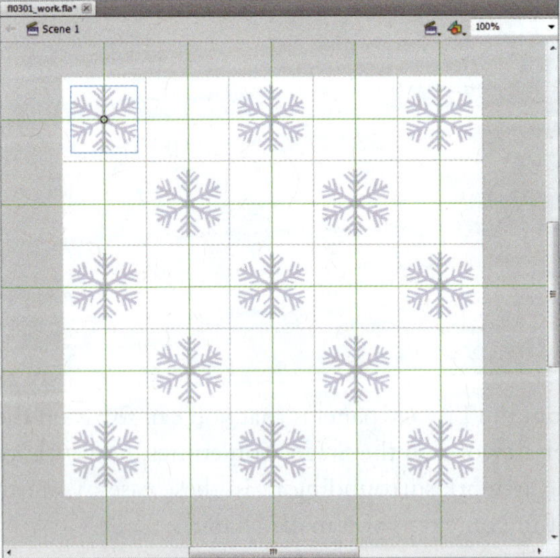

Figure 3-26: *Edit in Place allows you to see a symbol in the context of other items onstage.*

4. Choose File > Save to save your work.

Modifying individual symbol instances

What if you don't want a whole new look, but you just need to make a minor tweak to a single symbol instance? The link between the master symbol and its instances may seem constraining at times. The good news is that it doesn't have to be: Every instance of a symbol can be modified to take on its own color, dimensions, rotation, and transparency.

To resize or rotate a symbol instance, for example, select the instance on the Stage and use the Free Transform tool, Property Inspector, or Transform panel.

<table><tr><td>**Follow these steps to modify a symbol using the Transform panel**</td><td>**Step-by-Step**</td></tr></table>

1. Using the Selection tool (⬉), select a single instance of your Snowflake symbol on the Stage, and choose Window > Transform to open the Transform panel, which allows you to enter exact values and resize and rotate a single instance of the Snowflake symbol.

2. In the Transform panel, make sure the *Constrain* option is active, and type **80%** in either the vertical or horizontal scaling boxes at the top of the pane as shown in Figure 3-27. Press Enter (Windows) or Return (Mac OS).

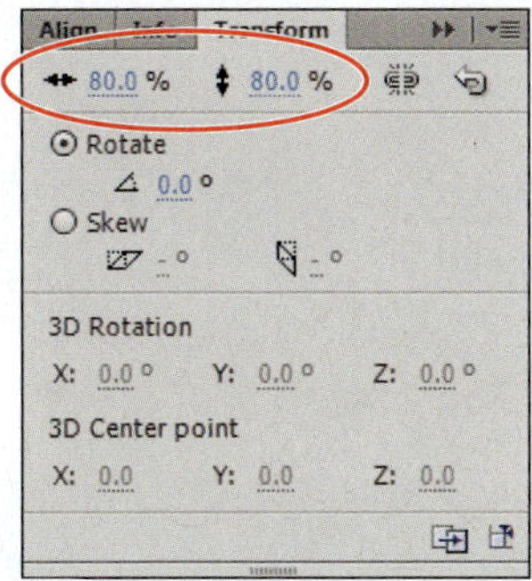

Figure 3–27: Resize and rotate a single instance of the Snowflake symbol.

3. Type **45** in the Rotate text field to rotate your snowflake, and then press Enter (Windows) or Return (Mac OS) to apply the transformations (Figure 3-28). This, combined with the scaling in step 2, creates a nice variation from the other instances on the Stage.

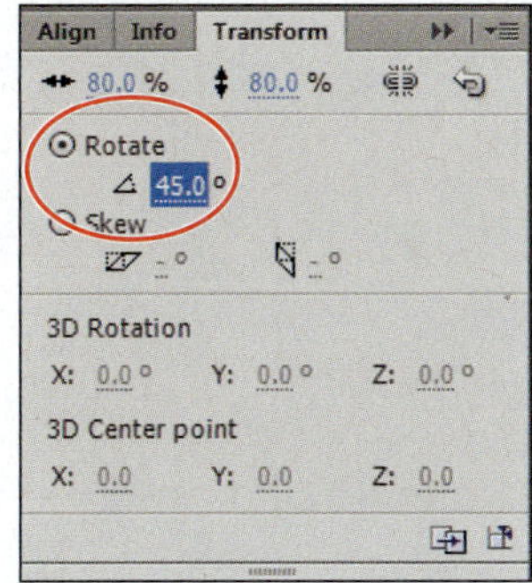

Figure 3–28: Set the rotation in degrees for the Snowflake symbol.

Modifying instance color

To modify the color of a symbol instance, you will use the Color drop-down menu in the Property Inspector, which lets you create interesting variations by applying color tints, brightness, and transparency. Try it on one of the ad banner's Snowflake symbols:

<table>
<tr><td>Step-by-Step</td><td>Follow these steps to modify the color of a symbol instance</td></tr>
</table>

1. Select the instance of the snowflake on the upper-left corner of the Stage. Make sure the Property Inspector is visible.

2. Open the Color Effect section of the Property Inspector by clicking on the triangle to the left of its label. From the Style drop-down menu, choose Tint as shown in Figure 3-29. This produces several options, including a color swatch and tint amount (percentage).

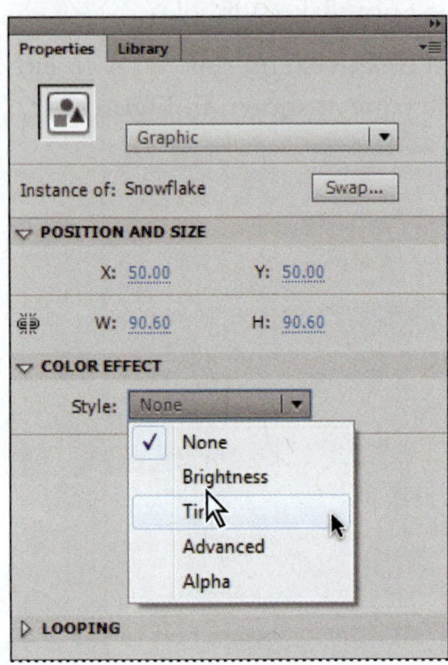

Figure 3-29: *You can apply a unique color tint to any instance of a symbol using the Property Inspector.*

3. From the color swatch, choose a blue as shown in Figure 3-30 (to match the example, use #0066CC). Set the tint amount to 100 percent by using the slider or typing **100** in the tint percentage text field. The symbol instance is now a darker blue, leaving the other instances and the master symbol unaffected. As you see, you can achieve some creative variations among your snowflake instances without modifying the original symbol in the library.

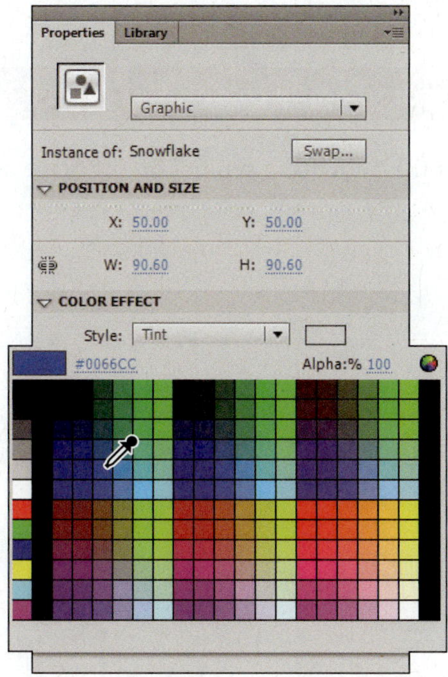

Figure 3-30: *Choose a color and tint percentage with the Color menu's Tint option.*

In the next exercise, you'll modify the background of your banner by changing the color and transparency of different symbol instances to create variety and texture.

Fine-tuning your background

You can take advantage of the unique characteristics that can be assigned to each symbol instance to add depth to your background. To make the snowflakes less obstructive to the type and additional artwork you'll add later, you can reduce the transparency (referred to as *alpha*) of all instances on the Stage. You can also use the Property Inspector to apply varying color tints to selected instances.

<table><tr><td>**Step-by-Step**</td><td>**Follow these steps to use the Property Inspector to apply color tints**</td></tr></table>

1. Choose Edit > Select All to select all instances of the Snowflake symbol on the Stage as shown in Figure 3–31.

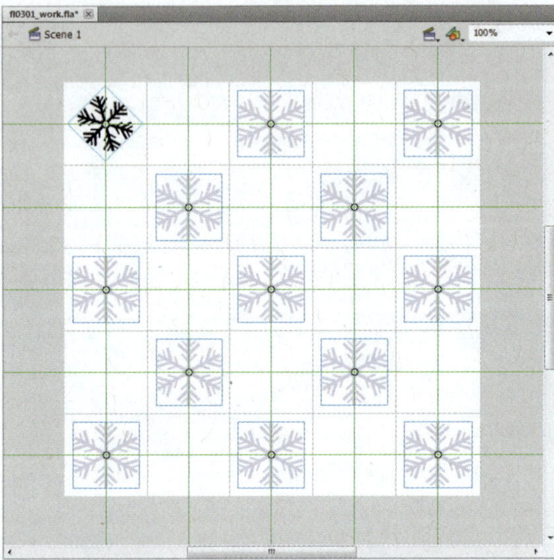

Figure 3–31: *To select everything on the Stage, choose Edit > Select All.*

2. In the Color Effect section of the Property Inspector, select Alpha from the Style drop-down menu as shown in Figure 3–32. The Alpha percentage and slider should appear, enabling you to set the transparency (in percent) of your symbols.

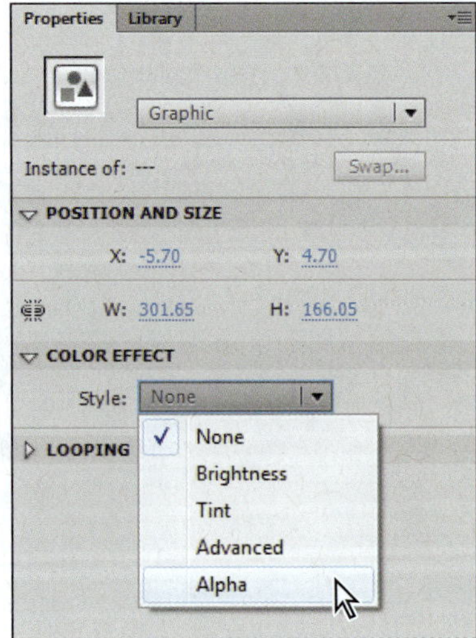

Figure 3–32: *The Alpha option is found in the Style drop-down menu in the Property Inspector.*

3. Using the Alpha slider, change the transparency of the selected symbols to 40 percent (Figure 3–33). Or, if you prefer, type **40** in the text field next to the slider. Notice in Figure 3–34 that the symbols immediately become more transparent on the Stage.

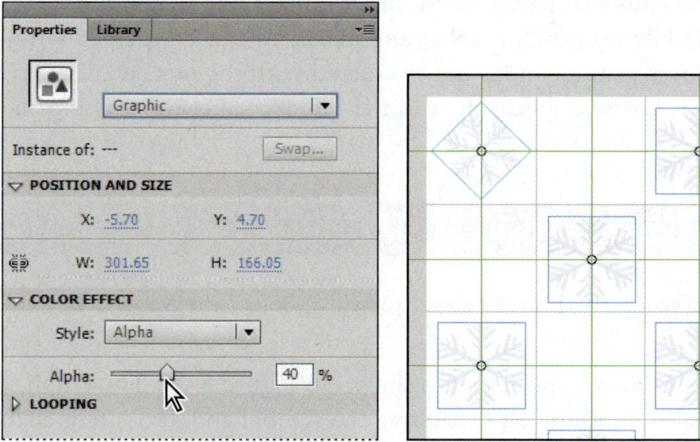

Figure 3–33: *Set the Alpha amount to 40 percent.* **Figure 3–34**: *The results show the decrease of opacity in the symbols.*

4. Choose Edit > Deselect All. Select only the snowflake instance in the lower-left corner. Adjust the Alpha setting in the Property Inspector to 90 percent (Figure 3–35) to darken this instance of the snowflake, setting it apart from the others as shown in Figure 3–36.

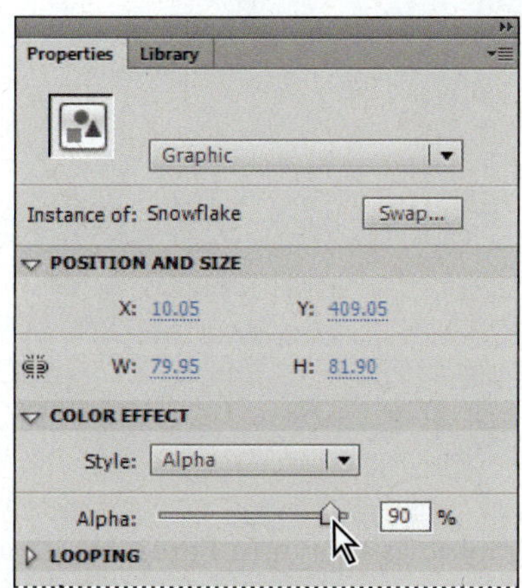

Figure 3–35: *Set the opacity amount to 90 percent.*

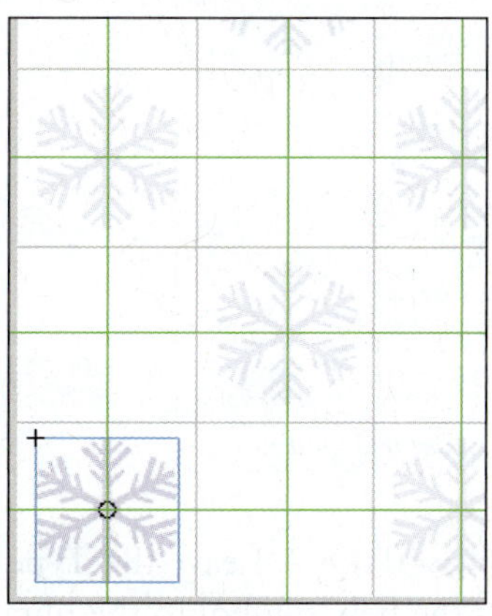

Figure 3–36: *The results show a darkened instance.*

Duplicating symbols

Sometimes a variation on a theme is the best way to explore other possible design ideas.
Perhaps you want to apply changes to a symbol beyond color or size (for instance, changing its
actual shape). Rather than make edits that compromise the original symbol, consider making
a duplicate of the symbol in the Library panel. Duplicating makes an exact copy of a symbol,
and the new copy becomes its own symbol and is not associated with the original. Try creating
a variation on the Snowflake symbol by duplicating it in the Library panel and making changes
to the new copy.

<table><tr><td>**Step-by-Step**</td><td>**Follow these steps to duplicate a symbol**</td></tr></table>

1. Click on the Library tab to bring the Library panel forward. Select the Snowflake symbol
   in the Library panel.

2. Choose Duplicate from the Library panel menu as shown in Figure 3–37. The Duplicate
   Symbol dialog box appears, prompting you to rename the symbol and, if desired, change
   the symbol type.

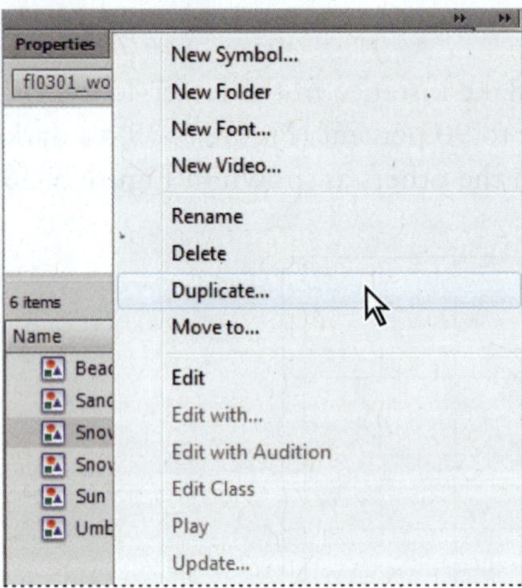

*Figure 3–37: Duplicate the symbol through the
Library panel menu.*

3. Name the symbol **Snowflake 2**. Leave the Type as Graphic as shown in Figure 3–38, and
   press OK. Flash adds the new symbol to the library. You can now use this symbol like any
   other, and it has no relationship to the original from which it was created.

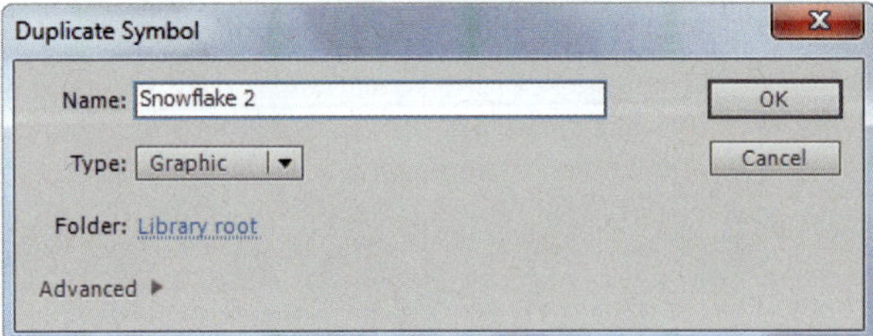

*Figure 3–38: Set the name for the snowflake copy in the Duplicate Symbol
dialog box.*

4. Double-click the new symbol in the Library panel to edit it. Add a different color, or use the Ink Bottle tool (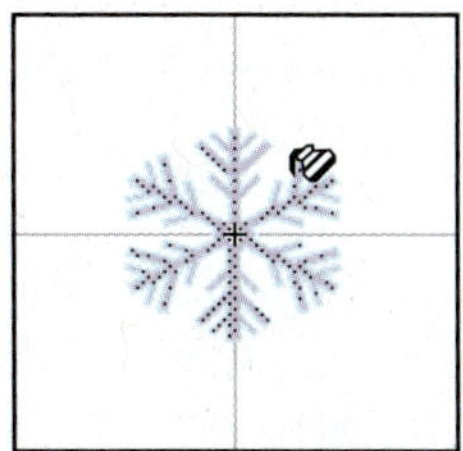) to apply an interesting outline (stroke) to it (Figure 3-39). Click on Scene 1 to exit the Edit mode for this symbol and return to the main Stage. Notice that the modifications made to Snowflake 2 don't affect instances of the original Snowflake symbol on the Stage.

Figure 3-39: Make some changes to distinguish Snowflake 2 from the original.

5. Choose File > Save to save your work.

   A duplicated symbol has no relationship to the symbol from which it was created. Modifications made to the duplicate will have no effect on the original or any of its instances. They are regarded as completely different symbols.

Adding graphics and text to your banner

With your background complete, you're ready to add the headline text and feature graphics to advertise your sale. For your feature graphic, you'll use the snowman drawing you added to the library earlier in this lesson. For the type, you'll use the Text tool and skills you learned in Lesson 2, "Getting Started with the Drawing Tools."

Follow these steps to add graphics and text   **Step-by-Step**

1. If it is not already selected, choose the Selection tool (▶) from the Tools panel.

2. Drag a copy of the Snowman symbol from the Library panel onto the right side of the Stage.

3. Toggle to the Property Inspector by pressing Ctrl+F3 (Windows) or Command+F3 (Mac OS). If it's not already selected, click the *Lock width and height values together* button (⬤) next to the W field to keep any adjustments to either the width or height proportional.

4. Type **350** in the H (height) field to resize the snowman. Type **350** for the X position, and **300** for Y position as shown in Figure 3-40.

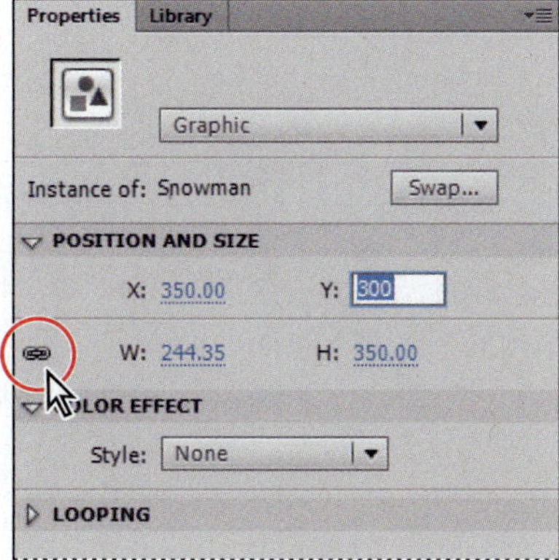

Figure 3-40: Use the Property Inspector to reposition and resize the snowman.

Adding graphics and text to your banner

5. Select the Text tool (T) on the Tools panel. Text-related options such as Font and Font size (in points) appear in the Property Inspector. Choose Times New Roman (or equivalent) for the font, and type **40** in the Font size text field (or use the slider). For now, set your type color to black using the Text (fill) color swatch (Figure 3-41).

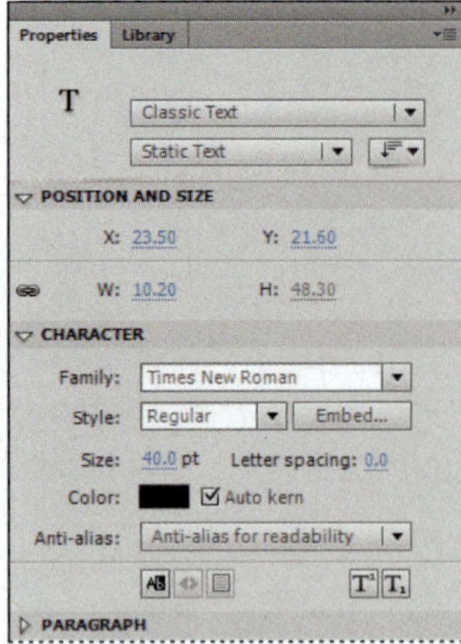

Figure 3-41: Use the Text tool and the Property Inspector to specify type options before creating the text on the Stage.

6. Click on the left side of the Stage, and type the words **SPACEY'S winter sale**, as shown in Figure 3-42.

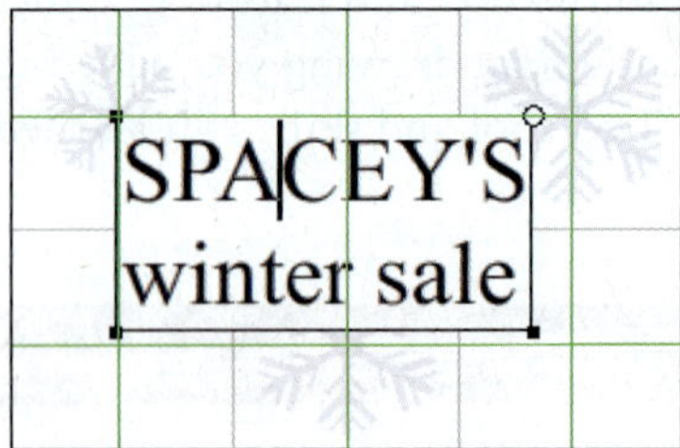

Figure 3-42: Type the words, SPACEY'S winter sale, on the Stage.

7. As shown in Figure 3-43, use the Text tool to select only the words *winter sale* inside the text area.

8. In the Property Inspector, set the color of the selected text to blue. To match the example, use the color labeled #003399. Choose Italic from the Style drop-down menu to change the style of the selected text to italics (Figure 3-44).

Figure 3-43: Selected text.

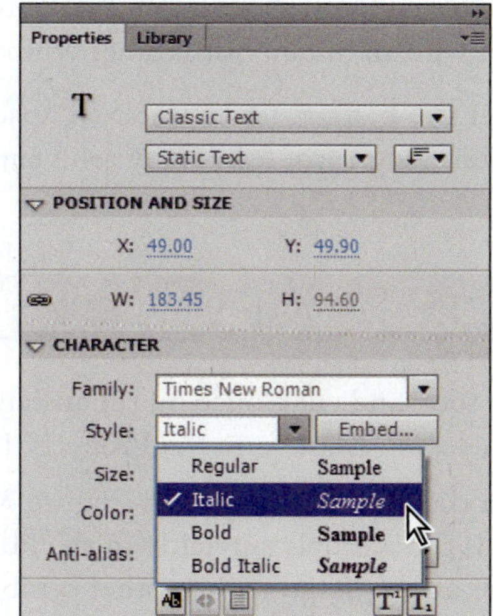

Figure 3-44: Use the Property Inspector to fine-tune the color and style of the selected text.

Your banner should be complete for the winter sale (Figure 3-45); choose View > Guides > Show Guides to toggle the guides off, and View > Grid > Show Grid to hide your grid. Creating and using symbols in this lesson allowed you to place and modify as many instances as you needed to complete your layout. In the next exercise, you'll discover how symbols can streamline your creative process even further.

Figure 3-45: Your completed banner, constructed using symbol instances.

Swapping symbols

Sometimes when you think you're finished, you're not—requirements change, new products are introduced, or those bright ideas you had in a late-night design session look dim the next morning. Symbols make such revisions easier; instead of starting from scratch, use the Property Inspector to **swap** any instance of a symbol with an instance of another symbol in the Library panel.

Consider your Spacey's winter sale banner, for example. If Spacey's wants a summer sale banner based on your successful winter design, you can easily reinvent your banner with a few quick symbol swaps.

Step-by-Step | **Follow these steps to swap a symbol instance**

1. Switch to your Selection tool, and click once on the instance of the Snowflake symbol in the upper-left corner to select it. Make sure the Property Inspector is visible.

2. Click the Swap button in the Property Inspector (Figure 3–46). The Swap Symbol dialog box appears, displaying all the symbols currently in the library. The Swap button lets you swap any symbol instance on the Stage with another symbol from the library.

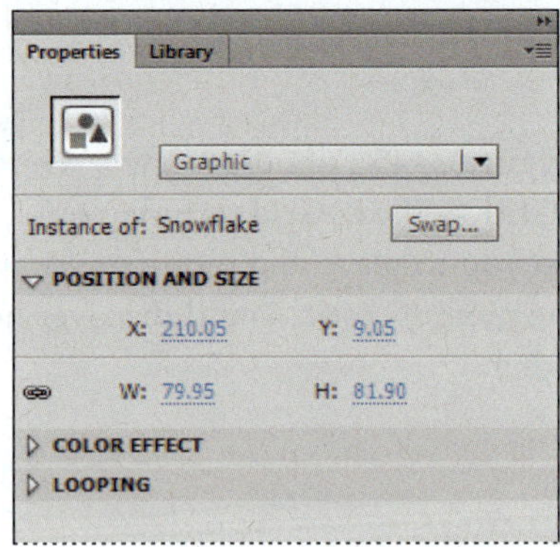

Figure 3–46: Swap any symbol instance on the Stage with another symbol from the library.

3. As shown in 3–47, select the Beachball symbol from the list and press OK, or double-click the Beachball symbol. A beachball replaces the snowflake in the upper-left corner. Swapped symbols inherit position as well as transformations.

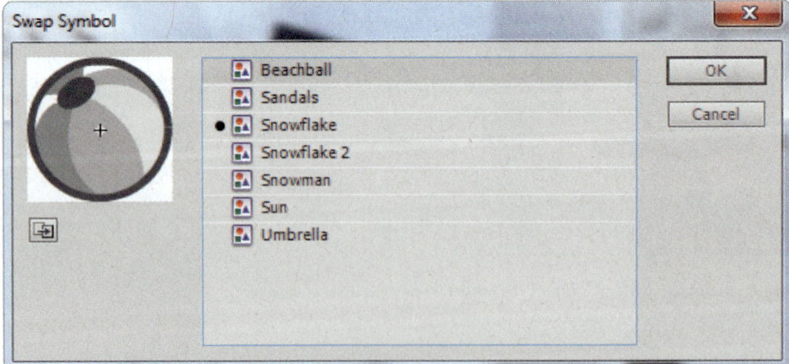

Figure 3–47: Select a different symbol from the library with which you can replace the current instance.

4. Repeat steps 1 to 3 for all remaining instances of the Snowflake symbol that appear in your background. If you'd like to change it up, try swapping some instances with the Sun or Umbrella symbols instead. Replacing each snowflake instance with other symbols in the library changes the whole theme. The best part is that positioning and other unique properties applied to the snowflake instances (such as Alpha) are maintained, even when a new symbol takes their place (Figure 3-48).

Figure 3-48: *Swap out all the snowflake instances.*

5. Select the Snowman symbol on the Stage. This is currently your feature graphic, which you need to replace with something that matches the new theme.

6. Click the Swap button to open the Swap Symbol dialog box, and double-click the Sandals symbol in the list that appears. An instance of the Sandals symbol replaces the snowman as shown in Figure 3-49. There is no need to resize the sandals, because the new symbol instance inherits size properties from the previous one.

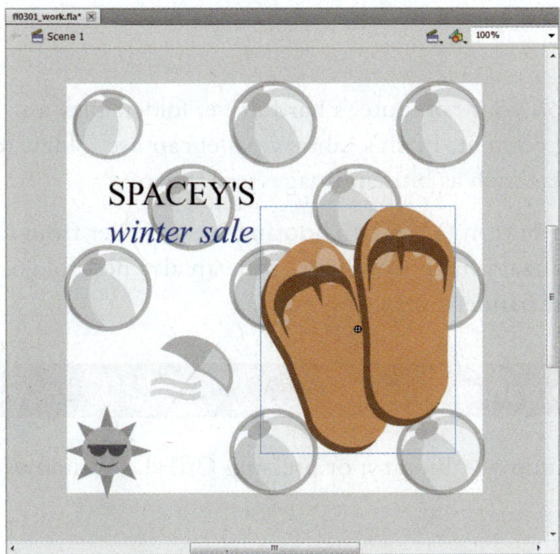

Figure 3-49: *Away goes winter as you replace the Snowman symbol with the Sandals symbol using the Swap button.*

7. Select the Text tool (T) from the Tools panel, and select the words *winter* inside the text frame to edit them.

8. Replace the word *winter* by typing **summer**, then select the words *summer sale*. Using the Property Inspector set the type color to orange (#FF9900).

9. Press the Escape key to commit the text changes (Figure 3-50). Choose File > Save to save your work.

Figure 3-50: *Your new summer sale banner.*

Swapping symbols is not only great for use for a single instance, but also can be taken further to change the feel of an entire movie or layout.

Managing the Library

As you use symbols more and more, you may find the Library panel getting a bit crowded. Even with the panel's sorting abilities, you'll definitely need to get a handle on things with a bit of organization. The Library panel features several ways to clean house and make sense of your assets.

Organizing symbols with folders

Whether for papers in a file cabinet or files on your computer's hard drive, folders play an essential role in categorizing and organizing content. Flash's Library panel can use folders to organize symbols, sounds, and imported assets such as bitmap images and video.

You can create folders using the New Folder button (■) or by choosing New Folder from the Library panel's menu. For very flexible organizational possibilities, you can also nest folders inside other folders. Practice organizing your banner project's symbols.

<table>
<tr><td>**Step-by-Step**</td><td>**Follow these steps to use folders to organize symbols**</td></tr>
</table>

1. Open the Library panel by selecting Window > Library, or pressing Ctrl+L (Windows) or Command+L (Mac OS).

2. Click the New Folder button in the lower-left corner to create a new folder in the Library panel. In the highlighted text field next to the new folder icon, type the phrase **Winter Graphics** to replace the default name, Untitled Folder 1 as displayed in Figure 3-51. Press Enter (Windows) or Return (Mac OS).

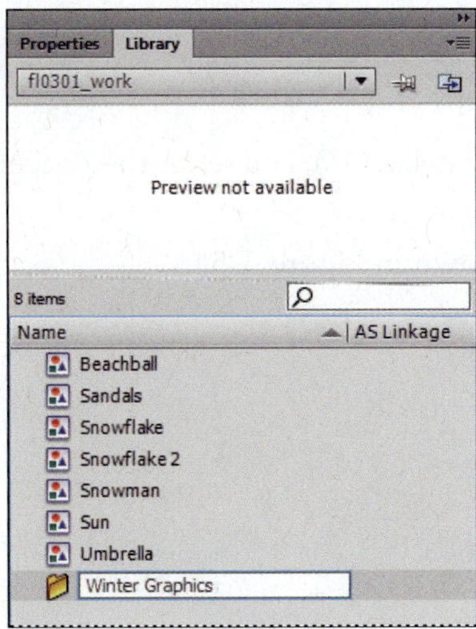

Figure 3-51: *Add a new folder for sorting symbols.*

3. Click and drag the Snowflake symbol into the new Winter Graphics folder as shown in Figure 3-52. Flash sorts it into the folder, and it appears indented under the new folder (Figure 3-53). Collapsed view hides the sorted symbols within their folders.

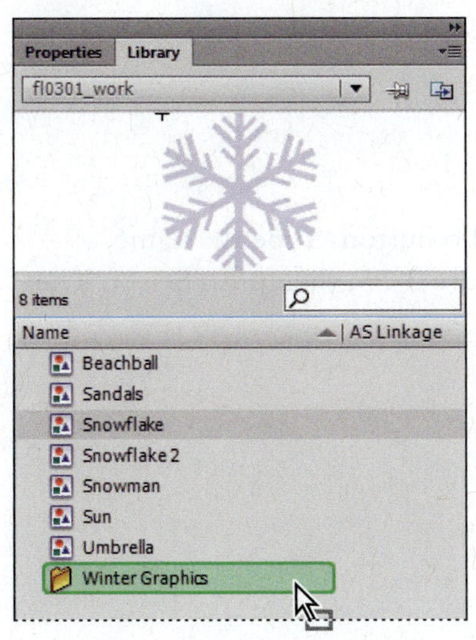

Figure 3-52: *Drag symbols to sort them into folders.*

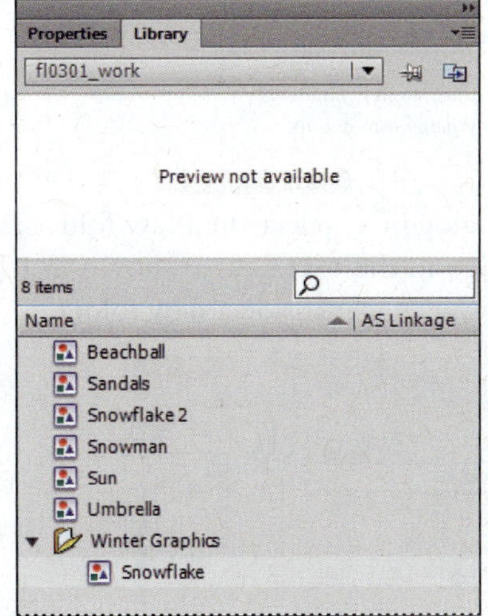

Figure 3-53: *The Winter Graphics folder (shown expanded) now contains a symbol.*

4. Repeat step 3 to add the Snowman symbol to the Winter Graphics folder.

The Move To command

A convenient alternative to these steps is the Move To command under the Library panel menu. **Move To** allows you to create new folders or move graphics to existing folders in one step. Sort the summer-themed graphics into a new folder to try it out.

 Follow these steps to use the Move To command

1. Hold down the Ctrl key (Windows) or Command key (Mac OS), and select the Beachball, Sandals, and Sun symbols together.

2. Choose Move To from the Library panel's menu as shown in Figure 3-54.

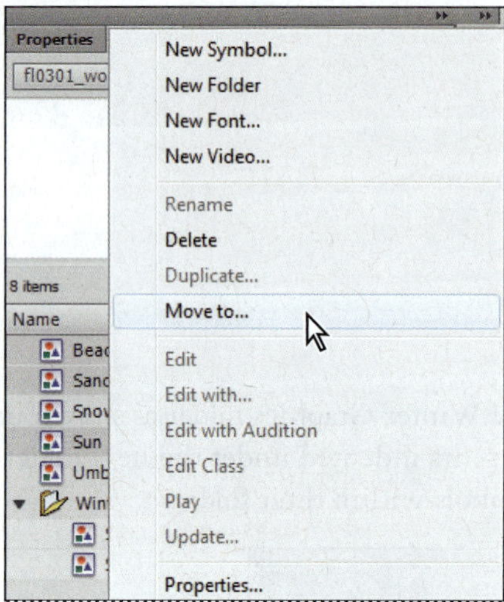

Figure 3-54: *Move To creates, names, and sorts selected items in the Library panel into a new or existing folder.*

3. In the Move To dialog box, select the New folder radio button. Type the name **Summer Graphics** in the text field as shown in Figure 3-55, then press Select. The selected symbols now appear inside a new folder.

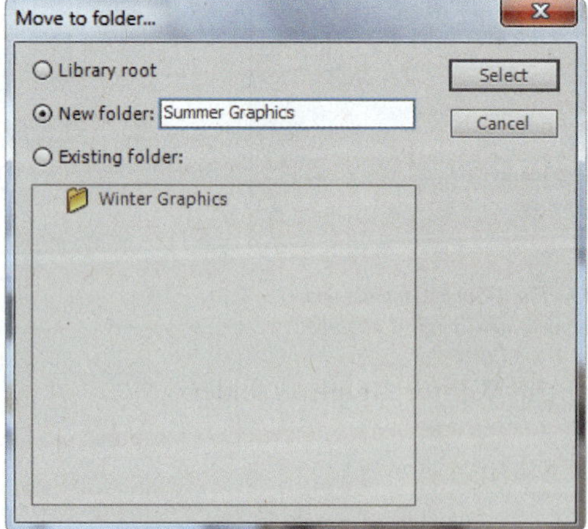

Figure 3-55: *Name the new folder Summer Graphics.*

4. As shown in Figure 3-56, click the arrow to the left of the folder or use the Library panel menu's Expand Folder option to show or hide the sorted symbols in the new folder.

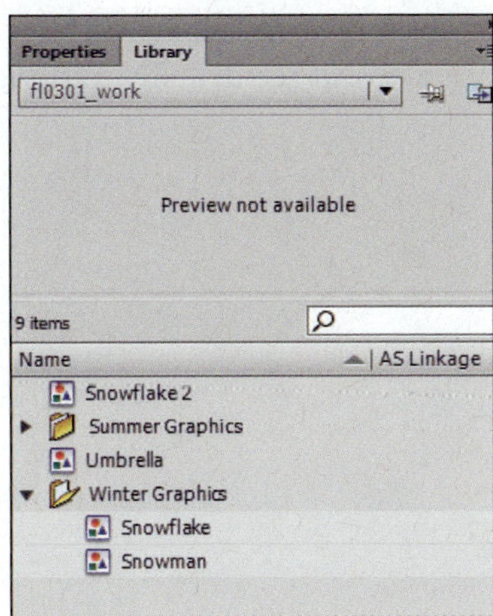

Figure 3-56: *The Summer Graphics folder, shown collapsed.*

5. Choose File > Save to save your work.

Take Note...
You can sort symbols into folders as you create them. The Folder option in the Create New Symbol and Convert to Symbol dialog boxes produces the Move to Folder dialog box, which you can use to sort the new symbol into an existing folder, and even create new folders on-the-fly.

Deleting items from the library

Over the life of a project, many symbols and assets may accumulate in the Library panel, some of which may not even be in use. If sorting your symbols is not enough to tackle this problem, you may want to select and trash unused items to eliminate clutter and reduce the size of your .fla file. Deleting unused symbols from the library is simple.

Take Note...
Keep in mind that a large amount of extraneous symbols and assets in your Library does not affect your final published movie size, only the size of your FLA file.

 | **Follow these steps to delete unused symbols from the library**

1. Open the Library panel, and choose Select Unused Items from its panel menu (Figure 3–57). Use this feature before you delete anything to avoid accidentally trashing items that are in use in your movie..

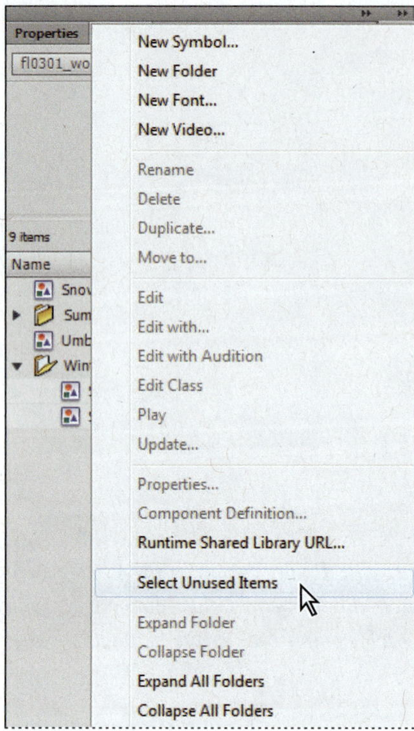

Figure 3–57: Choose Select Unused Items to reveal unused items in the library.

2. You should see the Snowflake, Snowflake 2, and Snowman symbols highlighted in the Library panel. Some of these symbols were never used; others, such as the Snowman, were retired when you changed the theme of your banner.

3. Delete the selected symbols by clicking the Delete button (🗑) at the bottom of the Library panel.

4. Choose File > Save to save your work.

Take Note...
Symbols that include other symbols create dependencies; one symbol can't be deleted without affecting the other. If a graphic symbol is composed of other graphic symbols, it requires those symbols to remain in one piece, like bricks that make up a wall. Always use the Delete Unused Items option to be sure; it accounts for symbols that are in use by other symbols.

Controlling library views

The Library panel's menu features some additional options you can use to adjust the appearance of contents in the library. If you combine this with the panel's sorting capabilities, managing and organizing the library will be easy, even with the most extensive Flash movies.

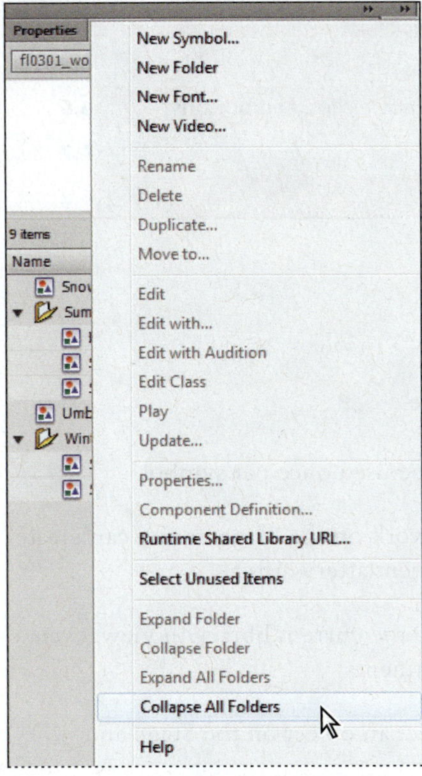

Figure 3-58: Collapsed and expanded views can be easily shown and hidden using the panel menu.

To expand all folders and view their contents, for example, choose Expand All Folders from the Library panel menu. To expand a single folder, select the folder and choose Expand Folder from the panel menu, or double-click the folder.

To collapse all folders and hide their contents, choose Collapse All Folders from the Library panel menu (Figure 3-58). To collapse a single folder, select the folder and choose Collapse Folder from the panel menu, or double-click the folder.

Choose File > Close to close the document.

Wrapping up

In this lesson, you've learned about the power of symbols, and how you can reuse, swap, and easily update artwork used throughout your design. As you'll see in later lessons, symbols also play an essential role in creating animation and adding interactivity in the form of buttons and movie clips.

Skill summary

In this lesson you learned how to:	Objective
Identify general and Flash-specific best practices for designing rich media content for the web, mobile apps, and AIR applications	2.1
Demonstrate knowledge of design elements and principles	2.2
Import and modify graphics	4.3
Create objects and convert them to symbols, including graphics, movie clips, and buttons	4.6
Understand symbols and the library	4.7
Edit symbols and instances	4.8

Knowledge Assessment

True/False

Circle **T** if the statement is true or **F** if the statement is false.

T **F** **1.** Symbols are not re-usable; they can only be used once per symbol.

T **F** **2.** Symbols can be created from existing artwork on the Stage or you can create blank symbols with the option to add content afterwards.

T **F** **3.** The Pin Current Library button will keep the current library in view, even when switching between other open documents.

T **F** **4.** One method to creating symbols is to select an object on the Stage and convert it into a symbol.

T **F** **5.** Don't confuse symbols with Drawing Objects. Although both appear inside bounding boxes, only symbols are stored in the library.

T **F** **6.** When editing a symbol, you cannot change the registration point after it's been established.

T **F** **7.** Symbols can only be edited directly from the Library panel, once they're placed on the Stage, they are no longer editable.

T **F** **8.** Instances on the stage cannot have their color changed unless you change the original symbol it's based on.

T **F** **9.** Duplicating symbols makes an exact copy of a symbol leaving the duplicate tied to the original so if you change the original, the duplicates update to reflect the change.

T **F** **10.** Symbols allow you to use the Property Inspector to swap any instance of a symbol with an instance of another symbol in the Library panel.

Multiple Choice

Select the best response for the following statements.

1. Each copy of a symbol is known as an:
   a. Instance
   b. Clone
   c. Symbol Copy
   d. Child

2. Which of the following is a type of symbol?
   a. Graphic
   b. Button
   c. Movie Clip
   d. All of the above

3. Which of the following symbol types are regarded as "super-symbols" and can contain anything from other symbols to full animation, even sounds and video.
   a. Graphic
   b. Button
   c. Movie Clip
   d. All of the above

4. Which of the following is the panel that symbols are stored in once they're created?
   a. Properties
   b. Timeline
   c. Library
   d. Snippets

5. Which is the reference point by which symbols are positioned on the Stage?
   a. Transformation Point
   b. Center Point
   c. Control Point
   d. Registration Point

6. Which of the following is not an option under the Snapping menu?
   a. Snap to Vectors
   b. Snap to Pixels
   c. Snap Align
   d. Snap to Objects

7. Which of the following color properties is used to change the transparency value of a symbol instance on the Stage?
   a. Brightness
   b. Alpha
   c. Tint
   d. None of the above

8. Which function allows you to create new folders or move graphics to existing folders in one step?

    a. New Folder

    b. Edit with...

    c. Move to...

    d. Edit Class

9. What feature is used to check for items that have not been placed on the Stage?

    a. Find

    b. Edit with...

    c. Select Unused Items

    d. Update...

10. The side benefit to trashing unused items in the Library panel is:

    a. Eliminating clutter

    b. Reducing file size

    c. Easier asset management

    d. All of the above

Competency Assessment

Project 3-1	Symbol Creation

There are a couple of ways to create symbols and organize them. It's good to understand these methods now so when the time comes to work on your big projects you're focusing on more important things like animation.

1. Create a new ActionScript 3.0 document in Flash.

2. Select the Oval tool in the Tools panel, make sure Object Drawing is turned on.

3. Select red for the fill and None for the stroke color values.

4. Draw a circle on the Stage and choose Edit > Deselect All.

5. In the Properties panel, change the fill color to green and draw a second circle on the Stage.

6. Choose the Selection tool from the Tools panel, click on the red circle and choose Modify > Convert to Symbol.

7. Name the symbol Red Circle MC and choose Movie Clip as the symbol type. Click OK.

8. Select the green circle and choose Modify > Convert to Symbol.

9. Name the symbol Green Circle GFX and choose Graphic as the symbol type. Click OK.

10. Save this file as **symbols.fla** and keep this file open for the next project.

<table><tr><td>**Symbol Storage**</td><td>**Project 3-2**</td></tr></table>

Symbols can pile up and get hard to manage when you start to get into a groove and end up creating a lot of them. Organize symbols using folders.

1. You should still have the **symbols.fla** file open from the previous project.

2. Choose Window > Library.

3. Click the New Folder button at the base of the Library panel. Rename the folder MC and place the movie clip symbol inside. Create another new folder called GFX and place the corresponding symbol into that folder as well.

4. Save the Flash file as **symbols_3.2.fla**, keep the file handy for the next exercise.

Proficiency Assessment

<table><tr><td>**Sharing Symbols**</td><td>**Project 3-3**</td></tr></table>

One of the great lessons with regard to Flash understands how to reuse and share assets among different projects you may be working on.

1. Create a new ActionScript 3.0 document in Flash.

2. Go to File > Import > Open External Library and find the **symbols.fla** file you created Projects 1 and 2. Drag the symbols you created to the new file's Stage and note how things will transfer from one Library to the other.

3. Keep the new file open for the last part of the exercise. Save it and name it **duplicates_3.3.fla**.

<table><tr><td>**Duplicating Symbols**</td><td>**Project 3-4**</td></tr></table>

Not only is being able to reuse symbols a power concept but so is repurposing them. You can do this easily enough by making a duplicate of the original symbol and then altering something like color but keeping the shape the same.

1. The **duplicates_3.3.fla** file should still be open from the previous project.

2. Select the movie clip symbol in the Library and from the Library panel flyout menu choose Duplicate.

3. Name the new symbol Blue Circle MC and change as needed.

4. Save the file as **duplicates_3.4.fla**.

Advanced Tools

Key Terms

- Deco tool
- Gradient Transform tool
- Inverse Kinematics
- Masking
- Spray Brush tool

Skill	Objective
Understand symbols and the library	**4.7**
Create masks	**4.9**

Business case

West Portland Homemade Textiles wants an animated version of their mascot Stevie the Silkworm. The silkworm needs to be designed in such a way that it shows some of the textile patterns that the company has available. The silkworm also needs to move in such a way that makes it look like the real thing with one segment of its body moving in conjunction with the others.

Starting up

Before starting, make sure that your tools and panels are consistent by resetting your workspace. See "Resetting the Flash workspace" in the Starting up section of this book.

You will work with several files from the fl04lessons folder in this lesson. Make sure that you have loaded the fllessons folder onto your hard drive from *http://www.wiley.com/college/sc/adobeseries*. See "Loading lesson files" in the Starting up section of this book.

The project

In this lesson, you'll be creating an ad for West Portland Homemade Textiles (WPHT). Their mascot, Stevie the Silkworm, showcases a multitude of WPHT's favorite patterns. Each segment in Stevie's body will feature a different pattern, which you will create using a combination of drawing tools. To see the finished file (Figure 4-1), navigate to the fl04lessons folder and open **fl0401_done.fla**. Keep this file open for reference or choose File > Close to close the file.

Figure 4-1: Stevie the Silkworm is a handsome beast!

Working with gradients

The first part of the silkworm that you will work on is his head. If you opened and viewed the finished file, you may have noticed the 3D appearance of this insect's visage. While this object is not truly 3D in the technical sense, a little fancy footwork with gradients can go a long way toward adding depth to your graphics.

Step-by-Step	Follow these steps to create a gradient

1. Choose File > Open. Navigate to the fl04lessons folder and select **fl0401.fla**. Press Open.

2. On the Stage is the West Portland Homemade Textiles logo and not much else. Choose File > Save As. In the Save As dialog box, navigate to the fl04lessons folder and type **fl0401_work.fla** into the Save As text field. Press Save.

3. Add a new layer for your caterpillar to separate him from the logo layer by clicking the New Layer button (⬚) at the bottom of the layers section of the Timeline. Double-click the name of the new layer and type **Stevie** into the text field that appears (Figure 4-2). Press Enter (Windows) or Return (Mac OS) to commit the change.

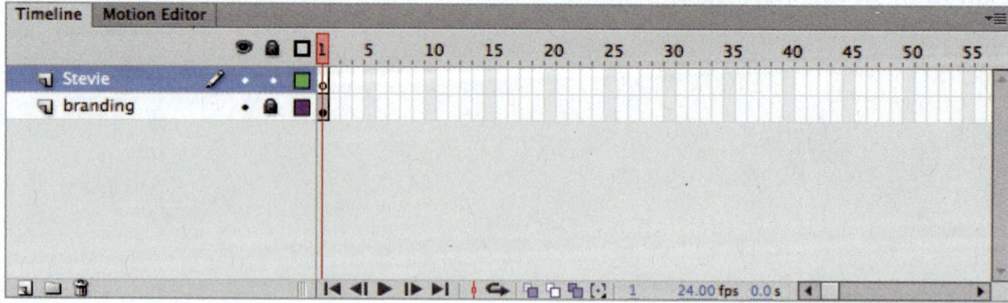

Figure 4-2: Create a new layer for Stevie.

4. Select the Oval tool (○) from the Tools panel. Make sure Object Drawing mode is enabled at the bottom of the Tools panel (the Object Drawing icon (◉) should be pressed in). Hold down the Rectangle tool (▢) to access the hidden Oval tool. At the bottom of the Tools panel, click on the Stroke color swatch to open the Swatches panel. Select None (⬜) from the top-right corner of the Swatches panel.

5. Click on the Fill color swatch to open the Swatches panel and select the black and white radial gradient in the bottom-left corner (Figure 4–3). You'll adjust this gradient after you draw the oval.

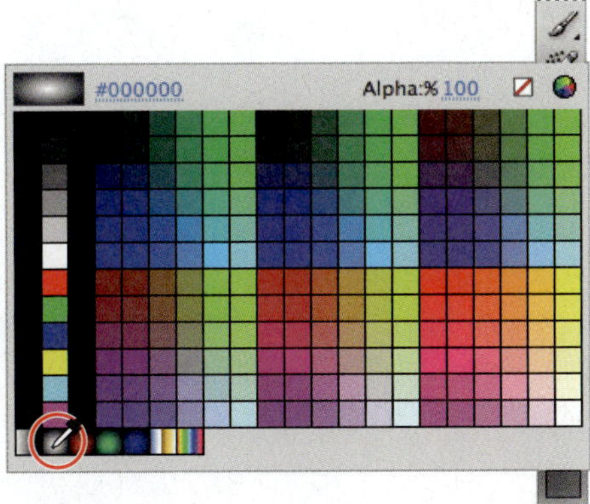

Figure 4–3: Select the radial gradient swatch.

6. While holding down the Shift key to constrain proportions, click and drag to draw a circle below the logo (Figure 4–4). If you need to move it, or draw it again, use the Selection tool (▸) to select it and then click and drag to move it, or press Delete on your keyboard to remove it.

Figure 4–4: Draw a circle below the WPHT logo.

7. Choose the Selection tool from the Tools panel and select the circle. Choose Window > Color to open the Color panel. This panel can be used to choose colors, save them as swatches, and modify gradients. In this case, you'll be doing the latter.

8. Make certain that the fill is selected, then click on the gradient stop on the right side of the gradient slider. In the text field above the gradient slider, type **E3E33E** to set the black to yellow (Figure 4-5). Notice that the sliders above this field change to reflect its hue and brightness. You can use these sliders to create custom colors for your own gradients.

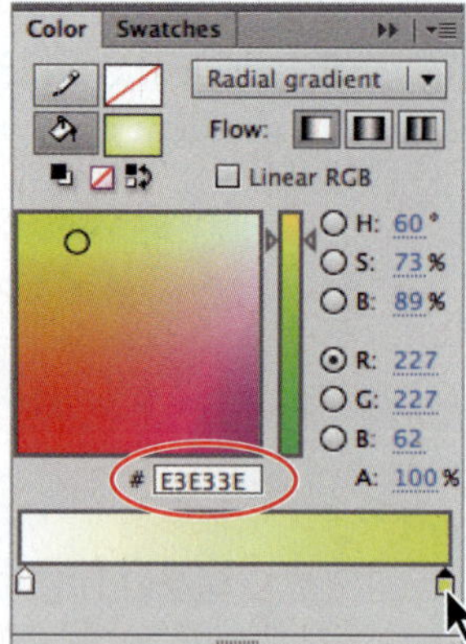

Figure 4-5: Set the black stopper to #E3E33E.

9. Close the Color panel and choose File > Save.

Adjusting gradients with the Gradient Transform tool

Gradients are pretty hip, but you'll probably want to customize more than just color. The **Gradient Transform tool** can help you exert some more control over the size, dimensions, and location of your gradient fills.

| Step-by-Step | Follow these steps to modify a gradient |

1. Hidden under the Free Transform tool (⬚) in the Tools panel is the Gradient Transform tool (▤). Choose the Gradient Transform tool, and click on the yellow circle on the Stage. Click and drag the center point down and to the right to offset the gradient as shown in Figure 4-6.

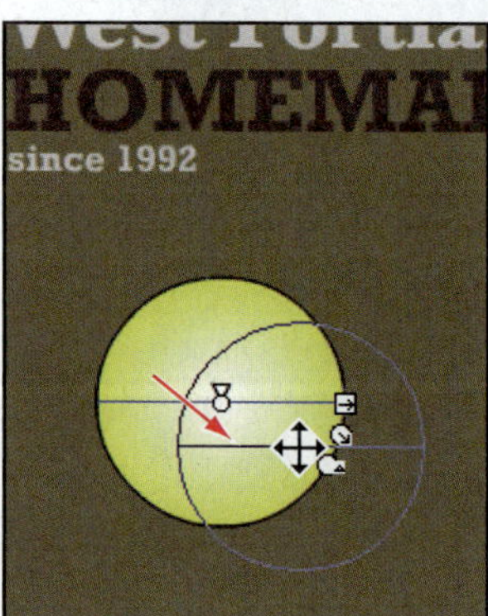

Figure 4-6: Drag the gradient off-center.

2. Click and drag the middle handle on the edge of the circle outwards to expand the size of the gradient (Figure 4-7).

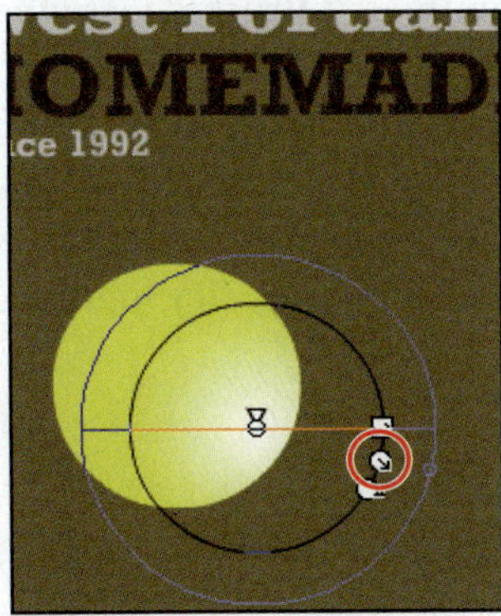

Figure 4-7: Use the handle in the middle to expand the size of the gradient.

Using the Gradient Transform tool to fine-tune gradients a bit can mean the difference between a convincing effect and a clumsy, amateurish effect. Keep it close at hand; it will serve you well.

3. For the finishing touches, drag out two instances of the eye graphic from the Library panel (Figure 4-8) and use the Selection tool (k) to position them on the circle (Figure 4-9).

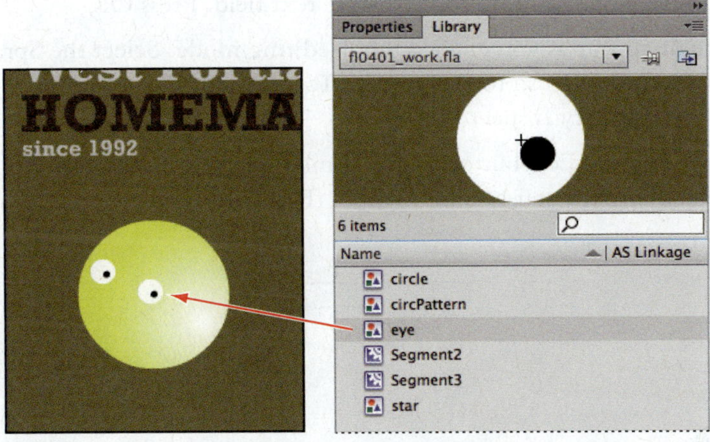

Figure 4-8: Position the eyes on the circle.

Figure 4-9: Drag out two instances of the eye graphic from the Library panel.

4. Now that the caterpillar has a respectable countenance, save it as a symbol. Use the Selection tool to click and drag a marquee around the circle and two eyes, and then choose Modify > Convert to Symbol. In the Convert to Symbol dialog box, choose Movie Clip from the Type drop-down menu, and set the registration point to the center. Type **head** in the Name text field and press OK.

5. Choose File > Save to save your work, and leave the file open for the next part of this lesson.

Flash CS6 tools for advanced drawing

Flash CS6 includes a number of tools that allow you to easily create effects that would otherwise be labor-intensive to create from scratch such as the Symmetry Brush effect when using the Deco tool, or even applying fill effects from the Properties inspector. In the next section, you'll use a few of these tools to create sections of the caterpillar's body. Perhaps more than any other features in Flash, these tools lend themselves especially well to experimentation. After you get a feel for the techniques in this section, you might find yourself staying up way past bedtime making strange compositions to astound your friends and family. It's highly recommended that you obey your impulses to do so.

Spraying symbols

Using the **Spray Brush tool** in Flash, symbols can be creatively "sprayed" onto the stage and the properties of the symbols can be adjusted.

For the first section of Stevie's body, you'll use the Spray Brush tool to create a field of stars, and then you'll mask out a circular section of this field.

Step-by-Step | **Follow these steps to use the Spray Brush tool**

1. Choose Insert > New Symbol. Much like the head, each segment of the body will be a Movie Clip symbol. In the Create New Symbol dialog box, choose Movie Clip from the Type drop-down menu and type **Segment1** in the Name text field. Press OK.

2. All the items on the Stage disappear as you enter symbol-editing mode. Select the Spray Brush tool (🖌), located beneath the Brush tool (✎) in the Tools panel. Click on the Properties tab to display the Property Inspector.

3. In the Property Inspector, press the Edit button in the Symbol section. In the resulting Select Symbol dialog box, choose the star graphic symbol (Figure 4-10) and press OK.

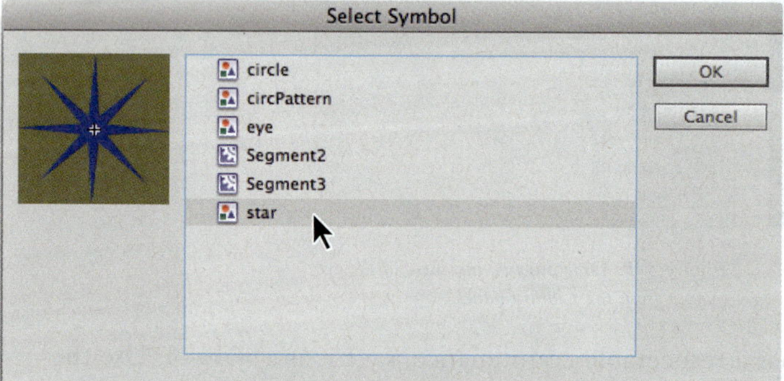

Figure 4-10: Select star from the Select Symbol dialog box.

4. In the Property Inspector, set the Scale width and Scale height to 50 percent. Make sure all three checkboxes at the bottom of the Symbol section are checked for Random scaling, Rotate symbol, and Random rotation. If you desire a more uniform effect, these checkboxes should be left unchecked, but in this case you're looking for maximum variety.

5. In the Brush section, type **200** in the Width and Height fields. Leave the Brush angle at its default setting (Figure 4-11).

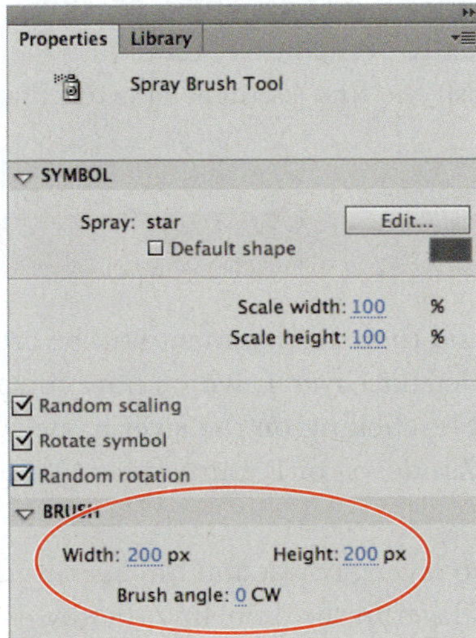

Figure 4-11: *Adjust the properties of the Spray Brush tool.*

6. Click and release in the center of the Stage. Each click sprays a number of symbols in a radius dictated by the brush width and height that you set in the last step. Clicking and dragging allows you to paint symbols onto the Stage.

7. Use the Spray Brush tool to create a field of stars (Figure 4-12). If you add too many stars, use the Selection tool to delete your work and try it again. In fact, try it a few times, even if you like the results of your first attempt. It's fun and easy, just like real spray paint, without the potential for legal trouble.

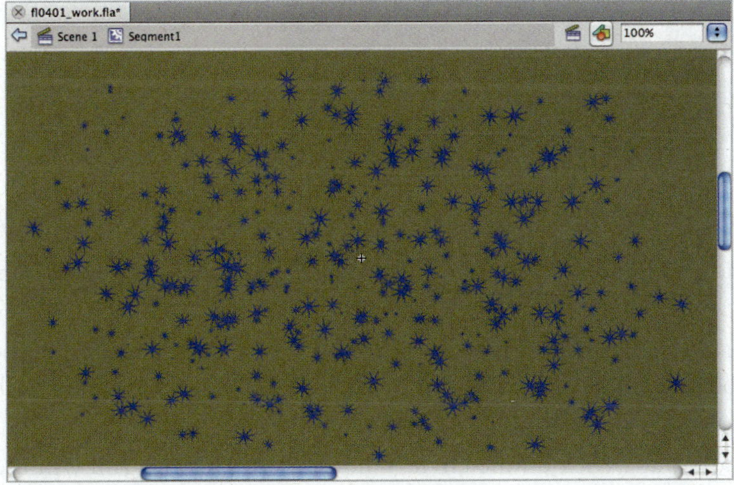

Figure 4-12: *Spraying symbols.*

Flash CS6 tools for advanced drawing

Masking

Most graphics programs support some form of masking. In Flash CS6, the implementation is fairly simple, but it can be a powerful tool, especially combined with animation. **Masking** is a way to conceal or reveal portions of artwork without actually permanently removing the artwork itself. Next you'll mask out the field of stars to finish the first segment of caterpillar Stevie's body.

Follow these steps to create a mask

1. Because you'll be working with more than one layer, and their arrangement will be crucial to success, you'll need to stay organized. Rename the default Layer 1, which now contains the field of stars you created in the last section, by double-clicking on the layer name and typing **stars** into the text field; then press Enter (Windows) or Return (Mac OS) to commit the change.

2. Press the New Layer button twice, then rename the two layers, **mask** and **background**, respectively. Drag the background layer below the stars layer in the Timeline (Figure 4-13).

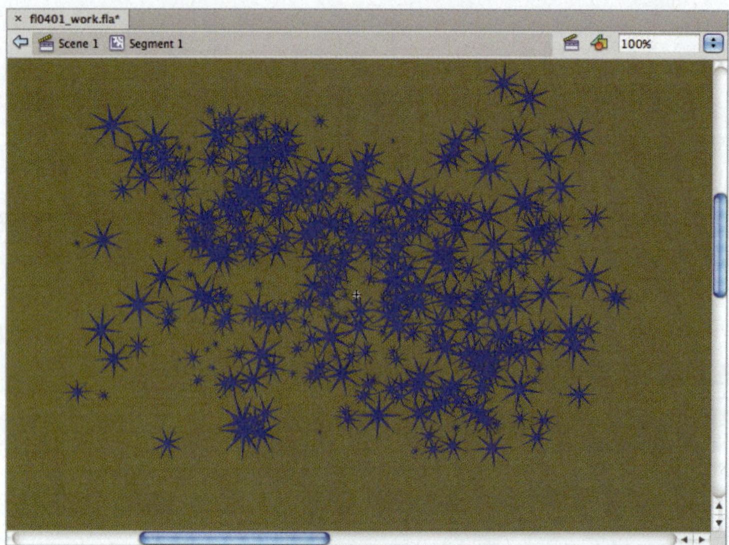

Figure 4-13: Add, rename, and rearrange layers.

3. Select the mask layer and choose the Oval tool (○) from the Tools panel. At the bottom of the Tools panel, choose none for the stroke, and set the fill to the blue labeled #6699CC.

4. Holding down the Shift key to constrain proportions, draw a circle over a section of the field of stars (use the crosshair as your guide as you paint). Any stars outside of this circle will soon be invisible, so if you've grown fond of them, adjust your circle accordingly.

5. Choose the Selection tool (↖) and click on the circle. Choose Edit > Copy. You will use this copy to populate the background layer in a couple steps.

6. Right-click (Windows) or Ctrl+click (Mac OS) on the mask layer in the Timeline and choose Mask from the context menu (Figure 4-14). Voila! Masking in Flash is just that easy.

Figure 4-14: Mask the stars you created with the Spray Brush tool.

7. Select the background layer and choose Edit > Paste in Place (Figure 4-15). If the circle disappears, click on the Stage to deselect the newly pasted shape. This particular technique is often used in conjunction with masking to give an object a background color if the masked content contains transparent areas.

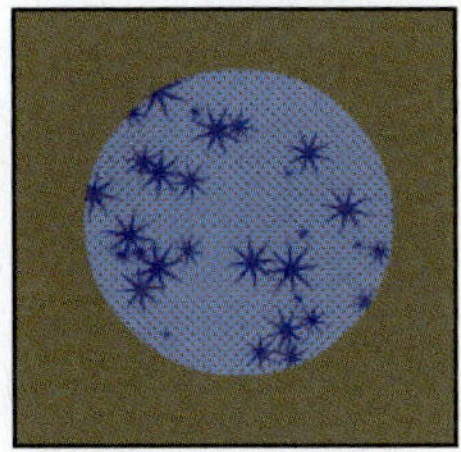

Figure 4-15: Paste the circle onto the background layer to give Segment1 a background color.

8. Return to the main Stage by clicking on the Scene 1 link in the Navigation bar above the Stage. From the Library panel, drag an instance of the Segment1 symbol onto the Stage. Don't worry if it isn't the same size as Stevie's head; you'll adjust that in the next step.

9. Click and hold the Gradient Transform tool (⬛) in the Tools panel and select the Free Transform tool (⬚). Click on the Segment1 symbol on the Stage. Holding down Shift to constrain proportions, click and drag any of the corner points of the symbol's bounding box toward the center or away from the center to make Segment1 about the same size as the head. Click and drag Segment1 into place, attached to the head as shown in Figure 4-16.

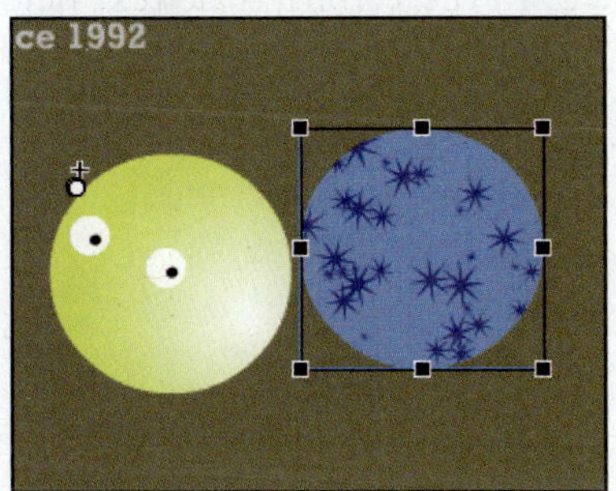

Figure 4-16: Use the Free Transform tool to get Segment1 sized-up and into place.

10. Choose File > Save and keep this file open for the next part of the lesson.

Introducing the Deco tool

The Spray Brush is a great way to throw symbols all over the Stage, but what if you want to distribute a number of symbols in a slightly more structured manner? Flash's **Deco tool** provides a number of customizable options for just this task. This tool allows users to decorate or paint using a number of different fill types while also allowing these fills to be animated.

<table><tr><td>**Step-by-Step**</td><td>**Follow these steps to use the Deco tool**</td></tr></table>

1. Click and hold the Oval tool (○) in the Tools panel and select the Rectangle tool (□). Draw a large rectangle on the Stage as shown in Figure 4–17. The dimensions are not too important, as you'll be using the mask technique from the last section to create this segment. This rectangle is just to contain the results of using the Deco tool.

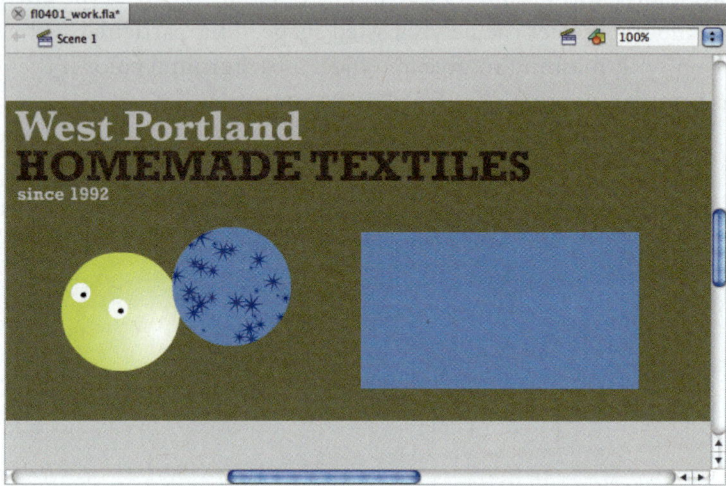

Figure 4–17: Draw a rectangle on the Stage to contain the next pattern.

2. Choose the Deco tool (🖌) from the Tools panel, then click the Properties tab to access the Property Inspector.

3. In the Drawing Effect section of the Property Inspector, choose Grid Fill. For Tile 1 press the Edit button and choose circPattern from the Select Symbol dialog box. Uncheck Tile 2, Tile 3 and Tile 4—you won't need these because we are using just one symbol for the pattern.

4. In the Horizontal and Vertical spacing text fields, type **2**. In the Pattern scale text field, type **60**.

5. Click inside the rectangle you created in step 1. A grid pattern is created inside this rectangle as shown in Figure 4-18. The Grid Fill effect of the Deco tool is a handy way to whip up a grid of symbols; just be careful to fill only within a shape unless you really want to coat the entire Stage.

Figure 4-18: *Fill the rectangle using the Deco tool. Note that fill results will vary from shape to shape.*

6. Using the Selection tool (⬉), click on the rectangle and press Delete to remove it. Click on the grid of circPattern symbols, and choose Edit > Cut. The rest of the segments have pre-created Movie Clips to streamline the process of finishing the project.

7. Double-click on the Segment2 Movie Clip icon in the Library panel to enter symbol-editing mode.

8. Select the content layer and choose Edit > Paste in Center.

9. Choose Window > Transform to open the Transform panel. This panel is the counterpart to the Free Transform tool (⬚). It's a bit more precise, as you can plug in specific values, but the Free Transform tool is often more convenient for quick transformations.

10. Type **25** in the Rotate text field to rotate the field of circles as shown in Figure 4-19. Close the Transform panel and view the change (Figure 4-20).

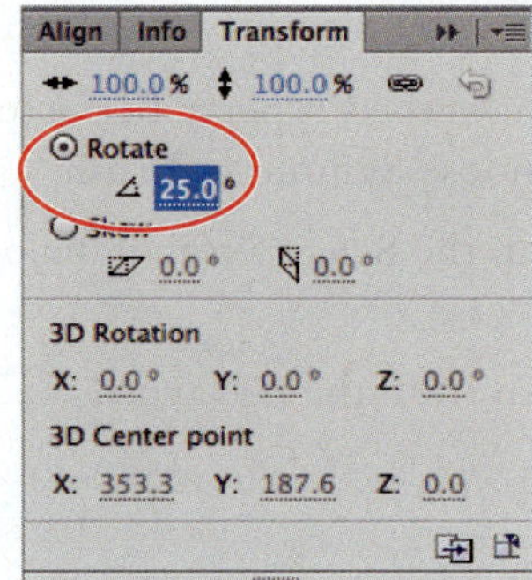

Figure 4-19: *Use the Transform panel to rotate the grid.*

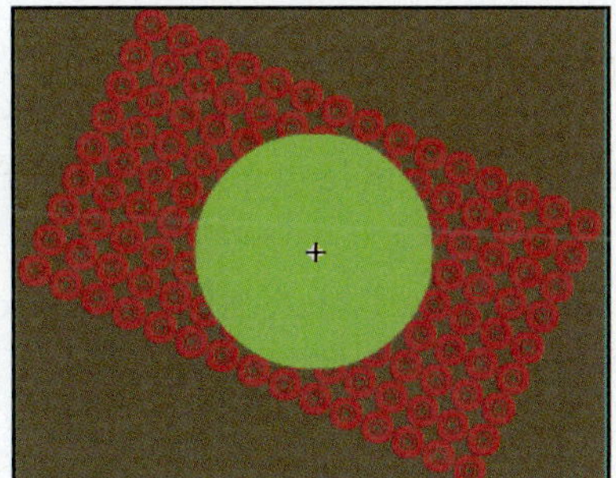

Figure 4-20: *View the object.*

11. Right-click (Windows) or Ctrl+click (Mac OS) on the mask layer and choose Mask from the context menu.

12. Click on the Scene 1 button in the Navigation bar to return to the Stage. Drag an instance of the Segment2 movie clip to the Stage, then reposition and transform your new segment with the Free Transform tool, if necessary (Figure 4-21).

Figure 4-21: Move Segment2 into place as the caterpillar's body.

13. Choose File > Save. Leave this file open for the next part of this lesson.

Advanced Deco tool techniques

Now that you're starting to get the hang of the new Deco tool, you'll take it to the next level, making the caterpillar's third body segment. In this exercise, you'll see how to make complex geometric patterns by piggybacking Deco tool features.

<table>
<tr><td>**Step-by-Step**</td><td>**Follow these steps to create a geometric pattern**</td></tr>
</table>

1. Once again, you'll be using a Movie Clip with mask and background layers already created to streamline the process. Double-click the Segment3 movie clip in the Library to enter symbol-editing mode.

2. Select the content layer. The other layers are locked and invisible to keep them out of the way until you need them.

3. Select the Deco tool (✍) and click on the Properties tab to access the Property Inspector. From the drop-down menu in the Drawing Effect section, choose Symmetry Brush.

4. Press the Edit button and select the circle graphic symbol from the Select Symbol dialog box. Press OK.

5. In the Property Inspector, make sure Rotate Around is chosen from the Advanced Options drop-down menu.

6. Click and drag outwards from the center of the Stage until eight circles appear as shown below in Figure 4-22. Be careful to not click at the intersection of the green lines. The Rotate Around option allows you to easily draw a circle of symbols.

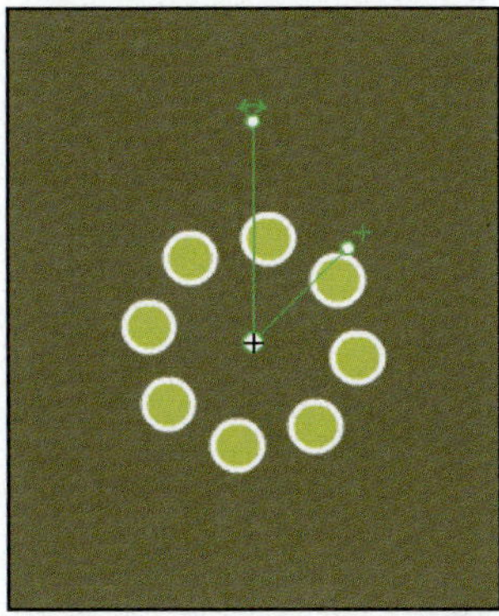

Figure 4-22: Drag to create a circular arrangement of eight circles.

7. Choose the Selection tool (➤) from the Tools panel. Click on the shape you created in the last step. You'll be using this shape to draw a more complex shape with the Deco tool, and so you'll need to convert it to a symbol. Choose Modify > Convert to Symbol. In the Convert to Symbol dialog box, choose Graphic from the Type drop-down menu, and type **halo** in the Name text field. Press OK.

Take Note...
When you draw with the Deco tool, you are creating groups. If you want to modify or swap parts of these groups, you can always choose Modify > Break Apart to break the group down to individual symbols.

8. Press Delete to remove the newly minted symbol from the Stage.

9. Select the Deco tool from the Tools panel. The Drawing Effect drop-down menu should still be set to Symmetry Brush. Click on the Edit button and select the halo symbol from the Select Symbol dialog box. Click OK.

10. In the Advanced Options section, choose Grid Translation from the drop-down menu. When the graph lines appear on the Stage, drag them by the intersection point to the center of the Stage.

11. Click and drag from this intersection point until four instances of the halo symbol appear (Figure 4-23). The Art Deco tool is very sensitive so place your cursor lightly on the green graph lines, small movements will create very different effects. We found putting the cursor on the horizontal axis of the green graph lines worked well.

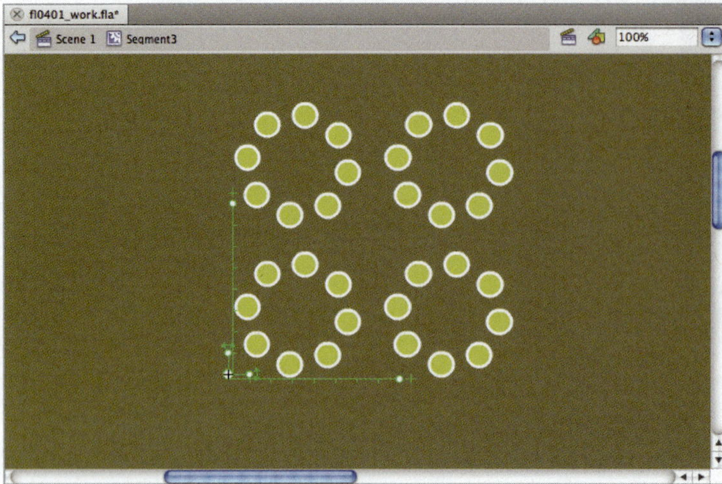

Figure 4-23: Drag four halos out onto the grid.

12. Change the Stage view to 50% by choosing 50% from the drop-down menu in the top-right corner of the work area.

13. Place your cursor on the circle on the far right of the horizontal graph line. Click and drag to the right to extend the graph line, as you do this, you create additional columns of the symbol, drag until there are four columns of circles. Now click and drag the circle at the top of the vertical graph line and drag upwards, this creates additional rows. Using these techniques you should make a 4-row by 4-column pattern. Now locate the small circle at the intersection of the graph, it has a small curved arrow. Drag this straight up to adjust the angle of the patterns (Figure 4-24).

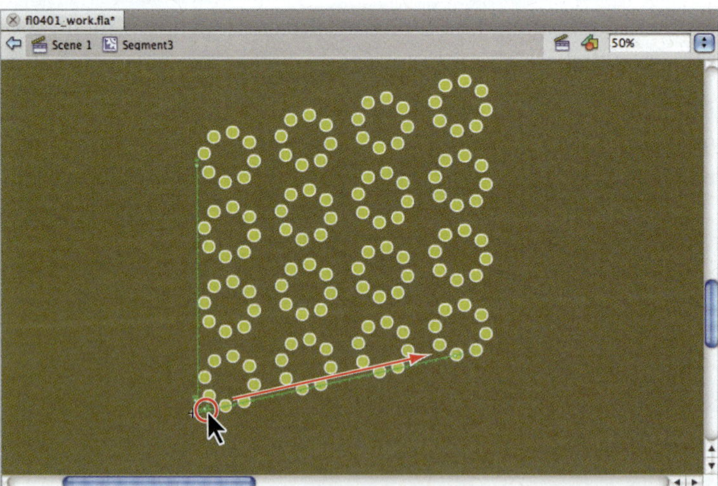

Figure 4-24: Use the grid handles to increase the size of the grid and skew the layout.

14. Choose the Free Transform tool (⊞) from the Tools panel. Drag to reposition the new grid in the center of the Stage, and then hold down Shift to constrain proportions and use the corners to resize the grid to about half of its original size as shown in Figure 4-25.

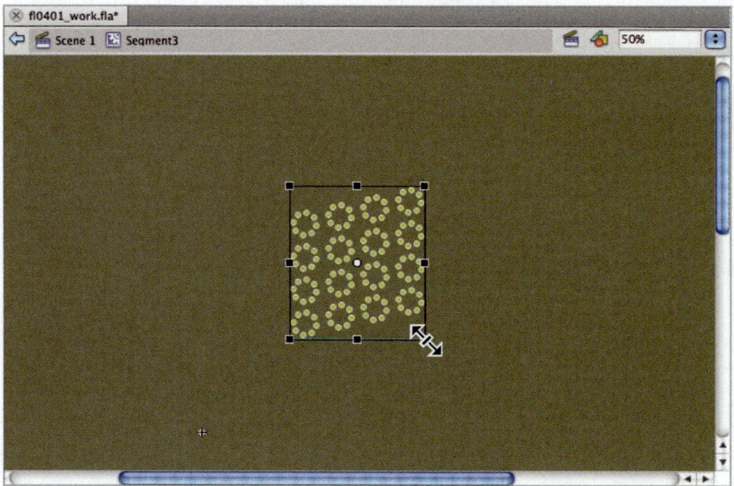

Figure 4-25: Use the Free Transform tool to reposition and resize the grid.

15. Make sure the halo graphic is centered on the Stage. If necessary, choose the Selection tool (▸) from the Tools panel and reposition it to the center of the Stage. Change the work area view back to 100%, then right-click (Windows) or Ctrl+click (Mac OS) on the mask layer and choose Mask from the context menu. Click on the red X's in the eyeball column of the mask and background layers to make them visible again and see the finished segment.

16. Return to the main Stage by clicking Scene 1, located above the Stage. Drag an instance of the Segment3 symbol out of the Library and move it into place to complete the caterpillar's body as shown in Figure 4-26.

Figure 4-26: Stevie the Silkworm with three segments.

The Deco Tool's new options

The Deco Tool has a number of creative and fun modes that include anything from drawing flames and flowers to landscapes decorated with random buildings. They are way too much fun to explain, so check them out by selecting the Deco tool and selecting a mode from the Property Inspector as shown in Figure 4-27.

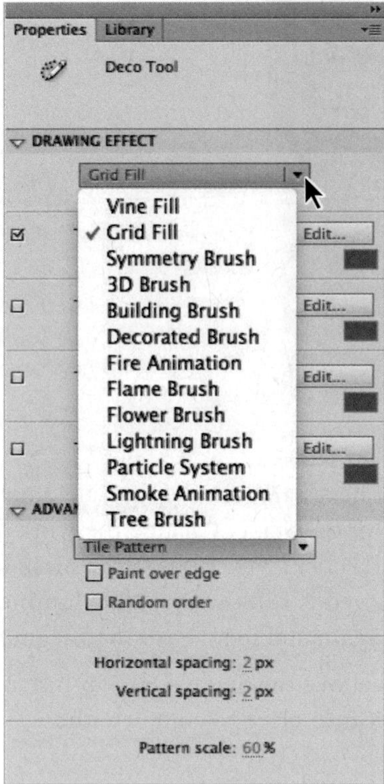

Figure 4-27: *The Deco tool options.*

Introduction to IK tools

Inverse Kinematics (**IK**) is used by 3D and character animators to help achieve more realistic motion, especially with jointed figures. Flash CS6 includes the Bone tool to add a skeletal structure to a group of symbols. In Lesson 6, "Advanced Animation," you'll explore animating with this feature; for now, you'll get your feet wet by making the caterpillar poseable.

<table><tr><td>**Follow these steps to use the IK tools**</td><td>**Step-by-Step**</td></tr></table>

1. Choose the Bone tool (⚙) from the Tools panel.

2. Click and drag from the center of Stevie's head to the center of Segment1. When you release the mouse, a bone is added, connecting Stevie's head to the first section of his bodyas shown in Figure 4–28. As you may know from personal experience, bones can be a great way to keep your body from falling apart.

Figure 4-28*: Use the Bone tool to connect Stevie's segments.*

3. Still using the Bone tool, click and drag from the end of the last bone, to the center of Segment2. Do the same from Segment2 to Segment3.

4. Choose the Selection tool (⬉) from the Tools panel. Click and drag the segments of Stevie's body. As shown in Figure 4-29, they are now joined together to allow easy posing for character animation.

Figure 4-29: *Stevie in all his glory.*

5. Choose File > Save, then File > Close.

Congratulations! You have completed this lesson.

Skill summary

In this lesson you learned how to:	Objective
Understand symbols and the library	**4.7**
Create masks	**4.9**

Knowledge Assessment

True/False

Circle **T** if the statement is true or **F** if the statement is false.

T **F** **1.** When using the Spray Brush tool, each click sprays a number of symbols in a radius dictated by the brush width and height.

T **F** **2.** In order to use a mask within Flash, the mask shape must first be drawn in Photoshop and then imported as part of another image.

T **F** **3.** The Deco tool will fill the entire stage unless you apply it to a shape to constrain the area that is filled as a result of using the tool.

T **F** **4.** When you draw with the Deco tool, you are creating groups of images.

T **F** **5.** The Deco Tool has a number of creative and fun modes that include anything from drawing flames and flowers to landscapes decorated with random buildings.

T **F** **6.** Inverse Kinematics (IK) is used by 3D and character animators to help achieve more realistic motion.

T **F** **7.** You can create your own symbols to be used in conjuction with the Deco tool, you do not have to use the pre-built brush patterns that are part of the tool.

T **F** **8.** Only movie clip symbols can be used in conjuction with the Spray Brush tool.

T **F** **9.** More than one symbol can be used as patterns for the Spray Brush tool.

T **F** **10.** Besides selecting your own symbols, the Deco tool has only 1 brush and 2 fill patterns to choose from.

Multiple Choice

Select the best response for the following statements.

1. Which tool can help you exert control over the size, dimensions and location of gradient fills?
   a. Free Transform
   b. Gradient Transform
   c. Gradient Fill
   d. Eyedropper

2. Which of the following is selected by default when using the Spray Brush tool?
   a. Random scaling
   b. Rotate symbol
   c. Random rotation
   d. All of the above

3. Which of the following is not an option under Drawing Effect when using the Deco tool?

    a. Vine Fill

    b. Grid Fill

    c. Fire Animation

    d. Neon Brush

4. Which tool is used when you'd like to connect one image to another so they move together like segments of a larger image?

    a. Bone tool

    b. Free Transform

    c. Sub-selection

    d. Link tool

5. When creating grouped images with the Deco tool, what step do you have to take to access the ability to edit each image individually?

    a. Edit > Cut

    b. Modify > Break Apart

    c. Modify > Transform

    d. Edit > Split

6. Which tool is best for distributing symbols in a structured manner as opposed to throwing symbols all over the Stage?

    a. Deco tool

    b. Spray Brush

    c. Brush tool

    d. Pencil tool

7. Which set of tools would be best to use when working with objects that include jointed figure points?

    a. Free Transform

    b. Brush tools

    c. IK tools

    d. None of the above

8. Which of the shape tools can be used to draw a mask shape?

    a. Rectangle

    b. Oval

    c. Polystar

    d. All of the above

9. Which of the following tools would be the best choice for making complex geometric patterns?

    a. Deco tool

    b. Rectangle tool

    c. Brush tool

    d. Pen tool

10. Besides the Bone tool, what other tool is part of the IK group of tools?

    a. Free Transform

    b. Bind tool

    c. Deco tool

    d. None of the above

Competency Assessment

Linear gradients	Project 4-1

As you can see, Flash offers a wide array of choices when it comes to working with gradients. The controls you use will vary depending on the nature of the gradient you're working with. You'll try out the linear gradient controls now to see how this varies from radial gradients.

1. Create a new ActionScript 3.0 document in Flash.

2. Select the Rectangle tool, leave Object Drawing turned on.

3. Choose Window > Color. From the color style menu choose Linear gradient.

4. Click and drag to create a rectangle that will include a gradient, don't worry about the colors.

5. Choose the Gradient Transform Tool and select the rectangle.

6. Drag the corner control to rotate, the arrow control to scale, and the registration point to change its position.

7. Save the file as **gradient.fla_4.1**.

Using the Spray Brush tool creatively	Project 4-2

The Spray Brush works great for spraying symbols but you can also use it with its native settings as a paint tool in its own right.

1. Create a new ActionScript 3.0 document in Flash.

2. Choose the Spray Brush Tool, change the color to blue and the scale to 250%.

3. Click and drag to start painting. Change the scale and color and continue to experiment with your painting. Be creative and create an interesting design or pattern using this tool.

4. Save the file as **spray_brush.fla**.

Proficiency Assessment

| Project 4-3 | **The Deco tool is out of control!** |

Painting within an object with the Deco tool is one thing, letting it run rampant and filling the Stage as a cool background is another.

1. Create a new ActionScript 3.0 document in Flash.
2. Select the Deco tool, make sure that Vine Fill is chosen in the Drawing Effect section of the Properties inspector and simply click on the Stage.
3. Save the file as **deco.fla** and keep the file open for the next project.

| Project 4-4 | **Manipulating the Deco tool's artwork** |

When you clicked in the previous project with the Deco tool, you ended up creating a graphic that filled the screen. The cool thing is that since its artwork, it can be manipulated.

1. With the **deco.fla** file from the last project still open, choose the Selection tool.
2. Double-click the artwork on the Stage, now double-click again and start adjusting visual characteristics in the Properties panel. Change the artwork to make it your own.
3. Save the file as **deco_custom.fla**.

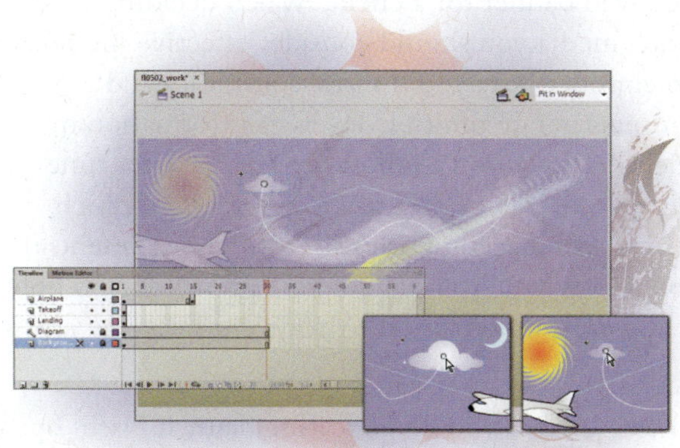

Creating Basic Animation

Key Terms

- keyframe
- layers
- morphing
- Motion Editor
- motion path
- motion tween
- shape tween
- Test Movie
- tween

Skill	Objective
Identify general and Flash-specific best practices for designing rich media content for the web, mobile apps, and AIR applications	2.1
Use the Timeline	3.3
Use the Motion Editor	3.6
Create animations (changes in shape, position, size, color, and transparency)	4.10

Business case

Now that you've learned the basics of animation, you'll need to learn how to refine animation so that you can control things like speed and direction to simulate more realistic movement in terms of how objects move in real life. In order to do that, you'll have to learn how to move objects along curved paths and how to control the animation in terms of speed and velocity.

Starting up

Before starting, make sure that your tools and panels are consistent by resetting your workspace. See "Resetting the Flash workspace" in the Starting up section of the book.

You will work with several files from the fl05lessons folder in this lesson. Make sure that you have loaded the fl05lessons folder onto your hard drive from *http://www.wiley.com/college/sc/adobeseries*. See "Loading lesson files" in the Starting up section of the book.

The project

In this project, you'll be creating an animated web banner for a client. When deciding if content should even be implemented using rich media you should consider effective methods to include audio and video in a project. Also consider how you'll show continuity and transitions of animations and how you might incorporate multiple levels of information in a transition to convey your message. The Timeline allows you to illustrate change over time and allows you to get layers of information from one side of the screen to the other which enriches graphical representations, consider how you'll accomplish this with your content. If you have 3-dimensional structures, think about how you'll visualize these on screen and how you'll attract attention to different elements and create interaction. Always consider any cross-platform issues as well.

To see a completed example of the animated web banner you'll be creating, launch Flash, open the **fl0501_done.fla** file, and choose Control > Test Movie > in Flash Professional to preview the final banner. Close the Flash Player and return to Flash Professional CS6 when you're done.

Introducing keyframes and the Timeline

One of the most important panels in the Flash workspace is the Timeline, which is where graphics, text, and media are sequenced and animation is created. The Timeline allows you to have items appear, disappear, or change appearance and position at different points in time, and also provides additional features for controlling an animation such as Onion Skin.

The Timeline consists of three main components: layers, frames, and keyframes.

Layers

Layers enable you to stack and organize your graphics, media, and animations separately from one another, thereby giving you greater control over your project elements. You can also lock content on a layer to prevent the accidental editing of content on that layer. If you've used other design applications such as Adobe Photoshop or Illustrator, it's likely that you've worked with layers before.

Flash also utilizes special types of layers for tasks such as tweening (animation), masking, and Inverse Kinematics, which you'll explore in this lesson and the next.

Frames and keyframes

On the Flash Timeline, time is represented by frames, which are displayed as small boxes across each layer of the Timeline and helps you to control the duration of an animation. Time is subdivided into frames based on your frame rate and the number for each frame can be seen at the top of the Timeline. In a document set to the default frame rate of 24 fps (frames per second), every 24 frames on your Timeline represent one second of playback in your movie.

The playhead, shown as a vertical red beam, passes each frame when a movie plays back, much like movie film passing in front of a projector bulb. You can drag the playhead sideways to scrub through an animation to see how it looks. To see several frames before and after the playhead while dragging, turn on the Onion Skin option at the very bottom of the Timeline by clicking on it. Click it again to turn it off.

When you decide you want to place a graphic, play a sound, or start an animation at a specific point along the Timeline, you must first create a keyframe. **Keyframes** are created to mark significant points along the Timeline where content can be placed. A keyframe can extend across the Timeline as long as you need it to keep its contents in view. By default, each new layer on the Timeline contains a single keyframe at frame 1. At times, you may also create a blank keyframe which is a keyframe that contains no artwork. This is useful in a number of different scenarios but one example would be if you are going to paste content on the blank keyframe instead of having artwork automatically appear there.

The best way to understand the Timeline is to dive right in and work with it. In this next exercise, you'll sequence some items across the Timeline and work with layers to get started.

<table>
<tr><td>**Follow these steps to work with keyframes and layers**</td><td>**Step-by-Step**</td></tr>
</table>

1. Choose File > Open, and locate and select the lesson file named **fl0501.fla** located in the fl05lessons folder. Choose Open to open the file.

    Examine the Stage, and you see an airplane graphic along with two pieces of text that read *Takeoff* and *Landing*. In addition to the background layer and diagram layer (which you'll use as a visual aid later on), each of these items sits on its own named layer.

    Note the frame ruler at the top of the Timeline, which marks frame numbers in 5-frame increments.

2. Choose File > Save As. In the Save As dialog box, navigate to the fl05lessons folder and type **fl0501_work.fla** in the Save As text field. Press Save.

3. Let's get a feel for sequencing items across the Timeline. Click directly on the Timeline on the Airplane layer at frame 15 to select that frame (it should appear highlighted in blue in Figure 5-1).

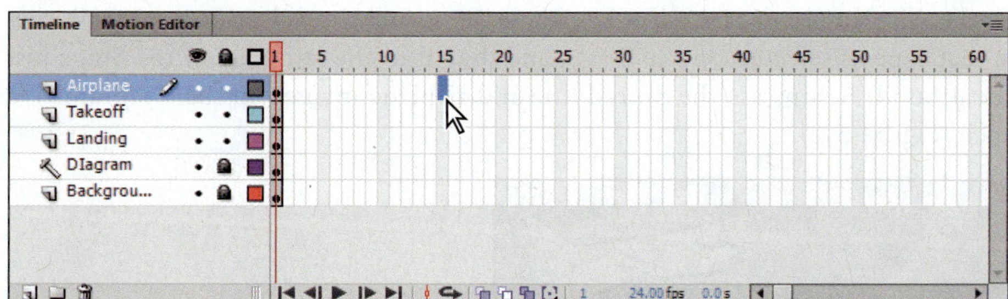

Figure 5-1: Select a frame directly on the layer to insert a keyframe at that position.

4. Right-click (Windows) or Ctrl+click (Mac OS) and choose Insert Keyframe to insert a new keyframe at this frame (Figure 5-2). The new keyframe appears with a border and bullet as shown in Figure 5-3.

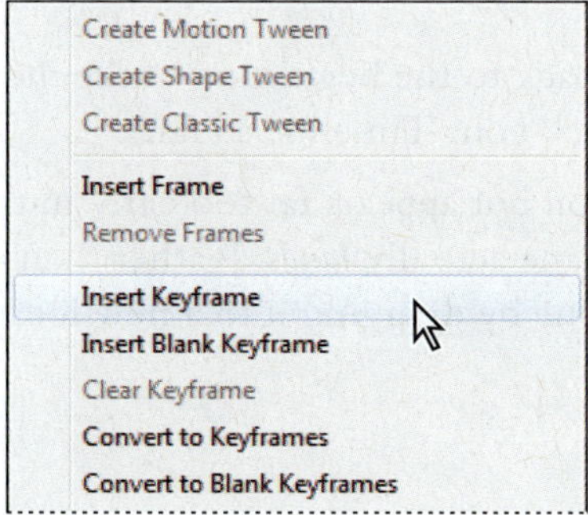

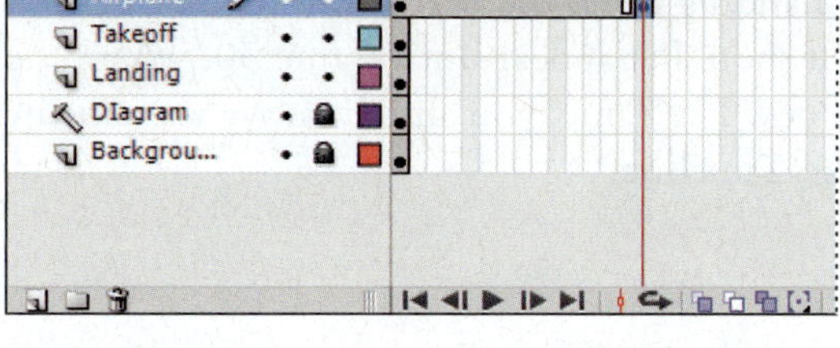

Figure 5-2: Insert a new keyframe.   *Figure 5-3: See the new keyframe on the Airplane layer.*

Notice that the airplane on the previous keyframe (frame 1) has been duplicated on the new keyframe—you can now reposition this airplane on the Stage. However, you first need to extend the Background and Diagram layers so you can use them for reference.

5. Select frame 30 on the Background layer, then right-click (Windows) or Ctrl+click (Mac OS) and choose Insert Frame from the contextual menu that appears. This extends the Background layer up until frame 30.

Repeat step 5 for the Diagram layer so that it also extends up until frame 30.

Here, you added frames on the Diagram and Background layer to extend them up until frame 30 as shown in Figure 5-4.

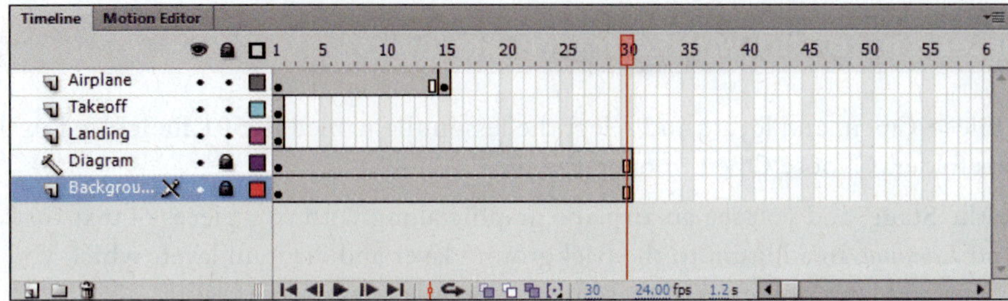

Figure 5-4: *Add frames after a keyframe to extend it further along the Timeline.*

6. Click on the Airplane layer and select keyframe 15. Using the Selection tool (➤), grab the airplane that appears selected on the Stage, and drag it to the top–middle of the Stage. Use the Diagram layer as a reference.

7. Select frame 30 on the Airplane layer. Right-click (Windows) or Ctrl+click (Mac OS) on the selected frame, and select Insert Keyframe to add a keyframe at this position. Once again, the airplane from the previous keyframe is duplicated on this new keyframe.

8. Click on the Airplane layer and select keyframe 30. Using the Selection tool, grab the airplane that appears selected on the Stage, and drag it to the left edge of the Stage just above the ground. Again, use the dotted line and airplane images on the Diagram layer as a reference (Figure 5-5).

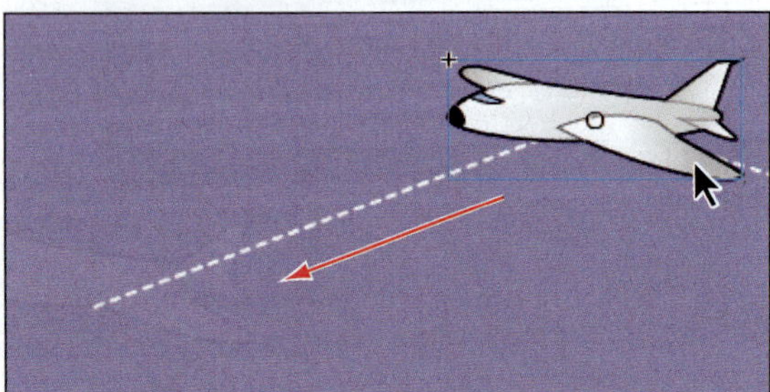

Figure 5-5: *Move the airplane along the Stage.*

9. Click on frame 1 of any Layer to bring your playhead back to the beginning of the movie. Press Enter (Windows) or Return (Mac OS) to play back your Timeline so far.

10. On the Landing layer, the text sits in the correct position but appears far too early in the movie. It shouldn't appear until frame 30, where the plane actually *lands*. Rather than create a new keyframe, you simply move the existing one by dragging it to a new location along the Timeline.

Click on the keyframe at frame 1 of the Landing layer to select it. Move your pointer over the frame again until a small white box appears below your cursor. Click, hold down your mouse button, drag the keyframe right, and release it at frame 30 as shown in Figure 5-6.

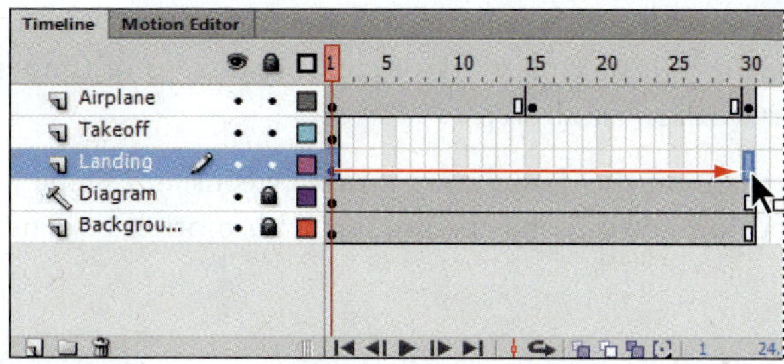

Figure 5-6: You can click and drag a selected keyframe to reposition on the Timeline.

11. The finishing touch is to ensure that the Takeoff text hangs out on the Timeline just a bit longer. You'll use the same technique you used to extend the Background and Diagram layers.

Click and select frame 15 on the Takeoff layer. Right-click (Windows) or Ctrl+click (Mac OS) on the selected frame, and choose Insert Frame to add a frame and extend the first keyframe up to frame 15.

12. Press Enter (Windows) or Return (Mac OS) to play your Timeline back. The airplane should appear in three different positions, and the text should appear and disappear at different points. Figure 5-7 shows the final Timeline as it should appear.

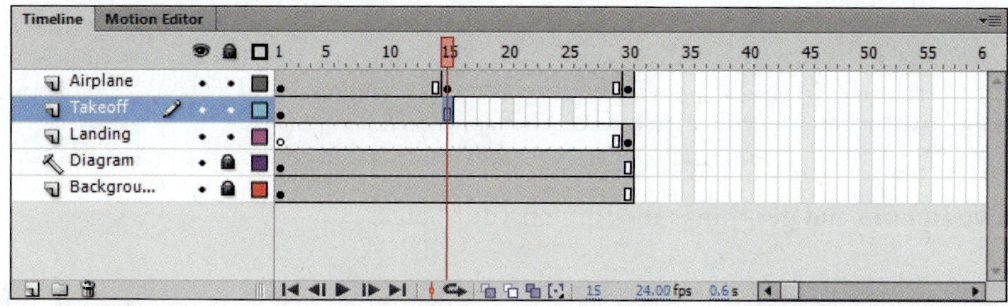

Figure 5-7: The final Timeline as it should appear in your file.

13. Choose File > Save to save your movie, then choose File > Close to close the file.

Take Note...
Keyframes can also be created using the F6 shortcut key or by choosing Insert > Timeline > Keyframe.

Building animation: Enter the tween

Flash's strength lies in its ability to create automatically generated animations, or **tweens**, making it easy and intuitive to get things moving on your Stage. You simply need to let Flash know where an object needs to start and where it needs to end using keyframes, and Flash draws the frames in-between, saving you the painstaking work of creating dozens of frames by hand and moving or manipulating the artwork in small steps.

There are two types of tweens you can create on the Timeline: motion tweens and shape tweens. In the following steps, you'll focus on getting objects moving with motion tweens and tween layers.

Tween layers and automatic keyframing

The animation engine in Flash is designed to make creating animation easy and intuitive for new and existing Flash users. The heart of animation in Flash is the *tween span,* a single sequence of frames that can include any number of movements and tweens on a single object. Flash can create both shape tweens and motion tweens, both of which are considered keyframe animation techniques.

Within a single tween span, you only need to move or modify an object at a certain point in time, and Flash automatically creates keyframes to mark those movements where they occur on the Timeline. A layer that contains one or more tween spans is called a *tween layer.*

New Term: Motion Tween

A **motion tween** is an automatic animation performed on a symbol instance that can incorporate changes in position, scale, size, color effects, and filters. To create a motion tween, you right-click (Windows) or Ctrl+click (Mac OS) a keyframe that contains a single symbol instance and choose Create Motion Tween from the contextual menu that appears.

It's time to dive right in and get things moving on your Stage:

Follow these steps to create motion tweens to animate an object

1. Choose File > Open and select the **fl0502.fla** file from this chapter's lesson folder.

   You'll notice some familiar graphics from the last exercise—except this time you'll get things moving with some fluid animation.

2. Choose File > Save As. In the Save As dialog box, navigate to the fl05lessons folder and type **fl0502_work.fla** in the Save As text field. Press Save.

3. Let's begin with the Airplane layer—you'll want to move the airplane as you did in the previous exercise, but have it animate its movement from place to place. Right-click (Windows) or Ctrl+click (Mac OS) on the first frame of this layer and choose Create Motion Tween as shown in Figure 5-8. A 24-frame tween span is created on this layer.

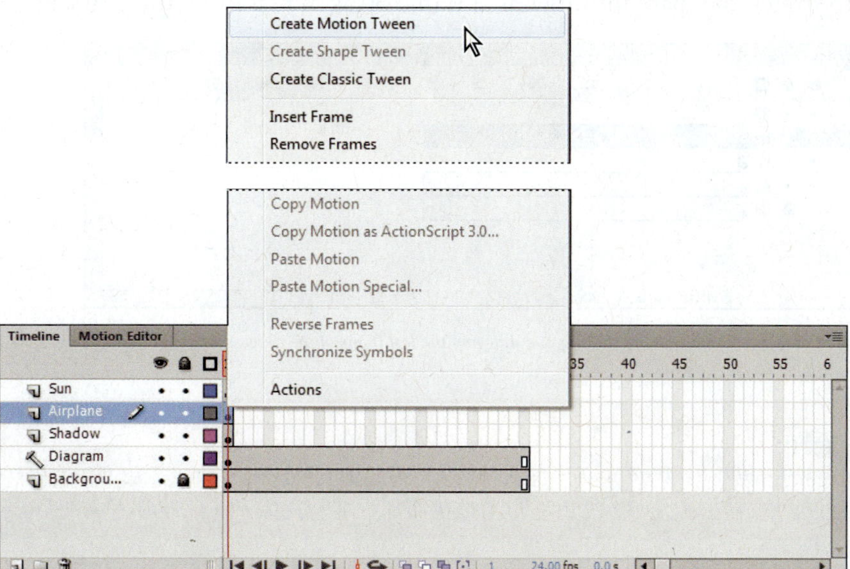

Figure 5-8: Right-click (Windows) or Ctrl+click (Mac OS) on a keyframe to create a motion tween.

4. To create animation, you simply need to move the playhead to a position on the Timeline and change the appearance or position of the graphic at that point in time. In this case, the goal is to get the airplane to the middle position at frame 15. To do this, click and drag the playhead to the frame 15 marker. Using the Selection tool (k), click and drag the airplane graphic to the middle position (using the diagram layer as a reference). Notice that a black dot marks an automatically created keyframe at this position.

5. You'll see a line appear on the Stage that outlines the motion of the airplane—this is referred to as a Motion Path. Click to select frame 1 on the Timeline ruler to return your playhead to the beginning of the movie, and press Enter (Windows) or Return (Mac OS) to play back your Timeline—you should see your airplane glide from one place to another (Figure 5-9)!

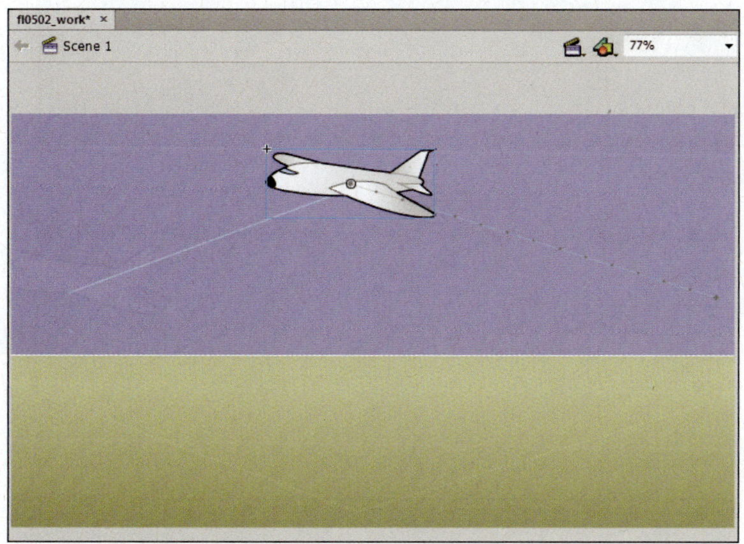

Figure 5-9: A motion path is created when you move an object within a tween span.

6. The next step is to get your airplane from the middle position to its final position on the left. To create an even number of frames for each movement, you're going to need to extend the tween span a bit. Move your mouse pointer over the last frame of the tween span (directly over the layer itself) until you see a double-arrow icon (↔). Click and drag to the right to stretch the span until it ends at frame 30 as shown in Figure 5-10.

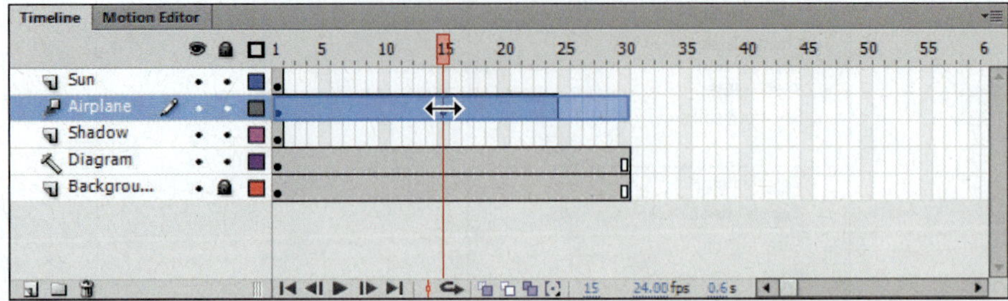

Figure 5-10: *Extend or trim a tween span by clicking and dragging the last frame of the tween span.*

Take Note...

You may notice that keyframe 15 moved slightly when you adjusted the length of the tween span. Keyframes shift as you readjust the length of a tween span; this is okay to leave as is.

7. On the frame ruler at the top, click on frame 30 to jump the playhead to this position. Select the airplane, being careful not to click on the small circle in the center and drag it to the left side of the Stage to the landing position (using the diagram layer as a reference). Another keyframe is created at this position in the tween span to mark the change.

8. Press Enter (Windows) or Return (Mac OS) to play back the Timeline, and you see your airplane glide from place to place.

9. You can view the finished Timeline in Figure 5-11. Choose File > Save. Leave the file open.

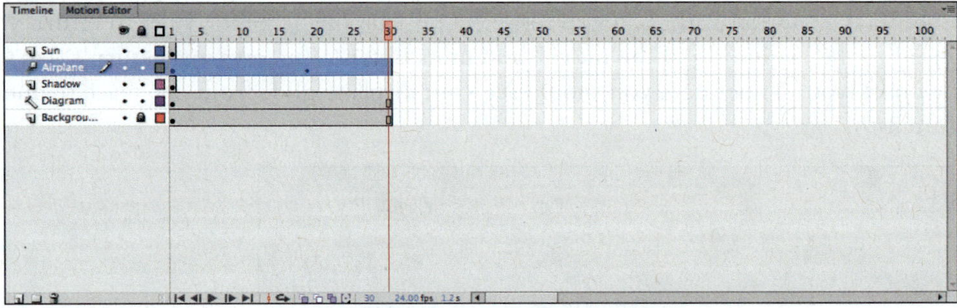

Figure 5-11: *The finished Timeline.*

The Tween rules

It most certainly does, but in this case, it refers to some rules that apply when creating motion tweens and tween spans on the Timeline.

- The length of any new tween span, by default, matches the frame rate of your movie. A movie at the default 24 fps frame rate will create 24-frame tween spans, and a movie at 30 fps will create 30-frame tween spans.

- To be included in a tween span, a graphic, text, or imported bitmap image must be converted to a symbol first. If you attempt to create a motion tween on a non-symbol, Flash will prompt you to convert the item to a symbol on the spot.

- Only one symbol or graphic can be tweened at a time. If you attempt to apply a motion tween to a layer with several objects, Flash will prompt you to convert the graphics to a single symbol.

- Tween spans can include changes to position, size/scale, color effects, and filters (for movie clips and buttons). To morph the shape of an object, you'll use shape tweens (discussed later in this lesson).

- Tween errors generally occur when you attempt to tween incorrect elements in Flash. A tween error is apparent when the tween in the timeline is dotted instead of a solid line. In the case of a shape tween, this usually occurs when you are trying to tween something other than a shape. In the case of a motion tween, you need to be working with symbols. To resolve the tween error, simply change the object to the appropriate type and the tween should repair itself. If it doesn't, delete the tween and recreate it.

Tweening multiple objects

To tween multiple graphics simultaneously, you simply need to place each one on its own individual layer. Each animated item will always need to have a dedicated tween span and tween layer. In this exercise you'll add layers to animate the shadow and text elements to complete the scene.

Follow these steps to tween multiple graphics

Step-by-Step

1. Select the first keyframe of the Shadow layer. Right-click (Windows) or Ctrl+click (Mac OS) on this keyframe and choose Create Motion Tween from the menu that appears. A tween span is created on this layer, and the shadow graphic is ready to be tweened.

2. Click on the Timeline ruler and drag the playhead to frame 15 as shown in Figure 5-12. At this frame, use the Selection tool (⬉) to select and move the shadow so it sits below your airplane (using the diagram as a guide).

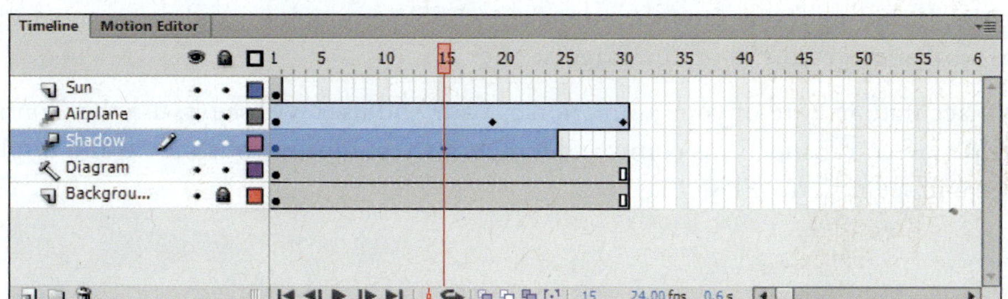

Figure 5-12: Create a tween span on the Shadow layer, and reposition the shadow on frame 15.

3. Move your mouse pointer over the last frame of the new tween span, and click and drag it to extend it to frame 30 (it should be as long as the airplane layer's tween span).

4. Click and drag the playhead to frame 30. On this frame, select the shadow once again and position it so it sits below the airplane in its landing position (using the diagram as a guide).

5. Press Enter (Windows) or Return (Mac OS) to play back your animation, and as displayed in Figure 5-13 you should see the shadow move in tandem with your airplane!

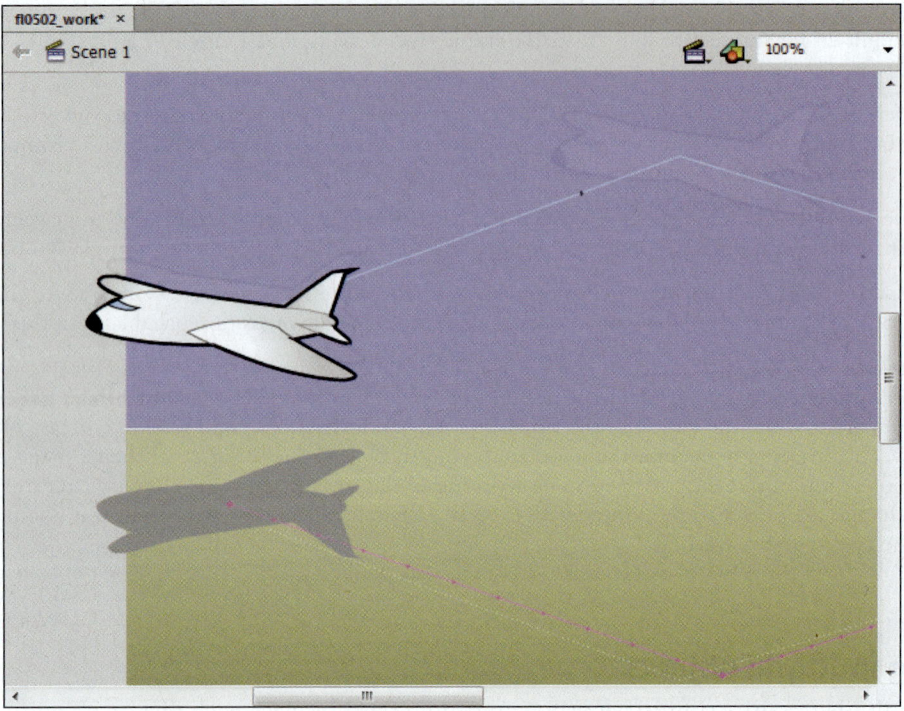

Figure 5-13: Reposition your shadow to match the movement of the airplane above.

6. Choose File > Save to save your work. Leave the file open.

Take Note...
A tween layer won't allow you to place or draw additional graphics on it once it's been created. You will get a warning dialog box if you attempt to add content to an existing tween layer.

Previewing animation with Test Movie

Pressing Enter (Windows) or Return (Mac OS) (referred to as Live Preview) is a quick way of seeing your animation as you build it, but the performance of your animation is based on many factors, including frame rate, the complexity of Stage graphics, and the number of simultaneous animations running on the Stage at once.

To get a more accurate picture of your animation as your end user will see it, use the Control menu's **Test Movie** command. This command temporarily publishes your movie and displays it as your user will see it in the Flash Player.

<table><tr><td>**Follow these steps to preview an animation**</td><td>**Step-by-Step**</td></tr></table>

1. With the current file open, choose Control > Test Movie > in Flash Professional.

2. The Flash Player opens, and displays and plays your movie. At this point, you can only stop the movie by using the Control menu in the Flash Player window. Choose Control > Stop.

> **Take Note...**
> *You may have noticed that your Diagram layer never shows in the final, published movie. The Diagram layer is a special type of layer called a Guide, whose contents are used strictly for visual reference and don't publish to your final movie. You can convert any standard layer to a Guide layer.*

Generally, performance will be better in the Flash Player as you're viewing a flattened and optimized version of your movie.

3. Close the Flash Player window and return to your file.

> **Take Note...**
> *You can use Ctrl+Enter (Windows) or Command+Return (Mac OS) as a shortcut instead of Control > Test Movie. This shortcut key combination will be used several times throughout the lesson.*

Moving and transforming tween paths

Once a tween has been created, you may decide that the entire animation needs to be repositioned or shifted. Thanks to the **motion paths** that appear on the Stage, this task is easier than ever. Because the motion paths are vector–based Bezier controls, they can easily be adjusted.

Certification Ready 3.6
What is a motion path and how can you modify them using Bezier controls?

<table><tr><td>**Follow these steps to move and transform tween paths**</td><td>**Step-by-Step**</td></tr></table>

1. Click the Shadow layer in the Timeline and locate the motion path that your shadow graphic follows along the bottom of the Stage.

2. Using the Selection tool (▸), click once on the motion path to select it in its entirety.

3. Click anywhere on the motion path and then drag it straight down—this moves the path and the entire animation along with it. Move it down until the bottom of the motion path touches the bottom of the Stage (Figure 5-14). Note that you can disregard the positioning shown on the Diagram layer at this point.

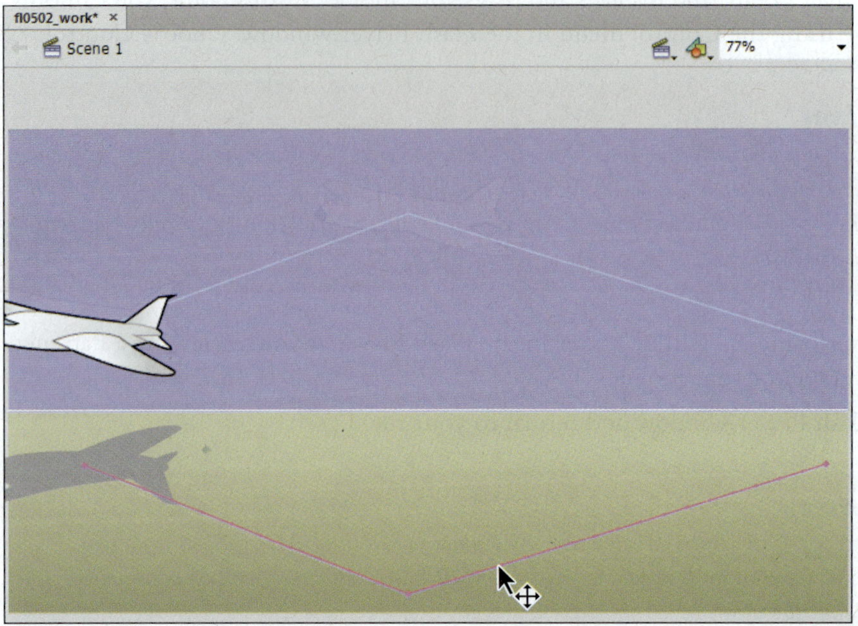

Figure 5-14: *Click and drag a motion path to move it and the animated objects that follow it.*

4. Leave the path selected, and choose the Free Transform tool (⌖) from the Tools panel. Handles appear on either end, and in the middle of, the motion path. You can transform the motion path just as you would a graphic to change its position or rotation.

5. Position your cursor to the bottom-right of the right handle and pull it upwards slightly to change the rotation of the path (Figure 5-15). You may notice that while the rotation of the path changes, the actual shadow does not!

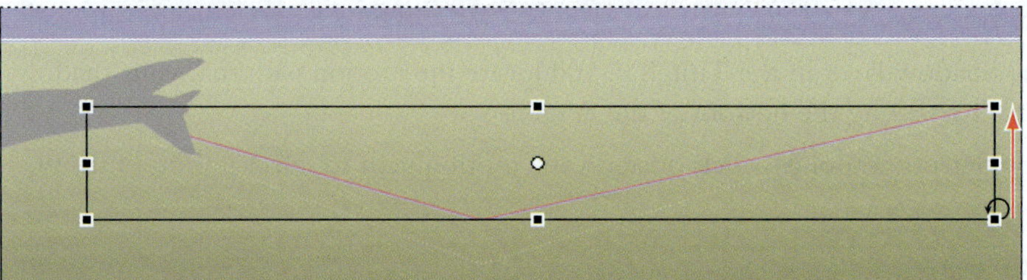

Figure 5-15: *You can transform a motion path just as you would a piece of artwork. This has no effect on the animated object that follows it, however.*

6. Press Enter (Windows) or Return (Mac OS) to play back your modified animation.

7. Choose File > Save to save your file.

Incorporating color effects and scaling

The cool thing about motion tweens is that you can have several properties of your graphic all animate at once, even within the same tween span. In addition to position, you can tween opacity (transparency), color tints, scaling, and rotation of an object to create more complex animation behavior.

For your airplane shadow, you'll want to manipulate the size and opacity of the shadow as the plane flies at different heights from the ground.

Certification Ready 4.10

How can you create effects such as fade in or fade out in an animation?

Follow these steps to modify the appearance of an object

Step-by-Step

1. Select frame 19 of the Shadow layer. This brings you to the part of the tween span where the shadow appears in the middle of the Stage. Because the plane is at a higher altitude, the shadow should appear lighter and smaller.

2. Choose the Selection tool (🢒), then select the shadow directly on the Stage at frame 19, and locate the Color Effect options under the Property Inspector panel on the right. If necessary, click on the arrow to the left of Color Effect to display the Style menu below it.

3. From the Style menu, choose Alpha, which controls the transparency of your symbol instance. Use the slider to set the Alpha back to 50 percent as shown in Figure 5-16. Leave the shadow selected.

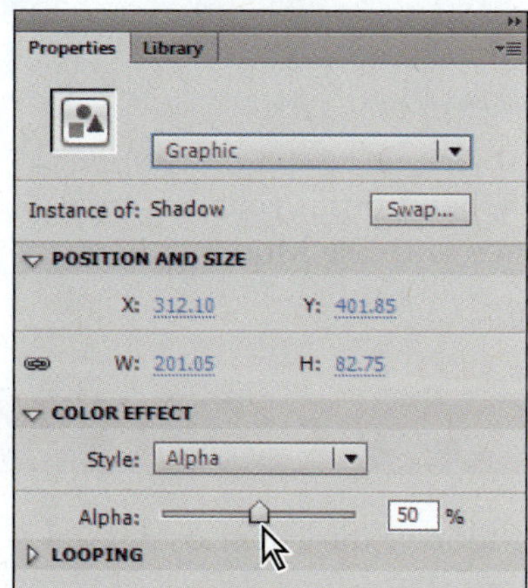

Figure 5-16: Select the shadow and use the *Color Effects* options to set its Alpha *(transparency) to 50 percent.*

4. Next, you'll reduce the size of your shadow slightly, as the airplane is higher off the ground. Choose Modify > Transform > Scale and Rotate. This opens the Scale and Rotate dialog box. Set the scale value to **60** percent, make sure the Rotate value is set to 0 degrees (Figure 5-17), and press OK.

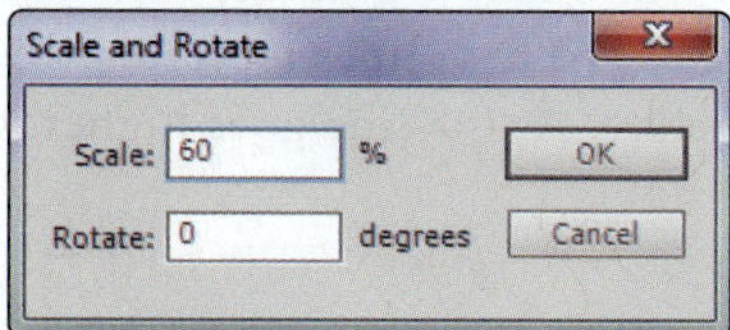

Figure 5-17: Scale the shadow graphic down *to 60 percent at frame 19.*

5. Drag the playhead to the beginning of the Timeline, and press Enter (Windows) or Return (Mac OS) to play back your animation—notice that the Alpha and scaling effects have been added to your tween!

   However, also notice that the size and Alpha of the shadow don't return to their original values when the animation reaches frame 30. You'll fine-tune this in the next lesson.

6. Choose File > Save to save your movie.

Introducing the Motion Editor

Certification Ready 4.10

What is the obect-based tweening model and the Motion Editor?

Docked behind the Timeline panel is the **Motion Editor**, a powerful panel that enables you to fine-tune and modify animation with precision (Figure 5-18). The Motion Editor displays all properties of a selected tween span in a graph-like format where you can adjust individual properties (such as position and Alpha) in a tactile, precise way. Because motion tweens are object-based, they can be easily manipulated and their properties can by copied and pasted easily.

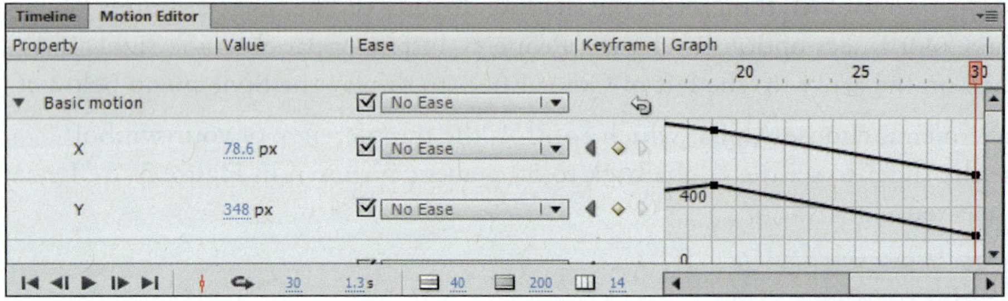

Figure 5-18: The Motion Editor is a powerful feature that allows you to see and adjust every aspect of your animation in a graph-like format.

Previous Flash users will find this to be a welcome addition, but if this is your first time animating in Flash, you'll also enjoy the flexibility that comes with the Motion Editor.

Let's take a look at the Motion Editor, and see how it works:

Follow these steps to use the Motion Editor

1. Click the Motion Editor tab to bring it forward. The Motion Editor appears docked behind the Timeline panel at the bottom of your workspace.

2. Before you can use or view properties in the Motion Editor, you'll first need to select a tweened object on the Stage. Click on the Shadow graphic on the Stage to select it and view its animation properties in the Motion Editor.

3. Each row across represents a different property that is either being tweened or can be tweened if desired. Use the vertical scroll bar on the right side of the Motion Editor to scroll down and see more properties.

   You should see that every property you've tweened for your Shadow graphic, such as x position, y position, and Alpha, all have lines running across. These lines represent the value of each property at different points along the Timeline. As the line goes higher, so does the value.

4. Within the Basic Motion category click on the X property to expand it. This expands the row to full height. Click on the X property again to collapse it to its original height. You can also make more room for the Motion Editor by dragging the divider in between the bottom of the Stage and the top of the Motion Editor/Timeline panels as shown in Figure 5-19.

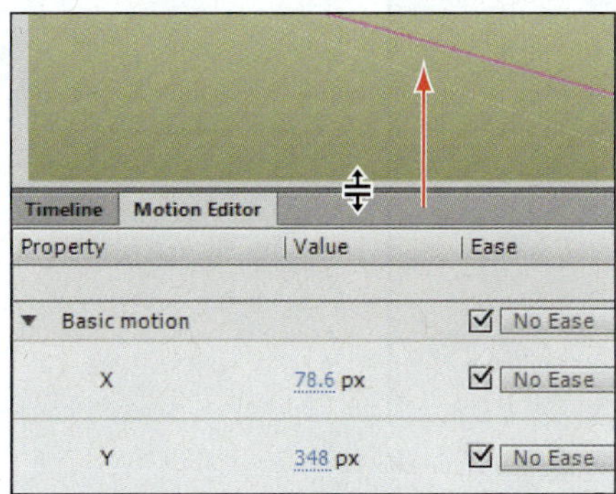

Figure 5-19: *Click and drag between the Motion Editor and the Stage to expand its height.*

5. Scroll down and take a look at the Skew X and Skew Y properties. These rows display dashed lines, which indicate that there is no value for these properties. You haven't applied any skewing to your graphic.

6. Leave the Motion Editor open for the next exercise.

Modifying the animation using the Motion Editor

Let's go ahead and put the Motion Editor to use by modifying the animation you created earlier.

You'll remember that the Alpha and scale values of your shadow didn't switch back even as the airplane returned to the ground in frame 30. You'll need to adjust these values to change later in the animation, and the Motion Editor will help you do that.

<table><tr><td>**Follow these steps to modify an animation**</td><td>**Step-by-Step**</td></tr></table>

1. If the Motion Editor is not already visible, click its tab above the Timeline to bring it forward. Note: If you accidentally collapsed the panel, you can reopen it by choosing Window > Motion Editor.

2. Using the Selection tool (▸), click to select the Shadow graphic on the Stage to reveal its properties in the Motion Editor. Scroll down if necessary and locate the Alpha/Alpha amount row nested inside the Color Effect category.

3. If necessary, expand the Alpha amount row by clicking on it. Use the horizontal scroll bar to scroll across, and watch as the line starts at 100 percent (top), dips down at frame 19 to 50 percent, and remains there. A dashed line appears from that point on. You'll need to add a keyframe along this line to change its value at a different point in time.

4. Scroll right until you reach the end of the Alpha amount line (frame 30). Right-click (Windows) or Ctrl+click (Mac OS) on the very end of the line, and select Add Keyframe from the small contextual menu that appears (Figure 5-20).

This creates a draggable point on the line at frame 30. From here, you can either drag the point up or down to change the Alpha value, or specify an exact value on the left.

Figure 5-20: Right-click (Windows) or Ctrl+click (Mac OS) at any point along a value line to add keyframes that you can use to adjust values.

5. Leave the point selected, and on the left side of the row, locate the Alpha amount value. Click and drag on the value until it reads 100 percent. You should see the point (keyframe) you created move to the top position on the right and the shadow on the Stage become opaque (Figure 5-21).

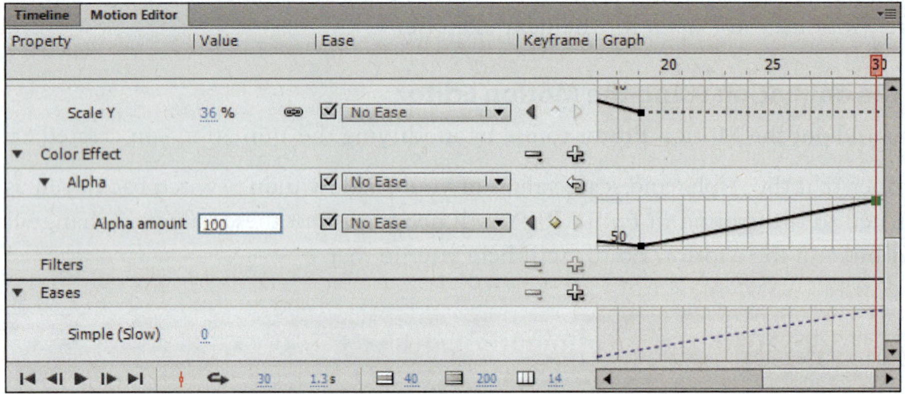

Figure 5-21: Adjust values of a selected keyframe using the slider/type-in box on the left side of a row.

Take Note...
To expand the height of the current row for a larger view, click on the row anywhere within the gray area on the left side of the Motion Editor.

6. Directly above the Alpha row, locate the Scale X and Scale Y rows, which affect horizontal and vertical scaling (respectively). You animated these properties when you scaled down the shadow earlier. Once again, scroll to the end of the row so that the end of the value line is visible.

7. At the end of the Scale X line, right-click (Windows) or Ctrl+click (Mac OS) directly on the line and choose Add Keyframe from the contextual menu that appears.

Note to make sure the Link X and Y property values button is not active so that you can set independent values for each axis.

Take Note...
Another way that you can create additional points along the value line is by holding down Ctrl (Windows) or Command (Mac OS) and clicking directly on the line. Add the Shift key to this combo to remove an existing point.

8. Click and drag the new point (keyframe) straight up until the value on the left reads 60 percent. The value is shown on the left side of the Motion Editor directly to the right of where it reads Scale X. As you change this value, you will also see the plane shadow scale.

9. The Scale Y value should have automatically scaled back up to 60% as shown in Figure 5-22. This is because Scale X and Scale Y values are linked together to maintain proportion. If you had disabled the Link X and Y Property Values button, repeat steps 7 and 8 for the Scale Y value, also returning its value to 60 percent at the end of the line (frame 30).

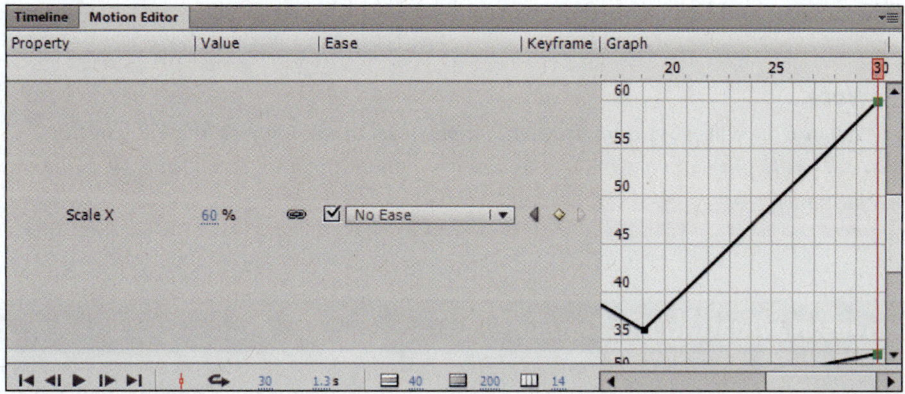

Figure 5-22: *Add keyframes to the end of the Scale X and Scale Y value lines and change their final value to 60 percent.*

10. Press Ctrl+Enter (Windows) or Command+Return (Mac OS) to preview the animation with the new adjustments you've made. You should see the shadow animate back to full opacity and its original size as the animation reaches its completion (Figure 5-23). Close the Flash Player once you've viewed your movie.

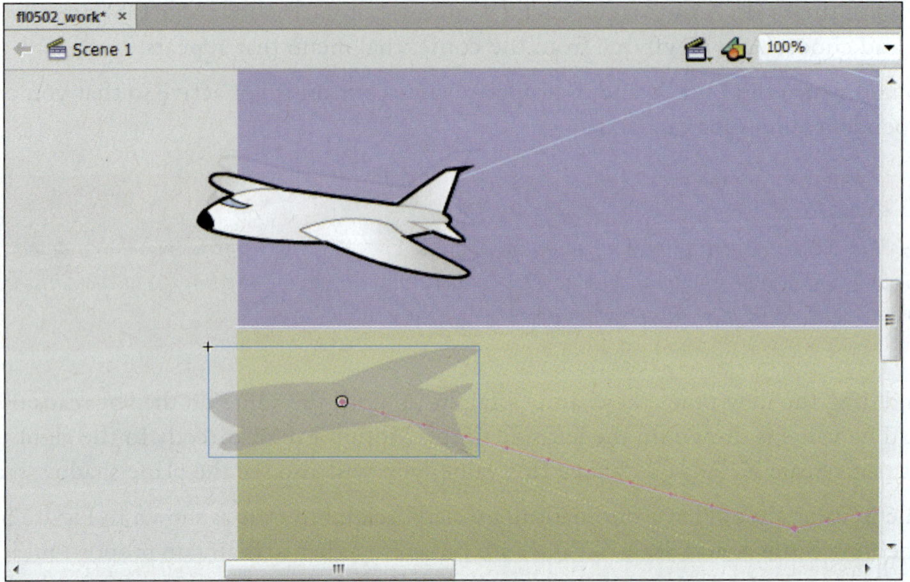

Figure 5-23: The airplane's shadow now returns to full size and opacity by frame 30.

11. Choose File > Save, and leave this file open.

Take Note...
The Motion Editor displays a frame ruler and playhead at the top just like the Timeline, so you can easily preview your changes as you go, without the need to switch back to the Timeline panel.

<table><tr><td>**Learning More**</td><td>**Making moves: Navigating the Timeline**</td></tr></table>

Now that you are working across several frames and tween spans across the Timeline, you'll want to be able to navigate the Timeline and view animation sequences in a number of ways.

Here are a few short tips for navigating the Timeline that you'll find useful:

Preview an animation by pressing Enter (Windows) or Return (Mac OS) to start playback of the Timeline and view an entire animation sequence.

Move frame-by-frame through the Timeline by using the , (comma) and . (period) keys.

Move in any direction at any speed by clicking and dragging the playhead back and forth across the frame ruler. This is referred to as *scrubbing*.

Rewind and jump to the beginning of the Timeline by choosing Control > Rewind or pressing Shift+, (comma).

Tweening rotation

If you need to incorporate one or more full rotations in a tween, you'll find that rotation has its own special option in the Property Inspector. Rotations may need to occur more than once (for instance, three full revolutions)—behavior that Flash can't figure out from a graphic's position alone.

In the following steps, you'll add a tween to the Sun graphic on your Stage, and rotate it using the Property Inspector's rotation menu.

<table><tr><td>**Follow these steps to add a rotation effect to an object**</td><td>**Step-by-Step**</td></tr></table>

1. Bring the Timeline panel forward by clicking its tab below the Stage, or by choosing Window > Timeline. Select keyframe 1 of the Sun layer on the Timeline.

2. Right-click (Windows) or Ctrl+click (Mac OS) on the keyframe and choose Create Motion Tween from the contextual menu that appears. The layer is converted to a tween layer and a new tween span is created.

3. Just as you did with the other tween layers earlier, move your pointer over the last frame of the tween span, and then click and drag it to the right until it ends at frame 30 as shown in Figure 5–24.

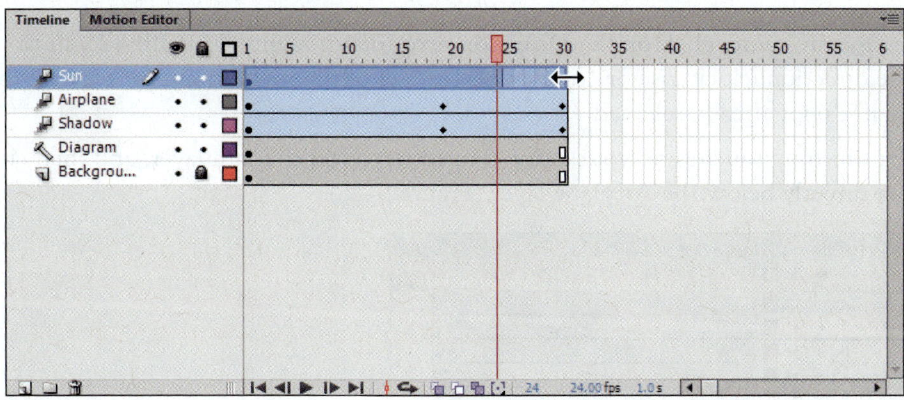

Figure 5–24: Add a motion tween to the Sun layer, and expand the tween span to frame 30.

4. Leave the frame selected, and locate (and if necessary, expand) the Rotation options in the Property Inspector on the right of your workspace.

5. Place your cursor over the 0 in the Rotate property and then click and drag to set the rotate count to 3 times. This sets the number of revolutions the sun will complete during the course of the tween span (Figure 5-25).

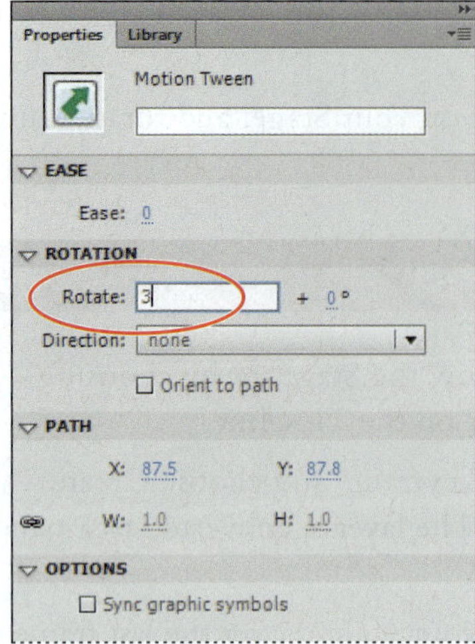

Figure 5-25: *Set the rotations to 3 on the Property Inspector. If necessary, set the direction to CW (clockwise).*

6. Under the Rotate value, click on the Direction drop-down menu. This allows you to choose the direction (clockwise or counter-clockwise) of the revolutions. Select CW for clockwise if it's not already selected.

7. To put the finishing touches on your animation scene, select the Sun layer, and then click and drag it directly below the Airplane layer (Figure 5-26).

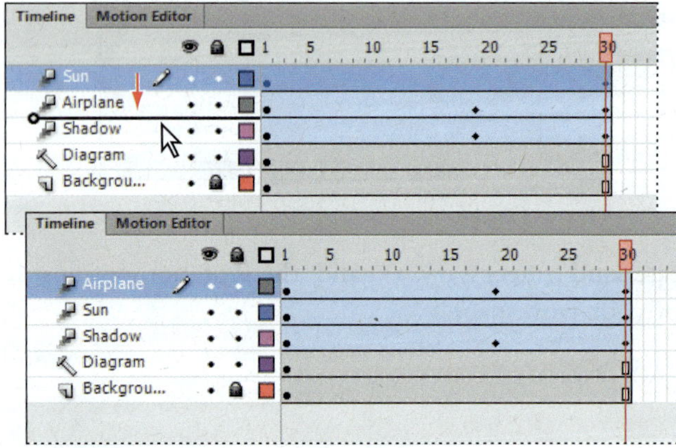

Figure 5-26: *Drag the Sun layer below the Airplane layer to complete the scene.*

Press Enter (Windows) or Return (Mac OS) to play back your movie, and you'll see the sun rotate three times clockwise! Experiment with different numbers of revolutions to increase the perceived speed of the rotation.

Take Note...
Remember, increasing revolutions without increasing the length of the tween span will result in faster rotation.

8. Choose File > Save to save your file.

New Feature: Rotation

The Rotation options feature the ability to add a specific number of degrees to the number of full rotations you've chosen. For instance, you can set three rotations and 45 degrees if you'd like! Previous versions of Flash only accepted whole number rotation values.

Controlling animation paths

You may have noticed how all the tweens you've created so far move in a straight line. While this may work in certain situations, there will certainly be a time when you want an animated object to follow a curved or unusual path.

To accomplish this, you can manipulate the motion path that your animated object follows. This motion path behaves much like any other path, and can be curved or manipulated using the Selection tool.

Follow these steps to modify a motion path

1. Select the Airplane layer in the Timeline. Choose the Selection tool (⬉), and move your pointer over the right half of the airplane's motion path (animation path). You should see a curved line appear below your cursor (⬉) when you get close enough to the line.

2. Click and drag up to bend the line into an upward curve, as shown in Figure 5-27.

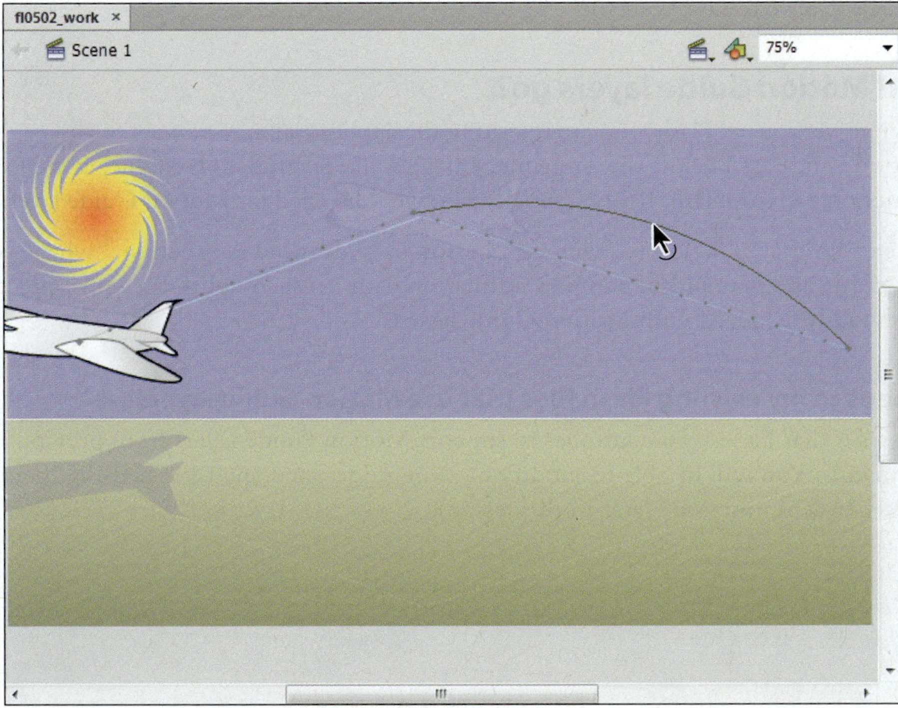

Figure 5-27: Click and drag over the middle of a line to bend it into a curve.

3. Move your pointer over the second half of the motion path (where the plane begins to fly down again) until the same curved icon appears below your cursor. Click and drag down to bend the line into a downward curve.

4. Press Enter (Windows) or Return (Mac OS) to play back your animation, and you'll see your airplane follow the new curve of the motion path (Figure 5-28).

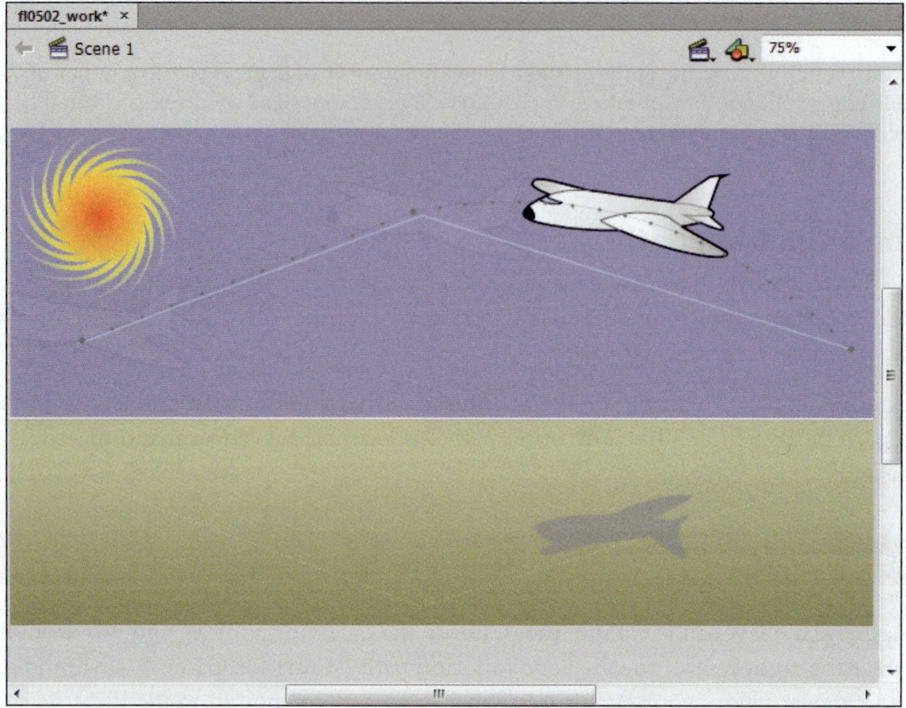

Figure 5-28: The airplane now follows the newly adjusted motion path.

5. Choose File > Save to save your file.

Where did Motion Guide layers go?

Users of previous versions of Flash who are revisiting the application may notice the absence of the Add Motion Guide icon below the Timeline. Changes in the animation engine, as well as the addition of motion paths in Flash, have essentially removed the need for Motion Guide layers.

More complex path manipulation is covered in Lesson 6, "Advanced Animation," where you will learn to create and manipulate complex animation paths to accomplish the same effect you may have previously achieved with Motion Guide layers.

What happens to my existing Flash files that use Motion Guide layers?

The good news is that Flash CS6 continues to support Motion Guide layers from previously created documents. You will be able to modify motion guides, and any tweens using them are treated as *classic* tweens (discussed later in this lesson).

How do I create a motion guide if I still want to?

Interestingly enough, despite the removal of the Add Motion Guide button, it is still possible to create a Motion Guide layer, but in a very non-obvious way. The Flash CS6 team thought enough to include a discreet way to create motion guides using standard guide layers.

Because traditional motion guides only work with classic (old-school) tweens, they are discussed in detail later in this lesson under "Legacy techniques: Creating classic tweens."

Morphing graphics and colors with shape tweens

So far, the tweens you've created have involved moving, scaling, or rotating symbol instances across the Stage. However, you may want to create some cool animations by having an object change its shape or color.

For these tasks, you'll explore shape tweens, which allow you to animate changes in shape and color between two graphics. You can also create cool **morphing** effects by having one object gradually transform into another. As a general rule, shape tweens work best with fairly simple shapes.

Shape tween basics

The good news for experienced Flash users is that the process of creating a shape tween has not changed. For new users, **shape tweens** differ in some important ways from the motion tweens you learned about earlier in the chapter.

Some major differences are:

- Unlike motion tweens, shape tweens don't work with symbol instances. You can only use mergeable artwork or drawing objects. Primitive shapes can be used, but they must be broken down first.

- Shape tweens require the creation of two keyframes to contain the starting and ending shapes of the tween.

- Shape tweens do not have motion paths, so their motion, if any, is always linear (they move in a straight line).

- The Motion Editor can't be used to adjust shape tweens.

In this section, you'll create a shape tween to transform a moon into a bird in your animation scene.

<table><tr><td>**Certification Ready 4.10**

What are some best practices for creating shape tweens?</td></tr></table>

<table><tr><td>**Certification Ready 4.10**

How do you insert, remove, manipulate and clear keyframes and frames?</td></tr></table>

<table><tr><td>**Certification Ready 4.10**

How do you create a shape tween?</td></tr></table>

Follow these steps to use shape tweens

Step-by-Step

1. Make sure the Timeline panel is visible by clicking its tab below the Stage, or by choosing Window > Timeline.

2. Select the Airplane layer and click the New Layer icon (⬚) below the Timeline to create a new layer; rename it **Shape Morph** (Figure 5-29). At this time, lock your other layers so you don't accidentally disturb their contents.

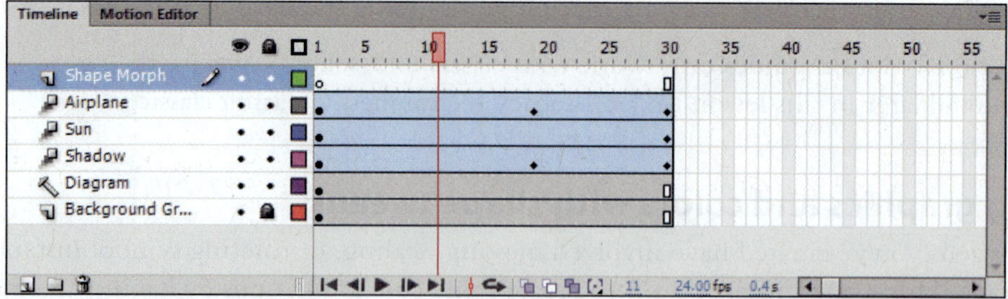

Figure 5-29: *Add a new layer and name it Shape Morph.*

Take Note...

To lock all layers except for the one you want to work on, hold down the Alt (Windows)/ Option (Mac OS) key and click the dot below the padlock icon on the layer you'd like to use. All other layers except for the selected one automatically lock.

3. Click and drag the playhead to the beginning of the timeline at frame 1. Bring the Library panel forward by clicking its tab—you'll find it docked behind the Property Inspector on the right. In the Library panel, locate the Moon graphic symbol, and drag an instance of it to the upper-right corner of the Stage. It is automatically placed on the new layer you just created as displayed in Figure 5-30.

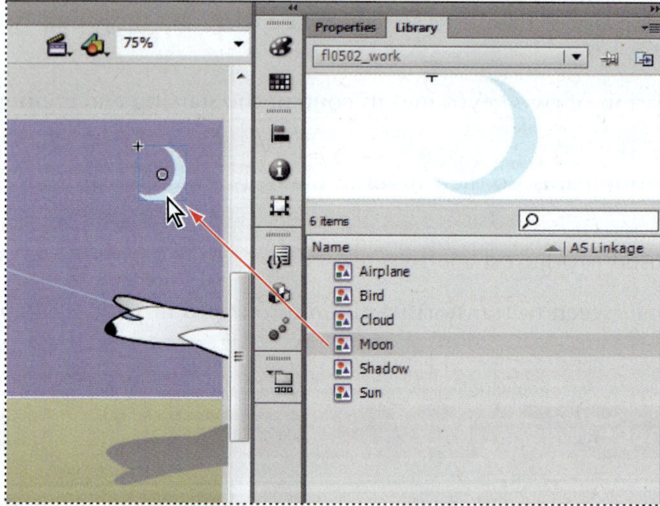

Figure 5-30: *Drag an instance of the Moon graphic to the Stage.*

Take Note...

You won't be able to drag a symbol to a locked layer, so if you're having difficulty, make sure that you have that Shape Morph layer selected on the Timeline, and that it is unlocked.

4. Because shape tweens can't work with symbol instances, you'll need to break this symbol back down to basic artwork again to use it in your shape tween. Use the Selection tool to select the new symbol instance, and choose Modify > Break Apart to break it down to non–symbol artwork (Figure 5-31).

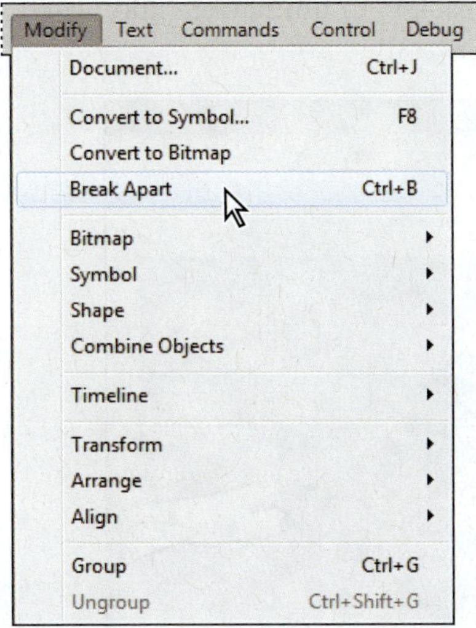

Figure 5-31: *Choose Modify > Break Apart to break a symbol instance apart and prepare it for shape tweening.*

5. Next, you'll need to add a second keyframe that will contain a new shape that your moon will transform into. Click and select frame 30 on the Shape Morph layer. Right-click (Windows) or Ctrl+click (Mac OS) on the selected frame and choose Insert Blank Keyframe to add a new empty keyframe at this position.

Take Note...
The only difference between inserting a keyframe or a blank keyframe is whether or not Flash copies the contents of the previous keyframe to the new one. For a shape tween, you generally aren't reusing the shape from the starting keyframe, so adding a blank keyframe is a better choice. At any point, you can select a keyframe and right-click on it to clear or remove a keyframe.

6. Click to select the new keyframe (30). Locate the Bird graphic symbol in your Library panel, and drag an instance of it to the middle of the Stage, slightly above the ground.

7. Once again, choose Modify > Break Apart to break the symbol instance down to basic artwork. Now that you have two unique shapes on keyframes 1 and 30, you're ready to create a shape tween to have one transform into another (Figure 5-32).

Figure 5-32: *Place and break apart the Bird graphic to prepare it for shape tweening.*

8. Click to select keyframe 1. Right-click (Windows) or Ctrl+Click (Mac OS) on the keyframe and choose Create Shape Tween from the contextual menu that appears. A green shaded area and an arrow appear between the two keyframes, letting you know that the shape tween has been successfully created.

9. Press Enter (Windows) or Return (Mac OS) to play back your animation, and watch as the first shape gradually morphs into the second! (Figure 5-33)

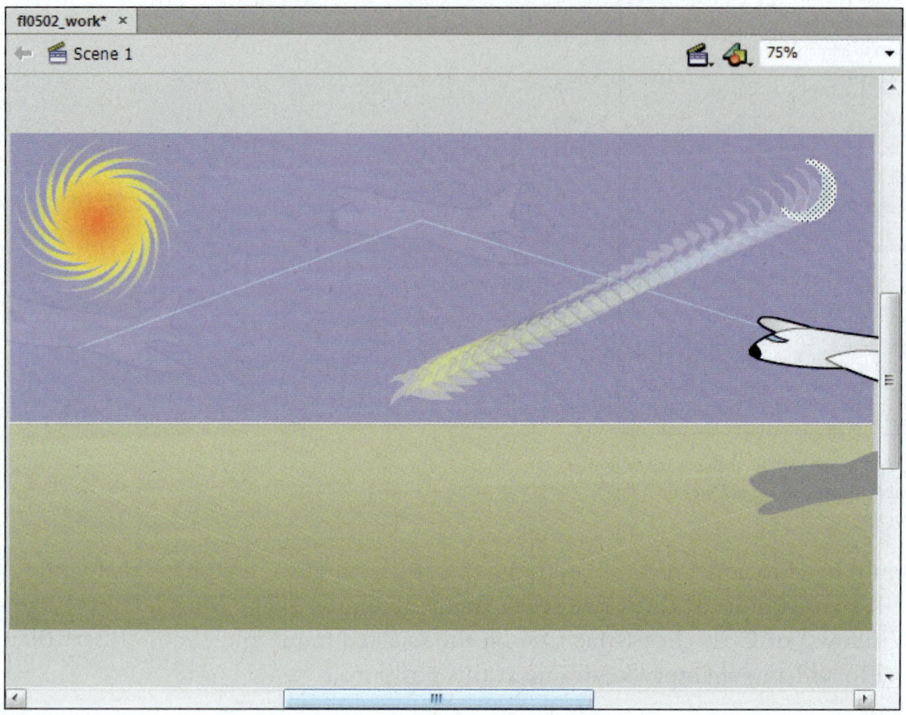

Figure 5-33: *Your completed shape tween. (Shown here in Onion Skin view)*

10. Choose File > Save to save your file.

Take Note...

If your tween displays a dashed line instead of an arrow, be sure to check that both pieces of artwork have been broken out of their symbol form. If either piece of artwork still exists as a graphic symbol, the shape tween can't be properly created.

Getting in shape: Making the most of shape tweens

Shape tweening is part technique, part luck of the draw. Every pair of shapes will yield a unique result, but in some cases the transition between two shapes may not be what you expect. In some cases, the transition may not be pretty at all. To get the best results from your shape tweens, here are some general pointers to consider:

1. Try using solid, whole shapes. For instance, if you have a face and two eyes, avoid trying to morph all three in a single shape tween. Consider breaking each element out onto its own layer for best results.

2. Try and keep the number of starting and ending shapes the same. Two shapes to two shapes, as opposed to two shapes to three shapes, will yield cleaner results.

3. If your starting shape includes a stroke, try to include one on the ending shape as well.

4. Use Shape Hints to fine-tune the quality of your shape tweens and anchor common points between starting and ending shapes (Shape hints are discussed in detail in Chapter 6).

Legacy techniques: Creating classic tweens

In previous versions of Flash, the process of creating motion tweens was very different. In fact, it was much more like creating shape tweens, whereby a set of keyframes had to be manually created to mark the beginning and end of a motion tween.

While it's highly recommended that you use the new tween model, there may be cases where you need to create or modify a *classic* motion tween within an older Flash file. The next lesson illustrates this technique for just those times.

Follow these steps to create a classic tween

1. Press the Insert Layer button (⬒) below the Timeline to add a new layer. Name this new layer Classic Tween.

2. From the Library panel on the right, locate and drag an instance of the Cloud graphic symbol to the first keyframe of the new layer. As shown in Figure 5-34, use the Selection tool (▴) to position it in the upper-right corner of the Stage.

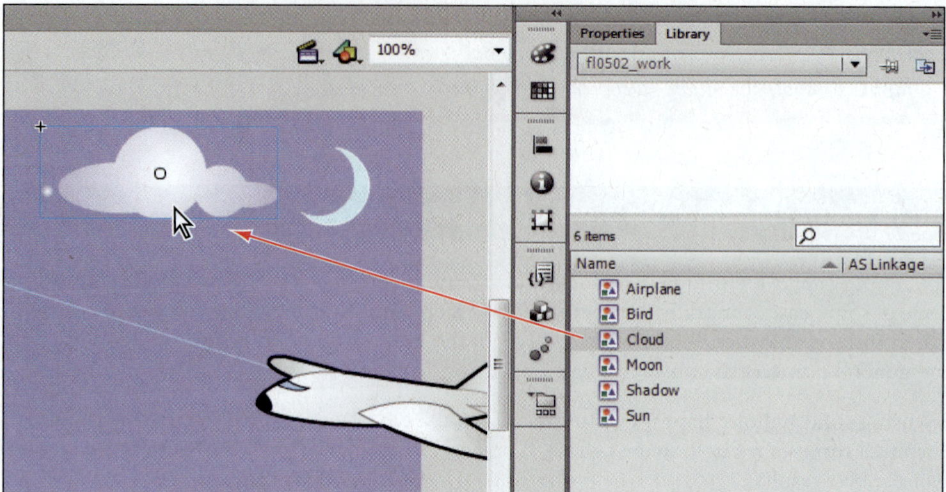

Figure 5-34: Drag instance of the Cloud graphic from your Library to the Stage.

3. Classic motion tweens require a starting and ending keyframe, so you'll need to create the ending keyframe further down on this layer. Select frame 30 of this layer, and press the F6 shortcut key (Windows) or choose Insert > Timeline > Keyframe (Mac OS) to create a new keyframe at this position.

4. The cloud from keyframe 1 has been duplicated onto this new keyframe—you'll change the position of this copy to mark where the cloud should go during the course of the animation. As shown in Figure 5-35, click and drag the cloud instance on keyframe 30 straight to the left so it sits beside the sun.

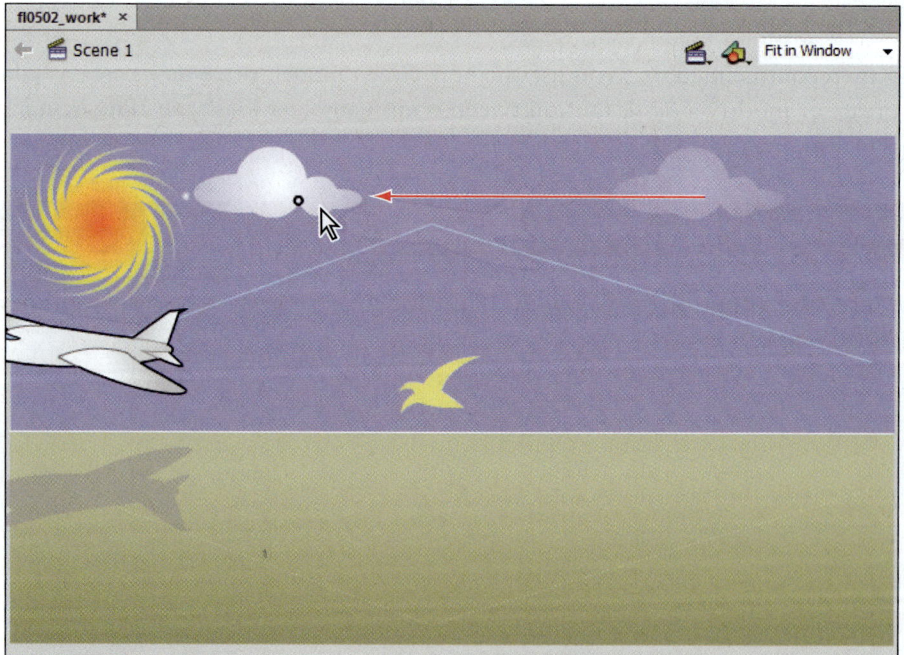

Figure 5-35: Move the cloud to the left to indicate where it will travel to (shown here in Onion Skin view).

5. Now it's time to finalize the tween. Click and select keyframe 1. Right-click (Windows) or Ctrl+click (Mac OS) on the keyframe and choose Create Classic Tween from the contextual menu that appears. A purple, shaded area and arrow should appear in between the two keyframes, indicating the tween has been successfully created.

6. Choose Control > Test Movie > in Flash Professional to preview your animation. The cloud moves to the left across the Stage!

7. Close the Flash Player, and choose File > Save to save your work.

Classic tween rules

As with tween layers and tween spans, classic motion tweens have some rules that need to be followed to ensure that they are created properly.

- Classic tweens require a starting and ending keyframe.
- Classic tweens can only use symbol instances.
- Both keyframes require an instance of the same symbol; you can't tween between two different symbol instances.
- Only one object can be tweened at a time on a single layer.

Adding color effects and scaling to a classic tween

When using classic tweens, you can animate several properties at once, just as you did with the airplane's shadow earlier in the lesson. By making changes to the starting or ending instance of the cloud, you can incorporate transparency, scaling, and other properties in the tween along with the existing motion.

Follow these steps to modify the appearance of a classic tween   **Step-by-Step**

1. If it's not visible, bring the Property Inspector forward by clicking its tab on the right side, or by choosing Window > Properties.

2. Click keyframe 30 directly on the Classic Tween layer to select it. The cloud on this keyframe should also appear selected on the Stage. Click once more on the cloud so it's active in the Property Inspector on the right.

3. Under the Property Inspector's Color Effect options, locate and click on the Style menu and select Alpha. When the Alpha slider appears, click and drag it to the left to set the Alpha value to 50 percent (Figure 5-36).

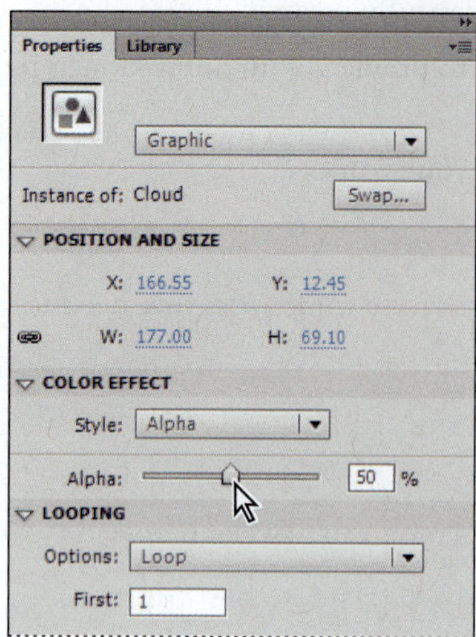

Figure 5-36: *Select the cloud on frame 30 and use the Color Effect options on the Property Inspector to set its Alpha to 50 percent.*

4. Leave the cloud selected, and choose Modify > Transform > Scale and Rotate. In the Scale and Rotate dialog box that appears, type **50%** for the Scale value, and press OK to apply the new value. View Figure 5-37 to see the changes applied.

Figure 5-37: *The cloud shown after color effects and scaling have been applied.*

5. Press Enter (Windows) or Return (Mac OS) to play back your Timeline, and watch as the cloud fades and shrinks as it moves across the sky.

6. Choose File > Save to save your file.

Take Note...
There is a big difference between selecting a keyframe and selecting the contents of a keyframe. If an object on the Stage appears selected, but you don't see its options in the Property Inspector, click once more on the object to make it active. This is sometimes referred to as focusing an object.

Take Note...
Unlike tween spans, classic tweens will not prevent you from adding other objects to the same layer. While this will not generate a warning, adding graphics or text to a layer that contains a classic tween will likely break the tween.

(Re)creating motion guides for classic tweens

Experienced Flash designers may have already noticed the apparent removal of the Add Motion Guide button below the Timeline, and, in turn, the ability to create Motion Guide layers. A technique still exists for creating *classic* motion guides when and if necessary. In the following steps, you'll change the path of animation for your classic tween using good, old-fashioned motion guides.

Certification Ready 4.10

How do you use a motion guide to animate shapes, text, and symbols along a path?

<table>
<tr><td>**Follow these steps to change the path of an animation**</td><td>**Step-by-Step**</td></tr>
</table>

1. Click and select your Classic Tween layer on the Timeline.

2. Click the Add Layer button (⬒) below the Timeline to create a new layer above the Classic Tween layer, and rename it **Motion Guide**. You'll use standard drawing tools, such as the Pencil tool, to create a random path that your cloud can follow.

3. Select the Pencil tool (✐) from the Tools panel, and make sure that you have a stroke color selected. In addition, make sure that Object Drawing is *not* enabled. The button at the bottom of the Tools panel, (◎), should be popped out.

4. On the new layer, use the Pencil tool to draw a single interesting path that starts about where the cloud begins, and ends about where the cloud ends on the left side of the Stage. This path, shown in Figure 5–38, is what your classic tween will follow in just a few moments.

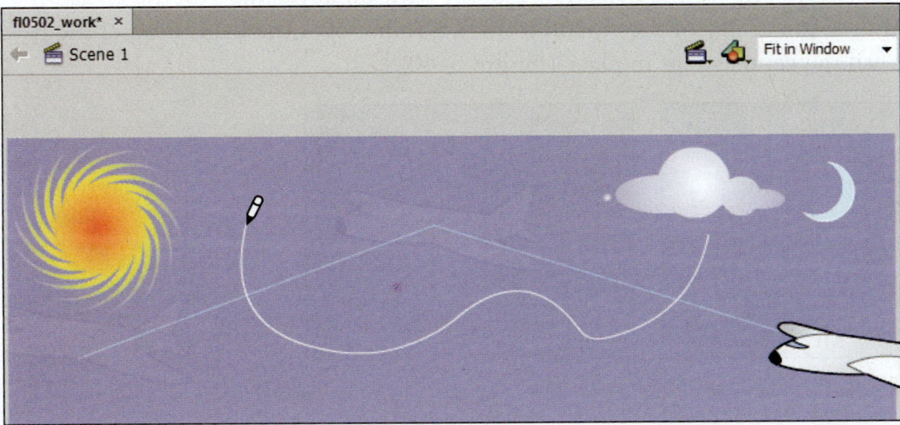

Figure 5–38: Use the Pencil tool to draw a path on the new layer you created.

5. The trick to making sure the classic tween will follow this path is to first convert this layer to a Guide layer. Right-click (Windows) or Ctrl+click (Mac OS) on the title area of the Motion Guide layer, and choose Guide from the contextual menu that appears. The layer icon is replaced by a T-square icon (✎), indicating that this is now a Guide layer.

6. Next, select the Classic Tween layer, and carefully drag it up and to the right below the Motion Guide layer until it appears indented underneath it (Figure 5-39). This lets the Classic Tween layer know to follow whatever path it finds on the Motion Guide layer above it.

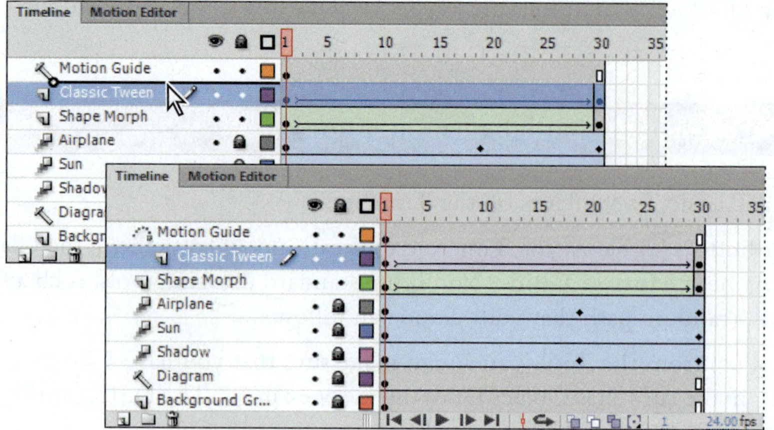

Figure 5-39: *Move the Classic Tween layer below and to the right of the Motion Guide layer to bind the two together.*

7. To get your cloud following the path, you'll need to snap the cloud instances at the beginning and end keyframes of the classic tween layer to the beginning and end of the path, respectively. Choose the Selection tool (ᐱ), click on keyframe 1 of the classic tween layer, and drag the center of the cloud on this keyframe over the beginning of the path you created until the center snaps in place (Figure 5-40).

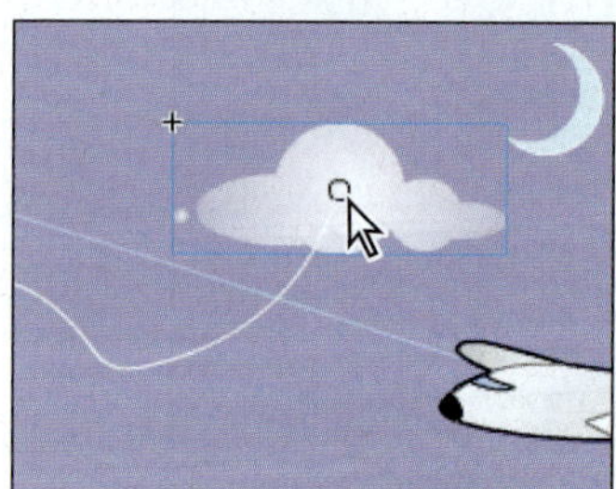

Figure 5-40: *Snap the cloud instance on keyframe 1 to the beginning of the path.*

Figure 5-41: *Snap the cloud instance on keyframe 30 to the end of the path.*

As shown in Figure 5-41, select keyframe 30 of the classic tween layer, and click and drag the cloud on this keyframe to the end of the path until it again snaps in place.

Take Note...

For symbol instances to properly snap in place to a path acting as a motion guide, make sure Snap To Objects is enabled. Choose View > Snapping > Snap To Objects to make sure it is checked.

8. Press Enter (Windows) or Return (Mac OS) to preview your animation—your cloud should now follow the path you created on the Motion Guide layer.

9. Choose File > Save to save your file.

Troubleshooting Motion Guides

Motion guides can be a bit tricky the first few times around. If your animation is not following the motion guide you created, use the following points to troubleshoot your animation:

- Make sure that both the starting and ending instance are snapped directly onto the path you created. If either instance is not seated properly on the motion guide, it will not work. Think of it as putting a train on the tracks.

- Make sure your motion path is NOT a drawing object, group, or symbol. Animations can only follow paths drawn in Merged Drawing mode. A telltale sign that you may not be using the right type of artwork is if your path appears inside a bounding box.

- Avoid using unusual stroke styles, such as dashes, dots, or ragged strokes. These occasionally cause unpredictable behavior if used on a motion path.

Adjusting animation with onion skinning

One of Flash's most useful visual aids is the Onion Skin, which allows you to view all frames of an animation at once on the Stage. This helps you make crucial decisions, such as how far to move or scale an object during the course of an animation. It also helps you see how your animation works alongside other items on the Stage as the Timeline plays back.

Onion skinning can be enabled for a single layer or multiple layers at once; simply unlock a layer if you want to view it as onion skins, or lock it if you don't.

In the following steps, you'll see how you can adjust your existing tweens in Onion Skin view.

<table>
<tr><td>Follow these steps to enable onion skinning</td><td>Step-by-Step</td></tr>
</table>

1. On the Timeline, lock all layers except for your Shadow, Shape Morph, and Classic Tween layers. If necessary, click and drag the playhead to the end of your Timeline to frame 30.

2. At the bottom of the Timeline, locate the cluster of five small buttons, and click the second button from the left, (⬚), to enable Onion Skin view. Two brackets appear on the frame ruler at the top of the Timeline as you can see in Figure 5-42. These brackets allow you to select the range of frames that you'd like to view in Onion Skin mode.

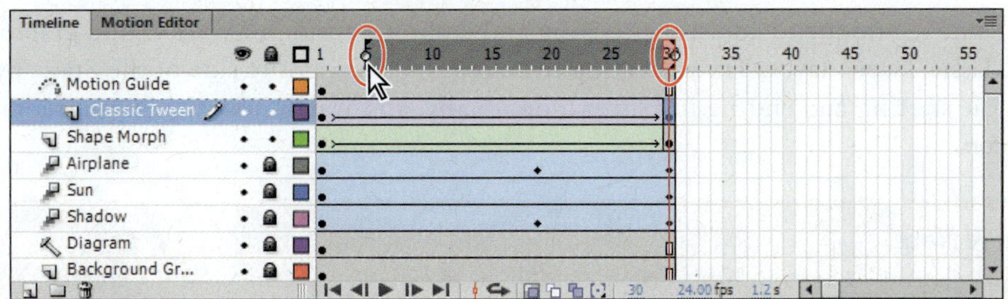

Figure 5-42: Adjust the brackets on the frame ruler to choose how much of the Timeline you want to reveal in Onion Skin mode.

3. Click and drag the left bracket to position it at the very beginning of the Timeline (frame 1). With the playhead at frame 30, the right bracket is at the end of the Timeline. You should now see all frames of animation on the unlocked layers (Figure 5-43).

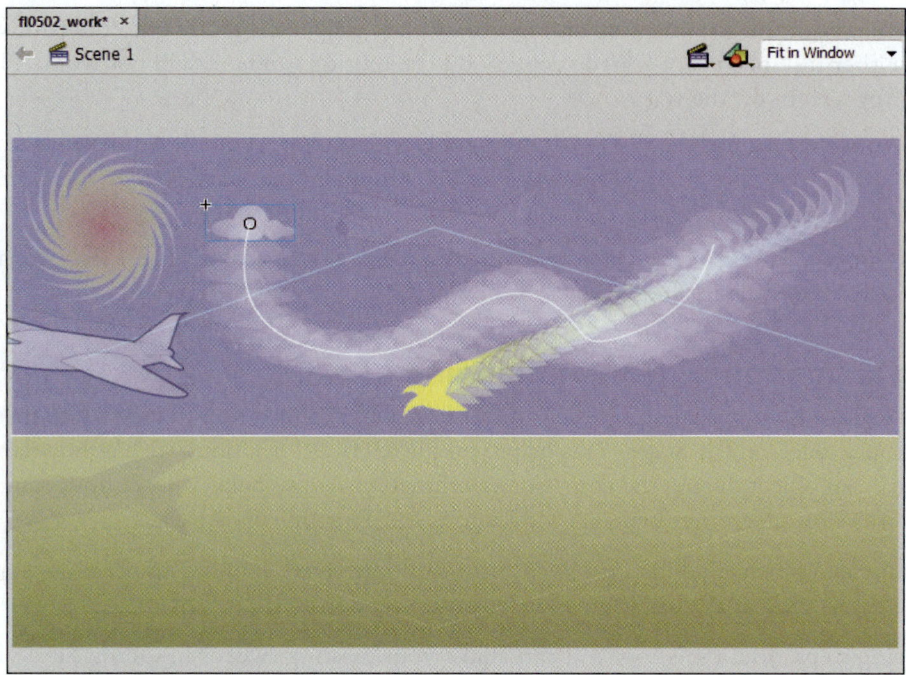

Figure 5-43: *With Onion Skin enabled, you can view all frames of animation on all unlocked layers.*

4. Click on the Timeline ruler at Frame 1 to return the playhead to the beginning of the Timeline. On the Shape Morph layer, select the moon shape and drag it slightly downward, click anywhere in the background and you will see the frames in between adjust automatically. Adjust the angle of the frames in between until you get the shape morph moving in a straight line from right to left.

5. On the Shadow layer, grab the starting shadow symbol instance on the right side of the Stage and drag it down slightly. You see the trajectory of the tween change, and the motion path readjusts as well.

6. Use the same technique to adjust the starting and ending position of your Cloud graphic on the Classic Tween layer. Try relocating the cloud to the opposite side of the Stage by moving the starting and ending instances individually, and watch how the frames redraw in between.

Take Note...
If the full-color frames in Onion Skin are difficult to look at, try Onion Skin Outlines. Click the button directly to the right of Onion Skin (third from the left in the button cluster below the Timeline). This displays all frames in an outline view that's easier to see in certain situations.

7. Choose File > Save to save your file, and choose File > Close to close the file.

Looking ahead

Now that you have a feel for creating basic animation and working with multiple layers of animation at once, you will move on to more advanced techniques in Lesson 6, "Advanced Animation."

You'll work more with the Motion Editor, learn to simulate gravity and inertia effects with Easing, and create more advanced motion paths. You'll also learn to incorporate 3D properties into your tweens, edit and align several frames of content at once, and create cool frame-by-frame animation using Flash CS6's IK (Inverse Kinematics) behavior.

Skill summary

In this lesson you learned how to:	Objective
Identify general and Flash-specific best practices for designing rich media content for the web, mobile apps, and AIR applications	2.1
Use the Timeline	3.3
Use the Motion Editor	3.6
Create animations (changes in shape, position, size, color, and transparency)	4.10

Knowledge Assessment

True/False

Circle **T** if the statement is true or **F** if the statement is false.

T   F   1. The Timeline is where graphics, text, and media are sequenced and animation is created.

T   F   2. In a document set to the default frame rate of 24fps (frames per second), every 24 frames on your Timeline represent one second of playback in your movie.

T   F   3. A layer that contains one or more tween spans is called a tween layer.

T   F   4. Having to animate frame-by-frame by hand is commonplace in Flash as opposed to using tweens.

T   F   5. Within a tween span, you must manually create additional keyframes if you wish to make changes to the animation.

T   F   6. With regard to tweens and inside a tween span, more than one symbol or graphic can be tweened at a time.

T   F   7. Tween spans can include changes to position, size/scale, color effects, and filters.

T   F   8. To morph an object, you'll need to use a motion tween.

T   F   9. With regard to motion tweens, you can only have one property of your graphic animate at a time.

T   F   10. Primitive shapes can be morphed in their native form and do not need to be modified for morphing.

Multiple Choice

Select the best response for the following statements.

1. The Timeline consists of which of these components:

   a. Layers
   b. Frames
   c. Keyframes
   d. All of the above

2. What is the term used to describe a sequence of frames that can include any number of movements and tweens on a single object?

   a. Motion Tween
   b. Classic Tween
   c. Animation Tween
   d. Tween Span

3. What is the term used to describe the line that displays how an object will travel from one point to another?

    a. Motion Path

    b. Animation Path

    c. Movement Path

    d. Travel Line

4. By default, the length of any new tween span matches length with what?

    a. The length of the last object set

    b. The frame rate of your movie

    c. One frame until you stretch it out

    d. None of the above

5. To tween multiple objects simultaneously, you simply need to place each object in its own:

    a. Graphic Symbol

    b. Library

    c. Flash movie

    d. Layer

6. What type of layer contains contents that are used strictly for visual reference and don't publish to your final movie?

    a. Motion layer

    b. Keyframe layer

    c. Guide layer

    d. Mask layer

7. Which of the features in Flash has been removed since it's not needed anymore?

    a. Blank Keyframes

    b. Motion Guides

    c. Masks

    d. Graphic Symbols

8. Which of the following objects can be morphed?

    a. Primitive objects

    b. Mergeable artwork and drawing objects

    c. Movie clips

    d. Buttons

9. Which type of tween requires that each keyframe require an instance of the same symbol?

    a. Motion tween

    b. Classic tween

    c. Shape tween

    d. All of the above

10. Which of the following Flash features allows you to view all frames of an animation at once on the Stage?

    a. View > Overlay

    b. Tween spans

    c. Tween layers

    d. Onion Skinning

Competency Assessment

<table>
<tr><td>Project 5-1</td><td>**Project 5-1: Animation Review**</td></tr>
</table>

In animation, you're often trying to replicate what the organic version of the object would really do in the real world. Many animators will study a subject for quite some time to take note of the physics and physical reactions of the object they're trying to recreate digitally. Let's start the process of creating a bouncing ball by doing some review.

1. Create a new ActionScript 3.0 document in Flash.

2. Select the Oval tool, set the fill color to blue, the stroke to none and make sure you're in Object Drawing mode. Draw a circle at the top of the Stage.

3. Choose the Selection tool and make sure the blue circle is selected on the Stage. Choose Modify > Covert to Symbol, save the symbol as movie clip named Bouncing Ball.

4. With the symbol still selected on the Stage, choose Insert > Motion Tween.

5. Make sure the playhead is at the end of the frame span and drag the circle down to the bottom of the stage.

6. Preview the animation of the circle by pressing Enter or Return.

7. Save this file as **bouncing_ball.fla** and keep it open for the next exercise.

<table>
<tr><td>Project 5-2</td><td>**Trying Out More Eases**</td></tr>
</table>

There are a lot of eases built into Flash. Some of them are already preset to simulate realistic animation of objects in the real world. Spring is one of those presets...

1. You should still have the **bouncing_ball.fla** file open from the last exercise.

2. Choose Window > Motion Editor.

3. Go to the Eases section at the bottom of the panel and add the Spring ease.

4. Return to the top of the Motion Editor and assign the Spring ease to the Y position value of your animation and preview the ball movement.

5. Save this file as **bouncing_ball_5.2.fla** and keep it open for the next exercise.

Proficiency Assessment

| **Animating Color** | **Project 5-3** |

Let's add to the bouncing ball by reviewing color animation. It's just another facet to animation that doesn't have to be about movement so much as it is about change.

1. You should still have the **bouncing_ball_5.2.fla** file open from the last exercise.

2. Return to the Timeline and go to the last keyframe.

3. Select the Bouncing Ball instance and choose Tint from the Color Effect menu in the Properties Panel.

4. Change the color to red and set the tint percentage to 100%.

5. The ball should now bounce and change color.

6. Save this file as **bouncing_ball_5.3.fla** and keep it open for the next exercise.

| **Eases Demystified** | **Project 5-4** |

Many people think eases only apply to physical movement, but as you'll see that's really not the case...

1. With the **bouncing_ball_5.3.fla** file still open from the last exercise, make sure your bouncing ball symbol is still selected. Choose Window > Motion Editor.

2. Go to the bottom of the Motion Editor and assign the Spring ease to the Tint Amount value and note the effect.

3. Save this file as **bouncing_ball_5.4.fla**.

Circling Back 1

There are numerous ways to add a curved movement to an object. Getting the Pen tool involved and creating Bezier curves is yet another method you can incorporate. If you're familiar with the Pen in Flash (or Illustrator) you may know it to be more of a drawing tool. In the next exercise you'll use it more as a manipulation tool.

| **Using the Pen as an Animation Modifier** | **Project 1** |

The company you're working for is asking you to design an animation that involves race cars on a race track that moves in an S shape. You need to mock up the animation to figure out how to replicate the movement of the cars on the track.

1. Create a new ActionScript 3.0 document in Flash.

2. Select the Oval tool, set the fill color to blue, the stroke to none and make sure you're in Object Drawing mode. Draw a circle on the left of the Stage.

3. Choose the Selection tool and make sure the blue circle is selected on the Stage. Choose Modify > Covert to Symbol, save the symbol as movie clip named race car.

4. With the symbol still selected on the Stage, choose Insert > Motion Tween.

5. Make sure the playhead is at the end of the frame span and drag the circle to the right so that it moves from left to right on the screen.

6. Preview the animation of the circle by pressing Enter or Return.

7. Go to the middle of the tween span to frame 12. Click on the symbol on the Stage and drag it up to create a diagonal movement.

8. Select the Pen tool in the Tools panel. Go to the keyframe point where the circle is. Hold down Alt (Windows) or Option (Mac OS) and click and drag down and to the right when you see the cursor change to the carat (<) symbol.

9. Use the Subselection tool to adjust the curve to form the S shape as needed.

10. Save this file as **race_cars.fla** and keep it open for the next exercise.

Project 2	**Refining the motion**

So now that you've got the path of the movement figured out. You'll need to figure out the speed that a car would travel given the circumstances regarding the shape of the track. Going back to the Motion Editor should help solve the problem of trying to recreate how organic objects move in the real world.

1. The **race_cars.fla** file should still be open from the last exercise.

2. Go to Window > Motion Editor. Navigate to the middle keyframe. Add the Simple (Slow) ease to the keyframe.

3. Go to the bottom of the Motion Editor panel and adjust the Simple (Slow) Value to -50.

4. Preview the animation to see the new kind of whip movement to the animation.

5. Save the file as **race_cars_5.2.fla**.

Project 3	**More morphing**

In addition to the car's movement for the race animation, you also have to recreate a car crash where the car will change shape when it impacts with another object. Shape morphs to the rescue! Practice the crash by practicing morphs!

1. Create a new ActionScript 3.0 document in Flash.

2. Select the Oval tool, set the fill color to red, the stroke to none and make sure you're in Object Drawing mode. Draw a circle on the Stage.

3. Click on frame 20 and insert a blank keyframe.

4. Using the Pen tool, draw a jagged shape on the Stage that might represent a car hitting an object.

5. Click the first keyframe in the layer and choose Insert > Shape Tween.

6. Add Shape hints and adjust as needed.

7. Save the file as **cars_5.3.fla**.

Advanced Animation

Key Terms

- 3D Rotation tool
- 3D Translation tool
- animated masks
- Copy and Paste Motion
- Easing
- IK poses
- motion presets
- rendering

Skill	Objective
Identify general and Flash-specific best practices for designing rich media content for the web, mobile apps, and AIR applications	2.1
Create animations (changes in shape, position, size, color, and transparency)	4.10

Business case

Learning efficient workflows with animation is key in Flash. Luckily there are methods such as copying and pasting and using presets that will help to streamline the process. Another aspect to animation is animating human figures in such a way that appears natural and not stiff and fake. Learning the IK tools is important to understand in order to achieve more realistic human-like movement.

Starting up

Before starting, make sure that your tools and panels are consistent by resetting your workspace. See "Resetting the Flash workspace" in the Starting up section of this book.

You will work with several files from the fl06lessons folder in this lesson. Make sure that you have loaded the fllessons folder onto your hard drive from *http://www.wiley.com/college/sc/adobeseries*. See "Loading lesson files" in the Starting up section of this book.

The project

You'll explore more complex animation techniques and new features by completing a complex ad banner for the skyPod portable music device.

Copying, pasting, and saving animation

As you develop more complex movies, you'll likely want to animate several objects in the same way throughout a single movie. Once you've created a tween span (or several), Flash gives you many options for copying and pasting animation between objects. Another more reusable option is motion presets. **Motion presets** allow you to capture, save and apply an animation behavior later onto any number of objects across objects or even different movies. Motion presets are discussed later in this chapter.

Using Copy and Paste Motion

The **Copy and Paste Motion** menu options enable you to copy animation behavior from one object and paste it to another. This means you can apply the same tween behavior to several symbols at once, or have two objects move in tandem with each other without having to manually recreate the same tween twice.

Copy Motion captures all aspects of a selected tween, including position, scaling, color effects, easing, and filters. You can paste motion as–is between two symbols, or use Paste Motion Special to pick and choose exactly which aspects you want to apply.

You'll use Copy and Paste Motion to create and apply the same tweening behavior to several text taglines in your skyPod banner.

<table>
<tr><td>Step-by-Step</td><td>Follow these steps to use the Copy and Paste Motion menu options</td></tr>
</table>

1. Choose File > Open and open the **fl0601_start.fla** file in the fl06lessons folder. Choose File > Save and name the file **fl0601_work.fla**.

2. On the Timeline, locate and expand the Tag Phrases folder by clicking on the arrow to the left. This reveals five layers: Jam, Dance, Skip, Bounce, and 65 Trillion, each of which contains a tag line that you'll animate.

3. On the Jam layer, right-click (Windows) or Control+click (Mac OS) on frame 1 and choose Create Motion Tween from the contextual menu that appears (Figure 6-1). This creates a new, 24-frame tween span (Figure 6-2). Move your cursor over the last frame of the new tween span, click and drag to the right, and expand the tween span to frame 40.

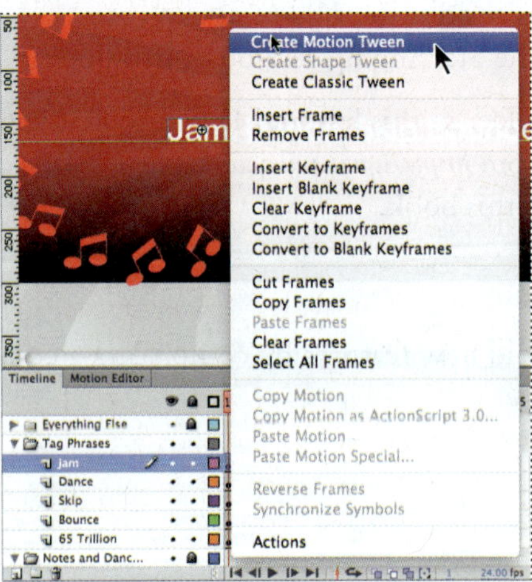

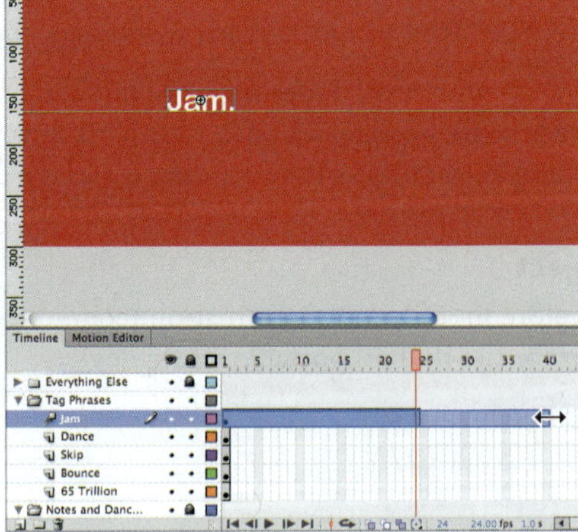

Figure 6-1: Create a new motion tween.   *Figure 6-2: Expand this tween span to frame 40.*

4. Drag the playhead to frame 1, and select the word *Jam* on the Stage, which is a movie clip symbol from your Library. On the Property Inspector, locate Filters. Click the Add Filter button at the bottom of the panel and select Blur from the filter menu that appears. Type **15** for the Blur X value to set a 15-pixel blur and press Enter (Windows) or Return (Mac OS). Choose High from the Quality drop-down menu.

5. Above the Filters options, locate the Color Effect options, and choose Alpha from the style menu. Use the Alpha slider that appears to set the alpha to 0 percent (full transparency)— the word *Jam* disappears (for now).

Next, you'll gradually fade the text back in, using a motion tween.

6. Position the playhead at frame 15, and reselect the word *Jam* at this frame (Figure 6-3).

Take Note...

If you are having difficulty finding fully transparent items, you can click the colored box to the right of the layer name to temporarily enable Outline view.

Figure 6-3: *Set a layer to Outline view for the layer to temporarily reveal transparent items.*

7. With the word selected, return to the Property Inspector and use the Alpha slider (under Color Effect) to return the alpha to 100 percent. Notice that a keyframe has been automatically created at frame 15 to mark the change.

8. Position the playhead at frame 40, where the tween span ends. Again, select the word Jam. Locate the settings you created earlier for the Blur filter (under Filters). Change the Blur X and Blur Y values to 0 pixels, then press Enter (Windows) or Return (Mac OS) to remove the blur.

9. Press Enter (Windows) or Return (Mac OS) to play back your animation so far. Notice that the word Jam fades in, and then gains focus as it reaches the end of the tween. Your next step will be to copy all the animation behavior you've just created, and paste it to the next word in the sequence: Dance.

10. On the Jam layer, click anywhere in the tween span to select it—all frames within the span should appear selected. Right-click (Windows) or Control+click (Mac OS) on the tween span and choose Copy Motion from the contextual menu that appears (Figure 6-4). The Animation behavior contained with the span, including motion, filters, and color effects, has been captured to memory.

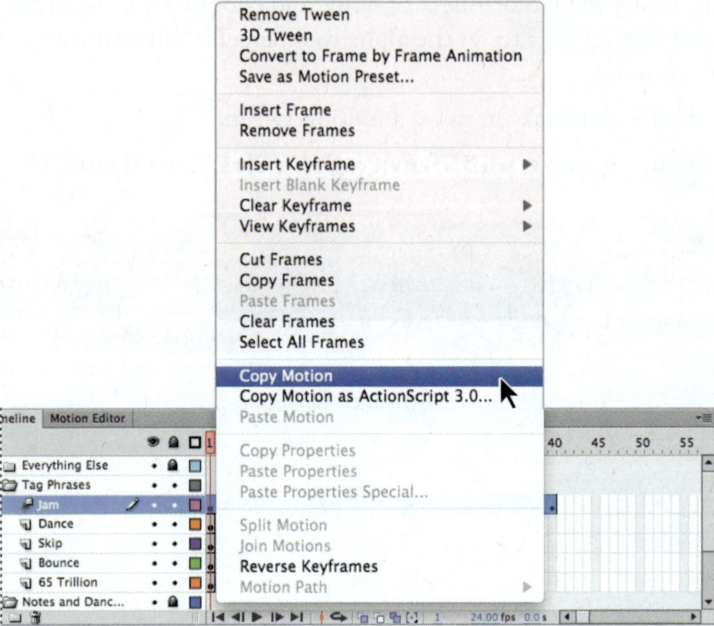

Figure **6-4**: *Right-click on a selected motion tween and choose Copy Motion from the contextual menu to copy its animation behavior.*

11. Select frame 1 on the Dance layer. Right-click (Windows) or Control+click (Mac OS) on the selected frame and choose Paste Motion from the contextual menu that appears. A tween span is created on the current layer of the same length, which includes all the same animation behavior and keyframes.

12. Press Enter (Windows) or Return (Mac OS) to play back the Timeline, and the word Dance now animates in the same exact way as the word Jam.

13. Repeat steps 11 and 12 for the Skip layer (Figure 6-5).

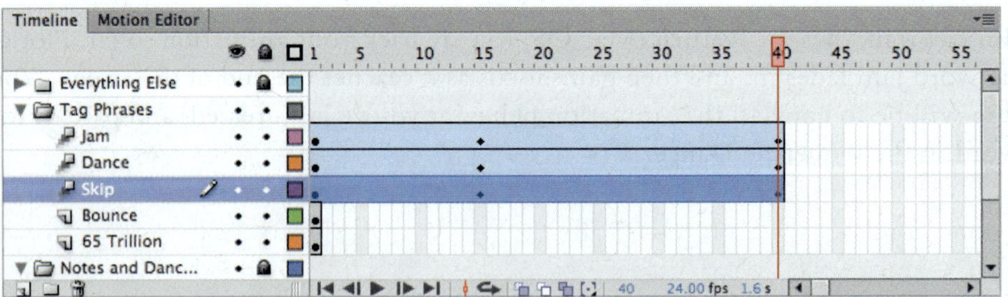

Figure **6-5**: *Paste the motion from the Jam layer to the Dance and Skip layers. All three now have the same tweens applied (as shown).*

Creating Motion Presets

As seen in the previous exercise, the ability to Copy and Paste Motion is a great way to quickly share animation behavior among multiple objects in your movie. However, if you'd like to apply animation behavior across multiple projects, or store an animation behavior for later use, Flash CS6 gives you the ability to capture animation behavior into motion presets.

Now you can save any existing tween (or series of tweens) into a motion preset, which can be recalled and applied from the Motion Presets panel. In addition, motion presets are saved in Flash itself (not to any specific file), and so they can be used across any number of Flash files.

In the following steps, you'll save the animation you designed in the last exercise to a new motion preset, and apply it to other objects in your movie.

<table><tr><td>**Certification Ready 2.1**

What are the benefits of using motion presets?</td></tr></table>

<table><tr><td>**Certification Ready 4.10**

How do you create a motion preset?</td></tr></table>

<table><tr><td>**Follow these steps to save an animation to a new motion preset**</td><td>**Step-by-Step**</td></tr></table>

1. Choose Window > Motion Presets to open the Motion Presets panel. As shown in Figure 6–6, it contains two folders, Default Presets and Custom Presets. Any new presets you create are added to the Custom Presets folder.

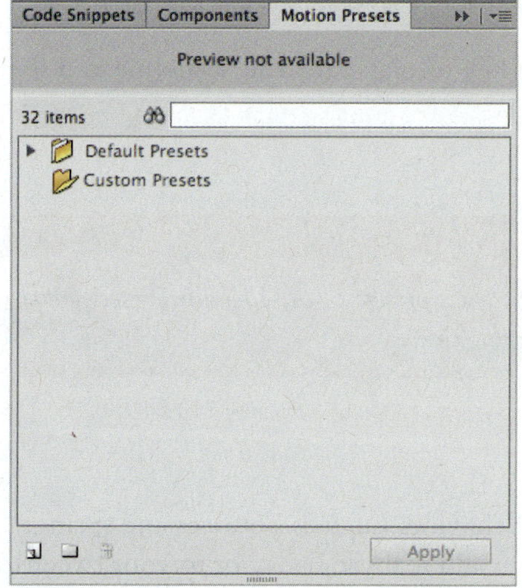

Figure 6–6: The Motion Presets panel stores saved animation behavior in named presets. You can apply any preset to any object from any file, at any time.

2. On the Timeline, click to select the entire tween span on the Skip layer. This tween contains animation that you copied and pasted from the Jam layer in the previous exercise. If necessary, reopen the Motion Presets panel.

3. At the bottom of the Motion Presets panel, click the Save selection as preset button to create a new motion preset from the selected tween. When the dialog box appears, type **Fade and Focus** for the new preset name, and click OK. The new preset now appears inside the Custom Presets folder.

4. Select the first keyframe of the 65 Trillion layer. This layer contains a graphic symbol with another tag line, and currently has no animation applied.

    If necessary, reopen the Motion Presets panel and select the new Fade and Focus preset you created, and click the Apply button at the bottom of the panel. The tween behavior is now applied to the 65 Trillion layer!

5. On the Timeline, expand the Everything Else layer. Locate the Logo layer, and turn its visibility back on (it's currently switched off). This reveals the skyPod logo in the middle of the Stage.

6. Select the first keyframe of the Logo layer. Click the skyPod logo in the middle of the Stage to select it. From the top of the Property Inspector, use the pull-down menu to choose Movie Clip. Keep the first keyframe of the Logo layer selected. In the Motion Presets panel, make sure your new Fade and Focus preset is selected, and once again, click the Apply button. This applies the animation behavior to the Logo layer (Figure 6-7), just like you did with the 65 Trillion layer.

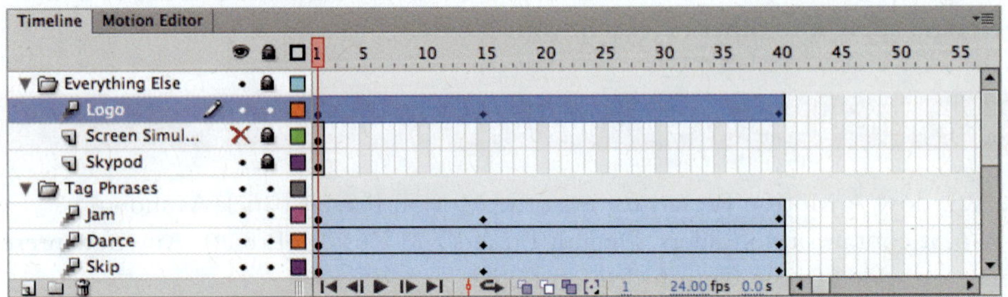

Figure 6-7: *Apply the animation in the Fade and Focus preset to the 65 Trillion and Logo layers with just a couple clicks.*

7. Press the Enter (Windows) or Return (Mac OS) key to play back the Timeline and see the new animations you created using Motion Presets.

8. Choose File > Save to save your work.

Take Note...
The Motion Presets panel includes many ready-to-use presets in the Default Presets folder. Try some of these to help you get up-and-running quickly.

Applying Advanced Easing Behavior

Flash CS6 provides many basic and advanced easing behaviors (such as bounces and springs), available from the Motion Editor panel, enabling you to add realistic behavior to your tweens. **Easing** is a setting in Flash that allows you to adjust how an animation begins or ends. You can ease into or out of the animation instead of an animation moving at a constant speed.

In the following steps, you'll apply some of the easing behaviors to a new tween using the Motion Editor panel.

Step-by-Step | **Follow these steps to apply easing behaviors to a new tween**

1. Under the Tag Phrases layer folder, locate and select the first keyframe of the Bounce layer.

2. Right-click (Windows) or Control+click (Mac OS) on the selected frame and choose Create Motion Tween from the contextual menu that appears. A 24-frame tween span is created on the Bounce layer.

3. Click and select the tween span, and move your cursor over the last frame of the span. Click and drag to the right, and extend the tween span out to frame 40 (it should end at the same point as the other tweens you've created so far).

4. Move your pointer over frame 40 of the new tween span. Right-click (Windows) or Control+click (Mac OS) and choose Insert Keyframe > Position from the contextual menu that appears. This captures the word Bounce in its current position in the middle of the Stage.

5. Click on keyframe 1 to return the playhead to the beginning of the tween span. Using your Selection tool (↖), drag the word Bounce on the Stage straight upward until it sits directly above the Stage in the pasteboard area as shown in Figure 6-8.

   A motion path appears on the Stage to show the direction the word Bounce will follow.

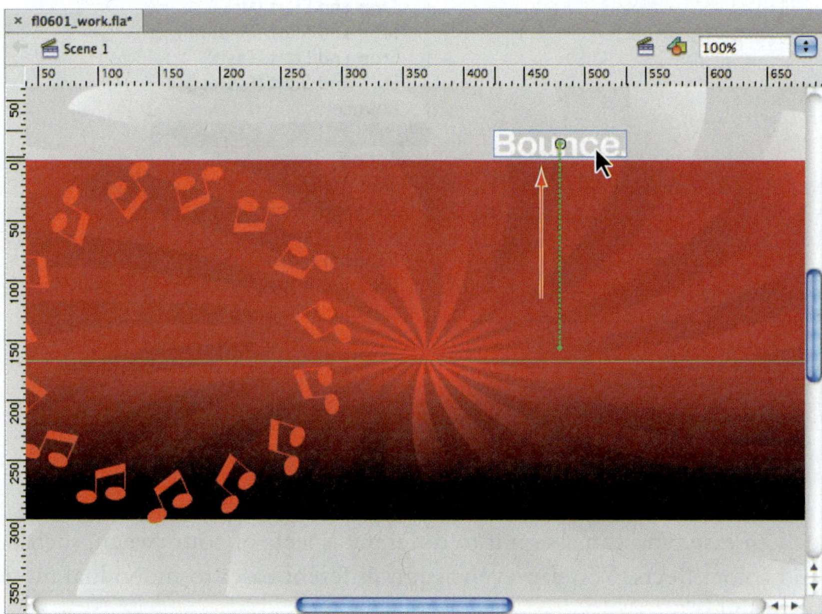

Figure 6-8: The Motion Tween you created sends the word Bounce from above the Stage back to the middle of the Stage alongside the other tag lines.

6. Press Enter (Windows) or Return (Mac OS) to preview the animation so far. The word Bounce moves from above the Stage and stops next to the other taglines to its left.

7. Now, you'll add some easing behavior to your new tween to make it more exciting. Click and select the entire new tween span you've created. Below the Stage, click the Motion Editor tab to bring the Motion Editor panel forward.

8. Scroll down to the bottom of the Motion Editor, and locate the Eases row, where you can add and modify easing behaviors to use on the selected tween. In the middle of the row, locate and click the Add Color, Filter, or Ease button (⊕). A menu appears with several ease behaviors—select the Bounce In ease behavior to add it to your current eases (Figure 6-9).

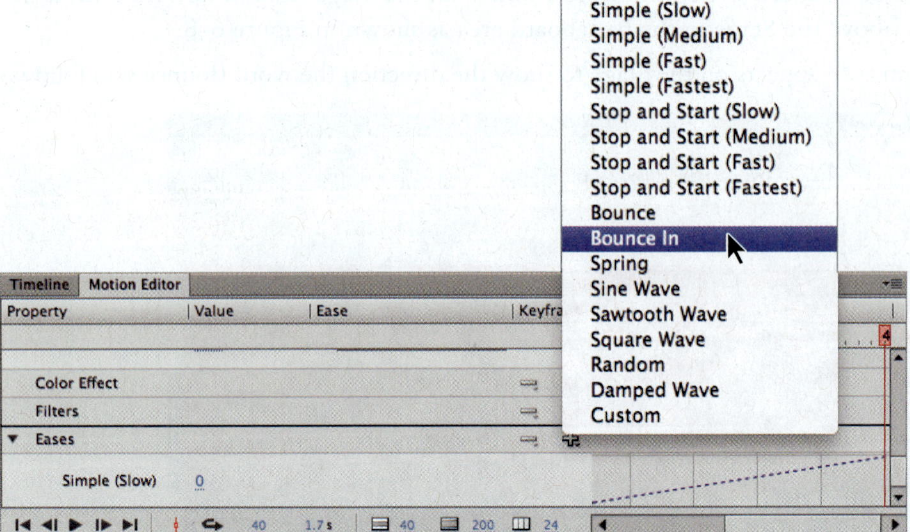

Figure 6-9: Add the Bounce In behavior to your list of active eases. You can now apply this to any properties in your motion tween.

9. Once you've added an ease, you can assign it to different aspects of your tween, such as motion, filters, and color effects. You can even assign different eases to individual motion properties, such as x and y.

   Scroll up in the Motion Editor so that you can see the Basic motion row. Locate the menu on that row that reads No Ease—this allows you to assign easing to all the Motion properties at once. From that menu, select the Bounce In ease you just added as shown in Figure 6-10.

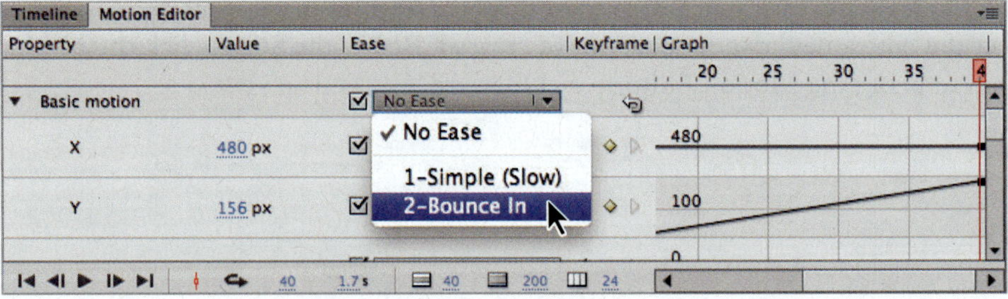

Figure 6-10: Apply the newly added Bounce In ease behavior to all the Position properties in your tween at once.

10. Choose Control > Test Movie > in Flash Professional to preview your work so far in the Flash Player. The word Bounce falls in from the top of the Stage and bounces when it reaches its final position in the middle.

11. Close the Flash Player and choose File > Save to save your movie.

Animating Masks

Masking allows you to hide and reveal selected areas of artwork on your Stage using a Mask layer and a chosen shape. You've learned the basics of this common design concept in Lesson 4, "Advanced Tools."

Now, you'll take masks a step further by incorporating tweens to create moving masks that add unique effects to your movies. **Animated masks** are the key to some common, cool Flash "tricks" that you may have already seen, such as magnifying glass and spotlight effects.

In the following steps, you'll have your skyPod device move across the screen, magnifying your tag line text as it crosses the Stage.

Follow these steps to create an animated mask	Step-by-Step

1. On the Timeline, expand the Everything Else layer folder, if necessary. Locate, unlock, and select the Skypod layer, which contains the symbol of the skyPod device you'll be tweening.

2. Click the New Layer button to insert a new layer above the Skypod layer, and rename the layer **Screen Mask**.

3. Return the playhead to frame 1, and drag an instance of the Screen Mask Movieclip symbol from your Library panel to the left of the Stage. Position it so it lines up and obscures the screen on the skyPod graphic below it (Figure 6-11).

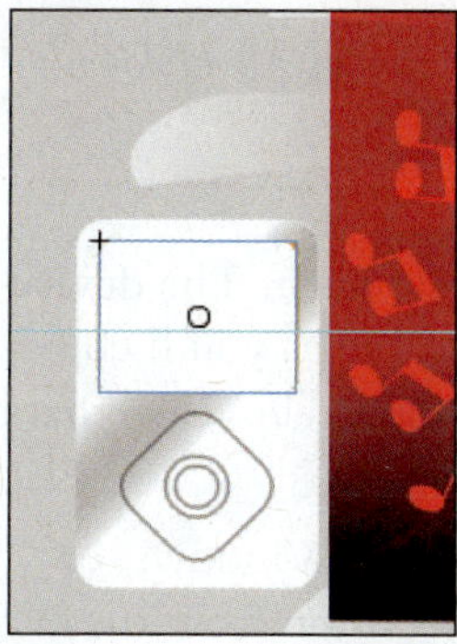

Figure 6-11: On frame 1 of the Screen Mask layer, add an instance of the Screen Mask movie clip to the Stage, and position it so it overlays the screen on the skyPod device.

4. Select keyframe 1 on the Skypod layer. Right-click (Windows) or Control+click (Mac OS) on the selected frame and choose Create Motion Tween from the contextual menu that appears. A new tween span is created.

5. Move your cursor over the last frame of the span, and click and drag to expand the tween span to frame 40.

6. Click on frame 40 on the Timeline ruler to advance the playhead to the end of the tween span. Drag the skyPod graphic from the left, and position it on the right side of the Stage as shown in Figure 6-12.

To match the completed demo file, use the Property Inspector to set its final position to X: **650** and Y: **200**. A motion path is created on the Stage to indicate that the skyPod device will be tweened from the left to the right.

Figure 6-12: A new motion path shows that the skyPod device will be tweened from left to right across the Stage.

Take Note...
To move an object in a perfect, straight path, either vertically or horizontally, hold down the Shift key while dragging it.

7. Press Enter (Windows) or Return (Mac OS) to play back your new tween. The device should glide in from the left side of the Stage and stop on the right. Next, you'll copy the motion from this tween and paste it to the Screen Mask in the layer above, so that it follows the exact same behavior.

8. On the Skypod layer, click on the new tween to select it. Right-click (Windows) or Control+click (Mac OS) on the selected frames and choose Copy Motion from the contextual menu that appears.

9. Select frame 1 of the Screen Mask layer. Right-click (Windows) or Control+click (Mac OS) on the selected frame and choose Paste Motion from the contextual menu that appears (Figure 6-13). A tween identical to the one on the Skypod layer is now added to this layer.

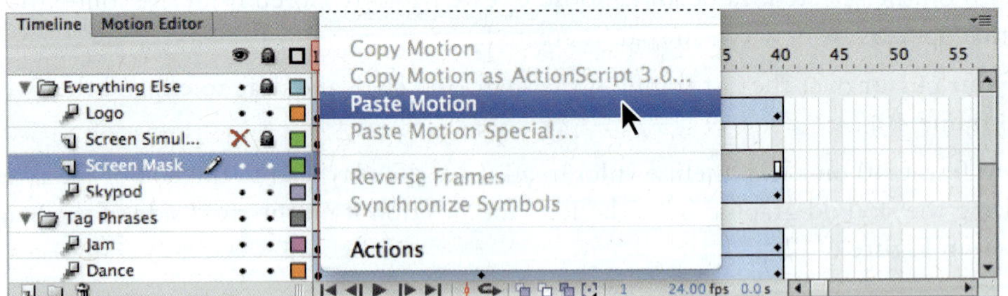

Figure 6-13: Paste the motion copied from the Skypod layer to the Screen Mask layer. The soon-to-be mask now follows the exact same animation behavior as the skyPod device so that the two move in tandem.

10. Press Enter (Windows) or Return (Mac OS) to play back your movie. The Skypod and Screen Mask layers should both animate exactly the same way. Next, you'll convert your Screen Mask into a mask, so that it reveals artwork as it moves across the Stage.

11. On the Timeline, drag the Screen Mask layer above the Screen Simulation layer. Unlock the Screen Simulation layer, and turn its visibility on. Click on frame 1 of the Screen Simulation layer. This reveals a graphic containing the same tag phrases that are already on the Stage. You'll reveal this behind the Screen Mask as it travels across the Stage.

12. Select and right-click (Windows) or Control+click (Mac OS) on the Screen Mask layer (next to its title). Choose Mask from the contextual menu that appears. This converts the Screen Mask layer, including its animation, to a mask that obscures the contents of the Screen Simulation layer below (Figure 6-14).

13. To complete the effect, select frame 40 on the Screen Simulation layer. Use the F5 shortcut key to insert a frame here and extend the contents of the layer to the end of the Timeline.

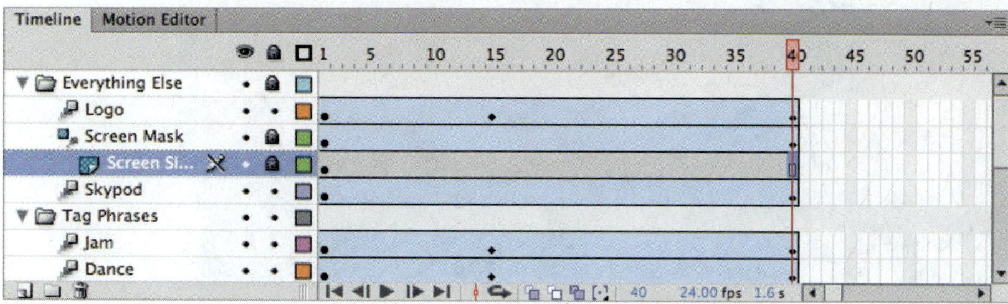

Figure 6-14: The Screen Mask layer now masks the Screen Simulation layer.

14. Press Enter (Windows) or Return (Mac OS) to preview the animation. The skyPod device moves across the screen, revealing digitized tag lines in its screen as it crosses the Stage!

15. Choose File > Save to save your file.

Take Note...
To enable a masking effect, both the Mask layer and the layer being masked must be locked.

Creating Animation with IK Poses

Two excellent tools for designers and traditional animators are the Bone and Bind tools, which allow you to create poseable, puppet-like Inverse Kinematics (IK) objects that can be animated with the same simplicity that you're accustomed to with motion tweens. You explored these IK tools briefly in Lesson 4, "Advanced Tools," and now you'll put your IK objects into motion by creating *poses*.

IK poses are very much like keyframes in a motion tween, and they store positions of connected IK objects at different points along the Timeline. Connected IK objects are grouped together on Armature layers, where you can create poses and animate the changes between each pose.

You'll reveal a pre-created IK object on the Timeline, and create poses to add a funky dancer to your banner.

Certification Ready 4.10

How can you animate symbols, shapes or objects by using Inverse Kinematics with the Bone tool?

<table><tr><td>**Step-by-Step**</td><td>**Follow these steps to create animation using IK poses**</td></tr></table>

1. Expand the Notes and Dancer layer folder on the Timeline as shown in Figure 6-15. Locate and unlock the Dancer layer, and turn its visibility on. Click on the dancer layer and then click on frame 1, if necessary. This reveals a series of connected IK objects on a single Armature layer, indicated by its distinctive icon (⚡).

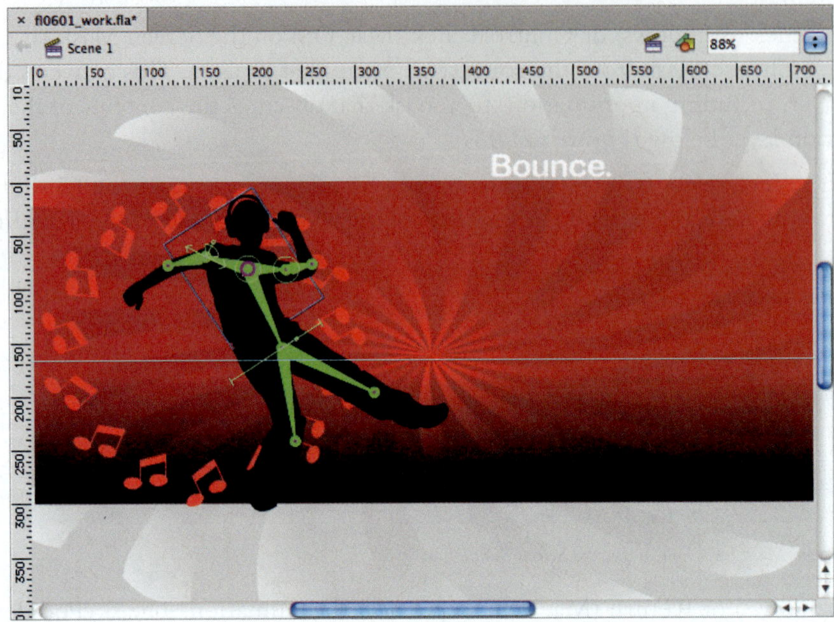

Figure 6-15: Select the poseable dancer on the Dancer layer to reveal the bones that connect its various pieces.

2. Select frame 10 on the Dancer layer. Right-click (Windows) or Control+click (Mac OS) on the selected frame and choose Insert Pose from the contextual menu that appears. A bullet (that looks much like a keyframe) is inserted at frame 10 as shown in Figure 6-16.

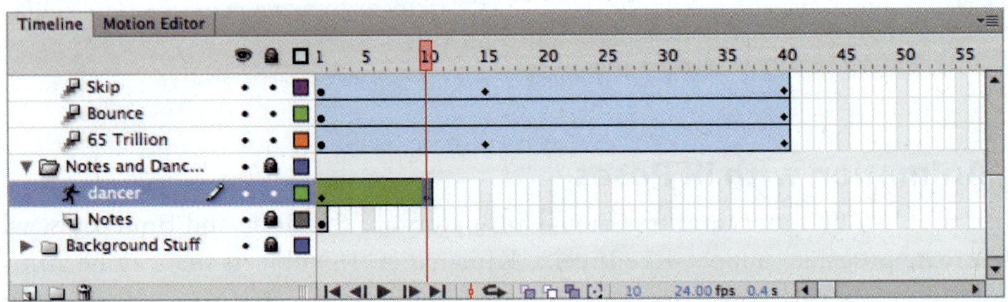

Figure 6-16: Right-click on a frame in an Armature layer and select Insert Pose to add a new frame where your IK object can be posed and positioned.

3. Choose your Selection tool (➤), and click on any part of the dancer; the bones that connect each limb are revealed. Click and drag each limb, and position it to make a new pose for your dancer.

4. Return the playhead to the beginning of the Timeline, and press Enter (Windows) or Return (Mac OS). Flash animates the changes between the original pose on frame 1, and the new one you created on frame 10!

Take Note...
Use Shift+, (comma) to rewind the Timeline and return the playhead to frame 1.

5. Select frame 20 on your Dancer layer. Right-click (Windows) or Control+click (Mac OS) on the selected frame and choose Insert Pose from the contextual menu that appears.

6. Just as you did on frame 10, use your Selection tool to position the limbs of your dancer in a new pose.

7. Repeat steps 5 and 6 to create new poses at frames 30 and 40 (Figure 6-17).

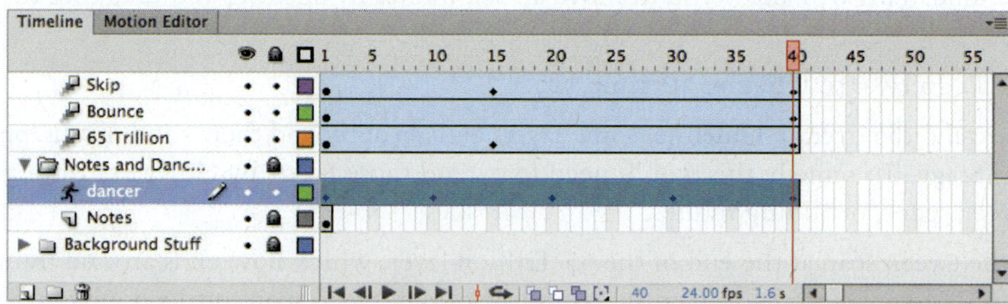

Figure 6-17: *The completed layer, with poses at frames 10, 20, 30, and 40. Flash animates the changes between each pose.*

8. Press Enter (Windows) or Return (Mac OS) to play back your animation. Your dancer animates through all four poses.

9. Choose File > Save to save your work.

Sequencing Animation

The true strength of the Timeline lies in the ability to sequence animation, graphics, and sounds across the Timeline to build more complex scenes. Now that you've added several layers of animation to your banner project, you'll work toward sequencing your movie so that every animation falls into its proper place. Think of it as writing a script for your first big movie—you've got the actors, you've got the Stage, and now it's time to orchestrate the scene.

Shifting, Moving, and Extending Tween Spans

Once you've created a tween span, you can easily slide it along a layer to reposition it at different points along the Timeline. This is an essential concept for creating well-planned scenes that get your message across.

You'll now begin to move a few things around to get your banner project closer to completion.

Follow these steps to shift, move and extend tween spans   **Step-by-Step**

1. Locate the Dance layer on the Timeline (under the Tag Phrases folder). Click anywhere on the tween span to select it.

2. Click and drag the entire span to the right. Release the span when the first keyframe is on frame 15. Fourteen empty frames now exist at the beginning of the Timeline.

3. Repeat step 2 for the Skip, Bounce, and 65 Trillion layers, repositioning their tween spans so they begin at frames 30, 45, and 120, respectively (Figure 6-18).

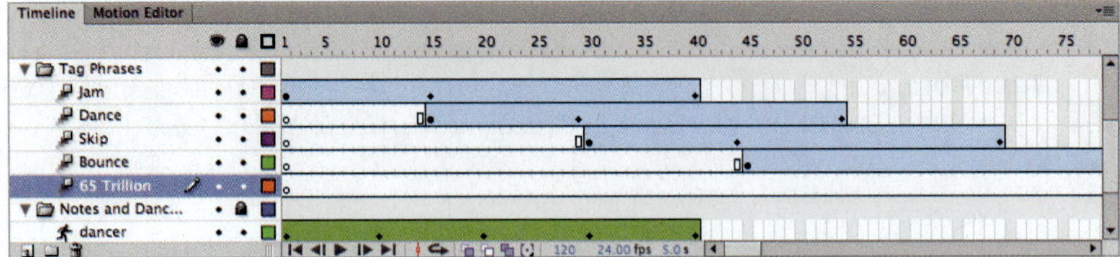

Figure 6-18: Select the frames on the Dance, Skip, Bounce, and 65 Trillion layers, and sequence them across the Timeline.

4. Under the Everything Else layer folder, reposition the Screen Mask, Screen Simulation, and Skypod layers so all three begin at frame 80. The Screen Simulation layer is not a tween span, in order to move it you should click on the first keyframe and then Shift+click the last frame. This will allow you to move all the frames by clicking and dragging the selection.

   Shift the Logo layer so it begins at frame 125.

   As you extend the overall Timeline, some layers end abruptly and their contents disappear from the Stage. To remedy this, you'll need to extend those layers by either expanding their tween spans, or adding frames.

5. Locate the tween span at the end of the 65 Trillion layer, which now ends around frame 159 or 160. Move your cursor over the last frame of the tween span until a double-arrow appears; click and drag to extend the tween span to frame 165 as shown in Figure 6-19.

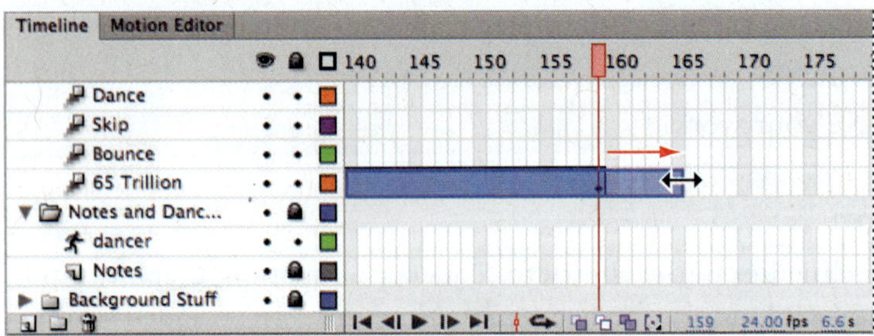

Figure 6-19: Extend the 65 Trillion layer to frame 165.

6. Locate the Skypod layer (under the Everything Else layer folder). Select frame 165 on the Skypod layer and use the F5 shortcut key to insert a frame at this position. This continues the layer's contents without disturbing the keyframes before it. Repeat this for the Screen Mask and Screen Simulation layers. You may not actually see the additional frames created on the layers contained within the folder unless the folder is expanded.

Take Note...
Keyframes in an existing tween span shift when the span is extended or trimmed. If you want to extend the duration of a tween layer without shifting keyframes, add frames to the layer using the F5 shortcut key.

7. Repeat step 6 for the Jam, Dance, Skip, and Bounce layers. As you can see in Figure 6-20, all layers should be extended to frame 165.

A nice shortcut when using layer folders is the ability to extend all included layers at once by extending the layer folder itself. You'll extend the layers within the Background Stuff layer folder using this shortcut.

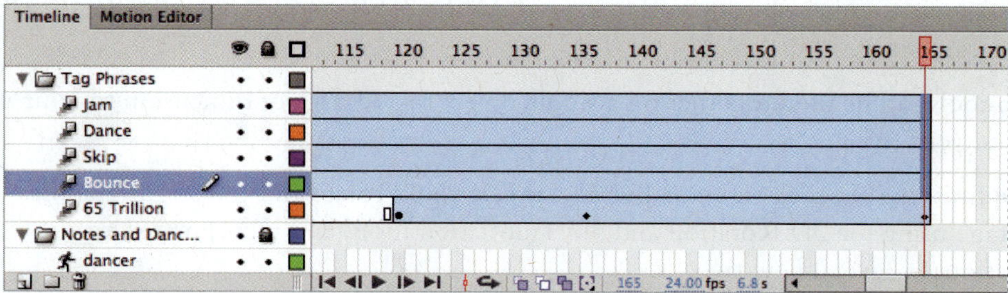

Figure 6-20: Extend tween layers by adding frames using the F5 shortcut key.

8. On the Timeline, select frame 165 on the Background Stuff layer folder. Press the F5 shortcut key; this extends the included layers (Twirl and Backing Box) so that the background artwork is visible until the end of the scene (Figure 6-21).

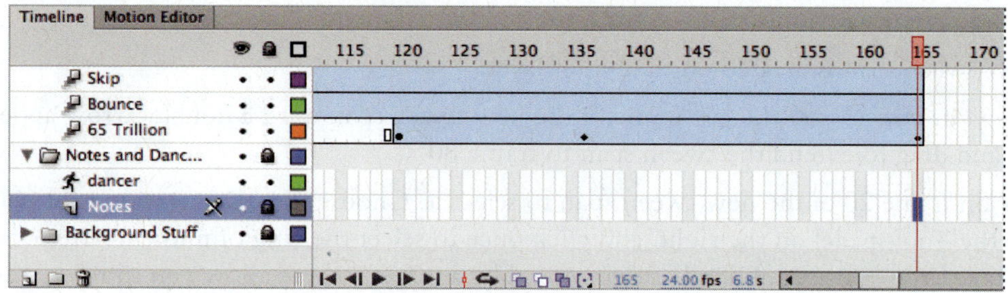

Figure 6-21: You can extend several layers within a layer folder by adding frames to the layer folder itself.

9. Choose File > Save to save your file.

Rendering and Animating in 3D

Web graphics have advanced a tremendous amount in recent years, with users demanding more than ever before. One aspect of this is the prominent use of 3D graphics across the Web to enhance the overall experience.

The 3D Rotation and 3D Translation tools give designers a way to take two-dimensional artwork and rotate, transform, and animate them in the 3D realm. This opens up the doors for unlimited creative possibilities and stunning effects through the use of movie clip symbols (covered in detail in Lesson 12, "Introducing Movie Clips"), and the 3D Rotation and 3D Translation tools.

Although you haven't yet explored the intricacies of movie clips, keep in mind that at this point, it's simply necessary for an item to exist as a movie clip symbol to take advantage of these 3D tools in Flash. This lesson file gets you started by providing you with several movie clips that you will use.

The 3D Rotation tool

The **3D Rotation tool** can be used to rotate and transform an object around an x-, y-, and z-axis, rendering 2D objects in the 3D plane. **Rendering** is a term often used when working with 3D objects to describe the generation of 3D elements and adjusting their properties. Every aspect of 3D rotation can be included in a motion tween, and modified using the Motion Editor.

The 3D Translation tool

In contrast to the 3D Rotation tool, which rotates movie clips *around* an axis, the **3D Translation tool** slides a movie clip *along* a specific axis to change its perceived distance and depth relative to other objects on the Stage. Like the 3D Rotation tool, all aspects of 3D Translation can be tweened.

These two tools can be used together on a single object to add a lot of dimension to your graphics and your tweens.

To add the finishing touches on your skyPod banner, you'll rotate and transform graphics on your Stage using the 3D Rotation and 3D Translation tools, and incorporate those transformations in several new tweens.

Step-by-Step	**Follow these steps to use the 3D Translation tool**

1. Locate and unlock the Notes layer (found under the Notes and Dancer layer folder). Right-click (Windows) or Control+click (Mac OS) the first keyframe of the Notes layer and choose Create Motion Tween from the contextual menu that appears.

   A new tween span is created on the Notes layer.

2. Move your cursor over the last frame of the new tween span until a double-arrow appears; click and drag to extend the tween span to frame 80.

3. Click on frame 20 of the new tween span to select it. Choose the 3D Rotation tool (⊕) from the Tools panel on the right, and click once to select the ring of musical notes on the Stage. You see a set of handles that resembles a target—these allow you to rotate the selected symbol around the x-, y-, and z-axes (or all at once).

4. Move your pointer carefully over the red beam that appears in the center—you should see a small *x* appear. This handle lets you rotate the symbol around the x-axis—click and drag to the left or right to rotate the symbol around the x-axis. Once you get a feel for this handle, click and drag slightly to the right to achieve the position shown in Figure 6-22. A new keyframe is created at frame 20 to mark the change in rotation.

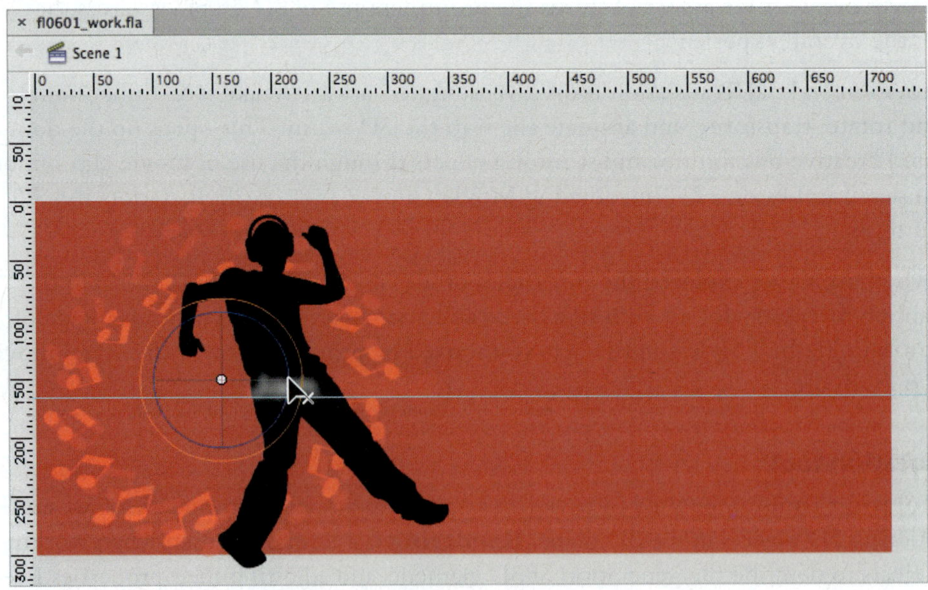

Figure 6-22: Rotate the symbol around the x-axis on frame 20. The change in position is marked by a new keyframe within the tween span.

5. Click and select frame 40 on the same layer, leaving the 3D Rotation tool active. Locate the blue circular handle that appears in the middle of the symbol; this is your z-axis handle. Click and drag on the handle to the right to rotate the symbol around the z-axis (Figure 6-23).

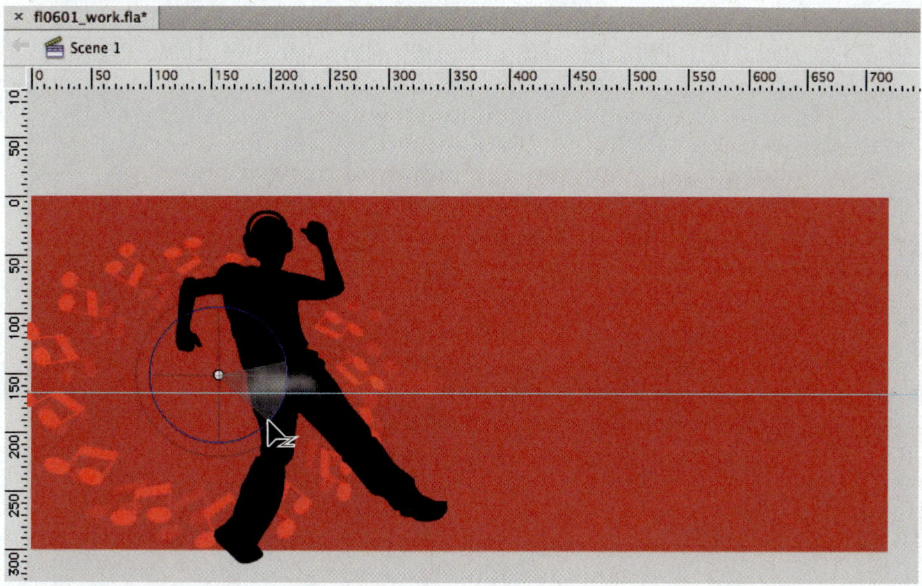

Figure 6-23: Rotate the symbol around the z-axis on frame 40.

6. Return the playhead back to the beginning of the Timeline (Shift+,) and press Enter (Windows) or Return (Mac OS) to see the tween that has been created so far. The rotations you added on frames 20 and 40 are now tweened from position to position!

7. Click and select frame 60 on the tween span, click and hold down the 3D Rotation tool and choose your 3D Translation tool (⊼) from the menu. Click on the Notes layer, if necessary. The rotation handles on your notes symbol are replaced by three arrows that you'll use to slide your symbol along the x-, y-, or z-axis.

8. Click and drag directly on the head of the red arrow—this moves items along the x-axis. Drag to the right until the notes touch the right edge of the Stage.

9. Click and select frame 80 on the same tween span, leaving the 3D Translation tool active. Click and drag the head of the green arrow, which controls movement along the y-axis. As shown in Figure 6-24, drag downward until the notes end up in the lower-right corner.

Figure 6-24: Slide the notes along the z-axis to the lower-right corner as shown.

10. Select frame 165 of the Notes layer, and use the F5 shortcut key to add a frame here—this is simply to extend the contents of this layer to the end of the Timeline.

11. Return your playhead to the beginning of the Timeline (Shift+,) and press Enter (Windows) or Return (Mac OS) to play back the entire tween span on the Notes layer. Your notes should rotate and slide their way to the lower-right corner of the Stage, creating cool depth and 3D effects along the way.

12. Choose File > Save to save your movie.

Fine-Tuning tweens with the Motion Editor

Once you've created a tween, you may want to adjust the degree or timing of how different properties (such as z–axis rotation) animate. The Motion Editor displays a selected tween and all its properties in an intuitive graph, where you can tweak, add, and remove as needed.

You may have noticed that the transformation you created using the 3D Translation tool is active throughout the entire tween span, even though it wasn't applied until around frame 60. Occasional side effects such as these can be easily fixed with the Motion Editor to control when a property changes during a tween span.

<table><tr><td>**Follow these steps to fine-tune a tween with the Motion Editor**</td><td>**Step-by-Step**</td></tr></table>

1. Click on the Notes layer to make it active and then click on frame 60. Bring the Motion Editor panel forward by clicking its tab.

Take Note...
You can increase the height of the Motion Editor by moving your pointer in between the Stage and the Motion Editor panel—when you see a double-arrow, click and drag upwards to vertically resize the Motion Editor panel. You can also undock the Motion Editor by dragging it out of the panel group by its tab, and resize it from the lower-right corner.

2. Locate and click on the Y row to expand it and view its graph.

Use the scroll bar at the bottom of the Motion Editor to scroll the graph to frame 60. Use the frame ruler shown at the top of the Motion Editor panel for reference.

3. Click the keyframe that appears on the graph line at frame 60 and then move the keyframe up or down to change the Y value at this frame (Figure 6–25). Watch the Stage to see how your changes affect the appearance of the notes.

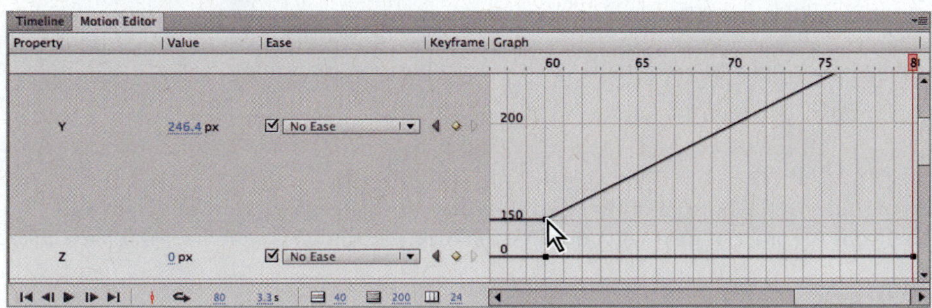

Figure 6–25: *Click and drag a keyframe up or down to change a property's value at that position.*

4. Using the vertical scroll bar on the side of the Motion Editor, scroll down and locate the Rotation X row. Click on it (near the title area) to expand it and view its graph.

5. Scroll horizontally until you reach frame 20. Right-click (Windows) or Control+click (Mac OS) and choose Add Keyframe from the context menu to insert a keyframe. Press the Shift key to keep the keyframe from moving left or right, and click and drag the keyframe down to the baseline (0.0) of the Rotation Z row. Then, again holding the Shift key, click and drag it to the right to frame 30 as shown in Figure 6-26. The z rotation now begins at frame 30.

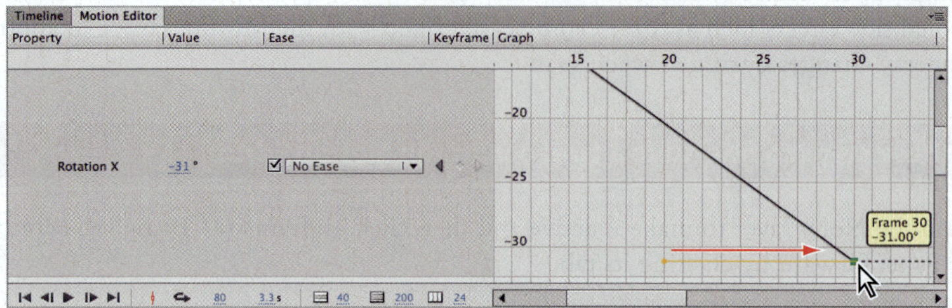

Figure 6-26: Hold down shift and drag left or right to move a keyframe horizontally without any vertical shift.

6. Bring the Timeline panel forward by clicking its tab, and return the playhead to frame 1. Press Enter (Windows) or Return (Mac OS) to play your movie and see how the edits you made in the Motion Editor have changed your animation on the Stage.

7. Choose File > Save to save your file.

<table>
<tr><td>**Learning More**</td><td>**Mastering the Motion Editor: tips and tricks**</td></tr>
</table>

The Motion Editor is a complex and powerful tool, so it helps to know a few shortcuts to make working with it easier.

Editing Graphs

Hold down Ctrl+click (Windows) or Command+click (Mac OS) on a graph to add a keyframe.

Hold down Ctrl (Windows) or Command (Mac OS) over an existing keyframe to delete it.

Click and drag left or right on a keyframe to change its position (in frames).

Click and drag up or down on a keyframe to change its value.

Changing the Display

Use the three sliders at the bottom of the Motion Editor to change your view of graphs and frames. The icons (in order of display) control Graph Size, Expanded Graph Size, and Viewable Frames.

Undock the Motion Editor by grabbing it by its tab and dragging it out of the panel group at the bottom. You can then resize it by its lower-right corner.

Adding shape tweens and shape hints

To wrap up your banner project, you'll add a basic shape tween to morph a musical note shape into the logo for Pineapple, Inc., the creators of the skyPod device. You explored shape tweens in Lesson 5, "Creating Basic Animation," and you will use the same techniques here. You will also learn shape hinting, a technique for fine-tuning shape tweens.

Before you explore shape hinting, you'll first create a new shape tween on your Timeline using some graphics from your Library panel.

| **Follow these steps to create a new shape tween** | **Step-by-Step** |

1. Locate and select the Logo layer (it can be found within the Everything Else layer folder on the Timeline). Click the New Layer button to insert a new layer above it. Rename the new layer **Pineapple Inc Logo**.

2. Insert a new, blank keyframe at frame 125 on the new layer using the F7 shortcut key (Figure 6–27).

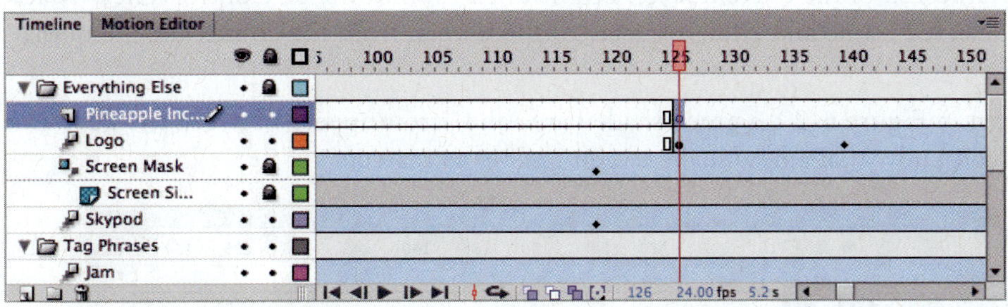

Figure 6–27: Add a blank keyframe at frame 125 of the new layer to set up for a shape tween.

3. In your Library panel, locate the Shape Tween Art folder and expand it. It contains two graphic symbols that you'll use to build your shape tween. Drag an instance of the skyPod Note graphic to the Stage. Position and center it directly on the screen of the skyPod player that sits on the right side of the Stage.

4. Using your Selection tool (↖), select the new symbol instance. Choose Modify > Break Apart to break the symbol down to mergeable artwork as shown in Figure 6–28. This will allow you to include it as part of a shape tween.

Figure 6–28: Use Modify > Break Apart to convert the symbol instance to basic artwork. This will make it possible to include the graphics as part of a shape tween.

> ***Take Note...***
> *Shape tweens can't use symbol instances, so in order to use artwork from your library, you need to first break it apart on the Stage by choosing Modify > Break Apart.*

5. Select frame 165 of the same layer, and use the F7 shortcut key to insert a new, blank keyframe at this position.

6. In your Library panel, locate the Pineapple Inc. Logo graphic symbol, which is located in the Shape Tween Art folder. Drag an instance of it to the Stage on the new keyframe. As you did with the skyPod Note, position it so it overlaps and centers over the skyPod player screen.

7. Leave the symbol selected, and choose Modify > Break Apart. This breaks the pineapple logo into mergeable artwork so that it can be included in the shape tween you're going to create.

8. Select frame 125 of the current layer. Right-click (Windows) or Control+click (Mac OS) on the selected frame and choose Create Shape Tween from the contextual menu that appears.

As shown in Figure 6-29, a green shaded area and arrow appear between the keyframes, letting you know that a new shape tween has been created.

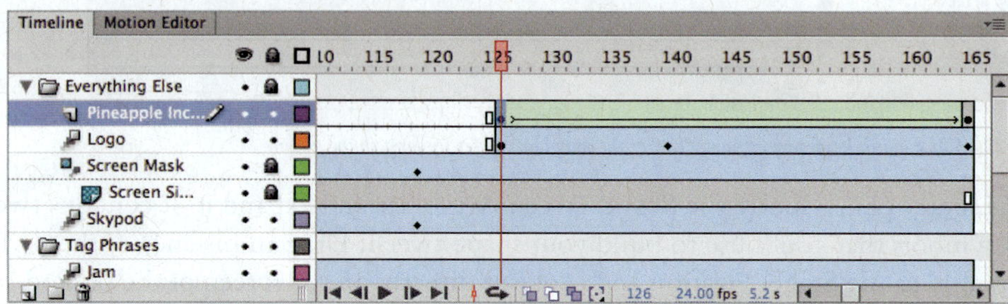

Figure 6-29: At keyframe 125, create a new shape tween to morph the note into the pineapple.

9. With the playhead positioned at frame 125, press Enter (Windows) or Return (Mac OS) to view the new shape tween. The note now morphs into the pineapple logo!

You may notice that while the shape tween is successful, the transition may not be as smooth as it could be. To perfect this, you'll explore the use of shape hints to finesse the new shape tween.

Creating Shape Hints

Depending on the shapes you choose for your tween, you may find that some transitions are smooth while others need some fine-tuning. For those that need a little help, you can make use of *shape hints*.

Shape hints tell Flash where it can find common points between two seemingly uncommon shapes. To use them, you place a matched set of small markers at important parts of the shapes on the start and end keyframes of a shape tween. The markers tell Flash that the indicated shapes and points are related, and should be preserved through the animation as much as possible. Say, for example, you're morphing a star into a square. You could place shape hints in the upper-right corner of each shape to match those points and keep the transformation as smooth as possible. You can place several shape hints, if necessary, to fine-tune a single shape tween.

Take Note...
Because shape hints are alphabetically labeled, Flash limits you to 26 shape hints per tween.

You'll use shape hints in this exercise to help Flash find common points between the musical note and pineapple logo for a better tween.

Step-by-Step

Follow these steps to create shape hints to fine-tune a tween

1. Select the Zoom tool (🔍) from the Tools panel. Click and drag to draw a marquee around the skyPod device on the right side of the Stage. This zooms in so that you can better see the transition between the two shapes.

2. Choose View > Show Shape Hints to make shape hints visible on the Stage (Figure 6–30). Nothing will appear until you add shape hints.

Figure 6–30: *Before making use of shape hints, make sure they are visible by selecting View > Show Shape Hints.*

3. Select keyframe 125 of the Pineapple Inc Logo layer. Shape hints must always be added (or removed) from the beginning of a shape tween. Choose Modify > Shape > Add Shape Hint. A new shape hint labeled *a* appears in the center of the note.

4. Click on the shape hint and drag it until it snaps into place at the very top of the musical note. This pins that point in place—you'll now match that point with a similar one on the pineapple shape at the end of the tween.

5. Click to select keyframe 165 (the end of the tween). You see the mate for the shape hint you just created, waiting to be placed. Click and drag the shape hint and snap it into place at the top of the pineapple shape. It should turn green, indicating the pair has been set.

6. Reselect keyframe 125, and choose Modify > Shape > Add Shape Hint. A new shape hint labeled *b* appears on the Stage. Click and drag the shape hint and snap it into place at the end of the note's attached flag.

7. Select frame 165, and locate the matching *b* shape hint. Click and drag it, and snap it into place at the top of the pineapple's right-most leaf.

8. Repeat steps 6 and 7 to add two more shape hints (*c* and *d*), and position them as shown in Figure 6–31.

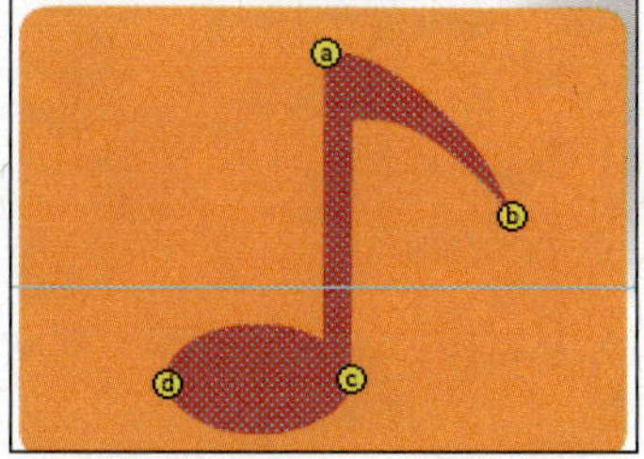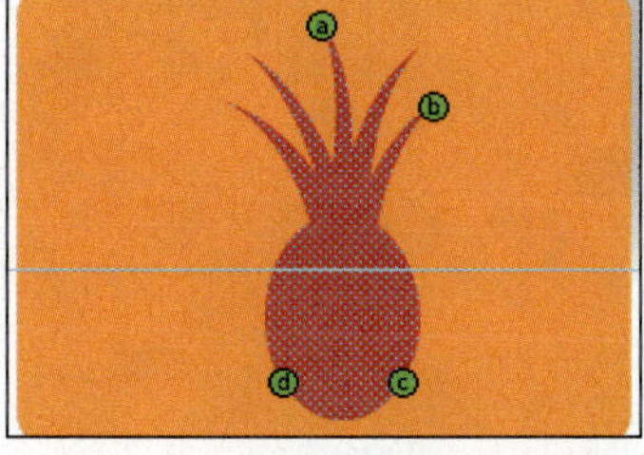

Figure 6–31: *Position the shape hints on frame 125 (left) and frame 165 (right) as shown.*

9. Position the playhead at frame 125, and press Enter (Windows) or Return (Mac OS) to play back your animation. You should see that the new shape hints you added have made a substantial difference in the smoothness and quality of the shape tween.

10. Choose File > Save to save your work.

Take Note...
To remove a shape hint, return to the beginning of the shape tween, right-click (Windows) or Control+click (Mac OS) on a shape hint, and choose Remove Hint from the contextual menu that appears.

Learning More

Hints for successful hinting

Adding shape hints is usually straightforward, but it can get a bit tricky with complex shapes. Follow these tips to create better shape tweens with a little less confusion:

Always enable Snap to Objects (View > Snapping > Snap To Objects). Although you can place shape hints without snapping, it's much more difficult.

Use shape hints in sensible places; although Flash doesn't make associations on its own, it can tell when a shape hint and its counterpart are not matched in a logical way. If the second hint remains red even after you place it, Flash is alerting you to a potential problem.

Avoid shapes that are broken into too many pieces; instead, try to tween between two whole shapes. Although Flash can tween between a single shape and a broken shape, the results are not always what you expect. If you need to tween between two multipart shapes, consider isolating each piece and applying to each its own shape tween.

Use Onion Skin view to assist you in placing shape hints. When you're having a hard time determining exactly what's happening in the course of a shape tween, turn on Onion Skin or Onion Skin Outlines view to follow the action and make better decisions on shape hints.

Sometimes less is more—gradually add shape hints and keep testing your animation as you go. Too many shape hints can sometimes have the reverse effect.

Sometimes it takes a few shape hint passes to get exactly the look you want. Try to fine-tune and complete the note-to-pineapple shape tween by adding some additional hints.

Skill summary

In this lesson you learned how to:	Objective
Identify general and Flash-specific best practices for designing rich media content for the web, mobile apps, and AIR applications	2.1
Create animations (changes in shape, position, size, color, and transparency)	4.10

Knowledge Assessment

True/False

Circle **T** if the statement is true or **F** if the statement is false.

T **F** **1.** You can copy and paste objects in Flash, you cannot copy and paste animations.

T **F** **2.** Filters cannot be animated within Flash, they are considered static effects.

T **F** **3.** Animations can be saved as presets for later use beyond your current project.

T **F** **4.** You can save any existing tween (or series of tweens) into a motion preset.

T **F** **5.** Masking allows you to hide and reveal selected areas of artwork on your Stage using a Mask layer and a chosen shape.

T **F** **6.** Masks are considered static and do not animate within Flash.

T **F** **7.** When converting a layer into a mask layer, animations that are applied to that layer are not included in the conversion process.

T **F** **8.** The true strength of the Timeline lies in the ability to sequence animation, graphics and sounds to build more complex scenes.

T **F** **9.** Keyframes in an existing tween span remain in place when the span is extended or trimmed.

T **F** **10.** Turning on the visibility of Shape Hints is found under the View menu.

Multiple Choice

Select the best response for the following statements.

1. Which of the following represents transparency values in Flash:

    a. Transparency
    b. Opacity
    c. Alpha
    d. Tint

2. Which panel allows you to add and edit advanced easing behaviors to an object?

    a. Motion Editor
    b. Properties Panel
    c. Transform Panel
    d. Actions

3. Which of the following is a choice when adding a new Ease:

    a. Simple (Slow)
    b. Sine Wave
    c. Spring
    d. All of the above

Knowledge Assessment

4. Which key needs to be held down to move an object in a single, straight path either vertically or horizontally?

    a. Alt/Option
    b. Control/Command
    c. Tab
    d. Shift

5. Which tools allow you to create pose-able, puppet-like Inverse Kinematics objects that can be animated?

    a. Transform Tools
    b. Bone and Bind Tools
    c. 3D Tools
    d. Deco Tool

6. Out of the following, which tool is used to rotate and transform an object around an x-, y-, and z-axis?

    a. 3D Translation Tool
    b. 3D Rotation Tool
    c. Bone and Bind Tool
    d. Free Transform Tool

7. What feature in Flash allows fine-tuning when transitioning from one shape to another?

    a. Motion Tweens
    b. Motion Editor
    c. Shape Hints
    d. None of the above

8. Shape Hints appear as what on the Stage?

    a. Squares with Numbers
    b. Circles with Numbers
    c. Circles with Letters
    d. Squares with Letters

9. Which of the following should be enabled when working with Shape Hints?

    a. Snap Align
    b. Snap to Objects
    c. Snap to Grid
    d. Snap to Pixels

10. What feature is helpful when placing shape hints?

    a. Onion Skin
    b. Motion Editor
    c. Actions
    d. Properties Panel

Competency Assessment

<table>
<tr><td>**Different Methods: Copy and Paste Motion**</td><td>**Project 6-1**</td></tr>
</table>

As you may have noticed, there are numerous ways to build an efficient workflow in terms of how you organize and reuse animation. Let's worry less about design this time and just review some of the functionality. You'll practice by creating some staggered animation in the Timeline using various methods.

1. Create a new ActionScript 3.0 document in Flash.

2. Select the Oval tool, set the fill color to yellow, the stroke to none and make sure you're in Object Drawing mode. Draw a circle on the top left-side of the Stage.

3. Choose the Selection tool and make sure the yellow circle is selected on the Stage. Choose Modify > Convert to Symbol, save the symbol as a movie clip named **Sliding Circle**.

4. With the symbol still selected on the Stage, choose Insert > Motion Tween.

5. Make sure the playhead is at the end of the frame span and drag the circle to the right. Preview the animation.

6. Make sure the playhead is on frame 1. Create a new layer and drag another instance of the Sliding Circle movie clip onto the Stage from the Library onto the new layer. Place the new instance below the other symbol already on the Stage.

7. Select the animated circle. Choose Edit > Timeline > Copy Motion.

8. Select the new circle in Layer 2 and choose Edit > Timeline > Paste Motion. Slide the circle's tween span in the Timeline so it starts at frame 5.

9. Preview and save your file as **animation_review.fla** and keep it open for the next exercise.

<table>
<tr><td>**Saving and Applying Motion Presets**</td><td>**Project 6-2**</td></tr>
</table>

Copying and pasting animation is convenient for immediate needs but what about a separate project? Motion Presets are the answer to that question. Let's expand on the last exercise.

1. The **animation_review.fla** file from the previous exercise should still be open.

2. If you haven't done so yet, stack the circles in the order they appear. Move the circle on Layer 1 to the top of the Stage, place the other circle just below so you have room for a third.

3. Create a new layer and drag another instance of the Sliding Circle movie clip onto the Stage from the Library onto the new layer. Place the new instance below the other 2.

4. Select the circle in Layer 1. Choose Window > Motion Presets.

5. Choose the New Preset button from the bottom left area of the panel. Name the new preset **slide to right**.

6. Click the new circle in Layer 3 and from the Motion Presets panel choose the slide to right preset in the Custom Presets folder and then click Apply in the bottom right portion of the panel. Slide the new circle's tween span in the Timeline so it starts at frame 10.

7. Save your file as **animation_6.2**. Preview the animation and keep the file open for the next exercise.

Proficiency Assessment

Project 6-3	**Sharing Your Motion Presets**

You may end up creating some pretty cool animations that you want to share with co-workers. Luckily, Flash offers an easy and convenient way to do just that.

1. The **animation_6.2.fla** file from the previous exercise should still be open.

2. Choose Window > Motion Presets if the panel was closed. Click on the slide to right preset you created earlier and go to the flyout menu in the upper right corner of the panel.

3. Choose Export and save the preset as **slide to right.xml**. Keep the file handy for the next exercise.

Project 6-4	**Importing Motion Presets**

Now that you've exported your presets, let's examine how to share them with other computers. You normally would need a separate computer with Flash installed, but we'll take a step to skip that part.

1. Go to the Motion Presets panel. Select the slide to right preset and click the Trash button at the bottom of the panel to remove it.

2. Go to the flyout menu in the upper right corner of the Motion Presets panel and choose Import.

3. Navigate to the **slide to right.xml** file and import the slide to right preset back in! As you can see, an easy way to share a preset with other users!

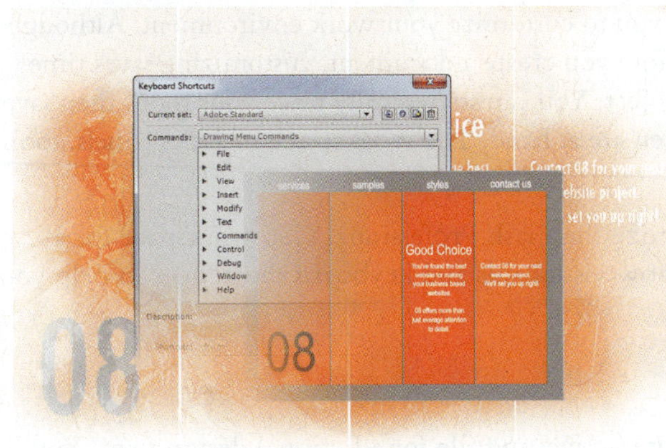

Customizing Your Workflow

Key Terms

- guides
- guide layers
- keyboard shortcuts
- rulers
- visual aids
- workspace

Skill	Objective
Demonstrate knowledge of design elements and principles	2.2
Identify elements of the Flash interface	3.1
Use Flash guides and rulers	3.5

Business case

There are quite a few panels in Flash for your use, unfortunately trying to manage them can be problematic if you're not used to dealing with all of them. Understanding workspaces can be really helpful in terms of managing the various panels and creating custom workspaces specific to your own personal habits and preferences. Besides panels, working with keyboard shortcuts can be another useful component to modifying your approach to using Flash in such a way that creates a faster and more personalized workflow when using the program.

Starting up

Before starting, make sure that your tools and panels are consistent by resetting your workspace. See "Resetting the Flash workspace" in the Starting up section of this book.

You will work with several files from the fl07lessons folder in this lesson. Make sure that you have loaded the fllessons folder onto your hard drive from *http://www.wiley.com/college/sc/adobeseries*. See "Loading lesson files" in the Starting up section of this book.

Customizing workspace layouts

Flash has many different features that enable you to customize your work environment. Although it means spending a little time organizing before you create a document, customizing saves time and headaches later when you're deep in a project. You can strategically place your tools, then save the workspace so the panels you use most often are at hand. The **workspace** includes panels, tools and their locations on the screen.

In this lesson, you will learn how to customize the Flash Professional CS6 workspace for a more efficient workflow. You'll also learn how visual aids and keyboard shortcuts can help you work smarter and faster.

Opening the completed file

This exercise involves assembling a small interactive .swf file for a fictional design firm. You'll place logos, text elements, and navigation buttons on the Stage with the help of guides, grids, and the align panel.

<table>
<tr><td>**Step-by-Step**</td><td>**Follow these steps to open the completed file**</td></tr>
</table>

1. Launch Flash CS6 Professional, if it is not already open.

2. Choose File> Browse in Bridge to open Adobe Bridge. Use the Folders tab in the upper-left of the Bridge workspace to navigate to the fl07lessons folder that you copied onto your computer. Adobe Bridge is used to navigate and open files in this lesson, but if you prefer, you can choose File > Open.

3. Once you have the fl07lessons folder open, double-click on the file named **fl0701_done.fla** to open it in Flash. A project file that includes a splash page for a mock design firm appears; you will reproduce this layout in the following exercises.

4. You can keep this file open for reference, or choose File > Close at this time. If asked to save changes, choose No.

5. Choose File > Browse to bring Adobe Bridge to the front. If you are not already viewing the contents of the fl07lessons folder, navigate to it now.

6. Double-click on the **fl0701.fla** file to open it in Flash.

7. Choose File > Save As. When the Save As dialog box appears, type **fl0701_work.fla** into the Name text field. Navigate to the fl07lessons folder and press Save.

Working with panels

Before getting started choose Workspace > Reset 'Essentials' to reset your workspace and return all panels to their default positions. The right side of the screen contains the Toolbar and two important panels: Library, and Properties. By default, the Property Inspector is in front of the Library as you can see in Figure 7-1. Many of the most common tasks in Flash can be easily achieved with this default layout; however, Flash includes a number of helpful panels that give you more sophisticated options to streamline your workflow.

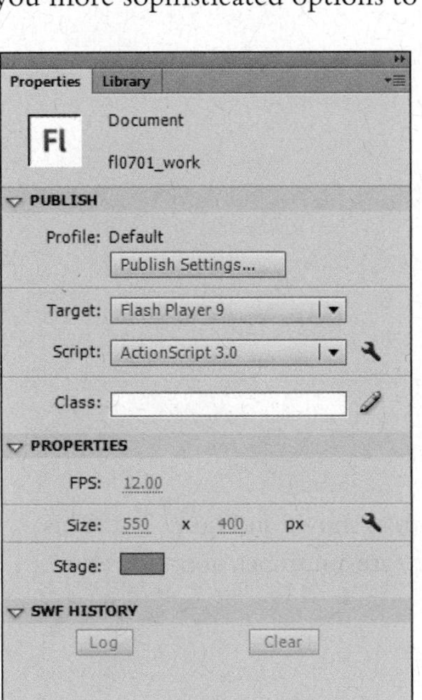

Figure 7-1: *The Properties and Library panels are open in the default workspace.*

Most panels are docked with other panels in the workspace by default. If you have a number of these panels open at the same time, they may become cumbersome to manage. Next you'll explore your options for docking panels in Flash CS6.

<table><tr><td>**Step-by-Step**</td><td>**Follow these steps to arrange panels**</td></tr></table>

1. Choose Window > Color to open the Color panel (Figure 7–2), which allows you to apply color to fills and strokes of objects in Flash.

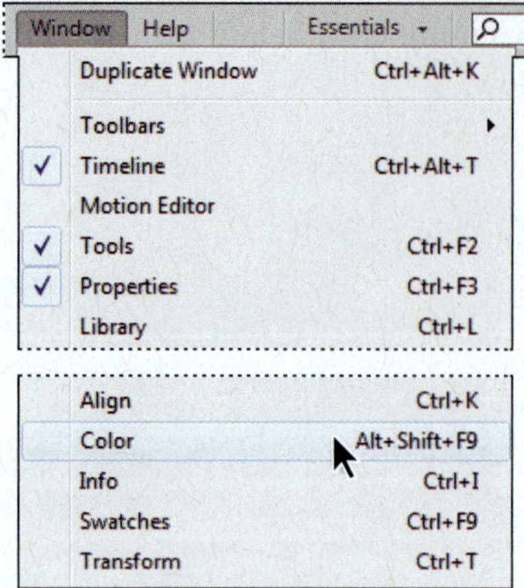

Figure 7–2: Open the Color panel through the Window menu.

The Color panel is docked with the Swatches panel by default as shown in Figure 7-3. This prevents you from having both panels open at once, but there are a number of options for repositioning them.

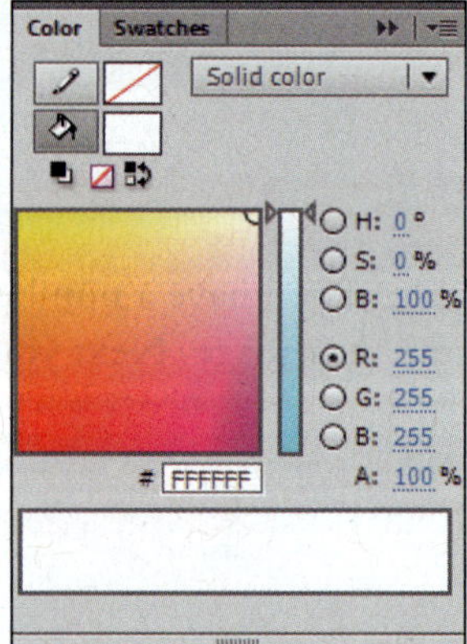

Figure 7–3: The Color and Swatches panels.

2. Remove the Color panel from the dock by clicking and dragging the Color title bar. Do the same with the Swatches panel to remove it from the dock.

3. Use the dark gray title bar to drag the Swatches to the bottom of the Color panel (Figure 7-4). When you get close to the bottom of the Color panel you should see the Swatches panel 'snap' into place below the Color panel. This helps you arrange panels in your workspace without overlap or misalignment.

Figure 7-4: Panels can be separated, positioned and docked back together by dragging them by their title bars.

Collapsing and storing panels

In addition to docking and snapping panels together, Flash CS6 provides a number of flexible options for maximizing screen space. By collapsing panels you can focus on only the features you need at any given moment, but keep within easy reach everything you might need during a session.

<table><tr><td>**Step-by-Step**</td><td>**Follow these steps to expand and collapse panels**</td></tr></table>

1. Double-click on the Color panel's title tab to collapse the panel. This option allows you to maximize vertical space. It's especially useful if you have several panels open at the same time. To expand the panel again, simply double-click the title tab again (Figure 7-5).

Take Note...

A panel that is docked into an icon bar will not collapse, but will minimize back to an icon in its respective panel group.

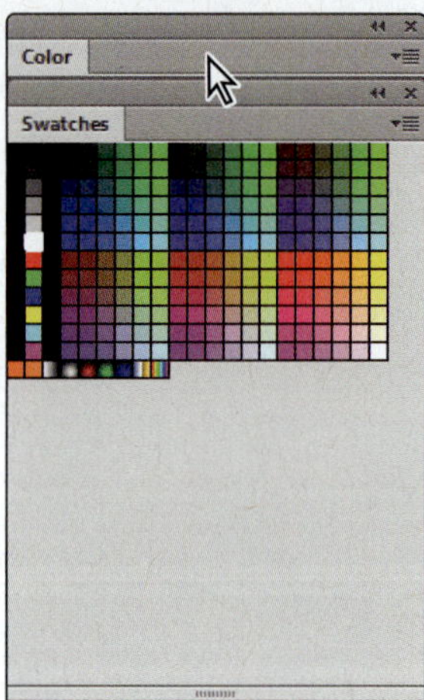

Figure 7-5: Collapse undocked panels by double-clicking on the gray bar above its title tab.

2. Double-click on the dark gray bar that sits at the top of the Color panel (above its title tab). This collapses the Color panel, as well as the Swatches panel into icon view.

3. Click on each icon to expand and collapse its panel (Figure 7-6). Notice that only one panel stays open at a time. Once you're familiar with the features of each panel, icon view can be a great way to hide panels when they're not in use.

Figure 7-6: *Reduce a group of panels to icon view by double- clicking the bar above its title tab.*

4. Click the double arrows at the top of the icon group to re-expand the panels.

5. Using the Color panel's title tab, drag it over the icon bar on the far right of the Stage (from where you originally pulled the color and swatches panels). When you see a blue line indicator at the top of that bar, release it (Figure 7-7). The Color panel will be redocked and its icon will appear again along with the others.

Figure 7-7: *Redock panels into groups by dragging them back into those groups.*

Managing workspaces

Once you arrange a layout that's ideal for your workflow, you can save it as a workspace for future use. You can save as many workspace layouts as you need, customizing them by task, project, or even for use among multiple users. Once you build up a collection of workspaces, Flash also offers controls for managing them.

Let's go ahead and set up your first custom workspace:

Step-by-Step | **Follow these steps to set up a workspace**

1. Choose Window > Workspace > New Workspace as shown in Figure 7-8.

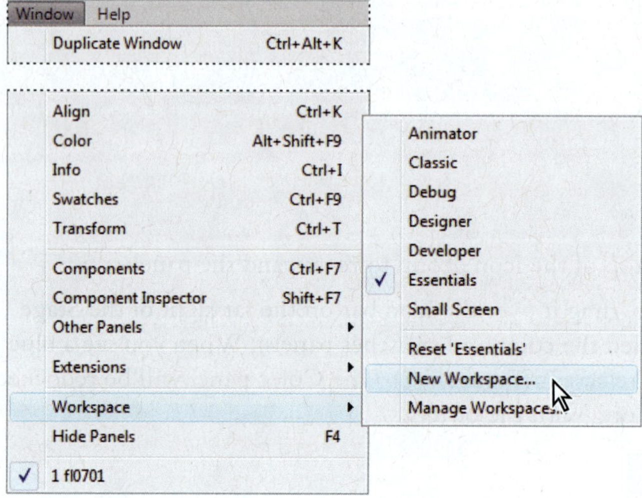

Figure 7-8: Choose New Workspace from Workspace in the Window menu.

In the resulting dialog box, type **Design Layout** in the Name text field (Figure 7-9), and press OK.

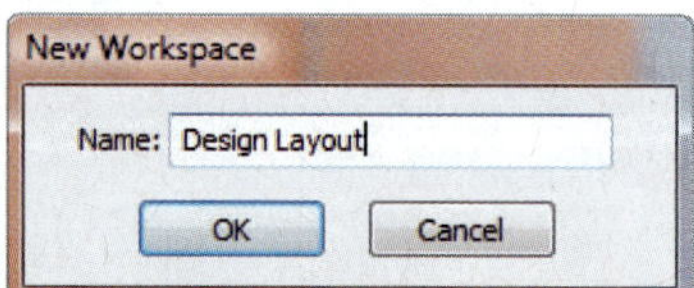

*Figure 7-9: Enter **Design Layout** in the New Workspace dialog box.*

2. Choose Window > Workspace > Reset 'Design Layout'. The panels reset to the default Flash workspace layout.

3. To restore your custom workspace, choose Window > Workspace > Design Layout as shown in Figure 7-10.

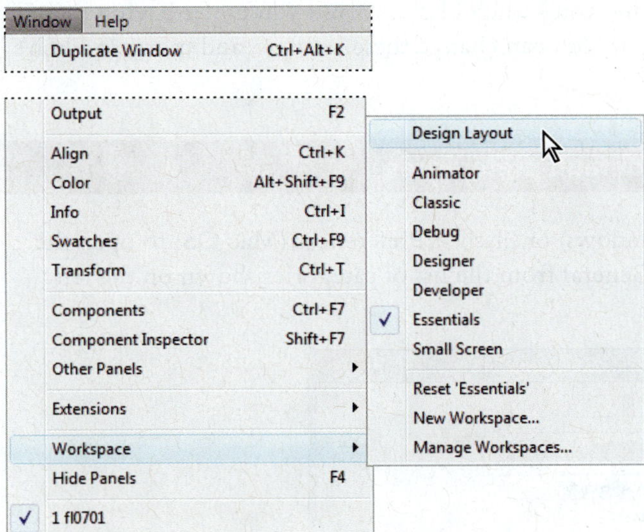

Figure 7-10: Access your saved workspace through Window > Workspace.

The panels and dock arrangement that you created in the previous exercise is now restored. Having multiple workspaces is very helpful for one person doing different types of projects or for multiple users who use the same machine. If you end up having multiple workspaces, you need a way to manage them.

4. Choose Window > Workspace > Manage Workspaces (Figure 7-11).

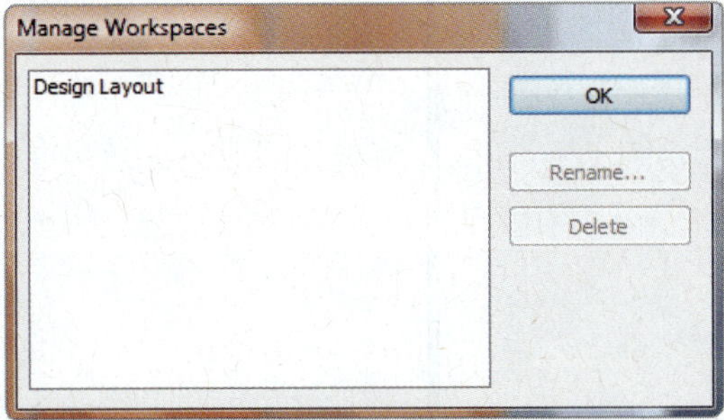

Figure 7-11: Manage your workspaces with the Manage Workspaces dialog box.

The Manage Workspaces dialog box lists all saved workspaces, including your newly created Design Layout. Even with a single saved layout, you can edit, rename, or delete it from here.

5. Choose the Design Layout and click the Rename button. Rename it **07 Design Layout** and press OK.

6. Press OK again to exit the Manage Workspaces dialog box.

Take Note...

You don't have to go to the menu area to switch workspaces. Click the Workspace drop-down menu on the right side of the main menu bar to see the same options available from Window > Workspace > Manage.

Setting preferences

Sometimes the little things can make the biggest difference in your workflow. Are you tired of seeing the Welcome Screen every time you launch Flash? Would you prefer having more levels of Undo or a different highlight color? You can change these settings, and more, in Flash's Preferences dialog box.

Step-by-Step | **Follow these steps to modify default preferences**

1. Choose Edit > Preferences (Windows) or Flash > Preferences (Mac OS) to open the Preferences dialog box. Select General from the list of categories shown on the left (Figure 7–12).

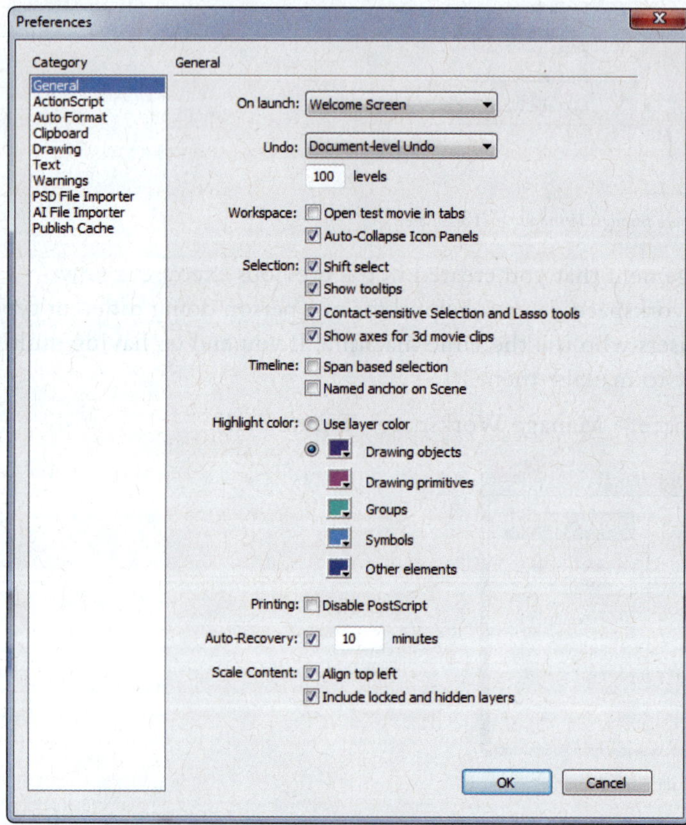

Figure 7–12: Options available in the General category of the Preferences dialog box.

2. To turn off the Welcome Screen, choose No Document from the On launch drop-down menu as shown in Figure 7-13. You could also choose to have the application open a new document or even the last document saved.

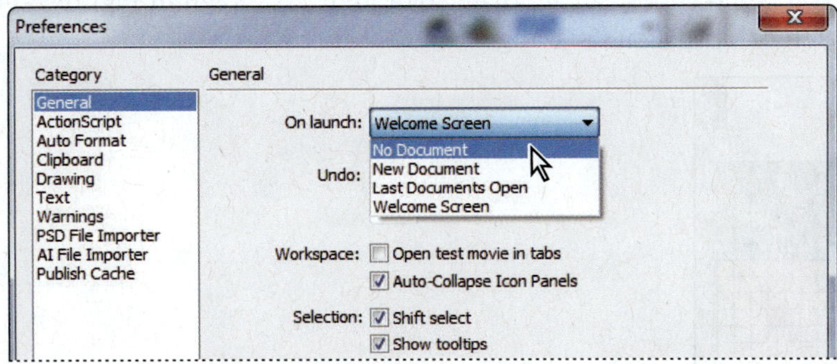

Figure 7-13: *Use the On launch drop-down to turn off the Welcome Screen.*

3. In the Undo section of the General preferences, the Undo levels are set to the default of 100. Type **150** in this text field. This increases the number of times you can Undo steps by 50. Flash supports up to 9999 undo levels, but this would likely slow down the performance of your system.

Take Note...

If you change your Undo preferences in the middle of a project, you will lose the history of the work you have done since you started your work session, which means you cannot go back and undo your previous actions. Object undos deal with tracking the separate steps performed on objects like the Stage, or symbols in the Library. Document undos deal with the series of linear actions you made in the current and open document like timeline changes, creating keyframes, and scaling.

4. Farther down in the General Preferences dialog box, you can set your preferred Highlight colors. You can change the default colors used for bounding boxes displayed around drawing objects, groups, or symbols. Click on the color swatch next the Drawing objects option and note that you could choose an alternate color here. As shown in Figure 7-14, click on the main swatch color to avoid making changes at this time.

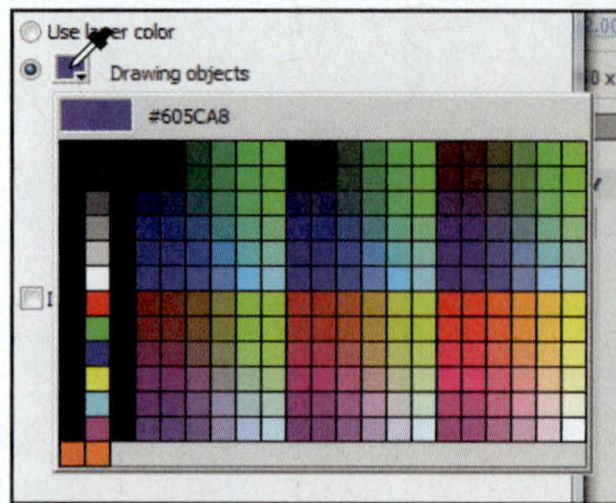

Figure 7-14: *Highlight colors can be customized in the General section of the Preferences dialog box.*

Take Note...

If you're a dedicated layer user, click the Use layer color button. This automatically sets bounding boxes to match the color assigned to each layer, so you'll know for sure to which layer a selected object belongs.

5. Press OK to commit the small changes made in this exercise.

Keyboard shortcuts

If customizing your workspace streamlines your workflow, then using keyboard shortcuts adds speed. Flash provides a window for you to view all the **keyboard shortcuts** in one location. You can do more than just identify shortcuts (Figure 7-15), however; you can also add, remove, and reassign shortcuts in one location, allowing you to truly customize the way Flash Professional CS6 functions (Figure 7-16).

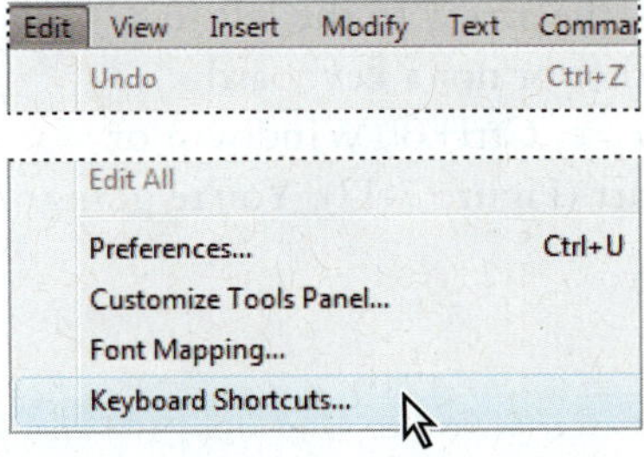

Figure 7-15: *Access the Keyboard Shortcuts dialog box.*

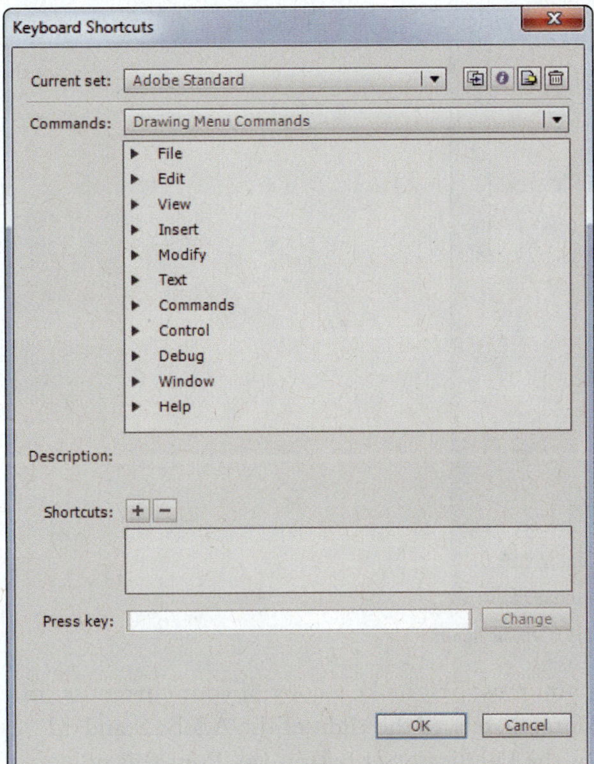

Figure 7-16: *View and customize all Flash's keyboard shortcuts with the Keyboard Shortcuts dialog box.*

<table>
<tr><td>Step-by-Step</td><td>Follow these steps to customize shortcuts</td></tr>
</table>

1. Choose Edit > Keyboard Shortcuts (Windows) or Flash > Keyboard Shortcuts (Mac OS). In the Keyboard Shortcuts dialog box, choose Drawing Menu Commands from the Commands drop-down menu if it is not already selected. Flash displays a list of all the commands specific to the Drawing menu below.

2. Scroll through the commands and locate Modify, then click the arrow to the left to expand the available menu commands. Flash indicates whether or not a keyboard shortcut is assigned to any given command already. In this case, Ctrl+B (Windows) or Command+B (Mac OS) is assigned to Modify > Break Apart (Figure 7-17). You're going to change this in the upcoming steps.

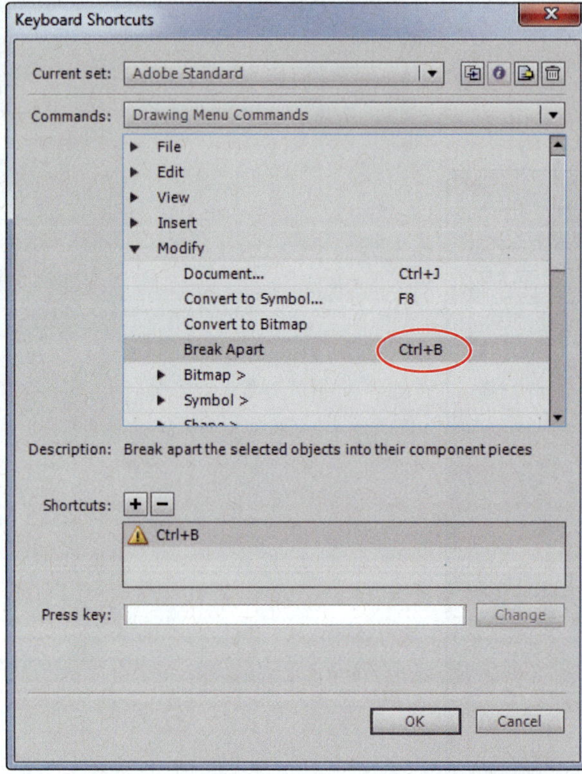

Figure 7-17: Find the keyboard shortcut assigned to Modify > Break Apart.

3. Before you can customize the shortcuts, you must first make a copy of your current set of shortcuts and save it with a new name. Immediately to the right of the Adobe Standard menu are four buttons. The first button is the Duplicate Set button (▣). Press this now to duplicate the current keyboard shortcut set.

4. In the Duplicate dialog box, type **Mine** as the name for the duplicate set (Figure 7-18) and press OK.

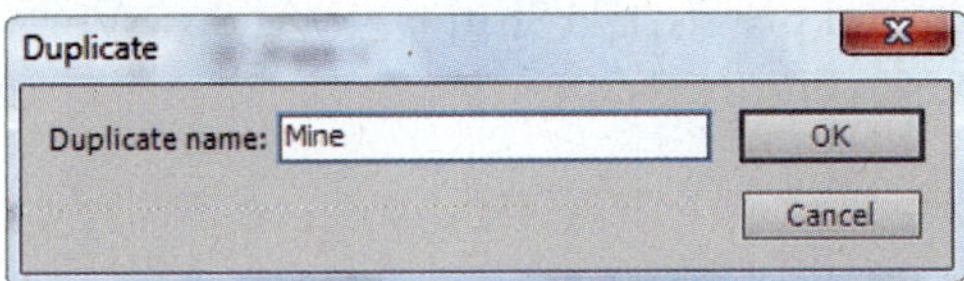

Figure 7-18: *Name your new set of keyboard shortcuts.*

5. Your new set, Mine, should appear selected in the Current set menu at the top as shown in Figure 7-19, but if not, reselect it from the Current set drop-down menu.

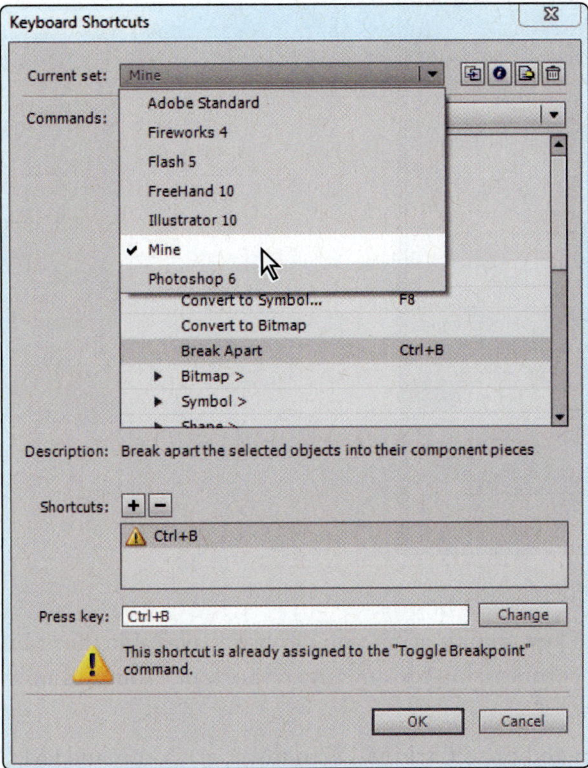

Figure 7-19: *If necessary, select Mine from the Current set menu.*

Take Note...
To rename a set of shortcuts, click the Rename Set button (◦) in the top-right corner of the Keyboard Shortcuts dialog box. To generate an HTML file listing every shortcut in the program, click the third button, Export Set as HTML, and then save the file to the desktop. You can open the file for reference at any time, or edit it with any standard text editor.

6. After saving the new shortcut set, let's edit the shortcut for Modify > Break Apart. Select the Break Apart command under Modify. Click once inside the Press key field at the bottom of the window to activate the field, and press Ctrl+Shift+9 (Windows) or Command+Shift+9 (Mac OS) on your keyboard (Figure 7-20).

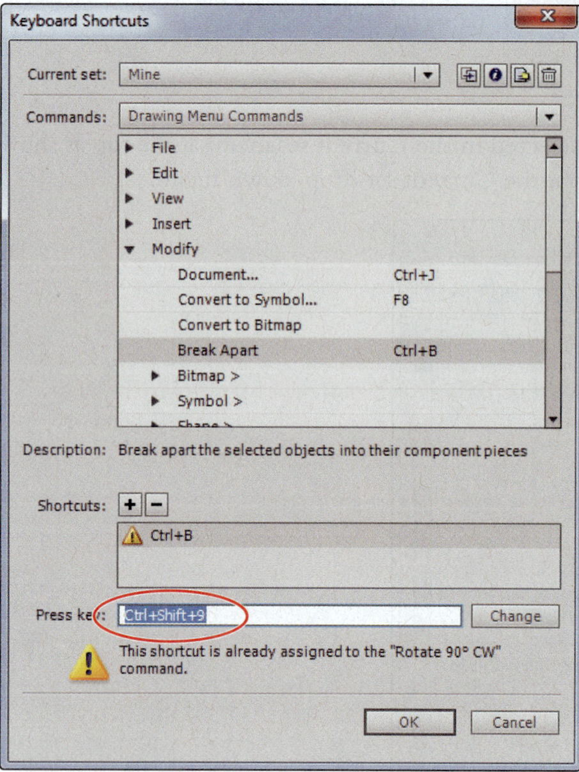

Figure 7-20: Enter the new shortcut in the Press key field.

The application can determine if the key combination you choose is available. For obvious reasons, you can only have one key combination for any given shortcut. You will now test this by trying different combinations.

7. Click inside the Press key field again and press Ctrl+M (Windows) or Command+M (Mac OS). You will receive no warning, therefore that combination is available. Now press Ctrl+K (Windows) or Command+K (Mac OS). A warning triangle appears, because that combination is the Align command's shortcut.

8. Press the Cancel button; you will not be modifying this keyboard shortcut right now.

Take Note...

To thoroughly customize your shortcuts, export the shortcut list as HTML, print it out, grab a pen, and circle the commands you use frequently. Choose the Shortcuts menu and try running a sequence of command keys until you find one that's usable, assign it to one of your frequently used commands, jot it down on your list, then try again for the next command.

Visual aids for alignment

Flash's **visual aids** streamline how you work on the Stage, whether it's drawing, placing objects, or aligning items in a layout. Rather than determining locations by eye, or placing graphics through trial and error, you'll take advantage of guides, rulers, grid, guide layers, and advanced alignment tools.

Rulers and **guides** work together to let the user place an item on the Stage at specific locations, providing an easy way for you to create symmetry, movement, and place objects including lines, in proximity to one another, while **guide layers** change artwork into a device that can be used for alignment and reference purposes helping you to balance and add contrast to your design. The grid functions much like graph paper, and appears superimposed on the Stage so that you can precisely place objects on the Stage. The Align feature and Flash's various visual aids allow for very precise positioning. To put these visual aids to use and explore their benefits, you'll put together a sample home page for a design firm.

When designing in Flash, remember to use good design techniques to add emphasis and unity to elements on the stage. Avoid designs that violate good design principles such as extraneous graphics, overcrowded layouts, and color that distracts from the main elements of the design. Utilize color and white space to make your design as appealing as possible. You can even use the visual aids in Flash to create a rule of thirds grid to aid in the visual balance of your project. Don't adapt the design to the page content, establish consistency in your design.

Rulers and guides

Rulers and guides work together to provide more precise placements in less time. Here's how they work.

Follow these steps to use rulers and guides

1. Choose the View menu. If there is a checkmark to the left of the Rulers option, the rulers are currently displayed (Figure 7–21). If there is no checkmark, select the Rulers option now. When activated, rulers appear on the top and left side of your work area.

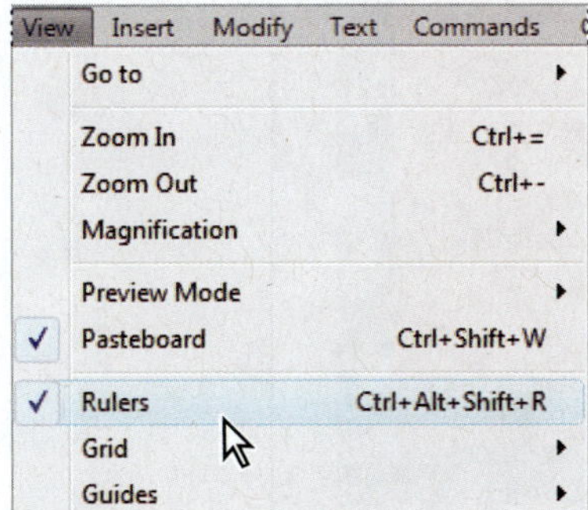

Figure 7–21: Rulers can be toggled on and off from the View menu.

By default, measurements on the rulers are displayed in pixels. You can easily change the unit of measurement in Flash CS6 Professional.

Certification Ready 2.2

What are some common graphic design elements and principles?

Certification Ready 2.2

What are some elements of page designs that violate design principles and best practices?

Certification Ready 3.5

How do you show and hide rulers?

Step-by-Step

2. Choose Modify > Document, then click on the Ruler units pull-down menu. You have the option to select inches, centimeters, millimeters, points, or pixels. Web pages and web graphics are typically designed using pixels, so select pixels if necessary (Figure 7-22) and press OK.

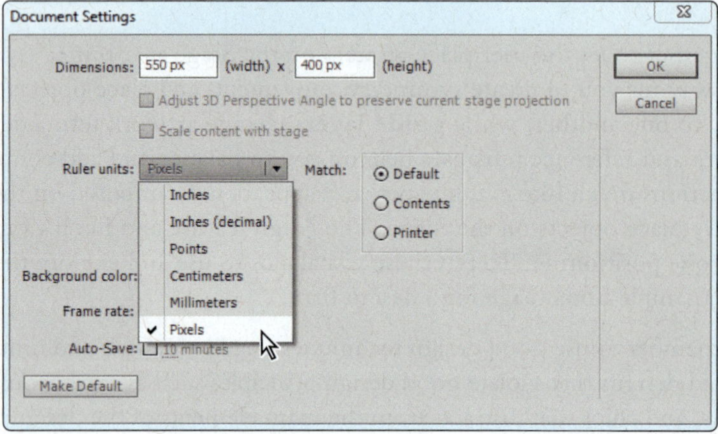

Figure 7-22: *Change measurement units from the Document Settings dialog box.*

3. Place your cursor on the horizontal ruler at the top of the Stage and then click and drag downwards. This pulls out a horizontal guideline from the ruler. Drag the guide to the 350-pixel mark displayed on the vertical (left-side) ruler as shown in Figure 7-23. Click and drag the guide again to fine-tune its position, if necessary. To remove a guide, simply click on the guide and drag it back to the ruler.

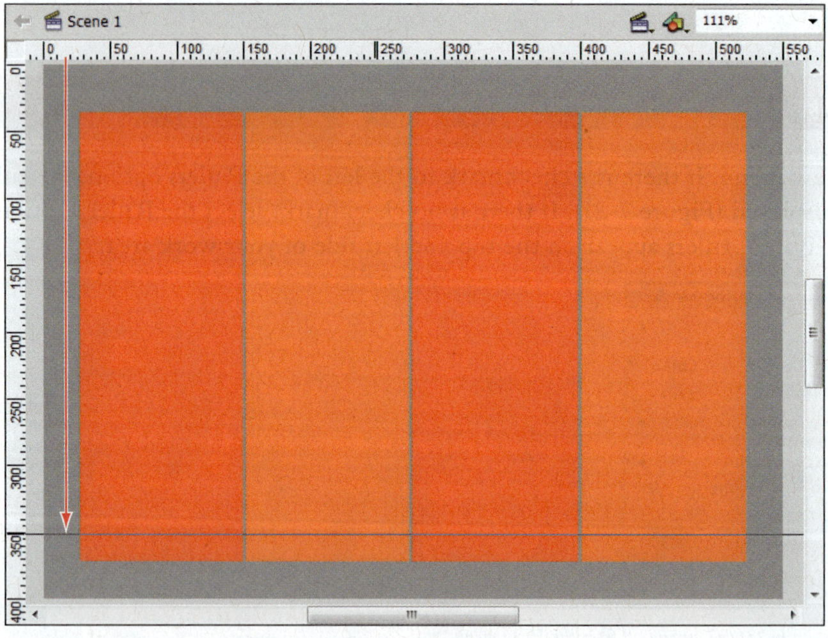

Figure 7-23: *Drag a new guide from the top ruler.*

Take Note...

By choosing View > Guides > Edit Guides, you have access to the guide properties. The guide properties provide control over aspects of guides such as locking and unlocking guides, and guide color. By choosing View > Guides > Snapping, you can control how objects snap to the guides as well as to the grid, objects and pixels in a document.

4. Click on the Library tab to bring the Library panel forward, and click on the graphic symbol named logo from the list as shown in Figure 7-24.

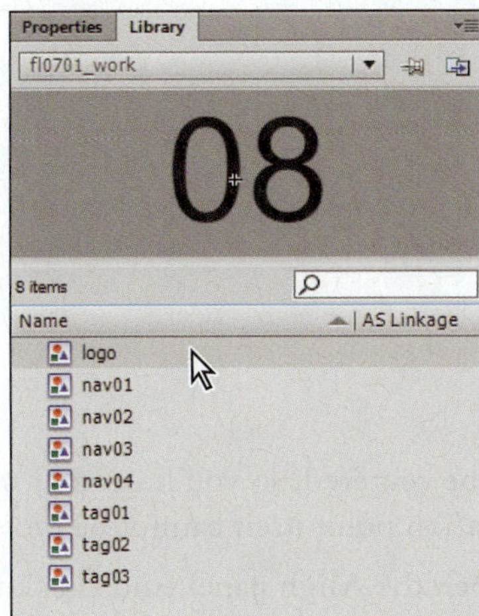

Figure 7-24: Select the logo graphic symbol.

5. Drag an instance of the logo symbol from the Library panel onto the Stage and drop it above the guide in the first orange column shown on the left (Figure 7-25). In the exact center of the logo is a small circle. This is the registration point, and you will now align it to the guide.

Figure 7-25: Drag the logo symbol from the Library.

6. Using the Selection tool (↖), grab the logo by its registration point and drag it downward as shown in Figure 7-26. When the registration point approaches the guide, it snaps to it.

Figure 7-26: The symbol's centered registration point snaps to the guide.

So, what if you wanted the bottom of the logo to snap to the guide instead of the center? To do this, you need to edit the registration point. In order to permanently change the registration point of any library item, you need to edit the original symbol.

Take Note...

If you're finding that objects aren't snapping into place as you expected, check to make sure Snapping is enabled for your document. Choose View > Snapping and make sure Snap Align, Snap to Guides, and Snap to Objects are all checked.

7. Double-click on the icon of the logo graphic in the library to edit it in place(Figure 7-27). Once you are in the item's edit mode, select the text box with the Selection tool (↖).

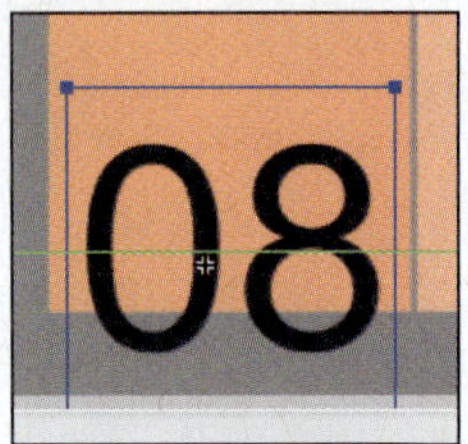

Figure 7-27: In the symbol's edit mode, use the Selection tool to select the text box.

The registration mark, shown as a crosshair, appears to be centered, so you'll need to move the content relative to the registration point (the registration point itself cannot be moved).

8. If it's not already visible, choose Window > Align to open the Align panel, and check the Align to stage checkbox at the bottom of the panel as shown in Figure 7-28. The Align panel's icon should appear on the right in the default "Essentials" workspace.

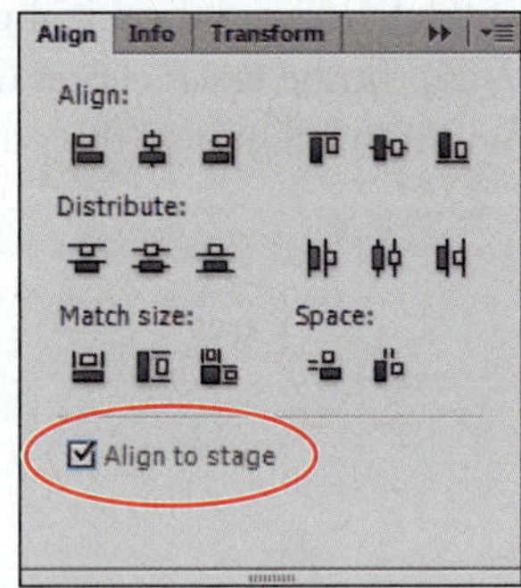

Figure 7-28: Click the Align to stage checkbox on the Align panel.

The top row of buttons grouped under Align heading are all the alignment choices available to you. Place your cursor over the first button and a box appears, indicating that this is the Align left edge option.

9. Place your cursor on the last button in the Align row, make sure the Align bottom edge box appears, and click once as shown in Figure 7-29. The text box will move upward and the registration mark is now aligned to the bottom of the text box. Close the Align panel.

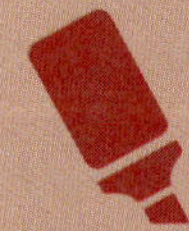

Take Note...

By default, the alignment, sizing, and distribution options on the Align panel work by comparing two or more selected objects on the Stage. Selecting the Align to stage checkbox sets the Stage itself as the ultimate point of reference, so results will be very different with this option enabled.

10. Click the Scene 1 link above the Stage to exit the symbol and return to the Timeline. You'll see that the logo now properly sits with its lower edge resting on the guide as shown in Figure 7-30. By default, guides always snap to the registration mark of an object.

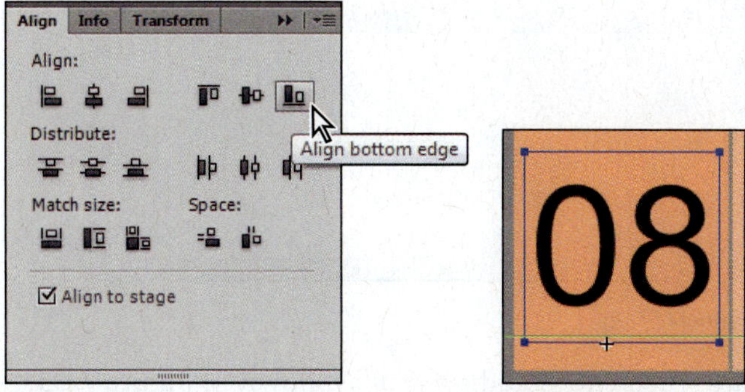

Figure *7-29*: Choose Align bottom edge.

Figure *7-30*: Logo is now properly placed.

Take Note...

If you prefer, you can change the default snapping behavior of guides. Go to View > Snapping > Edit Snapping, and uncheck Snap to Guides to prevent objects from snapping to guides.

Guide layers

Unlike standard layers, the contents of Guide Layers only appear during the design process, and are not published to your final movie

Important information to consider is that objects on guide layers will not export with your final movie; objects on a guide layer are only visible within the authoring environment.

Before you work with guide layers, however, you will first add the content to your current document.

<table><tr><td>**Follow these steps to work with guide layers**</td><td>Step-by-Step</td></tr></table>

1. Press the Insert Layer button (⬑) at the bottom left of the Timeline. Double-click the new layer name to rename it and type **Text** as shown in Figure 7-31.

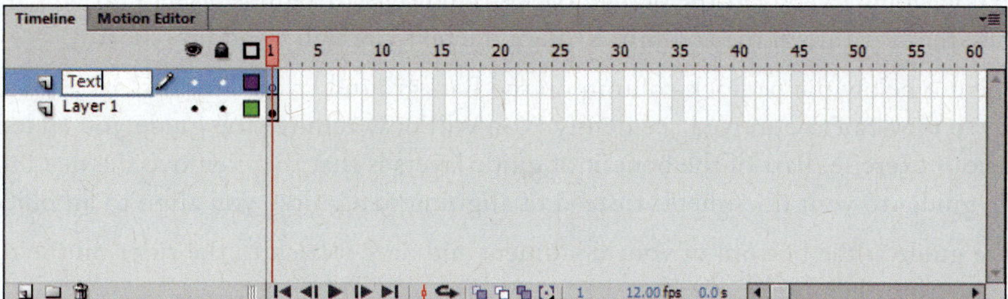

Figure *7-31*: Create a new layer and name it **Text**.

Visual aids for alignment ...sting layer 1 name, and rename this layer **Background** as shown

2. Double ... ...e. You will now move the logo you added in the previous exercise to the ... layer

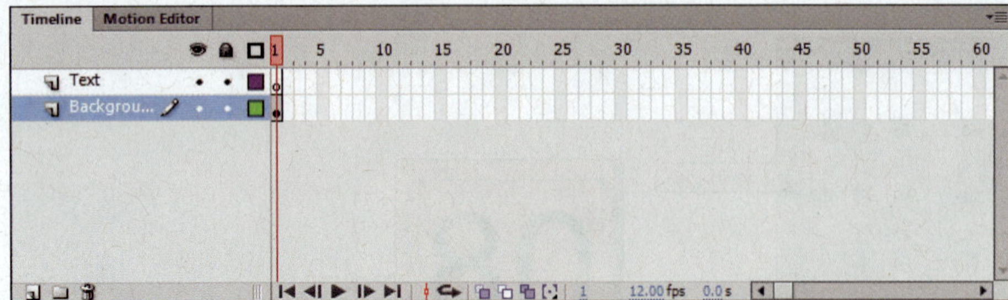

Figure 7-32: *Rename the bottom layer* **Background**.

3. Select the *08* logo on the artboard, then choose Edit > Cut as shown in Figure 7-33.

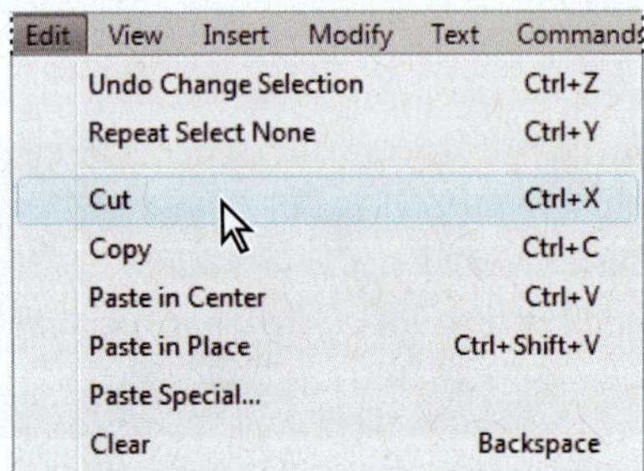

Figure 7-33: *Select the logo and choose Edit > Cut.*

4. Select the Text layer, then choose Edit > Paste in Place as shown in Figure 7-34.

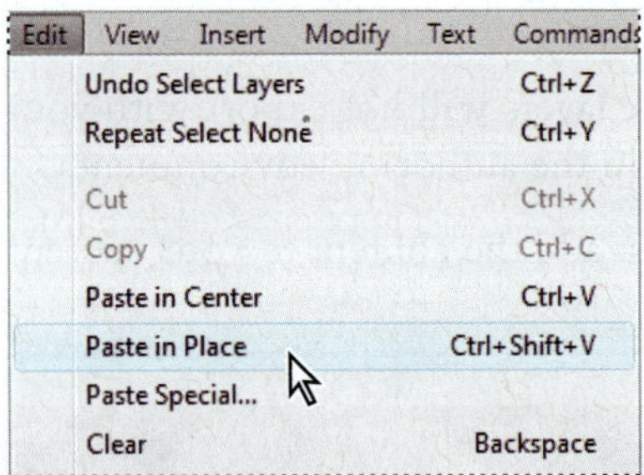

Figure 7-34: *Move the logo to the Text layer.*

The logo is placed on the new layer in the exact location it occupied on its original layer.

You are now going to convert the orange Background layer to a guide layer. This will allow you to use the structure of the columns to align the text you will be adding shortly.

5. Click the dot below the padlock column on the Background layer. This locks the orange columns so they can't be moved accidently. You will now remove the guide you added in the previous exercise. Part of the benefit of guide layers is that they remove the need to add multiple guides to your document. Instead of aligning to a guide, you align to an object.

6. Click the guide at the bottom of your document and drag it back to the ruler on the top. It is removed from the page.

7. Right-click (Windows) or Ctrl+click (Mac OS) on the Background layer in the Timeline, and as shown in Figure 7-35, choose Guide.

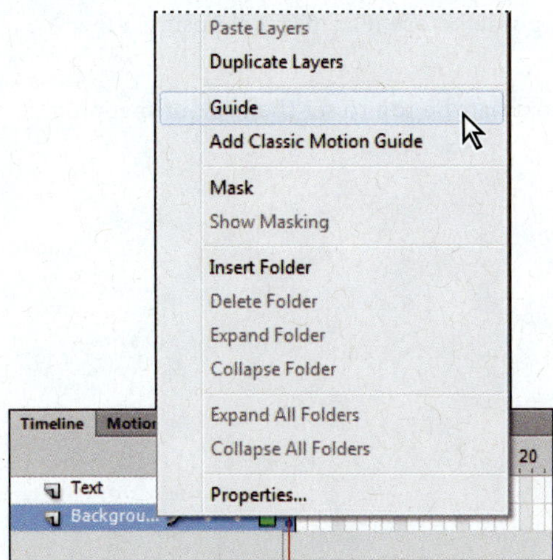

Figure 7-35: Choose Guide from the Background layer's contextual menu.

The standard layer icon converts to a T-square icon (), indicating that this is now a guide layer.

8. On the Text layer, select and drag the logo down to the bottom of the first orange column until the registration point snaps to the bottom of the column as shown in Figure 7-36.

Figure 7-36: Drag the logo down to the bottom of the orange column.

Learning More | **Sensitivity**

You can adjust how close a graphic needs to be to a guide before it snaps by choosing View > Snapping > Edit Snapping.

In the resulting dialog box, you can use the checkboxes at the top to set the type of snapping behavior you'd like to use (Figure 7-37).

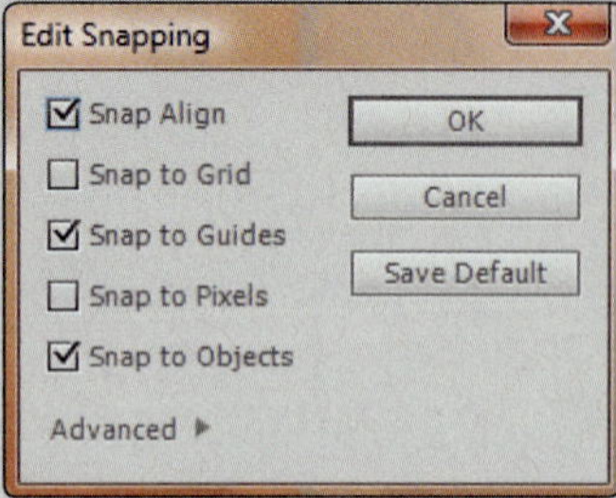

Figure 7-37: A number of options are available for snapping behavior.

To change the pixel distance, or tolerance, click the Advanced arrow to access the Advanced options. Stage Border is how close the graphic needs to be before it snaps; increase or decrease that number according to your feel for moving elements around the Stage.

The good thing is that you can save these settings by clicking Save Default just under the Cancel button on the top-right side of the dialog box. Your new settings become the standard setting for the entire program; not just the current document.

9. Now you'll continue using the guide layer to position more graphics on the Stage.

Select the Text layer so it's active. Select the nav01 graphic symbol in the Library panel and drag an instance of it onto the Stage within the first orange column on the left. Do the same to place nav02, nav03, and nav04 in the second, third, and fourth columns, respectively (Figure 7-38).

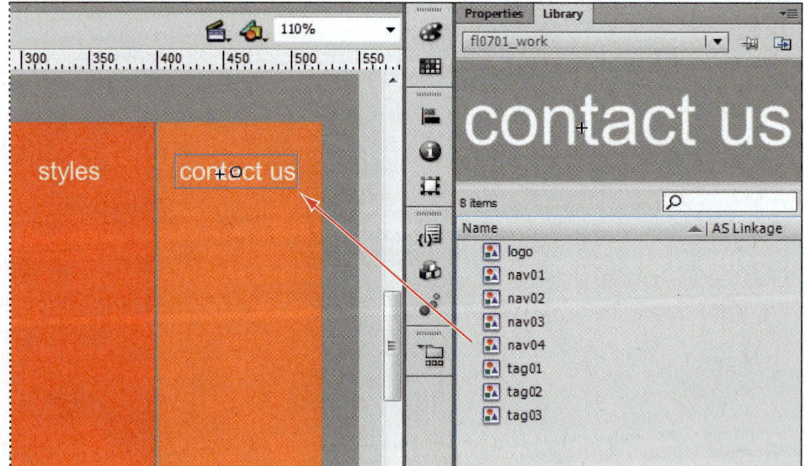

Figure 7-38: Drag and place the nav symbols onto the Stage.

10. To align the graphics, click and drag each one until its bounding box baseline is on top of its respective column, as shown in Figure 7-39.

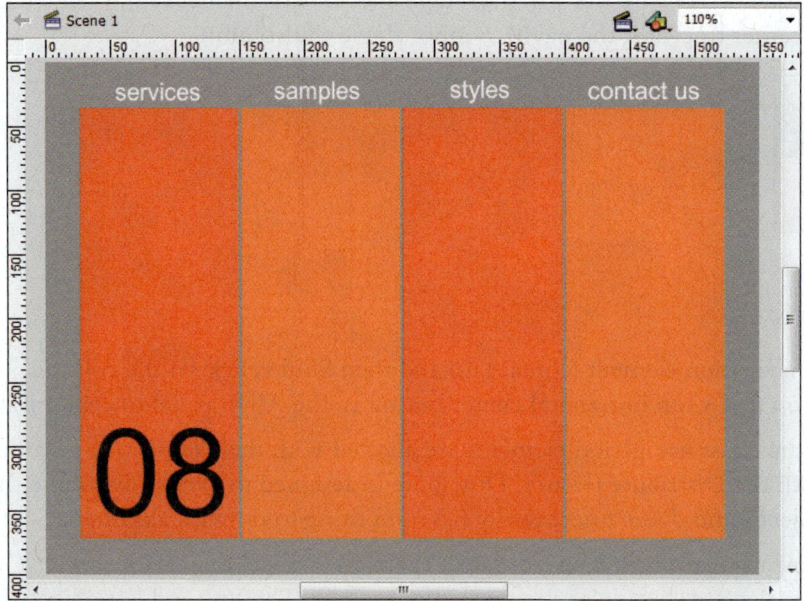

Figure 7-39: Place the nav symbols above their orange columns.

You will now convert the Background layer back into a standard layer.

11. Right-click (Windows) or Ctrl+Click (Mac OS) on the Background layer and deselect the Guide option. This converts this layer back to a standard layer.

12. Choose File > Save to save your work.

Advanced alignment

Because all four navigation elements are at the top of the columns, you will now properly align them, not just across the columns but also in spatial relation to each other.

Follow these steps to align elements on the page	**Step-by-Step**

1. Select the instance of nav01 (services) on the Stage and make sure it's centered above the column.

Take Note...
You can cycle through and select symbols on the Stage by using the Tab key.

2. Click on the padlock icon (🔒) to the right of the Background layer to unlock it. You will be aligning the navigation to the column and you need to be able to select the column.

3. Shift+click to select the orange column underneath the nav01 symbol instance you already have selected, so that both the symbol instance and the column are selected (Figure 7-40). Open the Align panel (make sure the Align to stage checkbox is unchecked), then click Align horizontal center to center the nav01 symbol above the column.

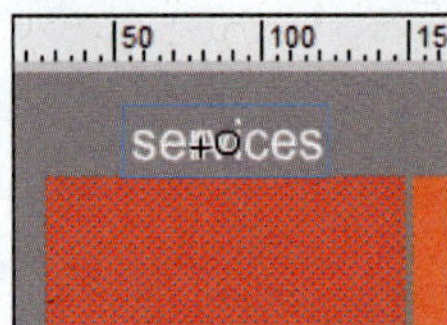

Figure 7-40: *Align the nav symbols with their respective columns.*

4. Click on the last navigation element (contact us) and then Shift+click on the column beneath it. Click on the Align horizontal center button in the Align panel to center it.

Now that the first and last navigation elements are aligned with their respective columns, you will work with the Distribute feature. Distribute is designed to evenly distribute the space between objects, and doesn't necessarily have anything to do with alignment.

5. Shift+click the four navigation elements to select them all at once, then click the Distribute horizontal center button as shown in Figure 7-41. The first and last objects are fixed and the second and third objects are now evenly distributed between them. Each element should be centered over its assigned column.

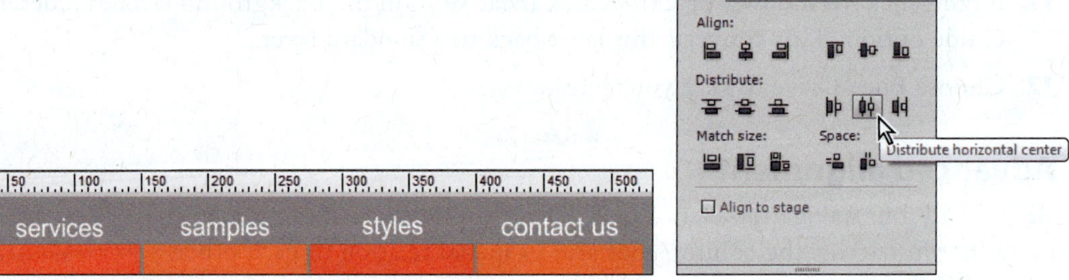

Figure 7-41: *Select and distribute all four nav symbols.*

Distribute looks at the registration point, not the bounding boxes, of each graphic. So, when you look at the four graphics, the centered registration marks are evenly distributed.

6. With all four items still selected, click the Space evenly horizontally button (⊣⊢)as shown in Figure 7-42. Notice how nav02 and nav03 shift a bit. It's the space between the bounding boxes, and not the center points, that becomes even. Distribute distributes the center points of graphics, while Space distributes the spacing between the bounding boxes of graphics.

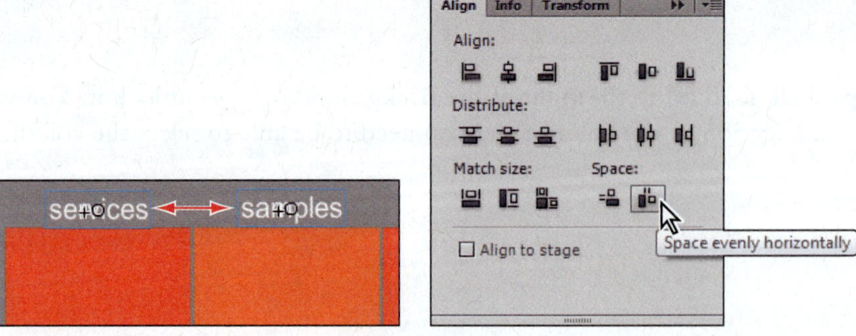

Figure 7-42: *Choose settings that even the spaces between the symbols' bounding boxes.*

7. The last few items you need to place on the Stage are the tag graphics. Drag the tag01 symbol from the Library panel to the Stage and position it in the top third of the third column.

8. Click and drag the tag02 text and place it in the third column beneath the tag01 text you just added. Drag tag03 and place it in the middle of the fourth column as shown in Figure 7-43. You will now be using the Align panel to center these.

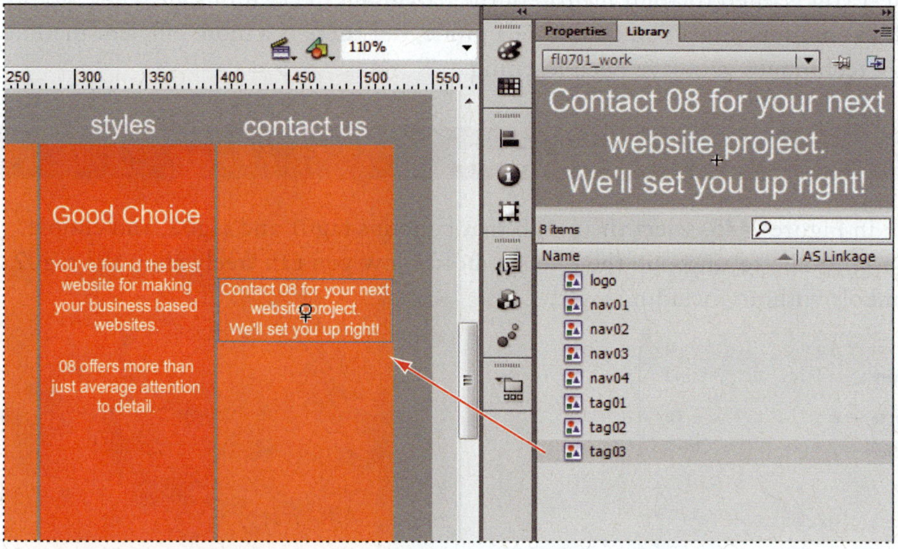

Figure 7–43: Drag instances of tag01, tag02, and tag03 into the second and third columns.

9. Shift+click tag01 and tag02 to select both graphics, press the Align panel button on the right to open it, then press the Align horizontal center button in the Align panel to center the two graphics. You will now group these two graphics so you can align all the text inside the third column.

10. Choose Modify > Group to group tag01 and tag02 together as shown in Figure 7-44. Grouping two objects together allows you to align the entire unit within the column.

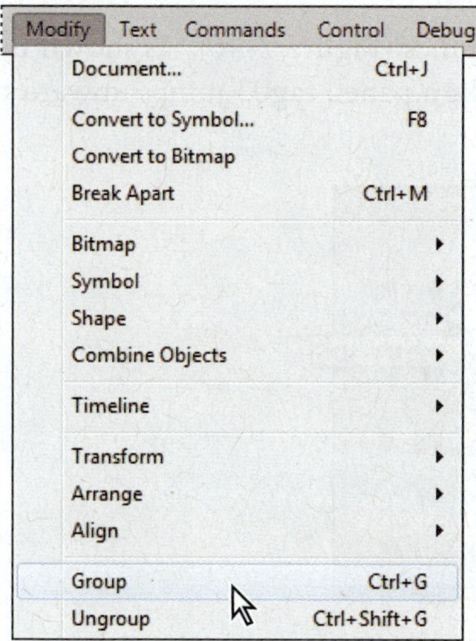

*Figure 7–44: After centering tag01 and tag02,
select Group from the Modify menu.*

11. Shift+click the third orange column to select both it and the grouped text, then press Align vertical center and Align horizontal center buttons in the Align panel.

12. Click on tag03 in the fourth column and then Shift+click the fourth column to select it as well. In the Align panel, press the Align vertical center button and the Align horizontal center button. Aligning your text in this fashion is much more precise than doing it by hand.

Refining your aligned objects

The devil is always in the details. Although you have been able to align tag03 within its own column, what if you wanted to align the top of the paragraph in column four with the top of the paragraph in column three? You could use a guide, but there is a more efficient method using the align techniques you have been learning.

<table><tr><td>**Step-by-Step**</td><td>**Follow these steps to refine aligned objects**</td></tr></table>

1. As shown in Figure 7-45, select the group that contains tag01 and tag02, and choose Modify > Ungroup to ungroup the two symbols. Now you can freely align the tag02 and tag03 symbols without including tag01.

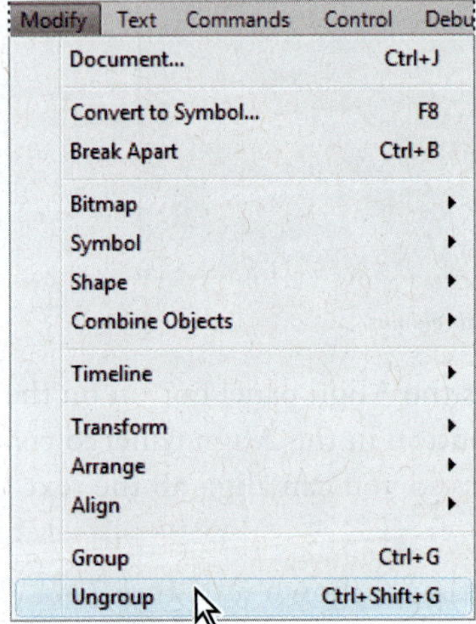

Figure 7-45: Ungroup tag01 and tag02.

2. Select tag03, then Shift+click tag02 to select both graphics (Figure 7-46). As shown in Figure 7-47, press the Align top edge button in the Align panel; tag03 jumps upward to align itself with tag02.

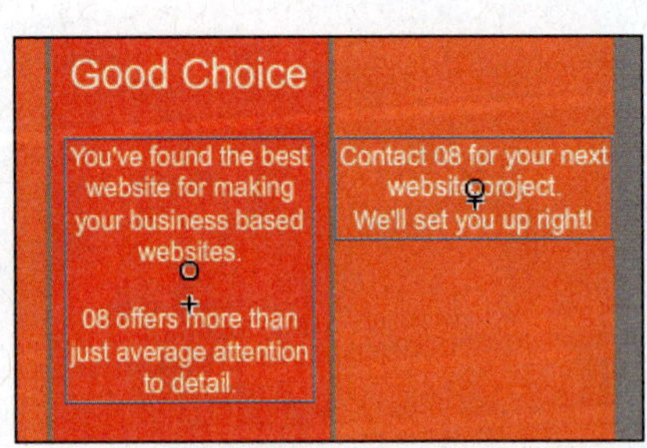

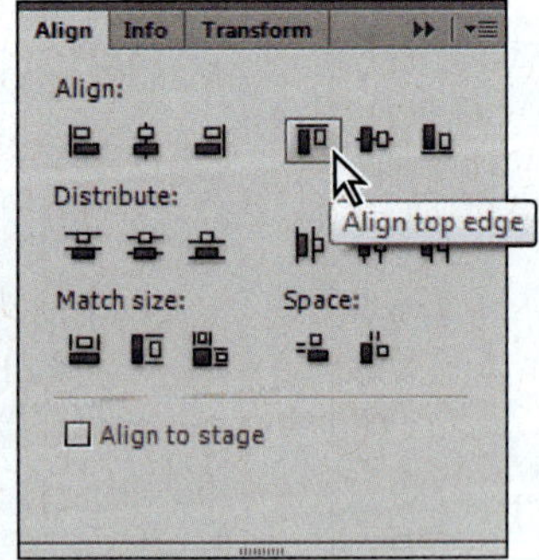

Figure 7-46: Select tag02 and tag03.

Figure 7-47: Press the Align top edge button in the Align panel.

3. Choose File > Save, then File > Close.

Congratulations! You have finished the lesson.

Grids

If you find that rulers and guides become too time-consuming for you, consider setting up a grid system to assist in placing graphics on the Stage. To turn on the grid behind the Stage, choose View > Grid > Show Grid.

To edit the grid details, such as color or increments, choose View > Grid > Edit Grid (Figure 7-48).

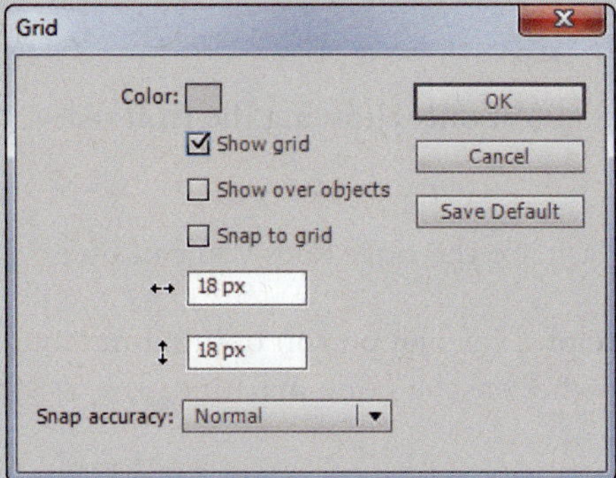

Figure 7-48: Grid options can be accessed by choosing *View > Grid > Edit Grid.*

In the Grid dialog box, you can choose to show or hide the grid, change the grid line color, and adjust snapping accuracy. It can be very frustrating to move a graphic onstage and see it randomly jump to a guide or grid line. Change snapping accuracy to suit your working style, and you'll have fewer surprises during layout.

Skill summary

In this lesson you learned how to:	Objective
Demonstrate knowledge of design elements and principles	**2.2**
Identify elements of the Flash interface	**3.1**
Use Flash guides and rulers	**3.5**

Knowledge Assessment

True/False

Circle **T** if the statement is true or **F** if the statement is false.

T F 1. By default, the Properties panel is in front of the Library.

T F 2. Most panels open as floating windows rather than being docked to other panels.

T F 3. Panels can be collapsed down to the point of only showing the icon that represents the panel.

T F 4. The workspaces that are built-in to Flash are the only ones you can use.

T F 5. Having multiple workspaces is very helpful for one person doing different types of projects or for multiple users who use the same machine.

T F 6. The maximum level of undos in Flash is 100.

T F 7. The more you increase the number of undo levels in Flash, the more it starts to slow down the performance of your computer.

T F 8. Bounding box colors in Flash are dictated by the layers the object is placed on, this cannot be changed.

T F 9. Flash includes shortcut sets from other programs such as Illustrator and Photoshop.

T F 10. The rulers for creating guides are found under the Edit menu.

Multiple Choice

Select the best response for the following statements.

1. Which panel is the Color panel grouped with when it's opened?
   a. Transform
   b. Properties
   c. Align
   d. Swatches

2. Which part of the panel should you click and drag on when you want to separate one panel from another?
   a. Bottom
   b. Title bar
   c. Left side
   d. Right side

3. If a panel is collapsed, what quick step is an easy way to open it back up again?

  a. Shift-click the title bar

  b. Shift-click the scroll bar

  c. Double-click the title bar

  d. Double-click the scroll bar

4. What is the color of the line indicator that shows up when dragging one panel on top of another?

  a. Yellow

  b. Blue

  c. Red

  d. Pink

5. Which of the following is not a workspace available in Flash?

  a. Animator

  b. Debug

  c. Classic

  d. Programmer

6. Which of the following is an available category in the Preferences?

  a. General

  b. Clipboard

  c. Warnings

  d. All of the above

7. What is the maximum number of undo levels in Flash?

  a. 100

  b. 5,000

  c. 300

  d. Infinite—as many as you want

8. If you change your Undo preferences in the middle of a project, what happens?

  a. Nothing, business as usual

  b. You will lose the history of the work you have done since you started

  c. A window opens asking you to save your preferences

  d. A warning dialog box opens asking if you are sure

9. Before you can customize keyboard shortcuts, what step should be taken first?

  a. Write down notes of your new shortcuts

  b. Export the current shortcuts

  c. Make a copy of the current set of shortcuts

  d. Open the Preferences

10. What type of file can be exported when exporting keyboard shortcuts?

  a. JPEG

  b. HTML

  c. .fla

  d. GIF

Competency Assessment

| Project 7-1 | **Playing with more preferences** |

There are a ton of different options in terms of how you can customize Flash and how it operates. These settings can even boil down to something as simple as the highlight color of an object when it's selected. There are several of these highlight colors that are kind of similar to each other, let's make them more distinctive.

1. Open Flash CS6 if it is not already running.

2. Choose Edit > Preferences (Windows) or Flash > Preferences if you are on a Mac.

3. From the General category go to the area that specifies Highlight color.

4. Try setting some different colors for the Highlight objects such as a red for Drawing objects. Choose darker colors that will contrast well against a white stage.

5. Create a new document. Create some shapes and symbols on the Stage. Note their highlight colors when you select them.

6. Save the file as **shapes**.

| Project 7-2 | **Printing shortcuts for reference** |

Given the vast amount of shortcuts throughout Flash, sometimes it's nice to have a printed list of shortcuts to reference.

1. Open Flash CS6 if it is not already running.

2. Choose Edit > Keyboard Shortcuts (Windows) or Flash > Keyboard Shortcuts if you are on a Mac.

3. Make sure your Current set is set to Adobe Standard.

4. Go to the buttons in the upper right corner of the Keyboard Shortcuts window and choose Export Set as HTML.

5. Save the file as **shortcuts.html**. Open the file in a web browser such as Internet Explorer or Firefox and print the file.

Proficiency Assessment

<table><tr><td>**More about guides**</td><td>**Project 7-3**</td></tr></table>

There's more to guides than meets the eye in Flash. You can change guide colors and snap accuracy from one window.

1. Create a new ActionScript 3.0 document in Flash.

2. Choose View > Guides > Edit Guides…

3. Alter the settings to your liking in the Guide dialog box.

<table><tr><td>**Aligning and Distributing on Stage**</td><td>**Project 7-4**</td></tr></table>

The Align panel is great for lining objects up next to each other, but it can also be used to place objects symmetrically on the Stage without the need for using a grid.

1. Create a new ActionScript 3.0 document in Flash.

2. Using the Oval tool in Object Drawing mode, draw a circle on the Stage and make 2 copies of it. Place them side by side horizontally.

3. Select all 3 circles and choose Window > Align. Select Align to stage. Use the Align Vertical Center button and the Distribute Horizontal Center button to place the circles automatically on the Stage.

4. Save the file as **align.fla**.

Working with Imported Files

Key Terms
- bitmap
- External Library
- still images

Skill	Objective
Import and modify graphics	**4.3**
Create animations (changes in shape, position, size, color, and transparency)	**4.10**

Business case

Your task in this assignment is to create a scary Halloween themed online card. Instead of creating the artwork yourself, you're being supplied artwork created by a different designer using Adobe Illustrator and Photoshop. There are some great tricks when it comes to importing and animating layered AI and PSD files that you'll explore as you create this project.

Starting up

Before starting, make sure that your tools and panels are consistent by resetting your workspace. See "Resetting the Flash workspace" in the Starting up section of this book.

You will work with several files from the fl08lessons folder in this lesson. Make sure that you have loaded the fl lessons folder onto your hard drive from *http://www.wiley.com/college/sc/adobeseries*. See "Loading lesson files" in the Starting up section of this book.

The project

In this lesson, you will work with a series of bitmap and vector images to practice importing and manipulating external files. First, you'll import a flat bitmap image and learn the techniques for modifying and updating it. Then, you'll move on to artwork in Adobe Photoshop and Illustrator native formats (.psd and .ai, respectively) to take advantage of Flash CS6's import features for these files.

Certification Ready 4.3

How do you import graphics?

Import formats

One of the strengths of Flash is its ability to import a wide variety of file formats. Flash can read and import a wide variety of common file types, including:

- Adobe Illustrator (.ai)
- Adobe Photoshop (.psd)
- Bitmap (.bmp)
- GIF and animated GIF (.gif)
- JPEG (.jpg)
- PNG (.png)
- Flash Player (.swf)

Adding the QuickTime Player plug-in (a free download for both Windows and Mac OS) adds the ability to import QTIF and TIFF images as well.

- For a full list of supported import (and export) file formats, refer to the Adobe knowledge base article located at *http://kb2.adobe.com/cps/402/kb402701.html*.

Import options

Flash offers four separate commands that enable you to import a variety of external media and control how they are treated once they're in Flash. Import to Stage, Import to Library, Open External Library, and Import Video all perform slightly different, but equally important, operations:

Import to Stage: Automatically places an instance of the imported file on the Flash Stage at the time of import.

Import to Library: Places the imported file in your library and allows you to manually place it onto the Flash Stage.

Open External Library: Allows you to open the library of any Flash file (.fla) and use its assets.

Import Video: Opens the Import Video wizard to walk you through the steps needed to bring your video files into Flash.

Take Note...
If you select a video file while in the Import dialog box for Import to Stage or Import to Library, Flash automatically opens the Import Video dialog box. The option you choose depends on how you want to work with Flash. Some users prefer to import everything into the library at once and then pull the content from there, while others prefer to import assets onto the Stage as they are needed.

Importing still images

Still images, such as photographs, scanned artwork, and graphics created in Photoshop, are some of the most common types of files that users want to bring into Flash. You can choose how to import images, and how you work with them once they are in Flash. Imported bitmap images can even be directly edited in an external application such as Fireworks or Photoshop. **Bitmaps** are one of two primary graphic file categories in which the file is composed of small squares or pixels.The images are then updated automatically without having to be reimported. Match the format to the content you'll be importing. Use JPEG images for photographs and GIF images for files with areas of solid color. PSD and AI are great native formats when importing source files from Illustrator and Photoshop.In the following exercises, you'll explore some of those choices.

<table>
<tr><td>**Certification Ready 4.3**

What are recommended graphic types to use when importing images to a Flash document?</td></tr>
</table>

Viewing the completed lesson file

<table><tr><td>**Follow these steps to review the finished file**</td><td>**Step-by-Step**</td></tr></table>

1. If you don't already have Flash Professional CS6 open, launch it now.

2. Choose File > Open and locate the file named **fl0801_done.fla** within the fl08lessons folder that you copied to your desktop. Press Open. This is the completed file that you will make in this lesson.

3. Choose Control > Test Movie > in Flash Professional to preview the final movie. Once you've taken a look, close the preview window and return the Flash CS6.

4. Keep the file open for reference, or close it by choosing File > Close.

Import a bitmap image

One of the easiest ways to import a bitmap image is with the Import to Stage command.

<table><tr><td>**Follow these steps to import a bitmap image**</td><td>**Step-by-Step**</td></tr></table>

1. Create a new Flash file by choosing File > New, or pressing Ctrl+N (Windows) or Command+N (Mac OS). When the New Document dialog box appears, choose ActionScript 3.0. Press OK.

2. Select File > Save As. In the Save As dialog box, navigate to the fl08lessons folder, and then type **fl0801_work.fla** into the Save As text field. Press Save.

3. As shown below in Figure 8-1, choose File > Import > Import to Stage to open the Import dialog box.

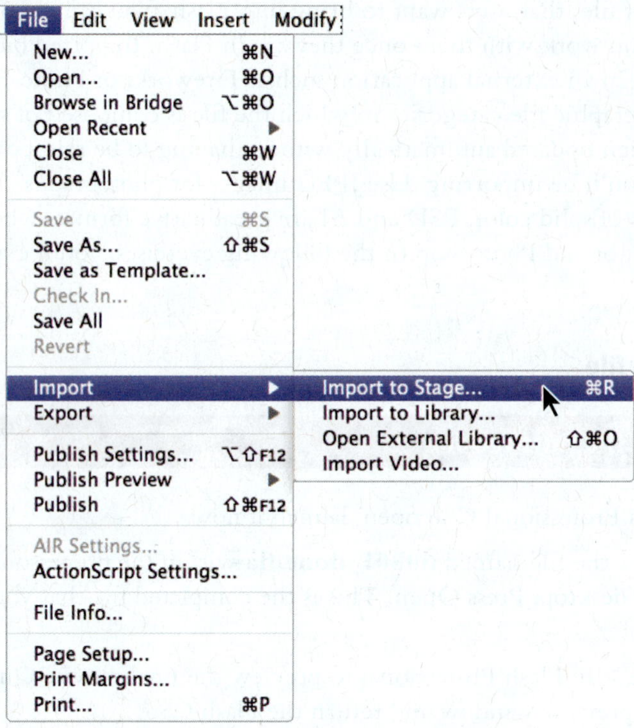

Figure 8-1: Import to Stage can be found under Import in the File menu.

Take Note...

The keyboard shortcut for Import to Stage is Ctrl+R (Windows) or Command+R (Mac OS).

4. In the Import dialog box, select the **fl0801.jpg** file from the fl08lessons folder. This is a black-and-white version of the final photo you will use as the background for this greeting card. Later you'll learn how to swap stand-in graphics for finalized artwork. Press Open.

5. Flash detects that the file you are trying to import may be a part of a sequence of images, and displays a dialog box asking if you want to import them all (Figure 8-2). Press No to import the selected image only.

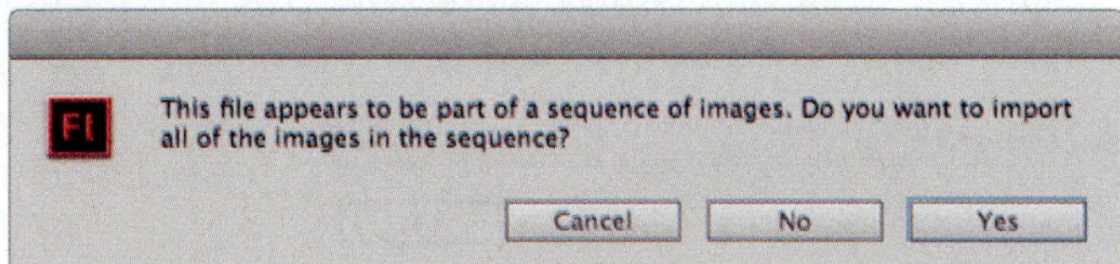

Figure 8-2: Flash detects a sequence of images in the folder containing fl0801.jpg.

Take Note...

When using Import to Stage, you can import individual still images or image sequences that have been manually created or exported from video editing and animation programs. If Flash detects that a sequence exists, it gives you the option to import the entire series of images. Flash can then place these images sequentially in consecutive frames on the Timeline.

The imported item appears in your Library panel, and Flash places an instance of it on the Stage as shown in Figure 8-3.

Figure 8-3: The library stores .jpg files as well as symbols.

Take Note...

The library doesn't store just symbols. All imported items, whether bitmap graphics, sound files, or video clips, appear in the Library panel.

6. Now that you have your stand-in image in Flash, you can begin to build the e-card around it. The graphic and the Stage are very different sizes, so the first order of business is to change the Stage to match the size of your image. Choose Modify > Document from the main menu. In the resulting Document Settings dialog box, type **600 px** in the (width) text field and **490 px** in the (height) text field (Figure 8–4). Press OK.

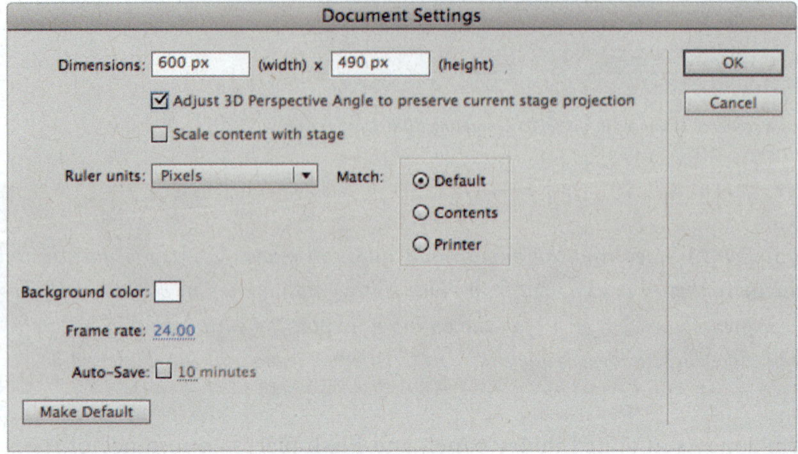

Figure 8–4: Change the dimensions of your document in the Document Properties dialog box.

7. Your image may not be centered on the Stage. To fix this, select the image with the Selection tool (↖). Choose Window > Align, or press the keyboard shortcut Ctrl+K (Windows) or Command+K (Mac OS), to open the Align panel.

8. Make sure the Align to Stage checkbox is selected (Figure 8–5) and select the Align horizontal center and Align vertical center buttons to center the image on the Stage.

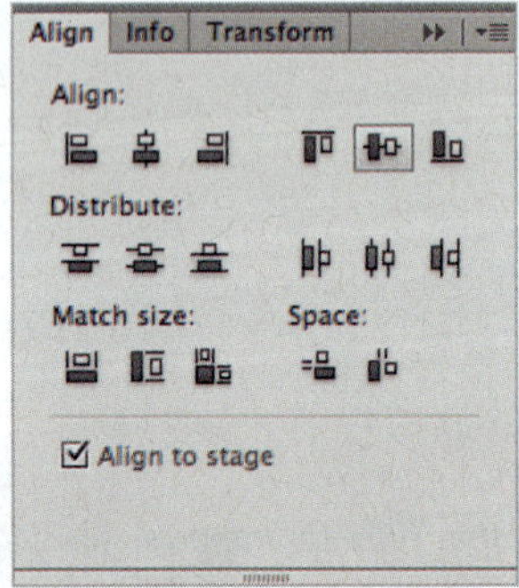

Figure 8–5: The Align panel allows you to align and distribute artwork on the Stage.

9. Choose File > Save to save your work.

Adding text

Flash CS6 allows you to animate text directly which provides for quicker editing of the text or the text can be converted to a symbol and animated as well. In the next section, you'll animate text from an imported Illustrator file.

Follow these steps to animate text from an imported Illustrator file

1. In the Timeline, double-click on Layer 1 to rename it **background**. It is always a good idea to change the default layer names to more descriptive names that help you identify content at a glance.

2. Click the space under the Lock or Unlock All layers button (🔒) to the right of the background text to lock this layer. This will make moving the rest of the objects you will use in this lesson much easier.

3. With the background layer selected, press the Insert Layer button (🗋) below the Timeline to add a new layer. Double-click on Layer 2 and rename it **text** as shown in Figure 8-6. This layer is where you will insert and animate the words Happy Halloween for your e-card.

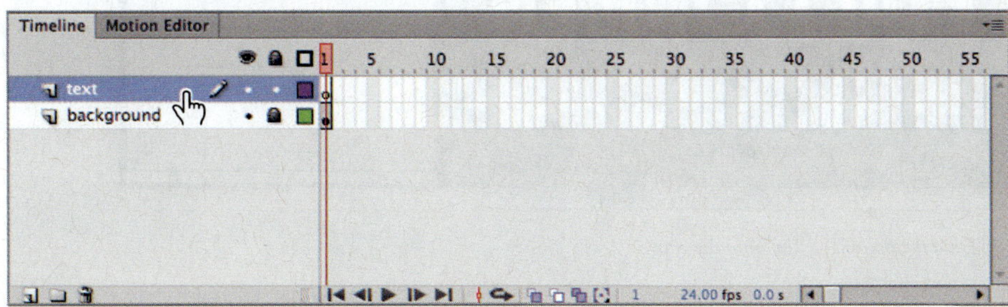

Figure 8-6: Layers can be renamed by double-clicking them.

The text you'll be using has been formatted, broken apart to a shape, and then saved as a movie clip. Flash provides a number of options for sharing symbols between .fla files. In this case, you'll use the Open **External Library** feature to access a movie clip that has been saved into the library of another file.

4. In the Timeline, select frame 1 of the text layer. Choose File > Import > Open External Library from the main menu. In the Open as Library dialog box, navigate to the **fl0801_library.fla** file located in the fl08lessons folder. Choose this file and press Open.

5. Drag the text movie clip from the external library onto the left side of the Stage, as shown in Figure 8-7. Afterwards, close the external library by clicking the X in the top-right corner (Windows) or the top-left corner (Mac OS) of the Library panel. It's important to realize that using symbols from an external library copies those symbols into your local library. After you copy them, it's good practice to close the external library to avoid confusion.

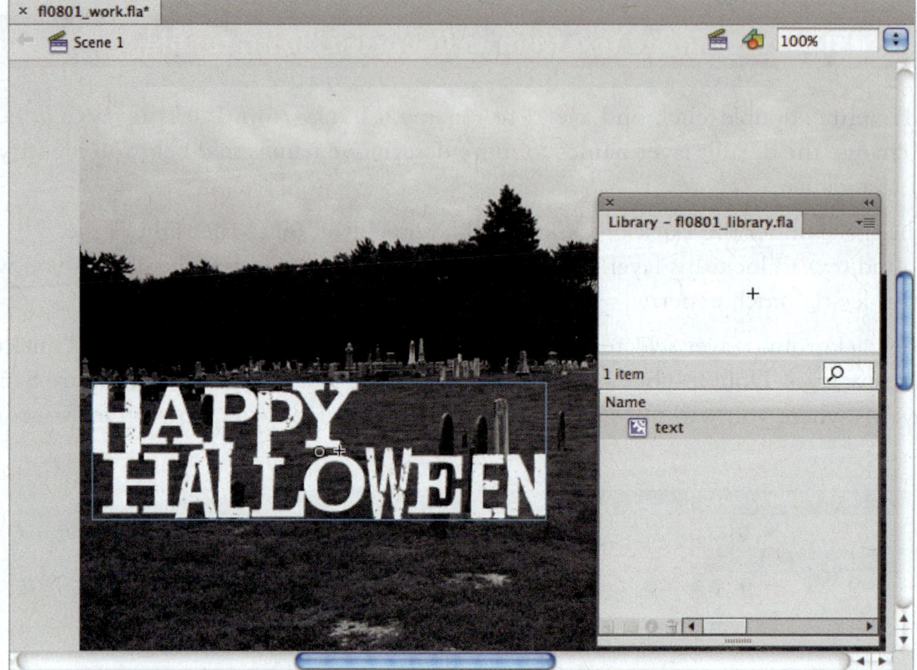

Figure 8-7: Drag the text movie clip onto the Stage.

6. Choose the Selection tool (⬆) from the Tools panel and select the text movie clip. In the Property Inspector, type **185** in the X text field and **265** in the Y text field to position the text to the left of the Stage.

Next you'll animate the text with a motion tween.

7. Right-click (Windows) or Ctrl+click (Mac OS) the Happy Halloween text movie clip. From the contextual menu, choose Create Motion Tween (Figure 8-8). The Stage appears to go blank, but try not to panic. Flash adds 23 frames to the text layer when you add a motion tween. You'll adjust this in a moment, and then extend frames on the background layer to make the white text visible again.

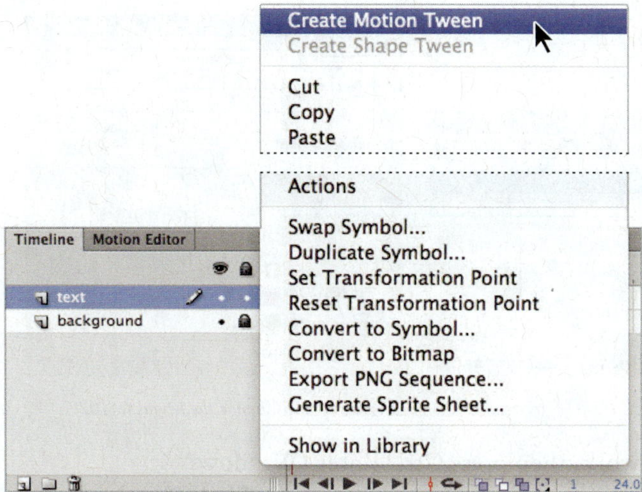

Figure 8-8: Choose Create Motion Tween from the contextual menu.

Take Note...
If you can't seem to get the contextual menu when you right-click (Windows)/Ctrl+click (Mac OS) on the text movie clip, make sure you're clicking on the letters. It's easy to click the background through the letters by mistake.

8. In the Timeline, scroll over to frame 120. Click on frame 120 of the text layer and choose Insert > Timeline > Frame to extend the text layer for 120 frames. Select frame 120 of the background layer and choose Insert > Timeline > Frame to extend this layer as well.

9. Now that you've got a little more room on the Timeline, click on frame 1 of the text layer. If you remember from previewing the finished file, this greeting card will feature text that shrinks down and snaps into place at the start of the animation.

10. Click on the Happy Halloween text movie clip. Make sure the Property Inspector is visible, and then make sure the link icon (∞) next to W and H is unlinked as shown in Figure 8-9. Type **800** in the H field and press Enter (Windows) or Return (Mac OS) to commit the change.

*Figure 8-8: Make sure the width and height are not locked together, and type **800** in the H field of the Property Inspector.*

11. Move the playhead to frame 15. Click on the Happy Halloween text movie clip on the Stage and then type **20** in the H text field of the Property Inspector.

12. Finally, move the playhead to frame 18 as shown in Figure 8-10, and with the Happy Halloween text movie clip still selected, set the H text field in the Property Inspector to **102.7** (Figure 8-11), which is the original height of the movie clip.

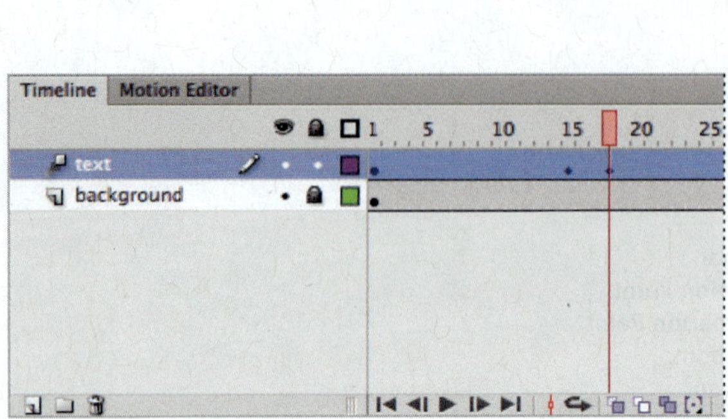

Figure 8-10: *Move the playhead to frame 18.*

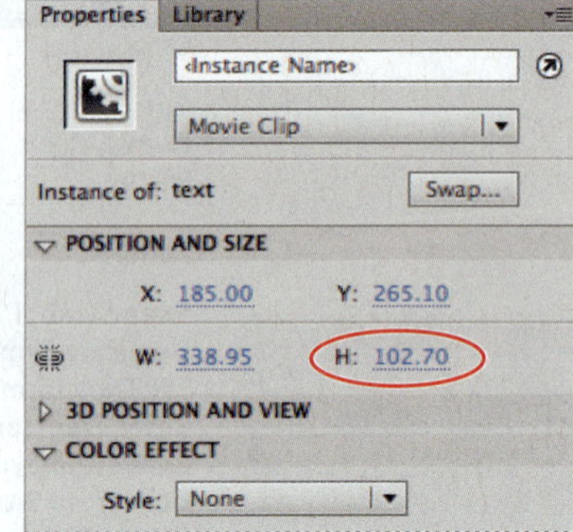

Figure 8-11: *Change the height to 102.7.*

13. Select File > Save to save your work, then press Ctrl+Enter (Windows) or Command+Return (Mac OS) to preview your animation in the Flash Player.

Swapping out an imported file

Certification Ready 4.3

What are some techniques to modify graphics?

The Library panel has the ability to replace one imported image with another. This is a very helpful feature when, for example, you want to use a stand-in image as a placeholder while the final artwork is still being developed.

Now you will swap out the basic image you imported from Photoshop with the image you will use in your final e-card.

Step-by-Step | **Follow these steps to replace one imported image with another**

1. Click the Library tab to bring the Library panel forward. Select the **fl0801.jpg** file in your Library panel and click the Properties button (●) at the bottom of the panel.

2. As shown in Figure 8-12, in the Bitmap Properties dialog box that appears, choose Import.

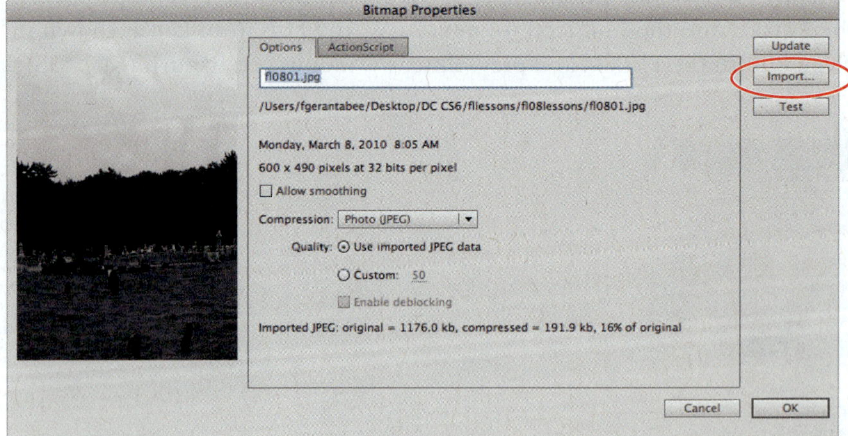

Figure 8-12: *Use the Import button to swap the selected target file for another image.*

3. In the Import Bitmap dialog box, select **fl0802.jpg** from the fl08lessons folder and press Open.

4. In the Bitmap Properties dialog box, press OK. As shown in Figure 8-13, the new image replaces the original **fl0801.jpg** wherever it occurs in your project.

Figure 8-13: A color-tinted image replaces the black and white image on the Stage.

5. Choose File > Save to save your work.

Modifying imported artwork

One of the advantages of working in Flash is that you can easily modify imported artwork using an external editor, and have the changes take effect in Flash. When you want to modify imported artwork, Flash gives you the option of opening the external editor directly from the Library panel. In this exercise, you will use Adobe Photoshop CS6. If you do not currently have Photoshop CS6 installed, you can download a trial version from *adobe.com,* or you can skip this step and jump ahead to the next exercise in this lesson.

Certification Ready 4.3

How do you trace a bitmap graphic?

Follow these steps to modify imported artwork

Step-by-Step

1. If necessary, open your Library panel by choosing Window > Library. Right-click (Windows) or Ctrl+click (Mac OS) on the **fl0801.jpg** file shown in the Library panel.

2. From the contextual menu that appears, choose Edit with (Figure 8-14).

    If Flash recognizes that you have Adobe Photoshop installed, then Edit with Photoshop appears above the Edit with option. You can use Adobe Photoshop to edit any standard bitmap image.

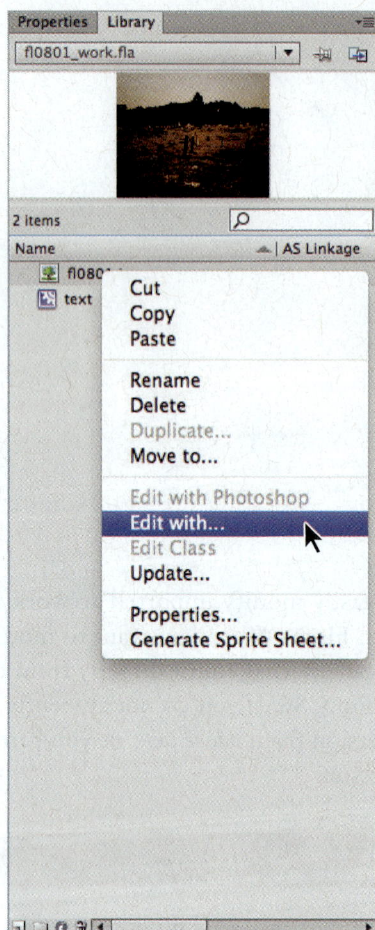

Figure 8-14: Right-click (Windows) or Ctrl+click (Mac OS) to use Edit with.

3. If necessary, from the Select External Editor dialog box that appears, navigate to the Photoshop CS6 application and press Open. The file open in Photoshop (Figure 8-15).

Figure 8-15: *Photoshop CS6 allows users to create and manipulate artwork.*

Take Note...
Except when using Photoshop, Adobe Flash Professional CS6 requires that you browse for your image editing application each time you want to edit a file.

4. In Photoshop, select Image > Adjustments > Curves to open the Curves dialog box. In Photoshop, curves are used to adjust the shadows, mid-tones, and highlights of an image. You will use curves here to darken the image to make it a little spookier.

5. Place your cursor at the middle point of the diagonal line, then click and drag down to create an arc (Figure 8-16). As you drag the curve deeper, the image becomes darker. Adjust the curve to your liking, remembering that you want it to look spooky but not so dark that you can no longer make out the image's details. Press OK.

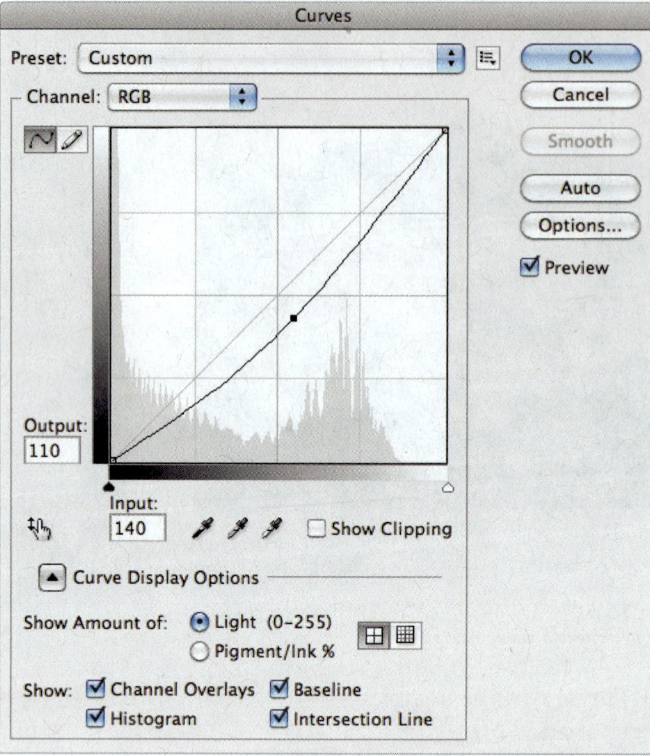

Figure 8-16: Make the image darker by adjusting the curves as shown here.

6. Select File > Save. If the JPEG Options dialog box appears, click OK to accept the default settings and choose File > Close to close the image. Choose File > Exit to close Photoshop. Return to Flash. Your image has been updated automatically.

7. In Flash, select File > Save. Do not close this file.

Take Note...
Bitmap images can be converted to shapes easily by choosing Modify > Break Apart. In addition, you can choose Modify > Bitmap > Trace Bitmap to convert the image to vector and control the appearance of the converted image.

Updating imported files

What if you forget to use Edit with, and you simply open Photoshop (or another external editor) and modify previously imported images? You may want to update those files in the Flash library without the time and trouble of reimporting them. Flash offers an easy solution.

<table>
<tr><td>Follow these steps to update imported files</td><td>Step-by-Step</td></tr>
</table>

1. Select the **fl0801.jpg** file in the Library panel.

2. Press the Properties button (◉) at the bottom of the Library panel to open the Bitmap Properties dialog box.

3. In the Bitmap Properties dialog box, press Update as shown in Figure 8-17. Changes you made to the imported image outside of Flash now become visible.

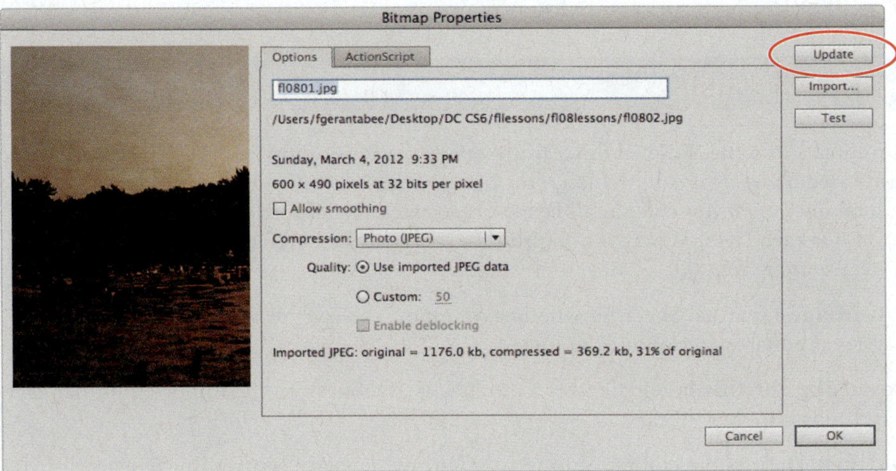

Figure 8-17: The Update button refreshes images modified in external editors.

4. Press OK to exit the Bitmap Properties dialog box. Keep this file open for the next part of this lesson.

Importing Photoshop files

In addition to importing standard bitmap image formats, Flash offers native import of Photoshop .psd files. This means you can import layered Photoshop files (including full support for Layer Comps), and choose which layers to import and how to treat each one as it's placed in Flash.

Importing a layered Photoshop file

To see how these settings work, import a layered .psd file:

Step-by-Step	Follow these steps to import a layered Photoshop file

1. With **fl0801_work.fla** still open, choose File > Import > Import to Library.

2. In the Import to Library dialog box, select **fl0803.psd** from the fl08lessons folder and press Open. The PSD Import Options dialog box opens.

Learning More	Photoshop import options

When you import a .psd file, Flash automatically opens the Photoshop Import dialog box, which is divided into two main areas: On the left, you choose which layers to bring into Flash from your Photoshop document (by default, all layers are selected for import). On the right, you set the import options for each layer. When you highlight a layer on the left, its options appear on the right. The layer options are:

Import this image layer as: Specifies whether to import the layer as a flat bitmap image or with layer styles as editable sections of the image.

Create movie clip for this layer: Creates a movie clip symbol from the imported bitmap layer at import, and adds it to your library.

Publish settings: Defines the compression setting with which each bitmap image is published. Flash uses two types of compression: the Lossy setting, which applies JPEG compression, and Lossless, which applies PNG compression. By default, the compression setting is the same setting as in your Flash file's Publish settings.

3. In the PSD Import dialog box, uncheck the checkbox next to the layer named sky_bg. Because you are importing this Photoshop document into a Flash movie, you do not need the background layer.

4. Shift+click on the three remaining layers: moon_highlights, moonshadows, and moon_base (Figure 8-18).

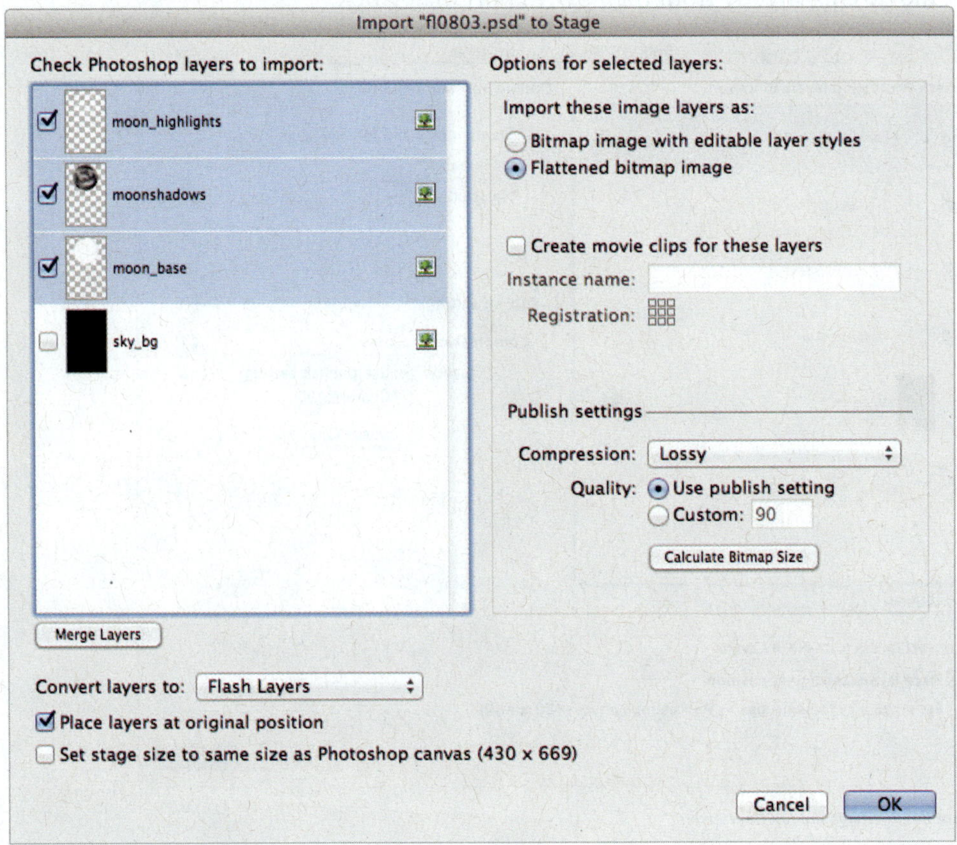

Figure 8-18: Select all three layers.

5. Click the Merge Layers button at the bottom of the list of layers as shown in Figure 8-19. This allows Flash to treat all three layers as if they were one. You will use this to create a new movie clip directly from the PSD Import dialog box.

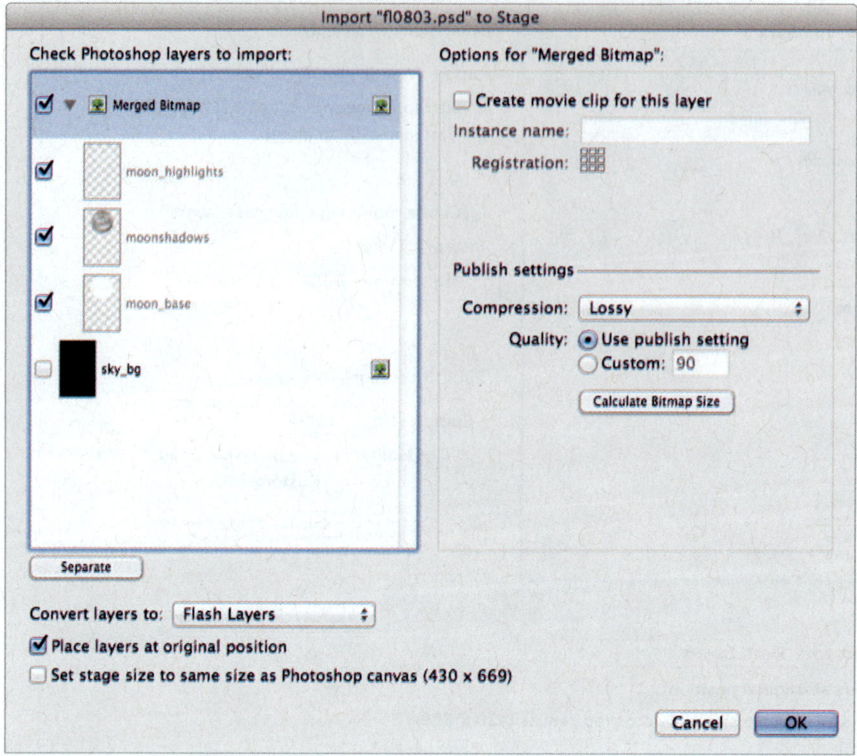

Figure 8-19: *Merge the top three layers.*

Take Note...
Selecting multiple layers is a great way to apply the same operation to all layers at once, or to merge layers into one object within the Flash environment.

6. Double-click on the name of the new Merged Bitmap layer and rename it **Moon**.

7. With the Moon layer selected, select the checkbox next to Create movie clip for this layer as shown in Figure 8-20. Center the movie clip's registration point. Leave all other settings as you find them, and press OK.

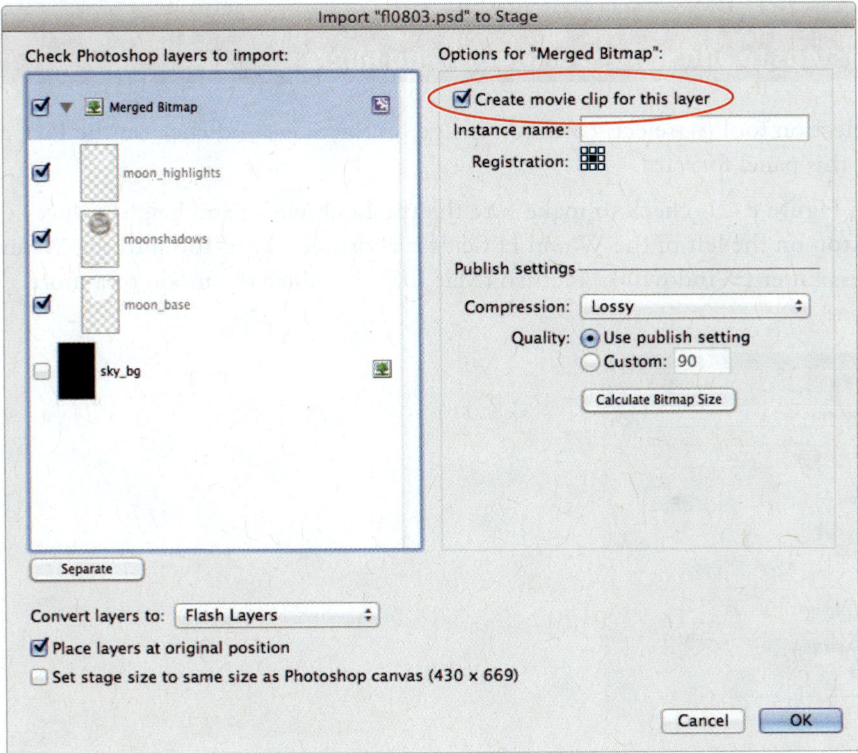

Figure 8-20: Select the Create movie clip for this layer checkbox and center the registration point.

8. You now have two new items in the library: a graphic symbol named **fl0803.psd** and a folder named **fl0803.psd** Assets. The graphic symbol contains all the objects that were in the Photoshop file in their original positions and their relation to each other, while the folder contains the individual imported bitmap layers (located in the Assets sub-folder) and the movie clips created during import.

In the Library panel, double-click on the **fl0803.psd** Assets folder to open it.

9. Click on the Insert Layer button (⊒) below the Timeline to create a new layer. Double-click on the layer name and rename it **moon**. Select the first frame of the new moon layer.

10. Drag the Moon movie clip symbol from the **fl0803.psd** Assets folder within the Library panel to the Stage. Do not worry about where you place it; you will deal with that in a few moments.

11. Right-click (Windows) or Control+click (Mac OS) on frame 1 of the moon layer and choose Create Motion Tween from the contextual menu. You'll use this tween to animate a filter applied to the moon.

Working with the Moon

Once a PSD has been placed into Flash, it can be edited like any natively created content. In addition, Flash has a variety of built-in filters that can be used to add style to your artwork.

<table><tr><td>**Step-by-Step**</td><td>**Follow these steps to add style to artwork using filters**</td></tr></table>

1. With the Selection tool (⬉), select the moon image on the Stage and click on the Properties tab to bring this panel forward.

2. As shown in Figure 8–21, check to make sure the the Lock width and height values together button on the left of the W and H fields is activated. Type **100** into the W text field and press Enter (Windows) or Return (Mac OS) to reduce the moon to a more reasonable size.

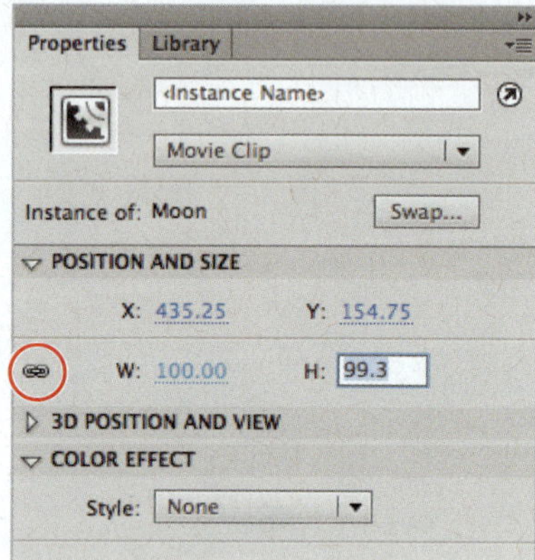

Figure 8–21: Use the Property Inspector to resize the moon.

3. In the Property Inspector, change the X position of the moon to **530** and the Y position to **65**. This positions it in the upper-right corner of the Stage.

4. With the moon still selected, expand the Display options in the Property Inspector and choose Hard Light from the Blending drop-down menu (Figure 8–22). You may be familiar with Blend modes from Photoshop. They're very similar in Flash.

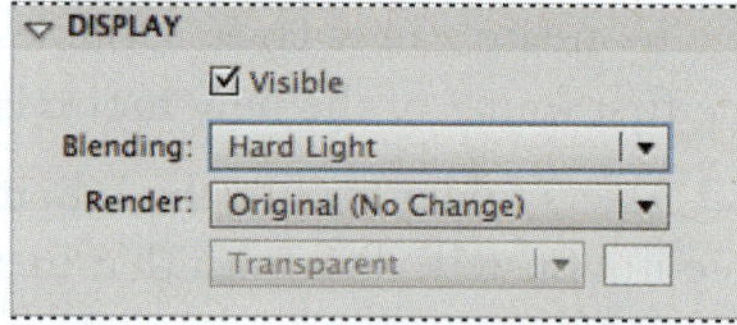

Figure 8–22: Choose Hard Light from the Blending drop-down menu.

5. With the moon still selected, click the Add Filter button (⬚) at the bottom of the Filters section of the Property Inspector. Choose Glow from the resulting menu. The default red filter is a bit too spooky even for this project. Select white for the color, and set the Blur X and Blur Y values to **100** as shown in Figure 8-23.

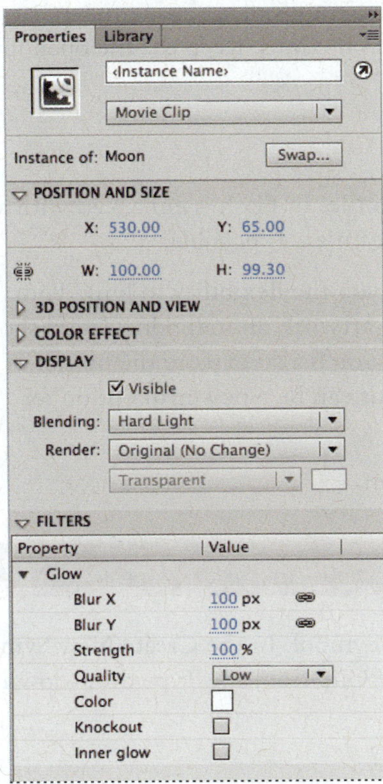

Figure 8-23: Setting up the glow for the moon graphic in the Filters panel.

6. A glowing moon is nice, but you could have done that in Photoshop just as easily. Fortunately, in the previous exercise, you created a motion tween for this moon. Let's put it to good use in the next step.

7. Choose frame 60 of the moon layer, and click on the moon to access the Filter options in the Property Inspector. As shown in Figure 8-24, type **250** in the Strength field.

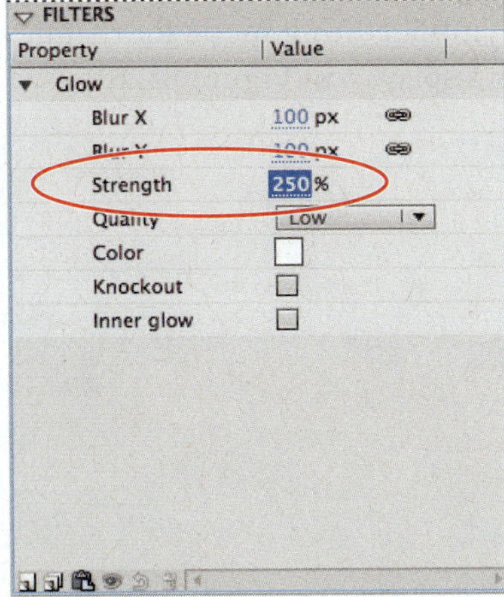

Figure 8-24: Change the Filter setting to animate the moon's glow.

8. Choose frame 120 of the moon layer, select the moon, and then type **100** in the Strength field you adjusted in the last step. This creates a loop where the glow gets more intense between frames 1 and 60 and then returns to its original strength on frame 120.

9. Choose Control > Test Movie > in Flash Professional to preview your Flash animation, then choose File > Save. The moon animation is subtle, but it's those little things that make your animation seem interesting without being obnoxious. Keep the file open for the next part of this lesson.

Importing Illustrator artwork

As with .psd files, importing and using native Illustrator .ai files in Flash is enhanced with a variety of features to make integration with Illustrator as seamless as possible.

Import options available in the AI Import dialog box give you the flexibility to build your layered projects in Illustrator, and then determine how the artwork on individual layers should be handled on import. In the following part of this lesson, you'll also explore the option of mapping Illustrator layers to keyframes in a movie clip. This can be a powerful option for quickly building frame-by-frame animations.

Let's import an Illustrator file to see these features in action:

Step-by-Step	**Follow these steps to import an Illustrator file**

1. With **fl0801_work.fla** still open, select Insert > New Symbol. In the Create New Symbol dialog box, rename the symbol **bat**, and choose Movie Clip from the Type drop-down menu (Figure 8-25). Press OK.

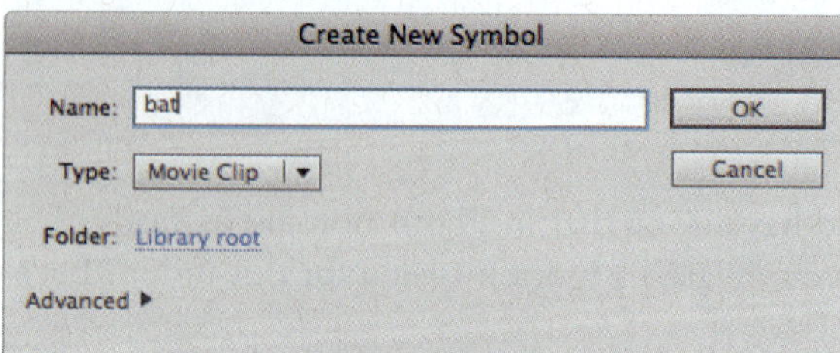

Figure 8-25: Create a new symbol named bat.

2. Don't be alarmed by the blank Stage. You may remember from Lesson 5 that creating a new symbol from scratch automatically places you in symbol editing mode for that new symbol. Notice the indication in the Navigation bar as displayed in Figure 8-26.

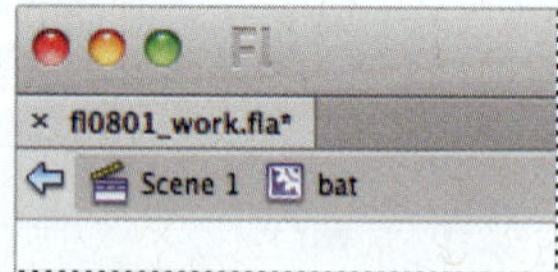

Figure 8-26: The Navigation bar indicates that you are editing your new bat movie clip.

3. Choose File > Import > Import to Stage.

4. In the Import dialog box, select **fl0804.ai** from the fl08lessons folder and press Open.

The AI Import dialog box opens with each layer and sub-layer of your Illustrator document represented. As you can see in Figure 8-27, the AI Import dialog box is divided into two main areas. On the left you select the layers or sub-layers you want to import, and on the right you specify the options for how Flash treats each layer.

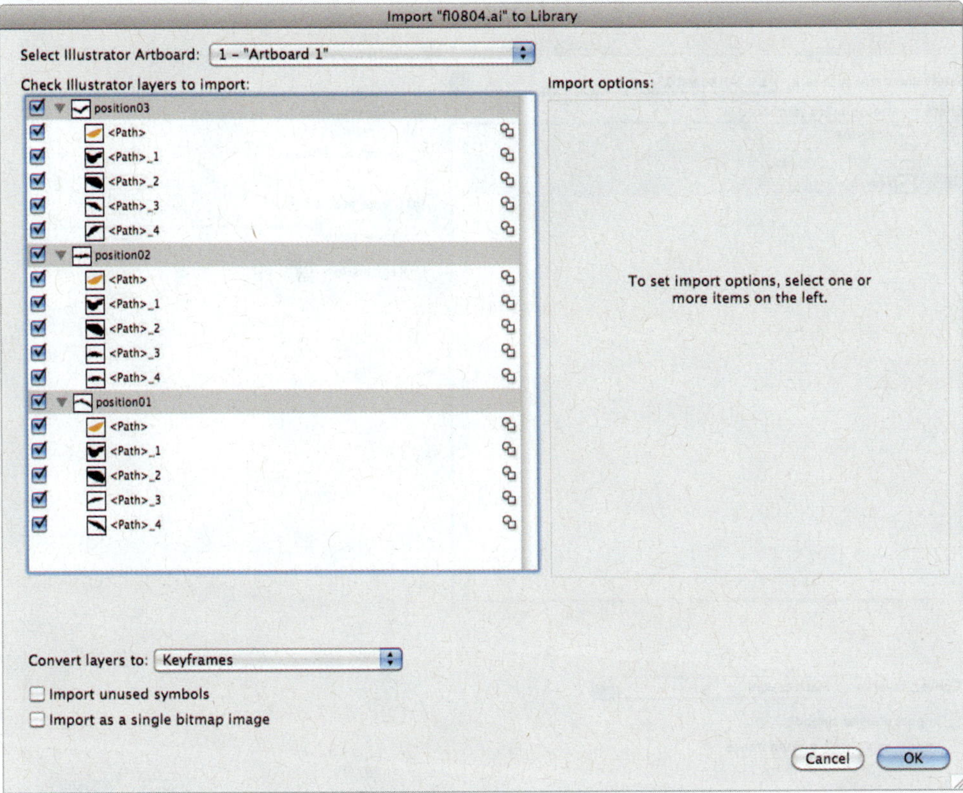

Figure 8-27: Every layer and sub-layer in your Illustrator file is visible in the Import dialog box.

5. To make viewing more manageable, collapse all the sub-layers by clicking the triangle icon to the left of the following three layer names: position03, position02, and position01.

Take Note...
To easily collapse or expand all layers at once, right-click (Windows) or Ctrl+click (Mac OS) inside the layer view on the left side of the dialog box and choose Collapse All/Expand All from the contextual menu that appears.

6. Select the Illustrator layer named position01. On the right, click the checkbox next to Create movie clip, and choose a centered registration point (Figure 8-28).

Take Note...

Setting the registration point of a movie clip is very important. The registration point determines how a movie clip is scaled, rotated, or otherwise transformed.

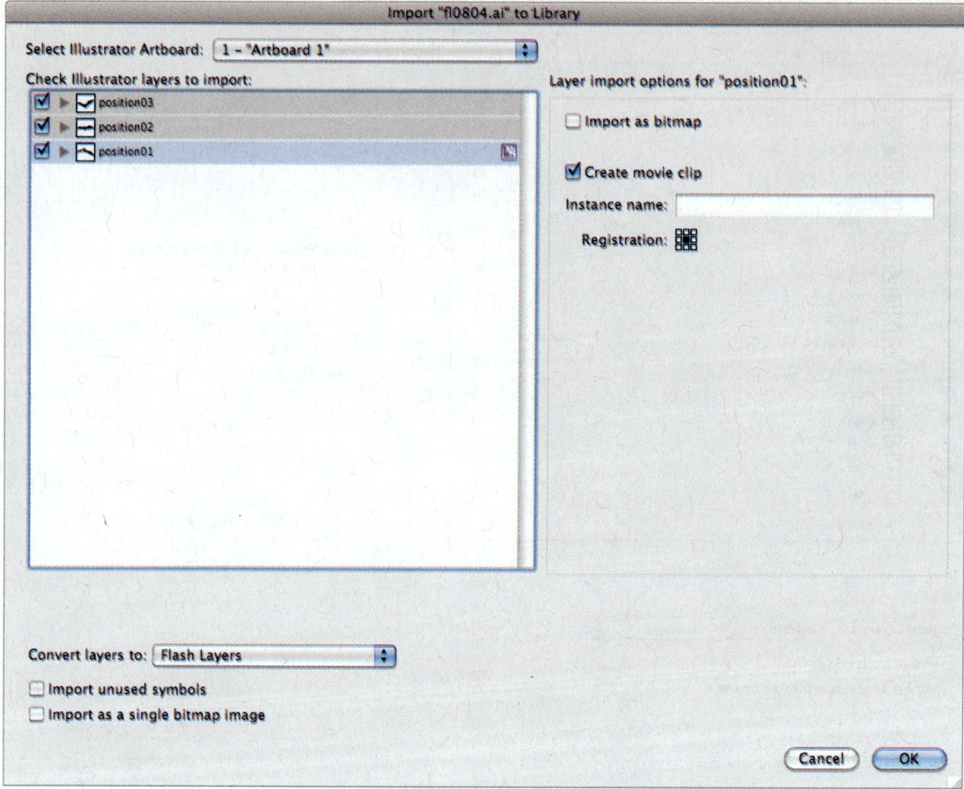

Figure 8-28: Convert primary layers to movie clips.

7. Repeat step 6 for the layers named position02 and position03.

Learning More

What's in an instance name?

When you import the contents of a layer as a movie clip, you have the option to specify an instance name. Instance names are used by ActionScript (Flash's built-in scripting language) to programmatically manipulate and animate movie clip instances on the Stage. This name serves as a unique identifier that ActionScript can use to target a specific movie clip instance on the Stage. Instance names for a movie clip instance can be set at any time from the Property Inspector.

8. At the bottom-left area of the dialog box, click on the Convert layers to drop-down menu and choose Keyframes. This imports each individual Illustrator layer as a separate keyframe. Because you used the Import to Stage command here, each keyframe is positioned on your movie clip's Timeline, providing you with a ready-made animation straight from Illustrator.

More Illustrator import options

The AI Import dialog box offers three additional options:

Import as bitmap: Converts vector artwork from Illustrator into a bitmap image on import.

Import as a single bitmap image: Converts all vector Illustrator layers into a single bitmap image on import.

Import unused symbols: Imports any unused objects from the Illustrator symbols panel into Flash.

9. Press OK to import the Illustrator file. As shown in Figure 8-29, the Illustrator layers should now occupy the first three frames of the bat Timeline.

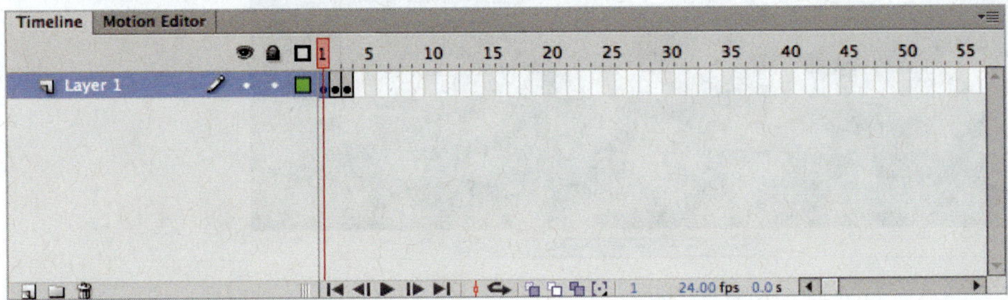

Figure 8-29: The Timeline now shows three keyframes for each layer added to the Stage.

10. Select the Scene 1 link on the Navigation bar above the Stage to return to the main Timeline. Click on the moon layer, and press the Insert Layer button (⊐) on the Timeline to insert a new layer. Double-click the new layer name and rename it **bat**.

11. Drag an instance of the bat movie clip onto the Stage from the Library panel. Don't worry about the position of the movie clip just yet.

12. Choose File > Save to save your work.

Animating the bat

Movie clips can be animated using basic motion tweens, just as the Happy Halloween text was animated.

Follow these steps to animate graphics using motion tweens

1. Select frame 1 of the bat layer. With the Selection tool (↖), select the instance of the bat movie clip that is on the Stage. Right-click (Windows) or Ctrl+click (Mac OS) and choose Create motion tween.

2. Bring the Property Inspector forward by clicking on its tab. Make sure that the link next to W and H is set to constrain proportions. Type **200** in the W field to size the bat down.

3. Set the X position to **600** and the Y position to **0**. The bat will start offstage, and then fly onto the scene after the text animation finishes.

4. Hover over the first frame of the bat layer in the Timeline. When your cursor turns into a double-headed arrow, click and drag the beginning of the bat animation to frame 20. Now that you've given the viewer some time to read the text, you can animate the bat.

5. Select frame 60 of the bat layer. Using your Selection tool, drag the bat to the center of the Stage (Figure 8-30). Switch to the Free Transform tool (⬚) and resize the bat as shown below.

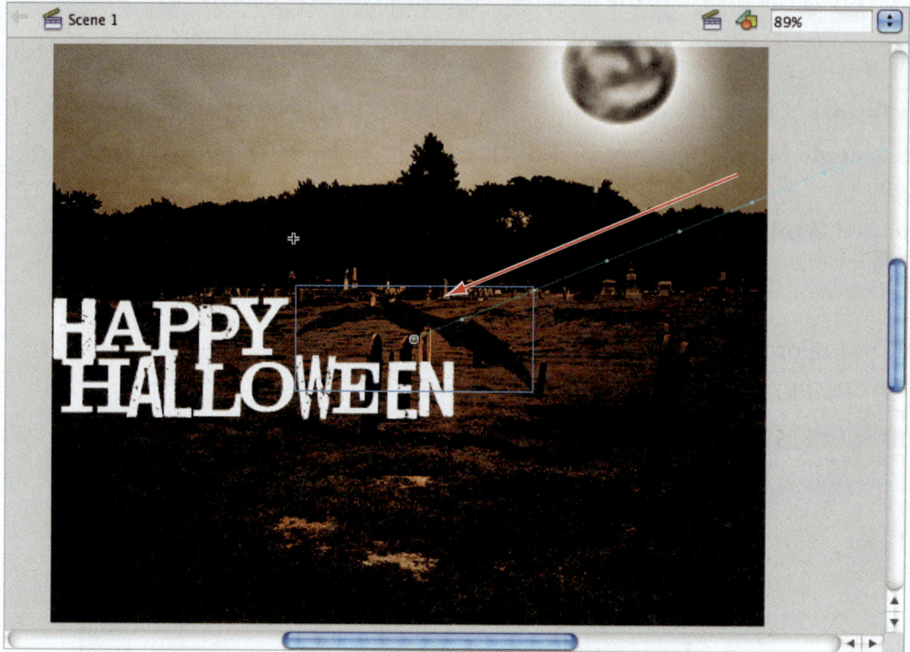

Figure 8-30: Move the bat to the center of the Stage.

6. Select the Free Transform tool, and hover over the corner of the bat movie clip until the cursor turns into a diagonal two-headed arrow. Hold down the Shift key to constrain proportions and drag toward the center of the bat movie clip to size it down as shown in Figure 8-31. When the animation is finished, this will give the appearance of the bat flying away from the viewer.

Figure 8-31: Resize the bat with the Free Transform tool.

7. Select frame 120 of the bat layer. Drag the bat off the Stage, and then size it up with the Free Transform tool as shown in Figure 8-32.

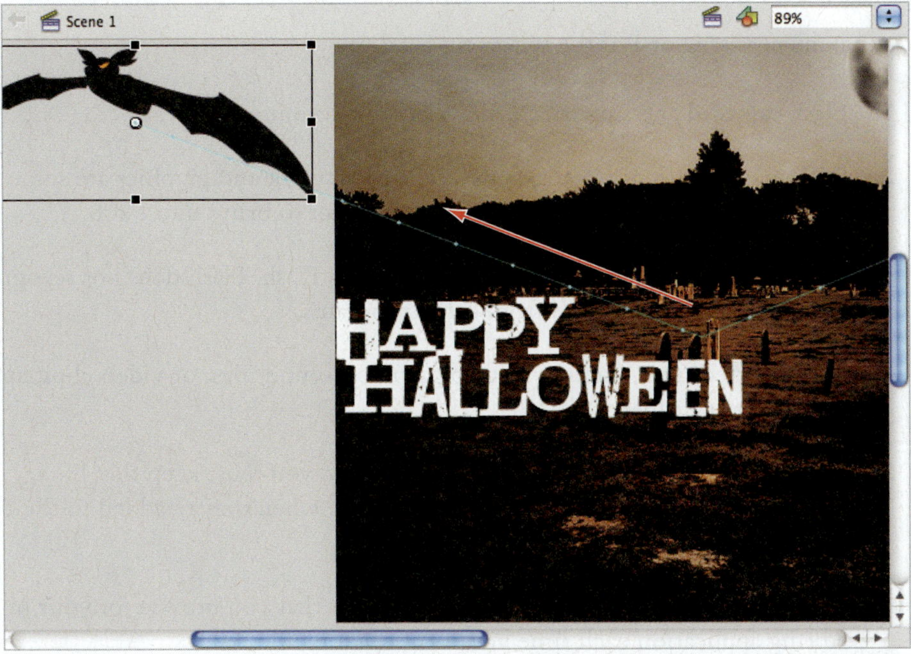

Figure 8-32: Reposition and resize the bat again to complete the animation.

8. Choose File > Save to save your work. Choose Control > Test Movie in Flash Professional to preview your Flash animation. The bat will swoop across the screen. It will appear to fly away from the viewer for the first half of the animation, and toward the viewer during the second half.

If you think the bat is moving a bit more gracefully than bats frequently do, feel free to add a few more positions inside that motion tween. In addition to scaling the bat, the Free Transform tool makes it easy to rotate the bat to put some pretty wacky daredevil flying into your animation.

Congratulations! You have finished the lesson. Choose File > Close.

Skill summary

In this lesson you learned how to:	Objective
Import and modify graphics	**4.3**
Create animations (changes in shape, position, size, color, and transparency)	**4.10**

Knowledge Assessment

True/False

Circle **T** if the statement is true or **F** if the statement is false.

T   F   1. Flash can read and import a wide variety of common file types.

T   F   2. Still images, such as photographs, scanned artwork and graphics are some of the most common types of files that users want to bring into Flash.

T   F   3. Only individual images can be imported into Flash. Flash does not recognize image sequences exported from other programs.

T   F   4. All imported files, whether bitmap graphics, sound files, or video clips, appear in the Library panel.

T   F   5. When using symbols from an external library, you must keep that library open since no copies of the symbols are made when they're added to the Stage from the external library.

T   F   6. Except when using Photoshop, Flash requires that you browse for your image editing application each time you want to edit a file.

T   F   7. Layered Photoshop files must first be flattened before importing the .psd into Flash.

T   F   8. Flash cannot flatten images during import, flattening must occur before the image is imported into Flash.

T   F   9. Flash includes Blend modes like those found in Photoshop.

T   F   10. When importing an Illustrator file, layers can be converted into keyframes.

Multiple Choice

Select the best response for the following statements.

1. Which of the following file types can be imported into Flash?
   a. Bitmap
   b. Animated GIF
   c. Flash Player
   d. All of the above

2. Which plug-in allows you to import QTIF and TIFF images?
   a. Windows Media
   b. Flash Player
   c. QuickTime
   d. Shockwave

3. Among the choices below, which one is not an import option?

   a. Import to Stage
   b. Import to Folder
   c. Open External Library
   d. Import Video

4. Which menu allows you access to the Document Settings window?

   a. Edit
   b. View
   c. Modify
   d. File

5. Which command from the Library panel allows you to open a file in an external program to make changes to it?

   a. Update...
   b. Move to...
   c. Edit with...
   d. Properties...

6. When you import a .psd file, which of the following options is not a choice in the Photoshop Import dialog box?

   a. Import this image layer as
   b. Automatically break apart
   c. Publish settings
   d. Create movie clip for this layer

7. At the bottom of which panel are the Filters available in Flash?

   a. Properties
   b. Library
   c. Transform
   d. Color

8. What serves as a unique identifier that ActionScript can use to target a specific movie clip instance on the Stage?

   a. ActionScript contained within the movie clip
   b. The keyframe the symbol is placed on
   c. The instance name established in the Property Inspector
   d. None of the above, this isn't a function

9. Of the options listed below, which one converts all vector Illustrator layers into a single bitmap image on import?

   a. Import as bitmap
   b. Import as a single bitmap image
   c. Import unused symbols
   d. None of the above

10. To animate an object automatically by converting layers to keyframes, you must first:

   a. Adjust the position of each object being animated so it simulates animation when converted to keyframes
   b. Flatten the image and then break it apart
   c. Make duplicates in Flash and then animate accordingly
   d. Use motion tweens

Competency Assessment

| Project 8-1 | Reverse cropping |

Merging bitmaps is a helpful way to manage images you'd like to merge. But what about controlling bitmap layers as separate images for the sake of animation and control?

1. Create a new ActionScript 3.0 document in Flash.

2. Choose File > Import > Import to Library.

3. In the Import to Library dialog box, select the **fl0803.psd** you used earlier from the fl08lessons folder and press Open. The PSD Import Options dialog box.

4. Select the checkmark button for each of the layers in the dialog box.

5. Choose Bitmap image with editable layer styles and Create movie clips for these layers, then select OK.

6. Animate the layers in different ways to take advantage of each layer being designated as a separate, controllable image.

7. Save the file as **psd_import.fla**.

| Project 8-2 | Importer preferences |

As you've experienced, Flash offers some pretty great options when importing native PSD or AI files. Maybe you have a consistent way you'd like to import these files but that's not the default. You don't have to choose individual settings every time if you play with the preferences a little...

1. Open Flash CS6.

2. Choose Edit > Preferences on Windows or Flash > Preferences on the Mac.

3. Go to the PSD File Importer category and alter the settings to your specifications. Do the same for the AI File Importer as appropriate.

Proficiency Assessment

<table>
<tr><td>**Swapping Symbols**</td><td>**Project 8-3**</td></tr>
</table>

The Swap feature in the Properties panel is another way to change images on the Stage without having to delete and re-position.

1. Create a new ActionScript 3.0 document in Flash.

2. Create 2 different movie clip symbols, one a blue square, one a red circle. Place numerous instances of the square on the Stage. Practice changing out the squares with the circles by selecting a square on the Stage and clicking the Swap button in the Properties panel.

3. Save the file as **swapping.fla** and keep the file open for the next part of the exercise.

<table>
<tr><td>**Another place instance names show up**</td><td>**Project 8-4**</td></tr>
</table>

Instance names are important when it comes to connecting ActionScript to symbols. There is another panel that can help you keep track of what instance is where and where your connections are going.

1. Make sure that the **swapping.fla** file from the last exercise is still open.

2. Using the Selection tool, click on a circle symbol on the Stage. Go to the Properties panel and add the name **circle_mc** in the Instance name field.

3. Go to Window > Movie Explorer and take note of the information.

4. Save the file as **instances.fla**.

Introducing ActionScript

Key Terms

- actions
- Actions panel
- ActionScript
- Code Snippets
- functions
- Script Assist
- stop()

Skill	Objective
Add simple controls through ActionScript 3.0	**4.11**

Business case

Animation is only the tip of the iceberg in terms of using Flash to its full capabilities. Learning ActionScript becomes really important when you want to take what you can do with Flash up a notch. Controlling objects and animation using ActionScript are just a couple of the many ways you can take advantage of the powerful code that's available within Flash.

Starting up

Before starting, make sure that your tools and panels are consistent by resetting your workspace. See "Resetting the Flash workspace" in the Starting up section of this book.

You will work with several files from the fl09lessons folder in this lesson. Make sure that you have loaded the fllessons folder onto your hard drive from *http://www.wiley.com/college/sc/adobeseries*. See "Loading lesson files" in the Starting up section of this book.

The project

You will learn how to stop, play, and loop an animation, using ActionScript to control the Timeline. To view the finished file, Choose File > Open and select the **fl0901_done.fla** file from within the fl09lessons folder. Choose Control > Test Movie > in Flash Professional to see how the finished movie behaves (Figure 9-1). Close the preview, and then close the file when you are finished, or keep the original FLA open as a reference if you'd like.

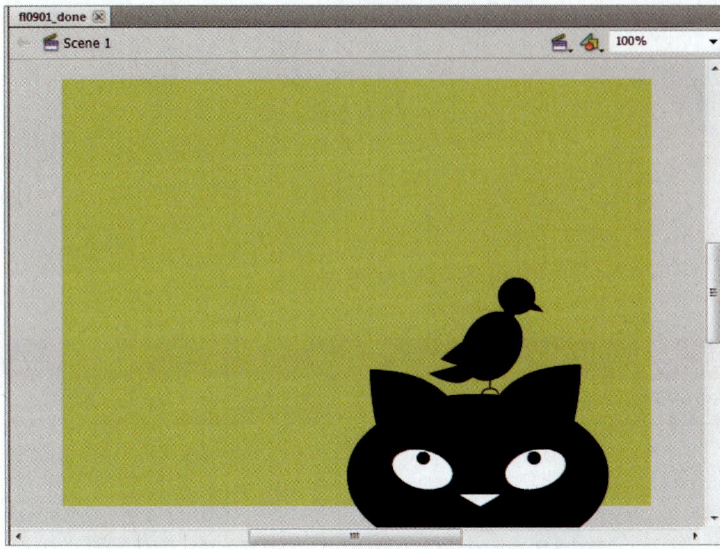

Figure 9-1: The finished file.

Exploring the lesson file

The lesson file features animation of a bird hopping across the Stage and onto the head of a cat. The scene is rife with tension. The bird animation uses the same techniques you explored in Lessons 5 and 6. In this lesson, you'll be using ActionScript to adjust the flow of this animation by starting and stopping the Timeline. While it would be possible to achieve a similar result with additional movie clips and a more complex Timeline, ActionScript allows you to streamline the process. Also, using ActionScript will increase the flexibility of your finished file and, in certain cases, decrease the size of your published movie.

<table>
<tr><td>**Step-by-Step**</td><td>**Follow these steps to open the project file**</td></tr>
</table>

1. Choose File > Open, and navigate to the fl09lessons folder.

2. Select the file named **fl0901.fla** and press Open.

3. Before you get started, choose File > Save As, type **fl0901_work.fla** in the Save As text field, navigate to the fl09lessons folder, and press Save.

4. Leave the file open, as you'll be using it in the next exercise.

What is ActionScript?

ActionScript is Flash's built-in object-oriented, scripting language and your way of sending instructions to the Flash Player and exerting more control over your movie. Using Flash's **Actions panel**, you can create and place lines of ActionScript code (often referred to as *actions*), in keyframes on the Timeline, or in external files. This code is interpreted and carried out by the Flash Player during playback. If the idea of typing code seems a little overwhelming, don't worry; you can use the Actions panel's Script Assist mode or the handy Code Snippets panel to help you create your first lines of code.

At its most basic level, ActionScript can control the playhead to fine-tune the behavior of animations or enable user controls for navigation of the Timeline (such as Stop and Play buttons). Beyond this, ActionScript is a powerful language that can manage virtually any object or piece of information in (and in certain cases, out of) your movie. It can even retrieve and display real-time data from databases, files, and web services.

Which version of ActionScript should you use?

Since you can work with several versions of ActionScript in Flash, the first step is sometimes deciding which version to use. Flash comes with both ActionScript 3.0, the latest version (and recommended), and 2.0, the previous version which was used predominantly with Flash Player versions 8 and earlier. You are also able to publish much older movies with ActionScript 1.0, but this is no longer recommended unless there's a good reason to do so.

The Flash Player continues to run ActionScript 2.0 and 3.0 side-by-side using two virtual machines (VM1 and VM2), with one dedicated to each version. At the time of this writing, ActionScript 2.0 is still in use (although much less frequently) and continues to be supported in both Flash CS6 and Flash Player 11. Version 3.0, however, not only adds many features and improvements in speed and performance but is considered the preferred standard for most movies.

ActionScript 3.0 is built upon object-oriented programming (OOP) concepts that make it modular and performance-oriented, which is essential for building large-scale Flash applications. In this book, you'll be working exclusively with ActionScript 3.0. It's important to note that if you are publishing to Flash Player 8 or earlier, you cannot use ActionScript 3.0.

Take Note...
If you are unsure which version to use, it's recommended that you stick with ActionScript 3.0. However, make sure that your project has no special requirements that would require you to publish for a much earlier version of Flash Player. Versions of Flash Player earlier than 9.0 do not support ActionScript 3.0.

Certification Ready 4.11

What are the basic concepts in object-oriented programming?

Where Do I Place ActionScript?

ActionScript is placed on keyframes along the timeline using the Actions Panel or the Code Snippets panel. Just as you would create a keyframe and place graphical content on it, you can add ActionScript code to a keyframe to have your movie do something at a specific point along the timeline.

In some more advanced and complex scenarios, you can also place ActionScript in external files that can be then referenced from your movie. Older versions of ActionScript (2.0 and earlier) also support placing ActionScript directly on symbol instances (although this widely considered to be a bad practice). For all the exercises in this lesson, you'll be placing ActionScript along the timeline as ActionScript 3.0 requires.

The Code Snippets Panel

While the capabilities of ActionScript are something every Flash designer should take advantage of, there is often a learning curve associated with any coding language, especially if you have limited scripting or interactive design experience. Flash CS6 helps to get you up-and-running quickly with the **Code Snippets** panel, which gives you one-click access to pre-created code blocks that handle everything from timeline navigation and animation tasks to loading and controlling audio and video.

These code snippets can be easily added to the timeline, saving you time as well as the need to create code by hand. You'll learn how to use the Code Snippets panel later in this lesson, and use it again in later lessons to help accelerate some common coding tasks. As you become more experienced with ActionScript, you can even add Code Snippets of your own.

An important note about Publish settings

You must adjust the ActionScript version as part of your Publish settings to match your preferred version of ActionScript.

<table><tr><td>**Step-by-Step**</td><td>**Follow these steps to adjust the Publish settings**</td></tr></table>

1. Make sure that no objects on the Stage are selected, and choose File > Publish Settings as shown in Figure 9-2.

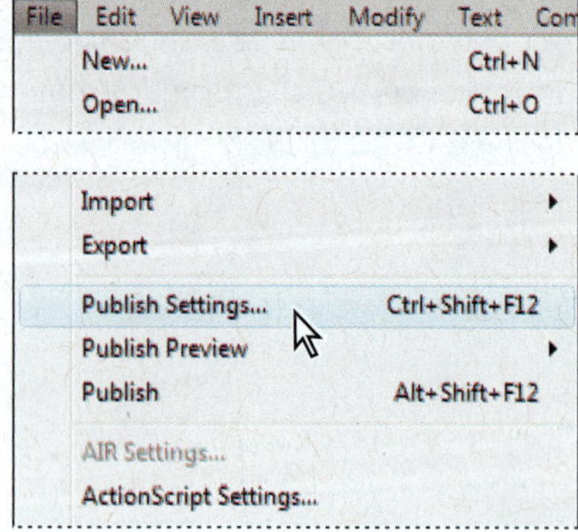

Figure 9-2: *Access your Publish settings through the File menu.*

2. From the Script drop-down in the top right corner, make sure that ActionScript 3.0 is selected (Figure 9-3) and press OK.

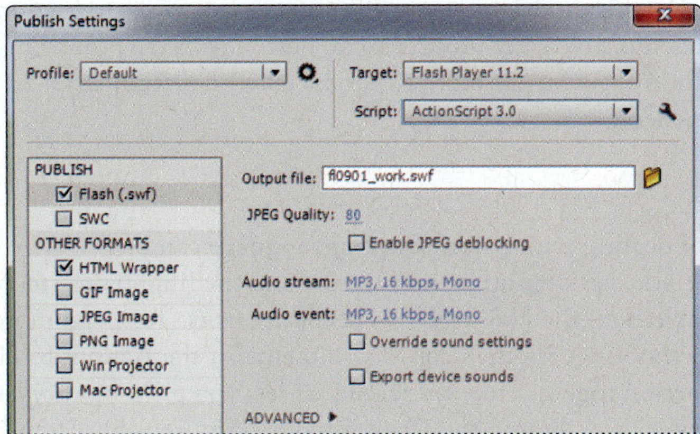

Figure 9-3: Set your ActionScript version using the Script drop-down menu in the Publish Settings panel.

Take Note...
You can also access the Script drop-down menu from the Property Inspector when nothing on the Stage is selected.

The Actions panel at work

The Actions panel is a script wizard, text editor, and code-checker, all in one (Figure 9-4). To open the Actions panel, choose Window > Actions, or press F9 (Windows) or Option+F9 (Mac OS). Note: On many laptops, you will need to add the function (fn) key: Fn+Option+F9.

Certification Ready 4.11

How do you use simple actions in Flash?

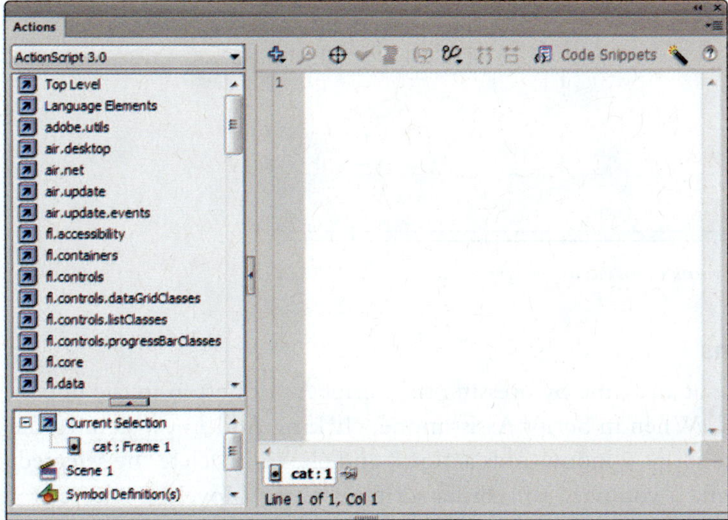

Figure 9-4: Open the Actions panel by choosing Window > Actions.

Here you build scripts (groups of actions) and place them in your movie. You can type scripts directly into the panel, choose scripts from drop-down menus, or use the Actions toolbox, which is a categorized menu of actions on the left side of the panel. To use the toolbox, double-click the script or click and drag it to the window on the right. You can use actions from the toolbox and drop-down menu in either standard or Script Assist mode.

The Actions panel at work

Standard (default) script editing mode

By default, the **Actions** panel opens up in a standard editing mode that lets you type freely in the Script window on the right. In this mode, you can still insert scripts from the Actions toolbox on the left, or by using the Add a new item to the script button (+) at the top. This mode is generally recommended for users who are more experienced with ActionScript or comfortable with typing code in general.

Using Script Assist

Certification Ready 4.11

How do you add simple actions to a movie using ScriptAssist mode?

For the novice user, the thought of dealing with a new scripting language can be overwhelming. Because ActionScript is very sensitive to both case and spelling, trying to type code freely before you're comfortable with the language can result in errors. To spend more time working and less time troubleshooting, try the drop-down menus or the Actions toolbox in **Script Assist** mode, which function together like a wizard that lets you pick, modify, and apply scripts without the need to type directly into the script window (Figure 9-5). After choosing your ready-made actions, you can tweak them with a series of form and menu controls at the top of the Actions panel. Script Assist is a great way to add simple actions to a movie to provide playback controls.

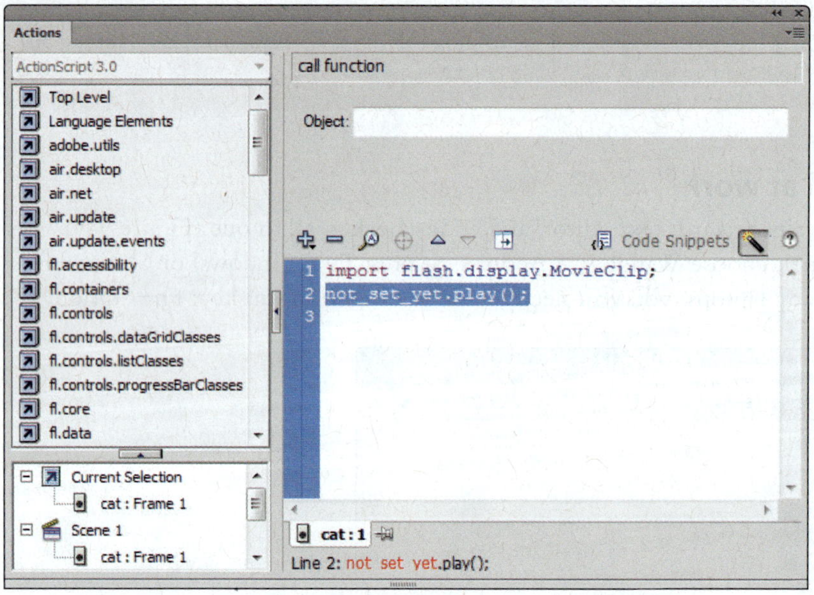

***Figure 9-5**: Script Assist mode lets you modify scripts with menus and type-in boxes.*

Adding and removing actions

You can enter Script Assist mode at any time by pressing the Script Assist button in the upper-right corner of the Actions panel. When in Script Assist mode, clicking Add a new item to the script button (+) at the top of the script window adds actions, and clicking Delete the selected action(s) button (−) removes them. If you need to reorder scripts, use the Move the selected action(s) up (▲) and Move the selected action(s) down (▼) buttons. You'll learn more about this mode later in this lesson.

As you highlight lines of code in the script window, menus will appear at the top of the Actions panel that let you adjust and set options for the selected action.

Adding actions to frames with the Code Snippets Panel

With a firm grasp of ActionScript fundamentals, you're ready to do some real work on the project. In this exercise, you'll use ActionScript to prevent the animation from looping, which is the default behavior of the Flash Player. Since you are most likely new to ActionScript, you'll get up-and-running quickly using the new Code Snippets panel to handle the heavy lifting for you.

Adding a stop() action

To stop a Timeline at a specific point, or prevent an animation from looping when it reaches the end, you use the `stop()` action. A **stop( )** action halts playback at the frame upon which you place it. When you test, preview, or publish a movie, the default behavior of the Flash Player is to loop playback; `stop()` actions override that behavior to ensure that the movie doesn't loop unnecessarily.

<table>
<tr><td>Follow these steps to add a stop action in the Timeline</td><td>Step-by-Step</td></tr>
</table>

1. If it's not already open, choose File > Open and open the file named **fl0901_work.fla**, which you saved earlier.

Take Note...
Although you aren't required to place actions on their own layer, it's a good practice to help avoid accidentally selecting a script versus an object on the Stage (and vice versa). Common practice is to keep a layer named actions at the top of the layer stack.

2. Select the cat layer in the Timeline, and click the New Layer button (⬰) to add a new layer above this one. Double-click on the layer name and type **actions** to rename the layer. It's considered a good practice to create a dedicated layer just for ActionScript.

3. Test the movie using Control > Test Movie > in Flash Professional. Notice that the animation continues to loop back to the beginning. Let's change that.

4. Like any object on the Stage, actions can be placed on keyframes only. As shown in Figure 9-6, select frame 42 on the new Actions layer, and create a new keyframe by pressing the F6 shortcut key.

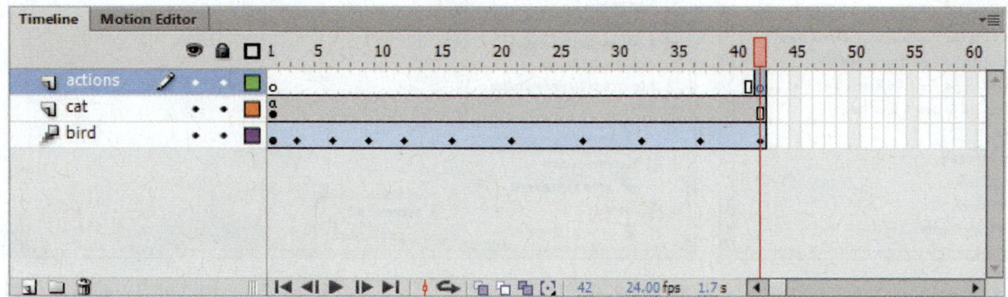

Figure 9-6: As a matter of good practice, always create a dedicated layer for your ActionScript.

5. Select the new keyframe, and open the Code Snippets panel (Figure 9-7) by pressing the Code Snippets button (img) on the right side of your workspace or by choosing Window > Code Snippets.

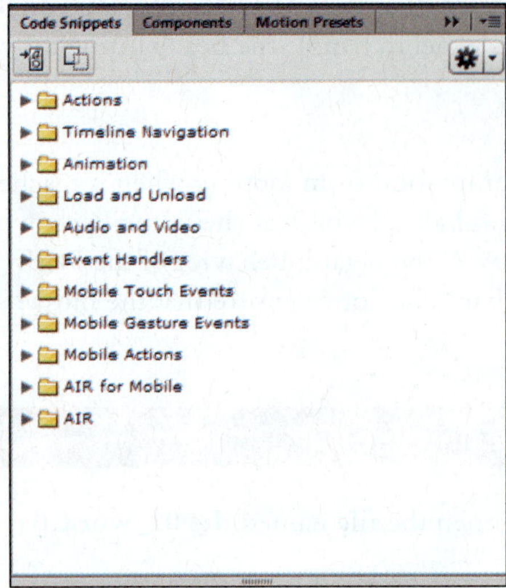

Figure 9-7: Once you've created a new keyframe, open the Code Snippets panel.

6. Within the Code Snippets panel, you'll see snippets organized into several named folders. Locate and double-click the Timeline Navigation folder to expand it as shown in Figure 9-8. Locate the snippet named Stop At This Frame, and double-click it.

The Actions Panel will launch, and the code from the selected snippet will be automatically added to Actions Panel at this keyframe (Figure 9-9). You should see a comment with some descriptive text and the statement `stop();` directly below it.

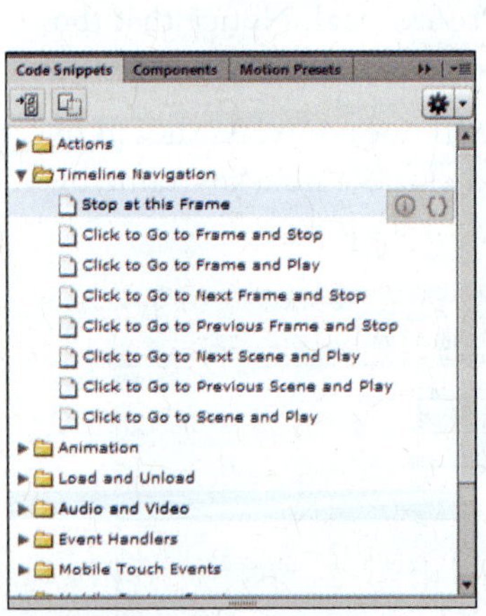
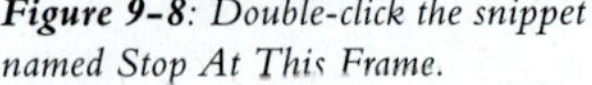

Figure 9-8: Double-click the snippet named Stop At This Frame.

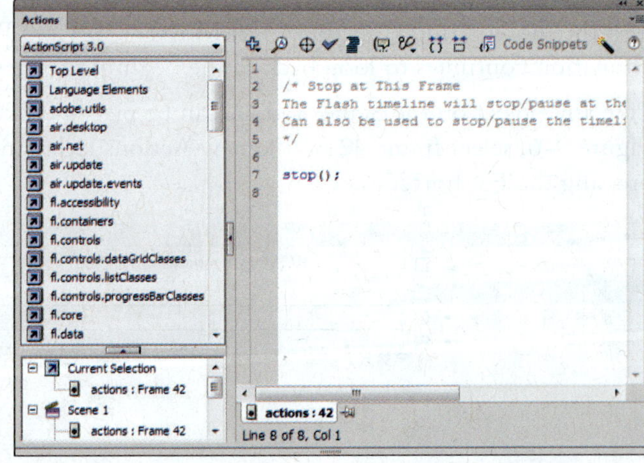

Figure 9-9: Placing a `stop()` action using the Stop At This Frame code snippet.

> ***Take Note...***
> *You may notice descriptive text in the Actions panel above or below certain lines of code. These are referred to as comments and are flanked by the characters /* and */ to separate them from real code and prevent them from being interpreted. You can use comments to annotate your code and describe its purpose and functionality.*

7. Close the Actions panel and look at the frame (Figure 9-10). The icon that looks like a lowercase *a* indicates that the frame contains actions that will run when the playhead passes it during playback.

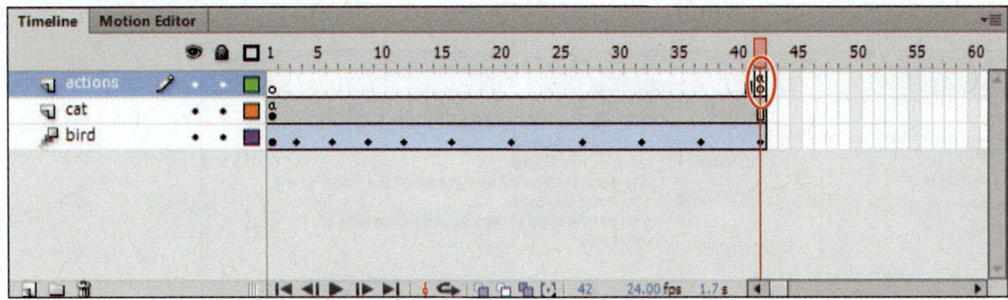

Figure 9-10: *The lowercase a icon indicates that actions exist on frame 42.*

8. Test your movie by choosing Control > Test Movie > in Flash Professional. The animation should play and stop abruptly at frame 42, exactly where you placed the action. The bird hops across the Stage and then perches on the cat. Close the preview.

9. Choose File > Save to save your work.

Placing a goto action using the Actions Panel

To make the playhead jump forward or backward to a specific frame, turn to the *goto* actions. The two variations—`gotoAndStop()` and `gotoAndPlay()`—jump to a specific frame, then stop playback and resume playback from that point, respectively. In this exercise, you'll explore these actions and get a little practice adding and subtracting actions.

This time, you'll be using the Actions Panel, and more specifically the Script Assist, which will help you build actions without hand-typing any code. This is a slightly different approach from the Code Snippets panel in the sense that you'll be building your own actions rather than using pre-created ones.

Follow these steps to add a goto action using the Actions panel	**Step-by-Step**

1. Select frame 42 on your Actions layer, and launch the Actions panel (Window > Actions). You must first remove the `stop()` action and comment created by the Code Snippets panel.

2. When the Actions Panel appears, press the Script Assist button in the upper-right corner. The top of the Actions Panel expands to indicate that you are in Script Assist mode.

3. Click in the Script window to select the comment above the `stop()` action. As displayed in Figure 9-11, click the Delete the selected action(s) button (➖) to delete the comment. Click the button twice more to remove the last two lines remaining in the Actions panel, including the `stop();` action, until the Script window is clear.

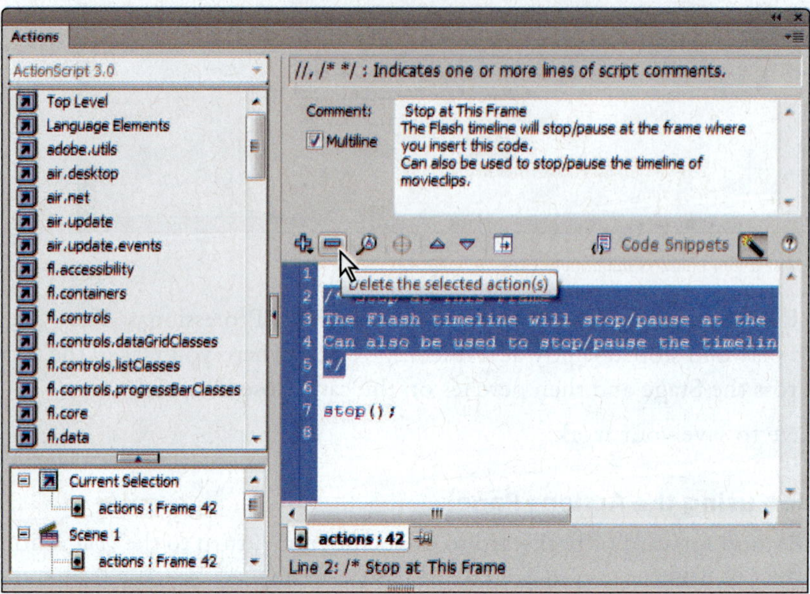

Figure 9-11: *Remove comments and* `stop()` *action on frame 42.*

4. Keep the Actions panel open. Press the Add a new item to the script button (➕) and choose flash.display > MovieClip > Methods > gotoAndStop. You may notice that `gotoAndStop()` and `stop()` are found in the same location. These are both methods of the MovieClip class. It's not too important to know exactly what that means, but simply put, it means that MovieClips can do things like stop, play, and go to specified points on their Timelines. Because ActionScript 3.0 is an object-oriented programming language, all the actions you add will be found grouped with the objects they relate to.

Take Note...

If you would like to further your knowledge of the key differences and new features in ActionScript 3.0, check out the articles and tutorials on Adobe's Developer Network site at adobe.com/devnet/.

5. In the Object text field, type **this**. Just like the `stop()` action from earlier, the this keyword tells Flash which Timeline you are referring to. A little later, you'll see how useful this field can be.

6. Right below the Object text field, type **20** in the frame text field (Figure 9-12).
ActionScript is very logical. If you're telling the Timeline to go somewhere and stop, you
have to tell it where to go and stop. You can use frame numbers, or add labels to your
frames. Close the Actions panel.

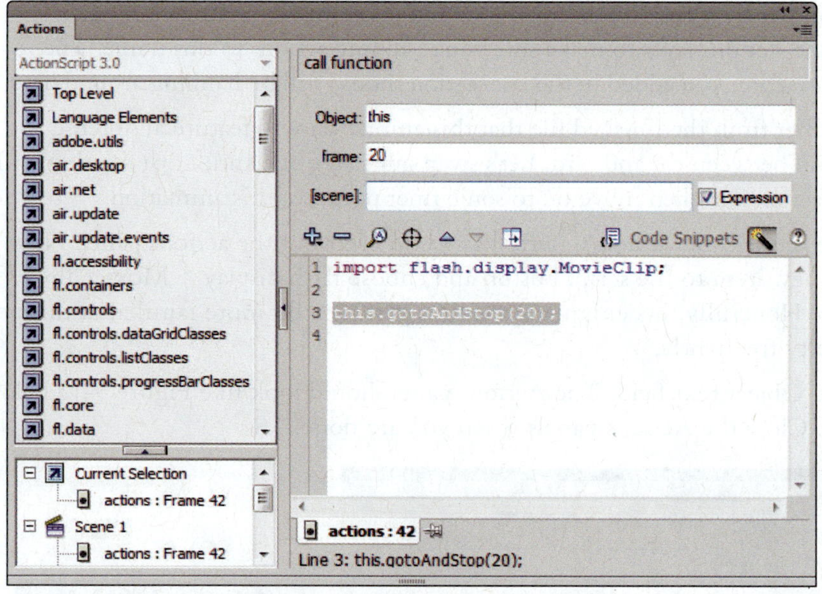

Figure 9-12: *Your script window with the* gotoAndStop() *action added.*

7. Choose Control > Test Movie > in Flash Professional to preview your movie. The bird
jumps onto the cat's head and then quickly changes his mind and jumps back to a safe
distance. Close the preview.

8. Choose File > Save and keep this document open for the next section.

Definition: Parameters	**Learning More**

You may see the word *Parameters* a lot in the Actions panel. Parameters are additional pieces of
information you feed to ActionScript functions to make them work. For instance, gotoAndPlay()
requires you to specify a frame number, a parameter it uses to complete its task. Many functions
in ActionScript take parameters, some that are required and some that are optional.

You enter parameters for selected actions using the menus and type-in fields that appear at the top
of the Actions panel in Script Assist mode.

Controlling Movie Clip Timelines

<table><tr><td>**Step-by-Step**</td><td>**Follow these steps to control Movie Clip Timelines**</td></tr></table>

1. Open the Actions panel by choosing Window > Actions from the main menu. Click on frame 42 of the Actions layer to make sure you're adding actions to this frame. The `gotoAndStop()` action you added in the last section should still be hanging around here.

   You may remember from the finished file that this animation will feature an intense and indefinite standoff between cat and bird. Let's swap out that `gotoAndStop()` action with a simple `stop()` action and then move on to some finer points of this animation.

2. Press the Delete the selected action(s) button twice to clear out the actions panel. Now click the Add a new item to the script button and choose flash.display > MovieClip > Methods > stop. Hopefully this enigmatic menu is getting a bit more familiar at this point. You'll use it pretty frequently.

3. Type **this** in the Object text field. The Actions panel should look like Figure 9–13 below when complete. Close the Actions panels when you are done.

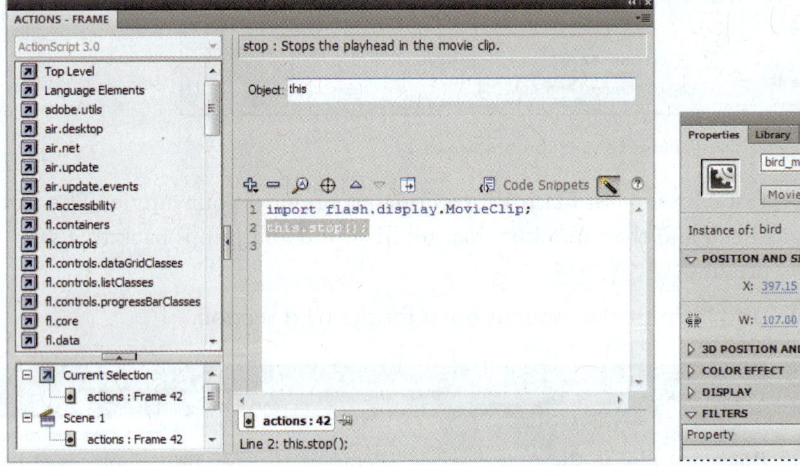

Figure 9–13: Swap out the `gotoAndStop()` action for a `stop()` action.

4. You may not have noticed, but the bird and cat are twitching and blinking respectively throughout the movie. It may be nice to hold off these movements until the bird has alighted atop the cat. You can stop and play the bird and cat Eye timelines the same way you stop and play the main timeline. But first you'll need a way to refer to each of these objects.

5. Using the Selection tool (⬉), click on the bird Movie Clip on the Stage as shown in Figure 9–14. Click on the Properties tab to make sure the Property Inspector is accessible.

> ***Take Note...***
> *The Actions panel often interferes with your access of objects on the Stage. Refer to Lesson 7 for tips on managing your workspace. Most Flash users who rely heavily on scripting create custom workspaces to help manage this sometimes cumbersome panel.*

6. At the very top of the Property Inspector, type **bird_mc** in the Instance Name text field as shown in Figure 9-15. Instance names are the way you refer to objects like Movie Clips and Buttons on the Stage. Remember that there can be multiple instances of these symbols in a movie. This is how you can tell one apart from another. Instance names are very important for writing ActionScript, in fact, you won't get very far without them.

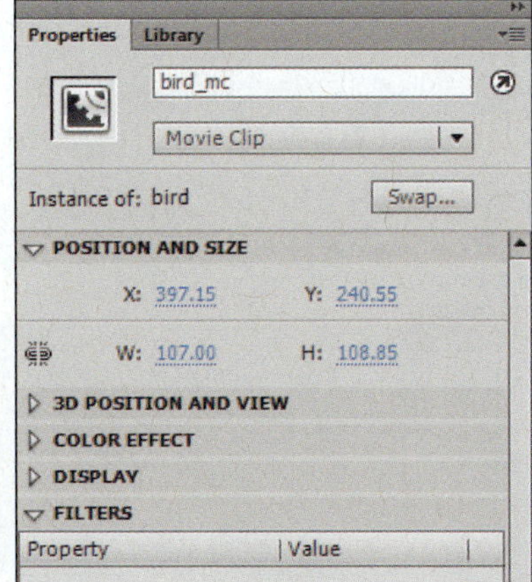

Figure 9-14: Select the bird Movie Clip.

Figure 9-15: Give it the instance name **bird_mc**.

7. Select Frame 1 of the Actions layer. If you closed the Actions panel to see the bird better, open it back up by choosing Window > Actions. Click on the Add a new item to the script button (⊕) and choose flash.display > MovieClip > Methods > stop.

    In the Object text field, type **bird_mc**. In this case you're not stopping the main timeline, you're stopping the bird timeline. For more information on Movie Clips and managing their timelines, refer to Lesson 12, "Introducing Movie Clips."

8. Choose Control > Test Movie > in Flash Professional. The bird no longer twitches. In the next section, you'll start the twitching animation at the end of the hopping animation on the main Timeline; first, get some practice by stopping the eye animation. In this case there are two eyes, so you'll have to do it twice.

9. Click on the cat's left eye and type **leye_mc** in the Instance Name text field of the Property Inspector. Then click on the cat's right eye and type **reye_mc** in the Instance Name text field of the Property Inspector.

10. Click the first frame of the actions layer. In the Actions panel, click the Add new item to the script button and choose flash.display > MovieClip > Methods > stop. Type **leye_mc** in the Object text field. Press Enter (Windows) or Return (Mac OS).

11. Click on the code section first to exit the cursor from the Object text field. Click the Add new item to the script button and once again choose flash.display > MovieClip > Methods > stop. This time, type **reye_mc** in the Object text field as shown in Figure 9-16.

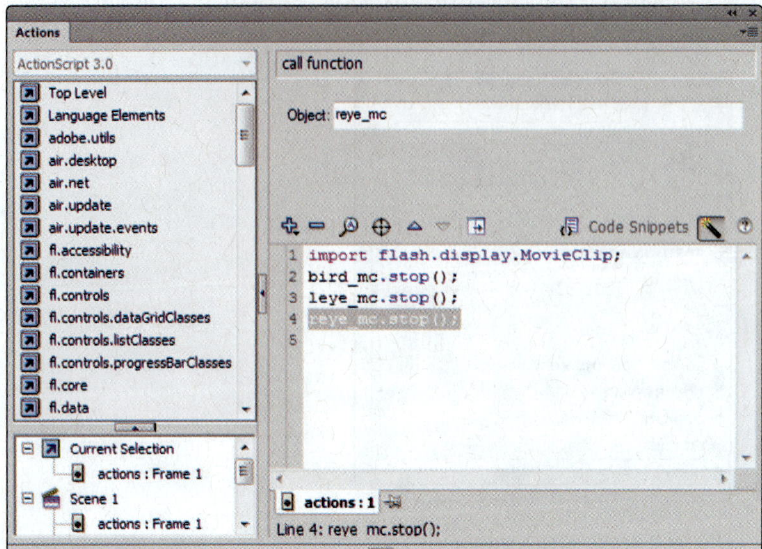

Figure 9-16: Add stop actions for the cat's eyes.

12. Choose File > Save, and then Control > Test Movie > in Flash Professional to see the results. The twitching and blinking should be all in the past.

Functions

In the next section, you'll use ActionScript to trigger the bird and eye animations after the bird hops onto the cat's head. There are a number of ways to make this happen, but in this case, you'll explore creating a reusable function to take care of this task.

Functions are one of a handful of elements that are common to almost every programming language. They allow you to group a number of statements together and then run them when needed. Imagine teaching someone how to change the toner in a copy machine. There are probably a handful of steps that never really change. Instead of posting your telephone number on the copier and walking people through the process every time it needs to be done, you could write up a set of instructions that they could follow on their own. The key to this concept is reusability. It may take a bit longer at the onset, but it will save you a lot of time in the long run.

In this exercise, you'll be removing the safety net by disabling the Script Assist, and coding this task entirely by hand. It's important to remember to follow the instructions carefully, and be conscious of case and spelling (ActionScript is pretty touchy about those things!).

1. Make sure the Actions panel is open with frame 1 of the Actions layer selected. You should see the actions you added in the last section. For this section, you'll turn off Script Assist and get your feet wet with a little hand coding. Don't worry, it won't hurt that much. You might even find it a bit easier than wading through the menus in Script Assist.

2. Click on the Script Assist button to turn off Script Assist (Figure 9-17). Writing in the ActionScript panel is just like writing in a text editor.

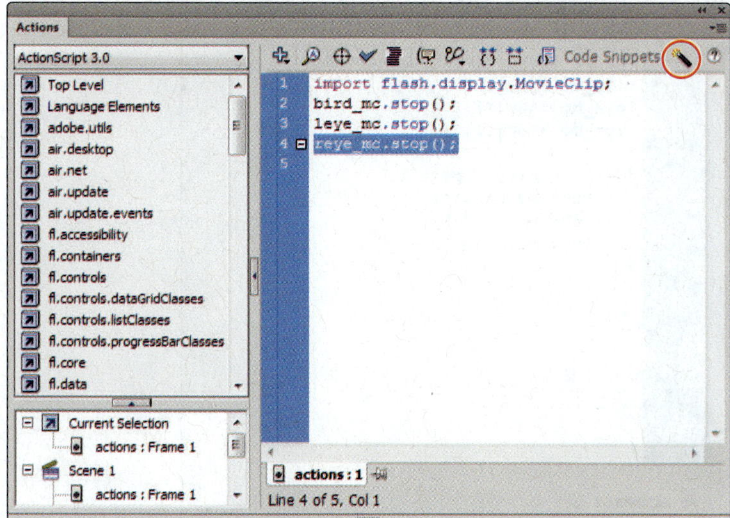

Figure 9-17: *The Actions panel with Script Assist disabled.*

3. Click at the end of line 4, after the semi-colon, and press Enter (Windows) or Return (Mac OS) twice. With the cursor blinking on line 6, type:

```
function playClips(){

}
```

As shown in Figure 9-18, be sure to include the space between function and playClips, the opening and closing parenthesis characters after playClips, and the opening and closing curly braces after the parentheses.

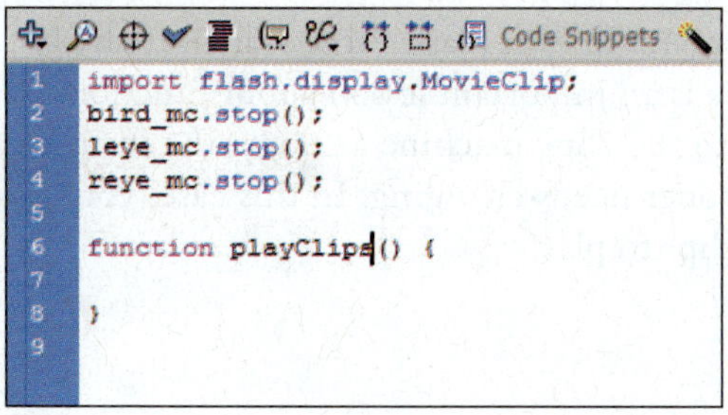

Figure 9-18: *Add a function named* `playClips` *in the Actions panel.*

4. Place the cursor at the end of line 6 and press Enter (Windows) or Return (Mac OS). Your cursor should be blinking and indented on line 7. Indenting the code inside functions is helpful for reading it later. Type the following lines to make the bird twitch and the cat's eyes blink:

```
bird_mc.play();
leye_mc.play();
reye_mc.play();
```

The Actions panel should look like the Figure 9-19 when you're finished.

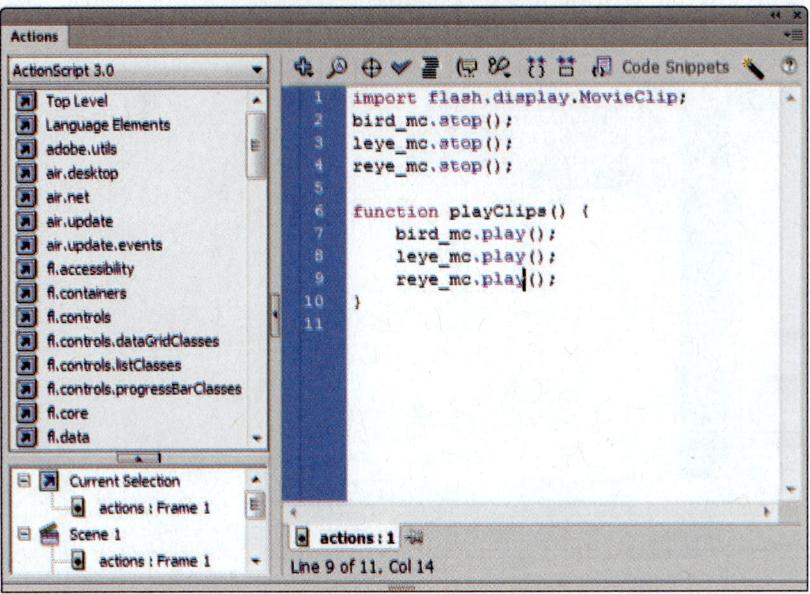


```
1   import flash.display.MovieClip;
2   bird_mc.stop();
3   leye_mc.stop();
4   reye_mc.stop();
5
6   function playClips() {
7       bird_mc.play();
8       leye_mc.play();
9       reye_mc.play();
10  }
11
```


Figure 9-19: *Add three statements inside the new playClips function.*

Take Note...

Curly braces define the beginning and end of one or more lines of grouped, or related code. The placement of curly braces on the same or following line after a function name is up to you, and is more a personal decision than anything. The code will work exactly the same regardless of whether you choose to keep curly braces and code on the same line or on dedicated lines, but in some cases spreading them out may result in more readable code.

5. Choose File > Save and then Control > Test Movie > in Flash Professional. It's a bit anticlimactic, but nothing has changed. This is an important lesson about functions. They must be called in order to run. Going back to the copy machine analogy, the instructions for changing toner only get used when the toner needs changing. In this case, you'll call the playClips function when you want the clips to play.

6. Click on frame 42 of the Actions layer. Place your cursor at the end of line 2 in the Actions panel and press Enter (Windows) or Return (Mac OS) twice to get to line 4. As shown in Figure 9-20, type the following line:

```
playClips();
```

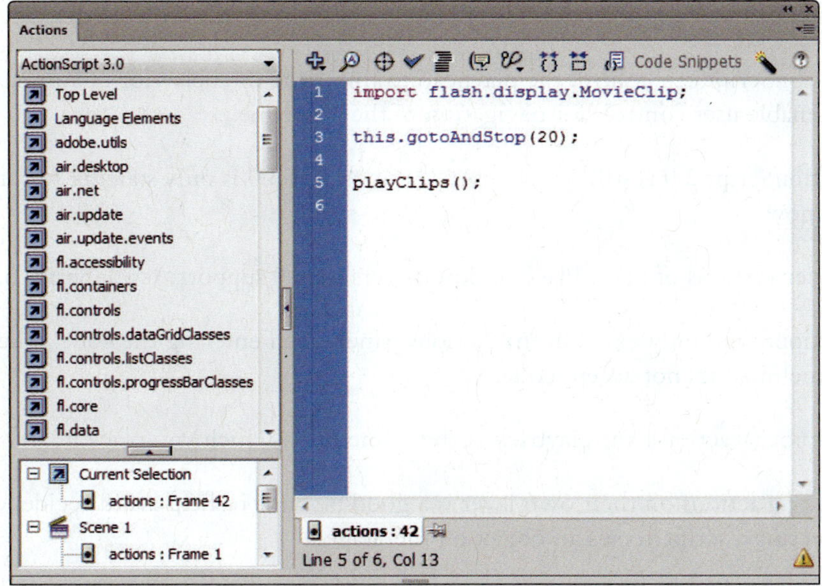

Figure 9-20: Call the `playClips()` function on the last frame of the animation.

Calling a function isn't so hard. Choose Control > Test Movie > in Flash Professional to see the fruits of your labor. The bird hops onto the cat's head and then they proceed to blink and twitch, caught in the immemorial struggle between the two noble species.

7. Choose File > Save, then File > Close.

Congratulations! You have finished the lesson.

Wrapping up

ActionScript offers a world of possibilities. Lesson 10, "Creating Navigation Controls," demonstrates how you can apply ActionScript to buttons to create controls and navigation. There you'll learn the power of another ActionScript staple: event listeners, and event handlers. Event handlers are specific functions that tell your movie what to do in response to a button or keyboard action. Because a button can be clicked, rolled over, released, or pressed and held down, event listeners help the button sort out when to perform which action, whether it's jumping to a frame on the Timeline, stopping playback, or launching a website in a browser window. Unlike frame-based actions, button-based actions can occur at any time, or not at all, based on what the user chooses to do.

Skill summary

In this lesson you learned how to:	Objective
Add simple controls through ActionScript 3.0	4.11

Knowledge Assessment

True/False

Circle **T** if the statement is true or **F** if the statement is false.

T F   **1.** The latest version of ActionScript (and the one that's recommended) is 2.0.

T F   **2.** ActionScript can control the playhead to fine-tune the behavior of animations or enable user controls for navigation of the Timeline.

T F   **3.** ActionScript 2.0 is still widely used, Actionscript 3.0 is only starting to catch up now.

T F   **4.** Older versions of Flash Player as low as version 6.0 support ActionScript 3.0.

T F   **5.** ActionScript only exists in the Actions panel when entering the code. The Timeline does not accept code.

T F   **6.** A `stop()` action halts playback at the frame upon which you place it.

T F   **7.** Placing actions on their own layer is a good practice to help avoid accidentally selecting a script versus an object on the Stage.

T F   **8.** Parameters are additional pieces of information you feed to ActionScript functions to make them work.

T F   **9.** Adding the extension _mov is a common practice when naming the instance of a movie clip.

T F   **10.** Functions are one of a handful of elements that are common to almost every programming language.

Multiple Choice

Select the best response for the following statements.

1. ActionScript is built upon what type of concepts that make it modular and performance-oriented?

    a. Control-Object Programming
    b. Object–Oriented Programming
    c. Control–Oriented Programming
    d. None of the above

2. Besides the Actions panel, what other panel will allow you to access pre-created code blocks?

    a. Properties
    b. Movie Explorer
    c. Output
    d. Code Snippets

3. Besides File > Publish, what panel offers the opportunity to access your project's Publish Settings?

    a. Output
    b. Movie Explorer
    c. Properties
    d. Info

4. Which feature allows you to modify and apply scripts without the need to type directly into the script window?

    a. Check Syntax
    b. Script Assist
    c. Code Hints
    d. Auto-Script

5. What programming element sometimes appears above or below certain lines of code and is flanked by /* and */ to separate them from real code?

    a. Annotations
    b. Notes
    c. Comments
    d. Snippets

6. Which set of actions will make the playhead jump forward or backward to a specific frame?

    a. jump actions
    b. navigate actions
    c. goto actions
    d. play actions

7. Which script command tells Flash which Timeline you're referring to?

    a. this
    b. that
    c. timeline.this
    d. timeline.that

8. In order to navigate the Timeline, Flash can be told to jump from one frame to another using frame numbers or frame...?

    a. Instances
    b. Keyframes
    c. Labels
    d. All of the above

9. You can enter in an instance name on an object in which panel?

    a. Info
    b. Movie Explorer
    c. Properties
    d. Snippets

10. Which of the following defines the beginning and end of one or more lines of grouped or related code?

   a. ( )

   b. { }

   c. [ ]

   d. / \

Competency Assessment

Project 9-1	Always more to learn — ActionScript

Flash comes with a bit of ActionScript built into it as you've discovered by now. Given the amount of code, it can be pretty challenging to figure out what it will do. The Help section in Flash comes with a built-in code dictionary that will help put things in perspective.

1. Create a new ActionScript 3.0 document in Flash.

2. Choose Window > Actions.

3. In the Actions panel, scroll down in the script portion of the panel in the upper left area.

4. Click on the Index category to reveal the scripts available.

5. Select one of the scripts, for example ACTIVATE (Event) and right-click or control-click to reveal the menu and choose View Help.

6. The Help viewer will open with a definition of the chosen script.

7. Save the file as **ACTIVATE.PDF** for future reference.

Project 9-2	Always more to learn — Code Snippets

Similar to the Help information, there's a more abbreviated and compact version of code definitions built-in to the Code Snippets panel.

1. Create a new ActionScript 3.0 document in Flash.

2. Choose Window > Code Snippets.

3. Go to the Animation folder and open it to see the snippets. Select the Move with Keyboard Arrows snippet.

4. Click the i button and then the {} button to learn more about the snippet.

5. After clicking on the {} button, right-click on the text and choose Copy Code Snippet.

6. Create a new text file on your computer and paste the Code Snippet text into the text file and save the file as **snippet.txt**.

Proficiency Assessment

<table>
<tr><td style="background:#b52025;color:white">Reviewing code preferences</td><td style="background:#b52025;color:white">Project 9-3</td></tr>
</table>

Don't forget that if you don't like how your code looks in the Actions panel that you can change it easily enough through the preferences.

1. Create a new ActionScript 3.0 document in Flash.

2. Select Edit > Preferences on Windows or Flash > Preferences on the Mac OS. Select the ActionScript category and choose the font and size you prefer for your ActionScript.

<table>
<tr><td style="background:#b52025;color:white">Automatic code formatting explained</td><td style="background:#b52025;color:white">Project 9-4</td></tr>
</table>

Flash likes to help you dot the i's and cross the t's. If you're a code enthusiast though, you may want to do that for yourself.

1. Create a new ActionScript 3.0 document in Flash.

2. Select Edit > Preferences on Windows or Flash > Preferences on the Mac OS. Select the Auto Format category and examine the options available for modification.

Circling Back 2

One of the great things about Flash is combining different methods to produce interesting animations without having to do a ton of code work or animation work. Once you learn the tools, you'll find ways to streamline the process of animation in more efficient ways.

<table>
<tr><td style="background:#b52025;color:white">Logo animation</td><td style="background:#b52025;color:white">Project 1</td></tr>
</table>

You need to create a new logo animation for the company. You've explained a couple of your animation ideas but your boss can't quite picture it. She's asked you to create a quick simulation before you go through the trouble of animating the logo. You need to come up with something quickly since decisions have to be made before a big meeting. The logo has a square–ish shape to it so you'll use a rectangle to simulate the logo as a placeholder.

1. Create a new ActionScript 3.0 document in Flash.

2. Select the Rectangle tool, set the fill color to green, the stroke to none and make sure you're in Object Drawing mode. Draw a rectangle on the Stage.

3. Choose the Selection tool and make sure the green rectangle is selected on the Stage. Choose Modify > Covert to Symbol, save the symbol as movie clip named **logo animation**.

4. With the symbol still selected on the Stage, go to the Properties panel. In the Instance Name field, enter the name **logo**.

5. Choose Window > Code Snippets.

6. Click on the arrow next to the Animation folder. You'll try a couple of options and compare.

7. Select the Fade In a Movie Clip animation. Click on the {} button and then the Insert button.

8. Preview the animation of the logo movie clip by choosing Ctrl/Cmd+Enter/Return.

9. Choose Edit > Undo three times to remove the Fade In action.

10. Keep the movie clip selected and select the animation called Rotate Continuously. Press the {} button and then the Insert button.

11. Preview the animation of the logo movie clip by choosing Ctrl/Cmd+Enter/Return.

12. Save this file as **logo_animation.fla** and keep it open for the next exercise.

Project 2	An easier approach to multiple choice

Undoing and redoing is all well and good while you're experimenting but what about during the presentation? Again, there are different ways to approach this but let's try one that involves enabling and disabling code just for practice.

1. The **logo_animation.fla** file should still be open.

2. You've already got the Rotate Continuously animation applied. Click on the keyframe in frame 1 of the Actions layer and choose Window > Actions.

3. Select the code from line 11 to line 16 and click the Apply block comment button in the top row of buttons to comment the code out and disable it.

4. Hide the Actions panel and reselect the logo animation movie clip on the Stage.

5. Go to Window > Code Snippets, then click on the animation called Fade In a Movie Clip. Press the {} and then the Insert button.

6. Preview the animation, the only one you should see is the fade in.

7. When you go into the presentation, show the fade in first. When finished, open the Actions panel, comment out the Fade in a Movie Clip code, reselect code lines 11–16 and press the Remove Comment button. Preview and demonstrate the rotation animation.

8. Save and keep this file open.

Project 3	Hey! That's a lot of code

Staring at a ton of code can start to bug your eyes out, especially if you're more designer and less coder. Let's clean up the code a bit and make it a little more manageable for our eyes.

1. The **logo_animation.fla** file should still be open.

2. Open the Actions Panel.

3. Select the code from line 1 to line 16. Click the Collapse Selection button.

4. Select the remaining code and click the Collapse Selection button again.

5. Click on the code blocks and the plus signs to the left to open and close as needed.

6. Save the final file as **logo_animation_final.fla**.

Creating Navigation Controls

Key Terms

- buttons
- events
- event handlers
- event listeners
- frame labels
- text-based buttons

Skill	Objective
Identify general and Flash-specific best practices for designing rich media content for the web, mobile apps, and AIR applications	2.1
Create objects and convert them to symbols, including graphics, movie clips, and buttons	4.6
Create animations (changes in shape, position, size, color, and transparency)	4.10
Add simple controls through ActionScript 3.0	4.11

Business case

Another major aspect to the use of Flash is creating projects that are interactive and navigational. Learning interactivity will allow you to create fully animated interactive websites that will transform your static projects into dynamic, moving, eye-catching pieces that instantly grab the attention of the viewer and keep them engaged enough to want to explore the rest of your site.

Starting up

Before starting, make sure that your tools and panels are consistent by resetting your preferences. See "Resetting the Flash workspace" in the Starting up section of this book.

You will work with several files from the fl10lessons folder in this lesson. Make sure that you have loaded the fllessons folder onto your hard drive from *http://www.wiley.com/college/sc/adobeseries*. See "Loading lesson files" in the Starting up section of this book.

The project

In this lesson, you'll be designing a mini–site project for the talkShop retail cellphone store. You'll build a few buttons, then link them to key points within the Flash movie and a sample website. For a preview of the final result, open the **fl1002_done.fla** file in the fl10lessons folder. Close the file when you are finished, or keep it open as a reference.

Working with button symbols

Buttons are one of three symbol types in Flash, and, like all symbols, they live in the library and are managed from the Library panel. Buttons are designed specifically to react to the user's mouse and keyboard actions. Like other symbol instances, each button instance can have its own transformation and color characteristics. In addition, button symbols have filter effects applied from the Property Inspector, and can be assigned instance names for ActionScript control.

To understand the anatomy of a button, you'll now open a sample file with a button instance so that you can explore a button symbol and its different components:

Certification Ready 4.6

What are the different states of a button symbol?

Step-by-Step

Certification Ready 4.6

What would be a use for a transparent or invisible button in Flash?

1. Choose File > Open. In the Open dialog box, navigate to the fl10lessons folder and open the file named **fl1001.fla**.

2. On the Stage, you see a single button. Double-click this button to enter its Edit mode, and to view its Timeline as shown in Figure 10-1.

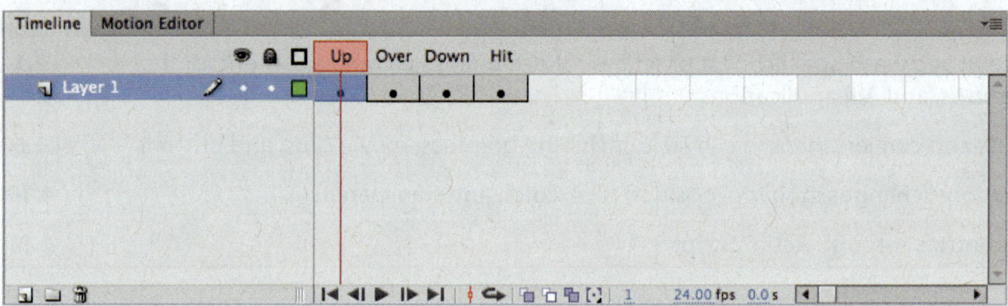

Figure 10-1: Button symbols have a unique, four-frame Timeline.

3. You'll see here that a button symbol has a unique Timeline featuring four main frames in each layer—Up, Over, Down, and Hit. Each represents a button's appearance in different states of use. Navigate through a button's frames by clicking on the frame ruler, or by using the < and > (comma and period) keys.

The Up state is the button's default appearance when it's just sitting on the Stage without any user interaction. By default, when you convert Stage graphics to a button symbol, they are automatically placed on the Up frame.

The Over state displays when the mouse pointer moves over a button. This indicates to the user that the button is a control that can carry out some action in your movie. You can characterize the Over state with anything from a simple color or text change to an animation or sound.

When the user presses down on the mouse button, the button symbol changes to its Down state. It remains in its Down state until the user releases the button. Because the Down state is visible only briefly during a typical mouse click, customizing a button's Down state with a long animation or sound is not the best idea.

The Hit area defines the *hot spot* where the button becomes active when the user moves over it (Figure 10-2). This state is never visible, and content placed on the Hit frame defines only the active area.

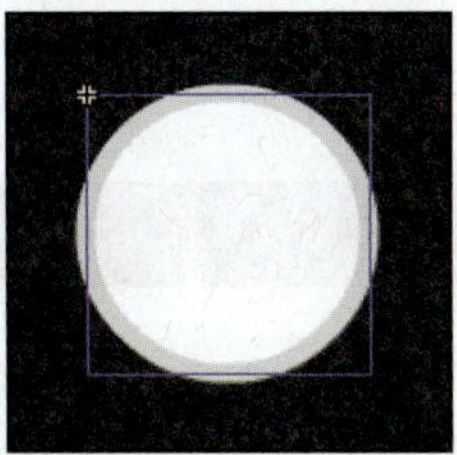

Figure 10-2: The contents of the Hit frame define the clickable, or 'hot,' area of a button.

This is especially crucial for buttons that are small, have an irregular shape, or contain only text with no underlying shape. Because the Hit area defines the active area of the button and is not visible, the size and shape of the content on the Hit frame matters most—color choice, for instance, has no effect on the button's operation. In fact, it's pretty common in Flash animations to create completely invisible buttons. Buttons that only have a hit state so that you can define a specific area of the animation as a clickable area.

Take Note...
What makes a good Hit state? The best Hit states are solid shapes that are generally as big as, or slightly bigger than, the visible states of the button. If your button changes shape from state to state, consider choosing a shape for the Hit state that is fairly neutral and encompasses as much of the visible area of the button as possible.

4. Choose Control > Test Movie > in Flash Professional to preview the button in the Flash Player. Move your mouse pointer over the button, and then click it to see how it switches between its various states as the mouse interacts with it (Figure 10-3). Then close the preview window.

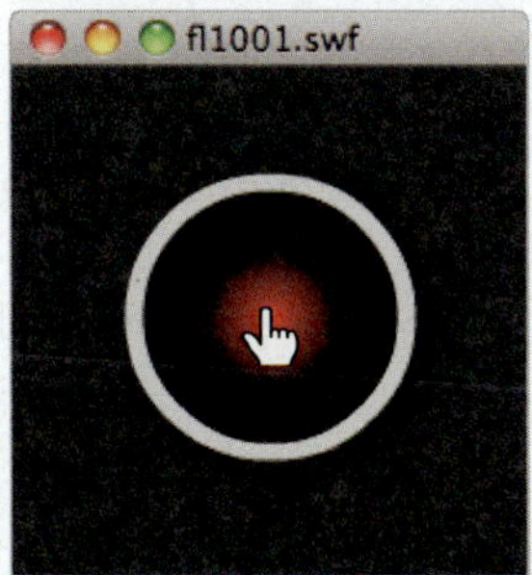

Figure 10-3: Button symbols display a hand cursor when the user moves their pointer over them.

5. Choose File > Close to close your movie. If asked to save changes, choose Don't Save.

Certification Ready 4.6

How do you add over, down, and hit states to a button symbol?

Building buttons

With a solid introduction to button symbol theory, you're ready to begin work on the project. The first step is to create a new button symbol and design its Up, Over, and Down states.

Step-by-Step

Follow these steps to create a new button

1. Choose File > Open and navigate to the fl10lessons folder. Select the **fl1002.fla** file and choose Open. In Figure 10-4 you see a mini-site project for the talkShop retail cell-phone store.

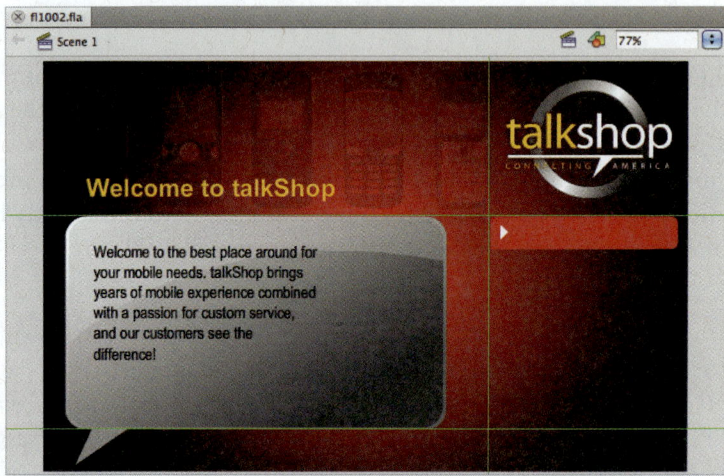

Figure 10-4: The talkShop project file you will be working with.

2. Before you modify this file, choose File > Save As. When the Save As dialog box appears, type **fl1002_work.fla** into the Save As text field. Navigate to the fl10lessons folder and press Save.

First, you'll create a button very much the same way you'd create any other symbol—from existing graphics on the Stage.

3. Click on the rounded rectangle and the arrow on the right side of the Stage under the talkShop logo. Choose Modify > Convert to Symbol. In the Convert to Symbol dialog box, type **Products Button** as the name, and set the Type to Button. Set the registration point to the upper left as shown in Figure 10-5, and click OK to create the new symbol.

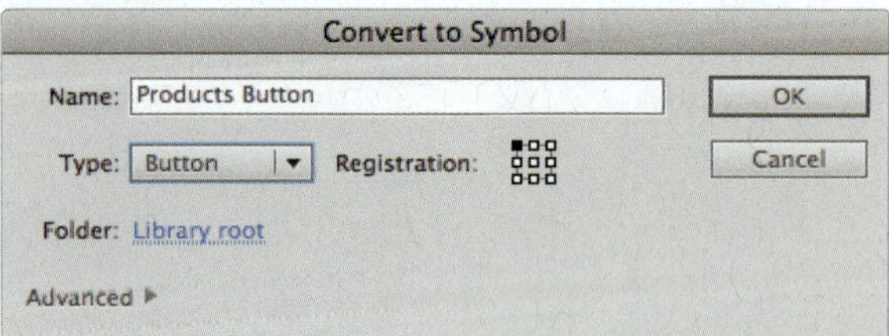

Figure 10-5: Select graphics on the Stage and use Modify > Convert to Symbol to convert them to a button symbol.

4. The next step will be to add to your button by designing the additional states (Over, Down, Hit). Double-click on your new button to enter its Edit mode.

5. The first state you'll design is the Over state, which is how the button will appear if and when the user rolls their mouse pointer over it.

Select Over frame directly on the layer. As with any other Timeline, you need to create a keyframe to put content here. Use the F6 shortcut key or choose Insert > Timeline > Keyframe to insert a keyframe here (Figure 10-6).

The graphics from the Up keyframe will be duplicated; take a moment to make some changes, such as color, to this copy, to make it distinctive from the Up frame. You may need to ungroup the box and the arrow graphics to change their colors individually. Select the graphics and ungroup by choosing Modify > Ungroup. Click anywhere in the background to deselect, then click on the button to select it. Click on the Fill color swatch and choose a grey color.

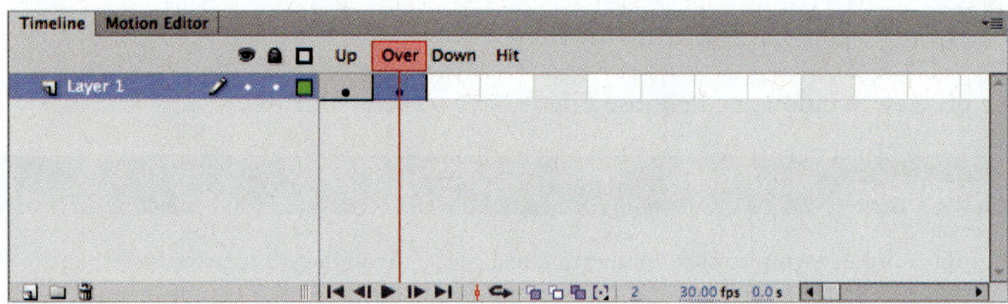

Figure 10-6: Add a keyframe to the Over state to design a unique look for your button when the mouse pointer rolls over it.

6. Next, you'll design the Down state, which is how your button appears when the mouse pointer is clicked and held down on it. Select the Down frame, and use the F6 shortcut key to insert a keyframe here.

Again, click anywhere in the background to deselect, and then click on the grey button to select it. Click on the Fill color swatch and choose an orange color.

7. Finally, select the Hit frame, and use the F6 shortcut key to create a keyframe here (Figure 10-7). The Hit frame is not visible, but determines the clickable area of your entire button.

For this reason, you should generally use a solid shape (color is unimportant) that is the same size as, if not bigger than, your button. In this case, you can use the graphics themselves to set the Hit state, as they accurately represent the size and shape of the button. Leave the duplicated graphics on this keyframe as-is (Figure 10-8).

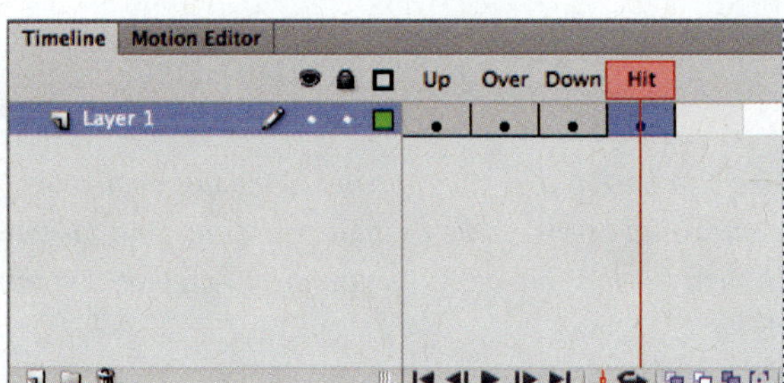

Figure 10-7: Create a keyframe on the Hit state.

Figure 10-8: Use the duplicated graphics from the Down state to set the Hit area.

8. Exit your new button by clicking the Scene 1 link above the Stage to return to the main Timeline.

9. Choose Control > Test Movie > in Flash Professional to preview your new button. Roll over and click with your mouse button to see the different states at work (Figure 10-9).

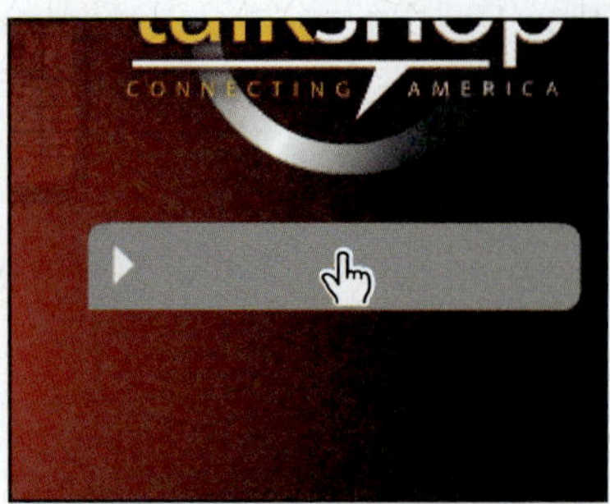

Figure 10-9: *Test your button design by choosing Control > Test Movie > in Flash Professional.*

10. Close the preview window, and choose File > Save to save your file.

Learning More

Certification Ready 2.1

What are some attributes of a website, game, mobile app, or rich internet application that demonstrate consistency?

Button design tips

When designing a project, you want to maintain consistency throughout the project so that the experience is familiar to the user. Providing consistent navigation, colors, and fonts helps to provide continuity in a project and making sure that the location of buttons and menus is intuitive provides the user with a familiar and enjoyable experience as well. When designing buttons, keep your users in mind and follow these guidelines:

• Aim for an interesting design that makes the navigation process easy for users to understand. An interesting-looking button may entice users to click on it.

• Make a button's purpose clear. Although you already know what all your buttons do, and where they'll lead, users aren't as familiar as you are with what's going on. Design buttons with familiar shapes (for example, a Play button that looks like a forward arrow), or label buttons with text if necessary.

• Make buttons easy to find. If the buttons are hard to pick out on the interface, or if their functions are unclear, your interactive project becomes a frustrating experience for the user.

Also, let the content drive the need for buttons. Know the sections you want to include in your project before you start to design the buttons. Developing content as you design your buttons can slow you down. A flowchart is a simple way to plan basic layout and navigation, and gives you a blueprint to work from when setting up your movie in Flash.

Take Note...

If a hit keyframe is not created (or empty), a button uses the contents of the last available keyframe as the Hit area. This works across all layers, so be cautious not to let your button use a non-graphic keyframe for its Hit area (such as an empty keyframe or one that contains a sound). The result may be a non-clickable button!

Adding text to a button

Like other symbols, and like the main Timeline itself, buttons can have multiple layers. Using layers helps you to create more complex designs and add more information while keeping everything carefully organized. In this exercise, you'll add a new layer to incorporate text into your button.

<table><tr><td>**Follow these steps to add text to a button**</td><td>**Step-by-Step**</td></tr></table>

1. Double-click your new button on the Stage to enter its Edit mode.

2. Press the New Layer button below the Timeline to add a new layer to your button as shown in Figure 10-10. Rename the layer **Text**.

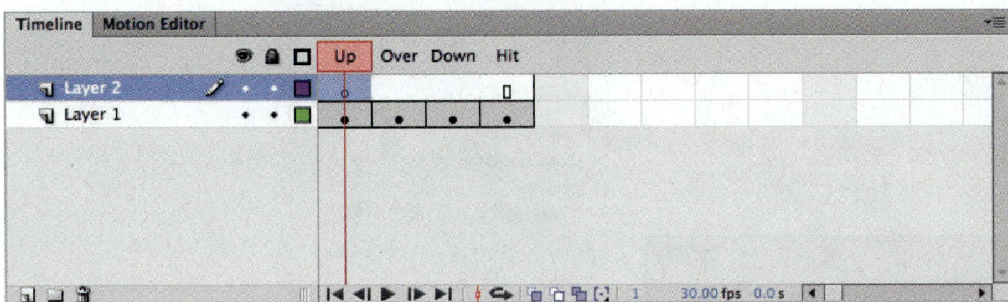

Figure 10-10: *Add a new layer and name it Text. You can layer graphics and content in button Timelines just like you can on the main Timeline.*

3. Select your Text tool (T) from the Tools panel. Make sure the new layer is selected, and click slightly to the right of the white arrow on your button. Type the word **Products**, and switch to your Selection tool (▶).

4. Leave the text frame selected, and locate the Character options on the Property Inspector on the right. Choose Arial from the Family drop-down menu, and set the Size value to 18 pt, and the color to White (#FFFFFF).

   If necessary, use your Selection tool (▶) or the arrows keys on your keyboard to reposition the text on the button (Figure 10-11).

5. The text should extend across all four frames of your button's Timeline (Figure 10-12). If not, select the Down frame on the Text layer and press the F5 shortcut key to extend the first keyframe and your text. This ensures that your text will appear across all three visual states.

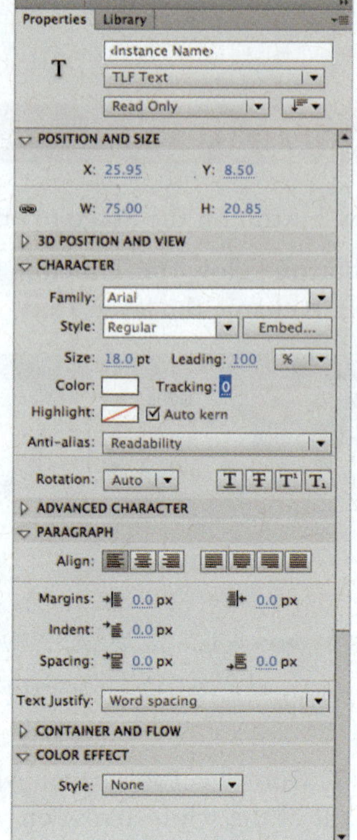

Figure 10-11: Add text to the new layer and style it using the Property Inspector.

Figure 10-12: Your text can (and should) extend across all frames on the button's Timeline.

6. Click the Scene 1 link above the Stage to return to the main Timeline.

7. Choose File > Save to save your file, and then choose Control > Test Movie > in Flash Professional to preview your movie. The new text should appear across all three states of your button as you interact with it. Close the preview window. That's one button down. The next button will be much faster and easier to create because you can build on what you've already done.

Duplicating and modifying buttons

Why build a completely new button when you can copy and modify an existing one? Using the Library panel's Duplicate command is faster, and it ensures that new buttons are consistent with those you've already created.

<table><tr><td>**Follow these steps to duplicate and modify a button**</td><td>**Step-by-Step**</td></tr></table>

1. In the Library panel, select the Products Button symbol. If necessary, choose Window > Library to open the Library panel.

2. Choose Duplicate from the Library panel menu as shown in Figure 10-13.

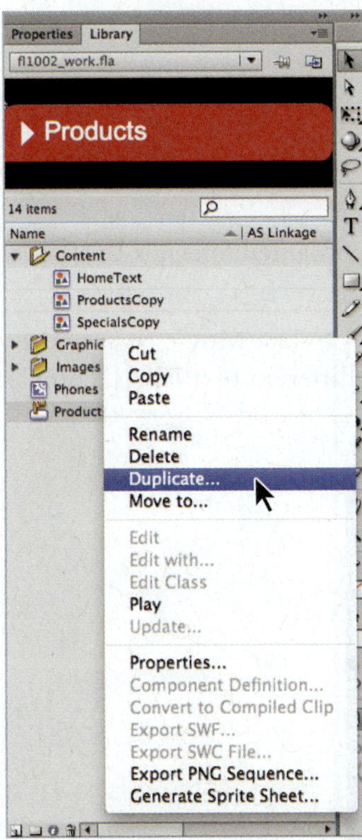

Figure 10–13: *Make a copy of your Products Button symbol in the library using its panel menu's Duplicate command.*

When the Duplicate Symbol dialog box appears, type the name **Home Button**. Leave the Type set as Button and press OK. A new copy of your original button, named Home Button, now appears in the Library panel.

3. Drag an instance of the Home Button to the Stage, and place it directly below your Products Button on the same layer. Double-click it to edit it in place.

4. Once inside the button, select your Text tool (T) from the Tools panel, then click on your existing text until you get the I-Beam. As shown in Figure 10-14, replace the word Products with the word **Home**. Click the Scene 1 link above the Stage to return to the main Timeline.

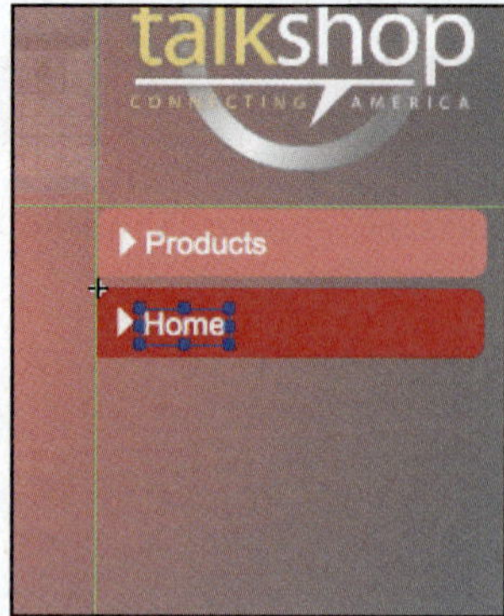

Figure 10-14: Edit the text on your button copy to read Home.

5. Repeat steps 1 to 4 to create a new duplicate of your button named Specials Button, and edit the text to read **Specials**.

6. Choose File > Save to save your work, and choose Control > Test Movie to preview your movie. You should now have three identical buttons with different text labels, completing your navigation menu as displayed in Figure 10-15.

Figure 10-15: The finished menu, created by duplicating your original Products Button.

Take Note...
Use your Align panel (Window > Align) to evenly align and space the three buttons on the Stage.

Learning More

Testing buttons on the Stage

Once you've added buttons to the Stage, you can conveniently test their behaviors and appearance directly within the authoring environment using the Enable Simple Buttons command. Enable Simple Buttons lets you quickly test button behavior without launching the Flash Player, and prevents you from selecting, moving, or editing buttons on the Stage.

To use Enable Simple Buttons:

1. Choose Control > Enable Simple Buttons.

2. Roll over and click your buttons as you normally would, to test their behavior.

3. When finished, choose Control > Enable Simple Buttons to toggle it back off.

Keep in mind that most ActionScript behavior is limited in this mode, and requires you to preview your movie using Control > Test Movie > in Flash Professional instead. In addition, you cannot move or edit button instances until Enable Simple Buttons is toggled back off.

Creating text-based buttons

Text-based buttons work differently because they are formed only from the character outlines that form your text, with no significant solid area or shape that defines them. A problem with text buttons is that if the mouse pointer is not precisely on a type character, the button remains inactive, appearing not to work. This is where the Hit area comes into play. By defining a hot spot in the Hit frame of your button, you create a solid and easy target for users to click.

Follow these steps to set a Hit area for a text-based button

Step-by-Step

1. Choose Insert > New Symbol.

2. When the Create New Symbol dialog box appears, name the symbol **Learn More**, and set the symbol Type as Button. Press OK. The main Timeline disappears, and you are brought into the edit mode for your new symbol. The Stage appears empty for now.

3. Choose the Text tool (T) from the Tools panel, then click on the Stage and type **Learn how to create sites like this**.

4. Highlight the text and use the Character options on the Property Inspector to set the text to Verdana, 10pt, white (#FFFFFF) type (Figure 10-16). Note that you can use the Zoom tool to zoom in on the Stage to make working with small text easier.

5. Choose the Selection tool (▶) in the Tools panel and select the text you just created. Open the Align panel (Window > Align) and click the Align to stage checkbox, if it's not already checked. Click the Align Horizontal Center (♣) and Align Vertical Center (♦) buttons in the Align panel to align the text to the symbol's registration point as circled in Figure 10-17.

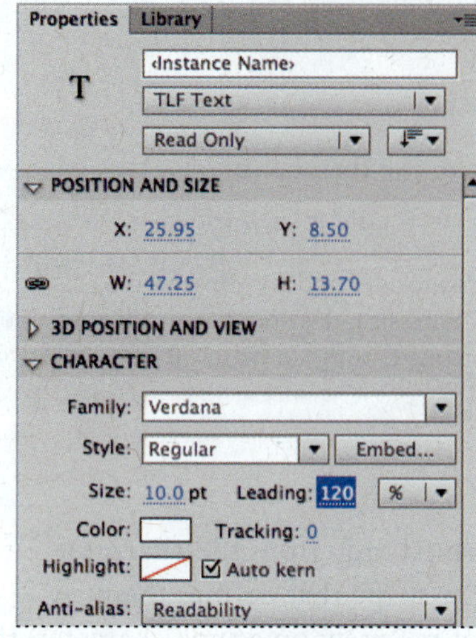

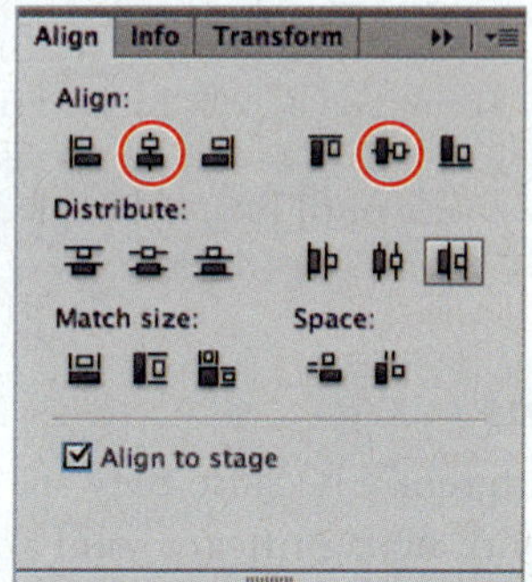

Figure 10–16: *Use the Property Inspector to text to the symbol's registration point on the Stage.*

Figure 10–17: *Use your Align panel to align the set its formatting.*

6. Select the Over frame and use the F6 shortcut key to create a keyframe. Using the Text tool, select the text and use the color swatch on the Property Inspector to set the color to light orange (#FFCC33).

7. Insert a keyframe in the Down frame. Select the text, and use the color swatch in the Property Inspector to set its color to pale grey (#CCCCCC).

8. Finally, you will need to set a Hit area for your button. Because the Hit area relies on solid areas, type will only be clickable on the characters themselves, making it difficult to interact with your button. Instead, you'll use a solid shape (such as a rectangle) to set the Hit area.

    Select the Hit frame of your button, and use the F6 shortcut key to insert a keyframe there.

9. Select the Rectangle tool (□) from the Tools panel, and use the Property Inspector to set a fill color for it (the color is unimportant). As shown in Figure 10-18, click and drag to draw a rectangle on the Hit frame that is larger than the text itself. Use the text duplicated on this keyframe as a reference, drawing the rectangle around it.

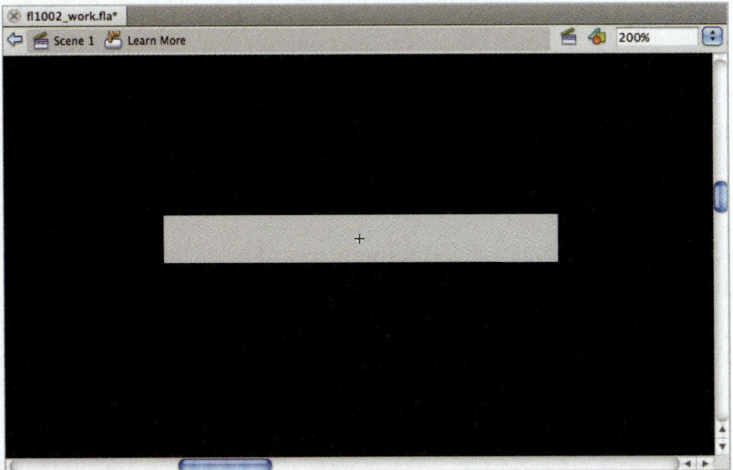

Figure 10-18: *Draw a solid, filled box larger than the actual button text to set the clickable area.*

10. Click the Scene 1 link above the Stage to return to the main Timeline (Figure 10-19). Locate your new Learn More button in the library, and drag an instance to the Buttons layer on the Timeline. Use your Selection tool to position it at the bottom center of the Stage.

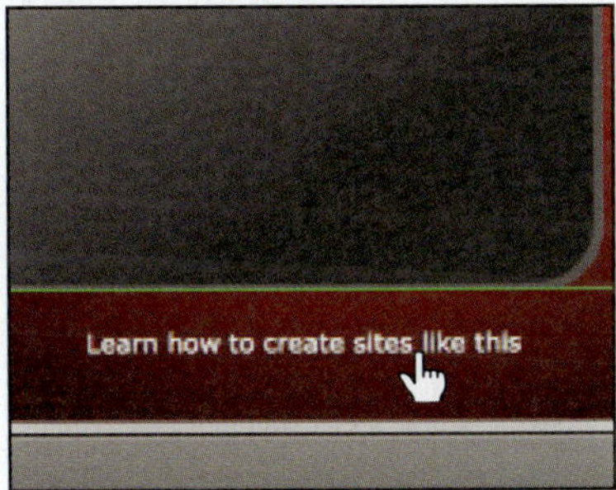

Figure 10-19: *Drag an instance of your new button to the Buttons layer, and position it at the bottom of the Stage.*

11. Choose Control > Test Movie > in Flash Professional to preview your movie. Move your pointer over your new button, and you should see it change colors.

12. Close the Flash Player and choose File > Save to save your work.

Creating frame labels for ActionScript

Now that you've built your navigation buttons, you'll learn to use ActionScript to have those buttons jump to different points on the Timeline that represent your different sections, such as Home, Products, and Services. To help you easily accomplish frame-to-frame navigation, you can name individual keyframes using *frame labels*.

Frame labels are a convenient alternative to using frame numbers for navigation, as they allow you to assign casual names (such as *home*) to a keyframe, and use that within ActionScript. In addition, labels as anchors reference labels in actions. Using frame numbers in ActionScript means that if you change the location of a piece of content along the Timeline, you'll likely have to change the frame number you're referencing.

Frame labels, however, travel with their respective keyframes, so it doesn't matter where the keyframe is along the Timeline, as long as the frame label remains the same. You can also use labels to add comments or notes for yourself directly on a layer in the Timeline. Labels help to organize content on the timeline more efficiently and can even be used to document information by typing content into the label.

Follow these steps to use frame labels

1. Make sure you have the Buttons layer selected, and click the New Layer button (⬚) to add a new layer. Rename the new layer **Labels.**

2. Insert keyframes at frames 5 and 10, using the F6 shortcut key—this lines up with the placement of the different content sections on the Timeline (Figure 10-20).

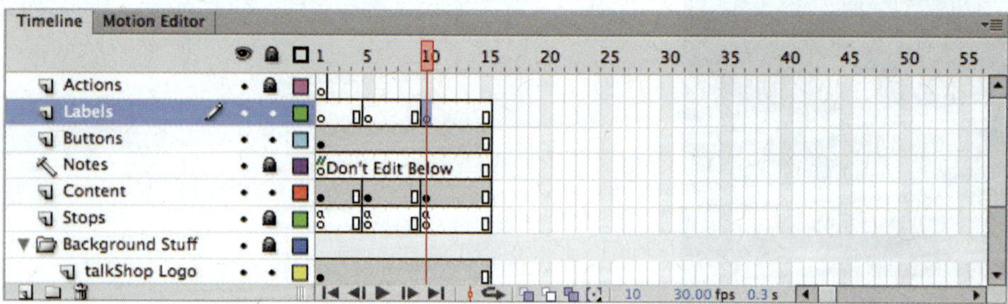

Figure 10-20: *Create a new layer named Labels, and add keyframes at frames 5 and 10, where you'll be creating frame labels.*

3. Click and select keyframe 1 on the Labels layer. In the Property Inspector, type **home** in the Name text field in the Label options area to set a frame label for this frame as shown in Figure 10-21. Press Enter (Windows) or Return (Mac OS). You should see a red flag icon (▸) appear inside the keyframe.

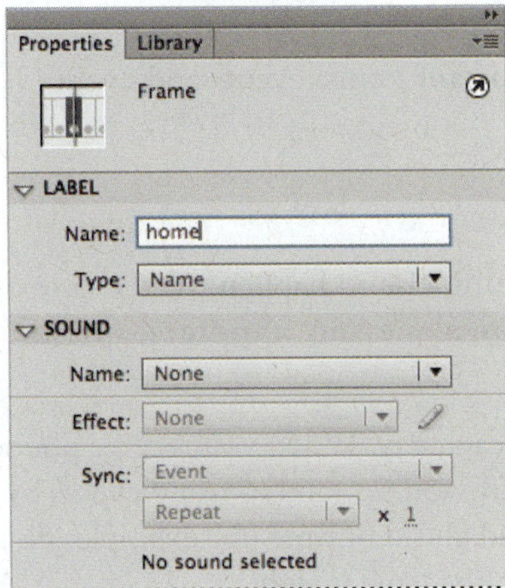

Figure 10-21: Type a frame label of home for keyframe 1 on the Labels layer. You'll add frame labels for keyframes 5 and 10 as well.

4. Repeat step 3, this time add the label **products** at frame 5 and the label **specials** at frame 10 (Figure 10-22).

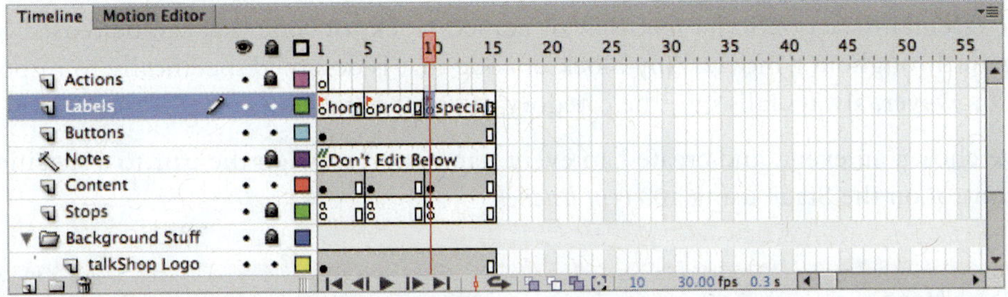

Figure 10-22: The finished layer, which now contains three frame labels that you can later navigate to.

Later on, you'll reference these frame labels in ActionScript to tell your navigation buttons where to send the playhead to view different sections of content across the Timeline.

Take Note...

The Notes layer is created using a frame label set as a comment. Comments place text across the layer itself and are useful for making notes directly on the Timeline, just like the lesson file does here. Please note, however, that comments cannot be used for navigation like frame labels. To set a frame label as a comment, type text in the Property Inspector's Frame text field and choose Comment from the Type menu.

Adding ActionScript: Events and event handlers

Certification Ready 4.11

What are some event-handling concepts in ActionScript 3.0?

You've already explored basic ActionScript in Lesson 9, "Introducing ActionScript," and learned to navigate the Timeline using frame-based actions. While working with buttons involves some similar code, there are some new concepts you'll need to familiarize yourself with to get your buttons up-and-running.

The process of scripting buttons revolves around two important items: events and event listeners.

Understanding events

Simply put, an **event** is an occurrence that triggers something else to happen. In the case of ActionScript, events occur, and blocks of ActionScript known as **event handlers**, run in response to those events.

If you are an employee at a company, you respond to events each day. When you receive phone calls, e-mails, or direct requests from managers and other staff, you respond to those events by carrying out certain tasks. Very often, those tasks are outlined ahead of time (for example, *file an expense report* or *design a logo*) so you're ready to respond when the time is right.

Some events you've become accustomed to during typical website navigation include mouse clicks, rollovers, and keyboard presses.

Responding to events with event handlers

An event handler is a block of ActionScript code that runs in response to an event. Event handlers are essentially ActionScript *functions*, or named blocks of code that can be reused over and over again throughout a movie. Any block of code that is designed specifically to respond to an event, however, always falls into the category of event handlers.

Once you've chosen an event, and created an event handler, you assign the pair to a specific button or control on the Stage using an *event listener*.

Take Note...

A detailed exercise on creating and using functions is included in Lesson 9, "Introducing ActionScript."

Tying it all together with event listeners

Event listeners assign a trigger event (such as a click) and an event handler to a specific button or control on the Stage. Every item in a Flash movie capable of triggering events (such as Button or Movie Clip symbols, and even the Stage) can be assigned an event/event handler pair using the `addEventListener()` method.

You can call this method from a specific button instance, and tell it what type of event to listen for, and what event handler to use if that event occurs:

```
mybutton_btn.addEventListener("click", myEventHandler);
```

To use the employee metaphor from earlier, you could think of your workflow represented in pseudo-code like this:

```
employee.addEventListener("boss calls", submitExpenseReport);
```

To code your buttons in the next exercise, you'll create an event listener function, and then attach that function to your button instances using the *addEventListener( )* method.

New Term: Method

A method is something that an object, or any copy of that object, is capable of doing. For example, a Movie Clip symbol, or any instance of any movie clip, can use its `gotoAndStop()` method to jump the playhead to a specific frame and stop.

Using metaphors once again, you can say that every human being has a `sleep()` and `eat()` method, and that methods can be called from any instance of a human being.

Linking buttons to specific frames

Now that you've set up frame labels across the timeline, you'll use ActionScript to link each button to a specific section within your movie. Each frame label corresponds to a specific section of the site, and the end result is when each button is clicked, users will be sent to that specific section within your movie.

Follow these steps to link buttons to specific frames

1. Click to select frame 1 of the Actions layer in the Timeline. Choose Window > Actions to open the Actions panel. Make sure that Script Assist mode is not active; you can disable it by clicking the Script Assist button in the upper-right corner of the Actions panel.

2. First, you'll build the event handler that will advance the playhead to the Products section. Type the following code on Line 1 in the right side of the Action panel to build the framework of your new event handler:

```
function gotoProducts() {


}
```

Here the function keyword is followed by an arbitrary name, creating a new block of code that you can call later on. The parentheses are a mandatory part of the language and the curly braces are used to group several lines of ActionScript together. You'll add code inside of these braces, which the function will run when called.

Take Note...
All ActionScript is case-sensitive. Be conscious of entering code exactly as it's shown in the steps here, including the same casing.

3. You'll now add the code necessary to instruct the playhead to jump to the Products section when called. On Line 2, in between the two curly braces, add the following line of code:

```
gotoAndStop("products");
```

The `gotoAndStop` action should be familiar to you already, except here you are adding it to an event handler that may be called at any time. The entire event handler should now read:

```
function gotoProducts() {
    gotoAndStop("products");
}
```

You may remember that "products" was the frame label you assigned to keyframe 5 on your Timeline, where the Products information is displayed. You could have also typed `gotoAndStop(5)`, but using the frame label is more flexible in the event that you decide to move content around on the Timeline.

4. Any function that will serve as an event handler (like your `gotoProducts` function) needs a few specific pieces of code to be fully complete. The first item you add lets ActionScript know that your function will not return any type of information, but will instead perform an action and shut down until it's next called.

Directly after the parentheses (no spaces), type **:void**, as shown here:

```
function gotoProducts():void {
    gotoAndStop("products");
}
```

The `:void` return type is just like saying *gives back nothing*. While your event handler will work without it, it's a good practice to include it. If nothing else, this visually distinguishes this function as an event handler, which can never return a value.

Watch your quotes. It's important to use only straight quotes and not curly quotes, sometimes called typographer's quotes. Only the straight quotes function properly.

5. Next, add the following code within the parentheses themselves:

    ```
    evt:Event
    ```

    The entire event handler should now appear like Figure 10-23:

    ```
    function gotoProducts(evt:Event):void {
        gotoAndStop("products");
    }
    ```

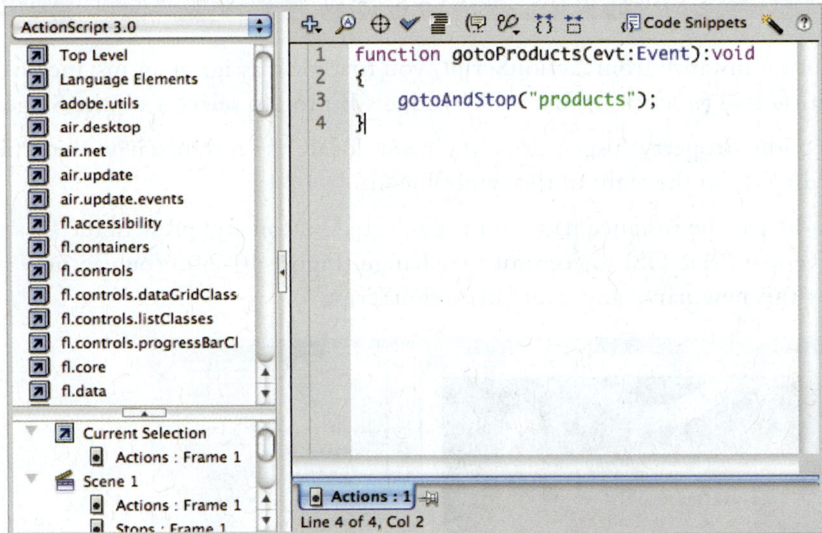

Figure 10-23: The code in the Actions panel should now display as shown above.

This little piece of code is referred to as a parameter, or parameter placeholder. It is designed to act as a container for any information passed into your event handler when and if it's called. While functions can generally be designed to take any number of parameters, event handlers are allowed only one, which is reserved to catch the event information itself.

Here, you've created a parameter named *evt*, which is designed to catch Event-type information.

Take Note...

The Event parameter passed to an event handler contains a number of pieces of useful information, such as the button/control that captured the event and the type of event (such as click) that occurred. At this stage, you won't use this information, but later on in your ActionScript travels, it may prove to be very useful.

6. You've completed your event handler for this one section, Close the Actions panel, then choose File > Save to save your file. In just a moment, you'll add more code to tie it all together.

Adding an event listener to a button

Once you've created an event handler, you'll need to assign it to a control within your movie, such as a button instance. This assignment first tells a button when to run an event handler, and then which event handler to run.

This assignment is created by the `addEventListener()` method.

Step-by-Step | **Follow these steps to add an event listener to a button**

1. To target any button instance from ActionScript, you first must assign it an instance name. Using the Selection tool (↖), click once on the Products Button to select it on the Stage.

2. At the very top of the Property Inspector on the right, locate the instance name text field box, which sits directly to the right of the symbol icon.

3. Type **products_btn** as the instance name for the selected button and press Enter (Windows) or Return (Mac OS) to commit the change (Figure 10-24). You can now refer to this button by this new name anywhere in ActionScript.

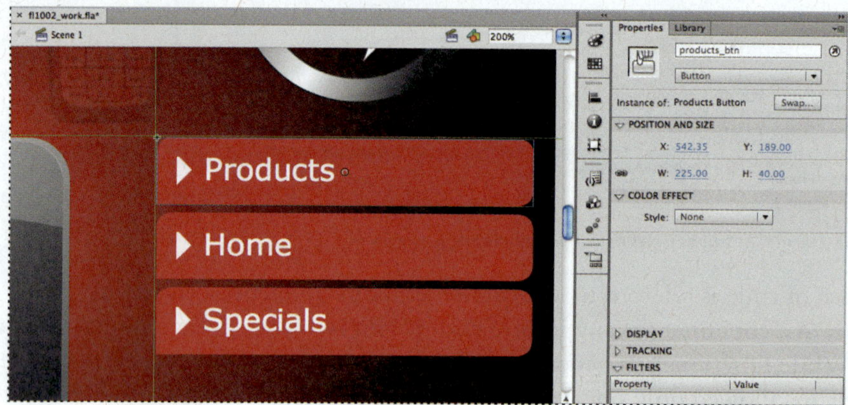

Figure 10-24: *Before you can assign ActionScript to a button instance, you first must assign it an instance name in the Property Inspector.*

4. Press Alt (Windows) or Option (Mac OS), then double-click on the first frame of the Actions layer in the Timeline to open the Actions panel.

5. Below the event handler you created in the last exercise, make a line of space, and add the following code as shown in Figure 10-25:

```
products_btn.addEventListener();
```

```
1  function gotoProducts(evt:Event):void
2  {
3      gotoAndStop("products");
4  }
5  product_btn.addEventListener();
```

Figure 10-25: *Insert a new, full line below your existing code and add the code that ties it all together.*

Here, you've targeted the Products Button by the instance name you just assigned to it, and called its `addEventListener` method. This method can be called from any button instance to assign it an event/event handler pair.

6. Next, you'll fill in the blanks and tell `addEventListener` two important things: first, what type of event this button has to receive to respond, and second, which event handler to use as its response.

Inside of the parentheses following `addEventListener`, type **"click"** (including the quotes), like so:

```
products_btn.addEventListener("click");
```

This lets the button know it's listening for a single click as its event, or trigger.

7. Finally, you will add one more piece of information inside of the parentheses, which is the name of the event handler the button should use as its response when and if it is clicked.

Within the parentheses, but after the click, add a comma and the name of the event handler you created earlier as done in Figure 10-26:

```
products_btn.addEventListener("click",gotoProducts);
```

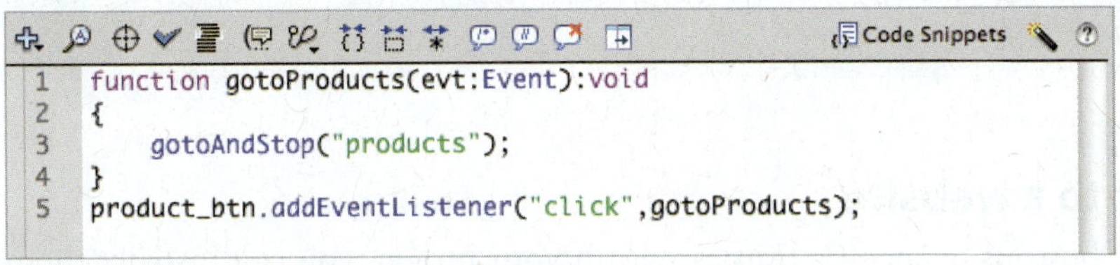

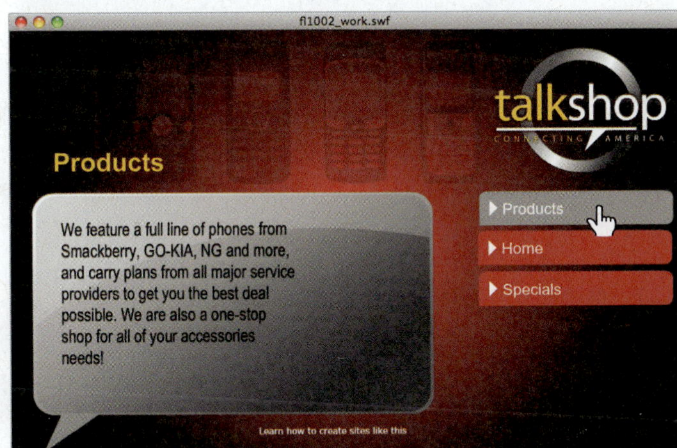

Figure 10-26: The completed code as it appears in your Actions panel.

8. Close the Actions panel, and choose Control > Test Movie > in Flash Professional to preview your movie. Clicking on the Products Button should now advance you to the Products section within your movie (Figure 10-27).

Close the Flash Player and keep the file open.

Figure 10-27: Your button should now advance you to the Products section when clicked.

Troubleshooting events, event handlers, and event listeners

Casing or spelling errors in your code may generate errors when you try and test your movie, and ultimately prevent your movie from working properly. If the Compiler Errors panel appears on preview or publish, and lists any errors, check first for the following:

1. Pay careful attention to the line numbers referenced in any errors that come up—they can be essential in finding out exactly where the error lies.

2. Use the Check Syntax button at the top of the Actions panel to check for any code errors on the spot. This will display a warning dialog if your code is not correct.

3. Review the code shown in the lesson steps to check for spelling, casing, or naming errors.

4. Make sure that the instance name you assigned your button exactly matches the instance name you're targeting in ActionScript. Even with instance names, a discrepancy in casing or spelling will be a problem.

5. Look for missing parentheses or curly braces. Curly braces and parentheses always work in sets—if you see a starting or ending brace or parenthesis without a mate, this could be your problem.

Linking buttons to a website

In addition to linking buttons to specific frames within your movie, you can instruct them to jump to a local web page, external website address, or file download.

In this exercise, you'll use the Code Snippets Panel to add the necessary code to have your button jump to an outside website. You worked with the Code Snippets panel in Lesson 9, "Introducing ActionScript." In this exercise, you'll work with it again as an alternative to coding this task by hand.

Introducing navigateToURL() and URLRequest()

The `navigateToURL` method was introduced in ActionScript 3.0, and is used to instruct your movie to open a local or remote web page in a browser or download a file. You can place `navigateToURL` directly on a keyframe to have it run at a specific moment in time or, like you're about to do here, add it to an event handler so a URL is opened in conjunction with a button click.

Take Note...

Experienced Flash users please note: `navigateToURL` *replaces ActionScript 2.0's* `getURL()` *method.*

When feeding a URL to just about any ActionScript 3.0 method, that URL first needs to be wrapped inside of a new `URLRequest()` object. Think of *URLRequest* as a fancy container that a URL must be placed in before handing it to ActionScript methods such as `navigateToURL`.

While `URLRequest` has many uses that go beyond the scope of this book, you'll get to use a single `URLRequest` object to get one of your buttons to launch an external web page in your system's default web browser. You'll see how the Code Snippets panel uses these two actions to make it all happen.

<table><tr><td>**Follow these steps to assign actions using the Code Snippets panel**</td><td>**Step-by-Step**</td></tr></table>

1. First, you'll need to select a button on the Stage and assign it an instance name so you can reference it in ActionScript. Click to select the Learn button instance at the bottom of the Stage. At the top of the Property Inspector on the right, type **learn_btn** in the instance name text field as shown in Figure 10-28. Note that if you do not create an instance name for your button, the Code Snippets panel will do it for you.

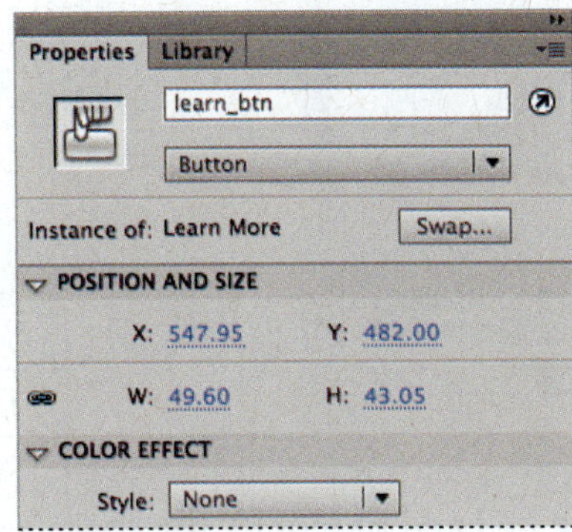

Figure 10-28: Assign the text-based button at the bottom of your Stage an instance name of learn_btn.

2. Make sure the Learn button is still selected, and expand the Code Snippets panel. If the Code Snippets panel is not visible, choose Window > Code Snippets to open it. Note that in the default workspace, the Code Snippets panel is collapsed into icon view on the right side of your workspace.

3. Within the Code Snippets panel, locate and expand the Actions folder. Locate and double-click the Click to Go to Web Page snippet as shown in Figure 10-29.

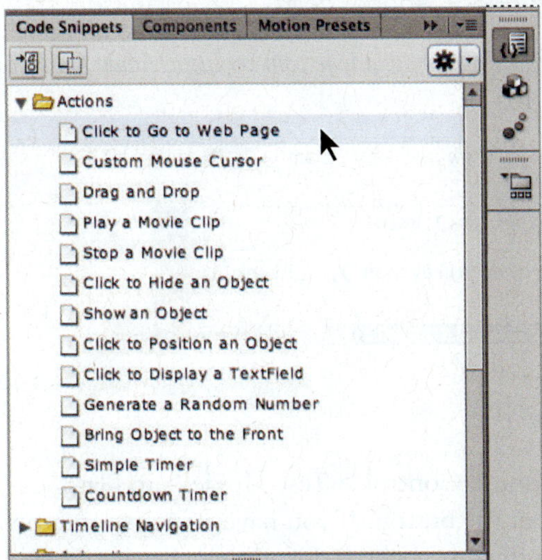

Figure 10-29: Add a new code snippet to open a web page.

The Actions panel will appear, and the new code will be placed below the existing code in the Script window as shown in Figure 10-30.

```
 1  function gotoProducts(evt:Event):void {
 2      gotoAndStop("products");
 3  }
 4  products_btn.addEventListener("click", gotoProducts);
 5  /* Click to Go to Web Page
 6  Clicking on the specified symbol instance loads the URL in a new brows
 7
 8  Instructions:
 9  1. Replace http://www.adobe.com with the desired URL address.
10     Keep the quotation marks ("").
11  */
12
13  learn_btn.addEventListener(MouseEvent.CLICK, fl_ClickToGoToWebPage);
14
15  function fl_ClickToGoToWebPage(event:MouseEvent):void
16  {
17      navigateToURL(new URLRequest("http://www.adobe.com"), "_blank");
18  }
19
```

Figure 10-30: Add a new event handler to open a web page.

Now, you'll use some of your experience creating code by hand to modify the code created by the Code Snippets panel. Specifically, you'll need to adjust the URL that you want the button to go to when clicked.

Take Note...

Be careful of the parentheses at the end. You should have two closing parentheses as shown here: one for `navigateToURL` *and the other for* `URLRequest`*.*

4. In the Actions panel, locate the line that reads:

```
navigateToURL(new URLRequest("http://www.adobe.com"), "_blank");
```

In the double quotes, change the URL from *http://www.adobe.com* to *http://www.wiley.com*. The resulting code should appear as Figure 10-31:

```
navigateToURL(new URLRequest("http://www.wiley.com"), "_blank");
```

```
15  function fl_ClickToGoToWebPage(event:MouseEvent):void
16  {
17      navigateToURL(new URLRequest("http://www.wiley.com"), "_blank");
18  }
19
```

Figure 10-31: Modify the code created by the Code Snippets panel.

Close the Actions panel.

5. Choose File > Save to save your work, and choose Control > Test Movie > in Flash Professional to preview your movie and try out the button. If you have an active Internet connection, the Wiley website should launch in your system's default web browser.

6. Close the browser window.

Skill summary

In this lesson you learned how to:	Objective
Identify general and Flash-specific best practices for designing rich media content for the web, mobile apps, and AIR applications	2.1
Create objects and convert them to symbols, including graphics, movie clips, and buttons	4.6
Create animations (changes in shape, position, size, color, and transparency)	4.10
Add simple controls through ActionScript 3.0	4.11

Knowledge Assessment

True/False

Circle **T** if the statement is true or **F** if the statement is false.

T F 1. There are three different types of symbols in Adobe Flash.

T F 2. Filters cannot be applied to button symbols; they can only be applied to movie clips.

T F 3. The color choice you make for the shape of your hit area is very important to the button's operation.

T F 4. You can create buttons from existing graphics on the Stage like any other symbol.

T F 5. Keyframes cannot be applied to the different button states like Up and Over.

T F 6. Buttons have multiple layers like movie clips and graphic symbols.

T F 7. Text cannot be applied within a button, it must be created on the stage and applied as a separate graphic.

T F 8. Frame labels are a convenient alternative to using frame numbers for navigation.

T F 9. Buttons cannot be tested on the Stage; you must test buttons using Flash Player.

T F 10. A method is something that an object, or any copy of that object, is capable of doing.

Multiple Choice

Select the best response for the following statements.

1. Which of the following is not a button state?

   a. Up state

   b. Over state

   c. Press state

   d. Down state

2. What is the name of the area that defines the hot spot where the button becomes active when the user moves over it?

    a. Active area

    b. Interactive area

    c. Hit area

    d. Code area

3. Which of the following is important when designing buttons?

    a. Interesting design

    b. Button purpose

    c. Easy to find

    d. All of the above

4. What should drive the need for buttons in terms of how many you include throughout your project?

    a. Staying trending with the maximum use of screen space

    b. The need for constant control to navigate anywhere at all times

    c. The nature of the content

    d. The designer's personal preferences

5. A problem with text buttons is that if the mouse pointer is not precisely on a type character, the button will remain inactive unless you incorporate a:

    a. ActionScript function

    b. Hit area

    c. Graphic background

    d. All of the above

6. What type of layer can be used to leave notes for yourself or another designer in the Timeline?

    a. Comment

    b. Guide

    c. Mask

    d. Masked

7. What is considered an occurrence that triggers something else to happen?

    a. Behavior

    b. Trigger

    c. Event

    d. Event Handler

8. What is considered a block of ActionScript code that runs in response to the correct answer for the previous question?

    a. Behavior

    b. Trigger

    c. Event

    d. Event Handler

9. What is the code element that actually connects the button to the code functions you're creating?

   a. Event

   b. Event Handler

   c. Event Listener

   d. Event Connector

10. Which of the following may generate errors in your code?

    a. Casing or spelling errors

    b. Color coding choices you make in the preferences regarding the code format

    c. Indenting

    d. Not deleting old comments

Competency Assessment

The Button Library	Project 10-1

Now that you've built some buttons from scratch, it's time to introduce some built-in buttons that may provide both convenience and design inspiration. Flash contains some pretty extensive choices to get you started with buttons when you may not have the time to come up with a design yourself.

1. Create a new ActionScript 3.0 document in Flash.

2. Choose Window > Common Libraries > Buttons.

3. Click and drag the scroll bar on the side to examine the various categories at your disposal.

4. Click on the arrow to the side of the folder called buttons tube.

5. Click and drag the tube blue button to the Stage.

6. To test the button's reaction when you mouse over it, go to Control > Enable Simple Buttons.

7. When you finish testing, once again choose Control > Enable Simple Buttons to disable the button preview.

8. Save the file as **buttons.fla** and keep it open for the next project.

The Button Library — Part Two	Project 10-2

The built-in buttons that come with Flash are great but can look a little stock. And what if you need to put in more specific information? No worries, you'll find the buttons easy enough to break down and manipulate...

1. The **buttons.fla** file should still be open from the previous project.

2. Double-click the Enter button on the Stage to open it in the symbol editor.

3. Unlock the layers and start to make adjustments to the various layer components as needed.

4. Save the file as **buttons_10.2.fla**.

Proficiency Assessment

Project 10-3	**Anything can be a button (well, almost anything)**

Remember the hit area in your buttons? That hit area is basically just an invisible, interactive zone, right? With that in mind, you can use that more strategically beyond just text buttons to create interactive elements such as pictures that have a specific interactive area rather than the whole thing being one big, button. You'll need a picture handy to work with for this next exercise.

1. Create a new ActionScript 3.0 document in Flash.

2. Import a picture into Flash or use the **fl0803.psd** file from the fl08lessons folder.

3. Create a new button symbol calling it **picture button**. Drop your picture into the Up state of the button. Add a blank keyframe to the Hit state. Draw a circle where you want the hit area to be on the picture.

4. Drag the new picture button to the Stage. Choose Control > Enable Simple Buttons and note the only time the mouse reacts to an interactive area is when you move to where the circle was placed in step #3.

5. Save the file as **hit_state.fla** and keep this file open for the next project.

Project 10-4	**Email links**

Linking to other websites is cool, but let's do another variation that's just as practical.

1. The file from the previous project should still be open.

2. Select the button picture on the Stage and apply the instance name picturebtn in the instance name field of the Properties panel.

3. Go to Window > Code Snippets. In the Actions folder, apply the Click to Go to Web Page action to the button.

4. Choose Window > Actions. On line 13 of the code, change "http://www.adobe.com" to **"mailto: youremailaddress@here.com"** to set up an email link to yourself.

5. Save the file as **flash_url.fla**.

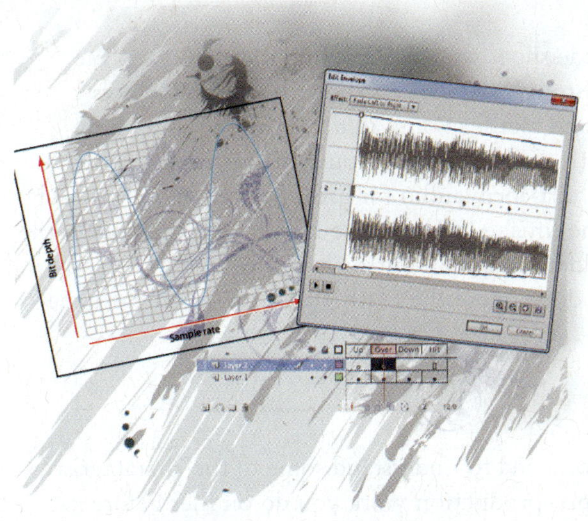

Adding Sound to Your Movies

Key Terms

- Event sounds
- looping
- MP3
- SoundMixer
- stopAll()
- Sync menu

Skill	Objective
Import and use sound	**4.12**

Business case

Sound is something that can take your projects to a whole new level in terms of dimension and experience for the user. Using music can help set the tone and "feel" of your piece while narration can share information and lend a personality to the experience as well. Learning how to control sound and how to use sound as an accentual element are important to using sound effectively and efficiently.

Starting up

Before starting, make sure that your tools and panels are consistent by resetting your workspace. See "Resetting the Flash workspace" in the Starting up section of this book.

You will work with several files from the fl11lessons folder in this lesson. Make sure that you have loaded the fllessons folder onto your hard drive from *http://www.wiley.com/college/sc/adobeseries*. See "Loading lesson files" in the Starting up section of this book.

The project

In this lesson, you will build an interactive slide show with background music to keep the listener engaged, narration to walk the user through the various slides, and sound effects to make the navigation feel more interactive and tactile. You will complete the slide show by importing and placing sounds included with the lesson files. You will also explore how Flash lets you optimize the use of long- and short-form audio for great performance, without sacrificing quality or presentation. To view the finished file, choose File > Open and select the **fl1101_done.fla** file within the fl11lessons folder. Choose Control > Test Movie > in Flash Professional to preview the movie, and when done, close the Flash player, and then close the .fla file.

Preparing sound files for Flash

Before bringing your audio files into Flash, you need to understand some of the characteristics and settings for digital audio files. The more pre-production work you do on files before importing them into Flash, the more likely it is that you'll get the results you want the first time around. In the next few sections, you'll explore the key properties of digital audio files along with some recommendations for preparing your files for import and use in your Flash movies.

Sample rate and bit depth

Digital audio is sound that has been converted from analog sound waves into a series of bits and bytes. The conversion takes place through the use of an A/D (analog-to-digital) converter. Your computer microphone jack contains a very basic converter; audio professionals use high-end units capable of reproducing sound at a much higher level of quality and accuracy. The quality of digital audio is determined by two important factors: sample rate and bit depth.

The *sample rate* refers to the number of samples of an audio waveform that the converter digitizes in one second, and it is analogous to the resolution of a digital photo. The more samples (or pictures) captured in each second, the more accurately the waveform is represented. Although the sample rate is specified when the sound file is recorded or converted, you can adjust it down or up later. As with digital images, however, if the detail wasn't in the original file, increasing the sample rate (or resolution) will not improve it.

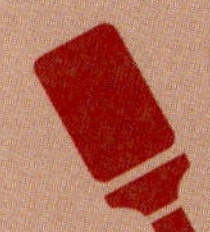

Take Note...

Always capture audio at a higher sample rate than you think you'll need. If necessary, you can downsample later to a lower sample rate, which reduces audio file size.

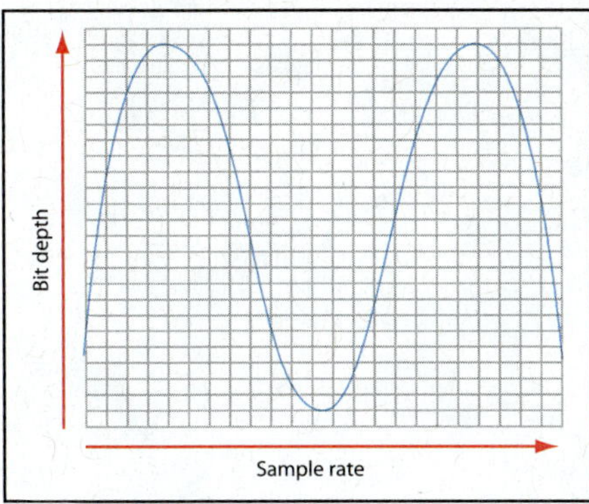

Figure 11-1: *An audio waveform representation of sample rate and bit depth.*

Bit depth determines the amount of information that each sample contains; think of it as similar to a digital photo's bit depth setting. The higher the bit depth of a photo, the wider the range of shades available to reproduce the original colors and details. In the audio world, bit depth is responsible for reproducing the amplitude (loudness) and dynamic range of an audio waveform. Low bit depth settings, such as 8 bits or less, produce poor recordings of limited quality, akin to a telephone answering machine (Figure 11-1). In contrast, a bit depth of 16 bits is sufficient for reproducing the wide range of instruments and vocals found in professionally recorded music.

For reference, audio on a commercial compact disc has a sample rate of 44.1 kHz (or 44,100 samples per second) and a bit depth of 16.

If you plan to record your own audio, pay attention to the sample rate and bit depth settings in your software and consider what they'll mean to the quality of the original sound. Mid- to professional-level audio applications, such as Avid Pro Tools, Steinberg's Cubase or Nuendo, Apple Logic, and Adobe Soundbooth all provide a range of options and tools for recording, importing, editing, and exporting digital audio into a variety of formats. If you'd prefer to let someone else do the recording, you can find many royalty-free sound effects and loops online in a variety of formats and quality settings.

Editing your audio

Although you can perform basic editing and trimming in Flash (Figure 11-2), to conserve space you should edit your sound files to some degree before importing them. Large audio files sitting in your library can bloat your Flash document (.fla file) unnecessarily. Why import unwanted, extra audio that you know will never be used in your movie?

If you need a basic sound-editing application, your choices range from low-cost shareware to full-featured professional programs. If you are creating original audio for your movie, consider an application that at least lets you trim, cut, copy, and paste, as well as export a variety of popular file formats. (You'll learn about Flash's built-in editing controls later in the lesson.)

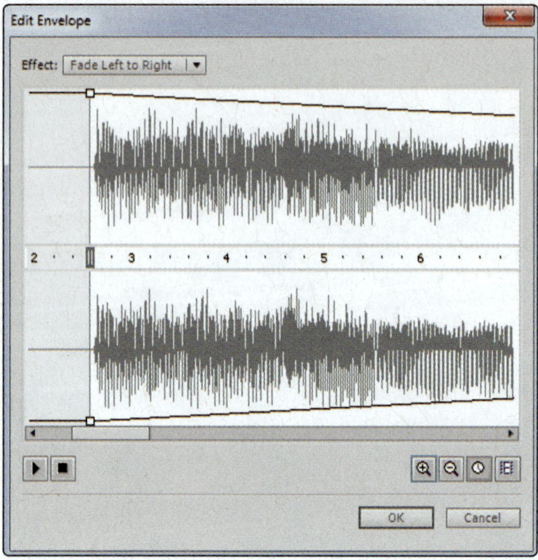

Figure 11-2: *Flash's Edit window provides basic trimming, pan effects, and volume editing.*

Mono or stereo

The nature of your source audio will determine whether you should stick with mono or stereo channels for your final output. Single-channel mono audio is a suitable choice for a solo recording of narration or voice. If you are working with prerecorded music or sound effects that pan from left to right, stereo is the best choice; with mono recording, you may lose a great deal of the perspective and placement (this is especially true with music). Keep in mind that stereo files include two channels (left and right), and will often take up twice as much storage space as a mono sound file at the same settings (Figure 11-3). Whether you record in mono or stereo, Flash has a series of built-in effects, such as fades and stereo effects, which you can apply to any sound you import.

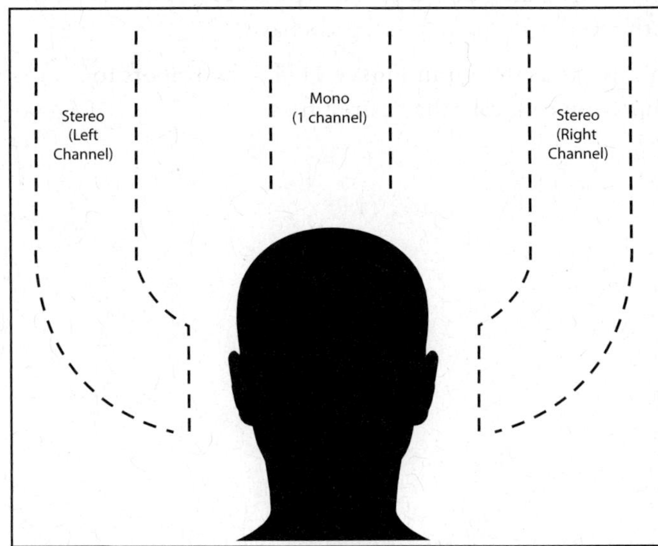

Figure 11-3: *Mono reproduces audio in a single channel, while stereo does it in two channels.*

Audio file formats

Flash imports three common file formats: Windows .wav, Mac OS .aiff, and .mp3. If you have QuickTime installed, you can also import additional audio file formats such as Avid's Sound Designer II format. The **.mp3** format differs slightly from the others because it compresses audio to facilitate file exchange and streaming over the Web. In addition, .mp3 files use a system of Kbps (kilobits per second) to determine overall quality. The average is 128 Kbps, but you can encode at a much higher level if your software supports it. For the highest quality, keep your source .mp3 files within the 128 to 192 Kbps range.

Which file format is the right one? The answer largely depends on your operating system, as well as the software you use to create and export audio. No matter which file format you start with, Flash performs its own compression on audio included in your movies and converts all the audio in your final .swf file to .mp3 format. You can set specific quality parameters in the Publish settings for your movie.

Certification Ready 4.12

What audio file types can be imported for use in a Flash document?

Importing sounds

To use a sound in Flash, you first must import it using the Import menu's Import to Library command. You'll import this lesson's sound files, so that you can begin to explore and place them on the Timeline.

Step-by-Step

Follow these steps to import sound files

1. Choose File > Open and navigate to the fl11lessons folder. Select the file **fl1101.fla** and press Open.

2. Choose File > Save As. When the Save As dialog box appears, type **fl1101_work.fla** into the Save As text field. Navigate to the fl11lessons folder and press Save.

3. Choose File > Import > Import to Library as shown in Figure 11-4. The Import to Library dialog box opens and prompts you to locate the desired files.

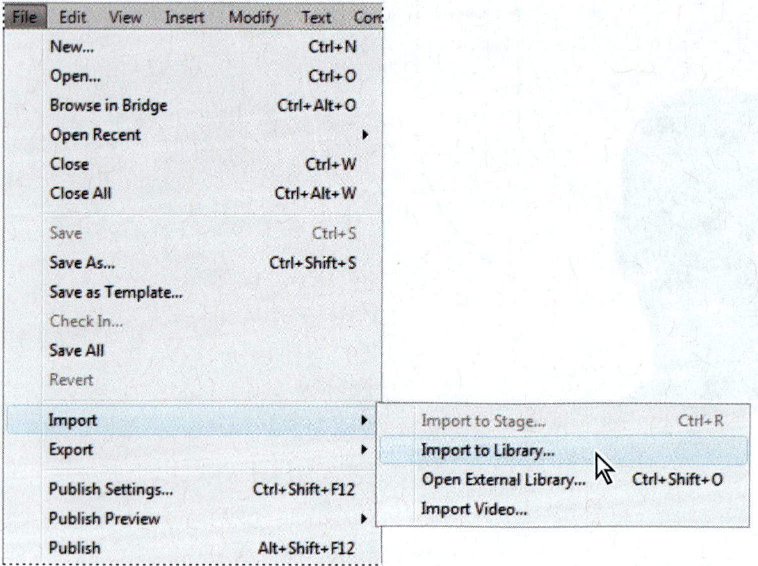

Figure 11-4: Use the Import to Library command to select and add sound files to your Flash movie.

4. Open the Sounds folder inside the fl11lessons folder. Hold down the Shift key, select the folder's nine .wav sound files, and choose Open to import the files directly to your Library panel.

5. If it's not already open, launch the Library panel by choosing Window > Library. The nine sound files appear as assets marked with a speaker icon as shown in Figure 11-5.

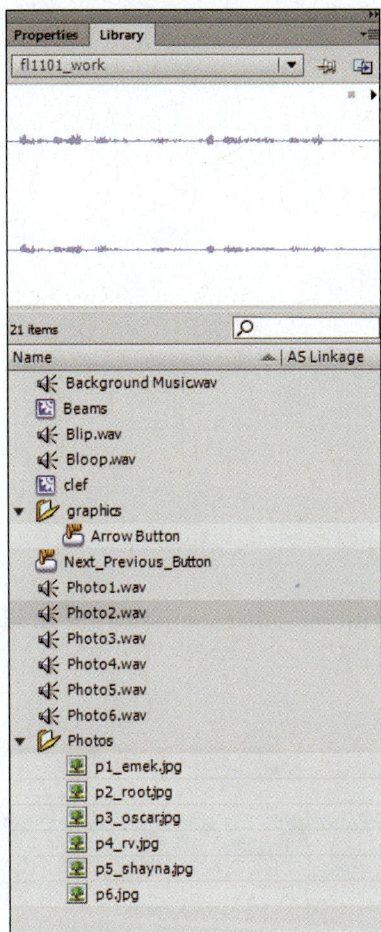

Figure 11–5: Each imported sound file appears in the Library panel with a speaker icon. You can use the Play button in the Preview pane at the top to listen to a sound.

6. In the Library panel, select the Blip.wav sound file. Notice that the Preview window (Figure 11-6) at the top of the panel now shows the sound as a waveform and also features small Play and Stop buttons in the upper-right corner.

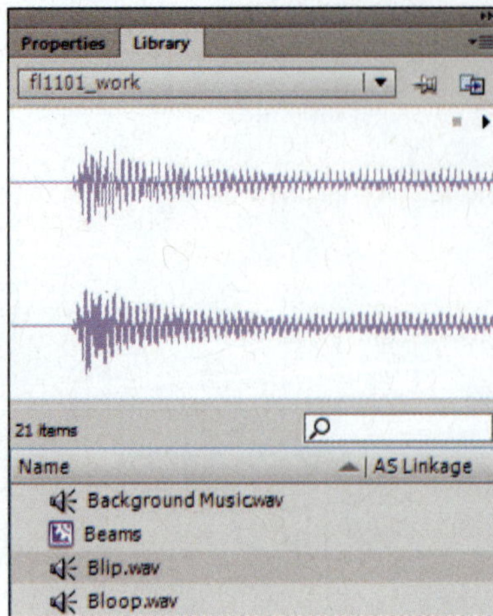

Figure 11-6: The Preview window displays the sound's waveform when selected.

7. Click the Play button to listen to the sound. Try this with the other sounds to get an idea of what each file contains.

8. Choose File > Save to save your work.

Take Note...
Use the techniques you learned in Lesson 3 to organize your imported sound files into a new folder if you'd like.

Placing sounds on the Timeline

To play a sound at a specific point in your movie, you place the sound on a keyframe on the Timeline. When the playhead reaches the frame where you placed the sound, you'll hear it. To place a sound, you'll select a keyframe and use the Sound options found in the Property Inspector.

You'll see in the following lessons how additional options in the Sound menu can loop sounds or create effects such as fades and pans. There are a few simple rules: sounds must be placed on keyframes, and you can place only one sound per keyframe (on a single layer).

Adding sound to your slide show project

The lesson file contains a photo slide show with six photos and captions arranged across the Timeline. Two buttons on either side of the photo let the user move forward or backward through the photos. You'll enhance this photo slide show by adding background music, a vocal narration for each photo, and subtle sound effects for the Next and Previous navigation buttons.

To begin, make sure your Property Inspector is visible by choosing Window > Properties.

<table><tr><td>**Follow these steps to add sound to a project**</td><td>**Step-by-Step**</td></tr></table>

1. Locate and expand (if necessary) the Sound layers folder on the Timeline as shown in Figure 11-7. Locate the empty layer titled Sounds. Select keyframe 1 on this layer.

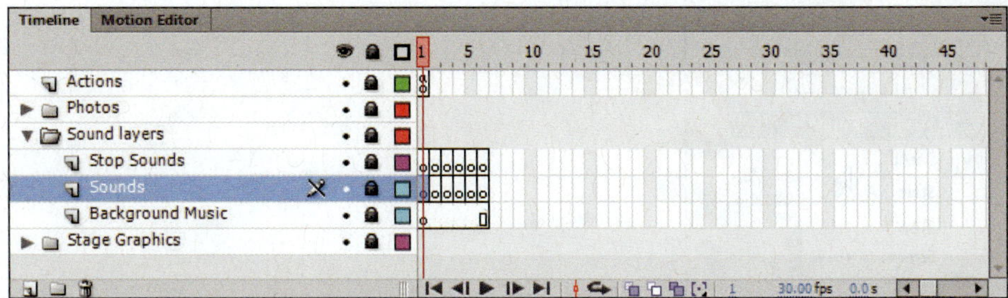

Figure 11-7: *A layer folder and individual keyframes are already created for you so that you can place sounds on the Timeline.*

2. With the keyframe selected, locate and expand the Sound options located in the Property Inspector. Click on the Name drop-down menu, which lists all the sounds available in the library. As shown in Figure 11-8, you should see all the sound files listed that you imported earlier.

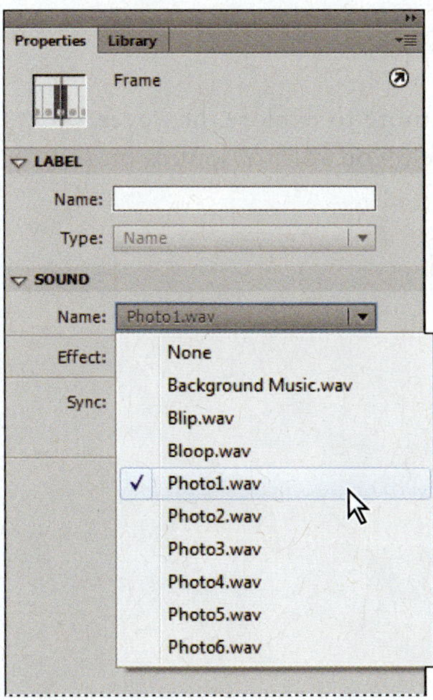

Figure 11-8: *Place a sound on the selected keyframe from the Name menu (located under Sound options).*

3. Select the sound named Photo 1.wav from the Sound menu to place that sound on the selected keyframe.

4. From the Sync drop-down menu right below, make sure Event is selected (Figure 11-9), which should be the default option. For an explanation of Sync options, see the sidebar, "Sync options and sound types."

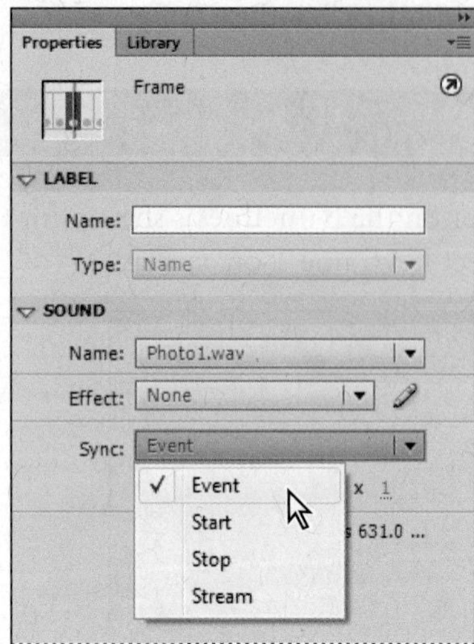

Figure 11-9*: Each sound's playback and loading behavior can be controlled with the Sync menu.*

By default, each new sound added to the Timeline has the Repeat option selected and set to 1. You will learn how to change this later on.

5. Press Ctrl+Enter (Windows) or Command+Return (Mac OS) to preview the movie in the Flash Player. You should hear the Photo1.wav sound play when the movie appears. Close the Flash Player and return to the main Stage.

6. Choose File > Save to save your work.

Adding a sound on the Timeline is that easy. There's more to explore, however. Next, you'll take a look at some of the sound options that help you control sounds on the Timeline.

Adding the remaining narration

You'll now add the remaining pieces of narration to their respective photos on the Timeline. Remember that these sounds should occur right when the playhead moves and the new photo is shown, so you'll need to set each one as an Event sound. The steps should be familiar to you.

<table><tr><td>**Follow these steps to add narration to a project**</td><td>**Step-by-Step**</td></tr></table>

1. In the Timeline panel, select keyframe 2 of the Sounds layer as shown in Figure 11-10. Use the Name drop-down menu in the Property Inspector's Sound options (Figure 11-11) to assign the Photo2.wav sound from the list. Note that you can also drag a sound file from the Library and drop it onto the stage to add sound to the Timeline.

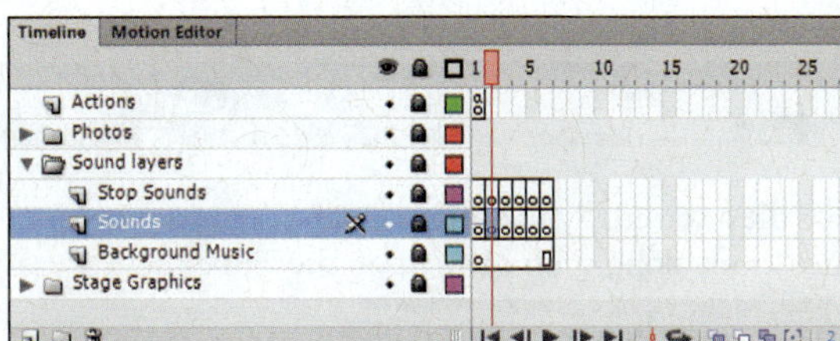

Figure 11-10: Begin assigning a sound to each sequential keyframe for all six photos.

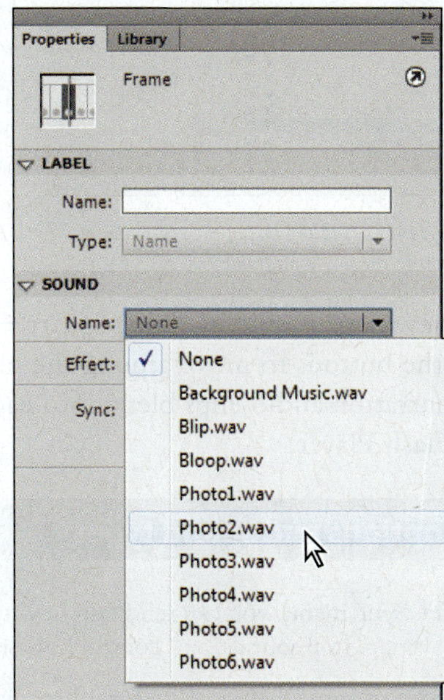

Figure 11-11: Use the Property Inspector.

2. Make sure Event is selected in the Sync drop-down menu. By default, Flash uses the last Sync settings chosen, so it's often unnecessary to reselect this option.

3. Repeat steps 1 and 2 for the remaining four photos as shown in Figure 11-12, setting the sound Photo3.wav on frame 3, Photo4.wav on frame 4, and so on, until you finally place Photo6.wav on frame 6 (Figure 11-13).

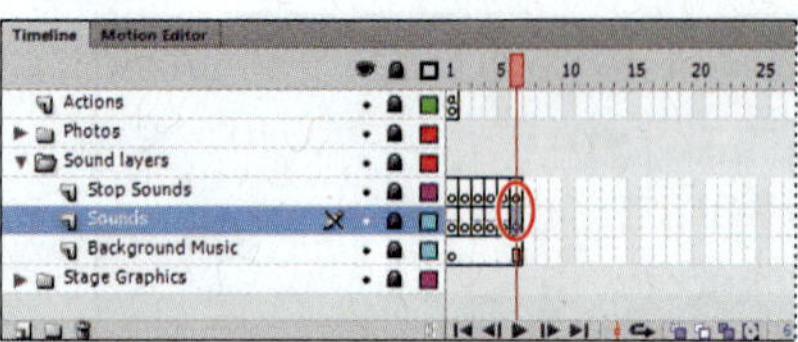

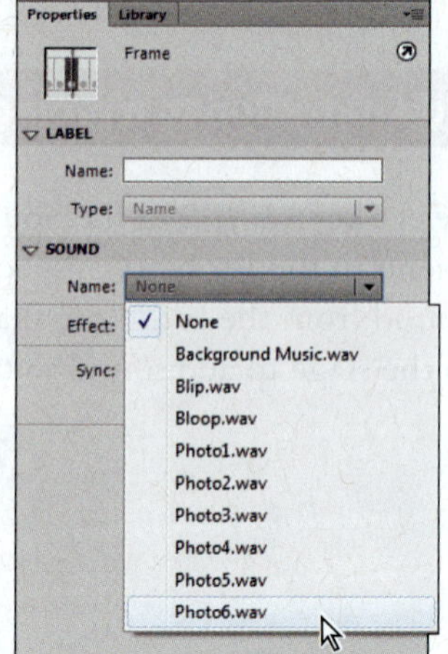

Figure 11-12: Add the last of the six pieces of narration to the photo on frame 6.

Figure 11-13: Use the Property Inspector.

4. Preview your movie by pressing Ctrl+Enter (Windows) or Command+Return (Mac OS). Use the buttons to move among the photos. You may notice that if you move too quickly, the narration audio clips blend into each other. You'll fix this later on in the chapter. Close the Flash Player.

Learning More	**Sync options and sound types**
Certification Ready 4.12 What do the terms stream and event mean?	From the Sync menu, you can tell Flash how to handle a sound. Sync options can be used to control sound overlap, stop sounds, and control how sounds work along with content on the Timeline. Event sounds must fully load before they play back, and they respond to events (such as the playhead reaching a certain frame, as in the previous exercise) or actions (such as a button click, as in the *Adding sound effects to buttons* section). Because you want the slide show narrations to occur in tandem with the user clicking the Next and Previous buttons, be sure to set them to Event sounds, as you did in the previous exercise. Stream sounds work best for long-form animation, as the audio is matched to the playback, like a soundtrack. Flash does everything it can to keep the sound in sync with the animation, including dropping frames if necessary. A continuous sound (such as a soundtrack or one continuous piece of dialog) that needs to sync with the Timeline from start to finish would be ideally set as a Stream sound. Start plays a sound so that no other instance of that same sound file can be playing at the same time. This makes Start sounds a great choice if you want to prevent unwanted overlap. A Start sound will play all the way through to the end, and can only be stopped by an instance of the same sound whose Sync is set to Stop. Stop sounds don't play a sound, but rather stop a specific sound. When choosing Stop for a selected sound, you will stop any instance of that sound that's already playing. Stop sounds can only stop instances of the same sound whose Sync is set to Start.

Adding sound effects to buttons

Sounds are a great way to enhance navigation, and they can make interacting with buttons feel more *real*. You learned about button symbols in Lesson 10, "Creating Navigation Controls." You know that buttons contain four frames, three of which correspond to the buttons' different visual states. The Over and Down frames of the slide show navigation buttons are the perfect locations to place Event sounds that will trigger on a rollover (the Over state) and click of the mouse (the Down state), respectively.

Placing Event sounds on button frames

Event sounds work independently of the Timeline and must be fully loaded before they can play back. The best example of this is a short sound placed on a button frame. Your user can click a button at any time, so an Event sound will be ready to respond to that click without any relation to other content on the Timeline. In this exercise, you'll place some sounds from your library on your Next and Previous buttons for both rollover and click actions. Both the Next and Previous buttons are instances of the Next_Previous_Button symbol in the library, so you'll only need to edit one to add sounds to both instances.

<table>
<tr><td>**Follow these steps to place Event sounds on button frames**</td><td>**Step-by-Step**</td></tr>
</table>

1. Expand the Stage Graphics layer folder on the Timeline, and, if necessary, unlock all layers under the Stage Graphics folder. Double-click the oval portion of the Previous (left) button to edit it directly on the Stage.

   In the button's Edit mode, you will see its four frames: Up, Over, Down, and Hit.

   You'll be placing sounds on the Over and Down frames, so that sounds will go off when a user rolls over or clicks on the buttons.

2. On the Sounds layer, as shown in Figure 11-14 select the Over keyframe and make sure the Property Inspector and Sound options are visible on the right.

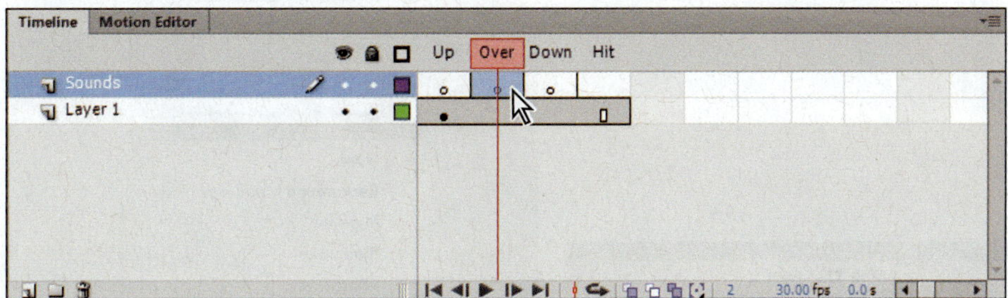

Figure 11-14: Assign the Blip.wav sound to the Over frame of your buttons.

3. From the Sound options on the right, choose the Blip.wav sound from the Name menu as shown in Figure 11-15. In the Sync drop-down menu, leave Event selected.

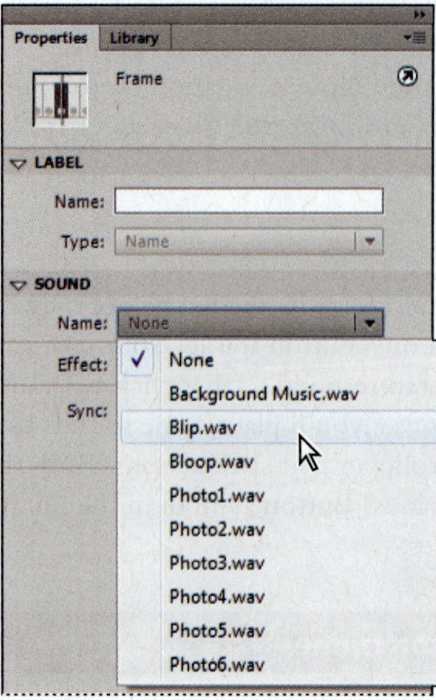

Figure 11-15: Assign the Blip.wav sound to the Over frame of your buttons.

4. On the Sounds layer, select the Down keyframe, and select the Bloop.wav sound for this frame (Figure 11-16). In the Sync drop-down menu, leave Event selected (Figure 11-17).

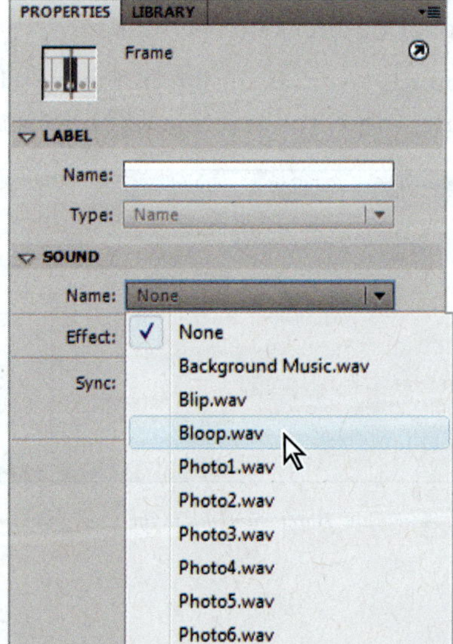

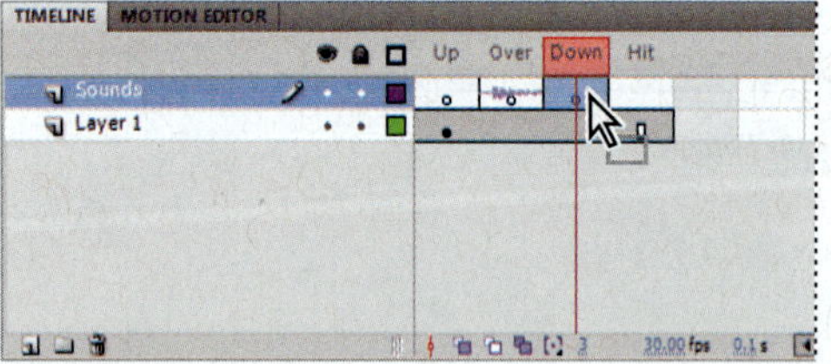

Figure 11-16: Assign the Bloop.wav sound to the Over keyframe of your buttons.

Figure 11-17: Leave Event selected.

5. Exit the button by clicking the Scene 1 link above the Stage, and return to the main Timeline. Because both buttons are instances of the Arrow button symbol, it's not necessary to edit the *Next* button on the right side of the Stage.

6. Press Ctrl+Enter (Windows) or Command+Return (Mac OS) to preview your movie. Rolling over the buttons should trigger a different sound than clicking them.

7. Close the Flash Player, and choose File > Save to save your work.

Editing sounds

If you find you need to adjust imported sounds, Flash offers some very useful tools for basic editing, effects, and sound manipulation. You'll explore these tools' options while adding the background music loop to your photo slide show.

Little audio dynamite: the Edit Envelope panel

When your sounds still need a little something extra, Flash's Edit Envelope panel offers you many ways to trim, fade, and pan your audio for the best possible soundtrack. The Edit Envelope panel is opened using the Edit button that appears on the Property Inspector when a sound on the Timeline is selected.

The Edit Envelope panel displays your sound as a waveform, or visual representation, of the length and volume of the sound as shown in Figure 11-18. Each channel of a sound displays its own waveform in the panel; a line above the waveform indicates the sound's current volume. You can edit volume by adding handles to the volume envelope to move the line up or down. By default, the line is all the way up (full volume).

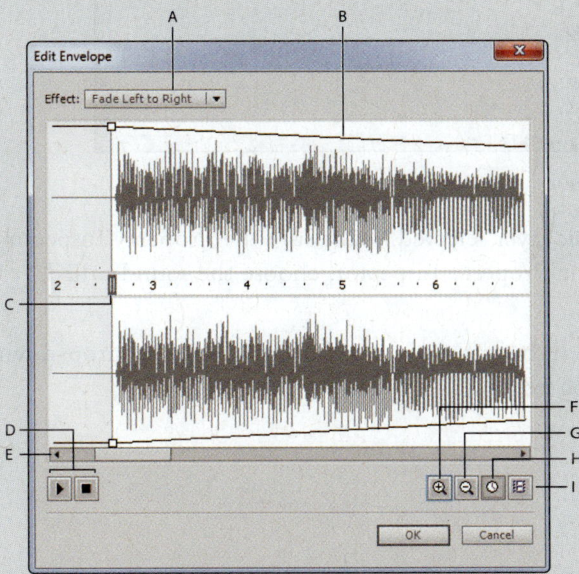

Figure 11-18

A. Volume/Pan Presets. B. Volume Envelope and handles.
C. Trim handle. D. Stop and Play buttons. E. Scroll bar.
F. Zoom In. G. Zoom Out. H. Seconds. I. Frames.

The lower-left corner features simple Play and Stop buttons so that you can preview your sound as you edit it. Scroll bars let you move through the waveform, and two magnifying glasses at the bottom-right corner let you zoom in or out to see more or less of the waveform in the window at one time.

The clock and filmstrip icons in the right corner let you toggle the Timeline between your waveforms to display in seconds or frames. Use the sliders on your Timeline (there are two) to trim the beginning and end of the sound to eliminate unwanted dead space or set specific in and out points for longer pieces of audio.

In the upper-left corner, a drop-down menu lets you choose from preset envelope and pan settings such as Fade In and Fade Out, Pan Left or Right, or Sweeping Left To Right (and vice versa). Any custom volume (envelope) edits automatically display as Custom in the Preset menu.

Trimming sound

Sometimes a sound contains a certain amount of silence or *dead air* before or after the material you need. Usually you want to minimize or eliminate this dead space to make playback as seamless as possible, especially if a sound needs to loop. Flash lets you trim sounds by adjusting their starting and ending points. This type of trimming can also be useful for selecting a small portion of a longer sound file for use. To edit a sound's starting or ending point, you'll first need to place it on the Timeline.

| Step-by-Step | **Follow these steps to trim a sound** |

1. Under the Sound layers folder, locate the Background Music layer and select the first frame (Figure 11-19).

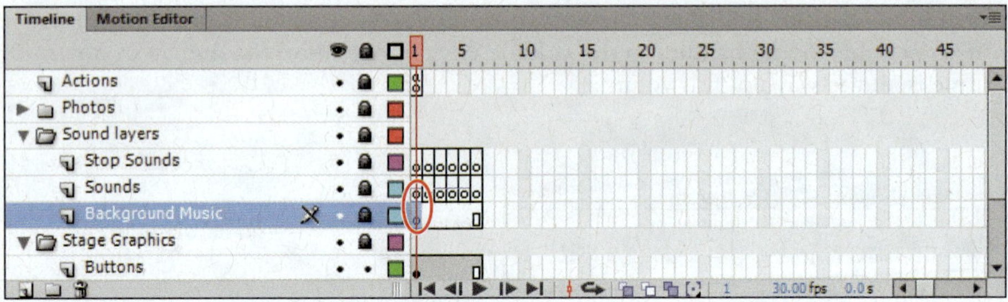

Figure 11-19: *Locate the layer that will contain background music that you'll add in a moment.*

2. With frame 1 of the Background Music layer selected, make sure the Property Inspector is visible. From the Sound menu on the Property Inspector, choose the sound called BackgroundMusic.wav.

3. As shown in Figure 11-20, click the Edit button (✐) to the right of the Effect drop-down menu to open the Edit Envelope dialog box.

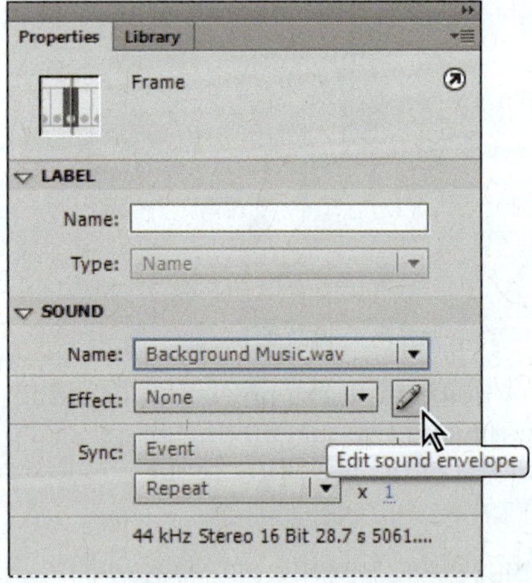

Figure 11-20: *Use the Edit button for a selected sound to edit that sound instance.*

Press the Zoom Out button (🔍) until the waveform becomes visible. Listen to the sound by clicking the Play button in the lower-left corner of the dialog box.

4. As shown in Figure 11-21, click and drag the marker in the Edit Envelope dialog box's middle ruler toward the right. The farther you drag it, the more you trim the beginning of the sound. Drag it as shown below, so that the sound starts when the waveform truly begins, eliminating the dead space at the beginning.

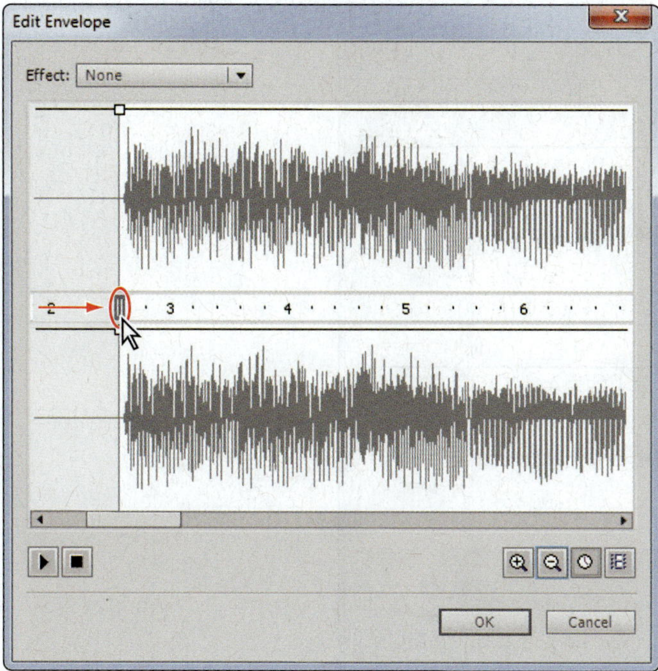

Figure 11-21: Use the slider between the waveforms to set the start and end points for your sound.

5. Use the scroll bar or arrows at the bottom of the Edit Envelope dialog box to move forward to the end of the sound, if necessary, where you'll find another marker. Click and drag this marker left to trim the end of the sound and adjust its length. As shown in Figure 11-22, click and drag it so that the sound ends just before the waveform stops, at about 24 seconds.

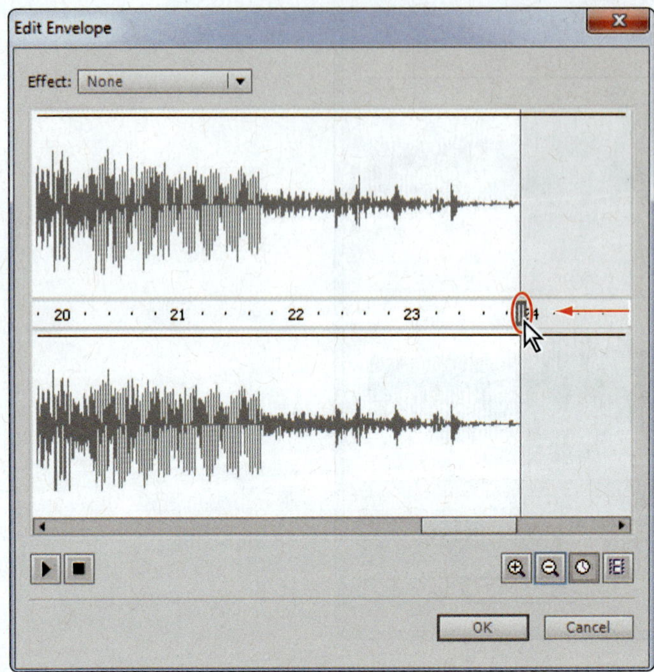

Figure 11-22: *Trim dead air from the end of your sound by moving the end slider as close to the end of the waveform as possible.*

6. Click the Play button to preview the sound. The sound plays between the adjusted start and end points.

7. Next, you'll bring down the overall volume of the track so the narration is heard clearly above it. Each waveform displays a line that represents the level of the track. Each time you click on this line, break points are created that can be dragged.

Scroll back the beginning of the sound, and grab the existing break point on the top (left) channel, and drag it so the line is close to the bottom but running straight across (Figure 11-23). Do the same thing for the bottom (right) channel, as shown in Figure 11-24.

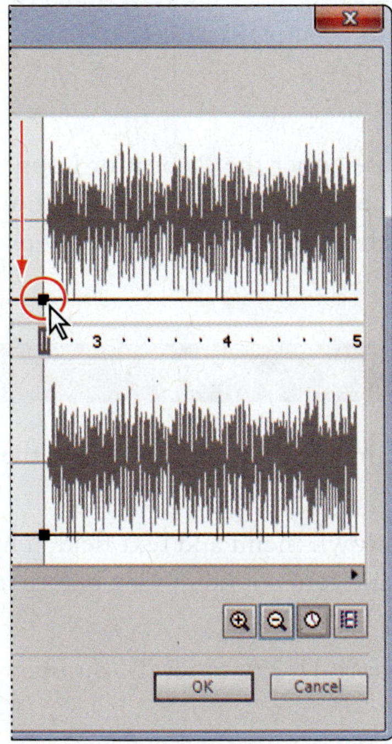

Figure 11-23: Drag the breakpoints shown to reduce or increase the volume of each channel in your sound.

Figure 11-24: Repeat this action for the bottom channel.

8. Press OK to close the Edit Envelope dialog box.

Now preview your entire movie. Press Ctrl+Enter (Windows) or Command+Return (Mac OS) to see how the music plays out. Don't use the buttons to navigate; just sit back and listen. The sound should play once without repeating.

9. Choose File > Save to save the file.

Take Note...
There have been reported issues of edits not behaving as expected when using imported .mp3 files. Where possible, use uncompressed (.wav or .aiff) audio for best results. Remember that all sounds imported in your movie and placed on the Timeline are compressed as .mp3 during the Publish process.

Controlling sounds

Once you've placed some sounds, you'll want to make sure you take the extra step to control the behavior of those sounds. Flash doesn't know when one sound should start and another should stop—it plays what you ask it to until the sound is done. This can result in a cacophony of sounds playing all at once if you don't set things up right. Sound control should be an essential part of adding sound, not simply an afterthought. One example is the narration that plays as you shuffle through photos in your slide show. If a user jumps to the next (or previous) photo before the current narration is done, the two overlap. The best solution here is to use a bit of ActionScript to stop any other sounds before playing the next one.

Repeating and looping sounds

When you want a sound to repeat more than once, you can use either the Repeat or Loop options under the Sound portion of the Property Inspector. **Looping** is when an animation plays in succession more than one time. Experiment with both options with your newly placed background music:

<table><tr><td>**Step-by-Step**</td><td>**Follow these steps to repeat a sound**</td></tr></table>

1. Select frame 1 of the Background Music layer, if it's not already selected, and locate the Sound options in the Property Inspector.

2. Under the Sound options, you will see the Repeat drop-down menu and text field. This option allows you to specify the number of times you want your sound to play before it stops. By default, all sounds are set to repeat at least once.

3. Drag over the Repeat value slider, or click and type **3** (Figure 11-25), to set the number of repeats to 3.

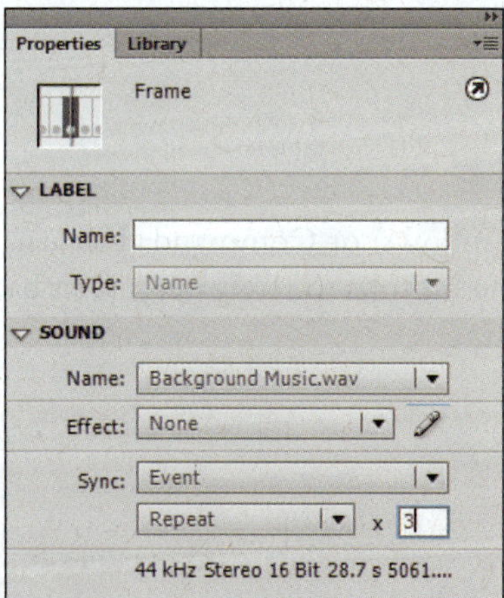

Figure 11-25: *Set the number of repeats for your sound.*

4. Preview your movie by choosing Ctrl+Enter (Windows) or Command+Return (Mac OS). The background loop should play three times and stop. Close the Flash Player.

Looping sounds

The Repeat option can be useful in situations where the sound needs to repeat in tandem with events on the Stage, or if you want to put a limit on the number of times a piece of music can repeat. If you are certain you want a piece of music or a sound to repeat continuously, you should choose the Loop option, which plays the sound repeatedly until the movie is closed down. This is a good choice for your background music loop, because you don't want the music to stop while the visitor is enjoying the slide show. Try Loop instead of the Repeat option to hear the difference.

<table><tr><td>**Follow these steps to loop a sound**</td><td>**Step-by-Step**</td></tr></table>

1. Select frame 1 of the Background Music layer, if necessary, and locate the Sound options under the Property Inspector.

2. As shown in Figure 11-26, select Loop from the Repeat drop-down menu.

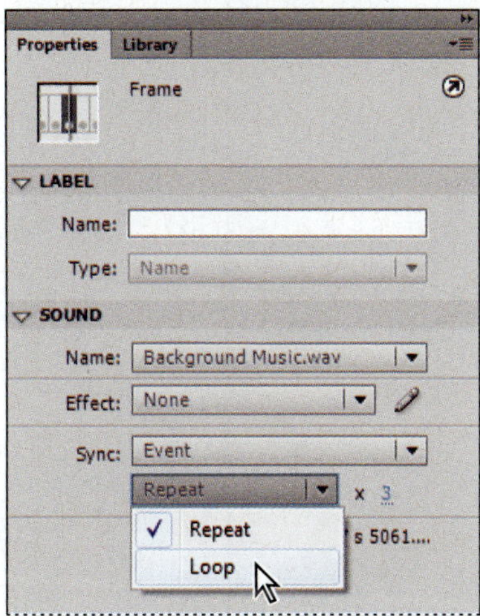

Figure 11-26: Set the Loop option to repeat forever.

   The Repeat text field disappears, as a loop is infinite and has no set number of repeats.

3. Preview your movie by choosing Ctrl+Enter (Windows) or Command+Return (Mac OS). The background loop should play continuously as long as the movie is open. Close the Flash Player.

4. Choose File > Save to save the file.

Introducing the SoundMixer and stopAll()

Introduced in ActionScript 3.0, the **SoundMixer** class controls the master sound output from your Flash movie, giving you global control over any and all sounds.

In this lesson, you'll focus on the use of one of the SoundMixer's many useful methods, **stopAll()**. This method does exactly what it says—stops all sounds in your movie—and serves as a quick-and-easy way to stop a sound before you begin playback of another.

In the following steps, you'll add the code necessary to stop the current narration from playing before starting a new one on the next photo. To do this, you'll add some code to your Next and Previous buttons to target the SoundMixer's stopAll() method.

<table><tr><td>**Step-by-Step**</td><td>**Follow these steps to stop all sounds in a movie using the SoundMixer**</td></tr></table>

1. Select the first keyframe of the Actions layer and open the Actions panel by choosing F9 (Windows), Option+F9 (Mac OS), or Window > Actions.

Take Note...
Add the function (fn) key to these shortcuts if you are on a laptop.

2. Look for the comment that reads, `//Moves backwards`, and locate the event handler below it named `prevPhoto` (Figure 11-27).

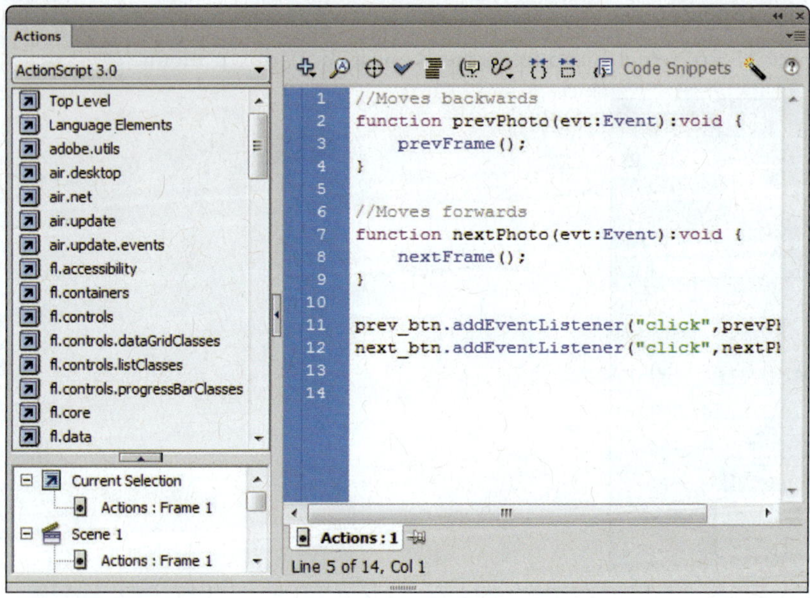

Figure 11-27: *The Actions panel shows the event handlers assigned to the Next and Previous buttons.*

3. Click to place your cursor at the beginning of the line that reads `prevFrame()`. Press Enter (Windows) or Return (Mac OS) to make a line of space and add the following script:

```
SoundMixer.stopAll();
```

As shown in Figure 11-28, the event handler should now read:

```
function prevPhoto(evt:Event):void {
SoundMixer.stopAll();
prevFrame();
}
```

Take Note...
As with all ActionScript code, this command is case-sensitive. Make sure you enter it exactly as shown above to avoid errors.

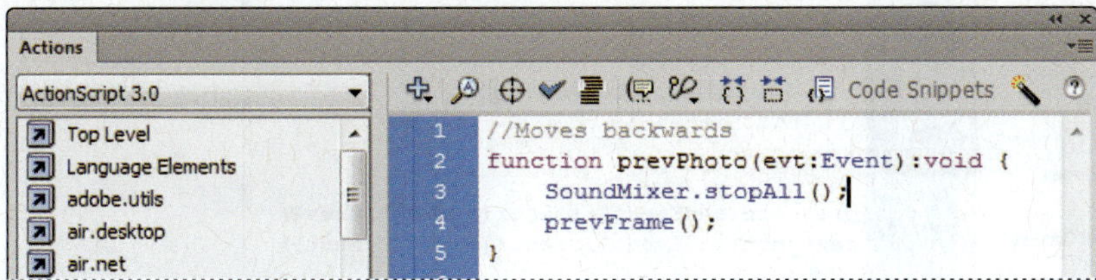

Figure 11-28: Add the `stopAll()` statement to the `prevPhoto` event handler.

4. Further down in the ActionScript panel, locate the comment line that reads, `//Moves forwards`. Directly below it, you should see the `nextPhoto` event handler. Make a line of space above the line that reads, `nextFrame();` and enter the following:

```
SoundMixer.stopAll();
```

As displayed in Figure 11-29, the code should now read:

```
function nextPhoto(evt:Event):void {
SoundMixer.stopAll();
nextFrame();
}
```

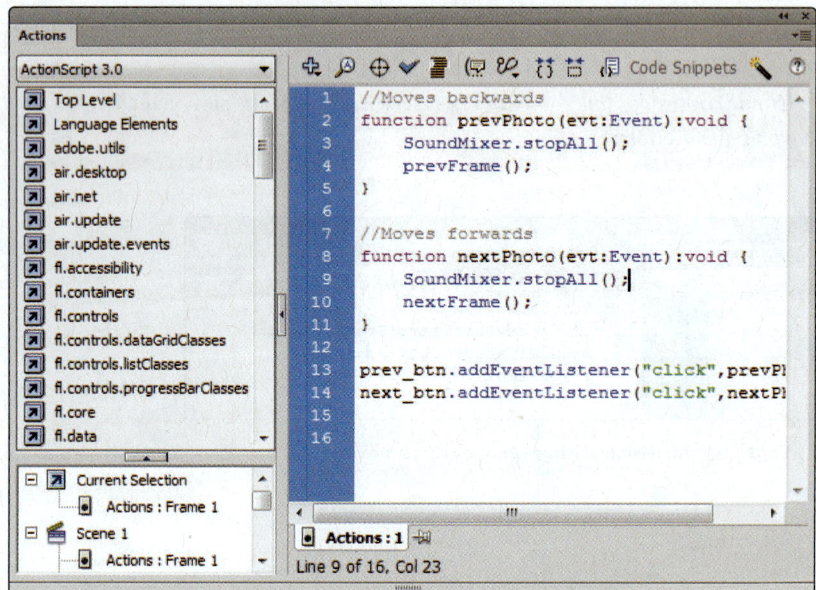

Figure 11-29: The final code, as shown in the Actions panel.

5. Close your Actions panel and preview your movie by pressing Ctrl+Enter (Windows) or Command+Return (Mac OS). The narrations should now properly stop and start without blending together when you move back and forth between photos.

Take Note...
If you are more comfortable using the toolbox on the left side of the Actions panel to add code, you can find the SoundMixer and its stopAll method under flash.media > SoundMixer > Methods > stopAll.

Learning More

It's all about the order

Ordering the ActionScript commands correctly on the mouse buttons is essential, because ActionScript executes sequentially from top to bottom. The sounds for each slide show photo are triggered when the playhead reaches their respective frames, so the current sound must stop before Flash advances to the next one. Had you reversed the command order in the exercise, the button would have moved you to the next photo, and played the new sound but immediately stopped it, because the `SoundMixer.stopAll()` function was called after the new sound began. Remember, although it seems that several lines of ActionScript run almost simultaneously, they are actually executed in order.

More sync menu controls: stop and start

You may notice that using the Previous and Next buttons stops your background music from playing. This is because both buttons contain a `SoundMixer.stopAll()` command, which is designed to stop any sound playing in a Flash movie at once. In the following lessons, you'll learn how to selectively stop the narration without affecting the background music.

Beyond Event and Stream, the **Sync menu** offers two more behavior options for sounds: stop and start. These options allow very fine control over the playback of specific sounds in your movie. You will use them now to fine-tune and complete your slide show. ActionScript allows for more powerful and granular ways to control individual sounds, but those techniques are beyond the scope of this book.

Start sounds

Because sounds placed on a frame are triggered when the playhead reaches that frame, you run the risk that a sound may overlap itself at some point. Consider your background music: you want to ensure that a user returning to the first frame to view the photo doesn't retrigger the background loop and cause it to overlap. To avoid this, set the Sync option for the sound to Start. Start sounds play only one instance of themselves at a time, thus preventing overlap. A Start sound also plays until the end and can only be stopped by a matching Stop sound (more on this in a minute). By setting the background loop as a Start sound, you can make sure it will not be retriggered unintentionally if it's already playing elsewhere in your movie.

<table><tr><td style="background:#b22;color:#fff;padding:6px">Follow these steps to start a sound</td><td style="background:#b22;color:#fff;padding:6px">Step-by-Step</td></tr></table>

1. Select frame 1 of your Background Music layer.

2. Choose Start from the Sync drop-down menu under the Property Inspector's Sound options (Figure 11–30). Leave the Loop options as they are.

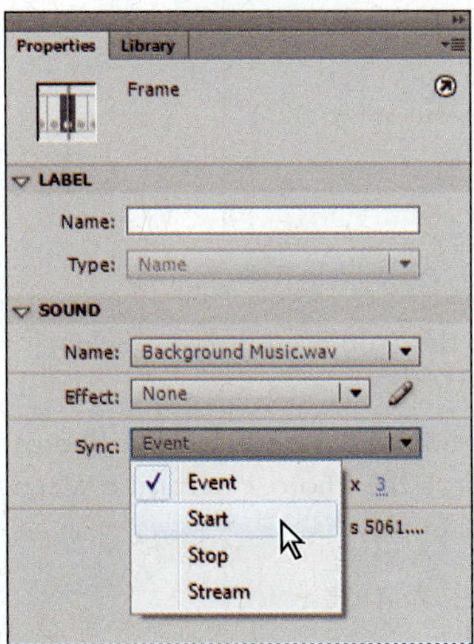

Figure 11–30: Switch the background music's Sync setting from Event to Start to avoid overlap.

3. Preview your movie by pressing Ctrl+Enter (Windows) or Command+Return (Mac OS), and return to the first photo using the Previous button. The background music should play properly without overlap. Close the Flash Player to return to the Timeline.

Stop sounds

The Sync menu's Stop option works with a single sound you specify through the Sound menu, stopping only that sound, if it is already playing. Stop is a great way to terminate any piece of audio narration without affecting the background music at all. As you've seen with the `SoundMixer.stopAll` action, it stops all sounds including your background music, which is probably not the intended effect. Let's put Stop sounds into practice for the slide show:

<table><tr><td>**Step-by-Step**</td><td>**Follow these steps to stop a sound**</td></tr></table>

1. Select keyframe 1 of the Actions layer, and open the Actions panel. Locate the two lines that read `SoundMixer.stopAll();`, and put a double backslash before each one to disable them, like Figure 11-31:

    ```
    // SoundMixer.stopAll();
    ```

    Close the Actions panel.

Take Note...

At the time of this writing, sounds using the start sync option would not playback when previewed or published in Flash Player 10. The issue has been noted and reported to Adobe, and future notes and workarounds will be posted on the Digital Classroom books website at digitalclassroombooks.com as they become available.

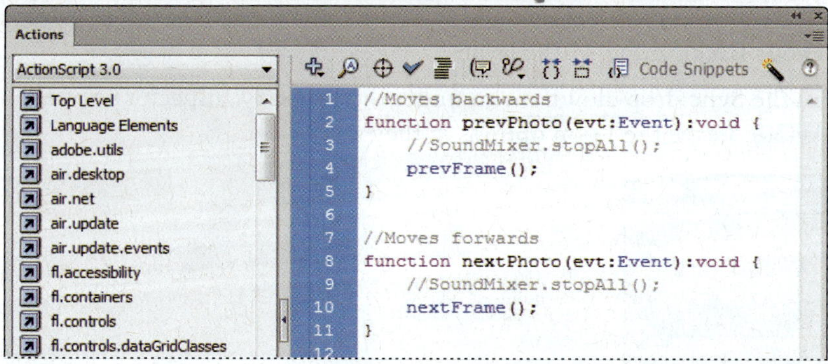

Figure 11-31: *Disable the* `SoundMixer.stopAll()` *action on the Next and Previous button event handlers.*

2. Under the Sound layers folder on the Timeline, locate the Stop Sounds layer. Select keyframe 2 on this layer as shown in Figure 11-32.

3. In the Property Inspector, use the Name menu (under Sound options) to select Photo1.wav. Although you are on the second photo, the goal is to stop the Photo 1 narration when switching to this frame so that the Photo2.wav sound can play.

4. With Photo1.wav selected, choose Stop from the Sync menu (Figure 11-33). Rather than play the Photo1.wav sound at this frame, it will stop any instances of this sound only, leaving other sounds unaffected.

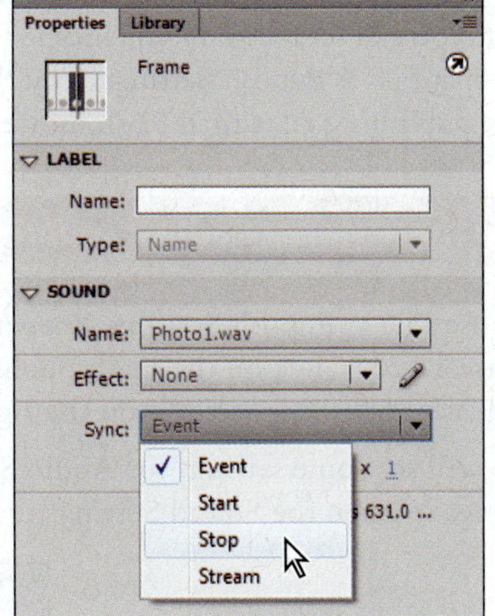

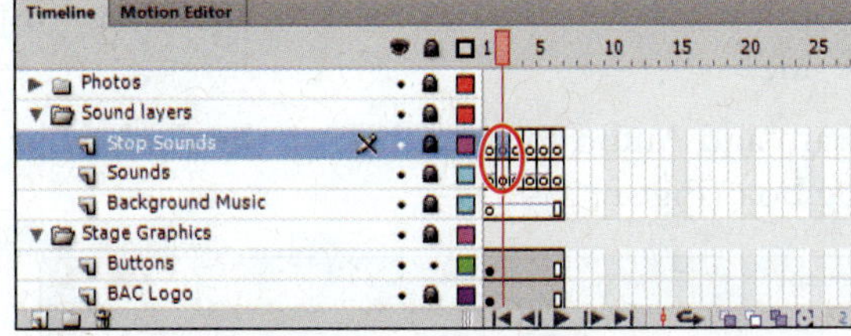

Figure 11-32: Select keyframe 2 on the Stop Sounds layer.

Figure 11-33: Set a Photo1.wav Stop sound in the Properties panel.

5. Choose Control > Test Movie to preview your movie. Move quickly from the first photo to the second. The Photo 1 narration should stop and the Photo 2 narration should begin, without interrupting other sounds in your movie.

6. Use the same methods outlined in steps 1 to 3 to place a Stop sound on each remaining keyframe in the Stop Sounds layer for Photo 2.wav through Photo 5.wav. These will stop any animation from the previous photo from running as you move ahead.

7. Choose Control > Test Movie to preview your movie.

Take Note...

You will notice that moving backward to previous photos, you will still experience overlap. There are a number of ways to alleviate this problem, but the limitations of Stop sounds may make this a better fit for an ActionScript solution.

8. Close the Flash Player, and choose File > Save to save the file.

Sound publishing options

When you publish your movie for final delivery to the Web, mobile, or other destination, you can adjust how Flash exports the audio and packages it with your movie. By default, Flash compresses sounds in your movie into the .mp3 format, regardless of the original file format. However, you can set the sound quality for both Stream and Event sounds in the Publish Settings dialog box at File > Publish Settings. You'll learn more about this, as well as other techniques related to publishing your final Flash movie, in Lesson 14, "Delivering Your Final Movie."

Step-by-Step | **Follow these steps to adjust sound publishing options**

1. Choose File > Publish Settings to open the Publish Settings dialog box as shown in Figure 11–35. Click on the Flash publish option on the left side of the dialog box to display the Flash publishing settings on the right side.

2. You will see some settings for Audio Stream and Audio Event. Click on the Audio Event settings to open the Sound Settings dialog box (Figure 11–34).

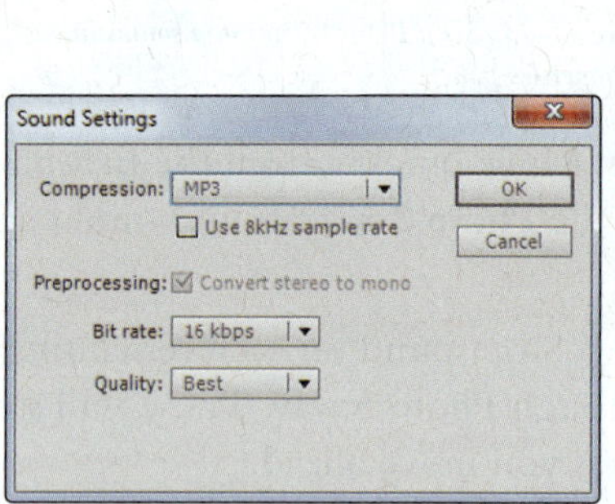

Figure 11–34: *Sound Settings dialog box.*

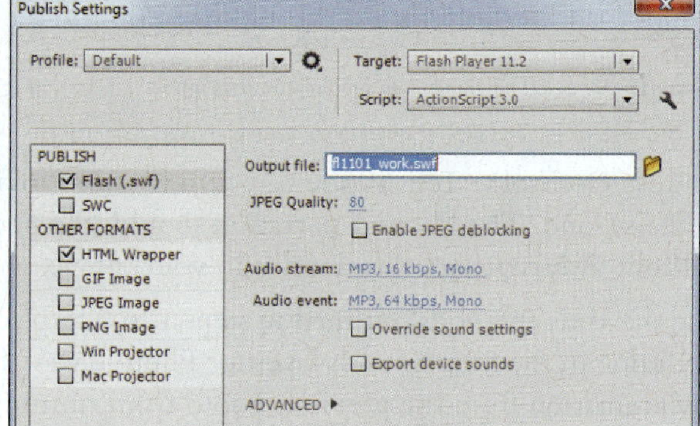

Figure 11–35: *You can set the quality and compression settings for sound in your movie from the Publish Settings panel.*

3. Leave or set the Bit Rate to 64 Kbps. MP3 quality is determined by bit rate. The higher the quality, of course, the higher the file size. Press OK to close the Sound Setting dialog box, then press OK again to close the Publish Settings dialog box.

Take Note...

MP3 applications such as Apple's iTunes encode MP3 files at a default bit rate of around 128 Kbps.

Take Note...

Remember that, just like quality settings for bitmap images, sound quality settings have a direct effect on the final file size. Before making a final decision, experiment with different quality settings for Audio Stream and Audio Event until you reach an acceptable quality level.

4. Choose File > Save to save the file, then choose File > Close.

Congratulations, you've finished the lesson.

Wrapping up

Sounds are a great way to enhance your movie, and, paired with ActionScript, the applications and ideas are limitless. Always plan carefully when working with sounds, as a certain level of preproduction on your original files will help guarantee the best possible results in Flash. Wherever possible, make sure the user has an option to discontinue or temporarily mute sounds.

Skill summary

In this lesson you learned how to:	Objective
Import and use sound	**4.12**

Knowledge Assessment

True/False

Circle **T** if the statement is true or **F** if the statement is false.

T F **1.** Analog audio is sound that has been converted from digital sound waves into a series of bits and bytes.

T F **2.** If you're lacking detail in the original audio recording, you can restore it by boosting the sample rate of the file.

T F **3.** Low bit depth settings, such as 8 bits or less, produce poor recordings of limited quality.

T F **4.** Flash has extensive audio editing capabilities and should be used in place of audio programs such as Soundbooth or Audition.

T F **5.** Single-channel mono audio is a suitable choice for a solo recording such as a narration.

T F **6.** Flash exports the audio in the same format in which it was imported.

T F **7.** Event sounds work independently of the Timeline and must be fully loaded before they can play back.

T F **8.** Sounds can be added to buttons to make the button click seem more organic.

T F **9.** You can edit the following sound characteristics in Flash: volume, balance (pan), start-stop points, frequency, and noise ratio.

T F **10.** Sounds can be set up to loop infinitely.

Lesson 11

Multiple Choice

Select the best response for the following statements.

1. What is it that refers to the number of samples of an audio waveform that the converter digitizes in one second, and is analogous to the resolution of a digital photo?

    a. Sample wave

    b. Sample rate

    c. Sample speed

    d. Sample frequency

2. What is the term that defines the amount of information that each sample contains, similar to the same information with regard to a digital photo?

    a. Bit depth

    b. Bit rate

    c. Bit speed

    d. Bit value

3. Which sound file type will Flash import?

    a. .wav

    b. .aiff

    c. .mp3

    d. All of the above

4. To play a sound at a specific point in your movie, you have to place the sound on a?

    a. Movieclip

    b. Keyframe

    c. Instance

    d. Button

5. Sounds can be placed from which panel?

    a. Transform

    b. Properties

    c. Audio

    d. None of the above

6. Which sync option works best for long-form animation like a soundtrack?

    a. Event

    b. Start

    c. Stream

    d. Stop

7. Which panel offers you ways to trim, fade, and pan your audio?

    a. Edit Envelope

    b. Edit Sound

    c. Library

    d. Audio

8. Which choice is best when setting up background music for your project?

   a. Loop

   b. Repeat

   c. Repeat × 99

   d. Repeat × 200

9. What is the code that stops all sounds in your movie?

   a. `stop()`

   b. `stopEvent()`

   c. `stopSound()`

   d. `stopAll()`

10. The higher the bit rate, the higher the quality, and the higher the:

   a. Sample rate

   b. Volume

   c. File size

   d. Frequency

Competency Assessment

The Sound Library	Project 11-1

Just like the buttons from the previous chapter, Flash offers a library full of royalty-free sounds and sound effects with the program. Music is still something you'll need to find on your own, but there are still plenty of choices for general sound effects that are here in Flash.

1. Create a new ActionScript 3.0 document in Flash.

2. Choose Window > Common Libraries > Sounds.

3. Find the sound called **Cartoon Human Male Laugh Evil Troll Laugh 01.mp3** and drag it into your Library panel.

4. Select the keyframe in Layer 1, frame 1.

5. Choose the Cartoon Human Male Laugh Evil Troll Laugh 01.mp3 from the name of the Sound source in the Properties panel. Test the movie to hear the sound.

6. Save this file as **sounds.fla** and keep it open for the next project.

Editing Sounds — A Review	Project 11-2

While Flash isn't built to be a major sound editing program, its fine for the quick, basic kind of editing you may need to perform, such as trimming a sound file.

1. The **sounds.fla** file should still be open from the previous project.

2. Select the keyframe in Layer 1, frame 1 so the sound is active in the Properties panel.

3. Click the Edit sound envelope button in the Properties panel.

4. Use the Trim handle to crop the Cartoon Human Male Laugh Evil Troll Laugh 01.mp3 sound so it starts right at the laugh and removes the brief pause beforehand.

5. Save this file as **sounds_11.2.fla**, but keep this file open for the next project.

Proficiency Assessment

| Project 11-3 | **Understanding More About Sound Compression** |

The publish settings of your .fla file can make a huge impact in terms of quality. The best way to understand more is to listen to different variations to the compression.

1. The **sounds_11.2.fla** file should still be open from the previous project.

2. Choose File > Publish Settings. Click on the Audio Event: settings. Change the compression from MP3 to Speech.

3. Publish different variations with each of the various sound compression choices and listen to each to compare. Examine the file size of each file as well. Save each published version as **sounds_<compression type>.fla**.

| Project 11-4 | **Beyond Flash** |

While Flash is OK for the basics, there are some powerful options out there such as Adobe Audition. If you don't have the budget for Audition, there is a free alternative.

1. Launch your web browser of choice.

2. Go to: *http://audacity.sourceforge.net/* to learn more about the free audio editing program Audacity.

Introducing Movie Clips

Key Terms

- blur
- ease
- filters
- movie clips
- movie clip timelines
- nest

Business case

Symbols are at the heart of using Flash in terms of creating artwork and manipulating that artwork through animation and code. Movie clips are perhaps the most important symbols to understand as they can help you consolidate frame space within the main Timeline, allow you to create looped animations, combine and nest symbols for a multitude of reasons including efficiency, and much more.

Starting up

Before starting, make sure that your tools and panels are consistent by resetting your preferences. See "Resetting the Flash workspace" in the Starting up section of this book.

You will work with several files from the fl12lessons folder in this lesson. Make sure that you have loaded the fllessons folder onto your hard drive from *http://www.wiley.com/college/sc/adobeseries*. See "Loading lesson files" in the Starting up section of this book.

The project

In this lesson, you will create an animation of a common, complex machine in motion: an airplane taking off. Using the power of movie clips, you'll break the airplane's various moving parts into individual animations. The graphics for the propellers and landing gear are provided; you'll simply put them all together while learning how to create complex yet manageable animations beyond the main Timeline.

About movie clips

Movie clip symbols have the same advantages as other symbol types: all instances of a movie clip remain attached to their master in the library, and you create new instances by dragging them to the Stage from the Library panel. Each movie clip instance can be modified with transformations and color effects, just like a graphic. The real power that sets **movie clips** apart is that each movie clip contains its own Timeline, independent of the main Timeline. Movie clip animation, therefore, neither depends upon, nor needs to synchronize with, anything happening on the main Timeline. Each movie clip can contain its own animation, which you can place on the main Timeline whenever and wherever you need it.

The lesson's airplane is a good analogy: it's a complex machine made of a lot of separate parts and smaller machines. Although the landing gear, turbines, and wing flaps make up the whole machine, each component has a different motion, rate, and function. Trying to build a plane out of one component would be impossible. Similarly, some complex animations can't be built on one timeline alone; they require the flexibility of separate parts. Each part needs to move at its own pace along its own Timeline. Movie clips allow you to break animations into separate manageable and reusable pieces.

Think about the airplane again: some smaller machines (like the engine) are built from a lot of smaller moving parts, but still need to be treated as one whole piece. Movie clips can contain other movie clips, so you can build a single movie clip from several others. They can also contain any number of graphic or button symbols.

Creating movie clips

As with graphic and button symbols, you create movie clips by choosing Insert > New Symbol, or by converting existing graphics or animations on the Stage by choosing Modify > Convert to Symbol. You'll get plenty of practice with this in the next exercise.

Laying the foundation: Your first movie clip

To begin your airplane animation, you'll build a propeller to power your plane.

Step-by-Step	Follow these steps to create a movie clip

1. Choose File > Open and navigate to the fl12lessons folder. Select the **fl1201.fla** file and press Open.

2. Choose File > Save As. When the Save As dialog box appears, type **fl1201_work.fla** into the Save As text field. Navigate to the fl12lessons folder and press Save.

3. Open the Library panel by choosing Window > Library, if it is not already open. Locate the Propeller graphic symbol displayed in Figure 12-1. This propeller blade is the foundation for an entire propeller assembly that you'll save as a movie clip symbol.

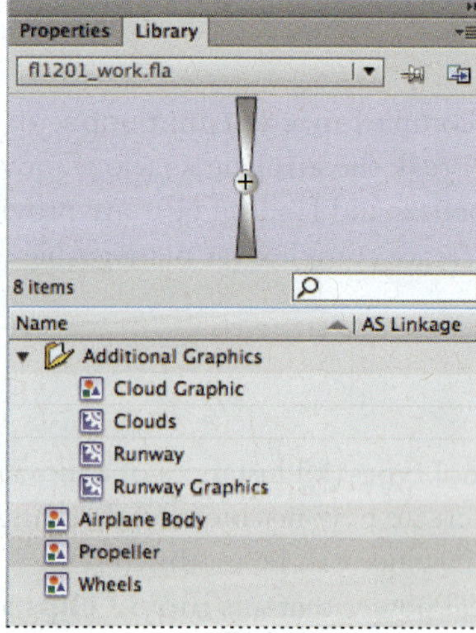

Figure 12-1: The Propeller graphic in your Library panel is the starting point for your first movie clip.

4. Choose Insert > New Symbol to open the New Symbol dialog box.

5. Name the new symbol **Propeller Animation**, and select Movie Clip for Type (Figure 12-2). Press OK. The blank Stage and new Timeline that you now see indicate that you're in Edit mode for the new symbol.

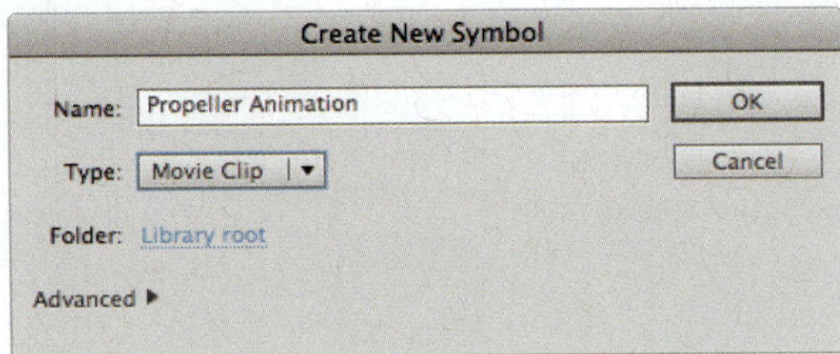

Figure 12-2: Create a new, empty movie clip.

6. Locate the Propeller graphic in the Library panel and drag an instance to the Stage. Choose Window > Align to bring up the Align panel. In the Align panel, make sure the Align to stage checkbox is checked, and then press Align Vertical Center (⊕) and Align Horizontal Center (⊕) to center the Propeller graphic on the Stage.

7. To add a motion tween to the propeller, right-click (Windows) or Ctrl+click (Mac OS) on the propeller instance on the Stage and choose Create Motion Tween from the contextual menu.

8. By default, Flash creates a tween span that is equivalent to one second of play time. The start file was set to 30 fps, so the tween span in this case is 30 frames. Click and drag the end of the tween span to reduce it to 20 frames as shown in Figure 12-3.

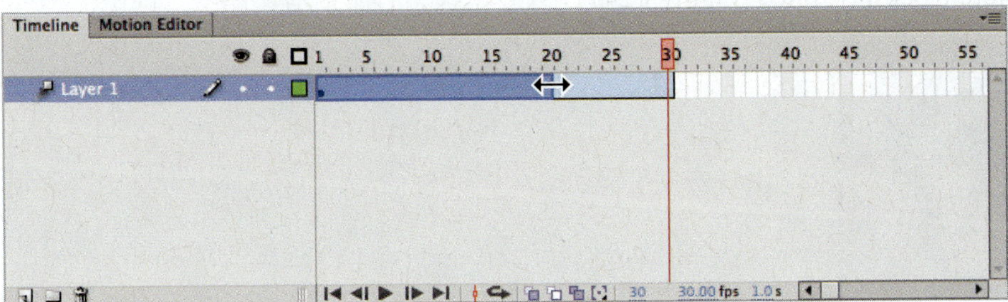

Figure 12-3: Add a motion tween, then reduce the tween span to 20 frames.

9. Bring the Property Inspector forward by clicking on its tab. If necessary, click on the tween span in the Timeline to make sure it is selected. As displayed in Figure 12-4, choose CW from the Direction drop-down menu in the Rotation section of the Property Inspector. The Rotate drop-down menu enables you to automatically apply rotation to the symbol in your tween. Here, you have applied one clockwise revolution.

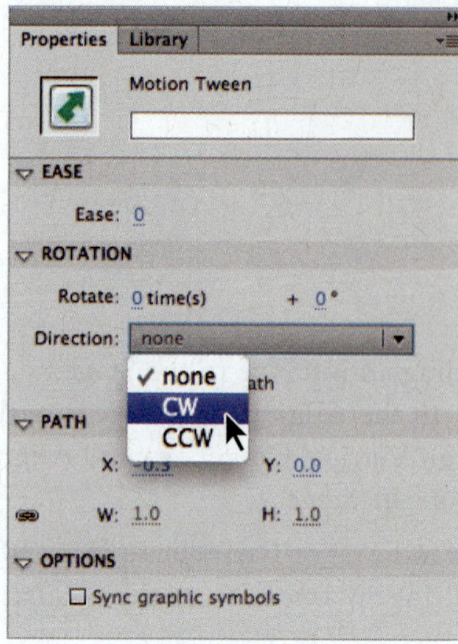

Figure 12-4: Choose CW from the Direction drop-down menu in the Property Inspector.

10. Press Enter (Windows) or Return (Mac OS) to play your animation. The propeller should now rotate clockwise once (Figure 12-5).

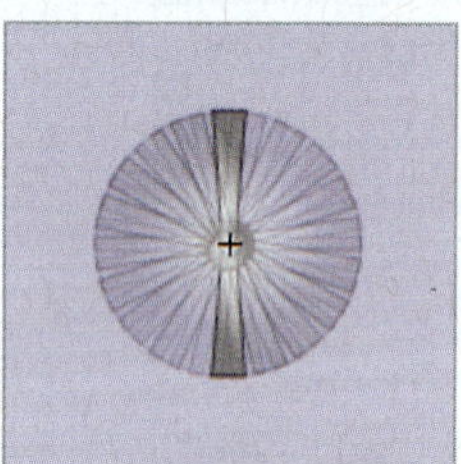

Figure 12-5: Watch the propeller spin clockwise once.

11. Exit the movie clip by clicking the Scene 1 link above the Stage to return to the main Timeline.

12. Choose File > Save to save the file.

Previewing movie clip animation from the main Timeline

Because movie clips each operate on their own timeline, it's not as easy as pressing the Enter (Windows) or Return (Mac OS) key to see them working on the main Timeline or along with other movie clips. You can view your movie using Publish Preview to see the clips play. Now you'll try placing some instances of your new movie clip on the Stage, and view them all in action.

<table><tr><td>**Follow these steps to preview a movie clip from the Timeline**</td><td>Step-by-Step</td></tr></table>

1. Locate the new Propeller Animation movie clip in the Library panel, and drag an instance to the Stage.

2. Press the Enter (Windows) or Return (Mac OS) key. Nothing happens, but that's OK; nothing is supposed to happen. You must view the movie in Publish Preview to see the movie clip play.

3. Choose File > Publish Preview > Flash, or go to Control > Test Movie > in Flash Professional, to export and launch your movie in the Flash Player (Figure 12-6). You should see your propeller moving now.

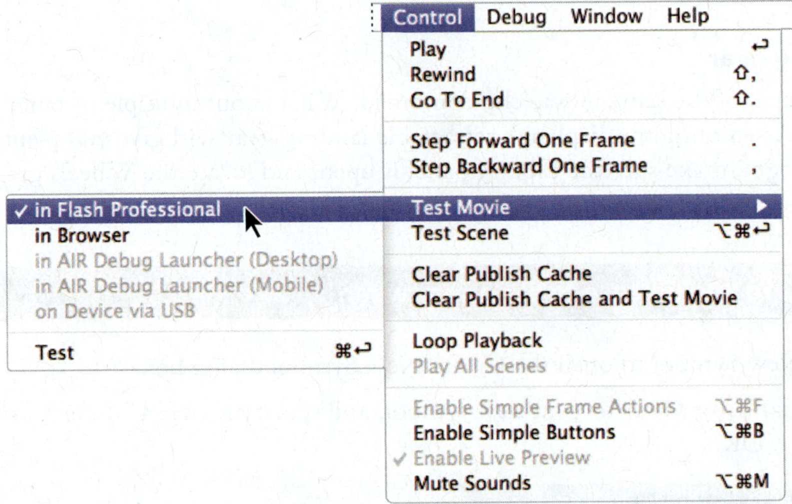

Figure 12-6: *Preview your movie using Control > Test Movie.*

4. Close the Preview window and return to the Timeline. Drag another instance of the Propeller Animation movie clip to the Stage.

5. Choose Control > Test Movie > in Flash Professional. As is Figure 12-7, you should see two propellers spinning at once. With movie clips, reusing animations are as easy as dragging and dropping them.

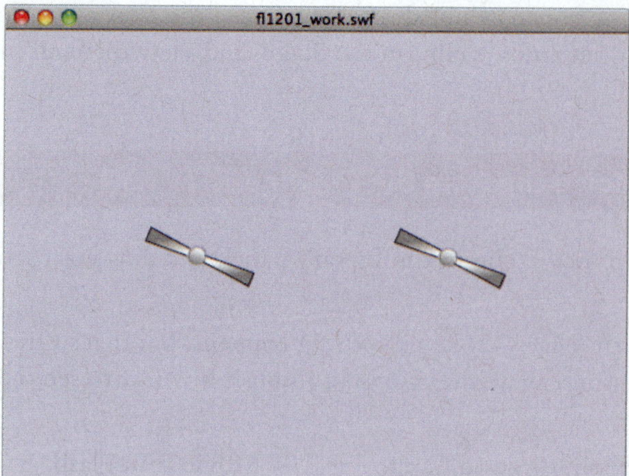

Figure 12-7: Two instances of the propeller turning simultaneously in Preview mode.

6. Close the preview window.

Creating the landing gear

You've seen two instances of the same movie clip combined. What about multiple instances of different movie clips? Assembling the airplane's retractable landing gear will give you plenty of practice. Before you begin, make sure the Library panel is open, and locate the Wheels graphic symbol.

Step-by-Step	Follow these steps to add an ease to a motion tween

1. Choose Insert > New Symbol to open the Create New Symbol dialog box.

2. Assign the name **Landing Gear** to your new symbol, and specify Movie Clip for its type (Figure 12-8). Press OK.

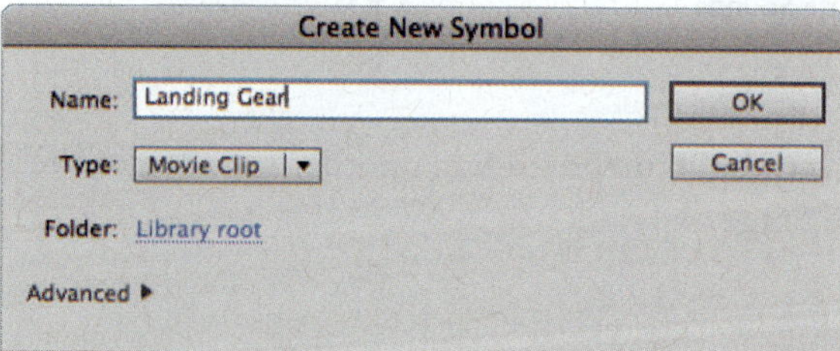

Figure 12-8: Create a new movie clip symbol.

3. Now you're in Edit mode for the new symbol. Drag a copy of the Wheels graphic from the Library panel onto the Stage, and position it so the top of it lines up with the crosshair in the middle of the Stage as shown in Figure 12-9.

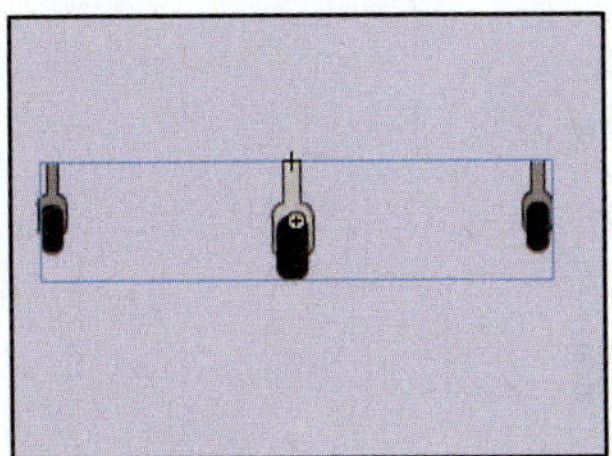

Figure 12-9: Position the Wheels graphic underneath the center of the crosshair.

4. Right-click (Windows) or Ctrl+click (Mac OS) on the instance of the Wheels graphic on the Stage, and choose Create Motion Tween from the contextual menu. Make sure the playhead is at frame 30, and that the wheels are still selected, and use the up arrow key to move them above the crosshairs as shown in Figure 12-10.

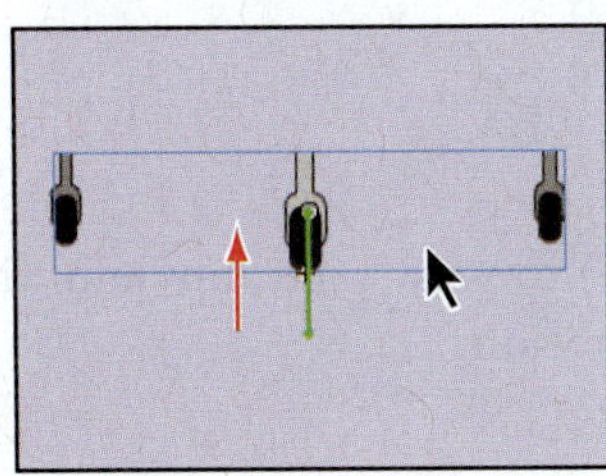

Figure 12-10: Animate your landing gear.

5. To add an **ease** to the landing gear animation and make it a bit more lifelike, click on the Motion Editor tab and scroll down to the Eases section. Click and drag the number 0 to the right until it reads 100 (Figure 12-11).

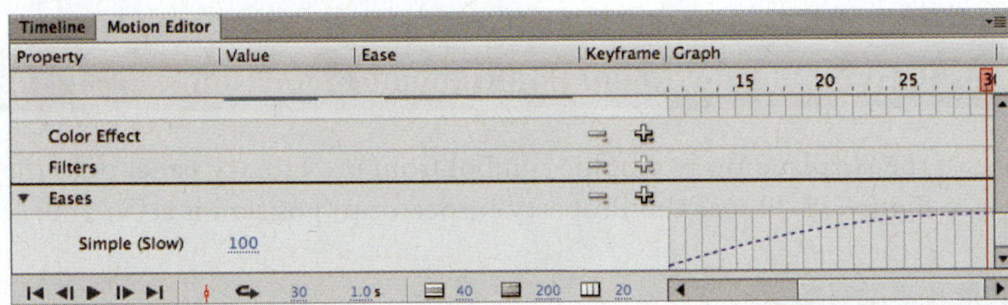

Figure 12-11: Adjust the Simple ease in the Motion Editor.

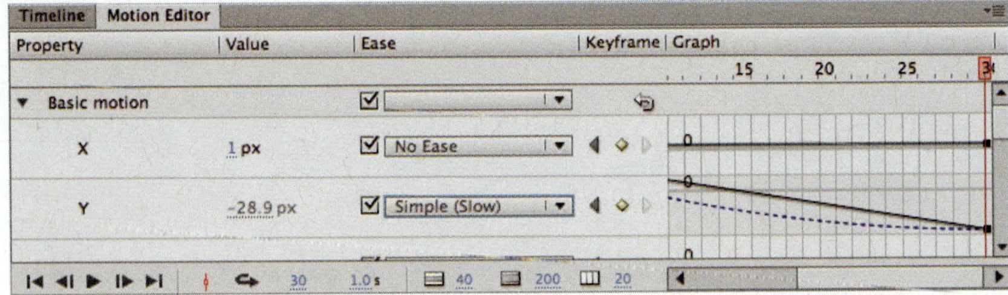

Figure 12-12: Assign it to the animation of the Y position.

6. Scroll up to the Y property in the Basic motion section and choose Simple (Slow) from the Ease drop-down menu (Figure 12-12). This applies the ease you just adjusted to the animation of the Y position of the wheels.

7. Exit the movie clip by clicking the Scene 1 link above the Stage to return to the main Timeline.

8. Locate and drag a copy of the new Landing Gear movie clip onto the Stage from the Library panel as shown in Figure 12-13.

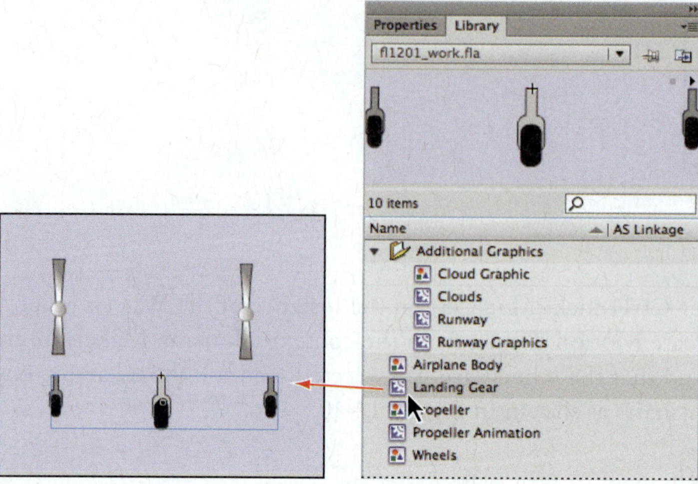

Figure 12-13: *An instance of your Landing Gear movie clip on the Stage.*

9. Press Ctrl+Enter (Windows) or Command+Return (Mac OS) to view your movie in the Flash Player and set both propellers and the landing gear in motion.

10. Close the preview window.

Combining movie clips and main Timeline animation

With some key parts in working order, you're ready to match the body of your airplane to these parts. Locate the Airplane Body graphic symbol in the library; you'll be placing this on the Stage in the next steps.

<table><tr><td>**Step-by-Step**</td><td>**Follow these steps to combine movie clips and Timeline animation**</td></tr></table>

1. Drag an instance of the Airplane Body graphic symbol from the Library panel onto the Stage. As shown in Figure 12-14, use the Property Inspector to position it at X: **260**, Y: **100**.

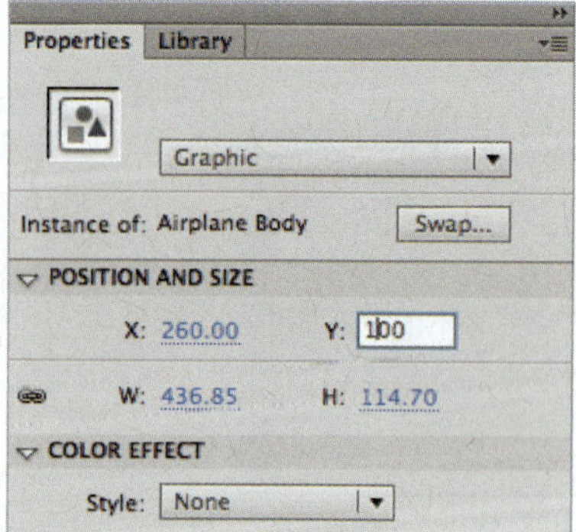

Figure 12-14: *Drag and position an instance of the Airplane Body graphic symbol on the Stage.*

2. Select the landing gear on Layer 1 and position it at exactly X: **260**, Y: **150**, using the Property Inspector. It should now be in its proper place at the bottom of the airplane body (Figure 12-15).

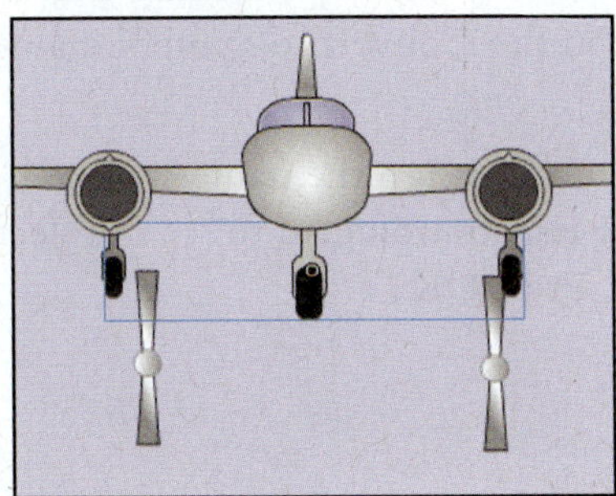

Figure 12-15: The landing gear is now in place at the bottom of the airplane.

3. Holding down the Shift key, select both instances of the animated propeller movie clip. You need to move these to the front of the stacking order to place them in position on the wings. Choose Modify > Arrange > Bring to Front.

4. Using the Property Inspector, move the left propeller to X:**147**, Y:**132**, and the right propeller to X:**373**, Y:**132** (Figure 12-16).

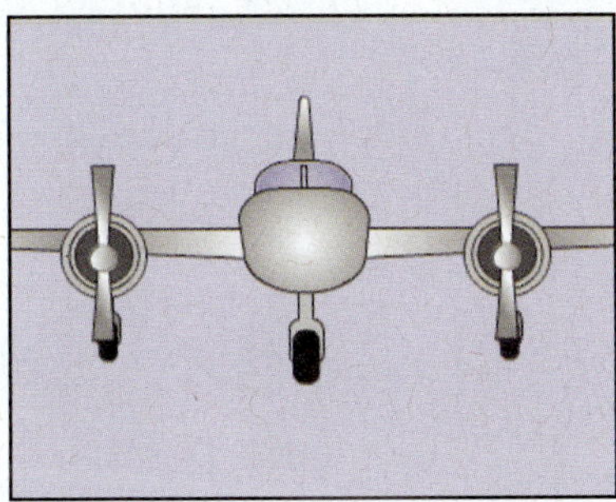

Figure 12-16: Bring the propellers to the front of the stacking list and position them on the wings.

5. Preview your movie in the Flash Player by selecting File > Publish Preview > Flash, or use the keyboard shortcut Ctrl+Enter (Windows) or Command+Return (Mac OS). The airplane should now be in full force with all parts moving.

6. Close the preview window, and choose File > Save to save your work.

Nesting movie clips

When creating complex animations, you can simplify your main Timeline by leveraging a movie clip's ability to **nest**, or to include movie clips inside other movie clips. In other words, you can create one single movie clip from several others. (Remember the engine analogy?) This gives you amazing flexibility, and the ability to drag and drop very complex animations to the Timeline as effortlessly as simple graphic or button symbols. Of course, you can modify and maintain movie clips as easily as other symbols by updating multiple instances of a complex movie clip from its master symbol in the library.

In this exercise, you'll convert the airplane and all its moving parts into a single movie clip symbol that you can tween, modify, or duplicate just as easily as any other symbol in your library. Movie clips can be created from existing movie clips, animations, or graphics on the Stage, using Modify > Convert to Symbol.

Step-by-Step | **Follow these steps to nest movie clips**

1. Select the Airplane Body, Propellers, and Landing Gear movie clips by choosing Edit > Select All. Choose Modify > Convert to Symbol to open the Convert to Symbol dialog box.

2. To convert the whole group into a single movie clip symbol, assign the name **Full Airplane** and set the Type as Movie Clip. Use the registration grid to set a perfectly centered registration point as displayed in Figure 12-17. Press OK.

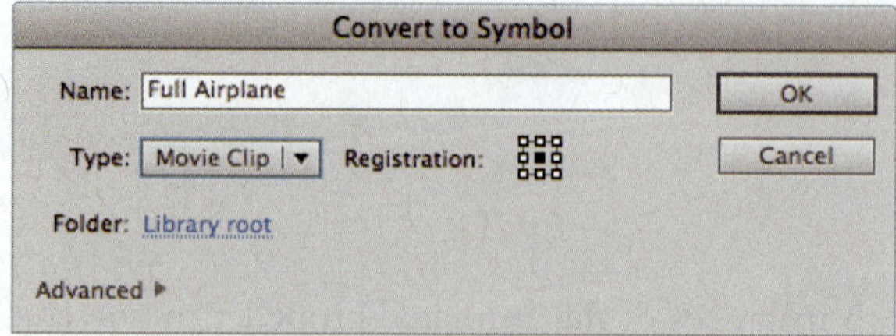

*Figure 12-17: Name the new movie clip **Full Airplane**.*

Notice that the group of parts appears on the Stage inside a single bounding box. You can now click and drag the movie clips around the Stage as one unit. Keep in mind, though, that the original movie clips must remain in the library (Figure 12-18), as the new movie clip depends on them.

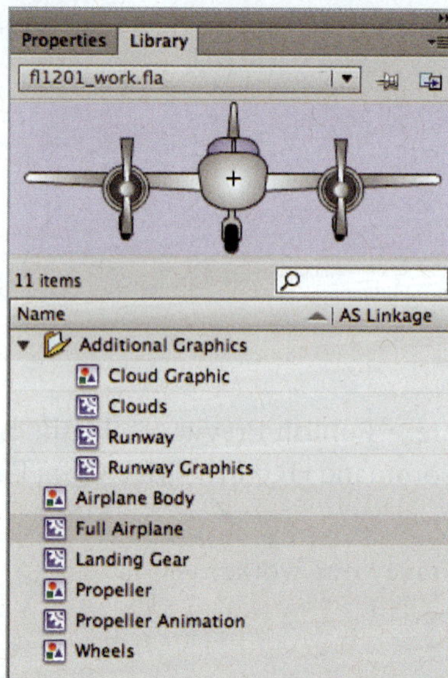

Figure 12-18: The new movie clip is created, and its individual components remain in the library.

3. Choose File > Publish Preview > Flash to view your movie in the Flash Player. It should play just as it did before.

As the exercise demonstrates, movie clips can contain not only other movie clips, but also graphics (such as the airplane body) and button symbols. This means that you can create entire animations inside movie clips without having to do anything on the Timeline.

4. Close the preview window, and choose File > Save to save your work.

Movie clip facts, myths, and legends

Now that you're pretty deep into movie clips, it's time to review some rules, dispel some myths about how movie clips work, and pass on some important facts you need to know.

Dependencies: When you nest one symbol (movie clip, button, or graphic) inside of another, you create dependencies. In other words, the highest-level symbol (for example, Full Airplane) depends on the symbols it contains (Airplane Body, Propeller Animation, and Landing Gear, in this case) residing separately in the library. Placing other symbols inside a movie clip doesn't copy them, but rather references them. If you remove any lower-level symbol from the library, it will disappear from the larger symbol. If, for instance, you remove Landing Gear from the library, Full Airplane will no longer be able to find it, and the landing gear component will disappear from the grouped movie clip.

Frame Rate: Although movie clip timelines are independent of the main Timeline, they can't use a different frame rate. Frame Rate settings are global to a Flash movie (.swf), and can't be modified from movie clip to movie clip. Changing the frame rate for one affects the entire movie.

Timeline Length: Because a movie clip works from its own timeline, its length is independent from the main Timeline's length or available space. You can place a 200-frame movie clip on the main Timeline, even if there's no more than one frame there. The movie clip will still play as it should. Many movies are built using the main Timeline as nothing more than a container for movie clips, and the main Timeline sometimes contains no more than the first frame of each movie clip.

Timelines: **Movie clip timelines** work just as the main Timeline does. Anything you can do on the main Timeline, from tweens and layers to ActionScript, you can use on a movie clip timeline. Here's a little-known fact: the main Timeline is a movie clip in itself.

ActionScript: ActionScript on a movie clip timeline has no effect on the main Timeline or Timelines of other movie clips (even included ones), and vice versa. ActionScript on a timeline, such as a stop or play action, affects only that timeline. This means you can use ActionScript across multiple timelines without a problem.

Adding ActionScript to movie clip Timelines

When you preview your movie, you may notice that a few elements need some adjustment. The landing gear, for example, retracts but then shoots back out again (and again, and again) because nothing is directing the landing gear to stop when it has fully retracted. The nature of movie clips is to loop until told otherwise. The default behavior of the Flash Player is to make a movie loop. To override these two behaviors, you'll use a little bit of the ActionScript that you learned in Lesson 9, "Introducing ActionScript."

Controlling movie clip playback

Because movie clip Timelines function just like the main Timeline, placing ActionScript on a movie clip Timeline is exactly the same as placing it on the main Timeline. Prove this to yourself by modifying the Landing Gear symbol so that it doesn't loop.

Step-by-Step	Follow these steps to control movie clip playback

1. In the Library panel, locate the Landing Gear movie clip symbol and double-click it to edit it. You should be in its Edit mode and see the tween you created earlier in the chapter.

2. Make sure you are viewing the Timeline by choosing Window > Timeline, then press the New Layer button () to create a new layer, and rename it **actions**.

> *Take Note...*
> *Although it's not required, separating ActionScript from frames that have content is a good practice.*

3. On the actions layer, click on the last frame (frame 30), and press F7 to create a new blank keyframe as shown in Figure 12-19.

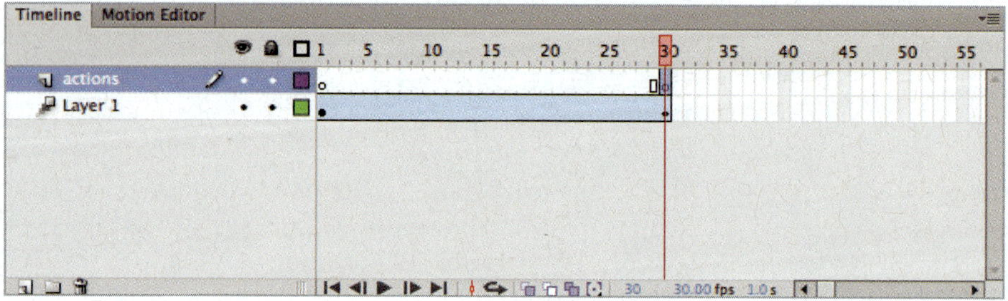

Figure 12-19: *Create a new layer and blank keyframe for the ActionScript.*

4. Choose Window > Actions or press F9 (Windows) or Option+F9 (Mac OS) to launch the Actions panel.

5. In the Actions panel, make sure that Script Assist is turned off. Type **stop();** into the Actions panel as shown in Figure 12-20.

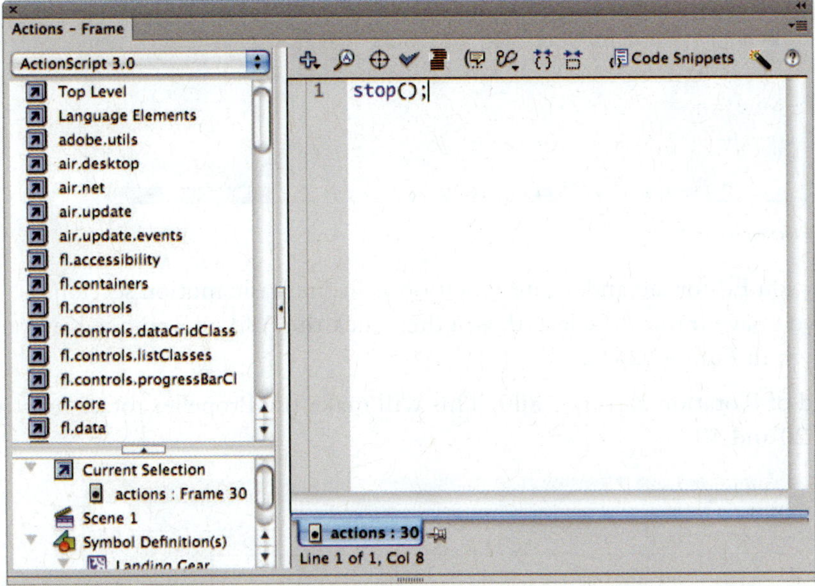

Figure 12-20: Add a stop() *action to frame 30.*

A lowercase letter *a* on the frame indicates that the frame now contains a script.

6. Close the Actions panel, then exit the movie clip by clicking the Scene 1 link above the Stage to return to the main Timeline.

7. Preview your movie, using File > Publish Preview > Flash. The landing gear should now retract and stay put without looping.

8. Close the preview window, and choose File > Save to save your work.

Adding some variation to the propellers

To make your animation a little more dynamic, you can add two stages of speed to your propeller's rotation. All you need is some additional animation and a little ActionScript. At the moment, the propeller has a single tween that keeps it rotating. Simply add another rotation tween with a higher rate of speed right after the existing one to give the viewer the impression that the propellers pick up speed. To keep them from slowing down and speeding up repeatedly, you'll add ActionScript to animate it over a selected number of frames.

<table><tr><td>**Follow these steps to modify an animation**</td><td>**Step-by-Step**</td></tr></table>

1. Locate the Propeller Animation movie clip in the Library panel, and double-click it to edit it (Figure 12-21). You should see that the Timeline for this movie clip contains a single tween.

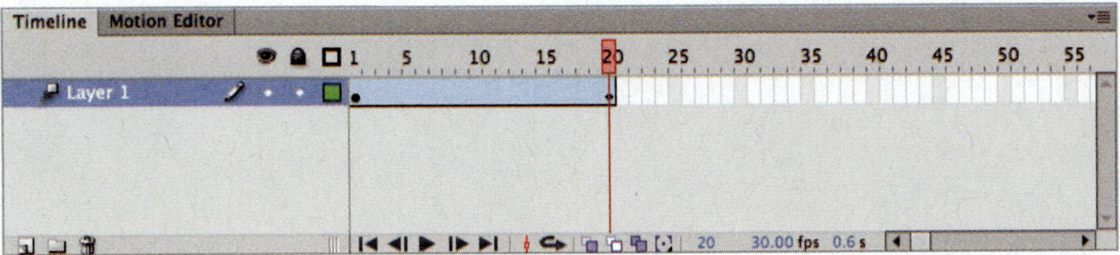

Figure 12-21: You'll work with tweens to better animate the propeller.

2. Right-click (Windows) or Ctrl+click (Mac OS) on frame 40 and choose Insert Frame (Figure 12-22).

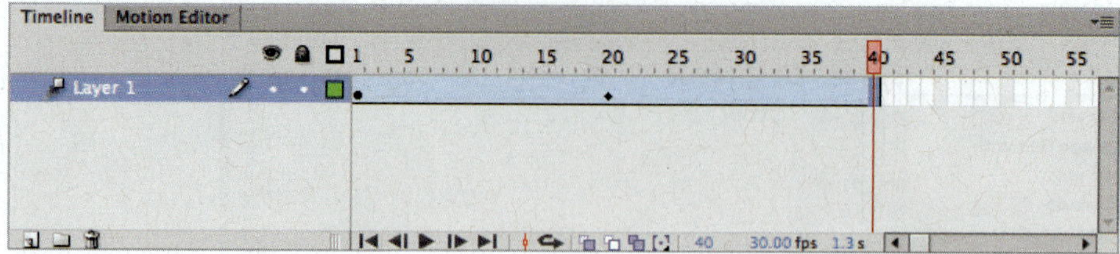

Figure 12-22: *Add a frame on frame 40.*

3. Click on the Motion Editor tab and locate Rotation Z in the Basic motion section. Make sure that you have frame 40 selected, and then click the Add or Remove Keyframe button (◦) as shown in Figure 12-23.

4. In the Value field of Rotation Z, type **1800**. This will make the Propeller rotate five times between frames 20 and 40.

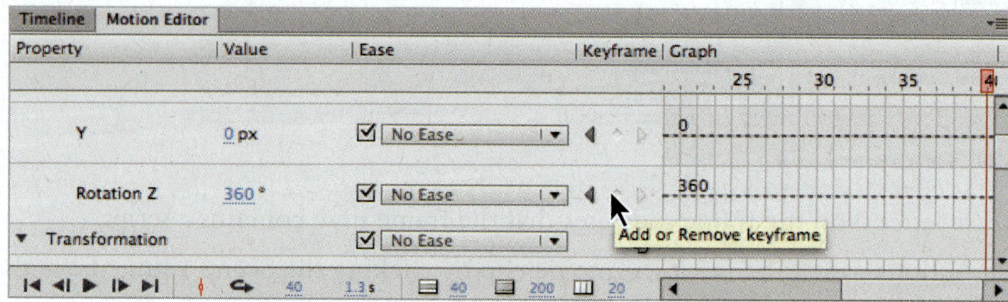

Figure 12-23: *Select frame 40 and click the Add or Remove Keyframe button.*

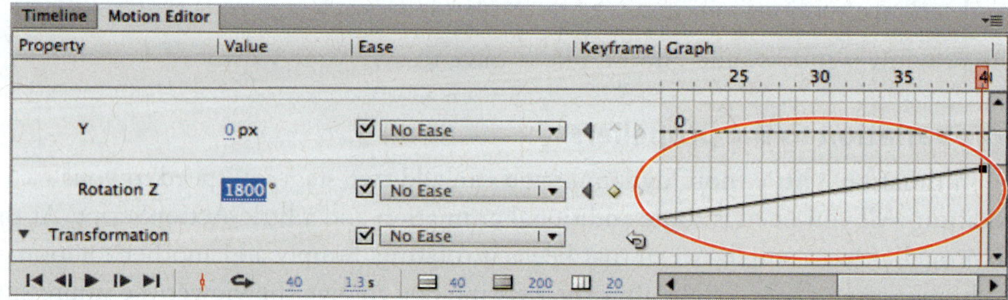

Figure 12-24: *Type **1800** in the Value field of the Rotation Z property.*

5. Click on the Timeline tab to bring the Timeline panel forward. With Layer 1 selected in the Timeline, insert a new layer using the New Layer button (⬏), and rename it **actions**. This layer will contain an action that forces the animation to loop.

6. Create a new blank keyframe on the Actions layer at frame 40 by pressing F7. Open the Actions panel (Window > Actions).

7. In the Actions panel, type **gotoAndPlay(21)**; as shown in Figure 12-25.. This method of the Movie Clip class instructs the playhead to jump to a frame or frame label and play. In this case, when the playhead reaches frame 40, it will jump to frame 21 and play. This will result in frames 1 to 20 playing once, and frames 21 to 40 playing indefinitely.

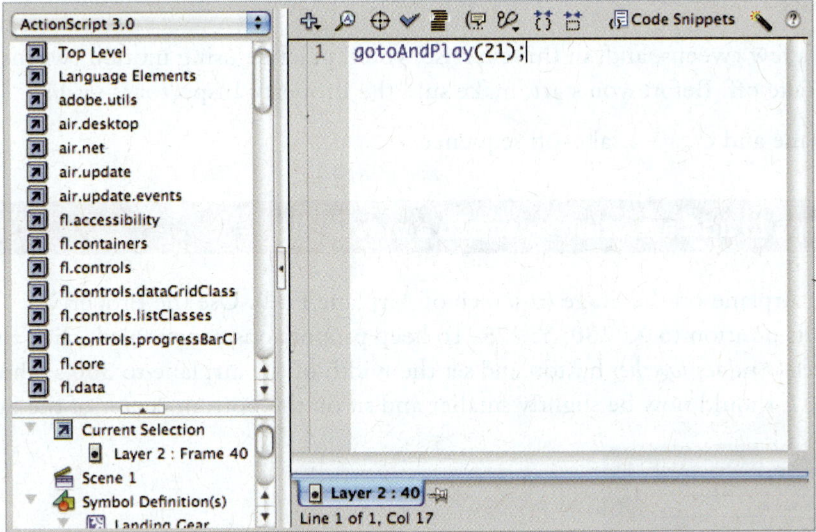

Figure 12-25: Add `gotoAndPlay(21)` *to frame 40 of the Actions layer.*

The loop starts later in the Timeline because you want the speed increase to occur only once and then have the propeller maintain a consistent speed as it loops. After the propeller picks up speed through the two tweens, the animation will loop continuously from frame 21, so the speed stays fast as the loop continues.

8. Close the Actions panel and select the Scene 1 link above the Stage. Preview your movie by choosing File > Publish Preview > Flash. The plane's propellers should appear to speed up and then rotate at a continuous rate. Because both propellers were instances of the same symbol, both automatically reflect the changes you made to the master symbol's animation.

9. Close the preview window, and choose File > Save to save your work.

Tweening movie clips

To make your movie clips glide, transform, or change their color tint, you can apply motion tweens to them just as you would to other symbols. Creating a tween with a movie clip is exactly the same as for graphic symbols, and several movie clips can be tweened at the same time on separate layers.

You've already used a few tweens, and, in this exercise, you'll practice using motion tweens to make your airplane take off. Before you start, make sure the Property Inspector is visible.

To tween your airplane and create a take-off sequence:

<table>
<tr><td>**Step-by-Step**</td><td>**Follow these steps to add a motion tween to a movie clip**</td></tr>
</table>

1. Select the entire airplane on the Stage (instance of Airplane Full). Use the Property Inspector to set its position to X: **280**, Y: **275**. To keep proportions constrained, click the *Lock width and height values together* button and set the width of the airplane to **300** as shown in Figure 12-26. It should now be slightly smaller and sit on the bottom center of the Stage.

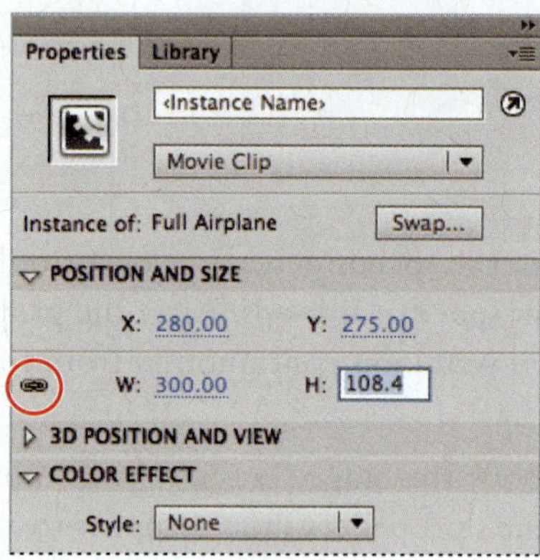

Figure 12-26: Reposition and shrink the airplane.

2. To animate the airplane taking to the skies, right-click (Windows) or Ctrl+click (Mac OS) on the instance of Full Airplane on the Stage, and choose Create Motion Tween from the contextual menu.

3. With the playhead on frame 30, use the Property Inspector to set the airplane's position to X: **280**, Y: **100** as shown in Figure 12-27.

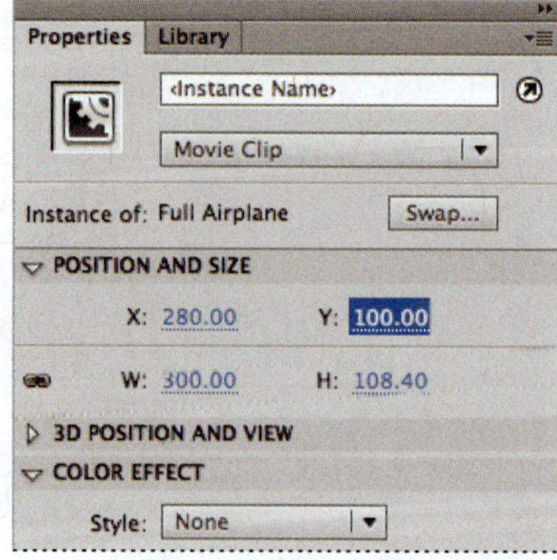

Figure 12-27: Use a motion tween to make the plane rise.

4. To create the impression of gravity pulling down on your plane as it takes off, add an Ease of –100 on frame 1. To do so, select frame 1, then click on the Motion Editor tab and scroll down to the Eases section. Type **–100** in the field to the right of Simple (Slow). Scroll up to the Y property in the Basic motion section and, if necessary, select Simple (Slow) from the Ease drop-down menu as shown in Figure 12-28.

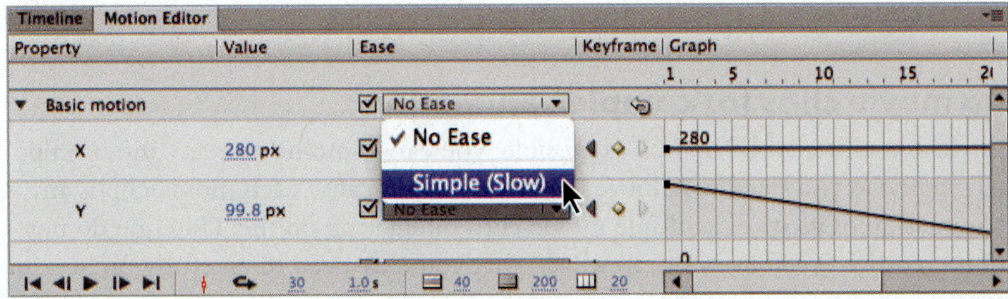

Figure 12-28: Add an ease to the airplane's new motion tween.

5. Preview your movie by choosing File > Publish Preview > Flash; your airplane should now lift off and make its way toward the top of the screen with propellers and landing gear in full effect.

6. Choose File > Save to save your work.

Adding a second tween

Now that you have your airplane taking off, you can elaborate further on your animation by making the airplane come toward you as it continues to fly. This will require a second tween after the one you just created.

<table><tr><td>**Follow these steps to add a second tween to a movie clip**</td><td>**Step-by-Step**</td></tr></table>

1. Click on the Timeline tab to bring the Timeline forward. Right-click (Windows) or Ctrl+click (Mac OS) on frame 60 and choose Insert Frame.

2. Click on the airplane and type **400** in the W (width) field in the Property Inspector (Figure 12-29).

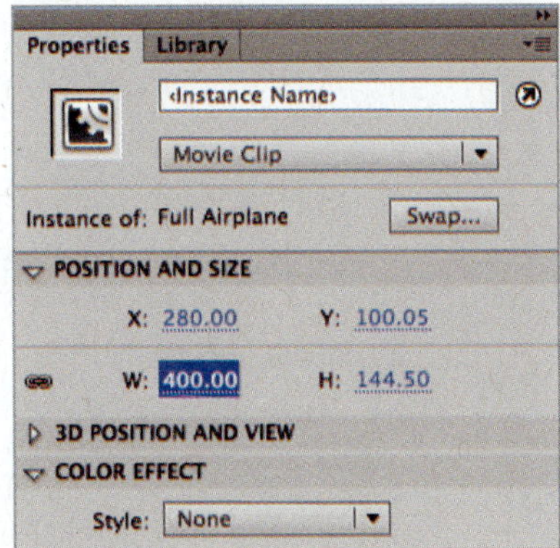

Figure 12-29: Resize the airplane.

3. Choose Control > Test Movie > in Flash Professional. The airplane takes off and appears to fly toward the camera. This effect may be a bit startling, so hold on to your seat.

    As you've seen in these steps, tweening a movie clip instance is very much the same as working with a graphic symbol; so transformations, color effects, and motion can all be applied. Because movie clips can contain entire animations, however, you can fully explore more complex and dynamic animations.

Combining movie clips for complex animation

To make a movie as realistic and dynamic as possible, you can combine as many movie clips on the main Timeline as you need to achieve the full effect. Because each movie clip is an independent animation of its own, multiple movie clips interacting on the Timeline do not interfere with each other. Keep in mind, however, that you may need to carefully orchestrate and sequence animation in different movie clips if one needs to interact with another.

Now that you have your airplane up-and-running, to make the scene more realistic, you'll add two things: a runway and some clouds. Both these graphics will have their own motion, especially as your plane moves off the runway and through the clouds. The movie clips for both of these have already been created for you in the library; all you'll need to do is place them on the main Timeline.

Step-by-Step | **Follow these steps to combine movie clips**

1. Rename Layer 1 **airplane**. Click on the New Layer button to create a new layer above this one and name it **clouds** (Figure 12-30).

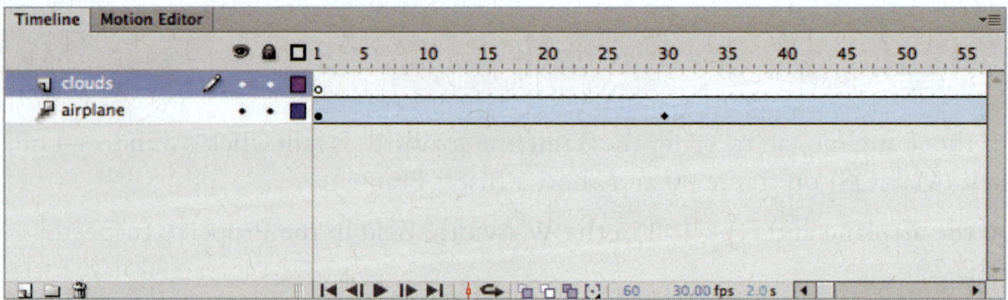

Figure 12-30: Create a new layer for the Clouds movie clip.

2. Click on the Library tab to bring the Library panel forward. Locate the Clouds movie clip in the Additional Graphics folder and drag an instance to the Stage (Figure 12-31).

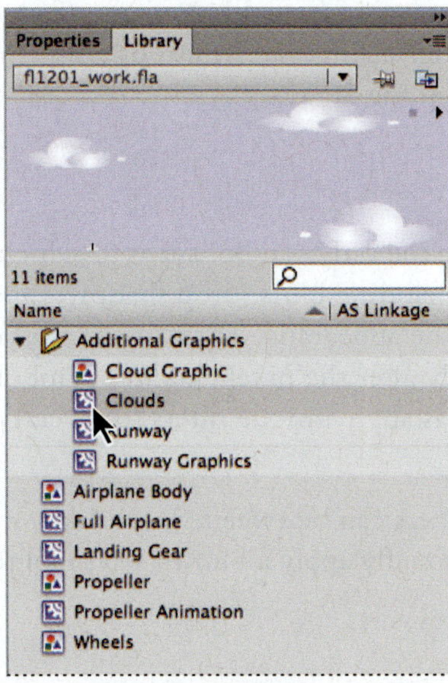

Figure 12-31: Drag an instance of Clouds to the Stage.

3. Use the Property Inspector to position the new Clouds instance at X: **100**, Y: **220**.

4. While still on the main Timeline, create a new layer and rename it **Runway**. As shown in Figure 12-32, drag this layer to the bottom of the layer stack below the airplane layer.

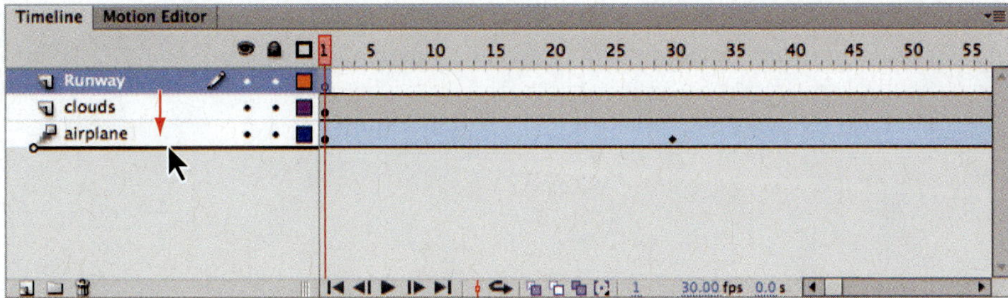

Figure 12-32: Create a new layer below the airplane tween to make room for your runway.

5. With the runway layer selected, locate the Runway movie clip in the Library panel in the Additional Graphics folder, and drag an instance of it to the Stage. Use the Property Inspector to position it at X: **275**, Y: **260**.

6. Test your movie by choosing Control > Test Movie > in Flash Professional. The newly added clips animate along with the airplane you created; you now have a full animation scene.

7. Close the preview window, and choose File > Save to save your work.

Exercise

To test your new skills, explore both the provided movie clips in Edit mode to see how they were created. Try making modifications to them and see how your overall movie is affected. Because these movie clips were built to work together, major changes in length or animation style may require you to also adjust the other movie clips on the Stage.

Adding filter effects to movie clips

Movie clips have another advantage: they (and buttons) are the only symbol types to which you can apply Flash's built-in, high-quality filter effects, including blurs, drop shadows, and bevels. A **blur** is a simple filter effect in Flash that softens the appearance of an object. Because the filter effects are nondestructive, they won't permanently alter the pixel data in a symbol, meaning that you can easily remove or edit filters, as well as apply unique filters to several instances of a movie clip.

Probably one of the coolest features to note is that Flash filters can be tweened, just like any other instance-specific property. For example, you can gradually apply a blur to a symbol to create realistic and artistic effects.

Take Note...
Some CS6 applications (most notably Adobe Photoshop) feature a variety of filter effects. If you're creating graphics in one of these applications, you may choose to apply filters then, or directly in the Flash environment after import. Because Flash natively supports importing Photoshop and Illustrator files, it converts most common filter types to Flash filters. The advantage of applying filters in Flash is that they can be easily edited without the need to switch applications and re-import updated files. In addition, you can manipulate Flash filters with ActionScript, which opens a world of dynamic filtering possibilities.

Using the Filters panel

In this exercise, you'll explore Flash filters by applying effects to the Clouds and Runway movie clips. Then you'll animate these effects with motion tweens to add more realism to the airplane animation.

Follow these steps to add a filter to a movie clip Step-by-Step

1. Select the instance of the Clouds movie clip on the Stage.

2. If necessary, bring the Property Inspector forward by clicking on its tab. Click on the Add filter button (⊒) at the bottom of the Property Inspector and choose Blur from the pop-up list of filters as shown in Figure 12–33.

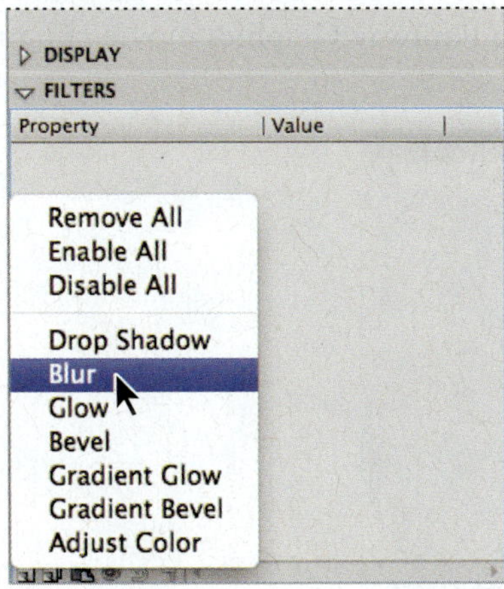

Figure 12–33: Add a blur filter to the Clouds movie clip.

The settings that appear to the right enable you to set the desired degree of vertical and horizontal blur.

3. Locate the Blur X and Blur Y text fields, and then type **10** in either field to set the blur amount for both.

4. Select Medium from the Quality drop-down menu. This is a good choice for making sure the effect looks clean without putting too much strain on the Flash Player (as filter effects are resource-intensive).

5. Preview your movie, using the shortcut key combination Ctrl+Enter (Windows) or Command+Return (Mac OS). Your clouds now have an interesting blur effect applied and, as a result, appear more realistic as the animation plays.

6. Close the preview window.

Creating a filter effect

Filtering an entire movie clip instance is a few clicks away using the Filters panel, but you can go a step further by combining tweens and filters to transition into a filter effect. **Filters** are several types of effects that can be applied to objects in Flash. Try this with your Runway movie clip by blurring the runway as the plane takes off, and climbs above the ground.

<table>
<tr><td>**Step-by-Step**</td><td>**Follow these steps to apply a filter effect to a movie clip**</td></tr>
</table>

1. Double-click the Runway movie clip on the Stage to edit it in place. You should see a basic motion tween that moves the runway down. The tween was created between two instances of a movie clip called Runway Graphics. (Graphics symbols cannot be used because you can apply filter effects only to movie clips or buttons.) Move the playhead on the Timeline to frame 30 and select the instance of the Runway Graphics movie clip on the Stage as shown in Figure 12-34.

Figure 12-34: The Runway movie clip at frame 30 in Edit mode.

Take Note...
You can apply filter effects only to movie clips, buttons, and dynamic text fields. If you want to apply a filter to a basic graphic, graphic symbol, or drawing object, you must convert it to a movie clip or button symbol first.

2. Click the Add filter button (⬚) at the bottom-left corner in the Filters section of the Property Inspector, and choose Blur from the resulting contextual menu.

3. Set the Blur X and Y values to **15**, and select Medium from the Quality drop-down menu as shown in Figure 12-35. Changing the Blur X and Y values to 15 from the default of 5 will automatically create an animation between frames 1 and 30. The effect will be applied for the entire tween span, but it will transition from the default value to the new value.

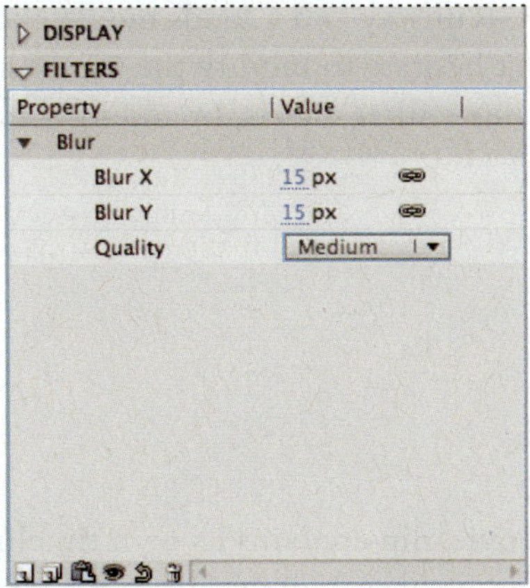

Figure 12-35: Add a blur to the runway, and then adjust the Blur X and Y values on frame 30 to create an animated filter.

4. To make the transition a bit more pronounced, drag the playhead back to frame 1, select the runway, and change the Blur X and Y values shown in the Property Inspector to **0**.

5. Press Ctrl+Enter (Windows) or Command+Return (Mac OS) to preview your movie.

6. If you like, return to the main Timeline and keep your airplane at cruising altitude by adding a `stop()` action on frame 60. Remember to insert a new layer for the `stop()` action and create a new keyframe at frame 60 before adding the action, to ensure it occurs in the right place. The provided runway and clouds already utilize a `stop()` action (Figure 12-36).

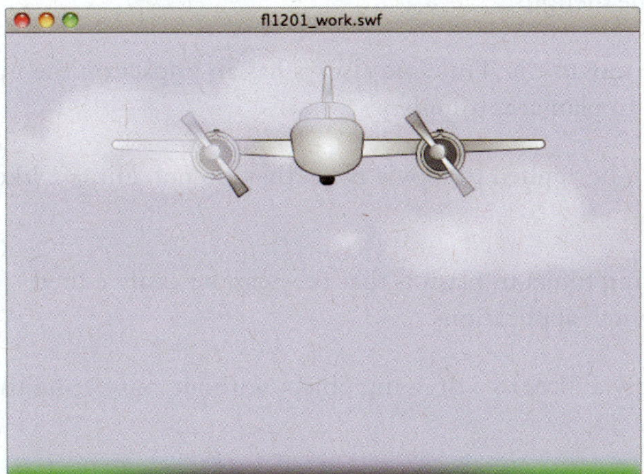

Figure 12-36: The preview shows the filters you've applied. Now you're flying!

7. Choose File > Save, then choose File > Close.

Congratulations! You've completed the lesson.

Wrapping up

Movie clips open a treasure trove of possibilities, and the best way to master movie clips is to use them—the more you do, the more ways you'll find to create innovative, complex, and eye-catching animations that far exceed what's possible on a single Timeline. To get ideas for your next movie clip, explore ready-made clips, such as the Runway and Clouds movie clips in your library, to understand how they were created. Don't hesitate to modify the movie clips in this exercise by adding keyframes, experimenting with more filter effects, or adding some additional graphics of your own.

Knowledge Assessment

True/False

Circle **T** if the statement is true or **F** if the statement is false.

T F 1. What sets movie clips apart is that each movie clip contains its own timeline, independent of the main Timeline.

T F 2. By default, Flash creates a new tween span to one second of play time. The length of the span will also be dictated by the frame rate.

T F 3. Movie clips cannot be dropped into other movie clips, they must be collectively assembled on the Stage.

T F 4. Although movie clip timelines are independent of the main Timeline, they can't use a different frame rate than the main Timeline.

T F 5. Because a movie clip works from its own timeline, its length is independent from the main Timeline's length.

T F 6. The ActionScript on a movie clip Timeline always has an impact on the main Timeline, so you have to plan accordingly.

T F 7. Only classic tweens can be applied to movie clips, they do not animate like other symbols do.

T F 8. An advantage of applying filters in Flash is that they can be easily edited without the need to switch applications.

T F 9. There is no way to apply a filter to a drawing object without converting to a symbol first.

T F 10. Filters cannot be animated.

Multiple Choice

Select the best response for the following statements.

1. Besides Transform, which panel allows you to set rotation values when rotating an object on the Stage?
    a. Properties
    b. Info
    c. Components
    d. Library

2. What concept and strategy is important to understand to simplify the main Timeline when creating complex animations?
    a. Layer naming
    b. Layer color coding
    c. Nesting
    d. Symbol naming

3. If a movie clip is combined with another movie clip, what must happen to the original movie clip in the Library?
    a. It must remain in the Library as a reference
    b. It can be deleted since all graphics are embedded within Flash
    c. A duplicate must be made
    d. None of the above

4. Which of the following is an important consideration when understanding how movie clips work?
    a. Frame Rate
    b. Timeline Length
    c. Dependencies
    d. All of the above

5. Which of the following blocks of ActionScript would instruct the playhead to jump to frame 20?
    a. `goto(20);`
    b. `gotoPlay(20);`
    c. `gotoAndPlay(20);`
    d. `gotoStop(20);`

6. To create a sense of space or distance between the viewer and an object on the Stage, which property can be very effective to animate?
    a. Position
    b. Scale
    c. Rotation
    d. Opacity

7. Which two symbol types can have filters applied to them?

   a. Movie clips and buttons

   b. Movie clips and graphic symbols

   c. Graphic symbols and buttons

   d. They can all have filters applied to them

8. When applying a filter and adjusting quality (for the Blur filter for example), what is the best quality choice to prevent putting too much strain on Flash Player but maintaining a clean look to the filter?

   a. Low

   b. Medium

   c. High

   d. It doesn't really matter

9. Besides symbols, what other object can have filters applied to it?

   a. Text fields

   b. Dynamic text fields

   c. Primitives

   d. Video

10. Which of the following is not a filter choice?

   a. Blur

   b. Glow

   c. Drop Shadow

   d. Stroke

Competency Assessment

Project 12-1	Exploring Filters

Filters are just one of the tools you can use to make a more dynamic, 3-Dimensional appearance to an otherwise 2-D, flat design. Programs like Photoshop have an impressive array of filters to accomplish this task; Flash also has some of the basic bells and whistles in there as well.

1. Create a new ActionScript 3.0 document in Flash.

2. Select the Rectangle tool and draw a rectangle on the Stage, set the color to blue and the stroke to none.

3. Convert the rectangle to a movie clip named blue rectangle.

4. With the movie clip selected, go to the Properties panel and click on the Add filter button at the bottom left corner. Choose the Drop Shadow.

5. The first portion of this exercise is complete. Instead of adjusting the Drop Shadow now, you'll animate it in the next exercise.

6. Save the file as **filters.fla** and keep the file open.

A Review of Animated Filters

Project 12-2

One of the advantages of applying filters in Flash is that you can change them over a period of time to enhance animation.

1. The **filters.fla** file from the last project should still be open.

2. Select the keyframe containing the blue rectangle movie clip and apply a motion tween.

3. Go to the first keyframe and select the movie clip on the Stage. Set the Drop Shadow strength value to 0%.

4. Go to the last frame of the tween span and set the Drop Shadow strength to 90% and preview the animation.

5. Save the file as **animated_filters.fla**.

Proficiency Assessment

Continuing to Practice with Buttons

Project 12-3

Movie clips aren't the only thing that filters can be applied to. Buttons are another candidate for filters...

1. Create a new ActionScript 3.0 document in Flash.

2. Create an oval button that contains a blue Up state and orange Over state. Name it **filter button**.

3. Place the button on the Stage. Apply the Bevel filter to give it a more raised appearance on the Stage.

4. Save the file as **buttons.fla** and keep this exercise handy for the next project.

Making the Button Pop

Project 12-4

Dimensional effects are nice but you can give it more impact by making it emerge from the screen by animating it.

1. The **buttons.fla** file from the last exercise should still be open.

2. Select the keyframe containing the button and apply a motion tween.

3. Go to the first keyframe and select the movie clip on the Stage. Set the Bevel strength value to 0%.

4. Go to the last frame of the tween span and set the Bevel strength to 100% and preview the animation.

5. Save the file as **animated_buttons.fla**.

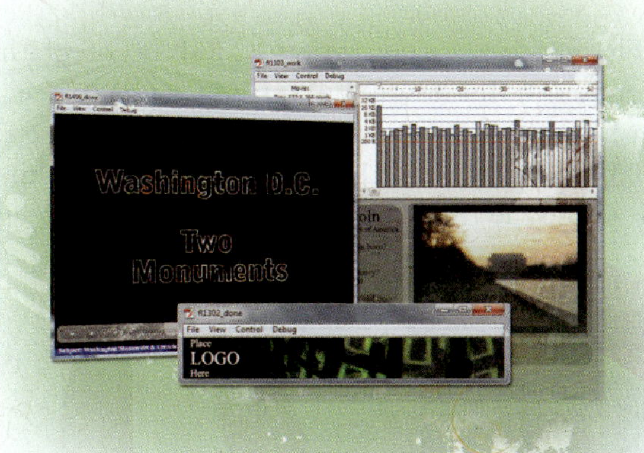

Working with Video

Key Terms

- Bandwidth Profiler
- codecs
- cue points
- embedded video
- linked video
- Live Preview
- Media Encoder
- skin

Skill	Objective
Understand Flash file types	3.7
Add simple controls through ActionScript 3.0	4.11
Add and export video	4.13

Business case

Video is everywhere these days and constantly at our finger tips through our phones, through the internet, and more. Understanding how to work with video in Flash is an essential part to understanding how you can incorporate videos into your interactive projects.

Starting up

Before starting, make sure that your tools and panels are consistent by resetting your workspace. See "Resetting the Flash workspace" in the Starting up section of this book.

You will work with several files from the fl13lessons folder in this lesson. Make sure that you have loaded the fllessons folder onto your hard drive from *http://www.wiley.com/college/sc/adobeseries*. See "Loading lesson files" in the Starting up section of this book.

The project

In this lesson, you'll import a video file into Flash and practice various methods of integrating it into your movies. Working through the exercises in this lesson will introduce you to the different ways to work with video in your Flash projects. To view the finished file, choose File > Open and select the **fl1302_done.fla**, **fl1303_done.fla**, and **fl1306_done.fla** files within the fl13lessons folder as shown in Figure 13-1. Close the files when you are finished, or keep them open as a reference.

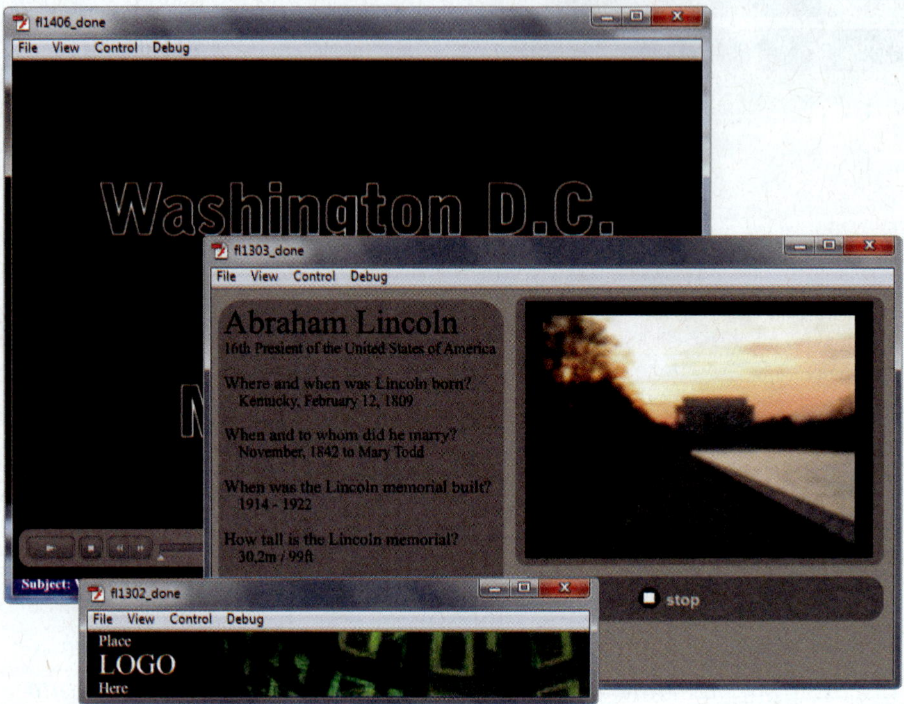

Figure 13–1: The finished files.

Video in Flash: formats and fundamentals

The first step toward importing video into Flash is to make sure you are equipped and ready. In addition to Flash CS6, you'll need the QuickTime player (at least version 7 for Windows or version 10 for Mac OS) installed on your system. You'll also need a source video file to import and convert (video is provided for the exercises in this lesson).

Understanding video

Like animations on the Timeline, videos are composed of a series of sequential still images played back very rapidly, sometimes with sound, and sometimes without. When played back very quickly, these images seem to form continuous motion. You need to keep two parameters in mind when working with video: frame rate, which is the speed, measured in frames per second (fps) at which the video plays, and frame size, which is the size, measured in pixels, of each frame of video. Both the frame rate and size contribute to the final file size.

Embedded versus linked video

There are two ways to work with video in a Flash (SWF) file: you can embed the video directly onto the Timeline, or have your movie reference an external, linked video file that resides on a server.

External video files can be streamed from a Flash Media Streaming Service, a Flash Media Server, a server solution optimized to deliver streaming or real-time media, or downloaded progressively from any standard web server, including the same one on which your Flash movie is hosted. Using external video keeps the SWF file size fairly small, and because the video file exists as an external video file on a server, the SWF container can be repurposed to dynamically display multiple video sources. In addition, because the FLV file exists outside the Flash movie, it can have a different frame rate from the SWF; this avoids messy issues where video and audio end up out of sync, which is common when working with embedded video files. For a comparison of the benefits of streaming versus progressively downloading, see the section, "Working with linked video."

Embedded video is placed directly on the Flash Timeline. This can significantly increase the SWF file size—potentially to unmanageable levels with longer clips. Additionally, because the video file and the Flash document can have two different frame rates, audio and video may end up out of sync when the movie is published. For this reason, embedded video is usually recommended only for short video clips, and even then usually only for short video clips without audio.

Another major difference between embedded and linked video is the way in which they are deployed for distribution. Because embedded video is a part of the SWF Timeline, it is automatically included when you publish the file. **Linked video**, however, exists independently and must be uploaded to the server in addition to your SWF and any other dependent files. In general, the goal of using linked video files is to create modular content than can be repurposed more easily than embedded video can, and to reduce the initial loading time of your SWF. In general, you should not import video into a Flash document when the publish target is HTML.

Flash Video formats: FLV and F4V

All video in Flash must be converted into the Flash Video format (FLV or F4V) or H.264 formats for playback in the Flash Player. This conversion can be performed as part of the process of importing video into a Flash document using the built-in Video Import wizard, or it can be completed before the import stage by using the Adobe Media Encoder or a video editing application such as Adobe Premiere Pro that can export Flash video.

There are two extensions used for Flash video files. The FLV format is supported by Flash Player version 7 and higher, while the newer F4V format is supported by Flash Player versions 9.2 and higher. The F4V format is intended to provide higher playback quality at lower files sizes than FLV can provide. The Flash Player version that you want to target will determine how you format your video. If you are publishing for the latest version of Flash Player (or even versions 9 or up), it's recommended that you convert video to F4V.

Understanding codecs

Codecs are software routines that compress video files small enough to be e-mailed, or viewed on the Web or mobile devices.

The video creator uses a codec to compress the video file for distribution; the files are then decoded by the viewer's video player using the same codec. Flash video (F4V specifically) supports three codec choices: Sorenson Spark, On2 VP6 (usually called ON2V), and H.264.

The Sorenson Spark codec is supported by files encoded in the FLV format for playback in Flash Player 7 and later. The On2 VP6 codec is the default setting for videos encoded for versions 8 and 9 of the Flash Player because it provides higher video quality than the older Sorenson Spark codec. MainConcept H.264 is supported by Flash Player versions 9.2 and later. The newer codecs provide better video playback quality at lower file sizes than the older ones do. This higher-quality video comes at the price of a slower encoding time and more use of system resources (such as RAM and connection speed) on the viewer's computer at playback time.

Understanding Adobe Media Encoder CS6

The Adobe **Media Encoder** is a stand-alone application that is installed when you install the Flash application. The encoder exists to convert video and audio media from one format to another. While often thought of as a tool for converting video into the Flash Video format, it can actually convert video into a wide range of formats, such as IPod video and video for sharing sites such as Vimeo and YouTube.

The Adobe Media Encoder can import video and audio in a wide variety of file formats. Some of the more common importable video formats are listed below:

- 3GPP/3GPP2 (.3gp, .3gpp)
- Digital Video (.dv)
- DV stream
- Flash Video (.flv, .f4v)
- QuickTime (.mov)
- MPEG (.mpg, .mpeg, .m2v)
- Windows (.avi)
- Windows Media (.asf, .wmv)

Take Note...

The QuickTime player is available as a free download from apple.com, *and is packaged with all versions of Mac OS X.*

The Adobe Media Encoder is divided into 4 main areas: the Queue, Encoding, Preset Browser and Watch Folders panes (Figure 13-2). The Queue is a list of the files you are going to convert, and the settings for each. From the Queue, you can choose the type of video you would like to output to, and the specific preset you would like to use for it.

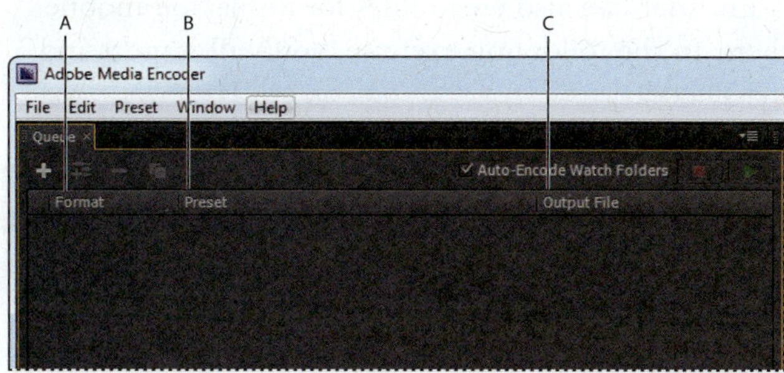

Figure 13-2
A. Format. B. Presets. C. Output file destination.

When the built-in presets aren't suitable for your project, you can open the encoder's Export Settings dialog box for greater control (Figure 13-3). The window gives you increased control over things such as output size, video and audio compression, and even the ability to upload directly to a web server. In addition to the output of your video file, the dialog box can be used to set cue points for Flash video and even perform basic editing by trimming the beginning or ending of a video file.

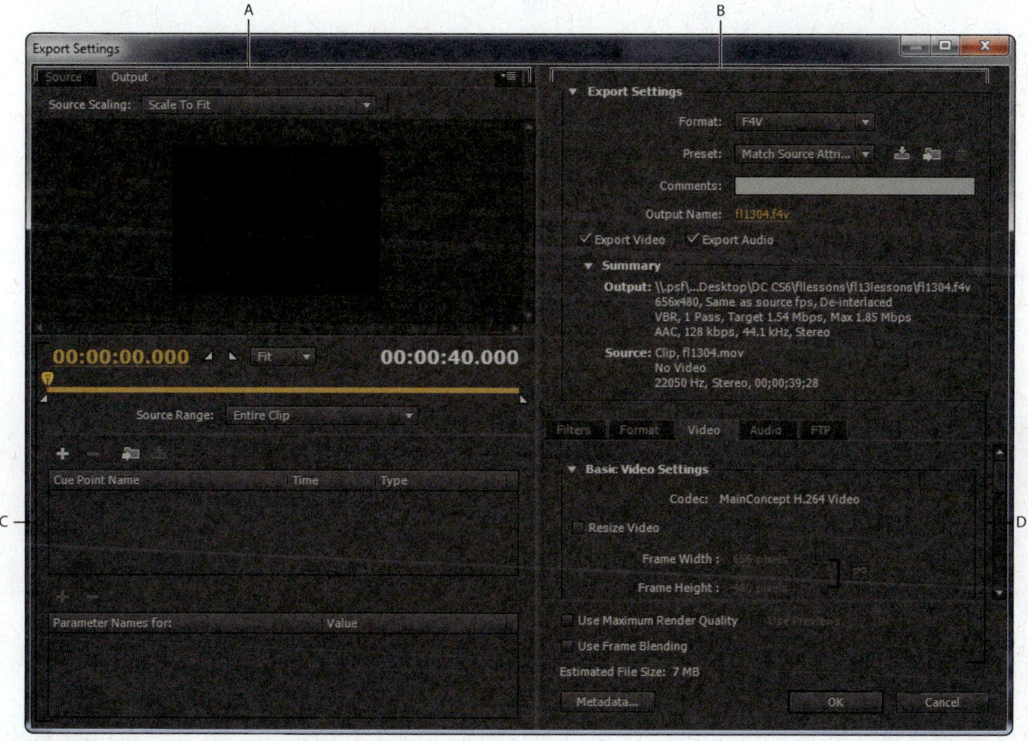

Figure 13-3
A. The Source and Output Monitor tabs. B. Provides a summary of the Export Settings. C. Location for setting cue points and trimming video. D. Tabs containing the specific settings for Video, Audio, and Format.

Converting video with the Adobe Media Encoder

The first phase is to prepare the video file that you will import into the Flash project using the Adobe Media Encoder. Technically, the Adobe Media Encoder isn't a part of Flash; it is a stand-alone video converter that can take video in one format and convert it to another. In addition to Flash video, the Adobe Media Encoder can also create files for display on mobile devices such as cell phones, iPods, and others. In the following exercise, you will import and convert a video file using the Adobe Media Encoder.

Step-by-Step | **Follow these steps to convert video using the Adobe Media Encoder**

1. Open the Adobe Media Encoder by choosing Adobe Media Encoder CS6 from the Start Menu (Windows) or Applications > Adobe Media Encoder CS6 (Mac OS).

2. In the Adobe Media Encoder, press the Add Source button. In the Open dialog box, navigate to the fl13lessons folder and select the **fl1301.mov** file. Press Open to load the video file into the Adobe Media Encoder.

Take Note...

You can also drag and drop files into the Adobe Media Encoder window from the Mac OS X Finder and Windows Explorer.

3. There are three editable fields for every file:

   - **Format**: Either Flash Video (.flv or .f4v), h.264 or mp3. The h.264 format is used when creating video for mobile devices, and video sharing sites like YouTube.

   - **Preset**: Once the format is chosen, AME allows you to select from a wide range of preset options for encoding the video.

   - **Output file**: Specifies the location and name of the new file that will be created.

   For Format, make sure that the drop-down menu displays FLV or F4V. For Preset, press the triangle button to open the menu and choose Match Source Attributes (Medium Quality). The Output file's location will automatically be set to match the location of the source video file.

Take Note...

As stated previously, if the F4V format is designed to provide better quality video, why are you using FLV-formatted video here? The reason is that for the first part of this exercise you will embed video directly into a Flash file. This procedure can only be done when using an FLV format.

4. Press the Start Queue button and the Encoder will convert your video.

5. Once the video has completed converting, close the Adobe Media Encoder by choosing File > Exit (Windows) or Adobe Media Encoder CS6 > Quit Adobe Media Encoder CS6.

Working with embedded video

Embedding video is the most straightforward method of adding video content to your movies. However, because it can enlarge the size of your SWF file and create issues where your audio and video are out of sync, it is best suited for adding short video clips. On certain projects, embedded video may be the only viable way to work with video in Flash. Often, when creating Flash banners or other advertising material, you have to deliver completely stand-alone SWF files without external links. Embedded video is also a very good way to create interaction or integration between video and Timeline animated assets, or to create a quick closed-captioning effect.

Adding embedded video to the Timeline

Once video has been converted to the Flash Video format, it is ready for use in Flash either as linked video that runs from a location outside your Flash movie (.swf), or embedded video that is placed directly into it. Once you have embedded the video file, the SWF that you create will be ready for deployment just like any other Flash movie. All you need to do is place it in a web page, and it will be ready to be viewed on the Web.

<table><tr><td>**Follow these steps to add embedded video to the Timeline**</td><td>**Step-by-Step**</td></tr></table>

1. Open Flash CS6. Choose File > Open, navigate to the fl13lessons folder, and select the Flash file **fl1302.fla**. Press Open. This file is a mockup for a banner advertisement.

2. In the Timeline, select the first frame of the Video Here layer, and then choose File > Import > Import Video.

3. In the Import Video dialog box, under the section labeled *Where is your video file?* make sure the radio button labeled On your computer is selected. Press the Browse button and from the fl13lessons folder, select the **fl1301.flv** file created in the previous exercise and press Open. Select the radio button labeled Embed FLV in SWF and play in timeline as shown in Figure 13-4.

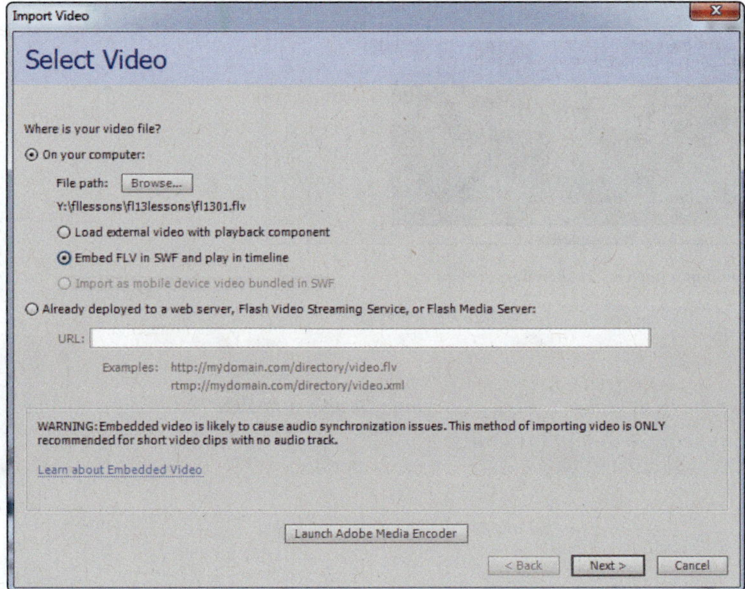

Figure 13-4: *The dialog box displays a warning that embedding video is recommended only for smaller video files and those without audio.*

4. Click Next. In the Embedding section of the Import Video dialog box, make sure Embedded video is selected from the Symbol type drop-down menu. Make sure that the Place instance on stage, Expand timeline if needed, and Include audio checkboxes are all selected (Figure 13-5).

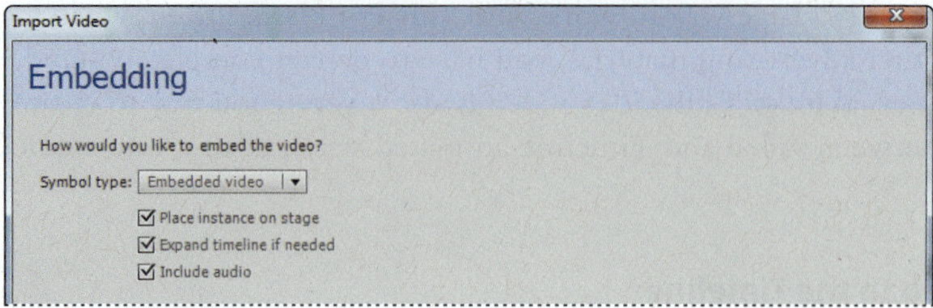

Figure 13-5: Increase the size of the Timeline to accommodate the new video.

5. Click Next. The Finish Video Import section of the Import Video dialog box provides a summary of the decisions you have made in the Video Import wizard. Press Finish to complete the import process.

6. Use the Selection tool (🖈) to position the video file so its left edge lines up against the second vertical guide to the right of the logo area, and it's vertically centered on the Stage (Figure 13-6). Lock the Mask and Video layers by clicking them below the padlock column in the Timeline panel. This fully activates the mask layer, and you should see only a portion of the new video revealed.

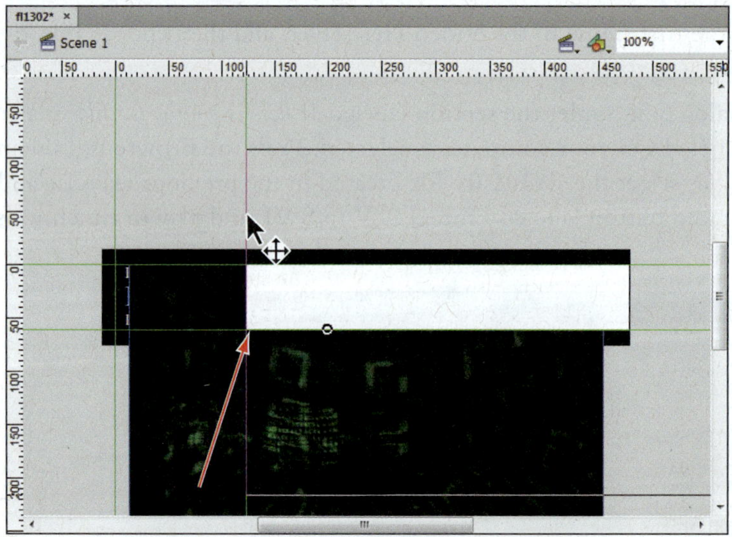

Figure 13-6: Position the video within guidelines as shown in the figure.

Take Note...
To make positioning the new video as easy as possible, make sure that snapping is enabled by choosing View > Snapping > Snap to Guides.

7. As the Timeline currently stands, the video on the Video Here layer plays for 1171 frames, but the theme, Mask, Logo, and Background layers only exist at Frame 1. You'll correct this in the next few steps by adding frames to the Timeline.

Click the Go to Last Frame button located at the bottom of the Timeline to advance to the end of the timeline at frame 1171 as highlighted in Figure 13-7. Click on frame 1171 in the Background layer on the Timeline. Hold down the Ctrl (Windows) or Command (Mac OS) key, and click on frame 1171 in the Mask and Logo layers as well, to select them all at once.

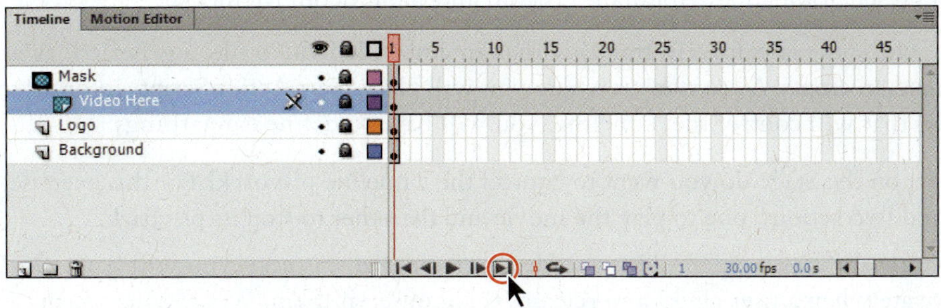

Figure 13-7: *Advance to the last frame of the timeline so you can extend the remaining 3 layers.*

8. Press the F5 key on the keyboard to add new frames to all three layers (Figure 13-8). This ensures that the content of the Logo and Background layers remains on the Timeline until the video finishes playing.

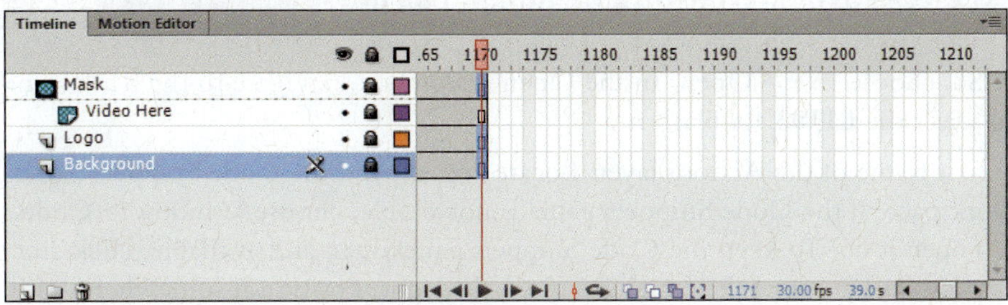

Figure 13-8: *Keyframes act as placeholders, extending the duration of the previous keyframe on the layer.*

9. Choose File > Save As. In the Save As dialog box, navigate to the fl13lessons folder, and then type **fl1302_work.fla** in the Name text field. Press Save.

10. Choose Control > Test Movie to preview your work so far.

11. Close the Flash Player preview window, then choose File > Close to close the FLA document.

Building controls for embedded video

Certification Ready 4.11

How can Code Snippets help you to program in Flash?

It is the standard behavior of the Flash Player to loop SWF files, but this may not be the effect you want. To prevent this continuous looping, you will use ActionScript 3.0 to control the Timeline and, in turn, the playback of the video. In this exercise, you will import and embed a short video file into a prepared Flash document and use the new Code Snippets panel to create functional Play, Pause, and Stop buttons to control it. The Code Snippets panel is a convenient and efficient way to program timeline navigation, actions, animation, audio/video control, event handling, and loading/unloading assets. The file you will be using for this section is a mock-up of a presentation about Abraham Lincoln and the Lincoln Memorial.

The Timeline of the file lasts for 915 frames. It has an embedded video file, a generic Play and Stop button, and an empty Actions layer where you will place your ActionScript. In order to create a button that will control the Timeline, you will have to define three things:

- Which object on the Stage do you want to control the Timeline playback? For this exercise, you will build two actions, one to play the movie and the other to stop its playback.

- When do you want it to happen? This is called an Event. In this case, you will have the buttons activate when a user clicks and releases the mouse on them.

- What do you want it to do? This is a special type of function called an Event handler. The Code Snippets panel will help you create event handlers that play and stop the movie's Timeline.

Step-by-Step

Follow these steps to build controls for embedded video

1. In Flash CS6, choose File > Open. In the Open dialog box, navigate to the fl13lessons folder and select the **fl1303.fla** Flash file.

2. Select the first frame of the Actions layer. Locate and expand the Code Snippets panel in your workspace; if the Code Snippets panel is not visible, choose Window > Code Snippets to open it up. To keep the Code Snippets panel open and available, click and drag it by its tab and pull it out of the panel group on the right. Position it somewhere within the left side of your workspace.

3. The first thing you will do is stop the movie's Timeline from playing automatically when the SWF file is loaded. Within the Code Snippets panel, locate and expand the Timeline Navigation folder (Figure 13-9). Double-click the Stop at This Frame code snippet to place it on the timeline. The Actions panel will appear showing that the code has been added to your project.

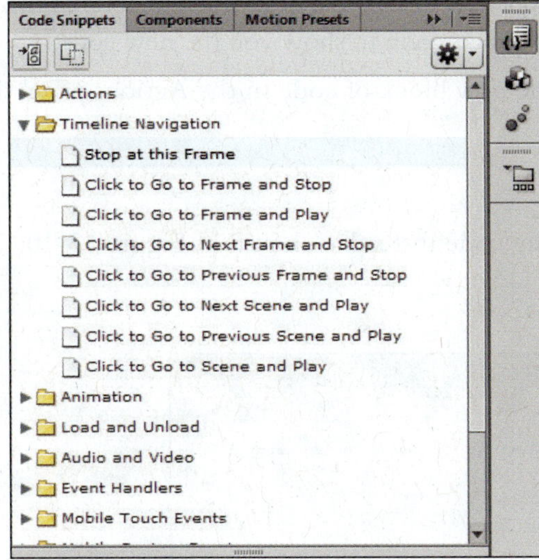

Figure 13-9: *The Code Snippets panel contains pre-created actions for timeline navigation.*

4. Select the button labeled Play on the Stage. You will notice when you look at the Property Inspector that the Play button has an instance name of play_btn.

5. With the Play button selected, once again return to the Code Snippets panel. This time expand the Event Handlers folder within this panel. Double-click the Mouse Click Event snippet to add it to the timeline. The Actions panel will appear again, showing you that the necessary code has been added to "wire up" your button for some type of click action.

6. In the Actions panel, locate the line in the new block of code that reads:

```
trace("Mouse clicked");
```

Replace this placeholder line with the following code instead:

```
play();
```

7. If necessary, drag the Actions panel out of the way, or collapse it by double-clicking its tab in the upper-left corner. Select the button labeled Stop on the Stage. Just as you did with the Play button, you'll add some ActionScript to the timeline to make this button do something when clicked.

8. Return to the Code Snippets panel. The Event Handlers folder should still be expanded. Double-click the Mouse Click Event code snippet again to add a new block of code to the timeline. The Actions panel will come forward once again to show you the new code.

9. Just as you did in Step 6, locate the line in the new block of code in the Actions panel that reads:

```
trace("Mouse clicked");
```

This time, replace this line with the following code instead as shown in Figure 13-10:

```
stop();
```

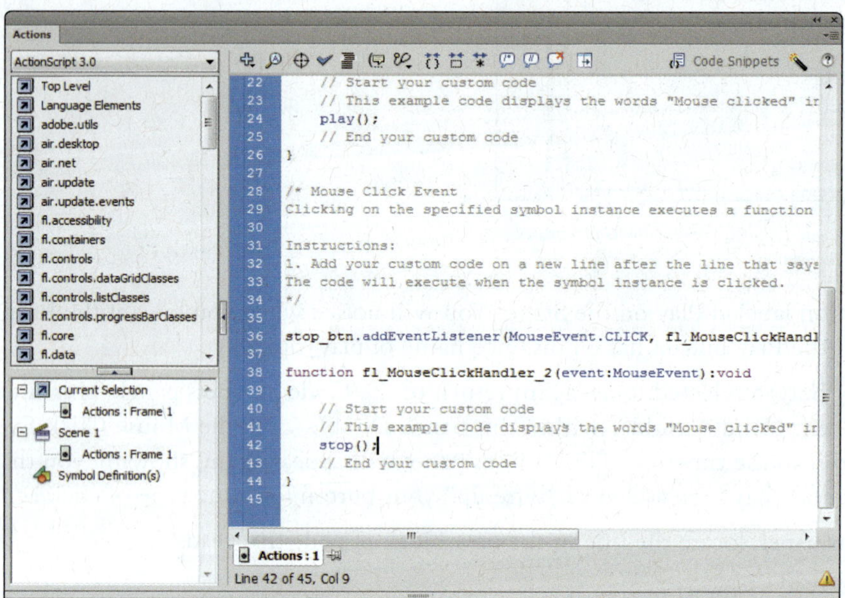

Figure 13-10: *The completed code as it should show in the Actions panel.*

10. With the help of the Code Snippets panel, you've added the appropriate code to the timeline that will instruct the Play and Stop buttons to play the current timeline, and stop it, respectively.

11. Close the Actions panel and choose File > Save As. In the Save As dialog box, navigate to the fl13lessons folder and type **fl1303_work.fla** in the Name text field. Press Save.

12. Choose Control > Test Movie to preview your Flash movie and test the buttons. Keep the Flash Player preview window open; you are going to use it in the next exercise.

The Bandwidth Profiler

The **Bandwidth Profiler** is a useful tool that can help you measure the impact of embedded video on your movie. Even if your movie plays well for you, how does it perform for your target viewers? The Bandwidth Profiler enables you to test your movie's download time under a variety of conditions, and gives you the ability to review the amount of data in each frame of your movie. Check how well your movies from the exercises stack up.

Follow these steps to use the Bandwidth Profiler   **Step-by-Step**

1. In the Flash Player window, choose View > Bandwidth Profiler (Figure 13-11).

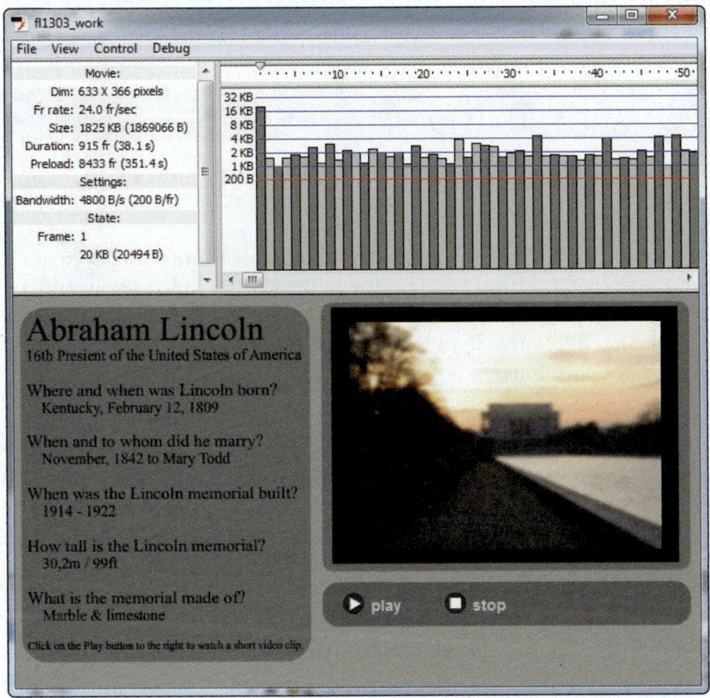

Figure 13-11: You can access the Bandwidth Profiler through the View menu.

2. Choose View > Frame by Frame Graph to see a breakdown of your movie's parameters on the left, and the size of each frame below that.

3. Choose View > Download Settings > DSL (32.6 KB/s) to see how your movie is treated if viewed over a DSL connection instead of a 56K dial-up connection.

4. Choose View > Simulate Download to preview what viewers experience when they watch your movie at the currently selected download settings.

5. Choose File > Close to close the Flash Player, then choose File > Close from the main Flash menu to close the file.

Working with linked video

If your video file is too large to embed into the SWF file, you should consider importing it as external video. External video remains separate from the SWF file that plays it, keeping the initial loading times for the SWF file fairly small. Linked deployment gives you the choice of three approaches: Web server, Flash Media Server, or Flash Video Streaming Service. Web server deployment enables you to use your current web server or hosting service plan to progressively download video into your Flash movie, using standard Hyper Text Transfer Protocols (HTTP). This allows users to begin watching a portion of your video while the rest of the file continues to load in the background.

Although progressively downloading a video clip from a web server doesn't provide the same real-time performance as using a Streaming Server, this approach requires minimal overhead and works easily with the same server that currently hosts your website.

Learning More

Video in the fast lane: Flash Media Server

For the fastest video delivery, consider deploying your video content to a Flash Media Server or Flash Video Streaming Service (FVSS).

The stream from a Flash Video Streaming Service for your Deployment option (available from the Deployment Options screen on the Video Import wizard) enables you to upload your video to a Flash Media Server and stream it directly into your Flash movie. Beyond just hosting, these servers also provide many other advanced features for adjusting bandwidth and quality and delivering high performance for large volume usage.

Such providers are often called CDNs (content delivery networks). The Video Import wizard's Deployment Options screen also displays a hyperlink to the Adobe website, *adobe.com*, where you can find a licensed FVSS. Choosing Stream from Flash Media Server on the Deployment Options screen allows you to stream your Flash video from a Flash Media Server that you host, and provides a hyperlink that takes you to the Adobe website to learn more about the Flash Media Server and how to license it.

For both linked approaches, you can use an FLVPlayback component with built-in navigation or ActionScript to control video playback and provide intuitive controls for user interaction.

To explore the linked video approach, you'll build a video player to display a short clip showcasing two presidential monuments in Washington, D.C. Because it is the most easily accessible method, this exercise focuses on progressive downloads from a web server.

Adding cue points in the Adobe Media Encoder

One of the benefits of using linked video is the ability to create navigational cue points and use skins to customize the appearance of the video player. Cue points are added when the Flash file is created in the Adobe Media Encoder, or within the Property Inspector in Flash CS6 (shown in a later exercise).

Cue points can be thought of as bookmarks, or chapter markers within a video. You can navigate through them using the seek buttons on the default Flash Video skins, or using your own mechanism created in ActionScript. A **skin** is a video interface added to a video file that often provides useful controls such as play, pause, stop, and the ability to scrub through the video.

<table><tr><td style="background:#a02820;color:white">Follow these steps to add cue points using the Adobe Media Encoder</td><td style="background:#a02820;color:white">Step-by-Step</td></tr></table>

1. Open the Adobe Media Encoder by choosing Adobe > Adobe Media Encoder CS6 from the Start menu (Windows) or Applications > Adobe Media Encoder CS6 (Mac OS). You may see videos that you're previously encoded (if any) appear here. If you want to clear out the display, you can highlight an entry and click Remove. It doesn't remove the files from your hard drive; it merely removes the reference to the file in the encoder.

2. Press the Add Source button on the left side of the workspace. In the Open dialog box, navigate to the fl13lessons folder and select the **fl1305.mov** file. Press Open to load the file into the encoder.

3. Under Format, make sure that the drop-down menu displays FLV or F4V.

4. In the Edit Export Settings dialog box, choose Web 640×480, Project Frame Rate, 4×3, 800kbps from the Preset drop-down menu as shown in Figure 13-12.

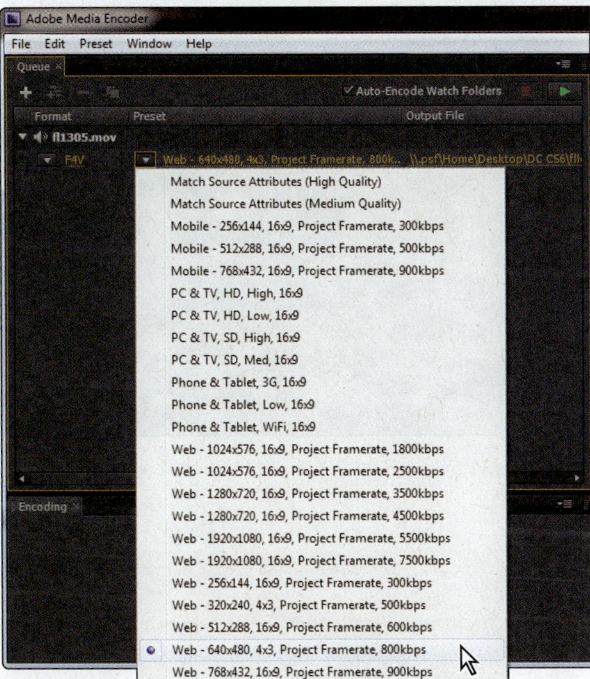

Figure 13-12*: The Preset drop-down menu allows you to select a base group of settings to start with.*

5. Click on the title of the newly selected preset in the queue to open the Export Settings dialog box.

6. Cue points are added in the area below the Source/Output monitors. The horizontal orange bar beneath the Source and Output monitors allows you to preview your video and add cue points. Slide the orange handle, called the Current Time Indicator, at the top of the bar until the time above it reads around 5 seconds (00;00;05;00) as shown in Figure 13-13. To get an even 5 seconds, you can click on the timecode and edit it by hand, or use the left/right arrow keys to move one frame at a time. This will move the playhead to 5 seconds, from the beginning of the video.

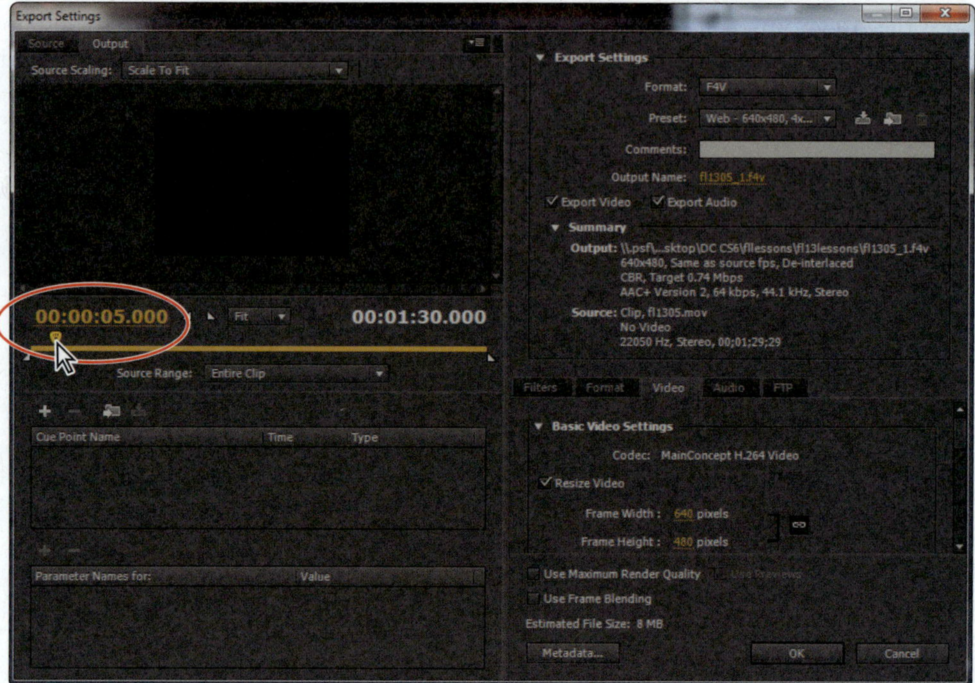

Figure 13-13: Specific times in a video are located using timecode, shown above. It is denoted by four sets of numbers separated by semicolons. The numbers indicate hours;minutes;seconds;frames.

Take Note...

If you are having trouble moving to a specific time in your video, you can use the left and right arrow keys on the keyboard to move left or right one frame at a time.

7. Press the Add Cue Point button (+) to add a cue point at the current time. In the cue point list, click on the name of the cue point and rename it **washington_monument**. As shown in Figure 13-14, choose Navigation from the Type drop-down menu.

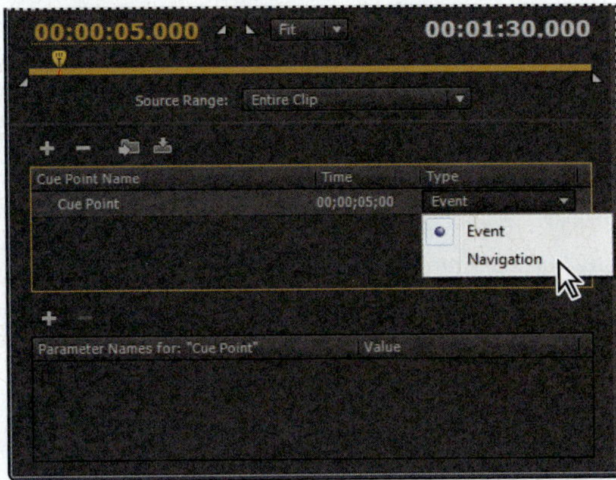

Figure 13-14: Set a cue point for the navigation.

8. Move the Current Time Indicator to 00:00:35:15. Click the Add Cue Point button. Rename this new cue point **lincoln_memorial** and choose Navigation from the Type drop-down menu.

9. Move the Current Time Indicator to 00:01:15:03. Click the Add Cue Point button. Rename the new cue point **website** and choose Navigation from the Type drop-down menu (Figure 13-15).

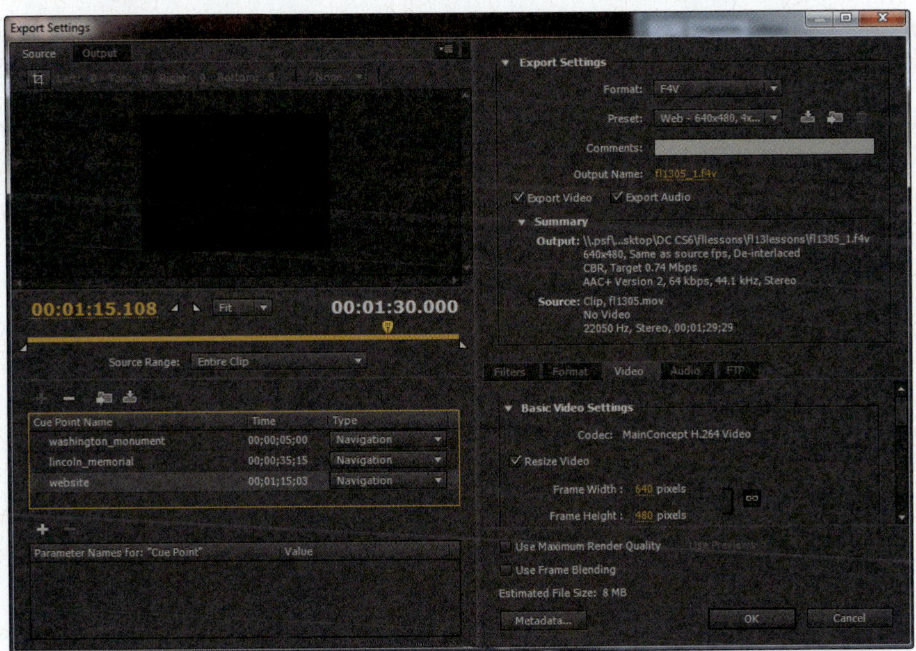

Figure 13-15: The completed cue points list.

10. Press OK to return to the Adobe Media Encoder. Press the Start Queue button to begin the conversion process. After the file finishes converting, close the Adobe Media Encoder by choosing File > Exit (Windows) or Adobe Media Encoder > Quit Adobe Media Encoder (Mac OS).

Take Note...

Video rendering is a very processor-intensive activity that can take quite a long time. The video included in this lesson could take anywhere from two to five minutes to complete the process. The longer a video file is, the longer the conversion process will take. For your convenience, all the video that you use in this lesson is included as pre-rendered Flash video files in the fl13lessons folder.

Adding linked video to the Timeline

Certification Ready 4.13

How do you create Flash video files (FLV)?

Once the video file is converted by the Adobe Media Encoder, the process for adding the file to the Flash Timeline is remarkably similar to the one used previously for embedding video.

Live Preview

Live Preview is a subtle but useful feature is the ability to preview linked video directly on the Stage within the Flash Professional CS6 environment. Previous versions of Flash required you to Test or Publish a movie first; now you simply use the included controls of the FLVPlayback component to play, rewind, and seek through your movie as you would in a published movie.

Step-by-Step

Follow these steps to preview linked video on the Stage

1. In Flash CS6, choose File > Open, and open the **fl1306.fla** file located in the fl13lessons folder. This contains a pre-created layout for your new video preview page.

2. Choose File > Save As. When the Save As dialog box appears, type **fl1306_work.fla** into the Name text field. Navigate to the fl13lessons folder and press Save.

3. Choose File > Import > Import Video to open the Video Import dialog box.

4. In the Select Video section of the Import Video dialog box, press the Browse button, navigate to the fl13lessons folder, and select **fl1305.f4v**. Press the Open button to return to the wizard. Make sure the radio button labeled Load external video with playback component is selected as shown in Figure 13-16. This option controls the download method of the video.

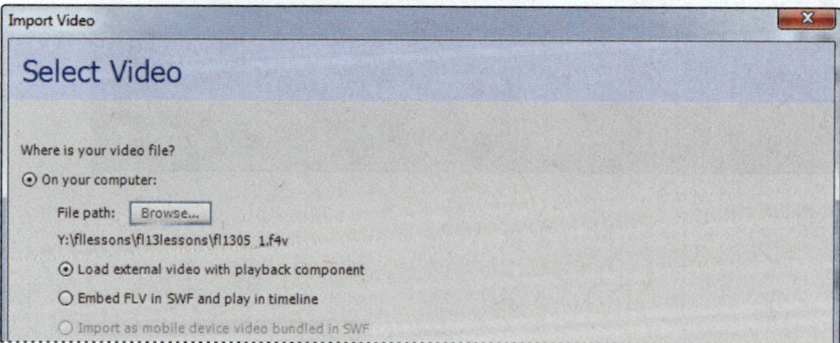

Figure 13-16: The video import dialog box allows you to embed or load external video.

5. Click Next. In the Skinning section of the Import Video dialog box, choose SkinOverAllNoCaption.swf from the Skin drop-down menu for the movie navigation. Press the Color button, and from the Swatches panel that appears, choose a color and alpha for the skin. In this exercise, the default dark gray was used as you can see in Figure 13-17.

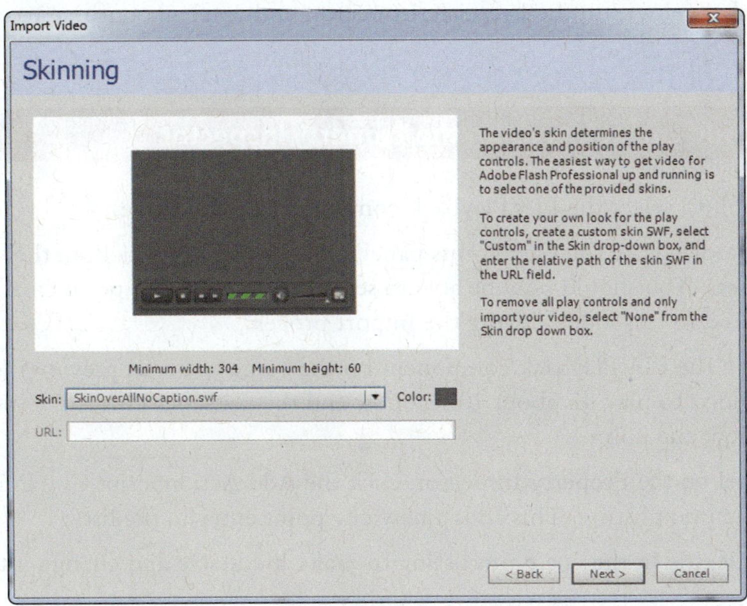

Figure 13-17: *The Skinning section of the Import Video dialog box allows you to control the appearance of the Video player interface.*

6. Click Next. The Finish Video Import section of the Import Video dialog box gives you a summary of the decisions you have made in the wizard. Press Finish to complete the video import.

7. Activate the Selection tool (k); then click and drag on the FLVPlayback component and move it to the top of the Stage area inside the guidelines (Figure 13-18).

Figure 13-18: *The positioning of your video should match what you see here.*

8. Choose File > Save to save your work.

Adding Cue Points in the Property Inspector

To make working with linked video easier, you can view and modify cue points directly within the Property Inspector in the Flash Professional CS6 environment. This eliminates the need to navigate through a series of complex dialog boxes. All the cue points of a selected video appear in a dedicated panel within the Property Inspector, and you can continue to edit and modify them as needed.

<table>
<tr><td>Step-by-Step</td><td>Follow these steps to add cue points using the Property Inspector</td></tr>
</table>

1. Using the Selection tool (⬉), select the FLVPlayback component on the Stage.

2. On the Property Inspector, locate the Cue Points panel, and expand it by clicking the arrow next to Cue Points. You should now be able to see a listing of all cue points that already have been created in this video during the import process.

3. Press the Play button on the FLVPlayback component on the Stage to begin previewing the video. Allow the video to play for about 10 seconds, and the pause it. This is the spot where you'll create a new cue point.

4. On the Cue Points panel on the Property Inspector, click the Add ActionScript Cue Point button (+) above the cue point listing. This adds a new cue point entry in the list.

5. Double-click the default title in the cue point listing to make it editable and change it to read **Chapter 1**.

6. Double-click the Time value for the new cue point to make it editable. Enter 00:00:10:00 to set the cue point at exactly 10 seconds from the beginning.

7. Repeat steps 5 and 6 for a different cue point listed. You can easily add, remove, or edit other cue points as needed directly from this panel.

8. Choose File > Save to save your work.

Working with the FLVPlayback component

The FLVPlayback component is a special Flash object used to control the playback of linked video in a Flash movie, and to provide the user with an intuitive set of controls for interacting with your video. For the most part, you can work with components in the same way you would with movie clips. However, components are far more complex, and you can edit several more parameters from the Property Inspector to control their behavior. In this exercise, you'll use the FLVPlayback component and its included controls for your movie's linked video.

Follow these steps to use the FLVPlayback component	Step-by-Step

1. Using the Selection tool (⬉), select the FLVPlayback component on the Stage.

2. Locate and expand the Component Parameters area within the Property Inspector to view the properties for this FLVPlayback component (Figure 13-19).

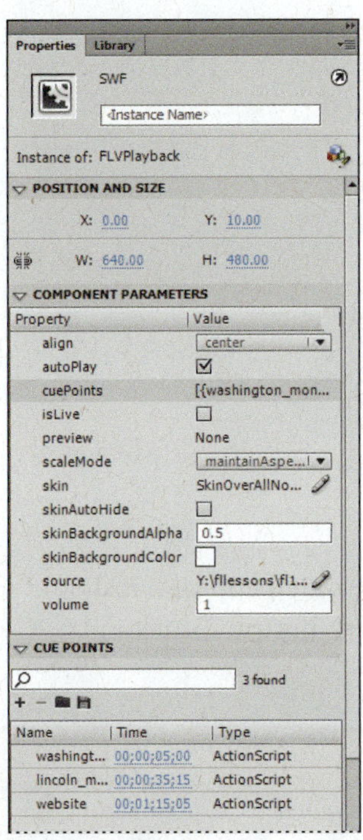

Figure 13–19: Components can be edited and fine-tuned using the Component Parameters on the Property Inspector.

Skill summary

3. By default, the autoPlay parameter is set to true, (the box next to it will appear checked), which sets the video to automatically play when loaded. Click on the checkbox to deselect it as shown in Figure 13-20. This sets the value to false, disabling the autoPlay behavior for this component.

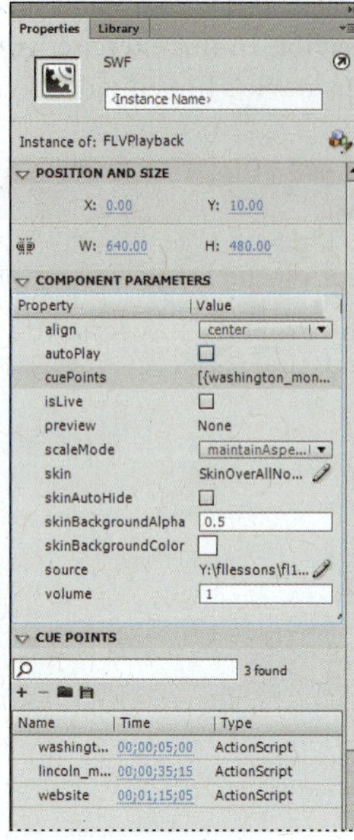

Figure 13-20: The Property Inspector offers access to most common properties of the FLVPlayback component.

4. Choose Control > Test Movie to test your movie. When the video appears, it should now be paused on the first frame; you will have to click on the Play button for it to play. Close the Flash Player.

Take Note...
You may notice a slight delay between the time that the Flash movie loads and the appearance of the video. This is normal and varies by the speed of a user's Internet connection. Some developers place an image or text on the layer below the FLVPlayback Component to entertain the viewer while the video loads.

5. Choose File > Save.

6. Close your project by choosing File > Close.

Congratulations! You have finished the lesson.

Skill summary

In this lesson you learned how to:	Objective
Understand Flash file types	3.7
Add simple controls through ActionScript 3.0	4.11
Add and export video	4.13

Knowledge Assessment

True/False

Circle **T** if the statement is true or **F** if the statement is false.

T F 1. Like animations on the Timeline, videos are composed of a series of sequential still images played back very rapidly.

T F 2. Video cannot be directly embedded onto the Timeline.

T F 3. When using linked video, it must be uploaded to the host server separately since it's not embedded in the Timeline.

T F 4. Codecs are software routines that compress video files small enough to be e-mailed or viewed on the Web or mobile devices.

T F 5. While exporting, a video can no longer be edited in any way whatsoever, the full video will play as is and there's no way to change that.

T F 6. Technically, Adobe Media Encoder isn't part of Flash; it's a stand-alone video converter.

T F 7. It's okay to embed long form video or short form video in Flash.

T F 8. By default, Flash is not set up to loop SWF files during playback, you have to establish that with ActionScript.

T F 9. You can simulate different download speeds while using the Bandwidth Profiler.

T F 10. If your video is too large to embed into Flash, you should consider importing it as external video.

Multiple Choice

Select the best response for the following statements.

1. The benefits to linking a video (vs embedding) include which of the following:
  a. A smaller SWF file
  b. Both the video and the SWF can have different frame rates
  c. You can avoid sync issues much easier
  d. All of the above

2. All video in Flash must be converted into which format for playback in Flash Player?
  a. MOV
  b. WMV
  c. FLV or F4V
  d. AVI

3. Which of the codecs below is not supported by Flash video?

   a. ProRes 422

   b. Sorenson Spark

   c. On2 VP6

   d. H.264

4. Which of the following is not a video format commonly imported into Flash?

   a. MOV

   b. DV

   c. DVI

   d. AVI

5. What term is used to define the area that lists files that are going to be converted in the Adobe Media Encoder?

   a. Queue

   b. Encoding

   c. Preset Browser

   d. Watch Folders

6. To embed video directly into Flash, the video must be in which format?

   a. FLV

   b. F4V

   c. H.264

   d. MOV

7. What feature in Flash can help you measure the impact of embedded video on your movie?

   a. Code Snippets

   b. Component Inspector

   c. Bandwidth Profiler

   d. Complier Errors

8. What are the items in Flash that can be thought of as bookmarks, or chapter markers within a video?

   a. Markers

   b. Cue Points

   c. Labels

   d. Keyframes

9. What section of the Import Video dialog box allows you to change the appearance of the video player interface?

   a. Formats

   b. Encoding

   c. Skinning

   d. None of the above

10. What is the name of the object used to control the playback of linked video in a Flash movie?

   a. FLVPlayback component

   b. FLVSkinning component

   c. MOVPlayback component

   d. F4VPlayback component

Competency Assessment

<table>
<tr><td>**More about the Media Encoder — Part 1: Getting to know the presets**</td><td>**Project 13-1**</td></tr>
</table>

Video compression is a bit of an art form and requires trial and error to get your file where you want it. You're essentially balancing quality and file size but it's a fine line sometimes between the two. Before rendering, you'll examine the settings first and then start to compare them.

1. Open Adobe Media Encoder CS6.

2. In the Media Encoder, press the Add Source button. In the Open dialog box, navigate to the fl13lessons folder and select the **fl1305.mov** file. Press Open to load the video file into Media Encoder.

3. Go to the Preset Browser portion of Media Encoder and click the arrow next to System Presets to open up the list and see the various settings.

4. Click the arrow next to the Broadcast category and then click the arrow next to H.264.

5. Note the various options available in terms of the settings you can apply. You'll typically target the native format options the video was shot in but there are times you have to jump to a different format.

6. Right-click on the HD 1080i 29.97 preset, choose Preset Settings to examine the preset settings a bit further.

7. Keep Adobe Media Encoder open to continue with the next project.

<table>
<tr><td>**More about the Media Encoder — Part 1: Trial and error**</td><td>**Project 13-2**</td></tr>
</table>

You'll want to continue to explore the various presets you have at your disposal in Media Encoder. There are quite a few so you'll probably want to do some research as far as what applies to you. In the meantime, let's set up a little comparison test to try some of them out...

1. Adobe Media Encoder CS6 should still be open from the previous project.

2. From the Broadcast category, go to H.264 and select the NTSC DV preset. Choose Apply Preset from the upper right corner.

3. Go to the Devices category and select DVD & Blu-ray. Go to the DVD sub-category and select the Match Source Attributes (High Quality) preset, apply it using the Apply Preset button to add it to the list.

4. Go to the Web Video category and choose the Flash sub-category. Select the Match Source Attributes (High Quality) FLV preset and apply it.

5. Keep Adobe Media Encoder open for the next project.

Proficiency Assessment

| Project 13-3 | **Understanding rendering** |

Processing video can be a very intensive function for your computer to perform. It can take a long time to finish the process so it's best to close all other programs besides Media Encoder and just wait for the computer to finish before doing anything else.

1. Adobe Media Encoder CS6 should still be open from the previous exercise.

2. You should have 4 presets applied and ready to compress your video. Click to the right of each one under Output File and save them to a new folder called Rendered Videos. Name each one according to the compression you're using. For example: Match Source F4V, Match Source FLV, H264, MPEG2.

3. Click the Start Queue button to start the process and take a break before going on to the next exercise since your computer will be busy for a little while.

| Project 13-4 | **Comparing results** |

After rendering, you'll want to take a look at the results and compare. You'll want to open each video you rendered and examine both the quality of the image the whole way through (which can actually change) and take note of the file sizes you end up with should you take the video to the Web or archive for storage as well.

1. Quit out of Adobe Media Encoder CS6.

2. Go to the Rendered Video folder you created in the previous exercise, open each video and examine both quality and file size.

3. Create a text, Word, or Excel document and outline the results of your tests. List the file size for each file, the perceived quality and any other observations that you've made.

4. Save the file as **Media_encoder_results**.

Delivering Your Final Movie

Key Terms

- Adobe AIR
- Android
- App ID
- digital certificate
- digital signature
- FTP
- iOS
- PNG Sequence
- Publish Settings

Skill	Objective
Understand options for producing accessible rich media content	**1.3**
Demonstrate knowledge of standard copyright rules (related terms, obtaining permission, and citing copyrighted material)	**1.4**
Identify general and Flash-specific best practices for designing rich media content for the web, mobile apps, and AIR applications	**2.1**
Identify general and Flash-specific techniques to create rich media elements that are accessible and readable	**2.3**
Identify best practices for managing the file size of a published Flash document	**3.8**
Publish and export Flash documents	**4.14**
Make a Flash document accessible	**4.15**
Conduct basic technical tests	**5.1**
Identify techniques for basic usability tests	**5.2**

Business case

Now that you've built animations and interactive projects, it's helpful to know what the options are in terms of delivering your projects to an audience. Flash offers ways to output your projects online, through mobile devices, and more! You'll need to explore these output options so you understand how to deliver your client's projects to their appropriate target audience and method of delivery.

Starting up

Before starting, make sure that your tools and panels are consistent by resetting your preferences. See "Resetting the Flash workspace" in the Starting up section of this book.

You will work with several files from the fl14lessons folder in this lesson. Make sure that you have loaded the fllessons folder onto your hard drive from *http://www.wiley.com/college/sc/adobeseries*. See "Loading lesson files" in the Starting up section of this book.

The project

In this lesson, you won't be creating a movie or even a piece of one. Instead, you'll be publishing existing movies so you can put your creations to work. You will also learn how to customize publish settings for a variety of output formats across web, mobile and desktop (AIR).

The publishing process

By now you should be very familiar with the Test Movie command. As you learned in previous lessons, the command generates an SWF file so that you can preview how your animation looks and how well its interactive elements behave.

Although Test Movie works very well for preview purpose and generates a temporary .swf file in the process, the Publish command gives you a much wider range of options. By default, the Publish command creates an HTML page with your SWF file embedded into it for display in a browser. You can also specify other file types such as HQX, SWC (for easier distribution of assets), web-ready image formats (JPEG/GIF/PNG), stand-alone projector files (self running applications in .mov format for mac and .exe format for windows), and more.

Publishing to the Web

For viewing in a web browser (the most common option), a Flash file must be embedded into a web page. Flash's Publish command does all the work for you by creating an SWF file, as well as an HTML wrapper file (web page) that has your SWF file contained within it. Once you have published these files you can easily upload them to your website to display your work to the world. Prior to publishing however, you should utilize best practices for reducing the size of your Flash document during the file creation process by using symbols as much as possible, limiting shape tweens, breaking apart bitmaps, using libraries, calling graphics or videos from outside the published .swf file, and even optimizing images prior to import.

Publishing a file is simple. With your FLA file open, select File > Publish. Flash then creates HTML, SWF, and any supplemental JavaScript files (for version checking and browser support), and saves them to the directory that contains the FLA file, or another directory that you specify.

Before you publish, you may want to explore, and work with, some of the Publish settings that can tweak the appearance and behavior of your movie, as well as generate any additional file types you may need.

A Note on Accessibility

It's important that when creating animations and projects in Flash to make sure that your project is accessible to the broadest number of people possible and to remember that not all users are experiencing content in the same way. There are a large group of users who have visual, auditory, and motor impairments who view content on the web using a screen reading device. Creating content that can be made accessible to users with these impairments is commonly referred to as accessibility.

Information provided to screen readers include dynamic text, movie clips, input text, buttons, Flash applications, and child objects in movie clips. Methods used to make Flash files accessible in rich media content include:

- Adding text equivalents for elements to provide a description of the image, link, graphic, or button.

- Allowing user reading order control of Flash content

- Add caption audio content for text when possible

- Placing the navigation scheme of the site on the page so that it is easily accessible.

- Use colors that provide significant contrast between elements on the page.

- Making looping elements inaccessible (because this can often cause a screen reader to reload the page and start reading from the beginning). You can hide objects from screen readers by unchecking the "make movie accessible" or "make child objects accessible" checkboxes in the Accessibility panel in Flash.

- Allowing users to control motion of an animation

- Ensuring controls for animations are keyboard accessible and providing keyboard navigation through shortcuts to allow for mouse-free navigation.

- Exposing the structure of complex Flash movies

- Exposing the state of the controls

- Using color wisely (incorporating colors that provide contrast with one another)

- Validate the accessibility of a document using a validation tool

- Allow tabbing between elements in a Flash animation

Objects are made accessible in Flash Professional using the Accessibility panel (Window > Other Panels > Accessibility). When you select an object that can be made accessible, options are displayed for that object. You can also set the accessibility properties for the entire document by making sure that no object is selected, then choosing the accessibility options in the Accessibility panel.

Learning More

Certification Ready 1.3

What are some elements of a SWF movie that can be read by a screen reader?

Certification Ready 1.3

What are examples of project requirements that result in accessible rich media content?

Certification Ready 2.3

What techniques can be used to make rich media content accessible to viewers with visual, auditory, and motor impairments?

Certification Ready 4.15

How do you set accessibility options for an entire document?

Certification Ready 4.15

How do you set accessibility options for individual objects or symbols in Flash?

Certification Ready 4.15

Why would you want to hide an object from a screen reader?

Certification Ready 4.15

How do you hide objects from screen readers?

Customizing the Publish settings

The default settings are fine for many situations, but you can customize the Publish settings for better results and to meet the needs of your target audience. Give it a try:

Follow these steps to customize the Publish settings

1. From the fl14lessons folder, open the file named **fl1401.fla**, which is an animated footer for a website.

2. Choose File > Publish Settings to open the Publish Settings dialog box. Along the left side of the dialog box, you can choose which formats to output. Make sure you are targeting the latest version of Flash Player by selecting Flash Player 11.2 from the Target drop-down in the upper-right corner (by default, the latest version of Flash player should be selected, but you can target any version of Flash that you wish including Flash Light versions). The dialog box will display available file formats on the left as shown in Figure 14–1.

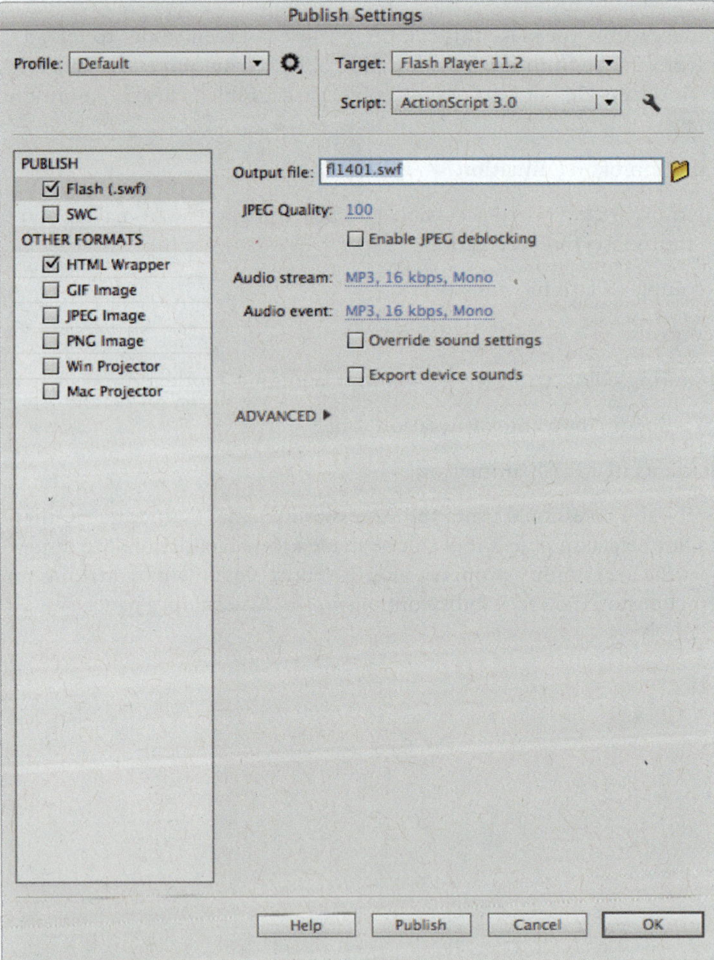

Figure 14–1: Open the Publish Settings dialog box through the File menu.

3. Under Publish on the left, click and select Flash (.swf) if it's not already selected, so that you display the available publishing options for this format on the right.

4. Here we can tell Flash how much to compress images used in our movie, which helps reduce overall file size. Click and drag to the left over the JPEG Quality value until it reads at about 85 as shown in Figure 14-2. This will increase the amount of compression on the bitmap images in your movie, and lower the file size with minimal sacrifice to image quality. Note that this is also where you can adjust the audio quality of the output file as well.

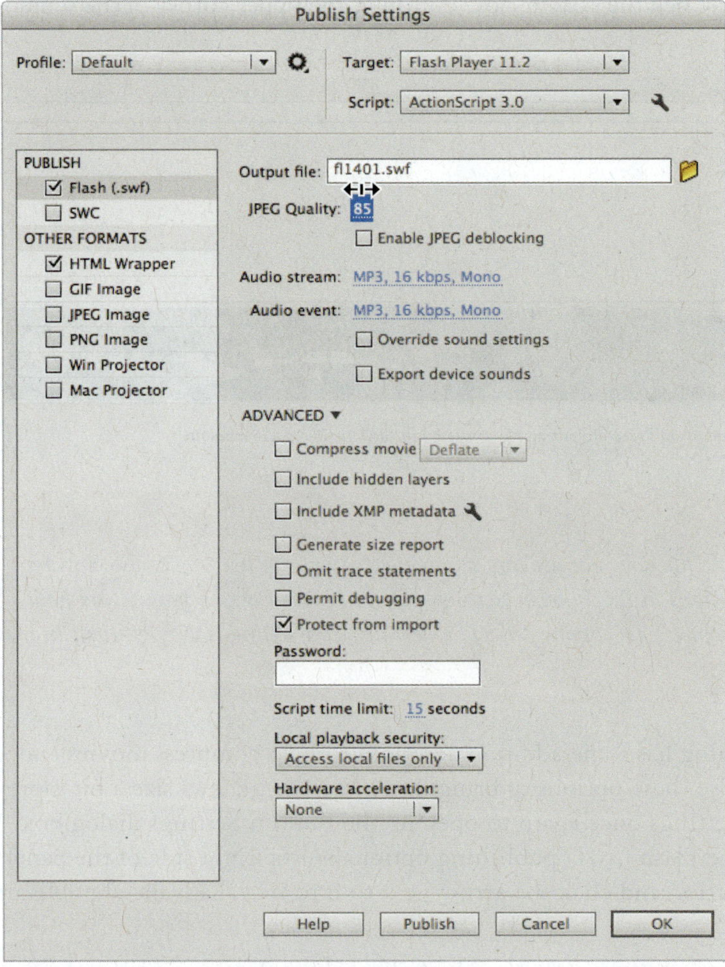

Figure 14-2: Drag the JPEG quality slider to 85.

5. At the bottom of the Publish Settings panel, click OK to apply the new settings and close the dialog box.

Take Note...
You can set many additional options for the Flash file export under the Advanced options. Omit Trace Action and Permit Debugging are specifically geared toward working with ActionScript, while Generate Size Report creates a text file that breaks down the size of each scene and symbol in your movie. You can also choose options such as "include hidden layers" which can be useful when exporting to HTML.

6. At this point, you can take a quick look at how your selected Publish Settings will affect the final movie. You can do this by using Test Movie and Bandwidth Profiler, both of which you have used previously in this book. Choose Control > Test Movie > In Flash Professional.

7. When the Flash player preview window opens, choose View > Bandwidth Profiler to open up the Bandwidth Profiler at the top of the window. Note: the Size should read about 42 kb as shown in Figure 14–3. Click the system close button in the upper corner of the window to close it.

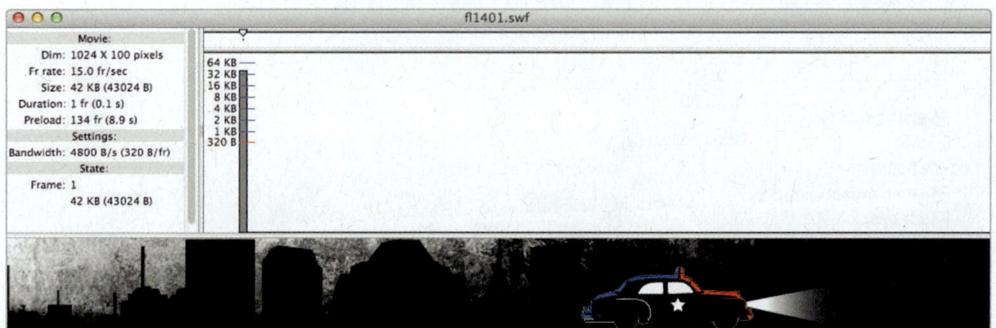

Figure 14–3: Note the statistics and overall size of your movie as shown in the left side of the window.

Take Note...
Although the example file does not use any audio effects, you can use the Audio Stream and Audio Event options in the Publish Settings panel to control audio quality and how those types of audio objects are compressed. The default MP3 setting is very efficient in most situations.

8. The Publish Settings dialog has some additional options to help compress movies and lower overall file size. Use these options to bring down the overall .swf size a bit more: choose File > Publish Settings once again to open up the Publish Settings dialog box. You should once again see the Flash (.swf) publishing options on the right side of the panel. Locate the Advanced section and click the arrow next to it to reveal advanced publishing options.

9. Locate the Compress movie option and check it. A drop-down list is enabled to let you select one of two efficient and loss-less (no information discarded) compression options: DEFLATE and LZMA. For now, choose LZMA from the drop-down list.

10. Click OK to exit the Publish Settings dialog box and apply the new settings. Repeat steps 6 and 7 once again; you should notice that the file size has decreased slightly to about 38Kb. Every byte counts, so this option can come in handy fairly often.

11. Once more, choose File > Publish Settings. Under the Other Formats category on the left, select the HTML Wrapper option to view the publish options for the HTML file that will contain your .swf file.

12. Locate the Size drop-down list and Width and Height values. By default, the Flash player is instructed to set your movie's dimensions to 100% of the browser window dimensions. This may cause some unwanted side effects, so if you want to keep your movie pixel-perfect, select "Match Movie" from the Size drop-down list. This will set the publish size to match the actual movie dimensions. You'll notice in Figure 14-4, you can't change the Width and Height to arbitrary values any longer. (Those fields are now disabled.)

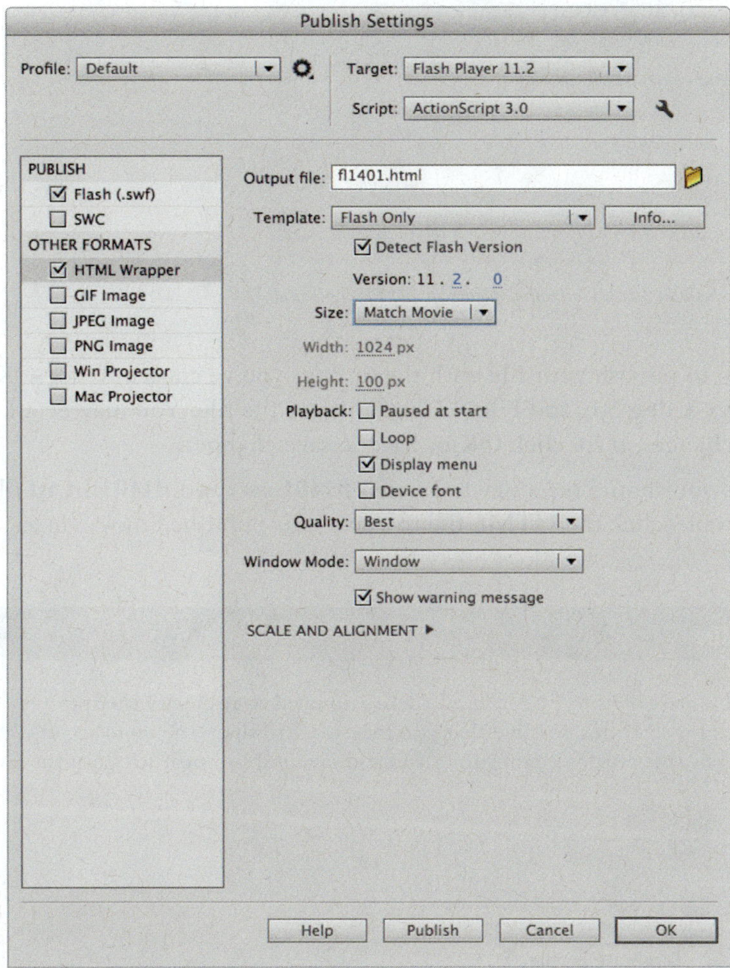

Figure 14-4: Modify size settings for the HTML Wrapper that will contain your movie.

13. Leave Window Mode, HTML Alignment, and Scale at the default settings. Window Mode controls the appearance of the box in which the SWF file appears; you can use it to create an SWF file with a transparent background. For now, leave this option set as Window.

Take Note...
Note that the example movie uses a nested movie clip symbol, the HTML tab's Paused at Start and Loop Playback options would have no effect; they target the main Timeline only.

14. Click the arrow next to SCALE & ALIGNMENT to reveal these options. Set Flash Horizontal alignment to Center and Flash Vertical alignment to Center (Figure 14-5), which will place the SWF file in the center of the browser window.

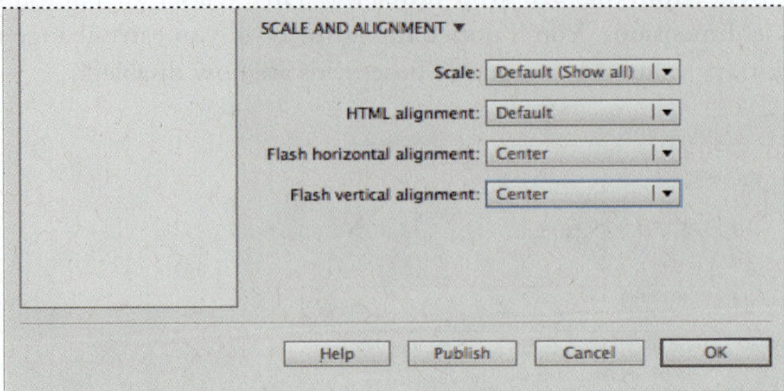

Figure 14-5: Choose Center from both the Flash Horizontal alignment and Flash Vertical alignment drop-down menus.

15. Click the Publish button to publish your file with the settings you've chosen. Click OK to close the Publish Settings dialog box and File > Close to close the file. You may be asked if you want to save the changes, if so, click OK or Save to save changes.

In the lesson files folder, you should see a newly created **fl1401.swf** and **fl1401.html** file sitting in this folder. Double-click the HTML file to view your published movie in a browser.

<table><tr><td>**Learning More**</td><td>## Creating Publish Profiles</td></tr></table>

Publish Settings are saved as part of your FLA file, so there's no need to respecify them in between authoring sessions. However, it's possible that you may want to share the same settings across multiple documents. For this purpose, you can create and save Publish profiles from the Publish Settings dialog box.

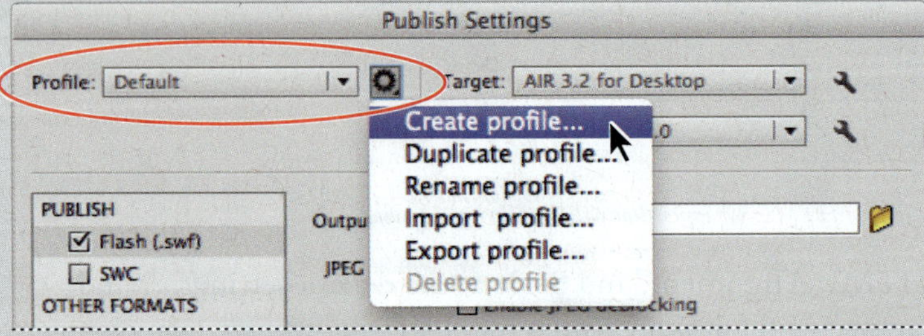

Figure 14-6: Create Publish profiles from the Publish Settings dialog box.

While in Publish Settings, once you've selected the settings you want, Click the Profile Options button next to the currently selected Publish profile (most likely Default, if you haven't created any before). Choose Create Profile, enter a Profile name and you're good to go! This is saved as part of your application settings, so you can call this profile up at any time within any FLA file.

Publishing for the Desktop with Adobe AIR

With all the capabilities Flash has to offer when it comes to building rich Internet applications, it seems natural that it has evolved to become a great tool for building desktop and mobile applications, as well.

The **Adobe AIR** runtime makes it possible to deploy your Flash movies (FLV or F4V)as full-blown desktop applications in a few clicks from your Publish Settings dialog box. Your movies will behave exactly as they do in a browser, and with a bit of ActionScript you can extend their capabilities to interact with the user's operating system, work with local files, and connect to outside services to get data.

The Adobe AIR runtime (in version 3.2 at the time of this writing), much like the Flash Player, is available as a free download from the Adobe website, and is a quick install for most users. Best of all, AIR applications are cross-platform, so there's no need to create separate installers for Windows vs. Mac OS platforms. One installer package can handle both.

Before you begin the next exercise, make sure you download and install the Adobe AIR runtime at *http://get.adobe.com/air/*.

Take Note...

You can also publish AIR applications from other applications in the Adobe Creative Suite. For example, Dreamweaver CS6 enables you to publish websites, including HTML, CSS and Javascript files, as AIR applications too.

> **Certification Ready 4.14**
>
> How do you publish to AIR for desktop, Android, and iOS?
>
> **Certification Ready 2.1**
>
> What are the benefits of authoring FLV files for Adobe AIR?

Follow these steps to work with Adobe AIR

Step-by-Step

1. Open the **WeatherMate_start.fla** file from the fl14lessons folder. This file contains the beginnings of a basic weather application widget. If you do not have the font used in this exercise, you may replace it with any other font on your computer. The exact font you use is not important for this exercise.

2. Choose File > Publish Settings to open the Publish Settings dialog box. Locate and click the Flash tab at the top to see Flash-specific publishing options.

3. From the Player drop-down menu at the top of the dialog box, select AIR 3.2 for Desktop (Figure 14-7), which will set the necessary publish options to deploy and install your movie as an AIR application on a user's computer.

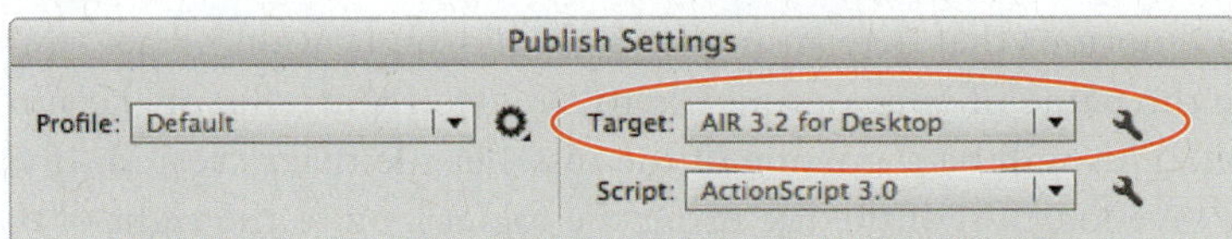

Figure 14-7: *Set up your Target as AIR 3.2 for Desktop. The Player Settings button sits next to the Target drop-down menu and allows you to open up additional dialog boxes to fine-tune your settings.*

4. Click the Player Settings button (⚒) next to the Target drop-down menu to open the AIR Settings dialog box as shown in Figure 14-8.

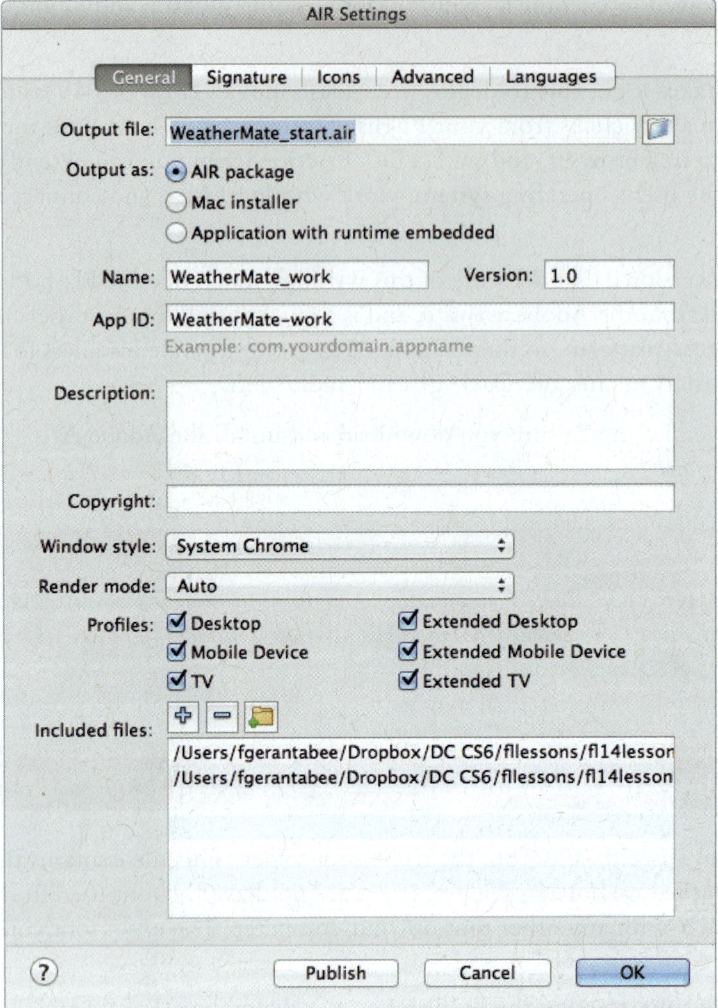

Figure 14-8: The Air Settings dialog box

Here you can set several options within this dialog box that will affect how your installer will be packaged, how it appears to the user, and how the application behaves on the desktop. You'll focus on the most essential ones for this exercise.

5. First, you'll set the general options that determine your file and application name. In the Output file field, change the name of your output file to **WeatherMate.air**; make sure to include the .air extension. This will be the name of the installer file that's created. If you'd like, you can change the save location of the file using the folder icon to the right of the field, but for the sake of this lesson, we'll leave the default save location which is the same folder as your original .fla file.

6. Under the Name and Version, enter **WeatherMate** and **2.0**, respectively. These specify your application's name as your users will see it, and a version number to correspond with the specific release you're offering. If you are not creating an official release, you can enter temporary information and set a default Version number. This is mostly to help your users identify your application.

7. Locate the **App ID** field; here you can enter a unique ID for your application to distinguish it from other applications the user may have installed on their system. The suggested convention is known as "reverse DNS"—which includes your company domain and application name. If your company is digitalclassroombooks.com and the application is Weather, the ID should read: **com.digitalclassroombooks.weathermate** as stated above. For now, enter this in the field.

8. Next, enter some descriptive text in the Description text field, and relevant copyright info in the Copyright text field as shown in Figure 14-9. These are optional, so you can leave them blank if nothing comes to mind at the moment. It is worth noting that in addition to this information, you can add additional information called metadata by choosing File > File info in Flash. This metadata can be read on mobile phones and is read by search engines when your file is posted to the internet to make it easier to find.

Certification Ready 2.1

What are the benefits of including metadata in a SWF file?

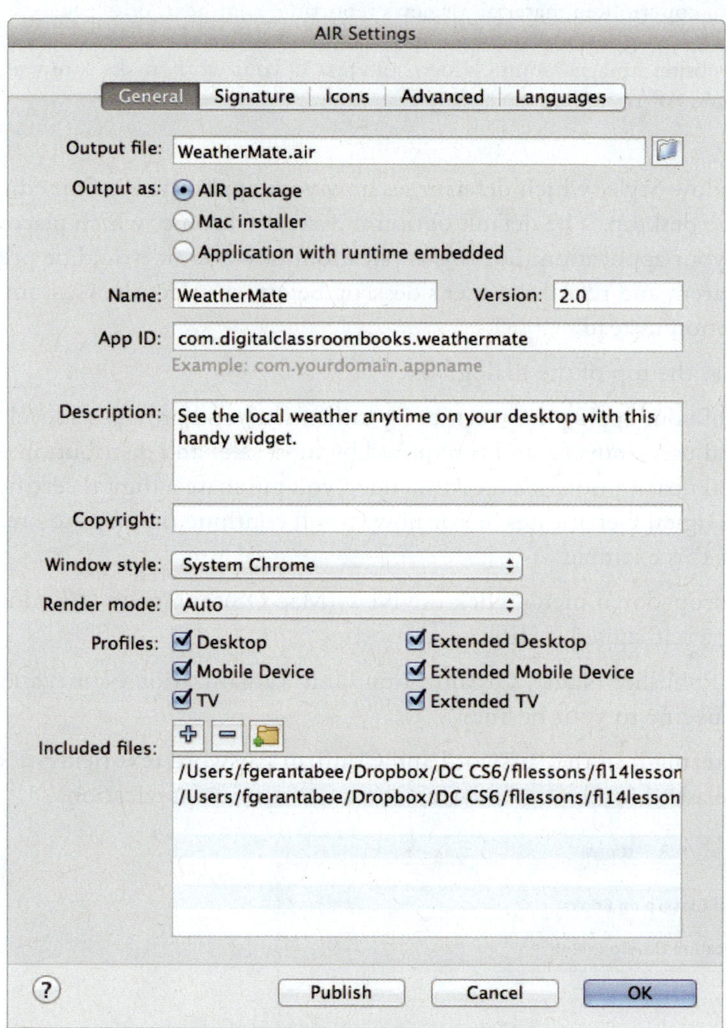

Figure 14-9: Enter important information about your application such as its name, App ID, description, and any relevant copyright information.

Copyright Considerations

Copyrighting of items is an important consideration for both you as an author and as a user of media in your projects. As you can see in the AIR Settings dialog box above, Flash provides an area where you can enter copyright information for you or your company to let people know that this is your work and that it's protected under the copyright law. The same rules apply when you are using images and artwork in your own projects. Always pay attention to the copyright status of artwork and images that you are using. Copyright status is usually indicated by the word "copyright" or a © symbol or the date of publication.

Permission should always be obtained to use copyrighted material in your work. This includes works of intellectual property (songs, literature, and artistic works), as well as derivative works (works that are based on original works but have been modified enough to constitute original work). With the exception of cases of fair use or instances that fall under the fair use doctrine (which provides for the use of copyrighted material for news reporting, comment, criticism, teaching, and research), if the copyright status is ever in question, assume that the work is copyrighted! When citing websites, images, sound, video, and text in your work, make sure you cite them properly using MLA, APA, or Chicago style writing.

9. Next, you'll set the Window Style, which determines how your application is framed, and how it appears on the desktop. The default option is System Chrome, which places a system window around your application. For this application, however, it would be pretty cool to have it be transparent and reveal the user's desktop below, so select the Custom Chrome (transparent) option instead.

10. Select the Signature tab at the top of the dialog box.

   The **digital signature** of your application verifies its authenticity and provides a level of confidence to your end users/buyers, and is required by most sales and distribution channels. For commercial distribution, it's recommended you purchase a digital certificate (see the section "About Digital Certificates"). For now, you'll continue the steps to create a self-signed certificate for this example.

11. Next to the Certificate drop-down menu, click the New (Mac OS) or Create (Windows) button to begin creating a self-signed certificate.

12. Fill in the text fields for Publisher Name, Organization Unit, Organization Name, and Country (these will be specific to your business).

13. Create a password by entering it in the Password and Confirm Password text fields (Figure 14-10). You'll be asked for this again later, when signing your application.

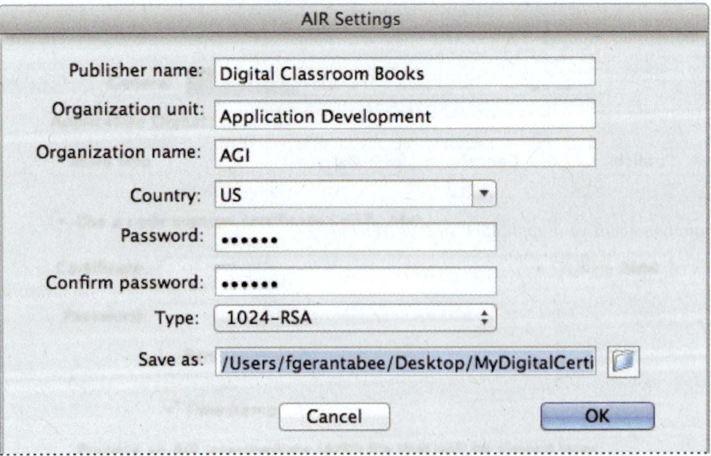

Figure 14-10: Creating a self-signed certificate allows you to install and run your application for testing or limited distribution.

14. Next to Save As, click the Folder icon and select a location on your computer to save the certificate in. Enter the file name **MyDigitalCertificate** for your new certificate, and click Save. Press OK to create the certificate and return to the AIR Settings dialog box.

15. The new certificate should be shown in the Certificate field. Enter the password you created for your certificate in the password text field, and for the sake of convenience, check Remember Password for this Session. Press OK to exit the Application & Installer Settings dialog box.

16. In the Publish Settings dialog box, press the Publish button to create your .air installer file. If you are prompted for your password, please re-enter the password for the self-signed certificate you created in step 12. When the process is complete, press OK to exit the Publish Settings dialog box. Note that you may be prompted to enter the password for your new digital certificate again—do so, and then click the Publish button once again, if necessary.

17. Choose File > Save to save your work, then close your document. If you return to the fl14lessons folder, you should see a series of new files created, including a file named **WeatherMate.air**.

About Digital Certificates

Digital certificates are used to verify the security and authenticity of a software application, and are commonly used for distribution of commercial and non-commercial applications. Depending upon your needs, you can purchase these certificates from vendors such as Thawte (*http://www.thawte.com*) and VeriSign (*http://www.verisign.com*).

While a self-signed certificate will work for testing and limited distribution, if you are considering making your AIR application available for sale, or wide distribution, a certificate can provide an extra level of confidence for your consumers.

Installing Your New AIR Application

Installing your new AIR application is an easy task, especially if you've already taken the time to install the Adobe AIR Runtime. Adobe AIR does the work for you, registering your new application on the system and making it available, just like any other application on your computer.

Take Note...

Make sure you have the Adobe AIR 3.2 runtime installed on your system. If you attempt to install an AIR 3.2 application on a system running an older version of AIR, you may receive an error message.

Follow these steps to install a new AIR application — **Step-by-Step**

1. From your Windows Explorer or Mac Finder, locate the **WeatherMate.air** installer file that you published to the fl14lessons folder.

. On Windows, if your extensions are hidden you may need look closely at each weathermate file and choose the Adobe Air application. If you are still unsure, select a file, right-click and choose Properties, then locate the type. You can double-click Adobe Air applications to open them.

2. Double-click the installer file; this will open the Adobe AIR installer dialog box.

3. The dialog box will confirm that you want to install the application. Press OK to begin installation. Note: You may get security warnings if you're using your own self-signed certificate as shown in Figure 14-11.

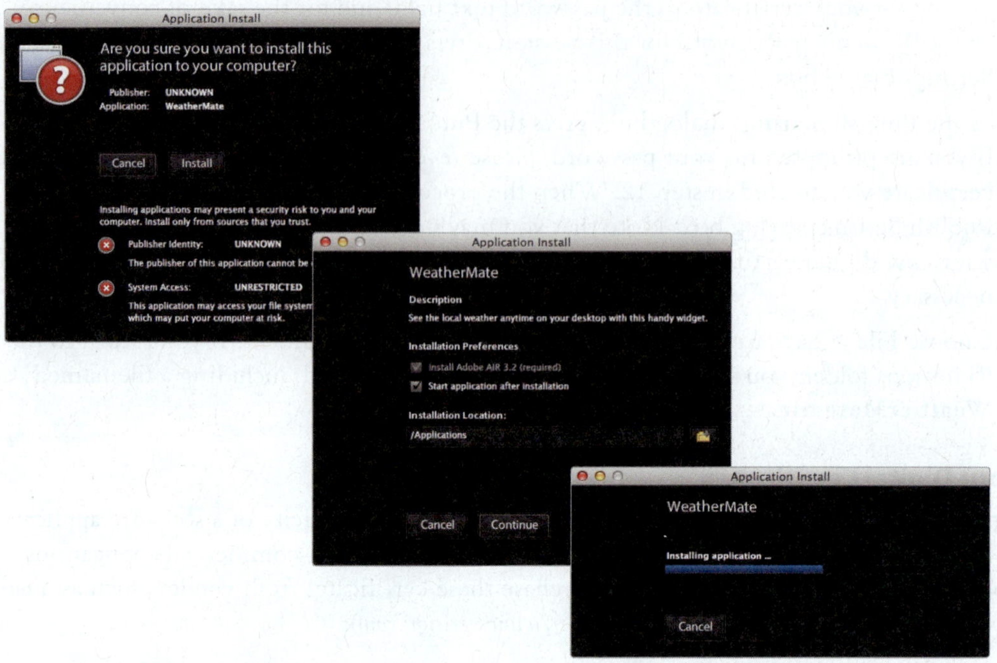

Figure 14-11: The various stages of installing your AIR application.

4. When the installation is complete, locate your new application under the Start menu (Windows) or the Applications folder (Mac OS), and launch it.

    You will notice that the WeatherMate application appears with no defined background or window; the desktop below, and only the application artwork itself shows. This is because you chose the Custom Chrome (Transparent) option in your publish settings in the previous exercise. Remember that a Flash movie is actually transparent, so the Stage will not appear in this environment.

Publishing for Mobile Devices

The Adobe AIR runtime has made it possible to take Flash beyond the browser and onto the desktop, and now you can author and publish native iOS and Android applications using the AIR for iOS and AIR for Android document and publish options.

There are many steps to take toward publishing stable and successful mobile applications: you'll need to become familiar with the respective SDKs and developer guidelines, set up developer accounts and testing devices, to name a few. These activities are beyond the scope of this book, but in this section we'll touch on the very basics for setting up your FLA for publishing to the iOS and Android platforms.

<table>
<tr><td>

Before You Begin

</td><td>

Learning More

</td></tr>
</table>

If you would like to get started with mobile application development, we suggest visiting the following resources:

The iOS Developer center on Apple.com Visit *http://developer.apple.com/devcenter/ios/index* to set up a new developer account and get started. You'll also need to make sure you have the SDK and the latest version of Mac OS X and the XCode tools installed.

The Android Developer center at Android OS at *http://developer.android.com/index.html* to get started and download the SDK.

As always, before creating or publishing an application for these mobile platforms, make sure you meet the development guidelines suggested by Apple and Android/Google. You can get started in the right direction by using one of the pre-sized documents from the Start Page or the New Document dialog boxes.

Publishing for iOS

The following steps take you through the basics of publishing an existing Flash document for installation on an **iOS** device such as an iPhone, iPad, or iPod touch. This assumes you are using the appropriately sized document template and have followed the basic guidelines suggested by Apple.

<table>
<tr><td>

Follow these steps to publish a Flash document for an iOS device

</td><td>

Step-by-Step

</td></tr>
</table>

1. Open the **fl14_iphone.fla** file from the fl14lessons folder. This file contains a simple movie based on the AIR for iOS document template.

2. Choose File > Publish Settings to open the Publish Settings dialog box. Next to the Target drop-down menu in the upper-right corner, click the Player Settings button (⚒) to open the AIR for iOS settings dialog box.

3. You'll start at the General settings tab (Figure 14-12). Fill in the appropriate name and output file for your app, as well as the appropriate settings for Aspect Ratio, Render Mode, and Device.

4. Select the Deployment tab, choose the certificate provided to you for iOS development as part of your developer account, and specify your provisioning profile.

Take Note...

These files and settings are available under the Apple Developer Center as part of your profile.

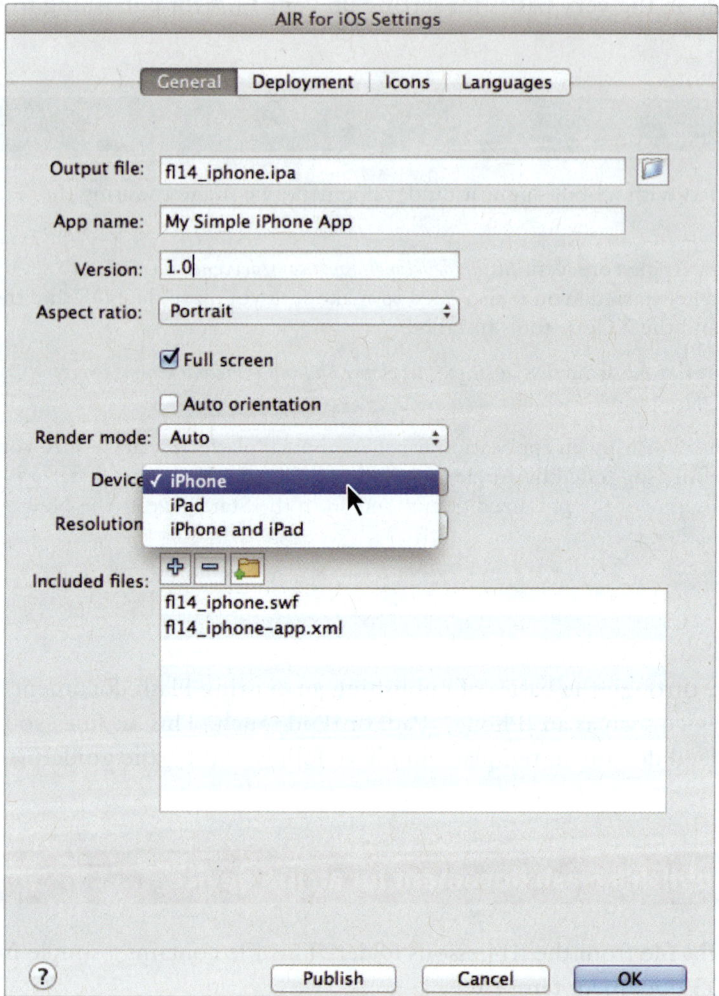

Figure 14–12: Enter important settings for your iOS application, such as name, certificate, and icons.

Take Note...

A provisioning profile is created as part of your iOS Developer Center account, and connects you and other developers in a group to test devices and to an authorized development group. If you work as part of a larger development team within an organization, it's possible that you can obtain this from your IT or development manager (or the person responsible for your company's developer account with Apple).

5. Choose the Deployment type, which determines how the app is packaged. You can package it for final App Store delivery or specifically for local testing and debugging. If you are still in testing and development, you may want to leave the default setting (Quick publishing for device testing).

6. Select the Icons tab. In each respective field, specify a graphic file for each of the required icon sizes, as shown. For specs and guidelines on preparing icons for an iPhone or iPad application, you can check the iOS developer center or this article at *http://developer.apple. com/library/ios/#documentation/userexperience/conceptual/mobilehig/IconsImages/IconsImages.html.*

7. Select the Languages tab, and choose the languages you will be targeting for your application. If you are targeting only North American and English speaking users, select English for now. If you are working as part of a team, make sure to consult the project lead or development manager to verify these settings.

8. Click OK to close the AIR for iOS Settings dialog box.

9. Click OK to close the Publish Settings dialog box and save your options, or click Publish to publish your application right away.

Take Note...

To save time, check out the "Creating Publish Profiles" sidebar earlier in the chapter to learn how to save your Publish Settings for reuse across other projects and files.

Publishing for Android OS

Just as with iOS devices, you can target and publish native applications for **Android** devices, and specify the appropriate settings in the Publish Settings dialog box. With Android devices, however, you have some added abilities to easily install and debug on a connected Android device, a feature added in Flash CS5.5, to make testing and setup a bit easier. Make sure to consult the Android Developer guidelines for creating an Android application and setting up testing devices.

<table>
<tr><td>**Follow these steps to publish a Flash document for Android devices**</td><td>**Step-by-Step**</td></tr>
</table>

1. Open the **fl14_android.fla** file from the fl14lessons folder. This file contains a simple movie based on the AIR for Android document template.

2. Choose File > Publish Settings to open the Publish Settings dialog box, and click the Player Settings icon next to the Target drop-down list in the upper–right corner. (It should read AIR 3.2 for Android.)

3. Under the General settings tab, enter the appropriate name and output file for your app. Make sure that settings for Aspect Ratio, Render Mode, and Device are correct for your specific application (Figure 14-13).

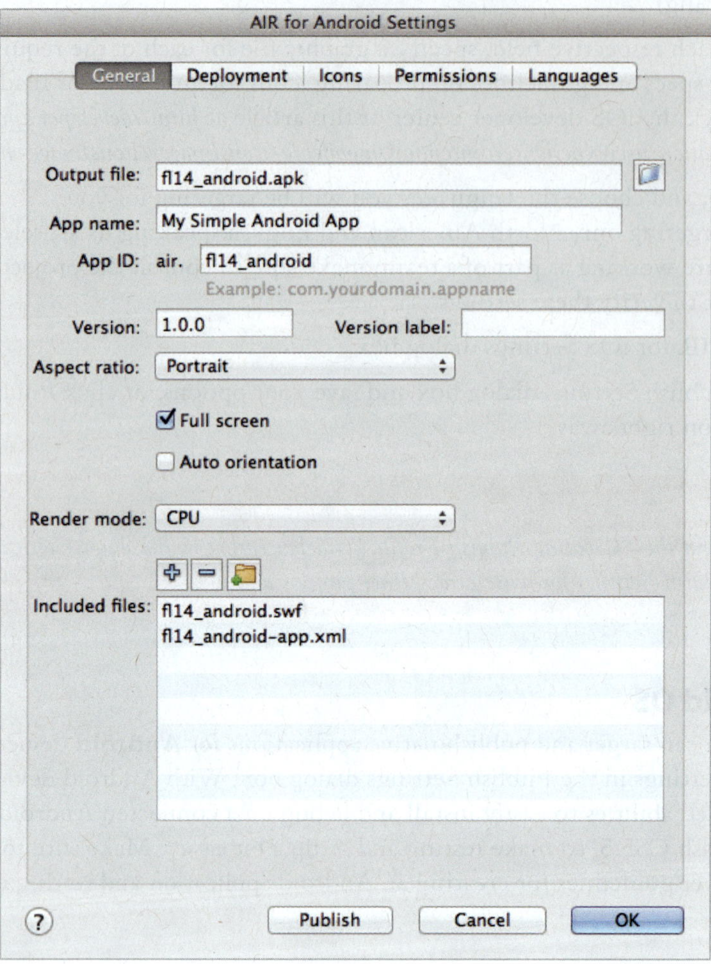

Figure 14-13: *Specify settings for your new Android application.*

4. Select the Deployment tab. Choose an .apk certificate provided to you for development, or create a self-signed certificate for temporary use and debugging by clicking the Create button. Certificates are essential for distribution in the Android Marketplace and installation on a test device. For more details and information about app signing, visit *http://developer.android.com/guide/publishing/app-signing.html*.

5. Select your deployment type (Figure 14-14). This will depend on whether you are creating a final app installer for distribution or a test build for debugging on a connected test device or emulator.

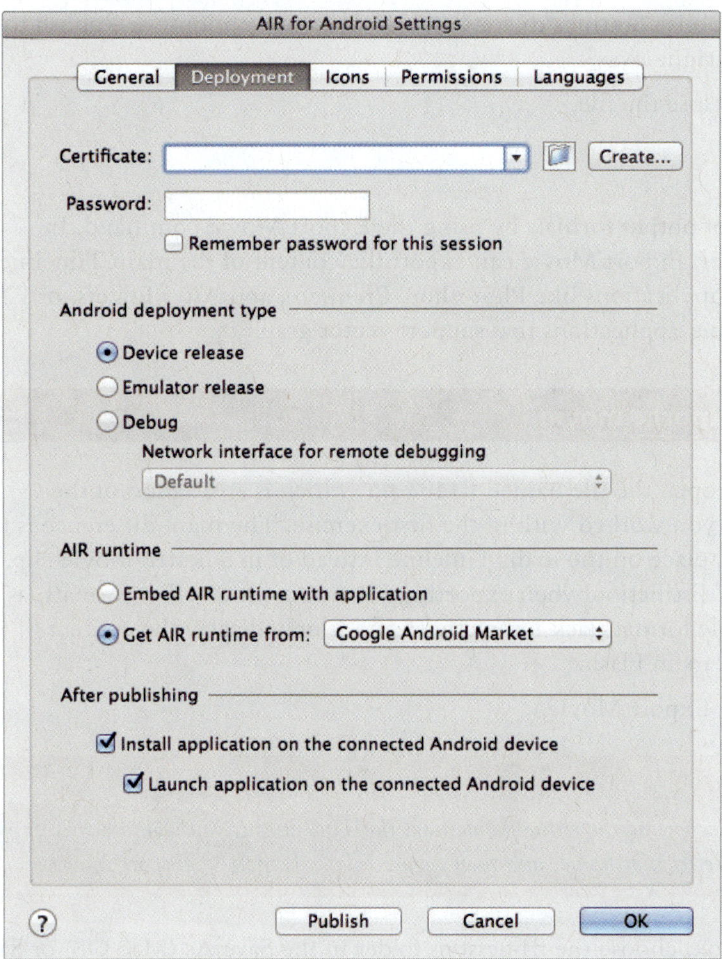

Figure 14-14: *Specify settings for your new Android application.*

6. Select the Icons tab, and specify the icon graphic files to use for each required size.

7. Select the Permissions tab, and specify the permissions necessary for your application to function properly. For example, if your application is designed to use the device camera, check 'CAMERA'.

8. Select the Languages tab, select the languages your application is targeting. If you are primarily focused on North American and English-speaking users, select English for now.

9. Click OK to close the AIR for Android Settings dialog box.

10. Click OK to close the Publish Settings dialog box and save your options, or Publish to publish your application right away.

11. Choose File > Close to close the file.

Using Export Movie

You can extend your range of output formats by using the Export Movie command. In addition to creating SWF files, Export Movie can export the content of the main Timeline to still images for editing in applications like Photoshop, Premiere, and After Effects, or FXG format for exchange with other applications that support vector graphics.

Step-by-Step **Follow these steps to export a movie**

1. In the fl14lessons folder, open the file named **fl1403.fla**, which is a variation of the animated website footer you worked with in the first exercise. The main difference is that here the animation takes place on the main Timeline instead of in a nested movie clip. This is a very important distinction when exporting Flash content to other formats, as the majority of the exportable formats lack interactivity and simply display the content of the main Timeline as it appears in Flash.

2. Choose File > Export > Export Movie.

Take Note...
This exercise covers exporting the entire movie from the Timeline. If you would rather export only a single frame, select that frame, and then choose File > Export > Export Image.

3. In the resulting dialog box, choose the fl14lessons folder in the Save As (Mac OS) or Save In (Windows) drop-down menu, if it is not already listed there.

4. Select QuickTime (.mov) in the Format drop-down menu. This creates a stand-alone QuickTime movie that can be played using the free QuickTime player, converted for display on such mobile devices as PSPs and iPods, or imported into video editing or motions graphics programs, such as Adobe Premiere or After Effects. Press Save. The QuickTime Export Settings dialog box appears.

5. Click the Quicktime Settings button in the lower-left corner; here you can fine-tune options for size, audio settings and other file-specific options. Press OK when you are done, to return to the QuickTime Export Settings dialog box.

6. In the QuickTime Export Settings dialog box, press Export to export your final QuickTime file (Figure 14-15).

> ***Take Note...***
> *Below the Render height field in the QuickTime Export Settings dialog box, you'll see the Ignore Stage Color checkbox. This generates a QuickTime movie with an alpha channel that you can then import into a video editing or motion graphics program, such as Adobe Premiere or After Effects.*

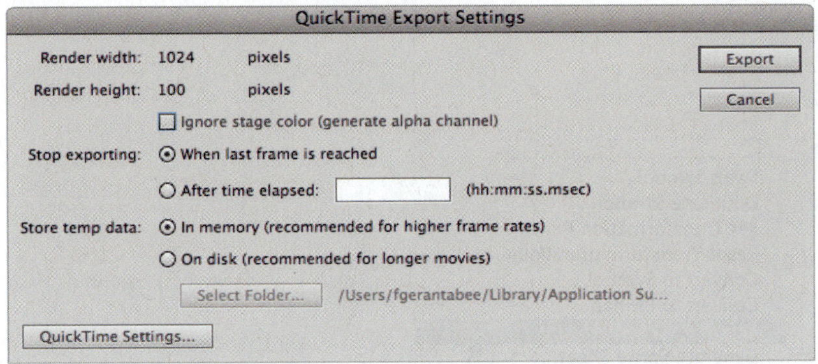

Figure 14-15: Dial in additional settings in the Quicktime Settings box, or just click Export in the QuickTime Export Settings dialog box to create your new file.

7. Minimize Flash and navigate to the fl14lessons folder. Double-click on your QuickTime movie to play it, and view the animation you have just exported.

8. Choose File > Save, then File > Close.

> ***Take Note...***
> *In addition to exporting your Flash project as a movie, you can also export a frame of your Flash project as an image using File > Export > Export Image.*

New: Export PNG Sequence

Sometimes it's handy to be able to export your animations in a way that can be used by other applications. If you need to export graphics for use within a website, mobile application or within a CSS or JavaScript based animation, you can now export a selected symbol as a **PNG Sequence.**

Follow these steps to export a symbol as a PNG Sequence **Step-by-Step**

1. In the fl14lessons folder, open the file named **fl1404.fla**. You'll see a single movie clip on the Stage.

2. Choose Control > Test Movie > In Flash Professional. You'll see an animation sequence of a small dot expanding into a word balloon. Close the window to return to the document.

3. Right click on the movie clip on the Stage. From the contextual menu that appears, locate the Export PNG Sequence option and select it as shown in Figure 14-16. You'll be prompted to save the sequence somewhere on your hard drive. Note: It's highly recommended to create a folder for the resulting images, as there may be quite a few! Choose a location to save the resulting images and click OK.

Figure 14–16: Right-click on any button, graphic, or movie clip symbol to select the Export PNG Sequence command.

4. The Export PNG Sequence dialog box appears. Here you'll see how many frames will be created (based on the length of the animation), and get a chance to adjust width, height and resolution. For now, leave all settings at their defaults and click Export.

5. Navigate to the folder or location where you exported the sequence; you should see a sequence of numbered PNGs, each of which represents a frame in your animation (Figure 14-17).

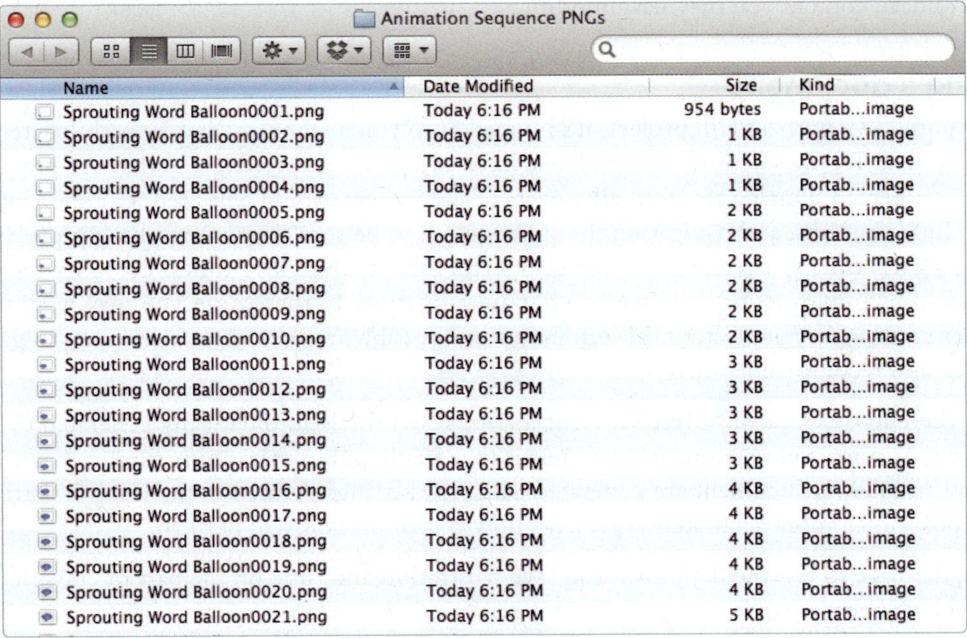

Figure 14-17: *PNG images generated by the Export PNG Sequence command.*

An overview of FTP

FTP is an acronym for the phrase File Transfer Protocol. These are the set of rules that allow different computers to connect to each other over the Web. Once you have created and published your Flash movie, you need to upload it to a web server in order to allow people to view it online. Whether this web server is one that you maintain yourself, one set up for you by your company's IT department, or space you rent from a web host, the publishing process is basically the same. While there are stand-alone FTP applications that allow you to connect to a web server, Adobe's industry-leading web design application, Dreamweaver, comes complete with an internal FTP engine that integrates very well with Flash content. The basic steps to follow when uploading Flash content for the Internet are:

<table><tr><td>**Follow these steps to upload Flash content for the Internet**</td><td>**Step-by-Step**</td></tr></table>

1. Create a Flash movie and publish it to your local hard drive.

2. Upload your Flash movie to your web server, along with any secondary content (HTML and JavaScript files) created by the publishing process. Your web hosting service or IT department can provide you with information on where to upload your files, as well as the login and password information you need to connect.

Take Note...
If you published a Flash movie with an accompanying HTML file, chances are that some additional JavaScript files were also created. It is essential that these files are copied with your .swf and .html files up to the web server in order for the Flash movie to appear properly.

3. If you want to make any changes to the movie, edit the file you published to your local hard drive, not the version on the web server.

4. Re-upload the edited version of your Flash movie to the web server, including any secondary content you may have modified.

Testing a document

Before going live with a Flash project, it's important to run a technical and/or usability test of the document. Doing so ensures that the end-user experience is positive and that the project works as expected. During this test, all aspects of the project should be tested. Components such as links, buttons, and navigation should be tested to be sure they are working properly. It's also a good time to check for ActionScript errors and analyze load times. Usability testing often requires employees or volunteers to test an animation. In these cases you may want to observer users as they are testing the animation and possibly even conduct interviews to gain feedback and recommendations.

When you choose Control > Test Movie in Flash, a .swf file is automatically generated to preview the animation. A more accurate test is to actually publish the animation so that a .swf and an HTML document are generated using the settings defined in the Publish Settings dialog box which more accurately represents how the animation will perform.

Taking the time to test the document can save frustration and time on the part of end-users and the developers as well.

Testing a Flash document against a storyboard

A storyboard consists of a number of pages that describe an animation, each page may have a list of related links, a functional description of the animation, images, text and some notes on content for the animation. You can do a comparison of your final animation to the storyboard by using it as a checklist of sorts. Does the functionality and content of the final animation reflect the functionality and content of the storyboard? If not, then why not? Was the content removed (or never delivered?) In the end, if the storyboards were well thought out, this step is a good measure of success. Were you able to include all the features you had originally planned? Maybe you ended up adding more, in which case you should ask for a raise!

Skill summary

In this lesson you learned how to:	Objective
Understand options for producing accessible rich media content	1.3
Identify general and Flash-specific best practices for designing rich media content for the web, mobile apps, and AIR applications	2.1
Identify general and Flash-specific techniques to create rich media elements that are accessible and readable	2.3
Identify best practices for managing the file size of a published Flash document	3.8
Publish and export Flash documents	4.14
Make a Flash document accessible	4.15
Conduct basic technical tests	5.1
Identify techniques for basic usability tests	5.2

Knowledge Assessment

True/False

Circle **T** if the statement is true or **F** if the statement is false.

T F 1. The test movie command generates a SWF file for preview.

T F 2. Increasing the amount of compression on the bitmap images in your movie has no effect on the file size.

T F 3. By default when publishing, Flash Player is instructed to set your movie's dimensions to 100% of the browser window dimensions.

T F 4. A SWF can be generated to include a transparent background.

T F 5. Publish Settings are saved as part of your FLA file so there's no need to re-specify them in between authoring sessions.

T F 6. Flash cannot be used to author native Android applications but can author to iOS.

T F 7. Creating a self-signed certificate allows you to install and run your application for testing or limited distribution.

T F 8. An app has to be first packaged for local testing and debugging before it can be packaged for the App Store.

T F 9. Export Movie cannot export still images, you can only do that from the Publish Settings.

T F 10. If you need to export graphics for use within a website, mobile app or within a CSS or JavaScript based animation, you can now export a selected symbol as a PNG sequence.

Multiple Choice

Select the best response for the following statements.

1. What type of file is set up by default to accompany the SWF when executing the Publish command?

  a. PNG
  b. HTML
  c. GIF
  d. FLA

2. In addition to the answer from the previous question, what other supplemental file type may be generated when publishing in Flash?

  a. ActionScript
  b. JavaScript
  c. XML
  d. CGI

3. Which of the following is not a format choice when publishing in Flash?

   a. TIFF

   b. JPEG

   c. PNG

   d. GIF

4. In the Publish Settings panel, which of the following options is geared toward working with ActionScript?

   a. Include hidden layers

   b. Permit Debugging

   c. Protect from import

   d. Include XMP metadata

5. What component of Flash makes it possible to deploy your Flash movies as full-blown desktop applications?

   a. Code Snippets

   b. AIR

   c. Component Inspector

   d. Movie Explorer

6. Which of the following is an option when publishing to AIR?

   a. App ID

   b. Copyright

   c. Render mode

   d. All of the above

7. When publishing to AIR, which feature verifies the authenticity of your application?

   a. Signature

   b. Name

   c. Copyright

   d. App ID

8. When determining a device for iOS app output, what device choice is available?

   a. iPhone

   b. iPad

   c. iPhone and iPad

   d. All of the above

9. What is the name of the profile associated with connecting you and other developers in a group to test devices?

   a. Provisioning profile

   b. Output profile

   c. Render profile

   d. Publishing profile

10. When exporting to video, which video format is available as a choice?

    a. DV

    b. Quicktime

    c. Realtime

    d. All of the above

Competency Assessment

Publishing options	**Project 14-1**

Publishing in Flash isn't necessarily only about the Web and mobile devices. There are other ways to deliver your project that incorporate CD-rom or desktop storage rather than being uploaded to the Web or a device.

1. Open Adobe Flash CS6 if not already running.

2. From the fl14lessons folder, open the file named **fl1402.fla**.

3. Choose File > Save As and save the file as **game.fla**.

4. Choose File > Publish Settings. Note that Win Projector and Mac Projector are already selected and ready to go. Projectors are self-contained applications specific to the Mac and Windows operating systems.

5. Click on each of the Projector formats and designate where you would like to save them.

6. Publish and take a look at the results on the platform specific to the computer you're using. The advantage to projectors is that they need no outside application (like Flash Player) to view them, they are their own players and software.

7. Keep the **game.fla** file open for the next project.

Dealing with older players	**Project 14-2**

Unfortunately not everyone updates their computer software on a consistent basis. Even though Flash Player is installed on upwards of 98% of all computers on the internet, not all versions of the player on each computer is the same. Inevitably, you will run into people who have older versions of the player; the good thing is that there's a way to force their hand a bit more in terms of getting them to update their software.

1. The **game.fla** file should still be open from the last project.

2. Choose File > Publish Settings. Click on the HTML Wrapper setting.

3. Click the checkbox that specifies to Detect Flash Version.

4. The default is Version 8. This is a good base but feel free to adjust as needed.

5. Keep this file open for the next project.

Proficiency Assessment

| Project 14-3 | Previewing on the fly |

Instead of choosing Control > Test Movie (which always generates a .swf file) you can preview with your final output file that may not be an actual .swf (such as a projector).

1. The **game.fla** file should still be open from the last exercise.
2. Choose File > Publish Preview > Default – (Project Projector).
3. Keep this file open.

| Project 14-4 | Exporting Specific Objects |

You can save your whole Flash movie as a flattened image but you can also be a bit more selective about the pieces of the artwork themselves and single things out you may want as individual graphics.

1. The **game.fla** file should still be open from the last project.
2. Select the plane on the Stage. Choose File > Export > Export Selection. Save the plane as **plane.fxg** and use it for other projects!

Circling Back 3

Complex programs like Flash often offer the opportunity to streamline your workflow through the use of presets. Presets come in handy when you're doing something consistently from one project through the next. You've already experienced some inherit presets such as the Code Snippets. Now, you'll create a new preset for the purpose of publishing your work.

| Project 1 | Setting Up a publishing template |

Your company has asked you to come up with a publishing preset for Flash that can be used company wide by all the Flash designers to ensure consistency when each designer publishes to the corporate website. Your first step will be to establish the settings for the template.

1. Create a new ActionScript 3.0 document in Flash.
2. Choose File > Publish Settings.
3. Click the Profile Options button at the top of the Publish Settings window. Choose Create profile.
4. Name the profile **Publishing Template**.
5. Click on the Flash (.swf) setting on the PUBLISH panel on the right of the window.
6. Set the JPEG Quality to 100. Click the checkboxes to turn on the following:

   Permit debugging

   Omit trace statements

   Protect from import

7. Select the HTML Wrapper option under OTHER FORMATS.

8. Click the checkbox for Detect Flash Version and set the version to 8.

9. Click the checkbox for Device Font.

10. Keep this window open for the next project.

Preparing to share
Project 2

Now that you've established the settings for your template, the time has come to make these settings accessible for everyone else that needs them.

1. Go to the Profile Options button and select Export Profile.

2. Save the file as **dc_preset.xml** someplace easy to access such as your desktop,

3. Keep this window open for the next part of the project.

Importing Publishing Profile into Flash
Project 3

Since you're flying solo here, we'll simulate the situation in terms of how the template you just created can be imported and shared from one computer to another.

1. Go to the Profile Options button and select Delete Profile to remove the Publishing Template.

2. To re-import it and simulate the experience for a different user, click on the Profile Options button and choose Import profile.

3. Navigate to the **Publishing Template.xml** file and re-import your publishing settings!

Adobe Rich Media Communication using Flash Professional CS6 Objectives

Skill	Objective	Lesson
Setting Project Requirements	1	
Identify the purpose, audience, and audience needs for rich media content	1.1	1
Identify rich media content that is relevant to the purpose of the media in which it will be used (websites, mobile devices, and so on)	1.2	1
Understand options for producing accessible rich media content	1.3	1, 14
Demonstrate knowledge of standard copyright rules (related terms, obtaining permission, and citing copyrighted material)	1.4	14
Understand project management tasks and responsibilities	1.5	1
Communicate with others (such as peers and clients) about design and content plans	1.6	1
Identifying Rich Media Design Elements	2	
Identify general and Flash-specific best practices for designing rich media content for the web, mobile apps, and AIR applications	2.1	1, 3, 6, 10, 14
Demonstrate knowledge of design elements and principles	2.2	3, 7
Identify general and Flash-specific techniques to create rich media elements that are accessible and readable	2.3	2, 14
Use a storyboard to design rich media elements	2.4	1
Organize a Flash document	2.5	2
Understanding Adobe Flash CS6 Interface	3	
Identify elements of the Flash interface	3.1	1, 5, 7
Use the Property inspector	3.2	1
Use the Timeline	3.3	1, 2, 5
Adjust document properties	3.4	1
Use Flash guides and rulers	3.5	7
Use the Motion Editor	3.6	5
Understand Flash file types	3.7	1, 13
Identify best practices for managing the file size of a published Flash document	3.8	14

Skill	Objective	Lesson
Building Rich Media Elements by Using Flash CS6	**4**	
Make rich media content development decisions based on your analysis and interpretation of design specifications	4.1	1
Use tools on the Tools panel to select, create, and manipulate graphics and text	4.2	1, 2
Import and modify graphics	4.3	2, 3, 8
Create text	4.4	2
Adjust text properties	4.5	2
Create objects and convert them to symbols, including graphics, movie clips, and buttons	4.6	3, 10
Understand symbols and the library	4.7	3, 4
Edit symbols and instances	4.8	3
Create masks	4.9	4
Create animations (changes in shape, position, size, color, and transparency)	4.10	5, 6, 8, 10
Add simple controls through ActionScript 3.0	4.11	9, 10, 13
Import and use sound	4.12	11
Add and export video	4.13	13
Publish and export Flash documents	4.14	14
Make a Flash document accessible	4.15	14
Evaluating Rich Media Elements by Using Flash CS6	**5**	
Conduct basic technical tests	5.1	2, 14
Identify techniques for basic usability tests	5.2	14

#

3D Rotation tool A tool in Flash that allows you to rotate and transform an object around an x-, y-, and z-axis, rendering 2D objects in the 3D plane.

3D Translation tool A tool in Flash that allows you to move a 3D object on the x, y, or z axis.

A

actions ActionScript commands added to a Flash animation that perform specific functions within an animation.

ActionScript Flash's built-in object-oriented, scripting language that allows you to control elements of an animation programmatically.

Actions panel A panel in Flash that is used to build and modify ActionScript code.

Adobe AIR Adobe Integrated Runtime provides a means for deploying Flash animations as desktop applications.

Anchor Points Vector-based objects are composed of paths that are connected using anchor points. Anchor points can be either smooth to draw curved lines or corner to draw straight lines.

Android A mobile operating system used to run devices from a variety of different manufacturers.

animation The process of using Flash or another animation program to create movement of objects on screen.

animated masks A mask is used to conceal and reveal certain portions of an animation. This mask itself can also be animated to create interesting effects.

App ID A unique identification number that that distinguishes an application from other applications.

B

Bandwidth Profiler A useful tool in Flash that can help you to measure the impact of embedded video in a Flash file.

bitmap One of two primary graphic file categories in which the file is composed of small squares or pixels.

blur A filter effect in Flash that softens the appearance of an object.

buttons Elements that provide a means for navigating a web site or animation.

C

codecs Software routines that compress video files small enough to be e-mailed or viewed on the Web or mobile devices.

Combine Objects This menu allows you combine multiple objects in a variety of different methods including union, intersect, punch, and crop.

Copy and Paste Motion The ability to copy the motion from one animation and paste the motion into another animation or object.

Code Snippets Pre-built sections of ActionScript code that can be applied to objects in Flash.

cue points Specific locations defined in a linked video file that can be referenced in Flash.

D

Deco tool This tool allows users to decorate or paint using a number of different fill types while also allowing these fills to be animated.

digital certificate Digital files used to verify the authenticity of a software application.

digital signature The component in Flash that uses a Digital Certificate to authenticate the authenticity of a software application.

Drawing Objects This command offers the ability to stack and arrange shapes within a single layer, providing a deeper level of ordering amongst multiple pieces of artwork.

E

ease A setting that controls how an object begins or ends an animation.

easing A setting in Flash that allows you to adjust how an animation begins or ends. Instead of an animation moving at a constant speed, you can ease into or out of the animation.

embedded video Video that is embedded inside of a Flash animation.

event An occurrence in an ActionScript that triggers something else to happen.

event handlers Blocks of ActionScript code that run in response to ActionScript events.

event listeners ActionScript code that assigns a trigger event and an event handler to a specific button or control on the stage.

Event sounds Sounds in Flash that trigger when an event occurs.

External Library A method by which you can make the assets available in one file to the Library panel of an open Flash file.

F

FTP (File Transfer Protocol) A common network protocol used to transfer files over the Internet.

filters Several types of effects that can be applied to objects in Flash.

Flash An application by Adobe Systems, Inc. that is used to generate vector-based animations, games, applications and web sites for use on the web and mobile devices.

Flash files Each file type has a very specific purpose in the process of creating or delivering Flash movies. They are generally identified by an extension appended to the file name.

Flash Player A stand-alone application found most often as a plug-in to popular browsers such as Internet Explorer, Safari and Firefox. It is used to play final Flash animation files (.swf files).

frame labels An identifier used to mark a frame so it can be referenced by that identifier.

functions A group of ActionScript statements that can be called upon in a script when needed.

G

gradient A gradual blend between two or more colors, and is often used for complex color transitions or to imply lighting effects.

Gradient Transform tool A tool used to apply a gradient to an object and adjust how the gradient is applied to the object. It allows control over the size, dimensions, and location of gradient fills.

guides Non-printing elements in Flash used for aligning objects on the stage. Guides also refer to motion guide used to control the movement of an object in a motion tween.

guide layers Layers used to create a custom guide to direct the movement of an object in a motion tween.

I

IK poses Using the Inverse Kinematics tools, you can create poses or positions of IK objects on the stage.

Inverse Kinematics IK is used by 3D and character animators to achieve more realistic motion, especially with jointed figures.

iOS An mobile operating system used to run Apple devices including iPhones, iPads, and iPods.

K

keyboard shortcuts Quick key commands that allow you to perform operations normally accessed from the menus.

keyframe A keyframe is a way to indicate a change in artwork over time in the Timeline.

L

layers Subdivisions of a document that provide for powerful organization of objects in a document.

Library panel A panel in Flash where imported artwork and symbols are stored.

Line tool A tool in Flash that draws straight lines in any number of directions.

linked video Video that referenced in a Flash animation but resides at an external location.

Live Preview A feature in Flash that allows a user to preview linked video on the stage.

looping When an animation plays in succession more than one time.

M

Masking The process of concealing certain areas of an object, while revealing others.

Media Encoder An application included with Flash Professional and other Adobe applications that encodes video files into various formats.

Merge Drawing A drawing mode whereby objects are merged together when they overlap each other. Think of Merge Drawing as having no stacking order between objects.

morphing An effect used with shape tweens where one object gradually transforms into another.

Motion Editor A powerful panel that allows a user to modify the properties of a motion tween with great precision.

motion path When a motion tween is created, a modifiable path is also created that indicates the path of movement of an object within a motion tween.

motion presets A saved motion setting that can be re-used on multiple objects with consistency.

motion tween An automatically generated animation between two keyframes that animates motion properties only.

Move To A Command in Flash that simplifies the process of organizing elements in the Library panel. Objects in the Library panel can be moved to specific folders using this command.

movie clips A symbol type that provides a Timeline that is independent from the main Timeline.

Glossary

movie clip timelines A Timeline within a Movie Clip symbol that is independent from the main Timeline in a Flash animation.

MP3 MPEG I or MPEG 2 audio layer III is a common audio format for consumer audio storage.

N

nest The process of placing a Movie Clip within another movie clip.

P

panels Small windows that provide specific options to control aspects of a Flash file. Some examples include the Library panel, Property Inspector and Timeline.

Pen tool A tool that draws vector-based Beziér curves and is the most precise drawing tool available in Flash.

PNG Sequence A sequence of still images that can be used within a website, mobile applicaton, or within a CSS or JavaScript animation.

Property Inspector A panel in Flash that is used to modify properties of the Flash document or the properties of a selected object.

Publish Settings The configurable options used to control the final published file in Flash.

R

rendering A term often used when working with 3D objects to describe the generation of 3D elements and adjusting their properties.

rulers Visual rulers provided at the top and left side of the Flash application window that provide for a quick view of the size of a document and access to guides that can be dragged to the stage.

S

Script Assist When writing ActionScript code, Script Assist provides an assistive mode that helps you to write ActionScript code in an intuitive way.

shape tween An animation in Flash between two shapes. During this tween, the properties of one object such as the shape and color will "morph" into the other shape.

skin A video interface added to a video file that often provides useful controls such as play, pause, stop, and the ability to scrub through the video.

SoundMixer An ActionScript class that controls the master sound output of a Flash movie.

Spray Brush tool Symbols can be creatively "sprayed" onto the Stage and the properties of the symbols can be adjusted.

Stage The visible working area of a Flash animation. During an animation, elements can enter and exit the stage to make them visible or hidden.

still images An image that does not contain animation or movement.

stop() An ActionScript action that stops an animation at a specific frame.

stopAll() A method in ActionScript that stops all sounds in a movie.

Swap One of the benefits of using symbols in an animation is that you can swap one instance of a symbol with another, replacing the artwork wherever the symbol is used.

symbols Reusable graphics, images and animations stored in the document's library. Symbols can be created from graphics or imported images on the Stage or from animations in the Timeline.

Sync menu A dropdown menu in Flash that controls each sound's playback and loading behavior.

T

Test Movie A command that generates a temporary .swf file so that you can test your animation quickly.

Text-based buttons Buttons created only from text. With these buttons, a hit state is required because without a hit state, only the characters of the text can be clicked on.

Timeline A panel in Flash where you create animations and sequence graphics with sound, video and controls.

tools Items used to create, select, or edit graphics on the Stage.

transform The process of modifying objects in various ways in Flash. Transformations include scaling, rotating, and skewing.

tween An automatically generated animation between two keyframes in the Timeline.

V

visual aids Non-printing elements that aid in the creation of animations. Non-printing elements include guides, rulers, grids, shape hints among others.

W

workspace The environment in which you work in Flash. The workspace includes panels, tools and their locations on your screen.

Index

Index

Index

On2 VP6 codec, 396
Onion Skin mode, 150, 181–182
onion skinning, 181–182
Onion Skin Outlines option, 182, 212
Onion Skin view, 212
On launch drop-down menu, 227
OOP (object-oriented programming), 285
opacity, 72–73
Open as Library dialog box, 257
Open command, 11
Open dialog box, 11, 398
Open External Library option, 252, 257
opening
  completed files, 218
  documents, 11–12
Open Recent Items column, 12
Option key, 25
Outline view, 191
Output file, 398
Output monitor, 408
Oval Primitive tool, 30, 58–59
Oval tool, 27, 41–43, 56, 72, 129, 134, 136
Over keyframe, 309, 345
Over state, 306

P

Padlock column, 78
padlock icon, 77, 241
Paint Bucket tool, 15, 29, 49, 52, 56
panel groups, 20–21
Panel menu, Library panel, 92
panel menu button, 74
panels
  collapsing, 222–223
  docking, 222
  keeping open, 42
  overview, 20–21
  resetting, 20
  storing, 222–223
  in workspace, 219
Paragraph option, 64
parameter placeholder, 323
parameters, 293, 323
parentheses, 322, 326, 328

pasteboard, 13
Paste Motion feature, 192, 198
pasting animation, 190–194
Pencil tool, 15, 41, 179
Pen tool, 15, 51–52, 187–188
Permit Debugging setting, 423–424
Photo2.wav sound, 343, 358
Photo3.wav sound, 344
Photo4.wav sound, 344
Photo5.wav sound, 359
Photoshop application, 50, 74, 261, 265–266, 384
Photoshop Import dialog box, 266
Photoshop (.psd) file format, 2, 266–272
piggybacking, 138
Pin Current Library, 92
Place instance on stage checkbox, 400
playClips( ) function, 297–298
Player drop-down menu, 427
Player Settings button, 428, 433
playhead, 150
PNG compression, 266
PNG Sequence, 439–441
Polystar tool, 43–44, 55
poses, 199
pound (#) sign, 50
Preferences dialog box, 226
Premiere application, 438
Premiere Pro application, 395
Preset drop-down menu, 407
Preset field, 398
prevFrame( ) method, 355
previewing
  animation with Test Movie, 158–159
  animation with Timeline, 166, 277
  movie clips, 369–370
Preview mode, 22
Preview window, 92, 370
Previous navigation button, 341
prevPhoto( ) event handler, 354

Primitive tools
  Oval Primitive tool, 30, 58–59
  overview, 58
Products Button symbol, 313
programming, 4
project management, 6–7
Properties, Library panel, 92
Properties button, 260, 265
Property Inspector
  adding cue points in, 412
  description of, 16–19, 64
  rotation menu, 167
  Timeline and, 19
Property Inspector panel, 161
provisioning profile, 434
.psd (Adobe Photoshop) file format, 2, 266–272
PSD Import Options dialog box, 266–269
Publish command, 420
publishing
  for Android OS, 435–438
  for desktop with Adobe AIR, 427–431
  for iOS, 433–435
  for mobile devices, 433–438
  sounds, 360
publishing movies
  overview of, 419–420
  to web, 420–426
Publish Preview option, 369
Publish settings, 266, 286–287, 422–426
Publish Settings dialog box, 360, 422, 424, 427, 431, 433, 435
Punch command, 56–57

Q

Quality drop-down menu, 191, 386–387
Queue, 397
QuickTime, 252, 337, 394, 396, 438–439
QuickTime Export Settings dialog box, 438–439

R

radial gradient, 70, 83
Rectangle Primitive tool, 58, 60–62

Rectangle tool, 16, 27, 129, 136, 317
red flag icon, 319
refining aligned objects, 244–245
registration mark, 236
registration point, 94, 96, 235, 274
Remove Hint option, 212
Remove Transform button, 82
removing actions, 288
Rename Set button, 231
rendering, 203, 410
Repeat drop-down menu, 352–353
repeating sounds, 352
resources, help, 32–33
reverse DNS, 429
revolution, increasing, 168
Rotate Around option, 138–139
Rotate drop-down menu, 368
Rotate text field, 105, 137
rotating arrow icon, 80
Rotation, 169
rotation, tweening, 167–169
rulers, 233–237
Rulers option, 233
Ruler unit, 9

S

sample rate, 334–335
sample template, 11
Save As dialog box, 24, 42, 46, 93, 128, 151, 154, 253
Save Default option, 240
Save dialog box, 10
saving
  custom colors, 74
  documents, 10–11
Scale and Rotate dialog box, 79, 161, 178
Scale field, 27
scale handle, 83
Scale X, 165
Scale Y, 165
scaling
  animation, 161–162
  classic tweens, 177–178
Screen Mask layer, 198–199, 202
Screen Simulation layer, 199, 202

All of the photos in this book were created by and printed with permission from the authors of the book.